Pelican Books

Introducing Economics

B. J. McCormick is Reader in Economics at the University of Sheffield.
G. P. Marshall is a Senior Lecturer, and P. D. Kitchin, A. A. Sampson
and R. Sedgwick are Lecturers at the same university.

# Introducing Economics

B. J. McCormick
P. D. Kitchin, G. P. Marshall,
A. A. Sampson, R. Sedgwick

Third Edition

Penguin Books

Penguin Books Ltd, 27 Wrights Lane, London W8 5TZ (Publishing and Editorial)
*and* Harmondsworth, Middlesex, England (Distribution and Warehouse)
Viking Penguin Inc., 40 West 23rd Street, New York, New York 10010, USA
Penguin Books Australia Ltd, Ringwood, Victoria, Australia
Penguin Books Canada Ltd, 2801 John Street, Markham, Ontario, Canada L3R 1B4
Penguin Books (NZ) Ltd, 182–190 Wairau Road, Auckland 10, New Zealand

First published 1974
Second edition 1977
Reprinted 1978, 1980
Third edition 1983
Reprinted 1985, 1987

Made and printed in Great Britain by
Hazell Watson & Viney Limited,
Member of the BPCC Group,
Aylesbury, Bucks
Set in Linotron 10/12 Times Roman by Syarikat Seng Teik Sdn. Bhd.

# Contents

# Acknowledgements

In the conduct of the seminars and the writing of this book we have had a great deal of help from our students, who patiently corrected our mistakes and tried to understand what we were getting at. In addition our colleagues at Sheffield and members of the Penguin Modern Economics Advisory Board gave us unstinting help. We are also indebted to Mrs Julia Galley who struggled to produce a coherent typescript from our chaotic handwriting. Good secretaries are more scarce than economists. For all the assistance we are grateful, though for any blunders still embalmed we are eternally responsible.

Western Bank, Sheffield
January 1983

# Note on the Third Edition

Two major changes have been made in preparing this revised edition of *Introducing Economics*. First, the discussion of the state has been moved to a more central position in the book in order to emphasize that the state and the market form competitive as well as complementary methods of allocating resources. Secondly, the macroeconomics has been overhauled in the light of the debate over Keynesian economics. There is now more discussion of aggregate supply and the behaviour of the price level as well as more discussion of policy.

Elsewhere we have taken the opportunity of making the text more readable. Isoquants have been introduced into the discussion of production and costs. The chapter on utility has been expanded in order to provide the reader with a thorough appreciation of why indifference curves are the least unsatisfactory tool of economic analysis. The section on mathematics has been enlarged in order to provide a discussion up to the problems of constrained maximization. Workers' control has been contrasted with public ownership. And throughout the text the opportunity has been taken to provide contemporary illustrations of economic problems.

# Preface

This book is an attempt to design an introductory course which reflects the changes in subject matter and techniques of analysis of modern economics. The contents of the book were tested with university students, some Open University students, extramural classes and sixth formers over a three-year period.

At the outset we were faced with the problem of how to approach economics. Three approaches suggested themselves – historical; market analysis; and non-market analysis.

## Historical

An historical approach could start with the relationship between men and natural resources, drawing upon the experiences of Robinson Crusoe to demonstrate the problems encountered at the beginning of civilization. But it would be more appropriate to indicate how the socio-economic problems of production, distribution and accumulation were resolved within the institutional framework known as *feudalism*. The tenant would hire land from the landlord or he would be employed directly as a wage-labourer. Irrespective of the contract in force he would receive a certain income and the remainder would go to the landlord for his consumption and for communal defence and accumulation. Because this agrarian system was dependent upon a power source – solar energy – which was uncontrollable by Man's actions, labour was often idle between spells of sowing and reaping, with the consequence that the system of feudalism had to cope with the problems of unemployment as well as the pressures of overpopulation spasmodically relieved by epidemics and drought. Yet the principal problem was that of the distribution of output between landlord and tenant.

Feudalism can then be depicted as giving way to industrialization as a result of the exploitation of fossil fuels and new technologies. By its release from dependence upon solar energy, innovations made in agriculture and the reduction of population pressure the industrial economy could become a fully developed *market economy* in which all resources are relatively scarce, and in which surpluses could be invested in all kinds of activities as a result of market mobility. In such an economy the distribution of output would somehow be determined by the market. In an industrial market economy the distribution of output is not between landlord and tenant but between capitalist and wage-earner. Should accumulation of capital over time increase the total amount of goods available, the conflict implicit in determining distribution might be reduced, but alternatively it would be heightened if capitalists attempted to increase their share. The conflict could widen and deepen into a triangular struggle between rentiers (those who financed economic activity), capitalists (those who directed economic activity) and wage-earners (those who endured economic activity) as specialization created a difference between owners (financiers) and controllers (directors). And, finally, the conflict could be shown to be world-wide as industrial economies destroyed agrarian economies in their pursuit of raw materials, new markets and new centres of production.

### Market analysis

Historical analysis has many virtues: it emphasizes the economic activity and stresses the uniqueness of different periods of time in terms of institutions and problems. But because it is a dialectical method it is apt to blur the differences; it does not allow the cutting edge of analysis to provide those deep insights which are so necessary to an understanding of how a particular economy works, or how an efficient economic system might be developed to deal with a particular problem. The dialectic is a barrier to measurement, since in emphasizing the qualitative it ignores the fact that many phenomena are capable of measurement. We murder to dissect but even post-mortem can advance understanding.

So an alternative line of advance would be to pick out the obvious in modern society – the market – and to analyse the way in which markets work, and from such an approach it would be possible to explain why markets sometimes break down.

## Non-market analysis

Much human activity is undertaken outside the market situation. We are born and live in families, go to youth clubs and attend churches, and receive innumerable benefits from a Welfare State. Moreover, some economies and about nine-tenths of the human drama has been enacted in non-market economies. It would therefore be interesting to begin with the assumption that the state makes all the decisions and takes responsibility for the organization of all economic activities, in order to see why markets might sometimes be useful.

## A compromise

Each approach has its merits. The historical approach brings out the importance of class and class conflict but tends to neglect the large element of co-operation in society. The market approach is class-less and ignores the importance of the state. A non-market approach would fail to emphasize the important rise in the use of the market over the last two hundred years. A compromise was necessary. We have dealt at greater length than most writers with the state, with non-market economies and the way in which theory has emerged out of historical problems. And to a basic approach we have fused the necessary mathematics because we believe that further advances in economics can be greatly assisted by the use of mathematics. Furthermore, we have introduced statistical testing as a necessary antidote to armchair theorizing and to indicate the scope and limitations of measurement. Finally, since economics is a moral science, we have not hesitated to introduce value judgements.

In Part One (*A Panorama of Problems*) the task of the economist is defined as being the analysis of the causes of the possibilities of civilization, the economist's role being that of aiding Man in his attempts to control his environment, and attain some satisfaction of his basic wants, so as to make possible the development of a culture. The indicators of material well-being and possibilities of civilization in the UK (national income) are measured over two centuries and explanations looked for to explain the variations in these indicators.

The nature of wants and the concept of a hierarchy of wants are discussed in connection with the indicators of society's ability to produce its material needs. From this the obvious step is made to study goods and their relationships with wants. Goods are classified as to whether or not property rights can be allocated to them, and it becomes apparent that although some goods can be privately produced, others require some form of collective action.

Following on from the initial discussion of the meaning of scarcity and the relationships between wants and the goods which satisfy them, a study is made of the processes and institutions used and devised by man to overcome the scarcity problem. Included in the illustration of the production problem is a discussion of over-population and pollution.

Production is not the only means of increasing a community's well-being: another is exchange and trade. The initial discussion concerns the world of barter exchange – the next stage is concerned with the institution of money as a means of further improving the material well-being of the trading partners.

'What is the function of money?' is a question answered primarily in terms of its use as a unit of account and medium of exchange. Finally the time dimension is introduced, and the concepts already developed used to show how the use of resources can be spread over time so that beneficial trade-offs can be affected between present and further consumption.

Part Two (*Markets, Demand and Supply*) turns the discussion from universal economic problems to something more specific –

how resources are allocated – and to the different methods man has adopted to do this. The market is viewed as a mechanism for allocation, treated as an information system and compared with a system of central planning. Analysis of the demand side of the market is carried out by reviewing the concept of a function and the relationships between individual and market demand curves; discussing the different treatments of private and collective goods; and exploring the important concept of elasticity. The supply side is treated in a similar way, illustrating volume and rate effects. Demand and supply are brought together to show price determination. The concept of equilibrium is discussed and ideas of consumer and producer surplus explained. Some potential consequences of state interference with market processes are considered with particular reference to housing and the labour market. The concept of a 'charity market' is considered, and the idea of expressing market relationships as a set of simultaneous equations is explained.

Relative price and output effects are considered in discussing the implications of shifts in market demand and supply curves. The impact of taxes and subsidies is illuminated by such current problems as stabilizing farmers' incomes via UK or EEC methods; manpower planning, etc. We complete our analysis of the market with some simple tests of the theory including a look at the identification problem.

Part Three (*Utility and Cost*) turns to the subjective base of economics to look behind demand and supply curves in order to explain the underlying behaviour of economic agents. The logic of choice will be developed in a way which indicates how economists create a theory and how they develop and generalize it. Utility or benefit is a recurrent theme and costs are presented as the loss of benefits from rejected choices – a sharp distinction is drawn between the economist's subjective theory of costs and the accountant's objective approach. The law of diminishing returns is strongly revived for the whole section.

Part Four (*A Mathematical Interlude*) is concerned with the mathematical tools used earlier in the book, but only implicitly. There are two reasons for doing this. The first is that having covered quite considerable ground in this study of economics, some revision should prove beneficial for the student. Secondly, the theory of the firm often involves simple mechanical relationships best expressed mathematically – and this is the next topic to be analysed.

The concept of a function is revised in this section, and total and marginal values reconsidered in the context of some simple differential calculus. The examples used draw heavily on the sections on production; demand and supply; utility and cost theory.

Part Five (*The Social Institutions of Production*) deals with the theory of the firm – really a continuation of the exploration of market behaviour. The firm is introduced as an alternative mechanism for monitoring the work of factors of production, particularly labour. Various firms – households, corporations and the State – are considered.

Part Six (*Market Structures*) begins with some general principles of organizational behaviour irrespective of market structure. All organizations need rules by which to attain their objectives and the rule stressed here is that, at the margin, expected benefits must equal expected costs.

Part Seven (*The Theory of Distribution*) uses the tools of demand and supply analysis to determine the prices of productive services in factor markets and complements the previous discussion of the pricing of goods.

Part Eight (*The State*) deals again with the market system which is seen to give rise to the under-consumption of some goods and the over-consumption of others. The intervention of the state and the alternatives of taxation, printing money and borrowing are analysed. The problems of poverty and inequality in a community are analysed. Finally we look at the problems of decision making in the state.

Part Nine (*Macroeconomics*) deals with the overall behaviour of the economy. It begins by drawing a distinction between an economy in which prices are rigid and quantities supplied respond to changes in demand without the stimulus of price increases and decreases, and an economy in which prices are flexible. There then follows a more detailed analysis of aggregate demand in a fixed price economy. This is followed by a discussion of money and enables us to round off our analysis of a fix-price economy in which money and goods co-exist – this is the ISLM model. Then follows a further analysis of a flex-price economy which leads into inflation. Next follows a consideration of monetary and fiscal policy. Finally, we consider some aspects of development and growth.

# Part One
# **A Panorama of Problems**

# Chapter 1
# The Wealth and Welfare of Nations

## Economics and economists

Inflation and unemployment, poverty and monopoly are examples of the types of problem which economists consider. But if there has to be a generalization of what economists study, a capsule definition, then it is that they study how men and women obtain their livelihoods. What constitutes a livelihood varies, of course, from country to country and from generation to generation, and economists try to provide some explanation of these differences. Furthermore, economists must also consider in a particular context the subtle relationship between livelihood, or 'life-style', and civilization – the life-style of some civilizations revolves around a bowl of rice, for others it centres on surfing. Economists do not pretend to study how a civilization is created, but they do believe themselves to be, in the words of Lord Keynes, 'the trustees of the *possibility* of civilization' (Harrod, 1951).

What does it mean to be the trustees of the *possibility* of civilization? First, it conveys the belief that only if men and women possess some control over their environment and have attained some satisfaction of their basic wants can they be said to enjoy the possibilities of a cultured life. Secondly, it indicates that it is the economists' task to seek out those methods of control over the environment which are most conducive to the development of the nobler arts of life. In a world of scarcity satisfaction of wants can be achieved through theft, rape and war, as well as production and trade. But the former methods lead to fear, suspicion and the degradation of the human spirit. It is, of course, the moral philosopher, the poet and the artist who create a civilization, but their work is made easier by the economist. So the economist sees himself as protecting and conserving the good qualities and he hopes that through his recommendations he can ultimately increase the virtues and eliminate the vices.

How do economists explore, create and sustain the possibilities of civilization? Some, the great economists, are possessed of powerful visions of the workings of society and they embody these visions in systems of thought which transcend their times. Late in the eighteenth century Scottish economist and philosopher, Adam Smith, delved into the causes of the wealth of nations. He was followed by a stockbroker and MP, David Ricardo, who inquired into the distribution of the rewards from economic activity, and the Reverend T. R. Malthus who warned of the dangers of overpopulation. In the middle of the nineteenth century came Marx with his penetrating analysis of the evolution of capitalist society. Towards the end of the century Alfred Marshall took the ideas of Smith, Ricardo and Malthus, infused them with additional insights and used sharper tools of analysis to produce a synthesis. At the same time Leon Walras captured the essence and interrelations of production, exchange and distribution in a few mathematical equations. In the twentieth century J. M. Keynes prescribed for slumps and A. C. Pigou for the problems of the affluent society.

But these are the great names. What of the ordinary, work-a-day economists, what do they do? Some work in government departments advising on such issues as unemployment, inflation, poverty and monopoly, the location of industry, and exports and imports. Others work in private firms on the problems of pricing products, appraising investment opportunities, forecasting sales and manpower planning. In international agencies economists can be found to be preoccupied with the diffusion of new technologies to developing countries, the flow of foreign aid, the stabilization of prices and incomes for producers of primary products such as cocoa and tin. In all these spheres, in all these inquiries into the ways by which men and women seek to obtain a livelihood, economists apply and create methods for the efficient use of resources.

In this chapter an examination is made of how the possibilities of civilization in the United Kingdom have altered over time. This enables us to isolate the causes of change in material living standards and thus to present a preliminary inquiry into the territory that forms the bulk of this book. The information obtained about the United Kingdom will then be used to throw light on the possibilities of civilization in other countries, a subject investigated by Adam Smith in 1776 and which served as the starting point of modern economics.

## The behaviour of the United Kingdom national output

One of the simplest methods of examining the foundations of civilization is to trace the behaviour of the national output, or national income as it is more usually termed. The national income measures the vast outpouring of goods and services that a country's citizens produce and *sell* during a given period, usually a year. The term 'sell' is important because sales records are the simplest means of checking that economic activity has been undertaken during a given time period; unpaid services, such as those performed by a housewife for the rest of her family, go unrecorded by the national income statisticians.

Statistics of the United Kingdom national income have been compiled for as far back as the middle of the nineteenth century. For earlier periods information is only available for Great Britain. In the nineteenth century the behaviour of the economies of Britain and Ireland diverged sharply: Britain underwent industrialization whereas Ireland was little affected by the Industrial Revolution; Ireland had a calamitous fall both in population (through deaths and migration) and in living standards as a result of the Famine whereas Britain did not. Of course, we must not expect that the recording of transactions in the nineteenth century was as rigorous and as accurate as nowadays and we do find great variations in both the quantity and the quality of information gathered over a century. These difficulties are compounded by the fact that there have been changes in the types of goods produced and consumed over the past one hundred and fifty years – motor cars and aeroplanes did not exist in 1800 and charcoal and candles have long since ceased to be significant items of consumption, save for those who enjoy barbecues and intimate dinners. But, despite the drawbacks, year to year changes can be compared and thereby, with some heroic assumptions, longer term comparisons can be made. Figure 1 shows the behaviour of the United Kingdom national income since 1855. National income is measured in money terms because money is a convenient common denominator: only by using monetary values is it possible to add the (annual) physical output of ice cream to the physical output of motor cars.

But there is a difficulty in using the money prices of goods and services which stems from the fact that money prices can change from time to time without there being any change in the volume of physical output. Last year a particular make of car

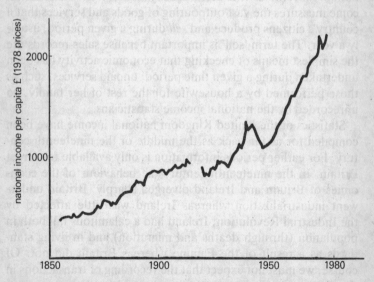

Figure 1  Real national income per capita, 1850–1980.
Source:  Deane and Cole (1960), *National Income Blue Books, Annual Abstract of Statistics*, 1981

may have cost £5000 and this year it may cost £6000. Some of the difference might reflect quality differences but a more likely explanation might be changes in the value of money. Ideally what we need to do is to have constant prices for all goods and services so that we can look at output in physical terms. We need to take the prices in one period and assume that these prices prevailed in all periods. In Figure 1 we assume that the prices which obtained in 1978 ruled in every year. This enables us to speak of national income in *real terms*.

In looking at the movement of national income figures over time we need to know how much income each person receives. We know what was available but we also know that the size of the population was changing. We must therefore divide the total real national income figures by the total population at various dates in order to get some idea of what the average standard of living was. This procedure is the best that can be done. We know that some people get more of the available goods than others but we have no reliable estimates of the disparities until recent decades. Dividing what is available by the number of potential recipients gives a measure of the standard of living that would have resulted if everyone had got equal absolute amounts of the goods and services.

So we have arrived at the real national income per head. And what we observe is the striking difference in the growth of living standards between the nineteenth and twentieth centuries, especially after 1950. Furthermore, there is evidence that the growth of real income is punctuated by fluctuations which seem to occur at regular intervals in the nineteenth century. During the twenties and thirties there was a catastrophic fall but the upward surge was resumed after 1950 until the end of the seventies.

## The shift in the composition of output

How was the increase in the total output of the United Kingdom brought about? First, there was the emergence of a surplus in agricultural production (a product of good harvests and new methods of production) which released labour for other activities. Secondly, there were the great inventions which enabled more and more goods and services to be produced with the same inputs of resources. Thirdly, there was the development of new lines of economic activity.

Let us not proceed further with the process of sub-dividing the total output into finer and finer classifications of industries. Instead, let us see what we can glean from the broad groups. The striking feature to note is the relative unimportance of agriculture, forestry and fishing, and government (see Table 1). By the middle of the twentieth century the contribution of agriculture is minute. The period under observation is one where economic activity is dominated by industry and trade, and mainly industry. What we see in Table 1 is the continuation of a process which began some time in the second half of the eighteenth century and which has been dubbed the Industrial Revolution.

Economic historians have long debated the significance and causes of the Industrial Revolution. Was it a Revolution, meaning thereby a sharp break with the past? Was it unique? Was it merely a revolution in industry and, if so, was it confined to particular industries? Some economic historians have pointed to a Neolithic Revolution which occurred around 4000 BC and brought about a shift from hunting and food-gathering to farming. Others have detected an industrial revolution in the thirteenth-century clothing industry and a later one in the six-

**Table 1** The composition of the British national product, 1801–1979 (percentages of the total national income)

|      | Agriculture, forestry, fishing | Manufactures, mining, building | Trade, transport, income from abroad | Government, domestic, other services | Housing |
|------|------|------|------|------|------|
| 1801 | 32·5 | 23·4 | 17·4 | 21·3 | 5·3 |
| 1851 | 20·3 | 34·3 | 20·7 | 18·4 | 8·1 |
| 1901 | 6·1  | 40·2 | 29·8 | 15·5 | 6·2 |
| 1979 | 2·3  | 39·0 | 28·0 | 24·7 | 6·0 |

Source:  Deane and Cole (1960), *Annual Abstract of Statistics*, 1981, table 1

teenth century connected with brass and glass. Thus, if there was a revolution in the eighteenth century then perhaps it was not historically unique.

The debate on the Industrial Revolution has also considered the question of whether the revolution was concentrated on cotton, coal or iron. Recent research has tended to reduce the importance of cotton and to emphasize the simultaneous revolutions in agriculture, industry, transport and communications. And even though it is conceded that there was some perceptible quickening in economic activity in the eighteenth century it is now considered to be the cumulation of many small changes that occurred from the seventeenth century onwards.

No doubt the debate concerning the Industrial Revolution will continue. If we wanted to single out any important feature it would be the factory system, and if we are to single out one important feature of the last fifty years then it must be the re-assertion of government relative to private enterprise. Before the Industrial Revolution the systems known as feudalism and mercantilism had stressed the importance of collective regulation of economic activity. This declined in the nineteenth century but collective regulation has now reappeared in a different form and is concerned with different issues.

The increases in output and the shifts in the composition of output were accompanied by changes in the size, composition and distribution of the labour force. The first marked change was the movement of labour from the land into urban factories. Attendant upon that shift were changes in methods of work and in attitudes towards work. The factory system introduced greater regularity into the working lives of its operatives. Seasonal influences, bouts of enforced idleness, began to disappear. There was also a great increase in the participation of women and children in the labour market.

Latterly, the shift towards a service economy is making itself felt in the decline in the relative importance of manual workers in manufacturing. Indeed by the year 2000 if present trends continue the manual worker will have become relatively unimportant as compared to the white-collar worker.

## Foreign trade

The task of feeding an increasing population has been partly met by increasing the output of domestic agriculture, but more so by exchanging our manufactures for the agricultural products of other countries. What we observe is a *substitution* of foreign produced foodstuffs for domestically produced foodstuffs. Presumably this must have represented a gain or it would never have been undertaken. The exploration of the gains from trade is the task of Chapter 4. What needs to be noted at this stage, however, is that if there were gains from trade, then their persistence has been due to a continual change in the kinds of goods that we export, the kinds of goods that we import and the countries from whom we import. The process of substitution is

**Table 2** Changing pattern of British exports, 1830–1977 (percentages of total exports)

|  | 1830 | 1850 | 1870 | 1910 | 1930 | 1977 |
|---|---|---|---|---|---|---|
| cotton yarn and cloth | 50·8 | 39·6 | 35·8 | 24·4 | 15·3⎫ | 3·6 |
| wool yarn and cloth | 12·7 | 14·1 | 13·4 | 8·7 | 6·5⎭ | |
| iron and steel | 10·2 | 12·3 | 14·2 | 11·4 | 10·3 | 8·6 |
| machinery | 0·5 | 0·8 | 1·5 | 6·8 | 8·2 | 25·0 |
| coal | 0·5 | 1·8 | 2·8 | 8·7 | 8·6 | — |
| vehicles | — | — | 1·1 | 3·8 | 9·0 | 13·0 |
| chemicals | — | 0·5 | 0·6 | 4·3 | 3·8 | 11·5 |
| electrical goods | — | — | — | — | 2·1 | 4·0 |

Source: Deane and Cole (1960), table 2, *Annual Abstract of Statistics*, 1979

**Table 3** Changing pattern of British imports, 1840–1977 (percentages of total imports)

|  | 1840 | 1880 | 1910 | 1977 |
|---|---|---|---|---|
| food, drink and tobacco | 39·7 | 44·1 | 38·0 | 16·1 |
| raw materials and semi-manufactures | 56·6 | 38·6 | 38·5 | 51·7 |
| manufactures and miscellaneous | 3·7 | 17·3 | 23·5 | 33·2 |

Source: Deane and Cole (1960), table 3, *Annual Abstract of Statistics*, 1979

continually occurring, as is well brought out in Tables 2 and 3. In the nineteenth century exports were dominated by textiles, coal, iron and steel, whereas the twentieth century reveals a shift towards machinery and vehicles. Likewise imports show a concentration on foodstuffs and raw materials, although manufactured goods have become important in the last fifty years.

*Inputs*

The material basis of civilization has been created by man working and wrestling with Nature and in the process creating and using what have been termed capital goods – machines, buildings, etc. Casual observation suggests that how much a man

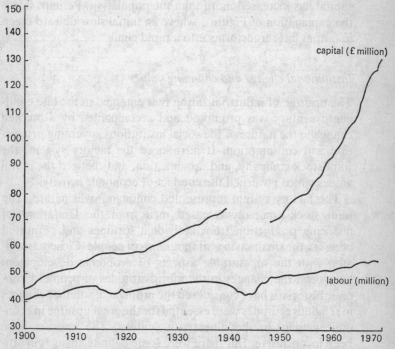

Figure 2  UK 1900–1970.
Source:  Times Newspapers (1971)

produces may depend upon whether he uses a spade or merely his hands. More generally we can say that what man produces is crucially dependent upon the amount of capital goods available. In Figure 2 we show the behaviour of population and the capital stock since 1900. Since capital is heterogeneous – machines, buildings, etc. – it is measured in money terms because, as we have seen, money is a common denominator. However, because prices change, we have assumed that the prices occurring in 1963 ruled throughout the period. It is the same measurement problem that we encountered with the national income. Although people do differ we follow the statisticians and Robert Burns and say: 'A man's a man for a' that'. There are assumed to be no measurement problems with people.

What emerges from Figure 2 is that over time the stock of capital has increased more than the population. Perhaps this is the explanation of Figure 1 where an initial slow upward creep in output later transforms into a rapid climb.

## Institutional change and changing values

The upsurge of industrialization that emerged in the late eighteenth century was promoted and accompanied by a marked change in the nature of the social institutions governing production and consumption. It introduced the factory system, the joint stock company, and urbanization, and changed the moral values which governed the conduct of economic activity.

The factory system represented command over nature. The joint stock company released men from the limitations of financing production from individual fortunes and permitted access to the small savings of thousands of people. Closely associated with the measurable aspects of economic development have been the changes in the moral attitudes of people. Economic historians have considered the problem of whether changes in religious attitudes were essential for the great upsurge in economic activity in the nineteenth century. The answers have been inconclusive. But there were some definite changes in attitudes, despite the fact that the new views on work, income and the accumulation of wealth were not the products of a smooth and gradual process. Men did not accept readily the doctrine of *laissez-faire*, a doctrine which may be defined as a belief that few restrictions should be placed on men's pursuit of wealth. Yet by the end of the nineteenth century there could be discerned a change in outlook. James Watt and his steam engine and Charles Darwin and the Beagle had done their work. The theory of evolution suggested that behind Nature lay not God but selective forces, and the steam engine was one means of controlling those forces.

## Other aspects of well-being

So far we have examined the changes in the output of goods and services and used those changes as an indicator of economic well-being and as a provider of a basis for a civilized life. We can, however, find alternative measures of well-being and an important one is the expectation of life. As Figure 3 shows, expectation of life has increased for all age-groups. Surely to generations succumbing to increasing scepticism about a life hereafter this must be counted as a blessing?

Two further aspects of well-being need to be noted. The first is that hours of work have declined over the period under

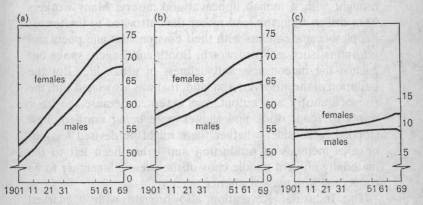

Figure 3 Expectation of life in Great Britain.
(a) At birth. (b) Five years old. (c) Seventy years old.
Source: *Social Trends*, no. 3, 1972, HMSO

observation. From fifty-four hours a week in the late nineteenth century they fell to around forty-six hours in the sixties. These changes have seen the elimination of Saturday and Sunday from the normal work-week. Leisure has in fact been an important indicator of the growth in well-being and since 1900 people have consumed more of both leisure and material goods. The second aspect has been the raising of the age at which young persons commence their working lives; they now enjoy longer periods in full-time education.

When obtaining our estimates of real national income per head we took into account changes in the size of the population. These changes in population have been considerable. Some economic historians have seen the problem of the eighteenth century as the task of feeding an increasing population and the Industrial Revolution as a solution to this problem. Others have questioned whether population change is a cause or consequence of economic prosperity.

## The social problems

The growth of output was not without its disadvantages. Not all output could be measured and some components of output that might have been measured were ignored. Industrialization brought with it human upheaval and misery. Many workers were driven from the land rather than attracted to the towns. People became careless with their environment and poets and reformers, such as Wordsworth, Booth and Engels, spoke out against the hideousness and ugliness of urban life. But the pollution of the air, rivers and land, that was associated with the rise of industry and output, was accepted because the basic wants of food, drink and shelter were being satisfied. Few stopped to consider whether there might be devised less obnoxious methods of production and it has been left to the materially affluent middle class of the twentieth century to be concerned with mass aesthetics.

The Industrial Revolution also brought with it marked fluctuations in economic activity. In agrarian societies such fluctuations were due to Nature and men attempted to insulate themselves from their effects by the social institution known as feudalism which permitted everyone a claim on what output was available. In industrial market economies, known sometimes as capitalist or *laissez-faire*, the fluctuations seemed to be due to forces within the system rather than to the forces without. Moreover, there seemed to be no methods of offsetting unemployment. Figure 1 shows some marked fluctuations per head. In the nineteenth century 8 per cent of the labour force could be reckoned to be permanently trying to find jobs, in the period 1919–39 the figure rose as high as 20 per cent (in 1931) and thereafter the proportion never rose above 3 per cent. What caused these variations is the subject of Part Nine. It is worth noting, however, that if we compare real income per head in the slump years of the twenties and thirties with that of the boom years of the nineteenth century, then the *employed* people were in some sense better off in the twentieth-century depressions. Why this should be so is a question of the causes of growth and progress, the subject of Chapter 46. It is also interesting to note that in the nineteenth century prices tended to be stable when unemployment was about 8 per cent; fell in the inter-war years when unemployment was around 12 per cent, and have risen with unemployment below 3 per cent in the post-war period. This suggests a theory relating the behaviour of prices to the level of unemployment which is explored in Chapter 40.

## Recapitulation

We started from a belief that changes in material well-being were conducive to the attainment of the good life and sought to measure such changes and isolated possible causes. We discovered that:

1 Changes in total output were accompanied by changes in the composition of output.

2 Some part of material well-being was created through foreign trade.

3 Change seemed to be accompanied by changes in mental and social attitudes.

4 Change seemed to have certain side effects – unemployment, pollution, etc. – whose significance has increased over time.

From a brief examination of the United Kingdom experience we now turn to ask the same questions of the rest of the world.

## Other countries

The trend of economic activity and of economic well-being in the United Kingdom poses the question: do other countries exhibit similar characteristics? This question is really three questions:

1 Do the poor countries of the world share the characteristics possessed by the United Kingdom of one or even two hundred years ago?

2 Do the rich countries have much in common with the United Kingdom?

3 Must the poor countries follow the same paths trodden by the rich countries?

### Lack of statistics

From the viewpoint of trying to measure national prosperity, the most notable feature of the poorer countries of the world is the lack of statistics. Some measures of national income are available but such figures tend to refer only to the sector of the economy where goods are bought and sold for money, to what is sometimes referred to as 'the market sector'. But a great deal of trade takes place in markets where there is little or no use of money and so the volume of trade is not recorded. And an enormous amount of production and exchange takes place within the family, which in poorer countries is frequently an extended family of considerable size. What economists sometimes do is to use the information from the market sector to make

**Table 4**  Indicators of economic development 1975

| | Gross product product per head US dollars 1975 | Per cent labour force in agriculture | Energy consumption per head kilogrammes coal equivalent | Literacy rate | Life expectancy (years) |
|---|---|---|---|---|---|
| *Developed market economies* | | | | | |
| USA | 7087 | 3·8 | 10 999 | 99 | 72 |
| EEC (6) | 5550 | 10·0 | 4355 | 99 | 72 |
| (total) | 5230 | 12·0 | 4922 | 99 | 72 |
| UK | 4689 | 2·4 | 5265 | 97 | 71 |
| West Germany | 6871 | 5·5 | 5345 | 99 | 71 |
| Japan | 4437 | 14·8 | 3622 | 98 | 74 |
| *Socialist countries* | | | | | |
| Eastern Europe | 2660 | 25·0 | 5412 | 98 | 69 |
| Russia | 2620 | 21·5 | 5546 | 100 | 69 |
| Asia | 330 | 63·0 | 734 | 75 | 67 |
| *Developing countries* | | | | | |
| Latin America | 1090 | 40·0 | 9427 | 75 | 62 |
| Africa | 370 | 70·0 | 197 | 20 | 50 |
| Asia | 310 | 55·0 | 306 | 50 | 55 |

Source:  UNCTAD, *Handbook of World Trade and Development Statistics, 1977 Supplement*

guesses about the subsistence sector. We need therefore to treat the national income data for poorer countries with caution.

## Gross domestic product per head

A crude measure is the gross domestic product per head which varies enormously – being one hundred and fifty times greater in the developed as compared with the developing countries.

## Agriculture

A simple method of determining the well-being of the country is to look at the proportion of its labour force employed in agriculture. The vagaries of the weather make agricultural output uncertain and threaten livelihoods so that agricultural communities tend to be poor communities – although there are exceptions, such as Denmark, New Zealand and Australia.

## Energy consumption

A highly significant indicator of development is fuel consumption; witness the voracious appetite of the Americans.

## Life expectancy

A further indicator of poverty is the low level of literacy in the developing countries. Literacy makes possible efficient communication between peoples and thereby leads to an increase in the output of goods and services.

## Alternative routes to affluence

An examination of the characteristics and problems of other countries serves to remind us how unique was the UK growth in prosperity. It was

1  Promoted by a revolution in farming methods.
2  The first major industrial revolution.

3 Accompanied by a removal of restrictions on trade.

4 Achieved with little or no foreign aid or investment although some have seen in slavery and piracy the foundations of UK glory.

5 It produced social and political changes without the extreme violence that occurred in some other countries.

The most significant feature of the take-off was the increase in productivity in agriculture – which released labour for the factories and ensured that the urban masses could be fed. Land reform and peasant emancipation were the prerequisites of European industrialization and it was lack of modernization of agriculture which has delayed the industrialization of the tropics until the second half of the nineteenth century.

The British experience is even more marked when contrasted with that of countries which began to industrialize in the second half of the nineteenth century. America and Germany imposed tariffs because they felt that their infant manufacturing industries would not be able to withstand the severe competition from the British economy. The British pattern of development was one which seemed to be associated with private enterprise and free trade. Today that association does not seem obvious to the underdeveloped countries. Some are inclined to follow the Russian example of centralized control of development with public ownership of the means of production, but even when the Russian pattern is rejected there is no acceptance of the UK example. There is, in fact, a tendency to imitate by example, if not intent, the French and German methods of state encouragement of industry as practised in the nineteenth century. But perhaps all countries, including the UK, have to follow a policy of state control in the preparatory and take-off stages and then allow a relaxation of controls at a later stage.

The problems of the poorer countries are of course tremendously difficult. Contact with the developed countries has created an immediate demand for Western standards of health, education and industrial relations. But these standards have been a relatively recent development in the West and their attempted introduction into the poorer countries may bring social tension and conflict and may inhibit social development. Moreover, the past experiences of colonialism have created a distrust of foreign investment and foreign aid.

## Questions

1 'The gross national product does not allow for the health of our youth, the quality of their education or the joy of their play. It does not include the beauty of our poetry or the strength of our marriage, the intelligence of our public debate or the integrity of our public officials. It measures neither our wit nor our courage, neither our wisdom nor our learning, neither our compassion nor our devotion to country. It measures everything, in short, except that which makes life worthwhile . . .' Robert Kennedy, *The Times*, 10 February 1968. Comment.

2 How should we measure the difference in the national income of Denmark and Eire created by the ability to buy pornographic literature in Denmark?

3 What conclusions would you draw from the following (hypothetical) observations:
(a) In 1980 the outputs of steel in China and the UK were each valued at 1 million US dollars.
(b) The cost of water supply in Kuwait was 20 US dollars per gallon as compared with 0·25 dollars per gallon in the UK.

4 Is the national income per head lower in Morocco than in Ireland because the former enjoys a warm climate?

# Chapter 2
# Wants, Goods and Property Rights

The characteristics of the UK national income over time have been those of changing size and composition. Why has this been so? It has occurred because what has been produced has been in response to the wants of the community and, through foreign trade, the wants of other communities. Economists, we said in the previous chapter, study how men and women obtain their livelihood. What we concentrated on in that chapter was the size and composition of the things that constitute that livelihood. But we said nothing about the *wants* that dictated the types of goods and services bought, nor did we say anything about *production* which is the process by which things, undesirable in themselves, are transformed into things which are desirable. Production is the mechanism by which resources are transformed into goods which satisfy wants. Evidently we cannot produce everything immediately, for that would imply that Neolithic Man should have had a motor car and an aeroplane. In fact production is dogged by scarcity of knowledge, of time, and of materials, and because of the scarcity there must be choice. Economics, we have said, is the study of how men and women obtain a livelihood but at a more philosophical level economics is the study of choice, of what methods are used to obtain what kind of livelihood.

### The economic problem

Economists study all kinds of decisions; taking jobs, getting married, buying a house or car. The techniques of economic analysis are general and it is a mistake to think of economics as a subject with a specific area of inquiry; its usefulness lies in the possession of a method for the solution of problems of choice. And choice arises because innumerable wants are constrained by limited resources. Without scarcity there would be no need for decisions, no choice and life might be meaningless.

Natural resources are essential to existence and comprise the potentialities of Nature. Such resources are limited because the earth is not boundless. But being limited is not synonymous with scarcity. Worn tyres are not scarce because they are *not wanted*. Water in the Indian Ocean is limited but it is not scarce. Only if everyone demanded a million gallons of water per day from the Indian Ocean might scarcity exist. Nor is scarcity a property only of physical things – time is a scarce resource and life is not eternal; time must be allowed for eating, sleeping, work and leisure and so a choice must be made as to how to allocate time.

Goods are the link between wants and resources. Goods are derived from resources and are necessary to satisfy wants. Goods need not be physical things and often economists use the more abstract term, 'services'. A symphony is a good even though it cannot be measured or weighed. Bread is a good, a motor car is a good and so are the words of the orator. Scarce resources are used to produce goods but which goods and hence which resources are used will depend upon choice, for people will attempt to obtain those goods which yield the greatest satisfaction from given resources. Alternatives are ranked according to their capacity to fulfil the objective of the individual, firm or country. Objectives can refer to 'satisfaction', 'well-being', 'utility', 'profit', 'national prestige' or 'duty'. In exercising choice an individual (or firm or country) will try to be consistent. If a man prefers a house to a car and a car to an aeroplane he will be inconsistent if he prefers an aeroplane to a house.

Sometimes contradictions or inconsistencies do occur or appear to occur. In complex situations fraught with uncertainty, apparently inconsistent choices are sometimes made. There is lack of complete information and what appears to be contradictory behaviour may often be experimentation, an attempt to obtain more information.

Choice links wants to resources through the selection of goods. Out of the myriad of wants some are given priority and given the limitations of time and other resources some goods are chosen to satisfy those wants. How is the choice made? According to the economist it is made through the principle of choosing the cheapest good to satisfy a given set of wants. If two cars will equally satisfy the want to travel then the cheaper is bought.

## Wants

Because wants are so important and occupy a key position in economics it is useful to explore their nature and see what problems they present for economists.

Some wants are obvious – the need for food and drink stems from biological requirements. Others appear to be culturally determined – eating in cafés, watching football matches, going to pop festivals. And sometimes curiosity is the source of wants. Undoubtedly, the exploration of the deeper recesses of human behaviour is the task of the psychologist, but the economist has an interest in some of the more obvious aspects of wants. Two things attract his attention. First, there are the *cultural determinants of wants*. Secondly, there is the apparent existence of a *hierarchy of wants*.

Although economists cannot say why Britons like cricket and Americans like baseball, the notion that within communities there are certain needs, concerning which there is such universal agreement that they must be satisfied, is of use to the economist interested in making policy recommendations. If there is a general belief that no one should live in poverty then an economist may confidently propose various policies which redistribute income from the rich to the poor. If no such consensus exists then an economist can only record the existence of poverty and hope to play an educative role. The existence of a consensus can enable an economist to bridge the gap between *positive economics*, concerned with 'what is', and *normative economics*, concerned with 'what ought to be'.

The second aspect of wants that interests the economist is the commonplace observation that wants can be ordered, that there is a hierarchy of wants. Some wants, such as the need for food and drink, must be satisfied before others can be considered. This means that there is an irreducibility of wants in the sense that we must first satisfy some wants before attempting to satisfy others. This notion helps to explain why Americans can contemplate space flights whilst Asians must be preoccupied with food production. In exercising choice an individual, firm or country attempts to satisfy the greatest number of wants starting with the most important and going down the hierarchy.

The links between the wants in the hierarchy and the goods which satisfy them are illustrated in Figure 4. For simplicity we can number a person's wants, $W_1, \ldots, W_n$. Let us assume that his first requirement is drink and can be satisfied by water $G_1$. If we join $W_1$ and $G_1$ then we can say that there is a one-to-one correspondence between $W_1$ and $G_1$. This need not always be so. Consider his second need, food. It can be satisfied by meat, $G_2$ and potatoes, $G_3$. Hence we can join $W_2$ to $G_2$ and $G_3$. Meat and potatoes may be thought of as a composite good created out of two other goods. In a similar manner, a blue car, $G_4$, can satisfy his need for transport, $W_3$, and colour, $W_4$. Here we can notice that the primary want is travel and so a blue house would be unacceptable whereas a red car or green car would satisfy the more pressing need.

Why should we emphasize a trivial point concerning a blue car? The answer is that when people are asked why they made a particular purchase they often give what is an apparently trivial reason – 'because it is blue'. Such a reply seems frivolous, yet to draw such a conclusion would be misleading for what the answer implies is that a *blue* car satisfies the lesser want.

The existence of a hierarchy of wants provides us with some reasons why a consensus might not exist. If individuals are seeking to satisfy different wants then, given the existence of limited resources to satisfy those wants, there will be a conflict of interest which may be difficult to resolve. If one group of stock-broker citizens want fast urban motorways in order to get to and from the office then they may require a motorway to be built close to the houses of those who wish to live in the towns. General agreement can usually be reached on basic needs – food and shelter – but conflict arises over the satisfaction of low-order wants. Should land be used for roads, or pony-trekking, or bird-sanctuaries?

We can go a little further in our exploration of wants by observing that the satisfaction of wants usually involves human services as well as inanimate objects. Suppose a man wants to live in a well-educated society. This want, $W_5$, can be achieved by combining schools, $G_6$, with other people $H_1, \ldots, H_n$.

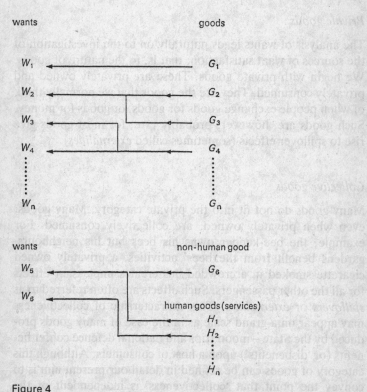

Figure 4

Again, we suppose that he likes congenial company, $W_6$, which can be satisfied by $H_2$, a one-to-one relationship which takes economics into the realms of love and marriage, and contrasts monogamy with polygamy, the aloof with the gregarious.

## The classification of goods

1 Private goods
2 Collective goods
    (a) Privately produced
    (b) Produced by the State
    (c) Free goods

### Private goods

The analysis of wants leads naturally on to the investigation of the sources of want satisfaction: that is, to the nature of goods. We begin with private goods. These are privately owned and privately consumed. They are the goods that we normally think of when people exchange goods for goods, or goods for money. Such goods are, however, probably rare, for most goods give rise to spillover effects (sometimes called *externalities*).

### Collective goods

Many goods do not fit into the private category. Many goods, even when privately owned, are collectively consumed. For example, the bee-keeper owns his bees but his neighbours' gardens benefit from the bees' activities; a privately owned cigarette smoked in a crowded bus creates unpleasant effects for all the other passengers. Such effects are often referred to as *spillovers* or *externalities*. This characteristic of collectiveness may appear on a grand scale as in the case of many goods produced by the State – moon trips and national defence confer benefits (or 'disbenefits') upon a host of consumers. Although this category of goods can be refined in detail our present aim is to convey the point that 'collectiveness' is independent of the actual number of consumers – the good may be consumed simultaneously by two consumers or by two hundred.

## Free goods

A special class of commodities is the so-called free goods. They cost nothing to produce and represent the free gifts of nature. But because they are free they are often squandered. Rubbish is dumped in rivers causing pollution and a scarcity of clean, pure water. Wild birds are slaughtered and wild flowers are picked indiscriminately. Into this category we also place the stately homes, English literature and other works of art, for they form, as much as the countryside, part of the cultural heritage which is shared by all. It is, in fact, interesting to observe the long line of distinguished economists who have sought to sustain the Arts largely through pressing for state financing and protection.

## Reality and the politics of economists

Where does reality lie? Does it lie in assuming that the world is dominated by private goods which are privately owned and privately consumed and traded through markets? Pick up almost any economics textbook and the impression given is of a world of private goods. This emphasis may be due to the fact that economics, as a distinct discipline, emerged at a time when the market was beginning to seem more important in everyday life. Moreover, it was also the period when individualism became the byword so that market economics tended to colour people's political and social thinking. Economists may be conservatives, but, if they are, then that arises not from their consciousness of the difficulties of making social changes, but from a presumption that reality is a world of private goods subject to some peripheral interference by the state.

Yet it is possible to see reality as a world of collective goods; a world in which people collectively seek to prevent standards of health, education and nutrition falling below certain social minima; a world in which many goods – neighbourliness, wonderful scenery – are not provided by markets, and where markets are continually crumbling under the forces prompting monopoly. Economic history suggests that the market economy has existed for only two hundred of the thousands of years of mankind's existence, and from such a vantage point an economist might become a socialist or a communist.

The fascination of economics lies in its unravelling of the ways in which people cope with the problems of spillovers. For two similar goods may be classified differently according to their immediate environments. Thus, the words on this page are private goods in so far as the owner of this book has established a unique property right. But if these same words were to be read aloud to an audience then, in that context, they would constitute a collective good (or 'nuisance' depending upon the tastes of the audience). Furthermore, the right to read this book may be disputed by some if it is felt to be seditious, pornographic and 'contrary to faith and morals'. Decisions concerning private and collective goods strike therefore at social behaviour and, in particular, at that faith known as liberalism which believes that each should be allowed to do that which enriches his own personality, but then discovers that this might mean subjugating the personality of another.

The simplest solution might be to deem all goods collective, the right to their use being vested in the community as a whole. But, of itself, that may be no solution. Should everyone have, for example, the untrammelled right to consume public property? But how should the state decide on the allocation of shares? And how should the international community deal with the radioactive dust which falls on one country when another explodes nuclear bombs?

The alternative is to deem all goods private, and hope that people find ways of coping with the spillovers. Thus, the enjoyment obtained from the view of a neighbour's garden may be obtained without having to pay for the privilege. And the neighbour may not be annoyed. Many delights in life are, in fact, obtained free of charge and life would be very intolerable if we had to pay for all pleasure. What would we think and feel about a world in which everyone put a high hedge around his garden? Tolerance of goods not paid for also extends to some nuisances which are received without payment. For most of the post-war period the Japanese have been more tolerant of smoke than the British. Evidently, the differences in tolerance are related to the hierarchy of wants. The Japanese have been prepared to put up with smoke in order to satisfy their higher wants. The British, having earlier solved the material problems of the nation, have sought to satisfy their desires for a healthy environment.

But when nuisances become intolerable then there will be private or collective attempts to eliminate them. Thus in the case of road accidents motorists may agree to compensate each other for injuries if the injured party can prove his claim. Or a householder may buy some waste land adjoining his house in order to prevent an ugly block of flats being built there. He may even pay the builder to build elsewhere. There are, however, more complex situations. Supposing the motorist fails in his claim for damages and, because of his injuries, cannot work. Should he therefore be allowed to starve? Not if the state is obliged to guarantee a minimum income.

In the bewildering assortment of options there will be a tendency to look for the least costly solution. Meanwhile we can classify some mechanisms for want satisfaction.

## Mechanisms for want satisfaction

Looking at the kinds of wants, and the goods which satisfy those wants, forces us to realize that the arrangements for obtaining those goods can also be complex. We can for simplicity list them and briefly consider their merits.

### Self-sufficiency

By self-sufficiency individuals can presumably satisfy their wants though they may do so in an inefficient manner. Indeed, in most cases self-sufficiency is inefficient. Who but the egoist can satisfy his own need for congenial company?

## Theft

Robbery can be a means of supplementing resources and imperialism may be its highest expression. But it is impossible to maintain a stable society when 'life is nasty, brutish and short'. Safety of personal possessions, including life, necessitates law and order and defence and involves making agreements with others.

## Charity

Suppose we wish to see other people as well fed and decently clothed as ourselves. We could give them the means to purchase food and clothing. Charity has always been a means of satisfying wants though it may not always be successful. Giving a poor man money may allow him to buy alcohol whilst giving him food might hurt his self-respect.

## Trade

This is the commonest method of satisfying wants when a person's own resources are insufficient. Such trade may be state or private, formal or informal, simple or elaborate. It can range from children swapping toys to millionaires buying diamonds.

Trade requires markets – means whereby buyers and sellers can make offers. Such markets may be physical locations – the schoolyard, the corner shop or the high street – but physical location and physical contact are not essential as long as communications can be established. The telephone links buyers and sellers in different countries and people can reply to newspaper advertisements in complete anonymity.

## Collectivization

Some of the wants we have examined cannot be satisfied by any of the methods we have so far considered. How can anyone buy a well-educated society? Slavery is not permitted in democratic societies and if someone provides education for others, how can he be sure that they will not migrate? Whilst if he gives them money they may spend it on alcohol. How can a community ensure that its countryside is preserved from speculative builders? These kinds of problems may require different solutions from those so far presented, they may require an institutional arrangement different from charity or the market.

Collectivization can imply compulsory consumption or an opportunity to reject the collective good. Fluoride in drinking-water cannot be avoided without at the same time abstaining from drinking water. On the other hand, for many collective goods their level of supply suggests that most people regard the costs of additional units as exceeding the costs of alternative private goods. Thus most people are willing to pay for a collective police force but still put locks on their doors. Similarly the provision of a public fire protection service is not a sufficient safeguard against fire and most people still check the safety of electrical and gas appliances and coal fires.

Collectivization need not imply the invocation of the State. Most communities abound in clubs – voluntary societies – through which citizens provide a limited number of people with collective goods. Golf clubs, football clubs, mothers' meetings and youth clubs are examples of such private institutions designed to provide collective goods such as friendship.

## Property rights and commitment

Goods and services can be allocated by a variety of methods. Some assign the rights to assets (*property rights*) to the state, some to individuals and some deny any right but that exerted by force. Which method is chosen to allocate goods and services depends upon people's preferences. There is a satisfaction from the methods by which goods are received which may be as important as the goods themselves. People may have a commitment to a particular economic and social organization and this commitment may be responsible for that organization's efficiency.

## Summary

We began from the proposition that wants are central to economic choice and consequently attempted to classify wants. We came to the conclusion that there was a hierarchy of wants – some wants had to be satisfied before others could be contemplated. From a classification of wants we were led to a classification of the goods which satisfy those wants. Here we distinguished between private and collective goods. Finally, and inevitably, we were led to an analysis of the means by which goods can be brought into contact with wants.

## Questions

1 What is the economic problem?

2 What is the hierarchy of wants?

3 Is Westminster Abbey a collective good?

4 'Medical care is a personal-consumption good and should not be made into a collective good.' Discuss.

# Chapter 3
# Production

All our wants cannot be satisfied unless the means are available and Andrew Marvell's rebuke to his coy mistress for her assumption that time and space were unlimited is as relevant to all other human activities as it is to love-making. There just simply are not enough resources to satisfy all our needs. Why study the movement of national income, population or foreign trade in a world of abundance? Consider Figure 5. It depicts the amounts of two goods, which a certain community produced, beer and cheese, or beer and education – it does not matter whether one is a private good and the other a collective good since resources will be necessary to produce both. With total resources available either $OA$ of beer or $OB$ of cheese can be produced. We might also suppose that various combinations of beer and cheese can also be produced and that the total number of combinations, the set of outputs of beer and cheese, which can be produced lie within the area $AOB$ or on the frontier $AB$. The line $AB$ is the frontier of production possibilities – *the production-possibilities curve*: it is impossible to produce beyond it at, say, $X$ or $Y$ because there are not the resources available to do so. Within $AOB$, therefore, is the set of all attainable combinations of beer and cheese that can be produced. Beyond $AB$ lies the set of unattainable production combinations.

It would be possible to produce *within* the frontier, say at $U$, but that would imply leaving some resources idle or in more

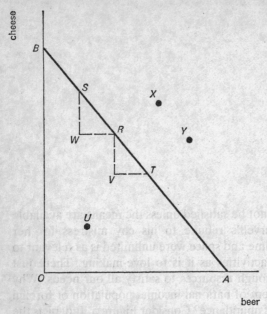

Figure 5  The production-possibility curve

general terms that resources were being used inefficiently. Even though the community's resources could take it on to the frontier, the actual output-combination produced may be that given by the point *U* because managers behave stupidly or workers are lazy, or because the institutional arrangements in society are such as to prevent the frontier being attained. Many countries, in fact, seem to be capable of producing more than they do. A glance at Figure 5 reveals that the United Kingdom has had over the post-war period unemployed labour which could presumably have been put to producing more goods, were the institutional arrangements for employing labour efficient. Just why idle resources do occur is a question which Part Four seeks to resolve.

But assuming that a community is on the frontier, say at *R*, what would be the implication of moving to either *S* or *T*? From Figure 5 we can see that such a move would mean a change in the amounts of beer and cheese produced and available for consumption. A move to $S$ would give rise to more cheese and less beer whilst a move to $T$ would mean more beer and less cheese. However, the interesting point about these switches of production is that they always result in a constant rate of transformation of one commodity into the other. Because line $AB$ has a constant slope then the resources that are capable of producing one pint of beer will always be capable of producing, say, one pound of cheese.

We can express this point a little differently. Starting anywhere on the frontier the cost of obtaining an extra bottle of beer or pound of cheese is the cheese or beer foregone. This cost in terms of the alternative foregone is known as *opportunity cost*. For the economist, cost is not the money spent on goods and services but the other goods and services that have been rejected.[1]

In terms of Figure 5 the giving up of $TV$ of beer enables the community to obtain $RV$ of cheese, and giving up an additional $RW$ of beer can result in the acquisition of $SW$ of cheese. Since the slope of $AB$ is constant then the opportunity cost of cheese in terms of beer is always constant (the ratios $RV/TV$ and $SW/RW$ are equal).

## Increasing cost

Constant costs are not found in all situations. It is in fact more usual to find increasing costs. Thus in Figure 6 the production-possibility curve is concave to the origin which means that in order to obtain additional units of beer successively more units of cheese must be sacrificed: hence $CD$ is longer than $AB$ even though the lengths $BC$ and $DE$ are equal. Why should this be so?

If we think about constant costs we come to the conclusion that it implies either that resources are equally efficient in all activities or that the proportions in which resources are employed are the same in all activities. Let us consider each of

1. Strictly speaking it is the benefits derived from consuming goods and services that are compared. This is gone into in some detail in Chapter 11.

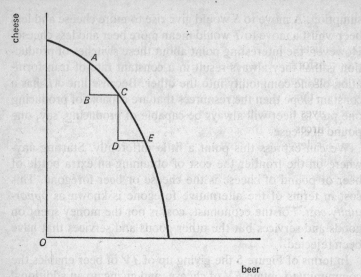

Figure 6

these assumptions in turn. It is unlikely that men employed in
breweries will be equally efficient in producing cheese. If the
community decides to give up beer in order to have more
cheese, then it may find that after a while the cost of obtaining
more cheese rises as the more skilful brewery workers move
into cheese production, and the losses of beer become cumu-
latively greater.

It is, however, unnecessary to assume that resources differ in
efficiency. Suppose that under ideal conditions beer requires
three men and two units of natural resources for hop production, whereas cheese requires two men and five units of natural
resources (cows and land), then whenever we switch from beer
to cheese we always have more men than we need (plus 1) and
too few natural resources (minus 3), and though we attempt to
substitute men for natural resources there is a limit to substitution. This problem lies at the basis of the celebrated 'law' of
diminishing returns. But let us examine this law in the context
of the general laws of production.

## Laws of production

Economists are interested in the efficiency with which resources are transformed into goods. This is partly a question of engineering, partly one of picking out the most efficient combinations – those that lie on the frontier – and then selecting the one which gives the desired combination of goods, given the prices of resources and the community's desires. For the moment, however, let us look at the engineering issue.

Economists tend to express the nature of the production process – the transformation of resources into goods – by means of a simple equation

$$Q = f(x_1, x_2, \ldots, x_n; T). \hspace{3cm} 1$$

This shorthand expression says that output, $Q$, is a function, $f$, of the inputs $(x_1, \ldots, x_n)$ and the prevailing state of technology or 'know-how', $T$. Both inputs and output are flows per unit of time. It may be that $x_1$ is a machine and we have therefore to imagine that so much of the machine is used up in each period. Accountants refer to this 'using-up' as depreciation and one of the accountant's difficult tasks is to measure this depreciation.

The most important item in the equation is the $f$-sign – representing 'function' – which tells us that there exists a systematic relationship between inputs and output. But what kind of systematic relationship exists? We can distinguish three general questions.

1 What happens to output as all inputs are increased by the same proportion?

2 Can the proportions in which inputs are employed be varied?

3 What happens to output when only some of the inputs are increased?

To the first question one is tempted to answer that if all inputs are increased by the same percentage then output will increase by this same percentage. But this sentence contains a trap for the unwary. 'Doubling' should not be confused with 'dupli-

cation'. It is always possible to double output by having two factories (instead of one) of the same size. But that is not what
doubling means in this context. Rather, it refers to the *scale* of
operations, that is, to an increase in the sizes of the inputs
rather than to an increase in the number of inputs of constant
size. We are interested in what happens when there is a *mor-
phological change* – of what happens if ants become ten times
their normal size, or the Soviet Union six times its present size.
What then happens if all inputs are increased in scale by the
same percentage? The answer to this question does not seem to
be clear-cut. If all the dimensions of a blast furnace are increased by the same percentage then the volume (and hence
output) increases by a greater percentage. If all the dimensions
of a plough are increased by the same percentage then the motive to pull it through the soil may have to be increased by a
greater percentage. The problem is whether or not constant
returns to scale exist.

If the scale of each input is increased by some proportion, $k$,
then *constant returns to scale* prevail if output rises by the same
proportion $k$.

In practice increasing or decreasing returns to scale may
occur because of the existence of fixed factors. If all the inputs
of a factory are increased tenfold we should expect to find workers eighteen metres high. The fact that we do not puts obstacles
in the way of a ready acceptance of the notion of constant
returns to scale. The ability to vary the proportions in which resources can be used is also something over which there is dis-
agreement. Taxis and taxi-drivers seem to be available only in
the proportion of one-to-one. But this may be an illusion since
it is possible to have one driver for day duties and one for night
duties. Variable proportions seem more likely if we allow
enough time to transform equipment. Bulldozers can be converted into spades if we decide not to replace worn-out bulldozers. If then we allow for variations in proportions what
happens to output as only one input is increased in amount?
This is the question answered by the celebrated *law of
diminishing returns*.

## The law of diminishing returns

We begin with a definition and the conditions under which the law is said to operate:

*If the input of units of one resource increases while the input of other resources remains unchanged then beyond a certain point output can only increase at a diminishing rate.*

*Conditions:*

1 Other inputs must be held constant, otherwise the problem is one of returns to scale.

2 The state of technical knowledge must not change.

3 The proportions in which resources can be combined must be capable of variation.

4 All units of the variable resource are homogeneous.

**Table 5**

| Men (a) | Total output (b) | Average product (b/a) | Marginal product |
|---|---|---|---|
| 0 | 0 | 0 | 0 |
| 1 | 8 | 8 | 8 |
| 2 | 22 | 11 | 14 |
| 3 | 37 | 12·33 | 15 |
| 4 | 50 | 12·50 | 13 |
| 5 | 60 | 12 | 10 |
| 6 | 68 | 11·33 | 8 |
| 7 | 74 | 10·57 | 6 |
| 8 | 80 | 10 | 6 |
| 9 | 85 | 9·44 | 5 |
| 10 | 90 | 9·00 | 5 |
| 11 | 88 | 8 | −2 |
| 12 | 84 | 7 | −4 |
| 13 | 78 | 6 | −6 |

The workings of the law are illustrated by Table 5. We assume that there exists an acre of land which is to be cultivated by an ever-increasing number of men. One man can produce eight bushels of wheat whilst two men can produce twenty-two bushels. In addition to the total product there are two other measures of output change which need to be observed. The first, *average product*, is self-explanatory. The second, *marginal product*, is a new concept and may be defined as the contribution which *each additional man* makes to total output. Generalizing, we may say: marginal product is the addition to total product caused by the addition of one more unit of the variable resources.

If we plot the data contained in Table 5 we can obtain Figure 7 which brings out three interesting stages in the operations of diminishing returns.

*Stage 1.* There is an increase in the product due to the increase in the number of men employed. This is because the area to be cultivated is large in relation to the number of men. Indeed, rather than attempt to cultivate the whole area the men might decide to farm a small portion. The first stage ends with the average product being at its maximum. Note that when the average product reaches its maximum, the marginal product – the increase in output due to an increase by one unit of the variable input labour – cuts the average product curve from above.

*Stage 2.* This comprises the section in which both the average and marginal product are falling though the total product is increasing. The second stage ends when the marginal product of labour is zero.

*Stage 3.* This is the opposite of stage 1, as there are now too many men, whereas in stage 1 there was too much land. Stage 3 is unlikely to occur in practice except by accident or ignorance.

The reason for the curves in Figure 7 not fitting perfectly to the description of production stages is that they are constructed

2. The use of a (discrete) arithmetic example causes the peak of average product not to coincide with the marginal intersection, and the total curve to fall before marginal product becomes negative.

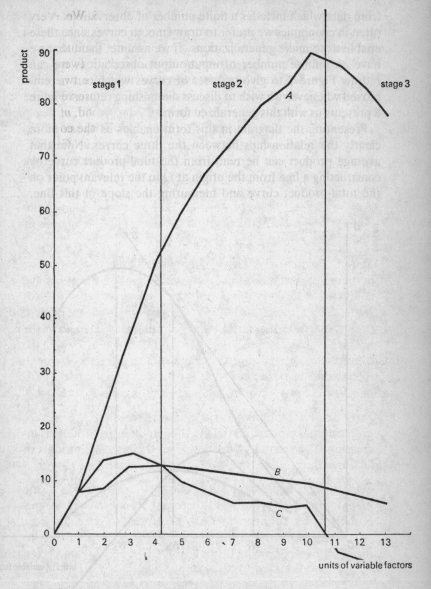

Figure 7 (a) Total-product curve. (b) Average-product curve.
(c) Marginal-product curve

from data which includes a finite number of observations. Very often in economics we prefer to draw smooth curves since these enable us to make generalizations. If we assume, then, that we have an infinite number of input/output observations we can redraw Figure 7 to give us a set of curves which can be employed whenever we wish to discuss diminishing returns. Figure 8 presents us with this generalized form.

Presenting the diagram in this form enables us to see more clearly the relationships between the three curves. Note that average product can be read from the total-product curve by constructing a line from the origin at $O$ to the relevant point on the total-product curve and measuring the slope of this line.

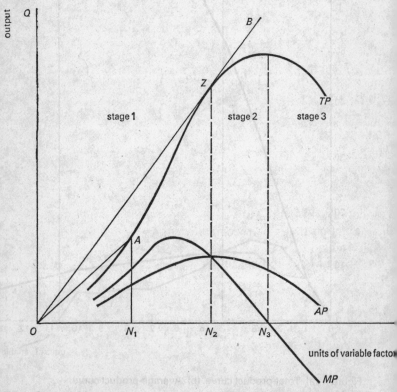

Figure 8

Thus if we wish to know the value of the average product when $ON_1$ units of variable factor are employed the tan of angle $AON_1$ gives the answer $AN_1/ON_1$ (equals total output divided by the number of variable units employed). Stage 1 ends, therefore, when the slope of such a line to the origin is at a maximum, i.e. when it is tangential to the total-product curve ($OB$ is tangential to $TP$ at point $Z$).

Marginal product, on the other hand, is given by the slope of the total-product curve itself, i.e. this slope is measured by a small change in output divided by a small change in the number of units of variable factor employed $\Delta Q/\Delta N$. Knowing this enables us to note the features of the ending of stage 1, direct from the total-product curve. Stage 1 ends at point $Z$ on the total-product curve and at this point the slope of the line $OB$ equals the slope of the total-product curve – average product equals marginal product.

Finally, we can also note the feature of the end of stage 2 direct from the total-product curve. Stage 2 ends when $ON_3$ units of factor are employed. At this level of employment the total-product curve reaches its maximum point and then turns downwards, i.e. at an employment level $ON_3$ the slope of $TP$ is zero – marginal product is zero.

### Indivisibility and fixed factors

At this point we should note an important qualification. A fixed factor should not be confused with an indivisible factor. It is perfectly possible for factors to be purchased in fixed amounts, lumps, but it is also possible for these lumps to be divisible. Thus, a field may contain 1000 acres but can be sub-divided and worked in one-acre plots. Hence, constant returns to scale may obtain with each acre being worked by one man. Increasing returns may occur when six men are applied to each acre and diminishing returns may not occur until ten men are employed on each acre. Similarly, a factory is divisible in terms of day and night usage. The effect of such divisibility in a fixed factor is to yield constant average and marginal costs over a considerable range of output and therefore to modify stage 1 of Figure 7.

The mechanics of the production function are interesting but at this stage we will confine our attention to two important applications of the diminishing returns principle. Later, we shall take up the implications of divisibility and fixity in the chapters on costs and the firm.

### Farm and factory

An understanding of the nature of the production function and the law of diminishing returns helps us to understand a phenomenon which intrigued economists who witnessed the emergence of the Industrial Revolution. They drew a distinction between agriculture, which they believed was subject to decreasing returns, and manufacturing, which they thought was subject to increasing returns. What was the reasoning behind this distinction? The principal source of energy in agriculture is the sun and two consequences follow from this dependence. First, the flow of solar energy cannot be varied by man because the stock inherent in the sun lies beyond his reach. Secondly, the flow of solar energy to the earth varies with the movement of the earth round the sun: only along the equator does the flow tend to remain constant. It follows from the variation in sunlight that man cannot alter the nature of the interdependence of the various agricultural activities. Sowing must precede reaping: sowing and reaping cannot be reversed in time sequence nor can they be carried on simultaneously. So increasing the number of men on the land may not have much effect on output because of the fixity of solar energy and the land receiving that energy. More men may simply mean more idle men.

Contrast agriculture with manufacturing. In manufacturing, the energy sources are coal and oil – fossil fuels whose stocks lie embedded in the earth and since the stocks are accessible and can be mined, then the flow of the energy input can be varied. As a result the various processes that go together to make a manufacturing product can be carried on almost simultaneously. In the car industry, tyres, batteries, wheels, bodies and upholstery are being simultaneously produced. It is in fact possible to see all the stages in the production of a motor car in one period of time – a possibility denied to the agricultural economist.

What made possible the simultaneous production of all parts, and the possibility of doubling all inputs and producing more than double the output? The switch to fossil fuels was one cause. The other was the level of demand. As the level of demand for manufacturing goods rose it became possible to increase the degree of specialization of production at each stage. Some workers, as Adam Smith observed, would specialize in producing pin heads whilst others would specialize in sharpening the points of pins. This specialization led to an increase in efficiency and output at each stage. Hence the famous dictum of Adam Smith: *the division of labour is limited by the extent of the market*. And the classic example was the cotton industry. As demand rose the interdependent stages of production – spinning, weaving and finishing – became detached and separate producing units were established.[3]

## Optimum population size and diminishing returns

One of the more obvious applications of the law of diminishing returns is to the question: how many people can be supported by a country's resources? The amount of resources available combined with the population and a given technology serve to determine a country's standard of living. Is it, then, possible to talk of an *optimum* population size? If so, then this optimum must be defined with reference to a subsistence living standard. Thus, given that subsistence is guaranteed, an optimum population size might be defined as one which maximizes output per head, i.e. average product. In terms of Figure 9, this population level would be *OM*.

An alternative definition might be in terms of the maximum

3. Note that it is the industry and not the firm which is subject to increasing returns. The firm will ultimately encounter diminishing returns for two reasons. First, individual technical units – boilers and so forth – will exhibit diminishing returns. Secondly, the firm as a whole will face diminishing returns because management (the decision-making unit) will be a fixed factor.

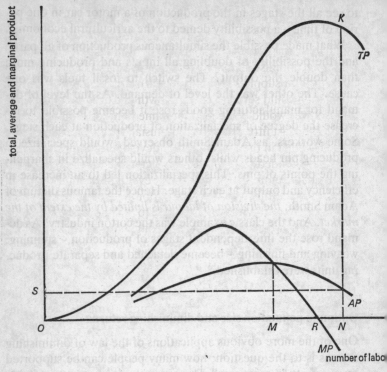

Figure 9

population that a country can support. This optimum would be reached when, on an equal sharing of community output, each worker receives a subsistence reward. If subsistence is less than maximum average product then population size will be greater than *OM* in Figure 9. However, a country which accepts this definition of 'optimum' may be courting social disaster. Suppose, for example, that the subsistence level for each person is *OS* in Figure 9. Permitting population to rise to *ON* then pushes marginal product below zero. Each newborn child will make a negative contribution to community output. In an economy where subsistence is the norm, social tension will be high and negative contributors are unlikely to be welcome.

How relevant to contemporary societies is the relationship

between population and resources that w have just explored? In the eighteenth and nineteenth centuries the spectre of over-population was a constant nightmare. Malthus, an eighteenth-century economist, had predicted that population growth would outstrip food supplies (Malthus, 1970). This tendency to over-population could serve to check growth and accumulation since all resources would be needed for immediate consumption.

Over the last fifty years the Malthusian spectre seems to have been dispelled in the UK and other developed countries. Inventions have tended to push the product curve upwards and outwards as in Figure 9. Recently, however, the quality of life in terms of space for living and recreation has come under attack and, looking to the future, imported food supplies may well be jeopardized as consumption rises throughout the world.

## Mauritius: a case study

It is, however, the underdeveloped countries which face the Malthusian problem in its original form. Consider Mauritius (Meade, 1961), a small island in the Pacific, which is virtually a one-commodity economy producing sugar. During the post-war period her population has expanded enormously, largely as a result of the reduction in the incidence of malaria. Migration is difficult since many countries now have immigration controls and so Mauritius is almost in the situation of having a population of *ON* as in Figure 9. For such countries population control is inevitable but there may still have to be an abandonment of a wage system (that is, of paying workers according to their marginal product as in Figure 9), and a move towards giving everyone some share of the total product.

## Marginal-product doctrine: a preview

In previous sections we have looked at the problem of over-population and the wage system. As we shall see later in Part Seven contemporary economic analysis tends to suggest that resources are paid in a wage system according to the value of the marginal product. In other words, if all men are alike then all men will be paid at the same rate as the last man employed since to pay more would be to incur losses. Now we have just seen that this doctrine breaks down when what a man might be paid would be less than the cost of his subsistence. This then is a criticism of the applicability of the doctrine. It says that in certain circumstances *men must be paid more than the marginal product*.

Later in Part Seven we shall encounter a body of theory that suggests that *men are paid less than their marginal product*. Briefly, the argument stresses the point that men are paid a subsistence wage whose value may be dictated by sociological factors, and that the difference between subsistence and the value of men's work constitutes a surplus or profit which goes partially to finance production before output emerges, and partly to the controllers of industry as their consumption. This theory raises many questions concerning the surplus which is necessary to finance production and development and these issues will be dealt with in Part Seven (notably Chapter 26). In the meantime it should be borne in mind that nothing has been said about the financing of production.

## Immigration

The law of diminishing returns is also useful in considering the problem of immigration. In 1968 the British Government passed an Act which proposed stricter control of the entry of Commonwealth immigrants into the UK. This Act occasioned a great deal of controversy both before and after its passage. Supporters of the Act pointed to the outbreaks of racial violence in America and to the social tensions in areas where immigrants have settled in Britain, notably London and the Midlands. On the other hand critics of the Act said that it discriminated against people from certain countries and that Britain should be free to all who wish to enter.

Although the question of immigration is fraught with ethical and political issues the economist can present some light on the problem. An influx of people operates to increase both the labour force and the consuming public. The question is which is the stronger force? Immigrants provide a source of immediate labour from adults but they also bring dependents. In attempting to acclimatize themselves and to ensure the care of their dependents, immigrants draw on the available private and social services such as housing, education and health. Moreover, since they often reside in working-class areas they may aggravate the existing problems of slum clearance, and the poor educational and health services that are available in such areas. On the other hand, they provide a willing labour force to cover shortages in transport and health services though this may prevent new thinking on the provision of these services by, for example, operating one-man buses and eliminating many unskilled jobs through mechanization. What therefore needs to be known is how important are these opposing forces, as well as the tastes of the population regarding the goal of a multi-racial society.

## Automation

Inventions are changes in technical knowledge which result either in the production of new commodities or new methods of producing existing goods. In the case of the latter, where it becomes possible to produce a commodity with fewer resources than previously, economists distinguish between three kinds of inventions:

1 Labour-saving inventions, where there is a saving in the amount of labour required to produce a commodity;

2 Capital-saving inventions which reduce the amount of capital needed to produce a good;

3 Neutral inventions which have no bias towards capital saving or labour saving but result in an overall reduction in the amounts of all factors required.

Most interest has been shown in the existence and strength of labour-saving inventions because they reduce the demands for labour. Indeed in the post-war period a particular form of labour-saving invention has been called automation because it is thought to dispense not merely with muscular strength but also with intelligence.

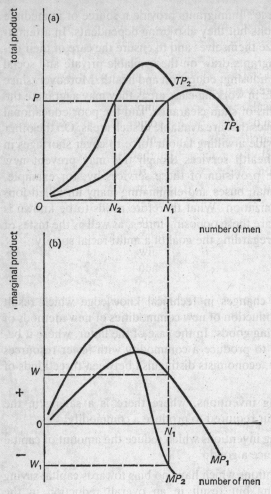

Figure 10

Figure 10a shows the vertical displacement of the total-product curve as a result of a labour-saving invention. So output $OP$ requires $N_1N_2$ fewer workers. In Figure 10b, the effect on the marginal-product curve is shown. The $MP$ curve is pulled towards the left. Now suppose that the labour force before the change was $ON_1$ and was paid at the wage rate $OW$. After the invention the labour force could only find employment at a wage of minus $OW_1$: in other words, workers would have to pay for the privilege of having a job!

Could such a state of affairs occur and what remedies could the economist recommend? In the early 1980s it would appear that technological or structural unemployment had occurred as a result of seven decades of technological change. The effects of prolonged research and development were masked in the twenties and thirties by the slump and in the fifties, sixties and seventies by inflation. New inventions reduced the demand for unskilled labour but governments kept up the demand for such labour by increasing aggregate money demand. The resulting full employment strengthened the forces resisting change in the developed countries but not in some of the developing countries, such as Japan, Hong Kong, Taiwan and South Korea. The result was that in the early 1980s when governments tried to reduce inflation and improve efficiency they found themselves saddled with obsolete industries and workers and also working populations swollen by the baby booms of the 1960s.

At existing wage levels it is difficult to employ all those seeking jobs. So the solution would seem to be to reduce wages. But if wages are reduced then there might have to be income supplements out of state social security schemes in order to prevent poverty. And even if wages were reduced it might be doubtful if many older workers would be re-employed. Hence, there is a problem of whether those in work could provide adequate pensions to those out of work and retired.

## Production and pollution

So far we have ignored a topic of the moment – pollution. Productive processes produce 'bads' as well as goods and how much importance we attach to bads depends upon which wants we are seeking to satisfy. When, as in the underdeveloped countries today or nineteenth-century Britain, people are seeking to satisfy basic needs then bads will be ignored and tolerated. However, once basic wants are satisfied then pollution –

the production of bads – is considered to be a problem. Moreover, the tremendous technological advances made in the Western World have now created a situation in which Man is very capable of exterminating himself. Of necessity, he must take account of the effect of his actions on the environment.

The production function, which was introduced at the beginning of this chapter, must be modified to take account of pollutants:

$$(Q_1, Q_2) = f(x_1, x_2, \ldots, x_n; T). \qquad\qquad 2$$

What we have done in equation **2** is to distinguish goods, $Q_1$, from bads, $Q_2$, which are jointly produced in the production process.

Figure 11 shows the typical system of production in an economy. This system is an *open system* in the sense that the production process delivers output to agents outside itself. Households demand goods and services from the production units, called firms, and households supply the firms with resources. In addition, both firms and households derive resources from the environment and deposit other materials (bads) into the environment. The environment is then conceived of as the repository of all free resources, that is resources not owned by anyone and which are initially in excess supply. Eventually, however, this state of affairs disappears. As economies progress, and production increases, the environment becomes depleted of resources which are useful.

The bads that are produced in advanced economies are in fact

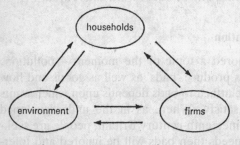

Figure 11

extraordinarily varied and complex: households may produce rubbish (paper, plastic containers), sewage, smoke and too many people! Firms may produce rubbish, noxious chemicals, scrap dumps, etc. How bads are reduced involves consideration of social institutions and rules of conduct that people develop. The citizens of a community may either tax or fine polluters; or cultivate good manners, implying that it is a social offence to have smoky garden fires and radios playing too loudly.

## Summary

We have examined the determinants of production and in doing so have implied limits to the consumption possibilities of a community. We might also have added that the laws of production also serve to limit the consumption possibilities of the individual since his skills dictate his output. But we observed in Chapter 1 that it was possible for a country (and presumably an individual) to go beyond their production possibilities through trade, and for them to enlarge their production possibilities through accumulation and growth. These two topics – trade and growth – are the subject matter of the subsequent chapters.

## Questions

1 What is the production-possibilities curve?

2 What arguments could you produce against the idea of constant returns to scale?

3 'But for the law of diminishing returns all the world's food could be grown in a flower pot.' Comment.

4 What are the main features of the three stages of production?

5 What relationships between the average and marginal products arise as output increases?

6 Is the concept of an optimum population ambiguous?

7 What effect will inventions have on the production function and the demand for labour?

8 Scotia has 1500 miners seeking employment in the three pits

still in operation. The total output of each pit depends upon the number of miners employed as follows:

| Miners employed | Total output (thousand tons) | | |
|---|---|---|---|
| | Pit A | Pit B | Pit C |
| 300 | 95 | 85 | 85 |
| 400 | 120 | 100 | 90 |
| 500 | 130 | 110 | 125 |
| 600 | 138 | 118 | 150 |
| 700 | 146 | 122 | 170 |
| 800 | 153 | 125 | 180 |
| 900 | 160 | 128 | 189 |
| 1000 | 165 | 130 | 195 |

What is the greatest output of coal that can be raised with an optimum distribution of the 1500 miners between the three pits?

9 If towns produce something called 'urbanism' and nations produce something called 'nationalism', what factors limit the size of towns and nations?

# Chapter 4
# Exchange and Trade

In the previous chapter we indicated that a country could not consume beyond its productive potential, as illustrated by its production-possibility curve. But we normally observe countries, and even individuals, consuming goods for which they do not have productive potential. The UK imports bananas, timber and oil in quantities which are larger than she might be able to produce. Teachers of economics possess motor cars even though they might lack the ability to produce such complicated pieces of machinery. Evidently then it is possible to escape the confines of the production-possibility curve through trade.

Trade arises for a variety of reasons and the simple explanation, put forward by David Ricardo (1772–1825) in the nineteenth century, is that trade arises because of differences in opportunity cost or *comparative advantage*.

Countries, and even individuals and regions, will produce and sell those goods and services in which they have a relative (comparative) advantage. They buy those goods and services in which they have a relative (comparative) disadvantage.

We can illustrate this thesis by means of a simple arithmetic example. Suppose that we have two countries which can produce differing amounts of food and clothing with their resources. Country 1, we may suppose, can produce *either* 600 units of food *or* 500 units of clothing *or* any combination of food and clothing as long as it is prepared to give up six units of food for five units of clothing. In contrast, Country 2 can produce *either* 1100 units of food or 600 units of clothing *or* any combination of food and clothing as long as it is prepared to give up eleven units of food for six units of clothing. These production possibilities are set out in Table 6 below.

These production possibilities can also be illustrated by means of the production-possibility diagrams we introduced in the previous chapter (Figure 12).

**Table 6**

|  | Production possibilities | |
| --- | --- | --- |
|  | Food | Clothing |
| Country 1 | 600 | 500 |
| Country 2 | 1100 | 600 |

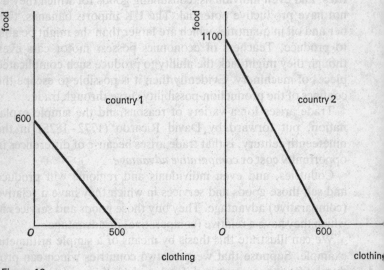

Figure 12

Three points should be noted. First, Country 2 can produce more of both food and clothing than can Country 1. Country 2 has an absolute advantage in the production of both goods. Secondly, the slopes of the production-possibility curves are constant: in Country 1 six units of food always cost five units of clothing, and in Country 2 eleven units of food always cost six units of clothing. Thirdly, though Country 2 has an absolute advantage in the production of both goods she has a relative advantage only in the production of food since one unit of food costs only 0·54 units of cloth, while in Country 1 one unit of food costs 0·83 units of cloth. Hence we can establish the following proposition:

Although Country 2 has an *absolute advantage* in the production of both goods she has a *comparative advantage* only in the production of food and so she may be prepared to trade with Country 1. Trade may be mutually beneficial.

The existence of different opportunity costs within each country means that it is possible for each country to gain through trade. If Country 1 could trade clothing with Country 2 at some rate which would give her more than six units of food for each five units of clothing, and if Country 2 could trade food with Country 1 at a rate which would give her more than six units of clothing for each eleven units of food, both countries would be better off. What this implies is that the rate at which they

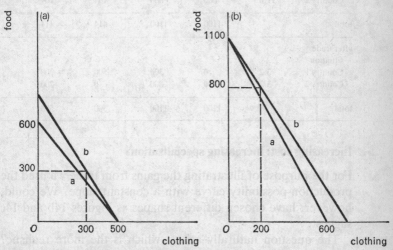

Figure 13 (a) pre-trade consumption possibilities.
(b) post-trade consumption possibilities

must trade goods should be different from the rates at which they trade domestically.

In Figure 13 we assume that both countries are willing to trade at a rate of three units of food for two units of clothing. This allows Country 1 to specialize in producing 500 units of clothing and exchanging some 200 units of clothing for 300 units of food. Country 2 specializes in producing 1100 units of food and exchanges 300 units for 200 units of clothing. The production and consumption possibilities before and after trade are set out in Table 7.

What Figure 13 and Table 7 indicate is that through trade both countries can consume more clothing and no less food than before trade so that there is an overall gain from trade.

**Table 7** Specialization and the gains from trade

|  | Opportunity cost | Food production | Food consumption | Clothing production | Clothing consumption |
|---|---|---|---|---|---|
| before trade situation |  |  |  |  |  |
| Country 1 | 6:5 | 300 | 300 | 250 | 250 |
| Country 2 | 11:6 | 800 | 800 | 164 | 164 |
| total |  | 1100 | 1100 | 414 | 414 |
| after trade situation |  |  |  |  |  |
| Country 1 | 3:2 | 0 | 300 | 500 | 300 |
| Country 2 | 3:2 | 1100 | 800 | 0 | 200 |
| total |  | 1100 | 1100 | 500 | 500 |

### Increasing cost: increasing specialization

For the purpose of illustrating the gains from trade we used the production-possibility curve with a constant slope. We could, however, have chosen different shapes as Figures 14b and 14c suggest.

The question naturally arises: which is the more realistic? From the previous chapter, where we discussed the law of diminishing returns, we can infer that Figure 14c is the most likely

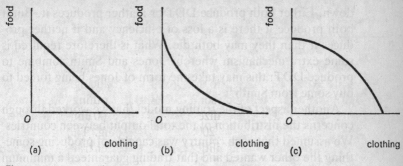

Figure 14

shape since it exhibits increasing cost. Such increasing opportunity cost implies incomplete specialization and casual observation indicates that most countries, regions and people do not indulge in complete specialization. We note, for example, that the UK imports and exports both food and manufactures. Figure 14b illustrates the case of decreasing opportunity cost, a state of affairs most unlikely to be widespread.

### Trade between countries: trade between people

The proposition that trade can be mutually beneficial applies to individuals as well as nations. A professor may be a good gardener, yet still find it advantageous to hire a gardener. Indeed, the internal characteristics of most countries exhibit trading between numerous individuals. Such specialization and trading can give rise to increased efficiency and greater consumption.

There is, however, one qualification to the extension of the analysis of trade to individuals. When we examine production and trading between people we become more conscious of the problems raised by collective goods. Suppose, for example, that we have two individuals, Smith and Jones, and that the goods are DDT (to kill malaria mosquitoes) and beer. If Smith specializes in the production of DDT he may find Jones refusing to buy it because he feels that there is no risk of malaria, Smith having sprayed the area with DDT. Trade therefore breaks down. Either both produce DDT or neither produces it. But if both produce it there is a loss of efficiency and if neither produces it then they may both die. What is therefore required is some extra mechanism whereby Jones and Smith combine to produce DDT: this may take the form of Jones being forced to buy some from Smith.

Another aspect of the trading model that we worked through concerns the distribution of the total output between countries. We assumed that each country was capable of producing something the other wanted and that trading guaranteed a minimum subsistence living standard. But if we look around we see people and countries who, through lack of resources, cannot survive even by trading. The problem of needs therefore cannot always be met by trade.

### The pattern of trade

Armed with our insight into the causes of trade we can now look at the actual pattern of world trade depicted in Table 8.

What Table 8 suggests is that:

1 The less developed countries tend to trade more with the developed countries than with each other. The developed countries tend to trade more with each other than with the developing countries.

These two basic patterns form the basis of many discussions of imperialism and the arguments for industrialization of the less developed countries. The facts have a historical foundation in that many of the less developed countries were formerly colonies of the developed countries of Europe. Hence, so the arguments run, the underdeveloped countries were, and are, dependent upon the growth of the developed countries. They were, and are, exploited. The only way therefore to break this dependence would be through industrialization. However, not all today's developed countries were colonial powers. Some, like Japan, were still underdeveloped at the time of the extensive and intensive colonization of the world in the nineteenth century, but with the weakening of the ties between the former im-

**Table 8** The pattern of world trade, 1976 (millions of US dollars)

| | World | Developed Countries | | | | | Socialist Countries | | Developing Countries | |
|---|---|---|---|---|---|---|---|---|---|---|
| | | UK | EEC | USA | Japan | All | Europe | Asia | Oil | Other |
| World | 999·1 | | | | | | | | | |
| Developed countries | | | | | | | | | | |
| UK | 46·3 | — | 16·9 | 3·4 | 3·2 | 32·9 | 1·2 | 0·2 | 6·2 | 5·9 |
| EEC | 326·4 | 19·1 | 145·9 | 18·2 | 3·0 | 250·7 | 14·0 | 1·5 | 27·4 | 31·1 |
| USA | 115·0 | 5·5 | 25·4 | — | 10·1 | 71·6 | 3·5 | 0·1 | 13·1 | 26·2 |
| Japan | 67·2 | 1·4 | 7·2 | 15·9 | — | 31·6 | 2·8 | 1·9 | 10·3 | 20·7 |
| All | 645·3 | 36·8 | 245·6 | 66·3 | 21·9 | 459·0 | 31·3 | 4·4 | 56·7 | 91·1 |
| Socialist countries | | | | | | | | | | |
| Europe | 87·0 | 1·8 | 13·8 | 0·9 | 1·2 | 24·5 | 48·0 | 2·5 | 2·8 | |
| Asia | 7·8 | — | 0·9 | 1·2 | 0·2 | 3·0 | 1·3 | n.a. | 0·6 | 2·9 |
| Developing countries | | | | | | | | | | |
| Oil states | 138·9 | 7·2 | 45·1 | 37·1 | 23·4 | 107·3 | 2·1 | 0·0 | 0·7 | 27·2 |
| Other | 112·1 | 8·3 | 26·5 | 27·5 | 10·7 | 75·6 | 7·4 | 0·9 | 6·8 | 20·3 |

Sources: UNCTAD, *Handbook of International Trade and Development Statistics*, 1977 IMF, *Direction of Trade*, 1977

perial powers and their dependents, other developed countries
have begun to establish trading links with the former colonies,
e.g. Japan with the Asian and African countries.

2 Since the developed countries tend to specialize in manufactures and the less developed concentrate on agricultural and
mineral products, there exist two clearly defined trade patterns
with two possibly different explanations of such trade. The
trade between the developed economies of the temperate zones
and the less developed economies of the tropics may have geographical origins. It may be possible to grow bananas in green-
houses in Scotland, but oil either exists or does not exist in
Scotland. Oil and other mineral products are the free gifts of
nature and their location owes nothing to human ingenuity.
Although bananas could be grown in Scotland, it seems foolish
to ignore the relatively lower production costs afforded to the
tropical countries by nature. On the other hand, most manufactured goods are footloose in the sense that they are not rigidly tied to particular climatic or geological conditions. Most
manufacturing countries produce motor cars so why do they
exchange them? Why does the UK import German Volkswagen
cars and Germany import Vauxhall Vivas? The explanation of
trade between manufacturing countries, therefore, seems complex, and certainly different from that put forward for trade
between manufacturers and primary producers. Perhaps it is all
due to differences in tastes even when comparative advantages
are similar.

3 The notable exception to the generalization that developed
countries tend to trade more with each other than with the less
developed has been the UK. The UK has always had extensive
trading relations with her former colonies but these have been
eroded in recent years and UK trade with Western Europe has
been growing rapidly.

4 Continental countries such as the USA and Russia and China
contain within their boundaries large developed and undevel-
loped areas and large manufacturing and agricultural regions.
Generalizations 2 and 3 may therefore apply to their internal
trade as much as to their external trade.

5 Countries tend to trade more with their neighbours than with *distant countries*. Transport costs and harmonious relationships are important in explaining these facts.

## The causes of comparative advantage

Table 8 has enabled us to go a little way behind David Ricardo's assertion that trade is based upon comparative advantages. We can now enumerate some of the causes of such advantages and disadvantages. In some cases there are initial resource disparities – the presence of precious minerals or possession of a favourable climate. In other cases it is know-how, technical knowledge or plentiful labour.

## Summary

Countries, regions and people can consume more than their productive potential by trade. Such trade is based upon differences in comparative advantage. Countries, regions and people will produce and sell those goods in which they have a comparative advantage and buy those in which they have a comparative disadvantage in producing. Underlying the comparative advantages are such factors as initial endowments of natural resources, climate and technical knowledge.

## Questions

1 'It is comparative and not absolute advantage that accounts for trade.' Discuss.

2 Is it true that a country can only gain from trade if another country loses?

3 America has an absolute advantage in the production of most goods as compared with the UK. Why then does she find it advantageous to trade with the UK?

4 Why have successive post-war governments attempted to introduce regional policies which interfere with the doctrine that

each region should specialize in the production of those goods in which it has a comparative advantage?

5 'Bananas must be grown where the temperature is 80°F and there is adequate rainfall.' 'Bananas will be grown where the opportunity cost is lowest.' Comment on these two statements.

# Chapter 5
# Money and Trade

We used money in Chapter 1 to measure the national income which was, in turn, used as a measure of economic well-being. We said that it was necessary to use money because it was the only way of adding one motor car to one ice cream. But in subsequent chapters money disappeared. Production was carried on without the use of money; exchange and trade were carried on without the use of money. So evidently we do not need money or, if we do, it seems to be only for the limited objective of calculating the national income. Yet we do use money extensively in society. Is money therefore important or is it a mere veil behind which the real action takes place?

## From a barter economy to a money economy

Let us begin by considering the structure and behaviour of a world without money, of a barter world. We may suppose that Smith has some butter which he wishes to swap for some bread. Hence, he must search for someone who has bread to offer in exchange for butter. But even when he has found another trader he still has to determine whether the bread is fresh or stale, and having ascertained the quality or characteristics of the bread, he has to strike a price, a ratio of exchange of butter for bread. Collectively, we can refer to these various costs – searching, evaluating and bargaining – as *transactions costs*. These costs increase as we increase the number of goods and traders. Thus, suppose that we endow each individual with one commodity, some of which he wishes to trade. The number of exchanges and exchange calculations will increase with the number of goods. Suppose that there are three individuals called Smith, Jones and Robinson trading three goods – bread, butter and wine, respectively – then three exchange calculations have to be made – bread: butter, bread: wine and butter: wine.

Adding another commodity, clothing, we have – bread: butter, bread: wine, bread: clothing, butter: wine, butter: clothing and wine: clothing. The addition of another good has added another three exchange calculations – transactions costs have increased more than proportionately to the increase in goods.

### Specialist trades: middlemen and merchants

It seems clear that faced with such severe transaction costs individuals would attempt to overcome the limitations of barter. One method would be for specialist traders to emerge. They would be skilled in judging the quality of goods – whether bread is fresh, butter is rancid or antiques are fakes. They could earn a living because of the differences in costs which might exist between two ignoramuses trading and an ignoramus trading with a specialist. The differences in costs would contribute a surplus or profit which a specialist could exploit and if there was active competition between specialists then this profit would be kept to a minimum.

In addition to judging the qualities of goods, middlemen could also hold stocks of goods and over time thereby iron out fluctuations in demands and supplies.

Indeed, given the obvious advantages of trading with specialists it would become rare for trading between ignoramuses to take place. We should expect to see a concentration of trading between specialists and ignoramuses and specialists and specialists.

### Trading posts and fairs

A second method of overcoming the limitations of barter would be to create trading posts or fairs – such were the origins of towns. These could reduce transaction costs by bringing people together at a central place on specified days. And because people would be brought together we should expect active competition between traders to reduce transaction costs.

## The money economy

Specialists and trading posts are means of overcoming problems of barter and are extremely useful in a modern economy. Yet they are as nothing compared with the introduction of a monetary economy. Thus, a specialist is unlikely to be knowledgeable about all goods and it may not always be convenient to get to the trading post. What the introduction of a money economy does is to create a commodity whose characteristics are known to everyone and are generally acceptable in exchange for other goods. Money overcomes the absence of a double coincidence of wants which can occur in barter, not in the sense of providing a commodity which everyone will immediately want in exchange but in providing something that is acceptable. We cannot eat money, sleep on it or ride in it, but we do know that in accepting money in exchange for some commodity there is a strong probability that we can dispose of it at a later date for some other commodity. Consider, for example, the case of a worker producing spades in a barter economy. If he is paid for his labour services in spades he has the problem of exchanging them for other goods. If, however, he is paid in money he knows that, although he does not want money, it is much easier to exchange it for goods. Everyone is skilled in buying and selling money but not everyone is skilled in buying and selling spades.

## Money and the division of labour

But observe: a monetary economy and specialist traders are not substitutes, they are complements. The willingness of everyone to accept money means that more people will be willing to become specialists because they know that they can exchange their skills for money; they are not under pressure to become knowledgeable about a lot of goods.

## The functions of money

Money then performs a variety of functions. It becomes the universal medium of exchange by virtue of its ready acceptability. It becomes the unit of account because all transactions are measured in terms of money and in this respect it reduces the number of calculations traders have to make. Thus, in a barter economy the number of combinations of exchange rates for goods is given by the formula $\frac{1}{2}n(n-1)$ where $n$ is the number of goods and, as we observed earlier and the formula indicates, the number of exchange rates increases more than proportionately to the number of goods added in a barter economy. Once a monetary economy is introduced then the formula reduces to $n-1$ because one good is chosen to be the unit of account. Thirdly, and by virtue of its acceptability in payment, money becomes a store of value. Finally, money becomes accepted as a standard for deferred payments – a unit of account over time to cover loans.

## The monetary commodity

Most of the gains from the introduction of money result from the introduction of the system rather than the nature of the commodity chosen. But once such a system has been introduced there will be an incentive to seek out cheaper commodities to use as money. It would, for example, clearly be wasteful to use foodstuffs as money. The attributes of a good money commodity came therefore to be recognized as:

Portability
Durability
Divisibility
Homogeneity

Given these characteristics there was a movement from commodity moneys whose face value was equal to their production costs – gold, furs, etc. – to paper money and bank ledger entries.

## Summary

A monetary system exists because money can fulfill many important functions in society. These functions are as a medium of exchange, a store of value, a unit of account and a standard for deferred payments. The benefits of a monetary system transcend the particular type of commodity used as money though once a monetary system has been introduced there has been a search for cheaper methods of producing the money commodity.

## Questions

1 What are transaction costs?

2 Why is the distinction between a monetary system and a money commodity important?

3 How does a monetary system reduce transaction costs?

# Chapter 6
# Production and Trading over Time

How much should a football manager pay for a player? Should the government expand the polytechnics rather than the universities? How can we explain the growth of the UK national income over the last two centuries? What factors should a person take into consideration when deciding to buy a house? What have these questions got in common?

*The football game*

Suppose we begin with the football manager's problem. We may suppose that our manager's team is in the running for the Football League Championship. The purchase of another star player could make success probable and ensure entry into the lucrative European football competitions. We may now suppose that the player he has in mind will only be released if his present club is paid £500 000, so what should the manager do? He estimates that the player has a playing life of seven years and that he will then retire. So there will be no resale price, at the end of seven years, to a club in a lower division. If there are any gains to be made they must be achieved within seven years. But what are the gains that might make the player a worthwhile buy? Briefly they are the extra receipts that might flow from his crowd-pulling power and from his ability to obtain for the club the Football League Championship and major European honours, which would of course bring even greater gate receipts.

Our manager assumes that the player will be an instant suc-cess and expects him to bring in £100 000 a year over the seven years. Hence the outlook is as follows:

| Season | 1 | 2 | 3 | 4 | 5 | 6 | 7 |
|---|---|---|---|---|---|---|---|
| outlay | 700 000 | — | — | — | — | — | — |
| receipt | 100 000 | 100 000 | 100 000 | 100 000 | 100 000 | 100 000 | 100 000 |

In seven years the player is expected to bring in £700 000 which is greater than £500 000 so it looks as though the deal should be clinched. But wait a minute! What could the club earn on £500 000 if it was put into a building society or stocks and shares? And is it really correct to assume that £100 000 earned in the seventh season is equivalent to £100 000 earned in the first season? Suppose that the player gets injured or suspended in the later season? Shouldn't the manager allow for such con-tingencies? Evidently like is not being compared with like, and some method of comparing sums at different points of time must be devised.

## Discounting

The process of comparing sums of money, or more generally benefits, at different points of time is known as *discounting*. Suppose an individual is faced with the choice of either spend-ing £100 today or lending this amount to someone else in return for a higher sum one year hence. What future amount would he demand as an inducement to make the loan? If he demanded £105 one year hence we could say that he attaches equal values to £100 today and £105 next year; that is, he values £105 next year as equivalent to £100 today. In other words, his valuation of current income is five per cent greater than his valuation of next year's income and he is only prepared, therefore, to fore-go present consumption (to lend) if the rate of return from doing so is at least five per cent. Thus the rate of interest is a means of relating present and future benefits and the discount-ing process is no more than the reverse of the compound-interest technique. In our example we have an individual only prepared to forego £100 today in return for £105 next year:

£100 (today) = £105 (next year) = 100(1 + 0·05).

This compound-interest expression can now be turned on its head to perform a discounting-function:

$$£105 \text{ (next year)} = £100 \text{ (today)} = \frac{105}{(1 + 0·05)}$$

## The dim and distant future

The further into the future are the potential benefits of deferred consumption the lower will be the value placed on these benefits. In our example £105 next year was worth £100 currently, but £105 in, say, five years' time is worth much less than £100 currently. People do tend to prefer present benefits to future benefits largely because of the uncertainty attaching to future events. Hence there will be an undervaluation of an income sum five years distant as compared with a sum to be received in only a year's time. The greater the time span between the present and the receipt of a future sum of income, the more heavily is that sum discounted.

To clarify the point made in the above paragraph let us again proceed via the principle of compound interest and then reverse the process. Again, let us assume that currently £100 is to be loaned to a borrower, and the lender demands a five per cent rate of interest. The table below shows the annual sums to which the original £100 accumulates over a span of $t$ years.

We can now collapse Table 9 into a general formula for the future value of the benefit derived from foregone current consumption

$$A = P(1 + r)^t, \qquad\qquad 1$$

where $A$ is the future value, $P$ is the initial sum (i.e. the amount of current consumption given up), $r$ is the rate of interest and $t$ is the number of years in the time span.

Now, returning to our primary task of calculating present

**Table 9**

| Initial sum (£) | Years' end | Accumulated sum at year's end (£) (5 per cent p.a.) |
|---|---|---|
| 100 | 1 | $100 + 0 \cdot 05 \times 100 = 100(1 + 0 \cdot 05)$ <br> $= 105$ |
| 100 | 2 | $100(1 + 0 \cdot 05) + 0 \cdot 05 \times 100 (1 + 0 \cdot 05)$ <br> $= 100(1 + 0 \cdot 05)(1 + 0 \cdot 05)$ <br> $= 100(1 + 0 \cdot 05)^2$ <br> $= 110 \cdot 3$ |
| 100 | 3 | $100(1 + 0 \cdot 05)^2 + 0 \cdot 05 \times 100(1 + 0 \cdot 05)^2$ <br> $= 100(1 + 0 \cdot 05)^2(1 + 0 \cdot 05)$ <br> $= 100(1 + 0 \cdot 05)^3$ <br> $= 115 \cdot 8$ |
| 100 | 4 | $100(1 + 0 \cdot 05)^3 + 0 \cdot 05 \times 100(1 + 0 \cdot 05)^3$ <br> $= 100(1 + 0 \cdot 05)^3(1 + 0 \cdot 05)$ <br> $= 100(1 + 0 \cdot 05)^4$ <br> $= 121 \cdot 6$ |
| ⋮ | ⋮ | ⋮ |
| 100 | $t$ | $100(1 + 0 \cdot 5)^{t-1} + 0 \cdot 05 \times 100(1 + 0 \cdot 05)^{t-1}$ <br> $= 100(1 + 0 \cdot 05)^t$ |

values of future benefits, i.e. discounting, we can simply rearrange equation **1** as

$$P = \frac{A}{(1 + r)^t}. \qquad\qquad 2$$

Equation **2** permits a simple calculation of the present value of a known future sum of income for a given rate of discount.

It is important to note that **1** and **2** are *general* expressions. Since a given amount of foregone consumption has alternative uses, each of which will yield a different level of future benefits, the present value of a future benefit could differ considerably from the amount of current consumption foregone (investment) in order to yield that benefit. Investment is thus likely to take place where the difference is positive, i.e. when the benefits (in present value terms) from investment outweigh the costs. For example, suppose a machine costs £$C$ and when operational will yield its owner £$a$ per annum for $t$ years. Furthermore, suppose that if £$C$ is used for any other purpose the best it can yield is $i$ per cent per annum. Since $i$ per cent represents the opportunity cost of tying up each £1 in the machine, it is used as the discount rate and the present value, $P$, of the future income stream, $a_1, \ldots, a_t$, is calculated as follows:

$$P = \frac{a_1}{1 + i} + \frac{a_2}{(1 + i)^2} + \frac{a_3}{(1 + i)^3} + \ldots + \frac{a_t}{(1 + i)^t}.$$

Now, as long as the present value of the income stream is greater than (or at least equal to) the initial opportunity cost ($P > C$) it is worthwhile investing in the machine.

The method of investment appraisal outlined above is termed the *net present value* method. An alternative route to the same answer is to calculate the *internal rate of return*. As its name suggests this method concentrates upon the *rate* of benefit rather than upon the net benefit in absolute terms. Using the same example again we can restate the appraisal problem by the rate of return method as follows:

$$C = \frac{a_1}{1 + r} + \frac{a_2}{(1 + r)^2} + \frac{a_3}{(1 + r)^3} + \ldots + \frac{a_t}{(1 + r)^t}.$$

In this expression $C$ and $a$ are known, therefore the object is to find the value of $r$ which satisfies the equation, i.e. to find the value of $r$ which will make the income stream at least equal to the initial opportunity cost. Thus, $r$ represents the minimum rate of return at which the machine is a worthwhile investment in terms of costs and benefits. Once $r$ is known it can be compared to $i$, the best alternative rate of return, and as long as $r > i$, the machine is the best investment.

*The easy way*

But we are not all mathematicians and provided we understand the rudiments of compounding and discounting then there is no sense in getting involved in laborious arithmetic. We can use simple tables provided for us by mathematicians.

**Table 10** Present value of £1: What £1 at the end of a specified future year is worth today at different rates of discount

| End of year | Discount rate (per cent) | | | | | |
|---|---|---|---|---|---|---|
| | 2½ | 5 | 7½ | 10 | 12½ | 15 |
| 1 | 0·976 | 0·952 | 0·930 | 0·909 | 0·889 | 0·870 |
| 2 | 0·952 | 0·907 | 0·865 | 0·826 | 0·790 | 0·756 |
| 3 | 0·929 | 0·864 | 0·805 | 0·751 | 0·702 | 0·658 |
| 4 | 0·906 | 0·823 | 0·749 | 0·683 | 0·624 | 0·572 |
| 5 | 0·884 | 0·784 | 0·697 | 0·621 | 0·555 | 0·497 |
| 6 | 0·862 | 0·746 | 0·648 | 0·564 | 0·493 | 0·432 |
| 7 | 0·841 | 0·711 | 0·603 | 0·513 | 0·438 | 0·376 |
| 8 | 0·821 | 0·677 | 0·561 | 0·467 | 0·390 | 0·327 |
| 9 | 0·801 | 0·645 | 0·522 | 0·424 | 0·346 | 0·284 |
| 10 | 0·781 | 0·614 | 0·485 | 0·386 | 0·308 | 0·247 |

Table 10 gives present values for a sample of years and discount rates. Each column shows how much £1 received at the end of various years in the future is worth today. For example, at 10 per cent £1 received two years hence is worth £0·826 to-

**Table 11** Future value of £1: What £1 would accumulate to at the end of a specified future year at various interest rates

| End of year | Interest rate (per cent) | | | | | |
|---|---|---|---|---|---|---|
| | 2½ | 5 | 7½ | 10 | 12½ | 15 |
| 1 | 1·025 | 1·050 | 1·075 | 1·100 | 1·125 | 1·150 |
| 2 | 1·050 | 1·103 | 1·156 | 1·210 | 1·266 | 1·323 |
| 3 | 1·077 | 1·158 | 1·242 | 1·331 | 1·424 | 1·521 |
| 4 | 1·104 | 1·216 | 1·336 | 1·464 | 1·602 | 1·749 |
| 5 | 1·131 | 1·276 | 1·436 | 1·610 | 1·802 | 2·011 |
| 6 | 1·160 | 1·340 | 1·543 | 1·772 | 2·027 | 2·313 |
| 7 | 1·189 | 1·407 | 1·659 | 1·949 | 2·281 | 2·660 |
| 8 | 1·218 | 1·478 | 1·784 | 2·144 | 2·566 | 3·059 |
| 9 | 1·249 | 1·551 | 1·917 | 2·358 | 2·887 | 3·518 |
| 10 | 1·280 | 1·629 | 2·061 | 2·594 | 3·247 | 4·046 |

day. Since £1 can be multiplied up to any amount we could have obtained the present value of £100, received two years hence discounted at 10 per cent, as £82·6. Turning the information round we could say £0·826 today would grow to £1 in two years' time at 10 per cent of rate interest. Table 11 is a table of compound interest which shows what sums will grow to in the future at different rates of interest.

## The football game again

We can now see how our football manager must deal with the problem of time. *Either*, his discount factor must make the sum of the present benefits greater than the outlay (as in the net present value method) *or* he must choose a discount factor which makes the sum of benefits equal to the outlay (the internal rate of return method) and then see if that discount rate is greater than the rate of interest he could get if he lent the money to someone else. Does a football manager think like this? Not explicitly nor so precisely although he is aware of the problem of cash flows at different points of time. Whatever he does, he must deal with time.

## The education problem[1]

Let us look now at another area where the discounting approach has been used to yield some interesting conclusions. The Minister for Education has a problem. Should he (or she) expand the universities or the polytechnics? Is a Ph.D. worth more to society than a B.Sc.? Is a B.Sc. worth more than an HNC? Suppose that we accept that what people are paid represents their worth to society, then we could obtain the earnings figures for various types of educated person as in Figure 15, and on the basis of this information both individuals and the state could make decisions. Thus an individual could assume that when he attains various ages he could earn what people of that age and with particular qualifications are currently earning.

1. Based on Morris and Ziderman (1971).

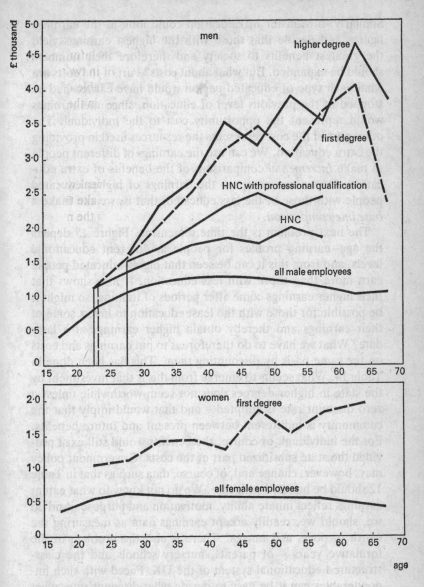

Figure 15  Mean annual income, 1966–67
Source: Morris and Ziderman (1971)

Similarly, a Minister of Education could look at the earnings figures and decide that those with the highest earnings yield the greatest benefits to society and therefore their numbers should be expanded. But what about costs? Part of the costs are what each type of educated person would have earned had he stopped at the previous level of education, since the earnings would represent the opportunity cost to the individual. The other part of the cost represents the resources used in providing the extra education. We can use the earnings of different people to make *incremental* comparisons of the benefits of extra education. Or we can compare the earnings of higher educated people with those of the less educated: that is, we can make a *base line comparison*.

The next problem is the time dimension. Figure 15 depicts the age–earning profiles for people at different educational levels, and from this it can be seen that highly-educated people earn more than those with less education. It also shows that their higher earnings come after periods of training, so might it be possible for those with the least education to invest some of their earnings and thereby obtain higher earnings at a later date? What we have to do therefore is to put earnings and costs on the same basis by discounting them. This has been done in Table 14. What seems to emerge from this is that investment by the state in higher degrees does not seem worthwhile unless a zero discount rate is adopted – and that would imply that the community is indifferent between present and future benefits. For the individual, of course, the benefits would still exist provided the state subsidized part of the costs. Government policy may, however, change and, of course, data such as that in Table 12 should be handled with care. We do not know to what extent earnings reflect innate ability, motivation and purpose. And do we, should we, readily accept earnings data as measuring the worth of poets and nurses? There is also the problem of the formative years – of parents, nursery schools and the class-structured educational system of the UK. Faced with such imponderables can it be easy to decide what discount rate, what measure of present and future benefits a society should adopt? We return to this issue in Chapter 11 and in Part Eight.

**Table 12** Comparisons of present values at age 15 of benefits net of costs (including research) between educational levels at various discount rates (£), 1966–7

|  | 0% | 4% | 6% | 8% | 10% | 12% | 16% |
|---|---|---|---|---|---|---|---|
| *Males* | | | | | | | |
| incremental comparison | | | | | | | |
| A-level/non-qualified | 17 950 | 3158 | 1188 | −144 | −743 | −1005 | −1308 |
| ONC/non-qualified | 9278 | 1592 | 761 | −40 | −322 | −473 | −614 |
| HNC/ONC | 18 410 | 5335 | 3156 | 2000 | 1310 | 893 | 444 |
| HNC-PQ/HNC | 8338 | 3062 | 1814 | 1073 | 633 | 370 | 113 |
| first degree/A-level | 46 084 | 10 392 | 4763 | 1880 | 373 | −425 | −1079 |
| master's/first degree | 1282 | −1876 | −2250 | −2314 | −2229 | −2078 | −1723 |
| doctorate/first degree | 3163 | −3218 | −3760 | −3754 | −3516 | −3198 | −2546 |
| base-line comparison | | | | | | | |
| A-level/non-qualified | 17 950 | 3158 | 1188 | −144 | −743 | −1005 | −1308 |
| ONC/non-qualified | 9278 | 1592 | 761 | −40 | −322 | −473 | −614 |
| HNC/non-qualified | 27 788 | 6927 | 3917 | 1960 | 988 | 420 | −170 |
| HNC-PQ/ non-qualified | 26 126 | 9989 | 5731 | 3033 | 1621 | 790 | −57 |
| first degree/ non-qualified | 64 034 | 13 549 | 5951 | 1735 | −370 | −1481 | −2384 |
| master's degree/ non-qualified | 65 315 | 11 673 | 3700 | −579 | −2599 | −3558 | −4109 |
| doctorate/ non-qualified | 67 196 | 10 331 | 2191 | −2019 | −3886 | −4678 | −4932 |
| *Females* | | | | | | | |
| first degree/ non-qualified | 25 133 | 4497 | 1195 | −546 | −1480 | −1980 | −2361 |
| first degree/A-level | 7974 | 749 | −384 | −941 | −1210 | −1325 | −1360 |

Derived from earnings survey (except: no qualification, A-level and ONC) and DES cost data

Source: Morris and Ziderman (1971)

## The larger issue

We can now turn to the larger issue of the growth of the UK economy. In an earlier chapter we saw that specialization and trade could increase the production and consumption possibilities at a point in time. But the principle also holds regarding such possibilities over time. Consumption possibilities can be increased over the long run as a result of the production of *capital goods*. The growth in the UK national income over the last 150 years has owed much to an increase in productive resources, particularly in durable capital goods such as plant and machinery.

## Investment and opportunity cost

Of course a community's decision to produce capital goods requires, as always, the acceptance of an opportunity cost. At some time in the middle of the eighteenth century, possibly earlier, there began to emerge a sizeable surplus of community income over customary consumption. This surplus could have been used to increase current consumption, but instead it was used to increase future consumption, i.e. it was used for investment purposes. Instead of being channelled into producing more goods by customary production techniques, the surplus was used to divert resources into production methods which could lead, in the long run, to even greater output. These production methods were initially time-consuming, which is why their benefits could only accrue over a lengthy time period, and for this reason they have been labelled 'roundabout' methods of production.

Roundabout production techniques are not confined solely to the UK's experience. Indeed the principle has been employed by all societies although the scale of operations may differ. It is true that the long-run output of manufactured products can be increased if some short-run output is sacrificed to the production of conveyor belts and heavy lifting gear; and it is equally true that primitive hunters can increase their long-run meat consumption by giving up a day's chase in order to make animal traps. The costs and benefits of roundabout production methods are represented by Figure 16, which is of course our familiar production-possibilities curve with re-labelled axes. If the community devotes all its current resources to the production of goods for current consumption, *OB* goods can be produced and consumed. However, if some resources were used to produce capital goods instead of consumption goods it is possible for the community's future (tomorrow) consumption to be increased by more than its present (today) reduction in con-

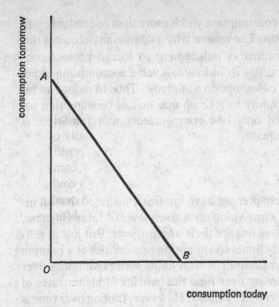

Figure 16

sumption, i.e. *OA* is greater than *OB*. In other words the benefits from roundabout production methods outweigh the opportunity cost involved, a unit of foregone consumption today yields more than one extra consumption unit tomorrow.

Whether or not future benefits will actually be pursued depends not only upon the possibilities of converting present consumption into future consumption, but also upon the community's willingness to do so, i.e. upon the community's relative *preferences* for present and future consumption. When the opportunity cost of future consumption in terms of present consumption matches the relative preferences of the community, then some capital goods are likely to be produced.

### 'Tomorrow is another day'

In the case of the community represented by Figure 16, production possibilities and community preferences could well coincide since the slope of *AB* is greater than 1, i.e. a unit of foregone present consumption yields more than one unit of extra future consumption. The reason why a community requires this positive rate of return as inducement to forego present consumption is that ordinarily individuals value consumption today more highly than consumption tomorrow. Thus to induce an individual or community to give up one unit of consumption today, a promise of only one compensatory unit tomorrow is likely to be inadequate.

## Trading over time

Throughout this chapter we have implicitly assumed that all individuals put the same value on a given level of future income, and that all investors finance their own projects. But just as self-sufficiency severely limits consumption possibilities at a point in time, as we saw in Chapter 3, so it limits such possibilities over time. Through *trading* over time the benefits of higher rates of economic growth can be realized. However, trading over time is only possible when there is a divergence between the evaluations made of present and future income by different groups in the community. When time preferences for income diverge some individuals are net lenders at a given rate of interest, and others are net borrowers. In this way investments can be financed out of borrowed funds.

Suppose, for example, that two individuals A and B differ in their relative abilities to transform present consumption into future consumption in the following way: A is able to produce two extra units of future consumption by giving up a unit of current consumption, whereas if B foregoes a unit today he can produce five units for tomorrow in return. Figure 17 shows the two production-possibilities curves. The preferences for current consumption compared with future consumption will determine whereabouts on his frontier each individual settles.

As with international trade in Chapter 4, we can demonstrate that both individuals can benefit by trading. In this case it is trading through time. If A concentrates all his efforts on producing for today's consumption and B concentrates all his efforts on producing for tomorrow (using his resources for pro-

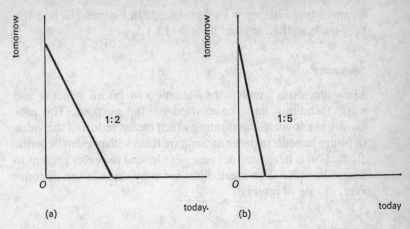

Figure 17 (a) *A*'s production-possibility curve.
(b) *B*'s production-possibility curve

ducing capital rather than consumer goods) then for the community of two $(A + B)$ they are each concentrating on the activity where they have a comparative advantage. The trade comes when *A* loans consumer goods *today* in exchange for a greater increase in consumption *tomorrow* than he individually could have managed. In our example they will both gain at any

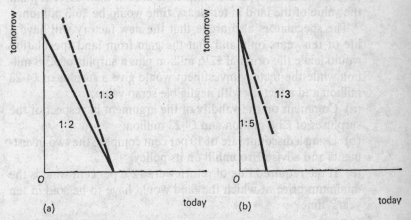

Figure 18

terms of trade between 1 : 2 and 1 : 5. In Figures 18a and 18b they trade to their mutual benefit at 1 : 3.

## Summary

Many decisions involve the valuation of future benefits and some technique must be devised for the purpose. The procedure is known as discounting which means reducing the value of future benefits in order to compare them with present benefits. Reduction is necessary because people tend to prefer present to future benefits. The mechanism for conversion is the discount rate, or rate of interest.

## Questions

1 Broomhill Ltd has £2½ million available to purchase a new factory. If Broomhill goes ahead with this project it is estimated that it will generate revenue (cash) flows of £270 000 in the first year, £360 000 in the second year and £450 000 each year thereafter. However, certain adventurous members of the firm have suggested that it might be better to purchase some land alongside the present factory, which has just come onto the market at a price of £2½ million. They believe that with the expected expansion of industry in the immediate area of their current plant the value of the land in ten years' time would be £6·3 million.

The speculators also argue that the new factory will have a life of ten years only and that the gain from land speculation would leave the original £2½ million plus a surplus of £3·8 million while the factory investment would give a surplus of £4·23 million and a factory with negligible scrap value.

(a) Comment on the validity of the argument in respect of the surpluses of £3·8 million and £4·23 million.

(b) Using a discount rate of 10 per cent compare the two investments and advise Broomhill on its policy.

(c) If the required rate of return were 12½ per cent what is the minimum price at which the land would have to be sold in ten years' time?

# Part Two
# Markets, Demand and Supply

Exchange may be effected through markets or a central planning bureau. A market need not be a physical location. It is any arrangement for bringing buyers and sellers together and in these days of teleprinter and radio satellite the market for any good may be the whole world. The lack of apparent form and structure often gives the appearance of chaos and haphazard happenings rather than spontaneous coordination. Unemployment, inflation, gluts and shortages force the claims of central planning.

## Planning

But consider the problems facing a planning bureau. Suppose it has to decide whether to use plastics or steel in the production of motor cars. How can it make the decision? It will have certain technical information at its disposal which may tell it that plastics are unsuitable for engine parts. But steel may be scarce and there may be claims to use steel in other uses. How can these competing claims be resolved?

### The aggregation and transmission of information

The fundamental problem facing a planning bureau is that it may not be possible to centralize all information. In any economy bits of information lie scattered. It is a characteristic of any economy that everyone possesses information about something but not about everything. Indeed, it may be the case that individuals are not aware of the knowledge they possess. It is the knowledge of particular place and circumstance that may not be available to the planner because it may not exist in a form capable of easy collection and assembly.

What the price system does is to aggregate and transmit the bits of information to everyone. The process of aggregation, of converting qualitative expressions into quantitative form, is achieved through the process of everyone casting money bids for the use of resources. Of course, the aggregation and trans-mission of information through the signalling mechanism of prices conceals an incredible amount of institutional detail which is necessary to make markets work. Thus, goods must be identified. Is a chair a Chippendale or a fake? Specialist dealers must emerge and property rights must be established. Only in a system of well-established property rights will individuals reveal their preferences. But if property rights are not clearly defined, if wants are collective rather than individualistic, then there may be a case for central planning. Indeed the case for central planning becomes most persuasive when the wants of the com-munity are few and acceptable to all. Thus, central planning may find a place in the take-off of developing countries. And there will always be a place in any economy for the intervention of the state to correct the mal-distribution of money votes, to interfere with the distribution of income and wealth.

# Chapter 7
# Demand

On one side of the market stand the buyers whose decisions to purchase serve to influence prices and thereby allocate resources. Demand by buyers in the market refers to the amount of a commodity which they are willing and able to purchase. It is *effective demand* and not mere wishful thinking or desire that constitutes demand. Furthermore, we can also distinguish between *ex ante*, or intended demand, and *ex post* demand or what is actually bought.

## The individual's demand curve

We can express the general forces influencing the demand of an individual for a commodity by a shorthand statement of the form:

$$D_a = f(P_a, P_b, \ldots, P_z; Y; T; r; u).\qquad\qquad 1$$

where $D_a$ is the quantity of a commodity $a$ demanded per period of time; $P_a$ is the price of $a$; $Y$ is money income; $T$ is tastes; $P_b, \ldots, P_z$ are the prices of other goods; $r$ is the rate of interest which is relevant in the case of durable goods; and $u$ is a term which summarizes all the unknown influences. Though equation 1 may be thought of as a convenient summary of the forces influencing demand we need to justify the variables we have included and the precise way in which demand is influenced by each of the variables in the right-hand bracket. What we shall now do is to take each of the variables in turn.

## *Income*

Generally, we would expect a positive relation between income and consumption (spending). But within this relation there lies an important distinction between *current income* and *permanent income*. Current income may be composed of a regular or permanent component – income which is fully anticipated and received on a regular contractual basis. Or, income received currently may comprise large transitory components – income which is not expected in the next period, having accrued due to circumstances beyond the recipient's control, income which is often 'out of the blue'. If we may offer stereotypes, Mr Pinstripe (civil servant) receives an income stream comprising mainly permanent components, while Mr Spats (amusement park owner) receives an income stream with several hiccups in it due to vagaries of weather, consumer tastes, etc. Hence, an individual might be expected to base his expenditures upon his permanent income and be slow to react to any changes in his income until he is certain that they are likely to persist. Thus, the true relationship between spending and permanent income may have a steeper slope than that between spending and current income. When, as in Figure 19, income increases beyond

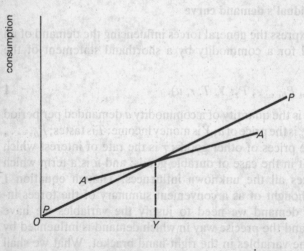

Figure 19

OY then an individual may move along the curve AA; he may not regard an immediate increase in income as a rise in permanent income. If the rise in income persists then he will move on to the line OP which is his permanent income-consumption line. If income falls below OY then he will move out along AA until the permanency of the fall in income and the exhaustion of his savings compels him to move down on to the line OP.

Later when we study macroeconomic variables, the distinction between permanent and transient income will become important in the determination of the *aggregate* consumption pattern. But now we turn to the relationship between income and the quantity demanded of a particular commodity. Figure 20 shows three possible relationships between income and the quantity demanded of some particular commodity. Curve 1 shows the quantity demanded rising with income until income level *b* is reached. Thereafter, the quantity demanded does not change as income rises. Curve 2 shows demand rising as income rises to *a* and falling thereafter. Curve 3 shows the quantity demanded continually rising with income.

Tables 13 and 14 throw some light on the relationship between demand and income. Two points about the data should

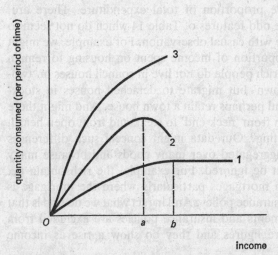

Figure 20

be immediately observed. First, the information refers to current income. Secondly, the statistics are derived from households and not individuals. Now the discrepancy between current and permanent income can be ignored if we remember that the data is collected from a large number of households, some of whom will be above their permanent incomes and some of whom will be below their permanent incomes, but averaging out across a group of households will yield a measure of permanent income behaviour. The second point can be dealt with by regarding a household as a single decision-making unit. How such single-mindedness arises lies outside the scope of our analysis.

1 The proportion of income spent on certain goods *falls* as income rises. This proposition does of course correspond to what might be inferred from the notion of a hierarchy of wants or, as the statisticians term it, Engel's law. Once basic necessities have been satisfied then any increases in income are spent on other goods. Tables 13 and 14 seem to confirm these ideas. For all households, housing, food and, in a modern society, transport form the bulk of expenditure but Table 14 also shows that as incomes rise, expenditure on some of these items becomes a smaller relative proportion of total expenditure. There are, however, some odd features of Table 14 which do not seem to be reconcilable with casual observation. For example, we might expect the proportion of income spent on housing to remain constant since rich people do not live in council houses or 'two-up and two-down' but migrate to detached houses in stockbroker belts and perhaps retain a town house. And might there not be a switch from 'neck end' to steak and from open hearth to central heating? Our data might conceal such differences because it is aggregated over many goods and because many subsidies might be ignored. For example, the rich obtain tax concessions on mortgages particularly where the mortgage is tied to a life assurance policy. And in fact what we do find is that mortgage payments and insurance policies are excluded from the expenditure figures and they do show a rise as income rises.

**Table 13** Household expenditure 1977

|  | Average weekly expenditure of all households | |
|---|---|---|
|  | £ | % |
| housing | 10·31 | 14·4 |
| fuel, light and power | 4·38 | 6·1 |
| food | 17·74 | 24·9 |
| drink and tobacco | 6·11 | 8·5 |
| clothing and footwear | 5·78 | 8·0 |
| household durables | 4·99 | 6·9 |
| other goods | 5·33 | 7·4 |
| transport and vehicles | 9·71 | 13·5 |
| services | 6·93 | 9·7 |
| miscellaneous | 0·56 | 0·8 |
| Total |  | 100·0 |

**Table 14** Household total weekly expenditure on goods and services by income size, 1977 (per cent)

|  | £25 but under £35 | £50 but under £60 | £90 but under £100 | £120 but under £150 | £200 or more |
|---|---|---|---|---|---|
| housing | 22·4 | 15·7 | 14·7 | 12·7 | 12·2 |
| fuel, light and power | 11·5 | 8·1 | 5·5 | 4·9 | 4·1 |
| food | 30·1 | 27·9 | 25·0 | 23·1 | 19·8 |
| drink and tobacco | 6·1 | 8·8 | 8·8 | 9·1 | 8·1 |
| clothing and footwear | 5·5 | 6·8 | 7·6 | 9·0 | 9·0 |
| household durables | 4·6 | 6·0 | 7·2 | 8·0 | 7·0 |
| other goods | 6·6 | 6·9 | 7·3 | 7·7 | 7·7 |
| transport and vehicles | 5·1 | 10·5 | 14·1 | 15·5 | 15·8 |
| services | 7·9 | 9·2 | 9·0 | 9·1 | 16·9 |
| miscellaneous | 0·2 | 0·1 | 0·6 | 1·0 | 1·1 |

Source: *Family Expenditure Survey*, 1977, HMSO, 1978

2 The proportion of income spent on some goods *rises* as income rises. Household durables, clothing, transport and vehicles, and services are good examples of this proposition.

## Price of the good

A relationship in which economists express a great deal of interest is that which exists between changes in the quantity of a good demanded and changes in its price, other things (tastes, income, the prices of other goods, etc.) being held constant. This is because they regard price changes as a signal for the re-allocation of resources. The belief that demand rises as price falls, and demand falls as price rises, seems to have a firm basis in everyday experience, though the precise circumstances under which it will be found to be true will be a matter for exploration in Chapter 11. For the moment however we will assume that the relationship be taken on trust or casual observation.

Table 15 is a demand schedule showing the numbers of cans of beans demanded at differing prices and the price–quantity information it contains can be plotted on a graph as in Figure 21. Price is measured on the vertical axis and the numbers of cans demanded (quantity demanded) are plotted on the horizontal axis. Each point on the graph represents the coordinates of a price–quantity combination and a line joining such points, the locus $D$, is called a *demand curve*.

**Table 15** A demand schedule

| Price per can (pence) | Cans of beans demanded (per unit of time) |
|---|---|
| 15 | 2 |
| 14 | 5 |
| 13 | 8 |
| 12 | 12 |
| 11 | 15 |
| 10 | 18 |

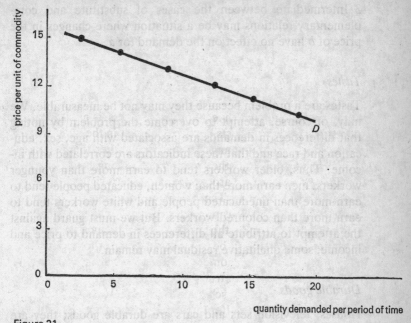

quantity demanded per period of time

Figure 21

## The prices of other goods

If the prices of closely-related goods fall then one of three possible changes in the demand for commodity *a* may occur:

1 If the price of commodity *b* falls then the demand for *a* may fall. If the price of *b* rises then the demand for *a* may rise. The repercussions on the demand for *a* of changes in the price of *b* arise because *a* and *b* are substitutes, that is, they are both goods which can satisfy the same want, e.g. butter and margarine.

2 If the price of *b* falls then the demand for *a* may rise. If the price of *b* rises then the demand for *a* may fall. The repercussions on the demand for *a* of changes in the price of *b* arise because *a* and *b* are complements, that is, *a* and *b* are jointly demanded in order to satisfy the same want, e.g. milk and cornflakes.

3 Intermediate between the cases of substitute and complementary relations may be a situation where changes in the price of *b* have no effect on the demand for *a*.

## Tastes

Tastes are a problem because they may not be measurable. We may, of course, attempt to overcome the problem by noting that differences in demands are associated with age, sex, education and race and that these indicators are correlated with income. Thus, older workers tend to earn more than younger workers, men earn more than women, educated people tend to earn more than uneducated people and white workers tend to earn more than coloured workers. But we must guard against the attempt to attribute all differences in demand to price and income; some qualitative residual may remain.

## Durable goods

Houses, television sets and cars are durable goods; they are stocks which yield a flow of services over time. The demand for such goods must therefore be regarded as an investment and the analysis of demand can be approached in terms of the discussion of Chapter 6. Thus, an individual will buy a car if the stream of services discounted to the present is greater than or equal to the price of the car. The minimum value of the services of a car at a point of time can be measured by what it would cost to rent a car for a day or a week or a longer period. Indeed, consumer durables present less of a problem to buyers than we might imagine at first sight. It is possible to rent or lease a house, car or television and it is always possible to use a laundrette. Similarly, firms can hire equipment such as cars, tractors and office space. All these possibilities represent substitutes to outright purchase.

## Market demand

So far we have attempted to isolate the factors determining de-

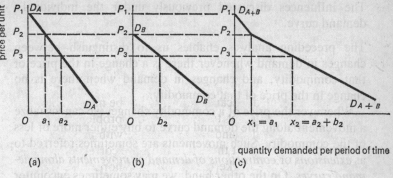

Figure 22

mand in terms of the individual. The usual material we deal with, however, is the sum of individual demand curves which constitute market demand. In order to obtain the market demand curve for a commodity we simply sum the individual demands for a commodity at each particular price.

Figure 22 shows how the market demand curve is derived as the horizontal sum of the individual demand curves.[1] The market demand curve is $D_{A+B}$ in Figure 22c and the individual demand curves are $D_A$ and $D_B$ in Figures 22a and 22b respectively. Thus, at market price $OP_3$ consumers demand $Ox_2$ of the commodity where $Ox_2 = Oa_2 + Ob_2$. For prices higher than $OP_2$, $A$'s demand constitutes the market demand; for example, at $OP_2$ quantity $Ox_1 = Oa_1$. The demand curve of consumer $B$ becomes effective at a price just below $OP_2$ (at $OP_2$, $B$'s demand is zero). Hence the market demand curve is kinked at price $OP_2$. When the number of consumers is large, so that each individual demand is small in relation to total demand, such kinks can be ironed out and the price–quantity relation becomes a smooth curve.

Market demand is influenced by:

The size and composition of the population;
The distribution of income within the population;

1. For simplicity, straight-line demand *curves* are assumed.

The influences discussed previously under the individual's demand curve.

The preceding analysis enables us to distinguish between changes in demand whenever there is a change in the price of that commodity, and changes in demand when there is no change in the price of that commodity.

Whenever the price of a commodity changes we can visualize a movement along the demand curve to buy either more or less of the commodity. Such movements are sometimes referred to as *extensions* or *contractions of demand* or *movements along demand curves*. On the other hand, we may sometimes encounter situations where the demand for a commodity changes even though price does not change. Such situations may be visualized as involving a shift of the demand curve. Figure 23 illustrates both possibilities. When the price falls from $P_1$ to $P_2$ there is a movement along the demand curve from $A$ to $B$. Now contrast this state of affairs with that which occurs when at price $OP_1$ there is an increase in demand from $A$ to $C$. This involves a shift of demand as a result of either:

An increase in income – more can be bought at the existing price;
A change in tastes;

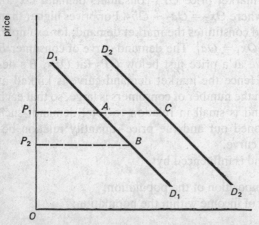

Figure 23  Quantity demanded per period of time

A fall in the price of a complementary good;
A rise in the price of a substitute good.

## The demand elasticities

Whenever any of the variables on the right-hand side of the equation changes, a change in demand occurs. One of the great interests of economists is how much does demand respond to changes in the variables. We shall now consider three measures of response:

Price-elasticity of demand;
Cross-price elasticity of demand;
Income-elasticity of demand.

### Price-elasticity of demand

The response of demand for a commodity to a change in price is termed the *price-elasticity of demand* and its formulation is as follows:

$$e = -\frac{\text{the percentage change in quantity demanded}}{\text{the percentage change in price}}$$

A minus sign is often placed in front of this expression to neutralize the effect of the price and quantity changes moving in opposite directions when the demand curve has a negative slope. It is a convention, although not one consistently adopted by economists. When a numerical measure of elasticity, based on empirical study, is given, the negative sign is retained. Thus $e = -2$ means that if price *falls* by 1 per cent demand rises by 2 per cent. Note also that $-2$ is a higher elasticity than $-1$ despite the negative sign; that is, the number is more important than the sign.

### Absolutes versus percentages

We must now underline the fact that the elasticity is measured in terms of proportional changes in price and quantity rather than absolute changes. The reason for this is that absolute changes can give different measures of response depending upon what units of measurement are adopted. For example, suppose we compare the demand schedules for butter for an individual consumer using two different sets of measurements, as follows:

**Table 16**

| Price of butter | | Quantity of butter demanded per annum | |
|---|---|---|---|
| *Pounds* (£) | *Francs* (F) | *Weight* (lb) | *Weight* (kg) |
| 1·00 | 500 | 50 | 22·50 |
| 0·90 | 450 | 55 | 24·75 |
| 0·80 | 400 | 65 | 29·25 |
| 0·70 | 350 | 70 | 31·50 |
| 0·60 | 300 | 75 | 33·75 |
| 0·50 | 250 | 80 | 36·00 |

Now suppose that our Englishman decides to calculate his price-elasticity of demand for butter when its price falls from 400 to 350 francs (we are assuming that £1 = 500F) on the assumption that elasticity is measured by

$$\frac{\text{Change in demand}}{\text{Change in price}}.$$

If he does the calculation in francs and kilograms, his result will be

$$e = \frac{2 \cdot 25}{50} = 0 \cdot 045.$$

On the other hand, if he does the calculation in English units of measurement, his result will be

$$e = \frac{5 \cdot 0}{0 \cdot 10} = 50.$$

The difference in the results is due to the fact that the units of measurement do affect the elasticity and in order to remove their influence the calculations must be in percentages. Thus

French $\quad e = \dfrac{(2 \cdot 25/29 \cdot 25) \times 100}{(50/400) \times 100} = \dfrac{0 \cdot 09}{1 \cdot 17} \times \dfrac{8}{1} = 0 \cdot 615,$

English $e = \dfrac{(5/65)}{(0 \cdot 10/0 \cdot 80)} = \dfrac{1}{13} \times 8 = 0 \cdot 615.$

There is one further problem to consider at this stage – for a given price the elasticity measure differs according to whether the original price was higher or lower than the new one. In the above example we considered a price *fall* from 400F to 350F which meant that the original price was 400F and the original quantity was 29·25 kilograms. Suppose, however, that we had considered a change in the opposite direction taking 350F and 31·50 kg as the original price and quantity. In this case a sharp rise of 50F would have yielded the following measure of elasticity:

$$e = \frac{(2 \cdot 25/31 \cdot 50) \times 100}{(50/350) \times 100} = \frac{2 \cdot 25}{31 \cdot 50} \times \frac{350}{50} = 0 \cdot 5.$$

In order to avoid such discrepancies when dealing with numerical elasticities we calculate an average measure, thus accounting for both the original and new levels of price and quantity, as follows:

$$e = \frac{\text{change in quantity demanded}}{\frac{1}{2}(\text{old quantity} + \text{new quantity})} \div \frac{\text{change in price}}{\frac{1}{2}(\text{old price} + \text{new price})}$$

Applying this formula to our numerical example yields

$$e = \frac{2 \cdot 25}{\frac{1}{2}(29 \cdot 25 + 31 \cdot 50)} \div \frac{50}{\frac{1}{2}(400 + 350)} = 0 \cdot 55.$$

### Elasticity and the slope of the demand curve

By grasping at the outset that elasticity refers to proportionate rather than absolute changes in price and quantity we can avoid the error of confusing elasticity with the *slope* of the demand curve. Let us take a closer look at the elasticity formula, representing it in symbols:

$$e = -\frac{\Delta Q/Q}{\Delta P/P},$$

where $Q$ represents the original quantity, $P$ represents the original price, and the changes in price and quantity are represented by $\Delta P$ and $\Delta Q$ respectively. Rearranging the symbols we have:

$$e = -\frac{\Delta Q}{Q}\left(\frac{P}{\Delta P}\right) \text{or} \quad e = \frac{\Delta Q}{\Delta P}\left(\frac{P}{Q}\right).$$

This latter formula is the most useful since it shows elasticity to depend upon two things: *the ratio of the changes in quantity and price* multiplied by *the ratio of the original price and quantity*. In other words, this formula reminds us that price-elasticity of demand does not depend solely upon the slope of the demand curve.

To further emphasize the point made in the previous paragraph let us consider a straight-line demand curve. We shall see

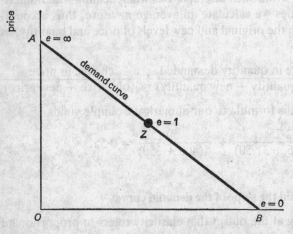

Figure 24

that although the slope of the demand curve does not change at each point on the curve, *elasticity does vary along the demand curve*. In Figure 24 the demand curve has been extended to meet the price axis at $A$ and the quantity axis at $B$. The demand curve is a straight line and so $\Delta Q/\Delta P$ is a constant (since $\Delta P/\Delta Q$ is a constant). But elasticity is not constant because $P/Q$ changes at each point on the demand curve:

1 As $P$ approaches $A$, quantity $Q$ approaches zero and $P/Q$ approaches infinity. Thus price-elasticity of demand approaches infinity as the demand curve approaches the vertical axis.

2 As $Q$ approaches $B$, price $P$ approaches zero and $P/Q$ approaches zero. Thus price-elasticity of demand approaches zero as the demand curve approaches the horizontal axis.

3 At the mid-point $Z$ of the demand curve, price-elasticity of demand is equal to unity. We shall explain this more fully a little later.

What happens when the demand curve is not a straight line? Again the $P/Q$ ratio is different at each point along the curve. But in this case the ratio $\Delta Q/\Delta P$ is also changing along the curve since the slope of the demand curve is different at each point. This means that our formula of elasticity gives an inaccurate measure when a discrete price/quantity change is taken along such a curve. At best our formula can only give an approximation to the true measure of elasticity, by providing an estimate of the average of the elasticities between any two points on the demand curve as shown in Figure 25. In this we depict a price change from $OP_1$ to $OP_2$. Our elasticity formula gives only an approximation to the elasticity measure since $\Delta Q/\Delta P$ is the reciprocal of the slope $\Delta P/\Delta Q$ of the *chord AB*.

It should be clear that the greater the price change considered the greater will be the elasticity error. To reduce the error very small changes in price and quantity must be considered. In fact we really need a measure of the elasticity for each *point* on the demand curve since elasticity differs at every point. It is this measure, *point-elasticity*, that economists usually refer to in their theoretical discussions, as opposed to the *arc-elasticity* which is

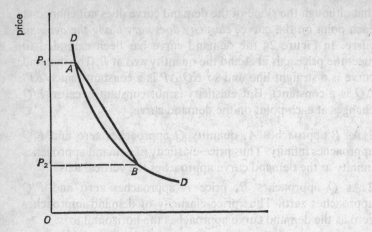

**quantity demanded per period of time**

Figure 25

the measure that we have adopted so far in this chapter. From now on, therefore, elasticity will always mean point-elasticity unless we state otherwise.

How is point-elasticity calculated? In Chapter 14 we derive point-elasticity with the use of the basic calculus, but meanwhile we can content ourselves with the use of similar triangles. Consider the straight-line demand curve in Figure 26 which meets the price axis at $A$ and the quantity axis at $E$. Let us calculate elasticity at price $B(= DC)$ using our earlier formula,

$$e = -\frac{\Delta Q}{\Delta P}\left(\frac{P}{Q}\right).$$

The ratio $\Delta Q/\Delta P$ is constant along $AE$ and, hence, is equal to $DE/DC$. The price $P$ is equal to $DC$ and $Q$ equals $OD$. Thus,

$$e = -\frac{DE}{DC}\cdot\frac{DC}{OD} = \frac{DE}{OD}.$$

But $OD = BC$ so that $e = DE/BC$ and since $ABC$ and $CDE$ are similar triangles,

$$e = -\frac{DE}{BC} = \frac{CD}{AB} = \frac{CE}{AC}.$$

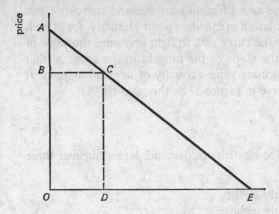

quantity demanded per period of time

Figure 26

Repeating this for any point on the demand curve gives us the same answer – that elasticity is measured by the ratio of the distance from the point to where the curve meets the quantity axis (*CE*), to the distance from the point to where the curve meets the price axis (*AC*). This explains why $e = 1$ at the mid-point *Z* in Figure 26.

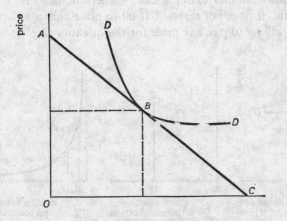

quantity demanded per period of time

Figure 27

Returning to the case of non-linear demand curves we can use this new formulation to calculate point-elasticity, for at each point we can treat the curve as a straight line since the slope of the curve equals the slope of the tangent to the curve at that point. We can calculate price-elasticity of demand at point $B$ on the demand curve in Figure 27 by the ratio $BC/AB$.

### Three special cases

Before leaving price-elasticity of demand, let us consider three special cases:

Demand is perfectly elastic;
Demand is perfectly inelastic;
Elasticity of demand is unity at all points on the demand curve.

Figure 28 shows all three cases. We have already seen that $e = \infty$ when a downward sloping demand curve meets the price axis. Figure 28a shows a demand curve where this is true at all points. Consumers are prepared to buy any amount at a unit price of $OP^*$ but nothing at all at a price just above this level. Extensive use of this case is made in our later discussion of a market structure named *perfect competition* (Chapter 18).

Figure 28b shows another extreme case – where demand is perfectly inelastic, it does not respond at all to price changes. Consumers are willing to pay any price for the quantity $OQ^*$.

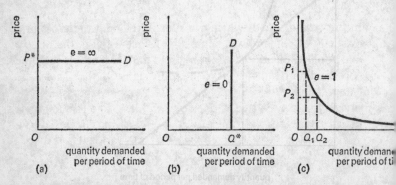

Figure 28

Such a case would exist in the cases of essentials of life, for example, water or heroin (in the case of an addict).

The third case, Figure 28c, is where elasticity is unity at all points. This means that every proportional price change is exactly matched by a proportional change in quantity demanded. Expenditure in such a case is constant and the curve is therefore a *rectangular hyperbola* – the area of any rectangle drawn from any point on the curve to the axes is always the same ($OP_1 . OQ_1 = OP_2 . OQ_2$ and so on). We make extensive use of this curve when considering the problem of farm incomes in Chapter 10.

We have spent a long time in considering the concept of price-elasticity. Our efforts will be justified because it is the most important elasticity concept in a world in which prices operate, and the most complex. The other elasticity measures will be dealt with more briefly.

## Cross-price elasticity of demand

This measures the response of demand for one good arising from a change in the price of another good.

$$e_x = \frac{\text{percentage change in the quantity demand of good } A}{\text{percentage change in the price of good } B}$$

$$= \frac{\Delta Q_A}{Q_A} \div \frac{\Delta P_B}{P_B} = \frac{\Delta Q_A}{\Delta P_B} \left(\frac{P_B}{Q_A}\right). \qquad \qquad 2$$

In the case of goods which are substitutes then the cross-price elasticity of demand will be positive, since a fall in the price of one good will lead to a contraction in the demand for the other good and both changes have the same sign. On the other hand, complementary goods will give rise to a negative cross-elasticity since a fall in the price of one good will lead to a rise in the demand for the other good.

## Income-elasticity of demand

The income-elasticity of demand measures the responsiveness of demand to changes in income,

$$e_y = \frac{\text{percentage change in quantity demanded of } A}{\text{percentage change in income}}.\qquad \mathbf{3}$$

For most goods an increase in income leads to an increased demand (i.e. a shift in the demand curve rather than a movement along the curve) and income-elasticities will be positive. For some goods, *inferior goods*, an increase in income can however lead to a downward shift in demand. Income-elasticity of demand may vary considerably as income varies through a wide range. Consider the case of housing. At low levels of income housing may account for a considerable proportion of income. As income rises this proportion may fall as households increase the range of goods they consume. But at very high levels of income the proportion of income spent on housing may rise as householders switch into Georgian and Tudor mansions.

### Taste-elasticity of demand

If we look back to equation 1 we observe that we have an elas-

**Table 17** Price-elasticity of demand

| The e measure | What it means | Technical term |
| --- | --- | --- |
| $e = 0$ | $Q$ does not change in response to changes in $P$ | perfectly inelastic |
| $e > 0$ but $< 1$ | $Q$ changes by a smaller percentage than $P$ changes | relatively (i.e. relative to 1) inelastic |
| $e = 1$ | $Q$ changes by exactly the same percentage as $P$ changes | unit elasticity |
| $e > 1$ but $< \infty$ | $Q$ changes by a larger percentage than $P$ changes | relatively elastic |
| $e = \infty$ | consumers are willing to buy all they can obtain at the given price but are unwilling to buy any at a slightly higher price | perfectly elastic |

ticity of demand for every variable except tastes. Is there, then, an elasticity measure for tastes? The answer is *no* because tastes are a qualitative phenomenon which are not amenable to measurement. There are some things which can be done with numbers and some things which cannot.

As a conclusion to the whole of the elasticities section, let us summarize some of the more important points in the form of Tables 17, 18 and 19.

**Table 18** Cross-price elasticity of demand

| The e measure | What it means |
|---|---|
| $e_x < 0$ | the two goods are complements |
| $e_x > 0$ | the two goods are substitutes |
| $e_x$ has a *high* positive value | the two goods are *close* substitutes |
| $e_x$ has a *low* positive value | the two goods are *not* very close substitutes |

**Table 19** Income-elasticity of demand

| The e measure | What it means |
|---|---|
| $e_y = 0$ | $Q$ does not change in response to changes in $Y$ |
| $e_y > 0$ | as $Y$ changes (proportionately) $Q$ changes in the same direction – *normal good* |
| $e_y < 0$ | as $Y$ changes (proportionately) $Q$ changes in the opposite direction – *inferior good* |
| $e_y > 0$ but $< 1$ | the proportionate changes in $Y$ and $Q$ are in the same direction but $Q$ change is less than the $Y$ change |
| $e_y > 1$ | the proportionate changes in $Y$ and $Q$ are in the same direction but the the $Q$ change is greater than the $Y$ change |

## Revenue

So far we have looked at the concept of elasticity of demand from the point of view of the consumers of a commodity. But we can also use it to illustrate some of the problems facing producers. Consumer outlay is the revenue of the producers and, hence, variations in consumers' outlay also mean variations in producers' incomes. *Total revenue* is easily read off from the demand curve since it is defined as price times quantity. *Average rev-*

**Table 20** The derivation of marginal revenue

| Quantity bought and sold | Price per unit (average revenue) | Total revenue | Marginal revenue |
|---|---|---|---|
| *(1)* | *(2)* | *(3)* | *(4)* |
| 0 | 100 | 0 | |
| | | | +90 |
| 1 | 90 | 90 | |
| | | | +70 |
| 2 | 80 | 160 | |
| | | | +50 |
| 3 | 70 | 210 | |
| | | | +30 |
| 4 | 60 | 240 | |
| | | | +10 |
| 5 | 50 | 250 | |
| | | | −10 |
| 6 | 40 | 240 | |
| | | | −30 |
| 7 | 30 | 210 | |
| | | | −50 |
| 8 | 20 | 160 | |
| | | | −70 |
| 9 | 10 | 90 | |
| | | | −90 |
| 10 | 0 | 0 | |

*enue* (*AR*) is similarly straightforward, being total revenue divided by quantity purchased and, hence, equal to price. However, to reach his output decision, a producer must know (for reasons fully explored in later chapters) his *marginal revenue* (*MR*) which is defined as *the change in total revenue resulting from a unit change in quantity sold*. Table 20 illustrates this concept.

Column (*4*) shows the values of marginal revenue calculated as the changes in total revenue which can be observed in column (*3*). Note that as the number of units bought increases, marginal revenue declines, and that marginal revenue is less than price (average revenue). Figure 29 shows these points more clearly. Both observations result from the fact that the demand curve slopes downwards from left to right – an extra unit of output reduces the price of all units. It should be clear that marginal revenue varies with the price-elasticity of demand since a change in total revenue means a change in consumer expenditure, the size of which is measured by the elasticity of demand. An interesting case which we can appreciate without knowledge of further techniques is where demand is perfectly elastic (Figure 28a). Since each unit sells at the same price, marginal revenue must equal price (average revenue).

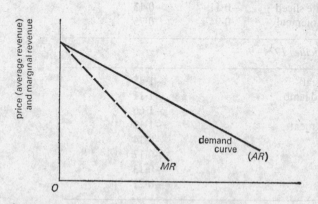

Figure 29

*Empirical measures of elasticities*

From the National Food Survey Committee Report for 1979 it is possible to obtain empirical estimates of income- and price-elasticities of demand. Two estimates of income-elasticities for each good are supplied. That the expenditure-elasticity is greater than the quantity elasticity indicates the extent to which consumers are buying a better quality product as their incomes rise. It is interesting that the elasticities for margarine confirm the commonplace view that it is an inferior good. This observation also applies to white bread though not to brown.

In the case of the income-elasticities, as the value of the elasticity falls the broader is the category as is shown by the values for all meats as opposed to beef or pork. Notice also that the signs of the elasticities for bread are negative which suggests

**Table 21** Empirical measures of elasticities

| Income-elasticities 1979 | Expenditure | Quantity purchased |
|---|---|---|
| cheese, natural | 0·42 | 0·40 |
| pork | 0·44 | 0·45 |
| beef and veal | 0·34 | 0·35 |
| butter | 0·22 | 0·22 |
| bread, white sliced | −0·11 | −0·13 |
| bread, wholemeal | 0·94 | 0·75 |

| Price-elasticities 1974−9 | |
|---|---|
| beef and veal | −1·45 |
| mutton and lamb | −1·11 |
| pork | −1·66 |
| all carcase meat | −1·17 |
| eggs | −0·14 |
| potatoes | −0·17 |
| white loaf | −0·13 |
| butter | −0·21 |

Source: *Household Food Consumption and Expenditure*, 1979, HMSO, 1980

**Table 22** Own- and cross-elasticities of demand for meat and poultry, 1972–9

| | *Elasticity with respect to the price of* | | | |
| | *Beef and veal* | *Mutton and lamb* | *Pork* | *Poultry* |
| --- | --- | --- | --- | --- |
| beef and veal | −1·60 | 0·23 | 0·08 | 0·03 |
| mutton and lamb | −0·53 | −1·41 | 0·12 | 0·13 |
| pork | −0·23 | 0·15 | −1·65 | −0·01 |
| poultry | +0·12 | 0·21 | −0·01 | −1·26 |

that people may reduce the quantity of bread bought when income rises though the fact that their expenditure rises may indicate a rising demand for 'real bread'.

All the price-elasticities are negative and consultation of the fuller list of elasticities in *Household Food Consumption and Expenditure* would reveal an absence of positive elasticities. This does not mean that they do not exist or that economists should not speculate on the implications of positive price-elasticities in order to check their reasoning about negative elasticities. In the eighteenth century, an economist and statistician, Sir Robert Giffen, thought he had come across an example in Ireland where, apparently, peasants reduced their consumption of potatoes when their price fell and bought more when their price rose.

## Cross-elasticity of demand

The price-elasticities we have looked at were *own*-price elasticities: that is, the elasticity of demand in response to a change in the price of the good. What may be more relevant however is the effect on the demand for a commodity if the price of another commodity changes, i.e. the cross-elasticity. In Table 21 are shown some cross-elasticities and we leave the reader to consider whether complements and substitutes exist.

## Statistics: a warning

The elasticity values we have quoted have been obtained from samples of household expenditures. They may therefore not be accurate measures of the whole population's response to price changes. When the reader has studied statistical theory he should consult the original sources of our data in order to examine the measure of the errors of the computations. Meanwhile, in this context we can remember that real world demand curves have to be constructed – they are not a free gift of nature! Economists and statisticians must collect data and they can plot their information on graphs. Such graphs are termed *scatter diagrams* and an example is given in Figure 30.

If the data collected and plotted are about a commodity which is assumed to be 'normal' and the economist's theory is correct then the scatter points would fall in the pattern shown in Figure 30. A visual interpretation of this diagram shows the price/quantity relationship to be generally downward sloping from left to right. The actual demand curve is obtained by finding the straight line (or curve) which is the best fit to the scatter points (by the technique known as *least squares regression*).

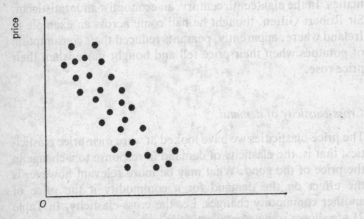

Figure 30

## Summary

This chapter has explored the demand for goods, concentrating on the case of private goods. The forces influencing this demand were seen to be the price of the good; the prices of other goods; consumer income; and tastes. It was assumed that people would buy more of a good as its price fell and the extent to which such a response occurred was known as price-elasticity of demand. Other demand-elasticities were also analysed. Finally, it was found that there were exceptions to the belief that people would buy more of a good if its price fell or if their income rose.

## Questions

1 Calculate the income-elasticities of demand for housing, transport, and services for different income changes from the data in Table 16.

2 If the price of *all* cars falls and an individual switches from buying a Volkswagen Golf to buying a Rover 3500, does this mean that Golfs are a Giffen good? Does this suggest that conventional statistical measures of elasticities fail to indicate the great importance of Giffen goods?

3 Comment on the following proposition: if we observe a rise in the price of a good accompanied by a rise in the amount bought then the demand curve of that good must be upward sloping.

# Chapter 8
# Supply

The supply of a commodity may be defined as the amount of that commodity which producers are willing and able to offer for sale. The stress on ability indicates that it is effective supply that is important.

## The determinants of supply

The determinants of supply can be summarized in a supply function or supply statement,

$$S_b = f(P_a, P_b, \ldots, P_z; P^f; O; T),$$

where $P_b$ is the price of the good which is to be supplied, $P_b, \ldots, P_z$ are the prices of the other goods; $P^f$ is the set of prices of the factors of production required to produce the good; $O$ is the objective(s) of the producer and $T$ is the state of technology.

### Producer's objectives

For some goods the amount supplied will depend upon whether the suppliers are attempting to obtain a large money income or a non-monetary income. A producer interested in maximizing universal goodwill or the sales of his product might be found to be providing more of a commodity than one who looked at the money income to be obtained from the sale of his good. The latter might cease producing the good if he felt that he could obtain a larger income from selling something else whereas the

saint, the universal fountain of good deeds, or the man who believes that everyone should eat Bono, would keep on providing
goods long after Mister Five Per Cent had given up.

## Price of the commodity

Other things being equal more of a commodity will be supplied
if the price rises as in Figure 31. This proposition follows naturally if we assume that producers are interested in money incomes. Higher rewards are necessary to induce producers to
incur the higher costs of increased outputs.

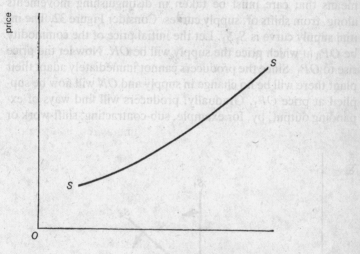

Figure 31

## Prices of other goods

If the price of another good rises then this will be a signal to
think about not producing the existing good and to consider
switching to the good whose price has risen. Another way of expressing this proposition is to say that as a result of the rise in
the price of the other good the opportunity cost of continuing in
the present line of business may be too high.

## Prices of factors of production

Since factor prices contribute to production costs then a rise in factor prices will cause an upward shift in production costs and hence in the supply curve.

## Technology

A change in technology brought about by an invention may lower costs and enable supply to be increased.

*Shifts and movements along supply curves.* The discussion so far means that care must be taken in distinguishing movements along, from shifts of, supply curves. Consider Figure 32. The initial supply curve is $S_1 S_1$. Let the initial price of the commodity be $OP_0$ at which price the supply will be $ON$. Now let the price rise to $OP_1$. Since the producers cannot immediately adapt their plant there will be no change in supply and $ON$ will now be supplied at price $OP_1$. Gradually, producers will find ways of expanding output, by, for example, sub-contracting, shift-work or

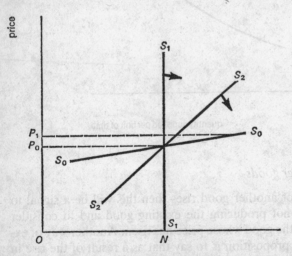

Figure 32

overtime working and they will expand output along $S_2 S_2$. Eventually, suppliers will fully adapt their plant by using known techniques which are more appropriate for the greater rates of output. This can be accomplished by recognizing that a greater output can be obtained by increasing the volume (capacity of the plant) and so enabling a movement along $S_0 S_0$. The distinction between the two supply curves $S_2 S_2$ and $S_0 S_0$ arises because in the case of the former a small plant can only increase a given output by increasing its *rate* of throughput, whereas the $S_0 S_0$ supply curve expresses the attempt to increase output by enlarging the volume of the plant as well as increasing the rate of throughput.

In Figure 33 we exhibit shifts of supply curves brought about by technical change. $S_3 S_3$ gives an overall increase in the supply of the commodity at all prices and lies below the curve $S_0 S_0$. On the other hand $S_1 S_1$ and $S_2 S_2$ yield improvements over certain ranges of prices. Thus the supply curve $S_1 S_1$ gives lower supply prices below $F$ and higher supply prices above $F$. Likewise the supply curve $S_2 S_2$ yields higher supply prices above $G$.

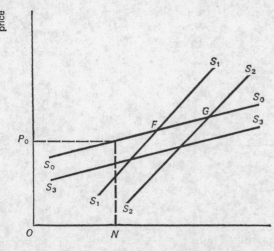

quantity supplied per unit of time

Figure 33

## Summary

In this chapter we looked briefly at the forces influencing the supply of goods. We took the view that supply would rise as price rose and that a price rise was necessary to overcome the tendency to rising costs caused by diminishing returns. Some causes of shifts in supply curves were also examined.

## Questions

1 In the previous chapter we discussed the price-elasticity of demand. Attempt a definition of price-elasticity of supply. What will be the main determinants of supply elasticity?

2 What are the causes of shifts in supply curves?

# Chapter 9
# The Market

## Introduction

With the information provided in the two previous chapters we can now continue the exploration of market behaviour which began in the introduction. Since the study of market behaviour has employed 90 per cent of economists' labours our discussion will be spread over two chapters. In this chapter we shall consider:

1 The implications of bringing the demand and supply curves together in a free market, i.e. one not subject to restrictions on entry or collusion by either buyers or sellers.

2 The possible results of interventions in markets.

3 Alternatives to the market.

4 Further mathematical properties of demand and supply curves. (This represents a more intensive exploration of the arguments of the section introduction using the simple technique of simultaneous equations.)

All the above subjects are discussed on the assumption that the demand and supply curves do not shift, i.e. only the price of the product changes. In the next chapter we shall look at situations where shifts occur.

Figure 34 brings the demand and supply curves for a commodity together. We notice three interesting features:

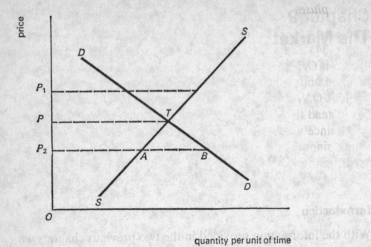

Figure 34

1 The two curves intersect once only because of the properties of the two curves. It might be possible for the curves to intersect more than once and we shall ignore such possibilities.

2 The two curves intersect at a *positive* price $OP$ – if this were not so then the good would not be scarce. This price is termed the *equilibrium* price since it is the only one which balances the market.

3 The market equilibrium is stable. Suppose there was a displacement of price from $OP$ to $OP_1$, then demand would contract and supply would extend. This would result in stocks piling up and in an endeavour to dispose of them producers would lower prices until the market was once more cleared at price $OP$. (Readers should now analyse the results from a change in price to $OP_2$.) Provisionally, we may conclude that stability exists because the demand curve slopes downward while the supply curve slopes upward. This conclusion will be modified in the next chapter when we shall observe situations (*cobweb cycles*) in which no equilibrium is reached following a shift of demand.

## *The surpluses*

Another unusual feature of the market situation is revealed by Figure 34. The price consumers pay for *all* units of the commodity is $OP$. Yet the price they would be prepared to give for individual units is given by points on the demand curve. Thus for the unit $ON_1$ consumers would be prepared to pay a price $OP_1$ but instead they get that unit for $OP$. This is a common occurrence since we normally find ourselves willing to pay more for some things than in fact we are asked. This state of affairs exists because it is rarely worthwhile for a producer to attempt to find out how much each person would in fact give for each unit he wished to consume, and it might be difficult for him to prevent a person who was prepared to pay a high price from getting it at a low price. There are costs of finding out what consumers will be prepared to pay. To get each consumer to pay exactly what he would be willing to pay, producers must be able to negotiate with each consumer separately and also be able to negotiate separately for every unit sold to each consumer. The difference

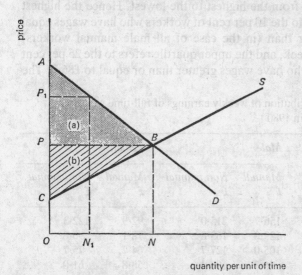

Figure 35 (a) Consumer surplus. (b) Producer surplus or rent

that exists between the outlay which consumers are willing to pay, area *OABN* under the demand curve, and what they have to pay, *OPBN*, is called *consumer surplus* and represents a gain to consumers equal to the area of the triangle *APB*. But this market result is mutually beneficial because there is also a difference between the revenue at which producers are willing to supply a good and the revenue they obtain; and this difference or gain is called the *producer surplus* or *rent*, represented by the triangle *PBC* in Figure 35.

### Intervention in markets

One of the most interesting areas where it might be considered that government intervention should take place is the labour market. Since poverty often arises because of low wages it seems sensible to raise wages. Table 23 reveals the full-time earnings of male and female workers in Great Britain in 1980. This distribution of earnings was obtained by ranking all workers' earnings from the highest to the lowest. Hence the highest decile refers to the 10 per cent of workers who have wages equal to or greater than (in the case of all male manual workers) £156·7 per week, and the upper quartile refers to the 25 per cent of workers who have wages greater than or equal to £86·3. The

**Table 23** Distribution of weekly earnings of full-time workers in Great Britain 1980

|  | Male | | Female | |
|---|---|---|---|---|
|  | Manual £ | Non-manual £ | Manual £ | Non-manual £ |
| highest decile | 156·7 | 215·0 | 92·9 | 122·3 |
| upper quartile | 129·0 | 163·8 | 78·1 | 96·6 |
| median | 105·0 | 127·7 | 64·7 | 75·7 |
| lower quartile | 86·3 | 100·4 | 58·8 | 61·0 |
| lowest decile | 71·8 | 89·3 | 45·6 | 51·4 |

Source: *New Earnings Survey*, 1980, HMSO, 1981

median is the wage of the worker whose earnings fall half-way along the distribution. The lower quartile and lower decile are defined in a similar way to the upper quartile and upper decile. The wage surveys reveal that:

There is a considerable spread of wages;
The earnings of women are consistently lower than those of men;
The earnings of manual workers tend to be lower than those of non-manual workers.

Now let us suppose that it is deemed undesirable for anyone to earn less than £100 per week. What would be the effects of such a policy? We can simplify the analysis by assuming as in Figure 36 that all units of labour are homogeneous. Figure 36 then shows the demand for and supply of homogeneous labour and indicates that the wage which will clear the market is $OW$. Now suppose that $OW$ is deemed to be too low and the government declares that no one shall work for less than $OW_1$.

The effect of a legal minimum wage of $OW_1$ is that $ON_2$ workers will try to get jobs but only $ON_1$ will be hired. Since $ON_1$ is less than $ON$ then the effect of the minimum wage will

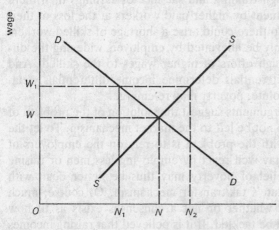

quantity per unit of time

Figure 36

be to reduce employment. Since there are now $N_1 N$ workers who previously had jobs without incomes, poverty has not been overcome despite the fact that workers who are employed receive higher wages. The effect of a minimum wage on employment will depend upon:

1 The elasticity of the employers' demand for labour. If the demand is relatively inelastic there may be a much reduced unemployment effect.

2 Whether or not higher wages lead to increased effort. If increased effort does result then the employers' demand will shift to the right.

It is conceivable that the distribution of receipts between employers and workers can be altered without any serious side effects; and that as a result of a wage increase morale might improve. But we do not know because no serious experiments on these hypotheses have been carried out. It may be that employers simply pass on wage increases in the form of price increases and governments cannot prevent them.

Once we relax the simplifying assumption of homogeneous labour then a further difficulty may arise. Since many skills are acquired through training and sacrifice of earnings then there may be resentment by higher paid workers at the loss of their differentials. So there could arise a shortage of skilled workers which could only be alleviated by employers widening the differentials through offers of higher wages to the skilled. And since wage differentials determine income differentials, relative, if not absolute, poverty may re-emerge.

The above arguments suggest that solution of the problem of poverty should not be left to the market mechanism. To let the market deal with the problem is to rely on the employers of labour, who may well react by employing less men or raising prices. The relief of poverty may thus be better dealt with through the state's tax/transfer mechanism. Of course, much depends upon whether or not a consensus exists as to how poverty should be tackled. If it is believed that raising incomes by direct intervention in the labour market is the best method (the question of commitment to a particular ideology raised in Chapter 2) then nothing more can be said. But if it can be demonstrated that other methods may be more efficient then people may accept them. The alternatives would seem to be:

1 Since unskilled workers earn less than skilled workers the state should subsidize training programmes.

2 Since poverty is linked to the number of dependents supported by one wage the state should introduce child allowances, tax reliefs and other low-income subsidies.

All such policies are, however, mere suggestions since we know so little about the actual effects of different policies. What we have done is to indicate the number of jobs that might be available after a wage rise and the redistribution of benefits that might then occur. These are the two predictive aspects of intervention that we considered in the previous section.

### Housing, health and education

Now let us look at another method of dealing with poverty. Suppose the State decided that instead of raising wages it would try to keep down the prices of the commodities which the poor buy. The most essential of these commodities are housing, health and education. Let us take housing services as an example. Figure 37 represents the market situation for rented housing services. Price (rent) has been established at $OP$ and $ON$ units of housing services are supplied. Now suppose the government fixes the price at $OP_1$. From our previous analysis we can predict that there will be an excess demand for housing. The supply of housing tends to be relatively fixed in the short run (which may be a considerable time period in the case of housing services) and we therefore depict the excess demand as $NN_1$ ($S^1$ $S^1$ may be considered the short-run supply curve and $SS$ the long-run curve). Later, as houses fall into disrepair because rents are insufficient to maintain them, or as houses are taken out of the controlled market by such loopholes as exist in the law, the supply of housing contracts to $P_1 A$ and excess demand

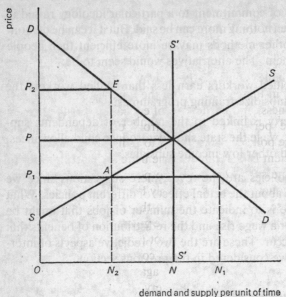

price

Figure 37

rises to $N_1 N_2$. Hence the conclusion follows that intervention has resulted in a shortage of housing.

But now let us look at who gets the available houses, $ON_2$. Having decided to interfere with market processes the state must take responsibility for allocation. Clearly in a situation of excess demand there might be several possible rationing rules. The state may operate a 'first-come, first-served' rule, or the state may decide that only those who would have been willing to pay a price $OP_2$ or more should get the houses. In the case of this group their consumer surplus would be $P_1DEA$ instead of the $P_2DE$ they would have obtained if they had had to pay $OP_2$. Notice also that the producer surplus would have been reduced to $SP_1A$. As a final case, suppose the government was intent on allocating the $ON_2$ houses available to those who could only pay $OP_1$ or more; in order to achieve its policy the government would have to discriminate on a non-price basis by such criteria as social need.

Some kind of objective similar to that outlined above seems to underlie much social policy. Health and education are provided at below market prices and there is evidence of excess demand. The state then expects its administrators to make these services available only to those who satisfy certain social criteria. Thus in the case of health the criterion is the seriousness of the illness, and in the case of education it is the proven ability of the person to benefit from educational courses. Whether these policies, which serve to redistribute income, are the most efficient is debatable. Some believe that it is better to provide income supplements to the poor in the form of non-transferable vouchers which can only be spent on the goods in question. These people also believe that by such methods the supply of such goods would be made greater whereas the other procedure implies that supply cannot readily be expanded and ignores the possibility that it might contract. They would also argue that in order to discriminate against the rich the state is forced to lower the quality of the service – 'who would go and live in a council house' and 'why wait six months for an operation' are expressions symptomatic of a lowering of quality. As in all issues of social policy we still do not know which are the most efficient methods. For some purposes, as when consumers are ignorant or short-sighted, the policies pursued may be the most efficient. But they do run the risk of making people dependent upon others and may not educate people into thinking for themselves. State policy is of course full of paradoxes when it comes to the question 'does the consumer know what he wants?'. It insists, for example, on compulsory education but not compulsory chest X-ray examinations.

## Rationing

What was suggested in the previous paragraph was that there are occasions when governments believe that physical rationing is better than rationing by prices. This presumption is even applied to the allocation of private goods under certain circumstances. In the Second World War the UK government introduced food rationing. Each person was allowed weekly fixed quantities of particular foodstuffs (sugar, butter, bacon, etc.). This rationing system worked tolerably well because the state was dealing with basic wants and these were reasonably homogeneous for all people. Hence the physiological needs together with the ethical climate ('we are all in this together') combined to make food rationing work. At a later stage the coalition government introduced rationing for tinned foodstuffs (fruit and meat) and clothing. For both these groups it was recognized that peoples' tastes varied. So each person was given a fixed quantity of $D$ coupons (for tinned foods) and clothing coupons which he could spend as he wished.

This war-time experience suggests that where needs are fairly simple and homogeneous a physical rationing system might work. Black markets, in which rationed goods were sold at higher prices but without coupons, did develop but they were never extensive enough to cause the system to break down.

## The market for blood

One of the most interesting commodities to be allocated by non-pricing methods in the UK is blood for transfusion purposes. Surgeons demand blood for numerous operations and blood is collected from donors by the National Blood Transfusion Service. The collection of blood and its use is remarkable both for the absence of the use of a price mechanism by which to reward donors and ration supplies to users; and for the absence of a central planning dictator who would forecast demands and command supplies from suitable people. On the supply side the only instrument used is moral persuasion, and on the demand side professional responsibility presumably safeguards against abuse and wastage.

## Allocation by non-profit institutions

Blood is a special case but it serves to introduce other interesting cases of allocation by non-profit-making private institutions. Sometimes a price is charged but it is less than that which could be obtained in a free market; sometimes no price is charged but another condition of qualification is imposed.

The price of tickets for the FA Cup Final is an example of prices charged which are below those which could be obtained in a free market. Each year a thriving black market operates in which tickets are sold for prices well above their nominal stated prices. Why does the Football Association not fix high prices? Why do they forego extra income? The usual argument is that the FA believes that the club fans who have loyally supported their teams throughout the season, perhaps standing on the terraces in rain and snow, should not be 'exploited'. Why should the rich man who seldom goes to a match be able to outbid the poor man for a ticket? The FA therefore operates as a charity and then seeks to prevent a black market emerging by controlling the issue of tickets.[1]

People sometimes prefer that some resources should be allocated according to merit and not income. University entrance is decided not by Mammon but by Jove; if a person possesses riches but not wisdom he cannot get in.

Do these examples contradict economic behaviour? The answer is No! Economics does not say how a man should maximize his welfare nor does it state that in pursuing his happiness a man should ignore the happiness of others. 'No man is an island' said John Donne, and most men, including economists, accept the truth of his dictum.

## Simultaneous equations: a useful digression

In the section introduction we suggested that the major difficulties confronting the central planner concerned the collection and the analysis of information. This we said involved the solution of vast numbers of equations. Now the mention of the word equations invites the use of mathematical techniques – a

---

1. Charities allocate resources outside the market and the number and variety of charities is endless. Indeed the law provides no definition of a charity, but prefers to test each claim (for tax exemption purposes) to charitable status on its merits.

thought which sometimes prompts consternation and dismay. Indeed many people feel that the introduction of mathematics into economics makes the subject more difficult than it needs to be, and also makes the subject impersonal.

Both the arguments against the use of mathematics fall to the ground if it can be shown that the use of mathematics illuminates the subject. In this section we shall use mathematics to explore the problem of market determination. The mathematics used will be the technique of simultaneous equations which is taught in O-level mathematics courses. We are all fairly familiar with the type of question which says: 'If two knives and three forks cost 45p and five knives and three forks cost 66p, what is the price of a knife and what is the price of a fork?' It is this type of mathematical reasoning that underlies the type of problem which we shall consider. From our earlier discussions we may recall two propositions:

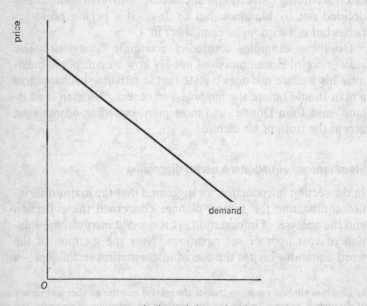

Figure 38

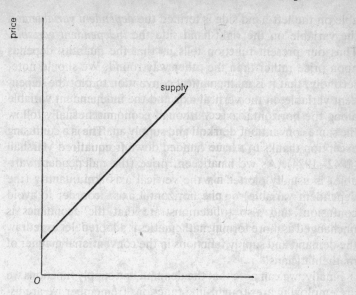

Figure 39

1 As the price of a commodity falls more of the commodity is demanded.

2 As the price of a commodity rises more of the commodity is supplied.

Both these propositions have been demonstrated with the use of graphs, as in Figures 38 and 39. Both graphs express a unique relationship between price and quantity (demanded or supplied). Such relations are called *functions*. An earlier example of such a unique relation was the production function of Chapter 3.

We shall explore the mathematics of functions more fully in Chapter 13 but we can note one or two points now. First, observe that the functions in Figures 38 and 39 are of the form:

$q = f(p)$

where $q$ represents quantity and $p$ represents price. The variable on the left-hand side is termed the *dependent variable* and the variable on the right-hand side the *independent variable*. Thus our present function tells us that the quantity depends upon price rather than the other way round. We should note, secondly, that it is mathematical convention to plot the dependent variable on the vertical axis and the independent variable along the horizontal axis. Although economists usually follow the same convention, demand and supply analysis is a confusing exception thanks to a habit handed down from Alfred Marshall (1842–1924). As we have seen, price (the independent variable) is usually plotted on the vertical axis and quantity (the dependent variable) on the horizontal axis. In order to avoid confusion, and also to demonstrate that the economics is unchanged as more formal mathematics is adopted, let us redraw the demand and supply functions in the conventional manner of mathematicians.

Finally, we can note that the demand and supply functions we are employing are straight-line functions (remember we are using such functions for simplicity only). Each one, therefore, can be represented by the equation for a straight-line function (the statistical problem of fitting a straight line to a set of real world data was mentioned in Chapter 7). Thus we may present the demand function as

$$q_d = a + bp, \qquad\qquad 1$$

where the parameter $a$ represents the intercept on the vertical axis (when $p$ is zero, $q_d$ is equal to $a$) and the parameter $b$ is the slope of the demand curve.[2] Note that when the demand curve slopes downwards, as in Figure 40, the slope coefficient will be negative. Similarly, we may present the supply function as

$$q_s = c + dp, \qquad\qquad 2$$

where the parameter $c$ is the intercept on the vertical axis and the parameter $d$ represents the slope of the supply function.

2. For those who may have forgotten, a parameter is a constant once its value has been specified for a particular function.

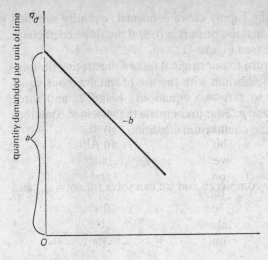

Figure 40 The demand function $q_d = a - bp$

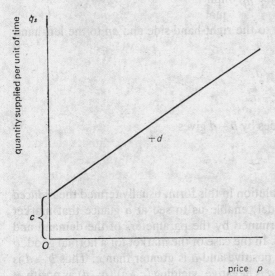

Figure 41 The supply function $q_s = c + dp$

Note that when the supply curve is normal, quantity supplied will be negative when the price is zero and the slope coefficient, $d$, will be positive (see Figure 41).

We can now return to our original task of illustrating the concept of market equilibrium with the use of simultaneous equations. We have, so far, two equations, **1** and **2**, and three unknowns $q_d$, $q_s$, and $p$. Thus to complete the system of equations we must include the equilibrium condition,

$$q_d = q_s. \qquad\qquad 3$$

Our model is now completed and we can solve for $q_d (= q_s)$ and $p$.

$$q_d = a + bp,$$

$$q_s = c + dp,$$

$$q_d = q_s.$$

Thus $a + bp = c + dp$,

and taking the $a$ to the right-hand side and $dp$ to the left-hand side

$$bp - dp = c - a,$$

or   $p(b - d) = c - a$.

Dividing both sides by $b - d$ gives

$$p = \frac{c - a}{b - d}.$$

Presenting the solution in this form, usually termed the *reduced form* of the model, enable us to see at a glance that market price, $p$, is determined by the parameters of the demand and supply functions. In the case of the market for a normal good, $b$ is negative, $d$ is positive and $a$ is greater than $c$. Thus $b - d$ is negative and $c - a$ is negative, yielding $(c - a)/(b - d)$ as positive, i.e. market price is positive.

Let us now try a numerical example:

$q_d = 710 - 15p,$

$q_s = -10 + 10p.$

Setting $q_d = q_s$ we have

$710 - 15p = -10 + 10p,$

or   $710 + 10 = 10p + 15p,$

hence   $720 = 25p,$

and   $28 \cdot 8 = p.$

Equilibrium price is $28 \cdot 8$. To find equilibrium quantity we may feed this value of price into either the demand function or the supply function since $q_d = q_s$.

$q_d = 710 - 15 (28 \cdot 8)$

$= 710 - 432$

$= 278,$

$q_s = -10 + 10 (28 \cdot 8)$

$= -10 + 288$

$= 278.$

Perhaps we should finally note that the mechanics of market analysis can also be employed by the planner. We must recall that the derivation of equilibrium prices and quantities have been obtained on the assumption that both demand and supply statements are available. A major task of any central planner would be to gather this information unless he assumed that everyone would enjoy what he wanted or what he thought they would want. The cost of collecting such information could be enormous. He would have to ask everyone what they wanted at different hypothetical prices for different goods, and he would have to add all the answers together to obtain a general market demand table. From this table or schedule he would then have to obtain a general demand statement. Similarly he would have to perform the same tasks for the production side of his economy. It is these prior costs of information (which can be colossal) which, added to the computer problems of solving millions of equations, make wholesale central planning seem difficult.

## Summary

In this chapter we looked at the market as a means of allocating resources. We found that there are circumstances in which the market gives results which society wishes to reject. The implications of interference in the market system were considered. It should not be assumed that interference is not warranted. What man has put together he can pull apart. The real issues are: what is the most efficient method of interference, and which method will give the least adverse effects?

## Questions

1 What implications follow from the fact that demand curves intersect supply curves from above, and slope downwards from left to right, whereas supply curves slope upwards from left to right?

2 Can a consumer get more than he pays for?

3 If instead of giving workers a minimum wage we give them a minimum income subsidy will they work? Why do economists tend to accept interference with people's willingness to work rather than interference with the employers' willingness to hire them?

4 The government is anxious to curb inflation and the TUC agrees to cooperate if a minimum wage of £90 per week is introduced together with a price freeze on all goods and services. Assuming the government accepts, what consequences might follow?

5 'If rationing of the necessities of life was considered the best way of controlling demand and allocating resources in wartime, there is surely good reason to do so in peacetime.' Discuss.

6 Comment on the relative merits of conscription and mercenaries (use of price mechanism) as methods of raising armies.

7 Why do we see queues forming at bus stops at peak periods? Why don't we see some people jumping the queue by offering to pay more? Are queues ever more efficient for rationing resources than prices? What goods and services are usually rationed by queues?

8 Why are city centres dominated by industry and commerce, and suburbs dominated by residential housing?

9 Traffic signals allocate road space and prices allocate some goods. Why don't we use prices to allocate road space at junctions?

10 In discussing low pay it was suggested that instead of raising wages it might be more efficient to increase family allowances, etc. Since these are subsidies, what might their possible effects be upon people's willingness to work? Illustrate by means of a diagram.

11  The government has a choice of policies for combating the housing problems of the poor. Either it can:
(a) give them money to buy houses;
(b) give them vouchers to be spent only on houses;
(c) provide them with houses.
Comment on the relative merits of these schemes.

12 By what non-price measures might a Government increase the supply of non-toxic blood?

13 In the absence of a system of rationing by price how should the National Health Service decide whether
(a) resources should be devoted to geriatric wards or to spina bifida treatment;
(b) Mr Smith should be supplied with a kidney machine instead of Mr Jones?

14 'If the government gives income subsidies to poor farmers this will remove rural poverty but promote labour immobility.' Discuss.

15 How does the market determine the optimum length of life for a motor car?

16 Calculate the equilibrium prices and quantities from the following market information:

(a)  $q_d = 35 - 8p$,
$q_s = -5 + 2p$,

(b)  $q_d = 10 - 2p$,
$q_s = 4 + 4p$,

(c)  $q_d = 16 - 8p$,
$q_s = 4 + 2p$.

17 Our previous questions devoted to the solution of simultaneous equations were confined to systems of *linear* equations; that is, demand and supply statements which yield straight lines. However, textbooks and casual observation suggest that perhaps we should analyse *curves*. The solutions of systems of curves involves the use of quadratic equations of the form $ax^2 + bx + c = 0$ as opposed to the linear equation, $ax + b = 0$. For the solution we can use the formula:

$$x = \frac{-b \pm \surd(b^2 - 4ac)}{2a}.$$

The $\pm$ indicates there will be two roots (solutions) and we reject the negative one. Why?

Now try the following:

(a)  $q_d = 100 - p^2$,
$q_s = 6p$

(b)  $q_d = 10 - 2p$,
$q_s = 5p^2$.

# Chapter 10
## The Market Continued

The previous chapter was concerned with examining situations where demand and supply curves remain fixed but where there might be possibilities of outside intervention. This chapter examines the more usual cases of markets where demand and supply curves shift. Shifts of demand can come about through changes in incomes, tastes or the prices of other goods; shifts in supply may come about through changes in technologies or factor prices.

Consider Figure 42. Initially demand and supply are in equilibrium at price $OP$ and quantity demanded and supplied $OQ$. Now let there be a shift of the demand curve to $D_1 D_1$ which puts the market in disequilibrium. If there is not an immediate response of supply then Figure 42 suggests price will rise to $OP_1$ to clear the market. But in practice the disequilibrium situation may be more complicated. Some firms may not raise their prices but attempt physically to ration available supplies at price $OP$. Other firms may raise prices to $OP_1$; some, uncertain of where the ultimate equilibrium price will be, might raise their prices by amounts varying between $OP$ and $OP_1$. *Hence, disequilibrium may be characterized by a dispersion of prices rather than a single price.*

The existence of price dispersion will indicate opportunities of gain to both buyers and sellers. Buyers will shop around to find the lowest price and suppliers will expand supplies as long as there is a possibility of profit. Thus, at some intermediate stage we may see an expansion of supply along the short run

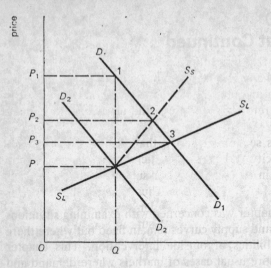

demand and supply per unit of time

Figure 42

supply curve SS and a contraction of price dispersion. And eventually, supply will have expanded along the long run supply curve and a single price established at *OP*.

Thus, a shift in demand (and the analysis of shifts in supply is similar) may provoke a variety of responses:

1 Immediate supply response – a run down of stocks or physical rationing of available supplies at the initial price or price rationing by means of a price rise.

2 Short-run response – increase supply and raise price to cover the cost of expanding supply.

3 Long-run response – increase supply until the market clears at a price which does not cause buyers and sellers to revise their plans.

How buyers and sellers respond to changes depends upon the information available to them and the nature of the goods. In the markets for manufactured goods it may be possible to cope with short-run changes in demand by raising and lowering stocks; such markets are known as *fix-price markets* and the apparent rigidity may owe nothing to monopoly power. In other markets, especially agricultural markets where goods are not easy to store, changes in demand may lead to immediate price responses; such markets are known as *flex-price markets*. Response will therefore depend upon the elasticities of demand and supply.

The previous section suggested that except in the cases of perfect inelasticity and perfect elasticity of demand or supply curves, a shift in either demand or supply would give rise to both a price and an output effect. Thus, if the supply were perfectly inelastic then an increase in demand would simply raise price; there would be no change in supply. Similarly, if supply were perfectly price-elastic then an increase in demand would simply cause an extension of supply. These two cases are shown in Figures 43 and 44 respectively.

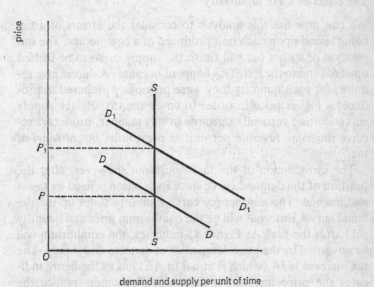

Figure 43 Pure price effect

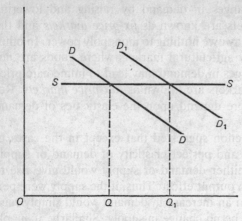

Figure 44 Pure quantity effect

## The effect of a tax or subsidy

We can now use this analysis to consider the effects of a tax being levied upon each unit produced of a commodity. The imposition of such a tax will cause the supply curve to be shifted upwards and to the left. This happens because producers now require, for each quantity they were previously prepared to produce, a higher price in order to cover the tax. By the supply curve shifting vertically upwards in this manner, producers receive the same revenue per unit as previously, but now *net* of tax.

The introduction of the tax should not, however, alter the position of the demand curve since its position is fixed by tastes and income. The new supply curve therefore slides up the demand curve. But what will be the equilibrium price and quantity sold after the tax? As Figure 45 indicates, the equilibrium will be governed by the price-elasticities of demand and supply. The tax increase is $JK$ (which is equal to $AE$) but as the figure indicates the price increase is only $CE$. Consumers reduce the amount they consume by $NM$ (which is equal to $BC$) but they cannot completely escape the tax and therefore pay $CE$ per

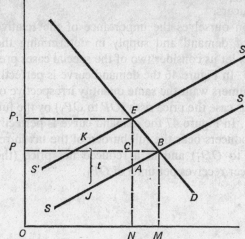

Figure 45

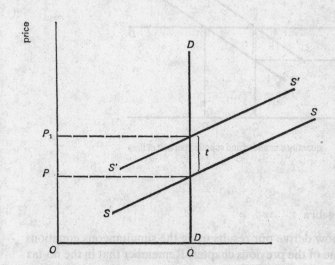

Figure 46

unit. The remaining portion of the tax increase, $AC$ per unit, is borne by the producers.

To impress upon ourselves the importance of the relative price elasticities of demand and supply in determining the effects of a unit tax let us consider two of the special cases previously referred to. In Figure 46 the demand curve is perfectly inelastic, i.e. consumers want the same quantity irrespective of the price and in this case the price rises ($OP$ to $OP_1$) by the full amount of the tax. In Figure 47 the demand curve is perfectly elastic and the producers bear the full burden of the tax in reduced sales ($OQ$ to $OQ_1$) and in a reduced net price (the amount the producer receives per unit) of $OP_1$.

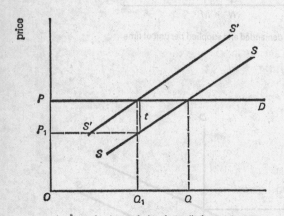

Figure 47

## Some algebra

Let us now derive our results using the simultaneous equations technique of the previous chapter. Remember that in the no-tax situation the reduced form of the market model was

$$p = (c - a/b - d).$$

What happens to the model when a unit tax is introduced? Since the tax does not affect demand, the demand function remains as

$$q_d = a + bp.$$

However, as we have seen, the tax *does* affect the supply function. Note that the price, $p$, in the supply function is a supply price, i.e. the quantity that the producer is *willing* to supply depends upon the return that he expects to receive for each unit. In the no-tax situation this return per unit is indeed the expected market price, but with the introduction of a unit tax any expected return per unit is reduced by the amount of the tax. Thus, the quantity that any producer is willing to supply now depends upon the expected return per unit *net of tax*. Representing the unit tax as $t$ the supply function has become, therefore,

$$q_s = c + d(p - t).$$

We can now solve for price and quantity.

In equilibrium $q_d = q_s$,

thus $a + bp = c + d(p - t)$,

$$= c + dp - dt.$$

Rearranging gives $bp - dp = c - a - dt$,

or $p(b - d) = c - a - dt$,

and dividing both sides by $b - d$

$$p = \frac{c - a}{b - d} - \frac{d}{b - d}(t).$$

Putting the tax result against the no-tax result we can readily see the impact of the tax as:

No tax $\quad p = \dfrac{c - a}{b - d}$, $\qquad\qquad\qquad\qquad$ **1**

Unit tax $\quad p = \dfrac{c - a}{b - d} - \dfrac{d}{b - d}(t).$ $\qquad\qquad\quad$ **2**

Equation **2** differs from **1** by the amount of $-\{d/(b - d)\}t$, thus $p$

varies with $t$ according to the expression $-\{d/(b-d)\}$. Now in the case of a normal good, $d$ is positive, $b$ is negative and $b-d$ is negative; thus $-d/(b-d)$ is positive (the tax raises the price).

Therefore $p$ varies with $t$ positively according to the relative slopes of the demand and supply curves (and not the intercept coefficients).

## The tax conundrum

The distinction between movements along demand and supply curves and shifts of demand and supply curves is so important that it is worth working through another example which illustrates the pitfalls that arise when ambiguous words like 'rise' and 'fall', 'increase' and 'decrease' are used. Consider the following statement:

'A tax on a commodity causes the price to rise and demand to fall. The fall in demand will then restore price to its original level.'

Now let us take this quotation sentence by sentence. The first sentence tells us that as a result of the tax the supply curve will be shifted upwards and the result is a rise in price. So far so good, the first half of the first sentence is reiterating what we have discussed in the previous section. But will demand fall? Demand may contract if the demand curve is price-elastic, but if we encounter a zero price-elasticity then there need be no fall in demand. Let us, however, assume that the demand curve is price-elastic and demand contracts; what then can we make of the final sentence? Here we encounter the ambiguity of the phrase 'fall in demand'. We are given no indication or evidence to suggest that a tax can shift a demand curve to the left or right, nor are we told that there has been a change in tastes or fall in incomes. So there is no reason to suppose that price will fall to its original level. Figure 48 sketches out the conclusions reached in the previous paragraph. As a result of the tax the supply curve shifts from $SS$ to $S_1S_1$. At the new price $OP_1$ demand contracts along $DD$ to $OQ_1$ from $OQ$. Price cannot fall to its original level unless the demand curve shifts to $D_1D_1$.

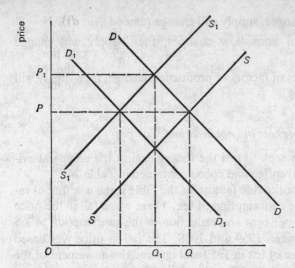

quantity demanded and supplied per unit of time

Figure 48

## Testing the theory

We are now in a position to make further applications of the theory of demand and supply. From previous discussions we know that the theory of demand makes certain predictions about the consumption of a good and certain key variables. These predictions are:

1 If price changes, demand will change (extend or contract) in the opposite direction;

2 If income changes, demand will normally change (shift);

3 If tastes change, demand will change (shift);

4 If the prices of substitutes change, demand will change (shift);

5 If the prices of complementary goods change, demand will change (shift).

Likewise the theory of supply predicts that when there are no monopolies or restrictions on markets, then:

1 If price changes, supply will change (extend);

2 If technical know-how changes, then supply will change (shift);

3 If the prices of factors of production change, then supply will change (shift).

### 'The cups that cheer but not inebriate' Cowper

We shall now seek to test the theory against the empirical evidence for tea, coffee and cocoa contained in Table 24.

The most noticeable feature of the table is the continuous reduction in the consumption of tea. There was a fall in the price of tea of 5·4 per cent and reduction in the consumption of 7·5 per cent between 1959 and 1968. The fall in price was based upon the price of tea in 1959 and ignored the movement of the prices of other beverages; the fall in relative price was even greater than the absolute price fall. From 1969 onwards the price of tea rose but so did the prices of all other beverages as a result of inflation. However, the price of tea *relative* to that of instant coffee fell by 8 per cent and consumption of tea declined by about 20 per cent between 1969 and 1977. The second noticeable feature of the table is the rise in the consumption of instant coffee despite the rise in its price relative to those of other beverages. Finally, there is the apparent constancy in the consumption of coffee beans and cocoa despite changes in relative prices.

The behaviour of tea consumption seems to refute our hypothesis concerning the normal relationship between price and demand. We should have expected demand to extend as price fell. So presumably something else happened to disturb the prediction. Now, real incomes rose over the period and therefore we can reject the hypothesis that a fall in incomes led to a fall in demand. There are, however, other possibilities. First, the price of some commodity complementary to tea, such as milk or sugar, rose in price. Secondly, tastes have changed. Thirdly, tea is an inferior good. Although we have not produced the evidence on the behaviour of milk and sugar prices

**Table 24** Average prices per lb and consumption per head in ounces per week of non-alcoholic beverages 1959–77

| Year | Tea | | Coffee (bean and ground) | | Coffee (instant) | | Cocoa | |
|------|------|------|------|------|------|------|------|------|
| | Price pence | Consumption oz | Price pence | Consumption oz | Price pence | Consumption oz | Price pence | Consumption oz |
| 1959 | 32·29 | 2·80 | 35·33 | 0·11 | 59·11 | 0·28 | 20·45 | 0·16 |
| 1960 | 31·83 | 2·80 | 31·25 | 0·10 | 99·33 | 0·29 | 20·25 | 0·16 |
| 1961 | 31·50 | 2·84 | 34·04 | 0·08 | 90·96 | 0·30 | 20·62 | 0·16 |
| 1962 | 31·42 | 2·79 | 35·91 | 0·10 | 87·95 | 0·20 | 19·95 | 0·16 |
| 1963 | 31·12 | 2·82 | 35·21 | 0·09 | 85·54 | 0·25 | 20·33 | 0·18 |
| 1964 | 30·95 | 2·69 | 37·46 | 0·11 | 92·17 | 0·23 | 19·88 | 0·18 |
| 1965 | 30·87 | 2·61 | 39·00 | 0·10 | 91·71 | 0·26 | 20·12 | 0·18 |
| 1966 | 30·75 | 2·64 | 39·81 | 0·10 | 92·86 | 0·29 | 19·10 | 0·19 |
| 1967 | 30·85 | 2·70 | 39·98 | 0·10 | 92·37 | 0·30 | 19·87 | 0·17 |
| 1968 | 30·55 | 2·59 | 42·63 | 0·09 | 89·33 | 0·36 | 19·45 | 0·18 |
| 1969 | 30·84 | 2·52 | 40·42 | 0·13 | 92·50 | 0·38 | 21·78 | 0·20 |
| 1970 | 32·40 | 2·59 | 48·78 | 0·09 | 94·14 | 0·42 | 23·12 | 0·20 |
| 1971 | 34·37 | 2·39 | 52·01 | 0·10 | 104·99 | 0·44 | 24·47 | 0·16 |
| 1972 | 34·48 | 2·23 | 52·23 | 0·12 | 100·91 | 0·46 | 23·42 | 0·16 |
| 1973 | 35·53 | 2·16 | 59·92 | 0·09 | 111·33 | 0·47 | 22·26 | 0·15 |
| 1974 | 38·97 | 2·24 | 67·61 | 0·10 | 121·20 | 0·51 | 28·78 | 0·17 |
| 1975 | 43·98 | 2·18 | 76·44 | 0·11 | 135·82 | 0·50 | 39·66 | 0·14 |
| 1976 | 50·25 | 2·06 | 106·07 | 0·10 | 186·01 | 0·50 | 45·88 | 0·15 |
| 1977 | 98·04 | 2·21 | 235·15 | 0·07 | 368·57 | 0·36 | 65·61 | 0·16 |

Source: *Household Food Consumption and Expenditure*, Annual Reports of National Food Survey Committee

there is no reason to think that they rose at an exceptionally fast rate over the period. Moreover, any changes in their prices would presumably have affected the demands for the other beverages – which does not seem to have occurred. But the second and third hypotheses seem plausible.

Casual observation does suggest that younger age groups consume less tea than their elders. (Indeed, there is now a noticeable swing towards soft drinks rather than tea or coffee.) But, in addition to the generation shift in tastes, there has also been a tendency, as real incomes have risen, to switch to 'convenience foods' and instant coffee falls into that category. So what we observe is a shift of the demand curve for tea to the left and a shift of the demand curve for instant coffee to the right. Note also that the fall in the demand for tea has occurred despite large advertising campaigns designed to promote the consumption of tea – particularly tea bags.

But how can we account for the fall in the price of tea? We have here an illustration of *the identification problem*. The statistics represent the interaction of demand and supply forces

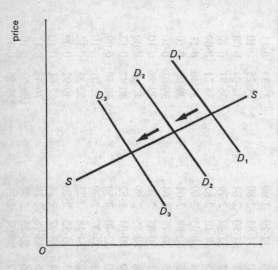

Figure 49

and we have assumed that they refer solely to demand. Hence, we have taken it for granted that a demand curve has shifted down a supply curve as in Figure 49. When consumption fell, as a result of a change in tastes, supply contracted until only those producers who were efficient at the lower prices remained in the market. There is, however, a second possibility shown in Figure 50 which reveals a shift in both demand and supply curves with the former shifting more than the latter so that the intersections of demand and supply (ringed) appear to fall along a demand curve. Finally, we have the curious case shown in Figure 51 where the supply curve is backward sloping. As demand falls producers expand their output in an endeavour to maintain their incomes (price times quantity demanded). The resolution of the identification problem requires additional information which is not available in the basic statistics, such as knowledge about tastes or climatic factors. These lie beyond our scope which has simply been concerned with making the reader aware of some of the problems involved in testing economic theories.

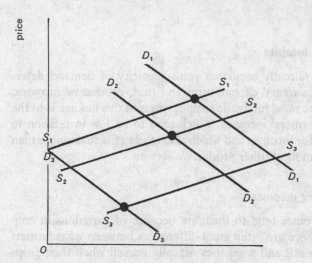

Figure 50

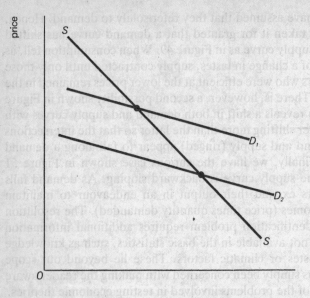

quantity demanded and supplied

Figure 51

## Farmers' incomes

We have already seen that price-elasticity of demand determines consumers' expenditures and thus, producers' incomes. One of the most interesting applications of this linkage is to the case of farmers' incomes, which tend to be low in relation to other sector incomes and which also tend to fluctuate more than incomes in most other productive sectors.

### Fluctuating incomes

Farm incomes tend to fluctuate because of variations in crop yields. There are often great differences between what farmers expect to sell and what they actually do sell when their crops have been harvested. Figure 52 demonstrates this point. The prevailing market demand curve is *DD*. The long-run supply curve, upon which farmers base their output plans, is *LRS*.

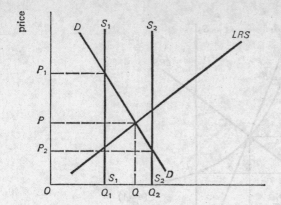

Figure 52

Farmers, therefore, intend to supply $OQ$ units of produce and expect to sell it at a market price of $OP$ per unit. Because of the perverseness of the weather their expectations are often not realized. For example, the actual short-run supply curve could be $S_1S_1$ in the case of say, a drought; or $S_2S_2$ if there is a bumper harvest. In the former case farm incomes are equal to $OP_1.OQ_1$ and in the latter case they are equal to $OP_2.OQ_2$.

## Policy

Farmers, like other income earners, prefer stable incomes since the more certain income is, the easier it is to plan expenditures. Farmers would, therefore, like to face a demand curve for their product of unit elasticity. Is there any means by which governments can help to provide such stability? Figure 53 shows how it might be done.

Figure 53 depicts the same basic situation as Figure 52 but a demand curve of unit elasticity has been superimposed upon the earlier figure. This curve shows how governments can maintain stability in farm incomes by buying up surplus harvests and selling off stocks in times of bad harvests. For example, suppose that $S_2S_2$ is again the unexpected short-run supply curve. The

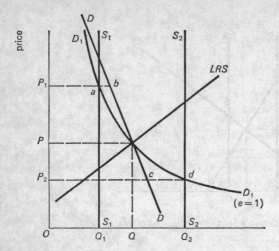

quantities demanded and supplied per unit of time

Figure 53

government maintains a price $OP_2$ by buying up what the market will not purchase – $cd$ units – and farmers' incomes are equal to $OP_2.OQ_2$ ($= OP.OQ$). Now suppose the unexpected short-run supply curve is $S_1S_1$. This time there is a market shortage of $ab$ and government again acts as a buffer against market forces by selling off an amount $ab$ of its agricultural stocks, thus maintaining a price of $P_1$. In this case farmers' incomes are equal to $OP_1.OQ_1$ which is again equal to $OP_2.OQ_2$ and $OP.OQ$ because $DD$ is a rectangular hyperbola. Thus, by making adjustments to the market process, government is able to provide stability in farm incomes.

## Low incomes

We now turn to the second observation – that farmers' incomes tend to be relatively low – and there are three major reasons for this. First, there is the fact that as real incomes grow, people do not demand proportionately more foodstuffs, but spend relatively more on manufactured goods and therefore the income-elasticity of demand for foodstuffs is low. Secondly, the mobility of farmers out of agriculture and into other sectors tends to be low. And thirdly, farming tends to be dogged by low productivity.

## Policy

What can the state do to alleviate the situation? Apart from measures to promote productivity the state can try to guarantee farmers a minimum income. (This raises the question of low wages and other problems dealt with in the previous chapter, but we shall now look at other issues.) In providing such a guarantee the state must face the problem of how to cope with any surpluses that might arise since these would threaten to pull down prices and incomes. These surpluses can be stored to cope with any shortages or they can be destroyed. Whatever policy is adopted, there is a cost in terms of the resources that could have been used elsewhere. Different procedures have been adopted in different countries and we shall consider those adopted by the UK (before entry to the EEC); and the EEC.

*The UK system (prior to joining EEC).* The UK traditionally pursued a cheap food policy by allowing food imports to enter without restrictions. To protect the livelihood of domestic farmers a deficiency payments scheme was employed whereby a guaranteed price was offered to home producers in the face of world competition. If the price received by the farmers in the market was less than the guaranteed price then the government made a cash payment to the farmers equal to the shortfall of price. The scheme is illustrated by Figure 54.

In Figure 54 the UK demand for foodstuffs is represented by the curve $D_{UK}$ and the long run supply curve is $S_{UK}$. The world supply of foodstuffs is represented by $S_W$, i.e. the supply curve of the world to the UK is perfectly elastic. Left to itself the market process would establish equilibrium at $OQ_3$ and price $OP_1$. At this equilibrium domestic consumers would enjoy a consumers' surplus equal to the area of the triangle $ZP_1H$. However, at this price UK farmers are only able to supply the amount $OQ_1$ yielding them an income of $OP_1.OQ_1$.

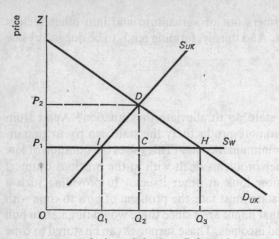

quantity demanded and supplied per unit of time

Figure 54

Suppose, then, that the government decides to guarantee domestic farmers the income they would enjoy in the absence of a foreign supply. This guarantee could be provided by a price of $OP_2$ per unit sold, enabling home producers to supply $OQ_2$ and enjoy an income of $OP_2.OQ_2$. The result of the scheme is that consumers can still buy $OQ_3$ and enjoy the benefits of the low market price of $OP_1$. An amount of consumer surplus is, of course, transferred to producers in the form of deficiency payments but domestic consumers are still better off than they would be in the absence of a world supply – by an amount of consumers' surplus equal to area $CHD$.

*The EEC system.* Let us now contrast the UK scheme with the EEC method of trying to solve the problem. In essence the EEC policy is to remove foreign competition by imposing tariffs on relatively cheap imported foodstuffs in order to raise the domestic price level and give domestic farmers adequate remuneration. The scheme is illustrated in Figure 55 where $S_W$ again represents world supply and $D_{EEC}$ and $S_{EEC}$ are the domestic demand and supply curves.

Free market forces would again establish equilibrium at price

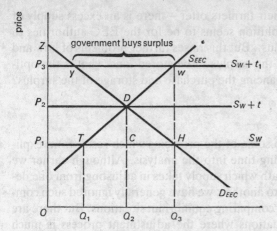

quantity demanded and supplied per unit of time

Figure 55

$OP_1$ and quantity $OQ_3$ giving rise to a consumers' surplus equal to area $ZP_1H$. At this price farmers in the EEC are able to supply only $OQ_1$, giving them incomes of $OP_1.OQ_1$. Suppose it is again decided to guarantee farmers an income of $OP_2.OQ_2$. The EEC method of promoting domestic production of $OQ_2$ is to guarantee domestic producers a market price of $OP_2$ by the imposition of a tariff (equal to $P_2 - P_1$), and by a readiness to buy any surplus output. This has the effect of shifting the world supply curve vertically to the position $S_W + t$. The result of this scheme is that the domestic consumption is reduced to $OQ_2$ and, while the transfer of $P_1CDP_2$ is no greater than in the UK example, the EEC method results in an excess loss of consumers' surplus equal to area $CHD$. Consumers are thus left with a surplus of $ZDP_2$ (this excess loss is a pictorial representation of the relative misallocation of resources resulting from the EEC scheme). Furthermore, suppose that the EEC farmers demand and succeed in getting a higher income guarantee than UK farmers. Suppose, for example, that they are guaranteed an income of $OP_3.OQ_3$. Such a guarantee requires the tariff to be raised to $t_1$ and the world supply curve shifted upwards to $S_W + t_1$. But at this higher price the EEC consumers will not purchase all that their farmers offer – there is an excess supply of *yw*. The only solution seems to be for the EEC authorities to buy up the surplus.. But this raises further problems of how and for how long is the surplus to be stored; and what is the optimum way of financing the purchase and storage of the surplus?

## Time

We turn now to some of the problems which result from explicitly incorporating time into the analysis. Although earlier we suggested the path which supply takes in adjusting from one demand situation to another, we have generally ignored such complications when comparing equilibrium situations. But there are some other situations where the adjustment process is much more complex. These cases arise when a change in supply takes a long time to take effect, i.e. when supply reacts with a definite time-lag. For example, what would happen in a situation in which supply takes some five years to hit the market? We can illustrate some possible consequences by looking at a manpower planning problem.

Figure 56 is meant to depict the demand and supply curves for accountants. Initially, there is equilibrium with $ON$ accountants being demanded and supplied per period of time at salary $OP$. But in recent years the demand for accountants has been rising faster than that for other groups of workers and they have experienced a rise in relative pay. We can illustrate this by supposing that the demand curve shifts to the right, $D_1D_1$, and pay rises to $OP_1$. Now let us look at the supply implications. Accountants cannot be produced overnight. There is a lengthy training period so salaries can stay high for some time. But this high pay will cause sixth formers to be attracted to accountancy. Universities and polytechnics will expand their accountancy departments. How many students will be attracted to accountancy? We do not know the answer to this question but we may suppose that everyone will be guided by the salary, $OP_1$, the signal of scarcity. However, everyone makes his own decision in isolation. Sixth formers in Manchester will not know how many of their contemporaries in London are contemplating account-

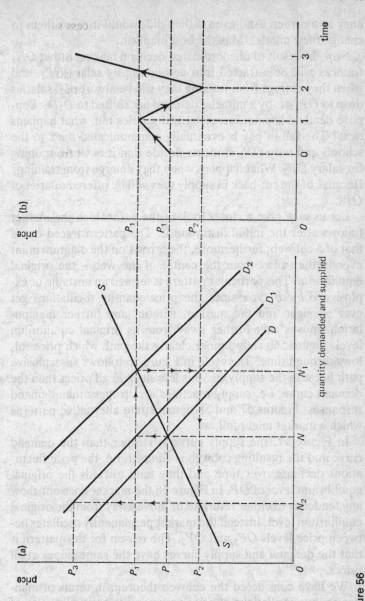

Figure 56

ancy as a career. And even if they did, would it cause them to change their minds? 'May the best man win.'

Now the result of uncoordinated decision making is that $ON_1$ trainees will be attracted into accounting by salary $OP_1$, and when they emerge from training they will be absorbed if salaries drop to $OP_2$ or, by a miracle, demand has shifted to $D_2D_2$. Suppose demand has not increased and salaries fall, what happens next? The fall in pay is eventually communicated back to the schools and only $ON_2$ students decide that it is worth training for salary $OP_2$. What happens when they emerge from training? Because of the cut-back in supply they will be offered salaries of $OP_3$.

Let us now take a closer look at the path which the market follows after the initial disturbance. The pattern traced out is that of a cobweb; furthermore, the arrows on the diagram point ever further away from the centre of the web – the original equilibrium. This particular pattern is termed an unstable or explosive *cobweb cycle* since the price/quantity oscillations get ever stronger and the market, without any further manipulation, moves ever further away from its original equilibrium level. Figure 56b shows more clearly the path which price follows through time. The cycle in Figure 56 follows an explosive path because the supply curve is less steep at all prices than the demand curve, i.e. supply reactions are stronger than demand responses. Figures 57 and 58 demonstrate alternative patterns which a market might follow.

In Figure 57, the supply curve is steeper than the demand curve and the resulting cobweb is *damped*, i.e. the price fluctuations decrease over time and they tend towards the original equilibrium level of $OP$. In Figure 58 the market does not show any tendency to either return to or move away from the original equilibrium level. Instead the market permanently oscillates between price levels $OP_1$ and $OP_2$. The reason for this pattern is that the demand and supply curves have the same slopes at all prices.

We have considered the cobweb theorem in terms of manpower, but oscillations of price and quantity are typical also of

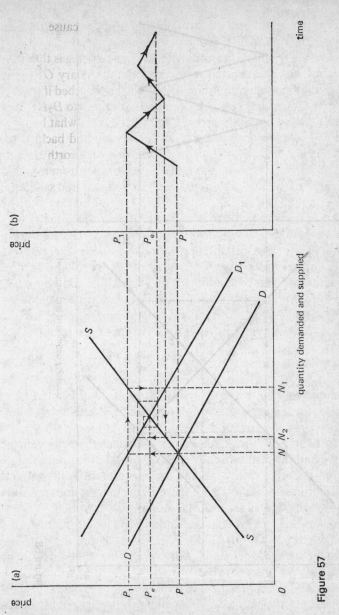

**Figure 57**

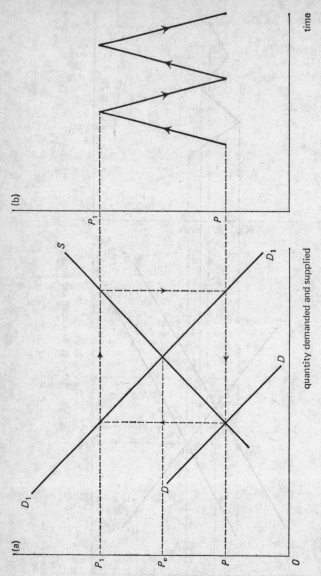

Figure 58

many agricultural products. Thus a cycle in pig production (the hog cycle) can be traced through time series data for the UK back into the nineteenth century. A cycle can also be found in natural rubber production.

In a wider context we can observe that most economies exhibit fluctuations in all prices and quantities and this broad fluctuation has been given the name *trade cycle*. Economists have long been interested in the trade cycle and though trade-cycle analysis lies outside the scope of this volume we shall in Part Eight look at some of the possible contributory factors. In the meantime our discussion of damped, regular and explosive cycles can provide some insights. Throughout the nineteenth century fairly regular oscillations in economic activity occurred. Their existence suggests that the demand and supply curves had the same slope at all prices. That would, however, be difficult to imagine; could we really expect such a state of affairs to last for 150 years? If we reject the miracle, however, we are left with either damped or explosive cycles. Damped cycles would require for their continual occurrence a series of outside shocks to occur at regular intervals. Harvest conditions, the opening up of the New World and sudden bursts of inventions might be the sources of such shocks. Explosive cycles seem out of the question: the evidence seems to be against booms getting 'boomier' and slumps getting 'slumpier'. Yet it might be possible to envisage explosive cycles constrained by a ceiling (created by full employment of all resources) and a floor (caused by some outside factor).

*Policy*

We cannot forecast the future and so it would seem that the only way of coping with fluctuations of the cobweb variety is to reduce the delay in the response of supply. This is difficult in agriculture, though stockpiling might help, but in manpower planning the lag can be reduced by altering the nature of the education system from one which emphasizes early specialization to one which insists upon giving people a broad education.

## Summary

In this chapter we have looked at market situations where demand and supply curves shift. This leads to a problem when examining data as to whether price and quantity changes have been due to demand or supply changes, or both. Shifting demand and supply curves also lead to problems when the state interferes in markets and add to the complications we noted in the previous chapter.

## Questions

1 In 1973 the school-leaving age was raised from fifteen to sixteen years. What does economic theory predict would be the effects of such a change on the labour market? Do the following statistics refute the predictions of the theory? What additional information do you think is needed to produce a more satisfactory analysis of the raising of the school leaving age (ROSLA)?

Basic statistics for Great Britain

| Year | Number of school-leavers entering employment | | Unemployment percentage (all workers) |
|------|---------------------|---------------------|----------|
| | Youths (under 18) | Girls (under 18) | |
| 1970 | 248 177 | 223 813 | 2·5 |
| 1971 | 242 122 | 220 409 | 3·4 |
| 1972 | 258 532 | 228 047 | 3·8 |
| 1973 | 140 532 | 107 047 | 2·6 |
| 1974 | 274 801 | 237 847 | 2·6 |
| 1975 | not available | | 4·3 |

Average weekly earnings

| Year | Youths (under 21) | Girls (under 18) | Men (over 21) | Women (over 18) |
|------|-------------------|------------------|---------------|-----------------|
| 1970 | 13·60 | 9·46 | 28·91 | 13·98 |
| 1971 | 15·17 | 10·33 | 31·37 | 15·80 |
| 1972 | 17·73 | 11·83 | 36·20 | 18·34 |
| 1973 | 21·60 | 15·21 | 41·52 | 21·15 |
| 1974 | 26·13 | 19·31 | 49·12 | 27·05 |
| 1975 | 32·87 | 23·15 | 59·74 | 34·22 |

Source: Department of Employment *Gazette*.
Note: Employment figures are calculated on the basis of a count of National Insurance cards. This count was discontinued in 1974 and meant that low-wage earners such as boys and girls have become excluded from the survey.

2 What do the following statistics reveal about the behaviour of buyers and sellers during the 1974 sugar shortage?

Sugar prices, purchases and consumption

| | Average quantity purchased per person per week (a) | Percentage of households which bought sugar during their week of participation in the survey | Average amount purchased at each transaction | Average number of transactions per buying household per week | Average price paid per lb |
|---|---|---|---|---|---|
| | oz | % | oz | no. | p |
| *1973* | | | | | |
| January–March | 14·23 | 72 | 45·1 | 1·30 | 4·51 |
| April–June | 12·50 | 68 | 43·0 | 1·31 | 4·74 |
| July–September | 13·98 | 71 | 45·7 | 1·34 | 5·10 |
| October–December | 14·03 | 71 | 45·8 | 1·32 | 5·20 |
| *1974* | | | | | |
| January–March | 14·06 | 70 | 45·4 | 1·32 | 5·24 |
| April–June | 13·80 | 69 | 45·2 | 1·34 | 5·27 |
| July | 15·84 | 71 | 46·2 | 1·45 | 5·83 |
| August | 12·19 | 66 | 34·8 | 1·54 | 6·72 |
| September | 11·53 | 68 | 33·7 | 1·43 | 6·92 |
| July–September | 13·21 | 69 | 37·7 | 1·49 | 6·49 |
| October | 10·90 | 71 | 35·1 | 1·28 | 7·60 |
| November | 9·88 | 67 | 33·8 | 1·34 | 9·71 |
| December | 13·04 | 69 | 39·4 | 1·44 | 11·08 |
| October–December | 11·04 | 68 | 36·0 | 1·34 | 9·30 |

(a) Averaged over all households in the sample, including those which did not buy any sugar during their week of participation in the survey.
Source: *Household Food Consumption*, 1974

# Part Three
# Utility and Cost

This is the high ground of economic analysis. This is where many of the great economists have established their reputations. In this century Nobel Prize winners, Samuelson, Hicks and Arrow, and the distinguished economist, Georgescu-Roegen, have fashioned and re-fashioned a beautiful, crystal-line structure of logic. Before them, in the nineteenth century, the Englishmen, Jevons and Marshall, the Austrian, Menger, the Italian, Pareto, and the Swiss economist, Walras, hammered out a foundation from the rudiments created by Smith, Ricardo, Mill and Gossen. And before them, reaching out over the centuries, come the ideas of the great philosopher, Aristotle. Therein lies the attraction, for utility theory is about choice and choice lies at the centre of the human drama. It is that area of economic knowledge which reaches back into that core of human inquiry we call philosophy.

The starting point of the analysis was the attempt to transfer the ideas of the natural sciences to the social sciences and this encouraged a search for a unit of measurement. In an agrarian society what a man produced on the poorest land might be considered to be his own creation and the excess of produce on superior land could be thought of as the free gift of Nature. Therefore, for early thinkers a labour theory of value seemed plausible and the fact that different men might produce different amounts on the poorer land could be dealt with by making superior men a multiple of ordinary men. Goods might exchange on the basis of the amount of labour they require to produce them. Of course, it would have been possible to produce a *land theory of value* by assuming that men could be produced at constant cost and that the produce of superior land is a multiple of the output of poorer land. But the social sciences need a social theory and not a theory based upon the outcome of natural forces. Hence, the attractiveness of a labour theory of value and eventually the basic idea, that goods exchange on the basis of their labour content, was transferred to the concept of an industrial society. If there were few machines at the dawn of the Industrial Revolution then output would be heavily dependent upon the exertions of labour. *Exploitation*, therefore, could be considered to be the extraction of the extra sweat exerted by the worker over and above the exertion required for his subsistence. In an agrarian society this surplus might be appropriated by the landlord and in an industrial society it might be appropriated by the capitalist. Here we have the germs of Marx's theory of value. But the labour theory of value had difficulties in dealing with heterogeneous labour and as machines became more plentiful it came to be accepted that capital, in the form of machines, was productive *irrespective of its ownership*. To this latter proposition could be added the growing conviction that a theory of value should say something about the demand for goods as well as revealing that the value of goods depended upon the cost of supplying those goods. Thus, some goods might have a high labour content and yet command only a low price; for example, road sweeping. There was also the problem of goods, such as antiques, whose actual labour cost of production might be low and yet they command a high price. Finally, there were goods, such as water, without which life could not exist but which seemed to command only a low price.

By analogy with 'attraction' and 'repulsion' it was assumed that satisfaction and dissatisfaction, *utility and disutility* as they came to be known, were capable of measurement. Unfortunately, the philosophical problems of measurement tended to be overlooked. There are, in fact, two methods of measurement. One method assumes that objects can be ordered according to some principle of 'greater or lesser' and this method is known as *ordinal measurement*. The second method assumes that we can say by how much one object is greater than another and this method is known as *cardinal measurement*. Now in order to proceed from ordinal to cardinal measurement the objects being compared must be capable of subsumption; that is, we must be able to consider them as qualitatively identical or homogeneous. For example, two pints of water are greater than one pint of water because we can pour them both into a pan which will indicate that the addition of the second pint will cause the depth of water to be twice what it was previously. And we can have no doubts about our result because it is impossible to distinguish the two pints within the pan – they have merged. **This was the basis of a *utility theory of value* – goods exchanged at prices which measured their utility to their purchasers.**

Now it seemed obvious that the things measured by physicists – heat, light and sound – were homogeneous, for theorems based upon cardinal measurement seemed to provide both understanding and prediction. Could, therefore, satisfaction and dissatisfaction be regarded as qualitatively homogeneous with dissatisfaction being merely negative satisfaction?

At first sight the answer seemed to be in the affirmative. Man makes choices and he must, therefore, possess within himself the common denominator which renders all things comparable. But a moment's thought suggests that this observation is too simple. The satisfaction derived from a cigarette at work may be different from the satisfaction derived from smoking a cigarette at home. Furthermore, people make choices for reasons other than the satisfaction they might derive. They choose to do things out of a sense of duty, altruism or because they have been taught to do a job in a particular way.

What this suggests is that there may be severe limits to the role of measurement in economics. For what economists had hoped to do was to obtain homogeneous units of utility which could be measured by means of a measuring rod of money. But if utility is not homogeneous then measurement is not possible. Yet we need not despair. After all, there are limits to measurement in the natural sciences. What has to be discovered is the area of choice which is amenable to measurement. It may turn out to be quite small. Definitive cost benefit analyses of Channel Tunnels may be illusory, but attempts must be made.

Utility is obviously a subjective concept, but it is not so obvious that cost is a subjective concept. We are used to thinking of costs in an objective sense – units of money, tons of steel and so on – yet costs, at the moment a choice is made, represent the lost benefits that might have been obtained from the rejected courses of action. These costs are subjective – they are based upon guesses as to the possible benefits from different courses of action. The costs which are objective are the consequences of the decision, the aftermath which may bear no relationship to those costs which were expected. And because costs are subjective the problems of comparing benefits (are they qualitatively identical?) bedevils analysis.

Production involves the creation of benefits, so benefits and costs are linked to productive processes. In the theory of production we found a curve of diminishing marginal product which, though couched in objective terms, could also be thought of in decision-making situations as expected marginal products giving rise to expected benefits.

We conclude this brief survey of the foundations of the theory of value with a short reference to money and collective goods. The value of a quantity of money is what it can purchase and for the purposes of Parts One to Eight, it is assumed that the quantity of money is constant. In Part Nine we shall examine some of the problems that arise when the quantity of money is varied and its implications for value theory. Also, for the time being we shall ignore the problems of collective goods. In the case of collective goods an individual's willingness to pay for the goods may depend upon the willingness or unwillingness of others to contribute. Both money and collective goods involve a more fundamental problem – uncertainty. In many situations uncertainty is not a problem. Nobody goes into a bookshop and comes out with a sack of potatoes. Uncertainty can be ignored or its effects calculated and the measuring rod of money applied. Thus, workers in dangerous trades may command high wages. But there may be situations where measurement may not be possible because uncertainty is not homogeneous. The foundation stone of value theory has been utility, but once we grasp that the utilities derived from goods may not be homogeneous then we perceive that the true foundation stone of value theory is the structure of wants upon which a superstructure of utilities may be erected. If the superstructure can be erected then it may be possible to measure utilities with a measuring rod of money and then make inferences about the satisfaction of wants, but it is important to examine the nature of the foundation stone.

# Chapter 11
## Consumer Behaviour

Economic analysis would be simpler if we could take the nature of the demand curve with its prediction about the relationship between price and consumption as something given, as an observable fact. Unfortunately we cannot, for there are odd occasions when the normal relationship breaks down. For this reason another problem for the economist has been to derive the conditions under which the statement 'as price falls demand will rise' holds true. **We shall begin this chapter with the approach known as *marginal-utility theory*. Some economists prefer the other approaches known as *indifference curve analysis* and *revealed preference* and we shall discuss them also.** We have examined the relationship between the differing viewpoints but have adopted a narrative approach, in order to show how economists have refined an original theory by reducing the number of restrictive assumptions. This should prove worthwhile, since the evolution of any theory is a fascinating subject. However, for those who prefer one theory or the other, we have endeavoured to keep the continuity links separate.

### Clearing the undergrowth

The simplest way of understanding the theory of choice is to observe its historical development. Economists noticed that as the prices of most goods fell people tended to buy more of these commodities, and when prices rose they bought less. The exceptions to this general tendency were twofold:

1 People sometimes bought more or less despite the absence of price changes.

2 People sometimes bought more as prices rose.

It was suggested that the causes of observation 1 could be put down to:

Changes in tastes;
Changes in income;
Changes in wealth;
Changes in the prices of other goods.

In these circumstances, shifts in demand may occur even though price remains constant. This case is illustrated by Figure 59 where demand increases from *M* to *N* without a change in price. Once the changes in 1 were eliminated, economists were left with a functional relationship between prices and quantities of a good. Causes of the behaviour described in 2 constitute a mixed bag:

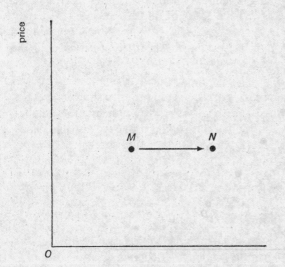

Figure 59

Speculative purchases;
Snob purchases;
Other possible causes.

Speculative purchases did not create analytical difficulties for economists since they could be explained in terms of the general observation about price–demand relationships: if consumers expected a price rise then immediate purchases represented a kind of purchase at a lower price. Snob purchases were deemed possible as when, for example, diamonds are bought as their price rises but such demand reactions were considered to be rare and insignificant. There remained the final category of 'other possible causes' to be dealt with. One relationship which seemed to require explanation was the observation by the noted statistician, Sir Robert Giffen, that in the nineteenth century very poor families would buy more potatoes in response to a rise in their price. Further investigations failed to produce any more cases of so-called 'Giffen goods' but it is possible for such instances to occur and economists needed to provide an ex-

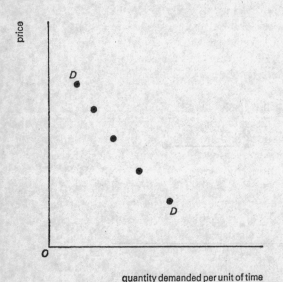

quantity demanded per unit of time

Figure 60

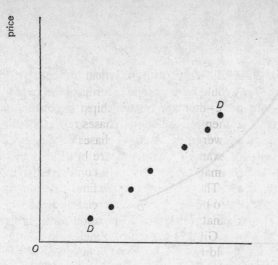

quantity demanded per unit of time

Figure 61

planation for their occurrence. (Later in this chapter an explanation will be provided but in the meantime we shall continue the development of marginal-utility analysis.)

In the meantime, having clarified the causes of *shifts* in demand curves there remained the relationship between price and demand. This relationship could be that of either Figure 60 or Figure 61. The next step involved an *abstraction*. Instead of dealing with the discrete price and quantity changes that are the real-life observations and are shown in Figures 60 and 61 economists chose, for convenience, to assume perfect divisibility of prices and quantities in order to obtain smooth curves.

There was a further step. The statistical relationship revealed in Figures 60 and 61 was a relationship concerning *market behaviour*; that is, the aggregate behaviour of all the individuals purchasing a particular good. The final step was one of *deduction*. What was observed to be true of the mass of consumers must be true of the majority of the individual consumers. The curves of Figures 62 and 63 could therefore be regarded as the statistical relationship for individual consumers. The way was

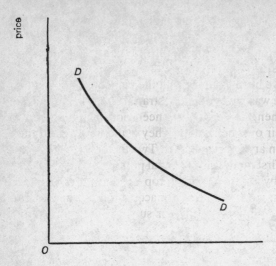

quantity demanded per unit of time

Figure 62

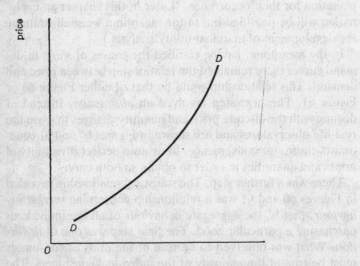

quantity demanded per unit of time

Figure 63

open, therefore, for a study of individual behaviour, which could mean that economists could study their own reactions to price changes, since they might regard themselves as representative buyers.

If it could have been assumed that the response of demand to changes in price was always that illustrated by the smooth curve of Figure 62, then the economists need not have bothered to think about their own behaviour. They could have rested their investigations on an observable fact. Two factors prevented this complacency. First there was the awful possibility that cases like that illustrated by Figure 63 might crop up. Secondly, there was curiosity. Whilst most people might accept a fact, some like to know its origin. Why did behaviour such as that portrayed in Figure 62 occur?

## Marginal-utility theory

The first theory produced to explain why a consumer buys more of a commodity when its price falls is known as the marginal-utility theory. This theory began by assuming that people derive satisfaction from the consumption of commodities, and economists referred to this satisfaction as *utility*. Since it is difficult to observe whether people derive satisfaction from the consumption of commodities, then it is apparent that this method of approach was based upon *introspection*. In other words, what economists knew or assumed about their own behaviour, they assumed to be true about the behaviour of others. From their observation of their own behaviour – their mental experiments – economists drew conclusions about the behaviour of others.

On the basis of these mental experiments economists came to the conclusion that a consumer with given tastes and money income, when faced by given prices for goods would, if he attempted to maximize his satisfaction from purchasing goods, be guided by a *law of diminishing marginal utility* whereby successive increments of a good would yield successively diminishing units of satisfaction.

What is important to note at this stage is that diminishing marginal utility is compatible with increasing total utility. As Figure 64 shows, total utility increases but at a diminishing rate. This implies that the additional utility added by each unit falls as is shown in the lower panel of Figure 64. The two parts of Figure 64 are linked because the slope of the total utility curve

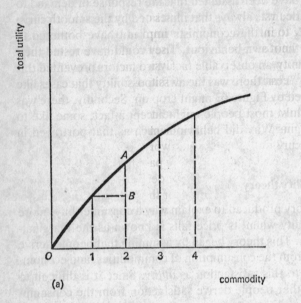

(a)

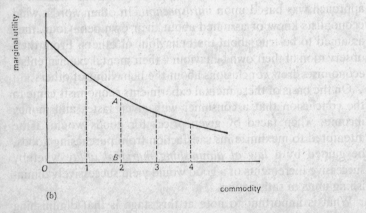

(b)

Figure 64

measures marginal utility. Thus when consumption rises from one to two units the increase in utility is $AB$.

There is, however, a snag. It may not be possible to apply the theory to necessities. Consider the utility derived from the first glass of water: it could be infinite. Now what is the utility derived from the first and second glasses of water? Is it possible to add anything to infinity? What this implies is that the total utility curve may not start at zero because the marginal utility curve starts at infinity. Hence utility analysis can only be applied to either non-necessities, or, to necessities if a suitable starting point is selected.

We can now resume the argument. Guided by the law of diminishing marginal utility, a consumer would purchase units of a commodity until the money's worth of utility he obtained from a unit was equal to the price he paid for that good. That is, the price paid measured the utility derived from the last unit. Price was perceived to be a guide for the consumer in allocating his expenditure:

$$\frac{MU_a}{P_a} = \frac{MU_b}{P_b} = \cdots = \frac{MU_z}{P_z} \qquad \qquad 1$$

Choice, however, involves the presence of at least two goods and the more general expression for consumer behaviour is contained in equation 1 (where $MU$ refers to marginal utility, $P$ to price, and the subscripts $a, \ldots, z$ refer to the commodities consumed). What equation 1 says is that if a consumer does maximize his utility then his equilibrium will be characterized by the ratios of marginal utilities to prices being everywhere equal. What does this mean? It means that if the utility from consuming an extra pound's worth of $a$ was greater than the utility from an extra pound's worth of $b$ then the consumer would reduce his spending on $b$ and increase his spending on $a$. The utility obtained from the last pound spent on each good must therefore be the same.

If the price of $a$ falls then the equation will be disrupted, and in order to restore the equality of the ratios of marginal utilities and prices, the theory assumes that the marginal utility of $a$ must fall, which means that more of $a$ must be bought.

## Income and substitution effects

At this stage we can notice an important assumption that has been slipped into the analysis. When the price of *a* falls then the consumer's *real* income has risen. Hence there is no obvious reason why he should spend his increased income on *a*; he could in fact spend it on more of the other goods *b, c, d, . . . , z*. Thus, suppose that commodity *a* was either cheese or beef. If it were cheese and its price fell from 18p to 9p a kilogram, then he might not buy any more cheese but instead spend the saving of 9p on, say, sugar. Or take the case of beef where, if its price fell from 36p to 27p a kilogram, he might spend part of the saving of 9p on buying more beef, but he might also spend some of it on buying more mustard – since beef and mustard are complementary goods.

When the price of a good falls there is evidently an income effect as well as a substitution effect. The substitution effect arises because the money's worth of utility from purchasing extra units of the good whose price has fallen is greater than the money's worth of utility that could be got from spending on any other good. The income effect looks odd because it suggests that more utility may be obtained from spending on the goods whose prices have not fallen. Indeed the income effect goes further, for we saw in Chapter 7 that with a rise in income he might buy less of a good, so the income effect could work in the direction of persuading the consumer to buy more of the good (whose price has fallen), or less of the good and more of other goods.

In order to arrive at its prediction that as the price of a good falls more will be bought, the marginal-utility theory had to rule out cases where demand might fall as the price falls and where the consumption of other goods might rise. The method by which this was done was to assume that only a small part of total expenditure was spent on the good. This meant that the income effect of a price change would be small and would be weaker than the substitution effect. What this might be taken to mean is that in terms of the hierarchy of wants, discussed in Chapter 2, the marginal-utility theorists looked at the wants which were just being satisfied and at essential wants that required very little to satisfy them, e.g. salt. When, however, the amount spent on the good was a large fraction of income then the 'Giffen good' case might occur; i.e. demand falls as price falls.

## Derivation of the demand curve

From equation 1 we can, by manipulation, obtain the following equation which holds for all pairs of goods:

$$\frac{MU_a}{MU_b} = \frac{P_a}{P_b} . \qquad\qquad 2$$

In effect this equation gives us a demand curve for it tells us that underlying a demand curve there is a marginal-utility curve with the prices and amounts of other goods being held constant. If the price of *a* falls then the marginal utility of *a* must fall if the denominators of both sides of the equation are to remain constant, and all income is to be spent both before and after the price change.

## The paradox of value

The marginal-utility theory enables us to resolve the paradox of value. A problem that perplexed early economists was why water, which obviously is essential to maintain life, commanded a lower price than diamonds. The answer is seen to lie in the distinction between total and marginal utility. Although the total utility of water is considerably higher than that of diamonds, its marginal utility is much lower because it is more plentiful.

Sometimes the paradox of value is explained by the fact that as we have more and more water we put it to less essential uses and thus we obtain a curve of diminishing marginal utility of water. We may use our first litre of water to slake our thirst, our second litre for washing and our fiftieth litre to wash down the car. But this approach may be misleading, for the different litres of water constitute different goods which satisfy different wants. The first litre of water possesses the technical properties of being able to sustain life, whilst the second possesses the characteristics of being a washing liquid. These characteristics serve to give rise to different goods which satisfy different wants; the fact that they are all characteristics possessed by water is irrelevant.

What we can think of is a curve of diminishing marginal utility for drinking water and a curve of diminishing marginal utility for washing water and so on. At some point the utility derived from an extra litre of drinking water will be lower than that derived from using water for washing and so an individual will reject any further drinking water. This suggests that *some* litres of washing water can be substituted for *some* litres of drinking water, but it is only some, for a person would not give up his first litre of drinking water for some more washing water. This is perhaps a fine point, for we usually envisage individuals operating in zones away from the boundaries of the hierarchy of wants. Yet there could be situations where people were moved from slums to a housing estate out of town and felt worse off because they ranked the delights of the countryside lower than the amenities of town centres. We should therefore guard against assuming that utilities are homogeneous.

In the indifference-curve approach discussed later, the fundamental hierarchy of wants is concealed by the assumption that there can be indefinite substitution of one good for another, but it is difficult to see how anyone would be willing to give up their last drop of water for any extra amount of bread or a number of Rolls Royces.[1]

## The labour theory of value

The third subject upon which marginal utility threw light was the labour theory of value. According to this latter theory commodities exchange according to the amount of labour embodied in them so that if the price of a good falls, it could be presumed that either the amount of embodied labour in other goods has risen

1. An alternative approach emphasizes that different goods possess different characteristics in different proportions.

or the amount embodied in the good has fallen. The trouble is that this theory cannot explain such goods as Old Masters whose prices rise even though there is no change in labour embodiment. Moreover, as soon as other resources, land and capital, are introduced into the discussion, then the simple labour embodiment thesis suffers further complications, since it is possible to have goods with the same labour embodiment but different capital endowments selling at different prices.

## Consumer surplus again

In Chapter 10 we drew attention to the fact that consumers frequently pay a price for goods which is less than that which they might be prepared to pay if they were subjected to an all-or-nothing offer. This gain we termed consumers' surplus and we illustrate it in Figure 65. Now it is evident that this gain is related to total utility and marginal utility. If all of the units of a commodity are homogeneous then a consumer will be prepared to pay a price for each unit which measures the utility derived from that unit. This is because all units are substitutable. Thus

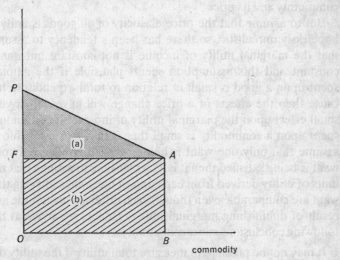

Figure 65 (a) Consumer surplus. (b) Total revenue

his total utility will be measured by the area $OPAB$ although his expenditure is only $OFAB$.

## A critical appraisal of marginal utility theory

Marginal utility theory depends upon the assumptions of a *quasi-constancy of the marginal utility of income* and the homogeneity of utility. These two assumptions are interrelated.

When the price of a commodity changes then the demand for that commodity may change. Suppose the demand for a good is price-inelastic; then if price falls demand will rise less than proportionately to the price change and there will be some saving of expenditure on the commodity. Real income will rise. But if real income rises then the marginal utility of income will fall and bring the possibility of changes in the demands for other commodities even though their prices have not changed. Conversely, if the price elasticity is greater than unity then spending on other goods would have to fall even though their prices would remain unchanged. So unless the price elasticity of demand is unity then it is not possible to hold other things constant in order to examine the relationship between the demand for a commodity and its price.

But to assume that the price elasticity of all goods is unity is hopelessly unrealistic, so there has been a tendency to assume that the marginal utility of income is not constant but quasi-constant and this assumption seems plausible if the amount spent upon a good is small in relation to total expenditure because then the effects of a price change will have only a very small effect upon the marginal utility of income. If the amount spent upon a commodity is small then it may be reasonable to assume that only one want is being satisfied. And if only one want is being satisfied then it is also plausible to assume that the units of utility derived from each unit of the good satisfying that want are comparable even though each differs in magnitude as a result of diminishing marginal utility. Hence, we arrive at the following conclusions concerning utility.

1 It may not be possible to measure total utility if the utility derived from the first unit is infinite. This applies to necessities.

2 It may not be possible to measure total utility if the amount spent on the good is large because the income effect may cause the demand curve to shift.

3 It may not be possible to add the utilities from different goods together because they may satisfy different wants.

4 It may not be possible to add the utilities derived by different people together unless they possess similar tastes. This means that national income statistics may be misleading.

## Indifference Curve Analysis

Suppose an individual is confronted with a set of quantities of two commodities, say apples and oranges, and he is asked how many oranges are needed to compensate him for the loss of one apple. We would expect the number of oranges required in compensation to vary according to the number of apples already possessed by the consumer. Table 25 shows a hypothetical set of combinations of apples and oranges which results from applying this principle of compensation.

**Table 25** Apples and oranges

| Apples | Oranges | Marginal rate of substitution of oranges for apples |
| --- | --- | --- |
| 10 | 3 | — |
| 9 | 4 | 1 |
| 8 | 6 | 2 |
| 7 | 9 | 3 |
| 6 | 13 | 4 |
| 5 | 18 | 5 |
| 4 | 25 | 7 |

Now the important implication to be drawn from the above example is that by varying the amount of compensation involved in the consumption of differing bundles of the two commodities it is possible to maintain a given level of consumer satisfaction. This means that within any set of combinations of the two com-

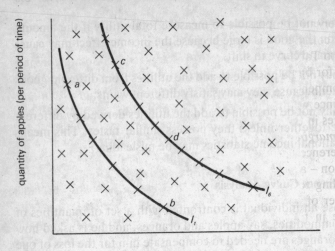

quantity of oranges (per period of time)

Figure 66

modities there will be several different bundles of goods which *yield the same level of satisfaction* to the consumer and there will be other combinations yielding higher or low levels of satisfaction. Figure 66 shows a sample of all the possible consumption combinations of apples and oranges with two locii constructed, one linking all combinations of the two goods which yield one level of satisfaction $I_1$ and the other joining all points yielding a higher level $I_6$.

The two curves $I_1$ and $I_6$ are examples of an *indifference curve*, so-called because the consumer is considered to be indifferent among the many combinations lying on the curve, since they all represent the same level of satisfaction (or *utility* if that interpretation is preferred). The term *indifference* is not meant to imply that the consumer does not care about the bundles of goods on offer but merely that he has no strong preference among the many combinations along any given curve. The reason for this lack of preference lies in the fact that although less of one commodity might be enjoyed at one point on the indifference curve than at some other point, there is adequate compensation for the consumer in the increased amount of the other commodity. We can see this more clearly by referring back to Table 25 where successive apples forgone are compensated for by extra oranges. The rate at which successive apples are compensated for in this way is termed the *rate of substitution* and since we assume that the rate can apply to very small unit changes in the quantity of one commodity we normally use the term *marginal rate of substitution* (MRS). Turning again to the indifference curve, its slope tells us the marginal rate of substitution – a steep slope signifies that the consumer is relatively unwilling to substitute oranges for apples (a relatively small number of oranges is required to compensate for a large decrease in the consumption of apples) while a relatively flat slope means that a relatively large quantity of oranges is required in compensation for a small decrease in apple consumption.

The indifference curves we have described tells us that an individual is better off if he is on a higher indifference curve than if he is on a lower one but they do not tell us by how much he is

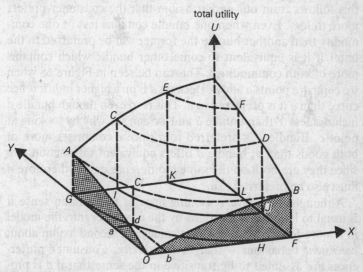

Figure 67

better off. If we want this additional information then we must introduce a third dimension in order to obtain a utility or satisfactions hill. Figure 67 shows such a hill of total utility measured from a base level, the contours on the hill join up points of equal satisfaction or indifference. If we consider the 'shadows' of these contours to be cast down on to the horizontal plane then we can reproduce that plane as the indifference map. *GH*, *IJ* and *KL* represent a sample of such curves being derived from *AB*, *CD* and *EF*; thus point *d* on the indifference curve GH derives from consumption of *Oa* apples and *Ob* oranges and is a 'shadow' of the contour *AB*, the lowest contour on the utility hill. Finally, observe that the curve *OA* is the total utility curve for one commodity and is similar to the total utility curve described in our analysis of marginal utility. Similarly, *OB* is the total utility curve for oranges.

## Characteristics of indifference curves

It is fairly easy to accept that bundles of goods on higher indifference curves are preferred to bundles on lower curves since this follows from our earlier axiom that the consumer prefers more to less. Even when one bundle contains less of one commodity than another bundle the former will be preferred to the latter if it is equivalent to some other bundle which contains more of both commodities. This can be seen in Figure 68 when we compare points *a* and *d*. Because *d* is on a higher indifference curve than *a* it is preferred to *a*. This is so even though bundle *d* includes less *Y* than bundle *a* and we can see why by looking at point *c*. Bundle *c* is preferred to *a* since *c* comprises more of both goods than *a*; bundle *d* offers equivalent satisfaction to *c* since they are both on the same indifference curve; therefore *d* must also be preferred to *a*.

Although the above reasoning appeals to common sense it is usual to build such reactions by the consumer into the model in a more formal manner by introducing a second axiom about *consistent* behaviour – that of *transitivity*. Consumer preferences are assumed to be transitive in the sense that if *a* is preferred to *b* and *b* is preferred to *c* then *c* cannot be preferred to

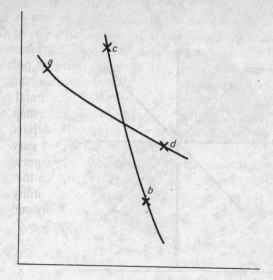

quantity of oranges (per period of time)

Figure 68

*a*. For this reason we can reach unambiguous conclusions regarding a comparison of points *a* and *d* in Figure 67 but if these points had been in the same position in the quadrant, *while lying on indifference curves which cross*, we could not have reached any conclusions since the transitivity rule would be broken. Figure 68 demonstrates the problem.

In Figure 68 points *abcd* from Figure 66 have been reproduced in their original locations but this time *a* and *d* lie on the same 'indifference curve' while *b* and *c* lie on another curve. Comparing *c* and *a* the consumer would prefer *c* since more of both goods can be enjoyed. Similarly, *d* would be preferred to *b*. However *a* and *d* are equivalent and so are *c* and *b*. Thus it cannot be that *c* is preferred to *a*, which is equivalent to *d* while *d* is preferred to *b*, which is equivalent to *c*. We conclude that *indifference curves cannot cross* since allowing them to do so defies the rule of transitivity.

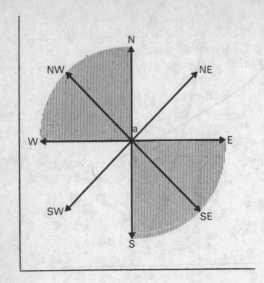

quantity of *X* (per period of time)

Figure 69

The axiom 'more is preferred to less' also explains why indifference curves slope downwards from left to right – any other direction would mean comparing points of more or less of one or both commodities. Figure 69 demonstrates this point.

Starting at point *a* in Figure 69 and comparing all of the routes radiating from that point, we can see that only two, NW and SE, involve a trade-off whereby one commodity is substituted for another. All other routes do not involve opportunity sacrifices – travelling due W, E, S, or N, involves either gaining more of one commodity without losing any of the other (W and E) or losing more and more of one while the quantity of the other remains fixed (S or W); while travelling either NE or SW involves either more and more of both commodities (NE) or, less of both (SW). Thus NW to SE is the only direction in which *indifference* could persist.

But why should the indifference curve be convex to the origin? This cannot be proved in any way since it does not follow from any axiom. Rather, the shape of the indifference curve results from our introspective interpretations of the real world. Individuals, in the main, are observed to have diverse preferences, variety being the 'spice of life', and the less of any one commodity possessed by an individual the less willing is that individual to forego any more units of that commodity. It follows that if any individual is to be induced to give up successive units of one commodity he must receive increasing amounts of some other commodity in compensation. So it is that in Table 25 the number of oranges required in compensation for the loss of each successive apple increases as the number of apples possessed decreases. We conclude, then, that the slope of the indifference curve, measuring the marginal rate of substitution, will flatten as the curve approaches the horizontal axis (and become steeper towards the vertical axis); in other words, the indifference curve shape characterizes a *diminishing marginal rate of substitution*.

To round off this section we present our three main conclusions about the characteristics of indifference curves.

1 Indifference curves slope downwards from left to right.

2 Indifference curves do not intersect.

3 Indifference curves exhibit a diminishing marginal rate of substitution between commodities.

### The budget constraint

So far we have concentrated on the preference map only. We have considered the relationship among various bundles of goods when the consumer's choice is unfettered by any purchasing constraint. However, the bundles of goods finally chosen must reflect not only subjective preferences but objective constraints of income and prices – how much can be bought depends upon how much the consumer has to spend and the prices at which he can obtain the goods. Suppose the consumer allocates £$Z$) of weekly income to the weekly purchase of goods $Y$ and $X$ and the market prices of these two goods are $P_y$ and $P_x$

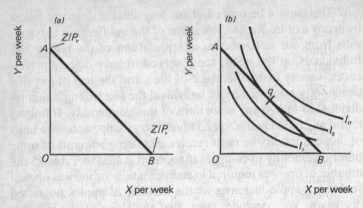

Figure 70

respectively. If the consumer decides to spend all of his weekly allocation on good $Y$ he can buy $Z/P_y$ per week and if he decided to spend all on $Y$ he can buy $Z/P_x$ per week. Thus, we can represent the expenditure constraint in the form of a *budget line* in the manner shown by Figure 70a.

In Figure 70a point $A$ represents the maximum amount of $Y(Z/P_y)$ which can be bought if no $X$ is purchased and point $B$ represents the maximum amount of $X(Z/P_x)$ if no $Y$ is bought. By joining $A$ and $B$ with a straight line $AB$ we can see the set of *combinations* of $Y$ and $X$ which can be bought with £$Z$ if it is spent on both commodities. Now, turning to Figure 70b we see the final result which combines the set of preferences with the set of constraints. The highest possible indifference curve which can be reached by spending £$Z$ on both commodities at prevailing market prices $P_y$ and $P_x$ is $I_5$ and the best consumption point is $q$. This point is 'best' in the sense that any other point along $AB$ must lie on a lower indifference curve, while any other point on $I_5$ is out of reach of the consumer given his constant of £$Z$. We can say that in the given set of circumstances the consumer is in equilibrium at point $q$ – only a change in circumstances will induce a move from this position.

Now let us take a closer look at this equilibrium point. The important thing to note is that it is a *point of tangency* – at $q$ the slope of the indifference curve is equal to that of the budget line. The slope of the indifference curve we have defined already as the marginal rate of substitution, but what of the budget line? The slope of this is given by $OA/OB$, however we know that $OA = Z/P_y$ and $OB = Z/P_x$, so we can write:

$$\frac{OA}{OB} = \frac{Z/P_y}{Z/P_x} = \frac{P_x}{P_y}$$

It would seem that the slope of the budget line is given by the ratio of relative prices of the two commodities. Thus we can define consumer equilibrium as being that position, in any set of circumstances, where the marginal rate of substitution between the two commodities equals the relative price ratio of the two commodities:

$$MRS_{yx} = \frac{P_x}{P_y}$$

What happens when circumstances change? Suppose, for example, that consumer income changes, or there is a change in the relative prices of the two commodities – how does the consumer react? Clearly as such changes occur the consumer is no longer in equilibrium and he will want to readjust his purchases until he is once again in a state of balance. We analysed a set of such reactions in the earlier section on marginal utility and the concepts introduced then continue to be relevant. Consumer reaction to a change in income we shall term an *income effect* and reaction to a change in relative prices we shall term a *substitution effect*. In terms of indifference curve analysis these effects are demonstrated by alterations in the position of the budget line. If consumer income changes while relative prices are unchanged the budget line will shift but its slope (measuring the ratio of relative prices) will not alter. On the other hand, a change in relative prices with consumer income unchanged, will alter the slope of the budget line. Figure 71a and b show what happens when only the income effect is operating.

In both diagrams of Figure 71 a series of budget lines *ab, cd, ef* and *gh* are shown, each representing a given level of income. The budget lines are parallel and represent differing levels of income with the relative prices of *Y* and *X* unchanged. Consumer

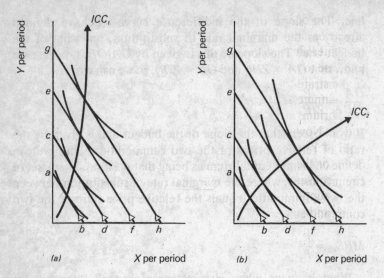

Figure 71

equilibrium in each income situation is where the slopes of the
budget lie and indifference curves are equal. In Figure 71a $ICC_1$
traces out the locus of such equilibrium positions while a similar
locus is traced out in Figure 71b by $ICC_2$. These curves show the
paths that consumption of $Y$ and $X$ (expenditure) follow as income changes and are termed usually *income consumption
curves*. Given the direction of the two curves it can be seen that
as income rises in the case of Figure 71a consumer expenditure
switches away from $X$ towards $Y$ while the preference map of
Figure 71b induces relatively greater quantities of $X$ to be
bought as income rises. In other words, in terms of expenditure
preferences $X$ is a relatively 'inferior good' in Figure 71a while
the same is true for $Y$ in Figure 71b.

In the case of price changes we must distinguish again between income and substitution effects and their relative
strengths. A change in relative prices renders one commodity as
the relatively cheap alternative and induces a substitution of
this commodity for the other one in the consumer's final consumption pattern – the substitution effect. In addition an

alteration of the price of one commodity, with the price of the other one unchanged, changes the real income position of the consumer and induces a change in his consumption pattern as a response to this alteration of circumstances. Figures 72a, b and c demonstrate three interesting cases of consumer reaction.

Beginning with Figure 72a we picture the consumer in initial equilibrium at point $a$ consuming $Ox_1$ units of $X$ per time period. Now suppose a fall in the price of $X$ (no change in the price of $Y$) pivots budget line $AB$ to $AC$. The new equilibrium point for the consumer on $AC$ is at $c$ where $Ox_3$ units of $X$ are being consumed now. But how does the consumer arrive at $c$? Let us suppose that we can view his thought processes frame by frame and study his reactions to the twofold change in circumstances. First we isolate the substitution effect by considering what the consumer would do if the fall in the price of $X$ were accompanied by a reduction in money income which would just permit him to maintain his original level of satisfaction, to remain on indifference curve $I_1$. In other words, how does the consumer react if his *real* position is unchanged, on $I_1$, but he is faced with a new price line, the slope of which reflects the new relative price ratio? Geometrically we show this by sliding $AC$ back towards $I_1$ until it just touches at a tangent – this final resting place is shown by the dotted budget line $A'B'$. Given this budget line the consumer would choose point $b$ and the move from $a$ to $b$ clearly results from the operation of the substitution effect – the consumer moves from $a$ to $b$ as a result of the change in relative prices and *for no other reason* since the income change has been effectively removed. Now suppose we restore the money income which we removed temporarily. We can see that as $A'B'$ moves towards $AC$ the consumer moves from $b$ towards $c$. Thus, from $b$ to $c$ is a move induced by the income effect and he consumes $Ox_2$ to $Ox_3$ more $X$ per period as a result of this effect.

In the initial situation depicted by Figure 72a both effects induce an increase in consumption of the commodity which has fallen in price – from $a$ to $b$ to $c$. Given the shape of an indifference curve we can say that the substitution effect will always result in more of the relatively cheaper commodity being bought

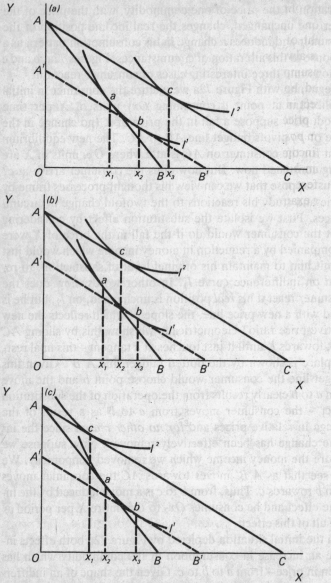

Figure 72 Possible consumer reactions to a change in budget circumstances

In terms of geometry it is not possible to find a tangency point on $I_1$ for a budget line which is later than $AB$ without looking to the right of point $a$. Thus we conclude that the substitution effect is always *positive* in the sense that there is an *increase* in the consumption of the relatively cheaper commodity. It should be noted, however, that some economists refer to this as a *negative* effect in the sense that the two changes are of opposite sign (*fall* in price and *rise* in quantity). The present authors prefer the term *positive* referring to the quantity effect only.

The income effect is positive also in Figure 72a since in moving from $b$ to $c$ more of commodity $X$ is consumed. However this effect may well follow the opposite direction. In Figure 72b for example, the substitution effect $a$ to $b$ remains positive but the income effect, $b$ to $c$ is negative. In other words the change in real income created by the fall in the price of $X$ induces a relative switch towards $Y$. However, this negative income effect is not strong enough to override the substitution effect and in the final position $c$ the consumer buys more $X$ ($Ox_1$ to $Ox_2$) although not as much as he would do in the absence of the income effect. It should be clear that this reaction occurs in Figure 72b because the consumer's relative preference for $Y$ is seen to be much stronger in 72b – the indifference curves are flatter indicating that the amount of $X$ he is willing to forego to obtain an extra unit of $Y$ is greater than in 72a. Commodity $X$, it would seem, is an 'inferior good' if the income effect is negative.

If we take this stronger preference for $Y$ even further we can envisage a situation in which the income effect is so negative that it overrides completely the substitution effect and the final net result is a reduction in the consumption of the relatively cheaper commodity. Figure 72c depicts this situation. Taking the initial equilibrium again and then allowing the price of $X$ to fall (budget line $AC$) we can trace the substitution effect as inducing a move from $a$ to $b$ (original indifference curve but new relative price ratio) and the income effect as inducing a move from $b$ to $c$. In this new 'final' equilibrium at point $c$ the consumer actually consumes less $X$ ($Ox_0$) than he did in the initial equilibrium at $a$. It would seem then that we have discovered a new method of defining the *Giffen good* – a commodity is a Giffen good if the (negative) income effect is strong enough to outweigh the (positive) substitution effect. In such cases the consumer buys less of a commodity when its price falls.

As a concluding piece to this section we can note that by altering the relative price of commodity $X$ and then measuring the effect on the consumer's purchases of $X$ we have been studying, in a sense, his demand reactions. For example, if we plotted a series of budget lines, each of which shows a different relative price ratio caused by a change in the price of $X$ only we could then find the point of consumer equilibrium on each curve and construct the locus of all such points. The resulting curve would show us the paths followed by the consumer's consumption of $X$ in response to changes in the price of $X$. Figure 73 adopts a preference map similar to that of 72b to demonstrate this. The resulting locus is termed usually a 'price consumption curve' (PCC) and its shape gives an indication of relative preferences – as the price of $X$ continues to fall in Figure 73 the absolute quantity of $X$ consumed increases but the relative quantity decreases.

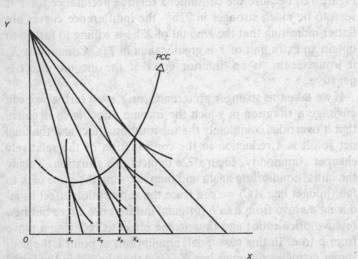

Figure 73

Note that the price consumption curve gives only an indication of demand response – it is not, by itself, a demand curve as we have defined it. In order to construct the latter we require price of $X$ on one axis and quantity of $X$ on the other, but we could derive such information from Figure 73 since that diagram provides a set of quantity responses ($Ox_1$, $Ox_2$, $Ox_3$, etc.) to a set of prices of $X$ (each budget line slope gives a ratio of relative prices with the price of $Y$ unchanged in each ratio).

## Critical appraisal of indifference curve analysis

Indifference curves assume ordinal and not cardinal utility. Using ordinal utility we can still derive hypotheses about an individual's response to price changes. Thus, to derive a demand curve, such as Figure 74, from an indifference map, we simply measure the quantity of $X$ purchased along the horizontal axis and the price of $X$ in terms of $Y$ along the vertical axis. The price of $X$ is simply $OB/OA$ and $OB'/OA$ and the points $S$ and $P$ are shown on the demand curve. And because the demand curve combines both an income and a substitution effect we can isolate a pure substitution (demand) curve by drawing a dotted

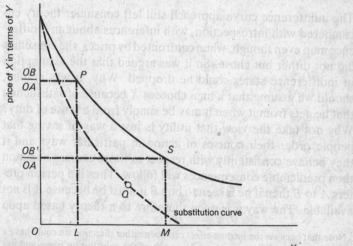

Figure 74

line – this would correspond to the demand curve that would be derived from a marginal utility map.[1]

But having noted the advantages of indifference analysis over that of marginal utility we should note that it still suffers from some of the disadvantages of the latter. We cannot assume that indefinite substitution of one good for another can be carried out so as to keep an individual on the same level of satisfaction. A dipsomaniac might be unwilling to give up his last bottle of whisky for any alternative. A pet lover might be indifferent between two dogs and two cats but would definitely reject the offer of a cat and a dog because they might be incompatible with each other. What we have to recognize, therefore, is that there may be a hierarchy of wants and that ordinal utility, like cardinal utility, tends to gloss over this point by assuming that all wants can be regarded as one homogeneous want which can be satisfied in innumerable ways; but a loaf of bread cannot quench thirst. Within this important limitation indifference analysis does have advantages over marginal utility by allowing us to deal with income and substitution effects.

## Revealed preference theory

The indifference curve approach still left consumer theory encumbered with introspection, with inferences about an indifference map even though, when confronted by prices, the consumer did not dither but chose. So it was argued that the assumption of indifference states could be dropped. Why, it was argued, should we assume that a man chooses $X$ because of satisfaction that he gets from it when it may be simply from a sense of duty? Why not take the view that utility is just a way of saying that people order their courses of action in particular ways and if they behave consistently with respect to those courses of action then predictable consequences will follow. Thus if a person prefers $A$ to $B$ then if he is seen to buy $B$ it must be because $A$ is not available. The way was open therefore to a theory based upon

[1] Note that because the income effect can go in either direction we could have a demand curve which was to the right or left of the substitution curve and not only to the right as in the diagram.

observations of choices made, a theory known as *revealed preference*.

The central proposition of the revealed preference approach is:

If a consumer is observed to buy more of a good when his income increases (the price of the good remaining unchanged) then he will buy more of the good if its price falls (and his income remains unchanged) because a price fall is equivalent to a real income rise.

This proposition is illustrated in Figure 75. The consumer is revealed to choose the combination of $X$ and $Y$ given by the point $P$ when his income and the relative prices of $X$ and $Y$ are given. He could have, in fact, chosen any combination of $X$ and $Y$ within the triangle $OAB$ but rejected all except that of $P$.

Suppose that the price of $X$ falls; then he could move to any combination within the larger triangle $OA'B$ but the fact that he had already rejected some combinations suggests that he will in fact be considering only those which lie inside the triangle $ABA'$.

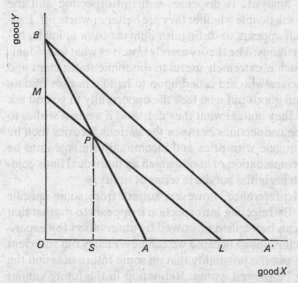

Figure 75

Before, however, ascertaining which combination he will choose, let us assume that whilst retaining the new relative prices we reduce his income so that he could still just purchase the combination $P$. In other words, through $P$ we draw a price line $LM$ parallel to $BA'$. Now which combination would he choose? We know that he would reject those lying along $MP$ since those were previously revealed to have been rejected in favour of $P$. Hence he will either continue to purchase $P$ or some combination along the line $LP$ which would imply buying more of $X$. Hence when the substitution effect is examined without the income effect working the consumer will never buy less $X$. Another way of putting the point is to say that the substitution effect is non-positive.

*Critical appraisal of revealed preference theory*

If elegance and simplicity of assumptions were the criteria by which we judge one theory to be superior to another then revealed preference theory would be judged superior to indifference curve analysis. It dispenses with introspection and the necessity to ask people whether they are better or worse off. Language, which appears to distinguish humans from animals, becomes superfluous. The theory merely observes what individuals do and as such is extremely useful to economic statisticians and econometricians who are called upon to handle masses of data on prices and goods but who lack the opportunity to go and ask people why they bought what they did. And if a purist wishes to trace out the connections between the various theories then he can simply juggle with price and income adjustments until he finds some combination of goods which an individual finds comparable with his initial bundle in terms of utility.

Revealed preference, however, suffers from some specific limitations. By rejecting introspection it appears to suggest that the theory can be verified or proved by observation (by experiment), which is not so because we can never carry out sufficient tests to rule out the possibility that on some future occasion the theory may be proved wrong. Refutation in the future cannot be ruled out. And in one particular aspect observation may be

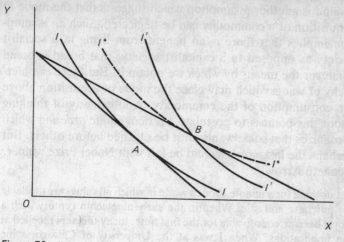

Figure 76

misleading because it does not exclude the possibility of a change in tastes. Thus, in Figure 76 we have no means other than by asking the individual whether, after the price change, he is on indifference curve $I'$ or $I^*$ which is part of a new preference map. There are also occasions on which an individual may not reveal his preferences, such as when collective goods are under consideration.

In addition to the specific criticisms of revealed preference theory advanced in the previous paragraph there are the more general limitations which we have noted about any economic theory of consumer behaviour which ignores the possibility of a hierarchy of wants.

## Final thoughts on utility theory

In presenting utility theory we have emphasized a movement towards simplifying assumptions and greater predictive power. But we have been continually reminded of the narrow scope of a theory which purports to measure utility by means of price. We have to remember that wants may not be homogeneous and therefore utility may not be homogeneous. And in the background is another assumption which suggests that the mode of acquisition of a commodity can be neglected. Such an assumption implies that there is no benefit from living in a socialist society as opposed to a capitalist society; that bread is bread whatever the means by which we obtain it. But there is a hierarchy of wants which may place the mode of acquisition above the consumption of the commodity. Another way of thinking about this point is to postulate a *lexicographic ordering* which recognizes that some wants must be satisfied before others. But perhaps the last words should be left with Nobel Prize winner, Kenneth Arrow.

Let us think for a minute about a world in which all values are available for purchase and sale. When in the early nineteenth century such a world became conceivable for the first time, many thinkers rebelled at the implications. When I was at the University of Chicago, some twenty-five years ago, the students put on a set of satirical sketches, one of which had as its main character the Rational Economic Man. He made no decisions without carefully consulting his slide rule (this was before the days of pocket computers, you understand). He was finally asked what price he would charge for murdering his grandmother. He thought about it for a minute, made some computations, and then looked up to ask, 'Do I have the right to sell the body?' Even in Chicago the indoctrination was not one hundred per cent complete.[1]

## Questions

1 A consumer spends his entire income on two goods $X$ and $Y$. His present position is as follows:

|   | Price per unit | Marginal utility |
|---|---|---|
| $X$ | 10p | 50 |
| $Y$ | 6p | 20 |

In order to increase his satisfaction should the consumer buy

(a) less $X$ and more $Y$;

(b) more $X$ and less $Y$;

1. K. J. Arrow, 'Why Profits are Challenged', in Benjamin Friedman, ed., *New Challenges to the Role of Profit*, Lexington Books, 1978, p. 54.

(c) continue with his present consumption pattern;

(d) more $X$ and the same amount of $Y$?

2 What is the paradox of value?

3 What is an inferior good? What is a Giffen good?

4 For a commodity like heroin, or even wine, the curve of marginal utility does not fall. Should we therefore abandon the theory or treat such goods as exceptional cases?

5 Comment on the following propositions:

(a) the theory of consumer behaviour assumes choice and ignores habit;

(b) the theory ignores uncertainty;

(c) the theory ignores advertising;

(d) the theory ignores the need to 'keep up with the Jones's'.

6 If the total utility derived from a good is at a maximum then the good is a free good and its marginal utility is zero. Do you agree?

7 A consumer with given tastes and money income confronted by two goods, $A$ and $B$, whose prices are fixed will maximize his satisfaction when

(a) $\dfrac{MU_a}{MU_b} = \dfrac{P_a}{P_b}$ or (b) $\dfrac{MU_a}{P_a} = \dfrac{MU_b}{P_b}$ or (c) $\dfrac{P_b}{P_a} = \dfrac{MU_a}{MU_b}$.

Give reasons for your answer.

8 Comment on the following propositions:

(a) increments of utility derived from particular goods are both intrinsically measurable and practically measurable with the measuring rod of money;

(b) totals of utility derived from particular goods are intrinsically measurable provided you reckon them from a sensible starting point;

(c) totals of utility derived from particular goods are not practically measurable unless the amount spent on the good is small;

(d) totals of totals, i.e. total utility of income in general is not practically measurable.

(Derived from Robertson, 1952.)

9 If the effect of the fall in the price of a good is not to have

repercussions on the purchases of other goods then the elasticity of the good whose price has fallen must be unity. Do you agree with this statement? Does it confine the usefulness of the theory? Could the theory be saved by assuming quasi-constancy of the marginal utility of money?

10 Construct an indifference map for a pair of complementary goods.

11 'I prefer to live in a town rather than the country.' Does this statement violate indifference curve analysis? Is it common for people not to buy some goods?

12 Does the theory of consumer behaviour predict that a 10 per cent rise in a person's income (all money prices remaining constant) will have the same effect on that person's behaviour as would a 10 per cent fall in all money prices (with money income held constant)?

13 Demonstrate that the substitution effect is non-positive.

14 The State can offer the poor subsidized housing *or* money. Which should the State offer if it wishes to ensure adequate housing of the poor? Which should the poor accept?

15 A rise in the price of milk leads to dairy farmers increasing their own consumption of milk and reducing the supply of milk to the market. Does this mean that milk is an inferior good?

16 Over time real incomes per head have risen but the numbers of domestic servants have fallen. Does this mean that domestic service is an inferior good?

17 Why is indifference curve analysis the least objectionable theory of consumer behaviour?

18 Is the following statement an example of lexicographic ordering? 'I prefer A to B if it provides more beer irrespective of how much bread it contains; but if it provides the same amount of beer as B I would prefer it if it provides more bread.'

19 Would you expect the hierarchy of wants to be the same for all people up to the point when basic wants were satisfied? Would you expect the hierarchy of wants in Britain to be the same for all its inhabitants but not for Britons and Spaniards?

20 Does it make sense to argue that taking a pound from a rich man and giving it to a poor man will make the community better off?

# Chapter 12
# Costs and Supply: Economic Costs

In the last chapter we looked behind the demand curve to find the reasons for its shape and position and we found a theory of choice which is more widely known as a theory of utility. We now look behind the supply curve to find reasons for its shape and position. We shall find a theory of choice but it is not called utility theory: instead it parades under the title of the theory of costs. There is no reason why it should not be regarded as a part of utility theory except the historical accident which led economists to designate that part of choice theory connected with consumption to be known as utility theory, and that part concerned with production as cost theory. But for a household, decisions to produce and decisions to consume are just decisions based upon choice among alternative courses of action. Let us however begin our analysis with a definition:

Cost in economics means opportunity cost: it is the value placed on resources in their best alternative use.

### Costs are benefits: costs are utilities

Definitions can be useful for examinations but their implications need to be fully explored if true understanding is to be achieved.

1 *Costs are rejected benefits*. Suppose that you are faced with the choice of going to a dance or watching television. If you decide to watch television then you must expect the benefits from

watching television to outweigh those that might accrue from going to a dance.

2 *Costs involve comparisons of net benefits.* Suppose you have to choose between digging in the garden and going for a run in the car. Digging in the garden brings the benefits of flowers, vegetables, a place of solace and contemplation *and* the possibility of a slipped disc. Should you then compare the benefits from the garden with the pain yielded by a slipped disc? The answer is: No. You should look at the net pleasures from the run in the car and compare them with the net benefits from the garden. So your balance sheet might look like this:

|  | Utils | Disutils |
|---|---|---|
| garden | 80 | 20 |
| car run | 60 | 40 |

Now the net benefits from gardening are not 60, i.e. 80–20 but 40, i.e. $(80-20) - (60-40)$.

3 *Disutilities may not be negative utilities.* The previous analysis glosses over the point that utilities and disutilities may not be comparable. If it is illegitimate to compare them, what are the alternatives? One method is to ignore them and look solely at the ultimate benefits, i.e. 80–60. This is a common approach in economics. Thus in Chapter 26 we shall look at how an individual allocates his time between work and leisure on the assumption that work yields only a benefit – income – which is compared with the benefits from leisure. Yet it must be apparent that many jobs yield disutility before they yield utility. The problem of disutility also occurs elsewhere in problems of time and leisure. Some writers, for example, assume that in buying washing machines and carpet cleaners, people are buying leisure whereas others would take the view that they are buying relief from dull, monotonous jobs. The problem may, in fact, be insoluble: utility and disutility may be inextricably mixed as are pain and pleasure. Throughout this book, however, we shall assume that it is net benefits, not gross benefits, that are compared.

4 It follows from what has been said so far that *maximizing utility means minimizing costs*; that is, the theory of costs is intimately linked with the theory of utility. Indeed it is another way of looking at the same problem. If the net benefits from digging in the garden were expected to be lower than going for a run in the car, then you would have said that the costs of digging were too high.

5 We can also see that the much bandied-about phrase *cost–benefit analysis* used in the evaluation of social projects, such as roads, railways and airports, means no more than a comparison of the benefits that might accrue from different courses of action. It could be called benefit–benefit analysis except that the rejected benefits are put under the heading 'costs'.

6 *Costs are subjective*. By 'subjective' we mean that the expected benefits from different courses of action are perceived and evaluated by the decision-maker and there may be no obvious objective criteria which an observer, an outsider, can point to as the factors influencing the decision-maker. This is important. It marks the difference between the businessman and his accountant. In making his decision the businessman will often be guided by intangibles, the 'feel of the market', those 'animal spirits' which prevent him from doing nothing. Contrast this with his accountant who regards as costs only those things which have bills of sale or receipts attached to them and who is forced to do so because the law requires him to measure income (the difference between receipts and costs) in an objective fashion by deducting the figures on one set of 'bits of paper' (receipts) from those on another set of 'bits of paper' (costs). But the businessman is not always guided by bits of paper: he may have only a hazy idea of the prices he will have to pay for resources at some future date and the receipts he will get at some future date.

7 Finally, we can now realize that *costs may be difficult to calculate*. Although we have drawn attention to the differences in the costing procedures of businessmen and accountants we can take the point further. For it is sometimes said that the decision-maker can enumerate his costs but not his benefits. This may

not be so, for his costs are all the benefits that might accrue from any of the numerous courses of action that he might have taken and some of which he may have overlooked or neglected.

## Costs and prices

Of course we normally expect costs, the foregone benefits, to be reflected in the prices paid for resources and in a world of perfect knowledge that would be true, because all the benefits from all courses of action would then be known. The subjective aspect of costs is strongest when decisions are 'once-and-for-all', for then there can be no recourse to past experience.

## Durable goods and the classification of costs

There is, however, one large class of goods for which price does not automatically record costs. These are the durable or capital goods whose services are not instantly consumed. Now in the case of a house, a car or a fridge the immediate resale price may be as much as 90 per cent of the purchase price and it is the difference between purchase price and resale price which measures cost or, to be more precise, *acquisition cost*.

Supposing you bought a car for £1000 and could immediately sell it for £990, then the acquisition cost would be £10. If you then kept the car for a year without using it you might get £800 and the *retention cost* or *depreciation* of the car would not be the difference between £1000 and £800, but the difference between £1000 and the present value of £800 discounted to the date of initial purchase. Recall that £800 next year is not the same as £800 now.

It would be most unusual for you not to run the car and we may suppose that at the end of the year you could get £500 for it. The difference between the discounted value of £800 and £500 represents the *operating cost* though you would have to add in (appropriately discounted) expenditure on petrol, oil and maintenance. And you could be unlucky in that, though you assumed you would get £500 for it on resale, the makers decide to bring out a new model which causes the resale price of your car to drop to £300. You would then regard the difference between the present values of £500 and £300 as *obsolescence cost*. We can set out the cost calculations as follows:

|  | *Expenditures (£)* | |
|---|---|---|
|  | *Now* | *End of one year* |
| purchase price | 1000 | |
| resale price | 990 | £800 or £500 or £300 |
| *Costs* | | |
| acquisition | 10 | |
| retention | 272·8 | (i.e. £1000 minus £800 discounted at 10 per cent for one year) |
| operating | 272·7 | (i.e. £800 minus £500 both discounted at 10 per cent for one year) |
| obsolescence | 181·8 | (i.e. £500 minus £300 both discounted at 10 per cent for one year) |

We have also established a set of cost components which are sometimes given other names in economics and accounting and it is useful to remember them.

**Table 26** Cost synonyms

| acquisition cost | fixed cost | instantaneous or |
|---|---|---|
| | overhead cost | inescapable |
| | unavoidable cost | benefits |
| | supplementary cost | foregone |
| operating cost | variable cost | |
| | direct cost | avoidable or |
| | avoidable cost | escapable |
| | prime cost | benefits |
| | running cost | foregone |
| | retention cost | |

Of the terms given above 'fixed' and 'variable' are fairly standard in the literature, though they do not always have the precision of 'acquisition' and 'operating' cost. We shall however use the terms 'fixed' and 'variable' so as to avoid confusion for readers of other books.

## Bygones are bygones

The distinction between fixed and variable cost is important because once a car, house, fridge or record player has been acquired then that cost cannot influence future decisions. The cost of running the car immediately after it was purchased is not £1000 (the historical cost) but £990 which could be obtained on resale. Similarly the cost at the end of one year is not £1000 but the resale price of £800, £500 or £300.

The point we are trying to make is important. Once costs have been incurred they can be ignored until the decision has to be reconsidered (as, for example, when an asset needs replacing). The only situations when initial costs or historical costs become important is, paradoxically, when prices are changing. Suppose a machine costs £1000 and through its use earns £3000, then net income is £3000 discounted to the time of the decision minus £1000. Let us take a year. Suppose at the end of the year the machine needs replacing but its price has risen to £1500 then the income of the old machine should be regarded as £3000 (discounted) minus £1500. Failure to allow for rising prices can lead to inability to replace assets because too much income has been consumed. Accountants are forced, by law, to measure income on the basis of historical cost, but sensible ones set aside contingency funds.

## Marginal cost

Having established a satisfactory definition of cost in terms of benefits foregone and drawn a distinction between fixed and variable costs we are now in a position to explore variable cost more fully. It is the cost that can be avoided that is relevant for decision-making and not the costs that have been incurred.

Indeed, any consequences that have flowed from a previous decision may have no bearing on the next decision. Thus a previous decision may have committed a firm to a blast furnace of a certain size whilst the next decision may cause the firm to abandon iron-making. What is relevant and important therefore is the decision that has to be made and not the decision that has been made.

A producer will have to make a decision if there has been a change in demand or a technological change making for a possible reduction in the costs of continuing along the present programmes. Such a decision will therefore cause a change in output and the simplest concept we can establish between cost and output change is marginal cost.

## *Marginal cost is the cost of increasing output by one unit*

Marginal cost is one of those concepts – along with marginal revenue, marginal utility and marginal product – which are fundamental in economics. All refer to small, incremental changes. In this case it is the change in cost associated with a change in output. Marginal cost can, however, be an ambiguous concept for there are a variety of methods of changing output and the output change can be effected quickly or slowly. We can set out some of the dimensions of marginal cost which need to be considered:

1 *The nature of the product*. In some cases the output of one good can only be increased if the output of another good is also increased. Joint products and joint costs are fairly common.

2 *Has the output to be increased quickly?*

3 *Is the increase in output to be permanent or temporary?*

4 *Does the decision include social as well as private benefits?*

## *Rate of output*

Suppose we have a firm with given resources. We may suppose that within a given time period, say a year, it can produce 5200 units. Now let us suppose that demand rises. How will the businessman react? If he decides to respond quickly then he may envisage a rise in costs. Thus if he hopes to produce 10 400 units in a year then overtime working or shift working may have to be introduced and workers will have to be paid higher rates of pay. Moreover, he may be forced to bid up the prices of raw materials, and bottlenecks may occur on the shop floor.

The expected behaviour of costs with respect to an increase in output from 5200 to 10 400 units a year can now be illustrated by means of Figure 77. In Figure 77 we show a cost curve for a plant capable of producing 5200 units in a year and we may envisage that the firm is producing at the point $A$, the lowest point on the cost curve, which is also a rate of 100 per week. Now when output rises the firm produces at $B$ which indicates that costs rise as the rate of output rises. (Note that since these costs are expected costs they are discounted to the time of the decision.) Note that the effect of rate changes is to cause costs to rise steeply. Costs may not rise so steeply if the plant is underutilized or if there is planned reserve capacity to take into account

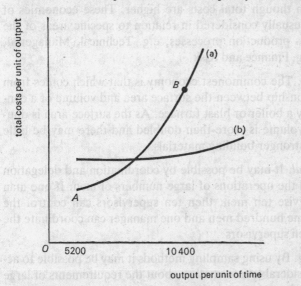

Figure 77

that output may swing between 5200 and 10 400 units per year, but note that spare capacity involves a cost and so the cost curve will be higher at low outputs and lower at high outputs than the curve initially considered (curve *b* is shallower than curve *a*).

The final point to note is that we can have a family of cost curves, one for each scheduled output and each rising as a greater rate of output is imposed. The cost curves for larger scheduled outputs will initially be above those for smaller plants but rates of change of costs tend to be lower for reasons we shall now explore.

## Volume of output

So far we have ignored the total output that is planned when a businessman assembles his resources. It is important to know whether output is scheduled to be 5200 units over one year or 10 400 units over two years. Although the annual rates are the same, the greater volume of output in the second case may give rise to considerable economies of scale and hence lower unit costs even though total costs are higher. These economies of scale are usually considered in relation to specific areas of the producer's production processes, e.g. Technical, Managerial, Marketing, Finance and Risk.

*Technical*. The commonest economy is that which comes from the relationship between the surface area and volume of a container, say a boiler or blast furnace. As the surface area is doubled the volume is more than doubled and there may be little need for stronger building materials.

*Managerial*. It may be possible by coordination and delegation to control the operations of large numbers of men. If one man can supervise ten men, then ten supervisors can control the work of one hundred men and one manager can coordinate the work of ten supervisors.

*Marketing*. By using sampling methods it may be possible to acquire considerable information about the requirements of large numbers of consumers.

*Finance*. It may be cheaper, in terms of brokers' fees, etc., to raise large sums of money.

*Risk*. With sampling methods it may be possible to exercise greater control over the quality of output.

**Table 27** Printing costs for an initial printing order for a 256 page book

| Number of copies printed (*thousands*) | Index of cost per copy including the cost of paper and binding | |
| --- | --- | --- |
| | Hardback | Paperback |
| 1 | 100 | — |
| 5 | 34 | 100 |
| 10 | 25 | 80 |
| 20 | 21 | 59 |
| 50 | 18 | 41 |
| 100 | — | 34 |
| 200 | — | 30 |

Source: Pratten (1971)

## Set-up costs

Economies of scale arise because of 'lumpiness' in the production process. Some reductions in costs per unit arise only by using certain production techniques which are only worthwhile when the volume of output is increased. Even where set-up costs increase there may be no proportional increase of costs with output. Lecturing to eighty students may be expected to involve no greater problems than are encountered when lecturing to sixty or forty students. Indeed it might be possible to reduce lecturing costs appreciably by means of television. As an example of the possibilities of the reduction in unit costs following an initial set-up cost we cite data obtained by Pratten. What Table 27 reveals is that cost per unit falls for both hardback and paperback books the greater the volume or 'run' of books and that production of low runs of paperbacks has a pronounced effect on the unit cost.

## Learning effects

Another source of cost reductions that occurs when it is expected to repeat a particular production run is learning effects. Adam Smith had noted in the eighteenth century that repetition brought with it increased dexterity and efficiency. Awkward operations become eliminated and workers 'filter' out the efficient methods of production. Such learning effects cannot be known in advance though they can be guessed at. Indeed one of the most controversial areas in government planning concerns the price-fixing arrangements for government contracts. Failure to allow for learning effects may be why private contractors make large profits and governments become involved in acrimonious debates over their ability to cost defence projects. There is also the general point that where learning effects are prevalent then workers will prefer to be paid by the number of pieces they produce (i.e. piece-work) whereas employers will prefer to pay workers either on time-rates of wages (with stringent supervision) or on piece-rate price lists which pay a declining price per piece as the number of pieces produced increases in order to capture some of the gains from learning for themselves.

*The effect on costs*. The effect of increased volume on costs will be to cause the expected costs for any given rate of output to decline as in Figure 78; the unit total-cost curve rises at a diminishing rate.

## The effect of rate and volume on costs

Now a common feature of most production processes is that the rate and volume of output increase together. This is because the length of the production period is unchanged in the sense that the market requires so many units of output per week, month or year. Thus to produce more in a given time period means an

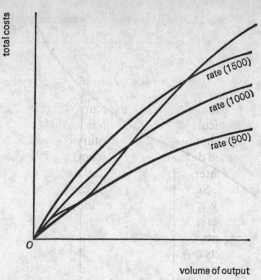

total costs

rate (1500)

rate (1000)

rate (500)

*O*

volume of output

Figure 78

increase in both the rate and the volume. For example, if output is doubled from 5200 to 10 400 units per year both the volume and the rate are increased. What happens to costs per unit depends upon the relative strengths of the volume and rate effects. For a given volume (capacity) the volume effect will be stronger than the rate effect when output is lower. As output increases unit cost will be falling. But after some output level has been attained the rate effect will outweigh the volume economies and unit costs will be rising. This is why the total cost curve has the curious shape shown in Figure 79.[1] From the origin to point *A* total costs increase but less than proportionately to the increase in output; from point *A* onwards total costs rise more than proportionately to the increase in output. From Figure 79 can be derived average and marginal cost curves as shown on the lower half of that diagram. The fact that the cost curves are U-shaped reflects both volume and rate effects. (The actual de-

1. The minimum point on the average cost curve occurs where the total cost curve begins to rise steeply beyond *C*. The minimum point on the marginal cost curve occurs at *A* where the total cost curve has an inflection point.

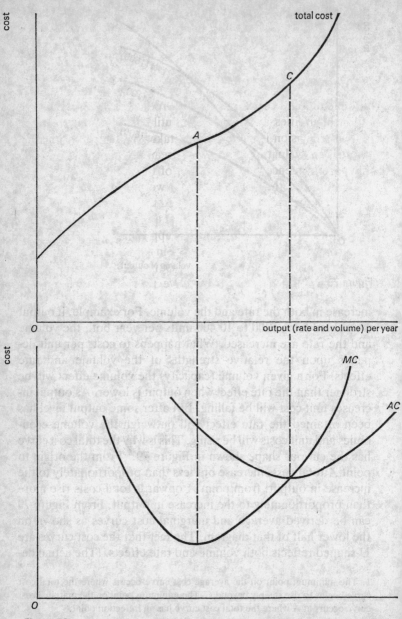

Figure 79

rivation of such curves will, however, be dealt with in the next section where we shall also relate the analysis of costs to the production function.)

## Production functions and cost curves

Production and costs are related. Production involves the creation of utilities and costs define utilities which are rejected. When a decision is made to undertake some economic activity there is an evaluation of different streams of benefits; these benefits are influenced by the nature of the production processes which created them. In Chapter 3 we analysed the nature of production processes and established the law of diminishing returns: the notion that output grew at a diminishing rate as more and more of a variable factor was applied to a fixed factor. In that chapter output was thought of in physical terms, as actual rather than expected. What we must now do is to interpret the production function in a subjective rather than an objective manner.

In Table 28 we outline the expected outputs from applying differing numbers of men in a factory. From the information, and given the expected wages of men and the price of the factory, we can obtain total costs, a variety of average costs and marginal costs. These cost categories are:

Average fixed cost (*AFC*), obtained by dividing total fixed cost by total output. Average fixed cost falls as the rate of output increases thereby confirming the commonplace saying that as output increases the overheads can be spread more easily. The average total cost curve is, of course, a vertical summation of the curves of average fixed cost and average variable cost and the reader might like to superimpose the relevant curves on to Figure 79.

Average variable cost (*AVC*), obtained by dividing total variable cost by total output.

Average total cost (*ATC*), obtained by dividing total cost by total output

**Table 28** Production and costs for a given production period

| Units of variable factor | Units of fixed factor | Total output | Total variable cost | Total fixed cost | Total cost | Average variable cost | Average fixed cost | Average total cost | Marginal cost |
|---|---|---|---|---|---|---|---|---|---|
| 0 | 10 | 0 | 0 | 50 | 50 | — | — | — | — |
| 1 | 10 | 5 | 5 | 50 | 55 | 1·00 | 10·00 | 11·00 | 1·00 |
| 2 | 10 | 12 | 10 | 50 | 60 | 0·83 | 4·16 | 4·99 | 0·71 |
| 3 | 10 | 24 | 15 | 50 | 65 | 0·62 | 2·04 | 2·66 | 0·42 |
| 4 | 10 | 39 | 20 | 50 | 70 | 0·51 | 1·28 | 1·79 | 0·33 |
| 5 | 10 | 50 | 25 | 50 | 75 | 0·50 | 1·00 | 1·50 | 0·36 |
| 6 | 10 | 59 | 30 | 50 | 80 | 0·51 | 0·85 | 1·36 | 0·56 |
| 7 | 10 | 67 | 35 | 50 | 85 | 0·52 | 0·74 | 1·26 | 0·63 |
| 8 | 10 | 75 | 40 | 50 | 90 | 0·53 | 0·67 | 1·20 | 0·63 |
| 9 | 10 | 80 | 45 | 50 | 95 | 0·56 | 0·63 | 1·19 | 1·00 |
| 10 | 10 | 84 | 50 | 50 | 100 | 0·60 | 0·60 | 1·20 | 1·25 |
| 11 | 10 | 86 | 55 | 50 | 105 | 0·64 | 0·58 | 1·22 | 2·50 |
| 12 | 10 | 87 | 60 | 50 | 110 | 0·69 | 0·58 | 1·27 | 5·00 |

*Points to note about marginal cost are:*

1 So long as marginal cost is below average variable or average total cost it is pulling average costs down. When marginal cost is equal to either average cost then that average cost is at a minimum level and when marginal cost is above either average cost then that average cost will be rising.

2 Marginal cost can be calculated as either the change in total cost or the change in total variable cost. Why? Because fixed cost will not be varying with output and so all changes in total cost must be changes in variable costs.

## The old and the new

In a previous section it was suggested that with an expansion of output it would be more efficient to operate a new plant of larger capacity. This need not always be the case. What we usually observe is the coexistence of old and new plants sometimes in different firms but often within the same firm. Why should this be so? The answer lies in the unimportance of the sunk costs of old plant. Those costs have been incurred and can be forgotten and attention needs only be paid to running costs. The choice can therefore lie between the variable costs of old machines and the total costs (fixed plus variable) of new machines. As long as the running costs of old machines are lower than the total costs of new machines, old machines will be retained. But for an output expansion the firm will supplement its stock of old machines with new ones since these will be relatively cheaper.[2] Sometimes 'old' technologies may be retained for stand-by purposes: e.g. coal fired power stations may be built to cope with peak demands for electricity whilst nuclear stations may serve the off-peak.

---

2. An alternative way of expressing this proposition is to say that a firm will use both old and new machines as long as the net present values of future earnings for the plants are equal. In calculating net present values the costs will be present values of operating and total costs respectively.

*Joint costs*

So far we have assumed that only one product is being produced. Many firms, however, produce more than one product. Indeed the number of one-product firms is probably small. Even Guinness produce sweets and toffees; launderettes offer semi-dry or dry clothing as products. The reasons for multi-product firms are of course not hard to discover.

1 Technology – it may be impossible to produce mutton without wool.

2 Risk-avoidance – it may be more efficient to produce a range of goods rather than run the risk of putting all 'the eggs in one basket'.

Whenever firms produce more than one product accountants encounter the problem of allocating overheads. Remember the accountant's task is to attach costs to the various goods produced in order to meet the requirements of company law and the tax authorities. He has to try to ascertain the income obtained from various products and to do this he must deduct costs from revenues. Now economists say that the apportionment of costs cannot be carried out in any meaningful manner. Suppose, say, our sheep farmer has the following receipts and payments position:

| Receipts | | Payments | |
|---|---|---|---|
| sale of wool | £5000 | wages | £2000 |
| sale of mutton | £2000 | materials | £1500 |
| | | buildings | £1000 |

Suppose that the farmer decides that half his outgoings shall be met from the sale of wool and half from the sale of mutton: then he will discover that the production of mutton incurs a loss of £250 whereas wool production shows a profit of £2750. If he decides to stop producing mutton he will automatically cease producing wool. What should he do? His overall position is one of a £2500 profit so there is no reason why he should stop sheep farming. The correct solution seems therefore to be to cover all the overheads out of total revenue. In other words, the problem of overheads is really a marketing problem of trying to get the maximum revenue from the sale of each product.

Of course, not all joint costs are so rigidly fixed. Sometimes the proportions in which products are produced can be varied and therefore marginal costs can be ascertained. But there is still no case for allocating overheads. There is no case for adding to marginal cost (or more usually average variable cost) a percentage to cover the overheads if that procedure results in a loss because the overhead has been fixed too high. As long as revenue covers marginal cost and some contribution can be made to overheads then production should be continued unless it can be shown that another product will bring in greater profit.[3]

## Collective goods

Joint consumption must be distinguished from joint production. In the case of jointly produced private goods the market can determine allocation issues as outlined in the previous paragraph; in the case of joint consumption, the collective goods case, the financing problems become more important since the good is made available to all consumers.

## Private and social costs

The final classification of costs is into private and social. A chemical plant, let us say, discharges noxious effluent into a river which flows by the plant. The cost to the chemical plant is the cost of pumping the effluent into the river (or more precisely the benefits foregone by pumping). If, however, the pollution reduces the incomes of others – fishermen and would-be bathers – then there are additional costs borne by others. The costs to

3. Not all accountants adopt the policy of trying to allocate overheads by apportioning a percentage to costs in order to arrive at price. Some, more recently, have adopted the *direct costing* approach which is a form of marginal costing. By this method products are priced on the basis of (marginal) direct cost and each product makes whatever contribution it can to overheads.

the firm are *private costs* whereas the total costs of waste disposal are called *social costs*.

Evidently the distinction between private and social costs depends upon the system of cost enforcement in operation. If the chemical firm has to compensate those whose incomes fall or has to introduce a system of waste disposal which has no spillovers then private and social costs would equate.

## Empirical aspects of costs

At various stages we have tried to relate our views on costs to the real world: most real-world studies of costs suggest that the U-shaped cost curve may not exist. Costs are usually depicted as either L-shaped or continually falling. Why should this be so?

1 Learning effects: the cost data show the effects of learning over time.

2 Volume effects: there may be changes in plant structure which give rise to economies of scale.

3 Wrong data. Accountancy data may contain biases because they were not designed to answer economists' questions.

4 Uncertainty: managers may build flexibility into plants. No one would build a steel firm to produce exactly 400 000 tonnes per year if demand was expected to fluctuate between 350 000 and 500 000 tonnes per year.

5 A different problem: the empirical results refer to the costs consequent upon decisions as recorded by the market but do not refer to the costs contemplated at the decision-making stage.

## Summary

Costs are the benefits foregone: the foregone utilities. As such they are subjective and may have no objective basis. When there is a change in tastes, income or the environment a decision will be made. This decision will involve a choice between various streams of discounted benefits and the highest valued stream of rejected benefits will constitute the costs of the decision.

The contemplated costs of a decision will vary with (a) the nature of the product; (b) how soon a decision has to be made; (c) the number of periods over which production will take place, i.e. the time horizon of the decision; (d) the presence or absence of technical change and (e) the social context within which decision-making takes place.

Costs are linked to production functions because it is productive processes that create utilities. But although production functions have an objectivity grounding in the inputs and products, often physical, that they involve, the production functions associated with costs are expected production functions. The empirical, or after-the-event, production functions show the consequences of decisions and may contain results different from those anticipated. As such they can only offer pointers to the likely outcomes of decisions based upon an extrapolation of past outcomes.

## Questions

1 'Costs are utilities.' Explain.

2 What are the implications of viewing costs as subjective opportunity costs?

3 What is the relationship between production functions and costs?

4 'If I can get enough to cover my running costs, I can produce and forget about my overheads, even though I make a loss for the time being.' Comment on this statement.

5 'Fixed costs do not exist in the long run and are irrelevant in the short run.' Explain.

6 In this country some electric power stations are conventional, fired both by coal and oil, some are nuclear and some are hydroelectric. How would you use economic theory to explain the coexistence of different methods of production for a homogeneous commodity?

7 The following equations express the relationship between costs and output:

$C = 3Q,$

$C = 10 + 3Q,$

$C = 10 + 3Q^2,$

$C = 10 + 3Q^3 + 3Q^2,$

where $C$ is total cost and $Q$ is output. Insert values (from say 1 to 100) for $Q$ and obtain values of $C$. What can you say about the nature of the cost curves? Which equation seems to express the relationship between costs and output as underlined by the law of diminishing returns?

# Chapter 13
# Costs and Production: Isoquants

In this chapter we shall pursue the connection between costs and production by means of isoquants. In Chapter 3 we analysed the problems of production by allowing one factor of production to be varied whilst holding another constant. But in a more general analysis we should allow for the possibility that the amounts of all factors can be varied. In Figure 80 we measure the amounts of labour, $L$, and capital $K$, being used within a given state of technical knowledge to produce

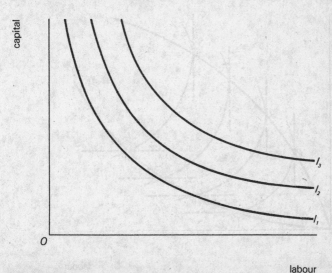

Figure 80

amounts of a commodity *X*. Along each curve, such as $I_1$, a given amount of *X* can be produced with varying combinations of labour and capital. The curves are called *isoquants* (equal output) curves. The curvature of the isoquants reflects the fact that one factor can only be substituted for another with difficulty. Hence, the slope of an isoquant at any point measures the *marginal rate of technical substitution* of one factor for another.

Not only does the isoquant slope downwards from left to right but also the slope tends to flatten. The reason for this flattening is that it becomes progressively more difficult to substitute one factor for the other and keep output constant. Eventually a point is reached where an isoquant begins to bend back and become concave to the origin and where the curve begins to bend back represents the limit to input substitution possibilities in that direction. Such points are marked as *pqrs* and *tuvw* in Figure 81.

Figure 81 shows clearly the range of substitution possibilities along each isoquant between pairs of points *pt*, *qu*, *rv* and *sw*.

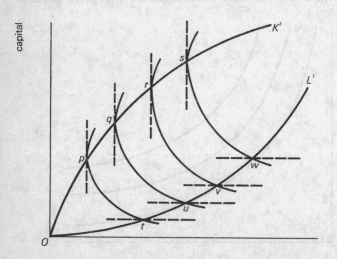

Figure 81

Outside these points each isoquant begins to bend on itself which means that output can be maintained at the level given by that isoquant if more of *both* inputs are employed. Within the range denoted by each pair of points, output can be maintained by substituting labour for capital (or vice versa) subject to diminishing marginal technical rate of substitution, but outside each pair the possibilities for substitution have been exhausted. The reason why this occurs relates to the effects on relative marginal products when factor proportions are changed and the technicalities of this warrant further investigation.

To understand more fully the relationship between factor input substitution and relative marginal products consider Figure 82 which looks closely at one chosen isoquant.

Figure 82 depicts the isoquant for 1250 units of output of commodity *x*. No matter what combination of *K* and *L* is employed along the isoquant, 1250 units of *X* is always the resulting output. Consider a move from point *a* to point *c*. Such a move entails using *ab* less capital and *bc* more labour. Now, since output is unchanged the output of the extra labour em-

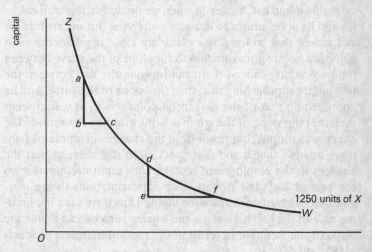

Figure 82

ployed at $c$ must compensate exactly for the output lost by the reduction in the employment of capital. Using the symbol $\Delta$ to denote 'change in', $\Delta q^k$ to represent 'change in quantity of $X$ due to change in capital employed' and $\Delta q^L$ to denote 'change in quantity of $X$ due to change in labour employed', we can write

$$ab \cdot \Delta q^k = bc \cdot \Delta q^L \tag{1}$$

where the left hand side product is negative (a *reduction* in output due to employing *less* capital) and the right hand side product is positive (an *increase* in output due to employing *more* labour).

Rearranging **1** we can write

$$\frac{ab}{bc} = (-)\frac{\Delta q^L}{\Delta q^k} \tag{2}$$

Now, a closer look at $ab/bc$ reveals it to be the slope of the isoquant between points $a$ and $c$. Strictly speaking, of course, the slope of the isoquant at any point is given by a tangent *to the curve* at that point. We shall be pursuing such concepts in considerable detail in Chapter 14 when we discuss differential calculus and its applications to economic analysis. But meanwhile we can accept that so long as $a$ and $c$ are close together the ratio $ab/bc$ is a good approximation to the slope of the curve between the two points. Indeed if we can imagine the gap between the two points approaching zero then the 'slope of the curve' will be approaching that of the tangent at point $a = c$. It would seem then that the slope of the curve is being given by the ratio of the changes in output that result from the changes in inputs. Again, if we assume that $a$ and $c$ are very close together, so that the changes in the employment level of each input are minute, we can regard $\Delta q^L$ and $\Delta q^k$ as close approximations to the marginal products of each resource input. Thus if we take the limiting case of the gap between $a$ and $c$ being zero we can define the slope of the isoquant in terms of the ratio of marginal products ($MP^L$ and $MP^K$)

$$\frac{ab}{bc} = \frac{MP^L}{MP^K}$$

Indeed we can go a little further since the ratio *ab/bc* tells us also the rate at which labour (*bc*) is being substituted for capital (*ab*) and if we assume that *a* and *c* are only an infinitesimal distance apart we can define the marginal rate of technical substitution of labour for capital ($MRTS^{LK}$) as the slope of the isoquant which, in turn, can be defined as the ratio of marginal products. Thus at point $a = c$:

$$\text{Slope of isoquant} = \frac{MP^L}{MP^K} = MRTS^{LK}$$

This analysis can be repeated for all points along the isoquant; it is not restricted to point *a* or point *c*.

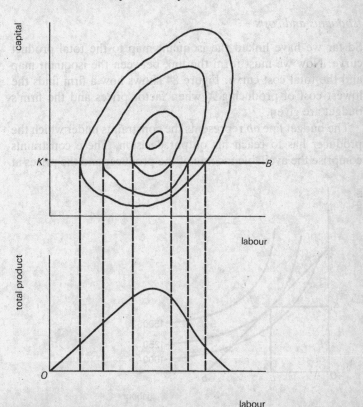

Figure 83

## Isoquants and the total product curve

We can now use the preceding analysis to derive the total product curve of Chapter 3. In Figure 83 the amount of capital is held constant at $K^*$ and the amount of labour is increased. As we move along $K^*B$ output increases and successively higher isoquants are crossed. But observe that the spaces between the isoquants are increasing as a result of the flattening out of the isoquants. Eventually output reaches a peak and then falls – there is a descent down successively lower isoquants. In the lower half of Figure 83 the total output curve, derived from the traverse of the isoquant map along $K^*B$, is drawn.

## Isoquants and costs

So far we have linked the isoquant map to the total product curve. Now we must form the link between the isoquant map and the total cost curve. Figure 84 shows how a firm finds the lowest cost of producing $X$ when factor prices and the firm's budget are given.

The budget line *ab* represents the constraints under which the producer has to reach his output decision. These constraints comprise the available income of the producer and the prices at

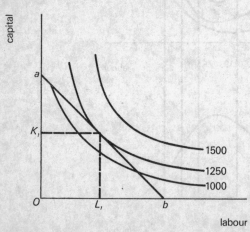

Figure 84

which he is able to acquire supplies of the resources which he employs in the production process. Suppose, for example, that the producer has £$Y$ to spend on resources and that the prices of capital and labour are $P_K$ and $P_L$ respectively. If the producer decides to spend the full amount of $Y$ on capital and labour he can do so subject to the constraint $Y = P_K.K + P_L.L$ where $K$ and $L$ represent quantities of the two respective inputs. Now given this constraint and the earlier assumption about the producer's objectives, he tries to reach the highest isoquant compatible with the constraint. In terms of Figure 84 the best point for the producer is where the budget line is tangential to the isoquant which represents 1250 units of the final commodity. Clearly, given the shape of the isoquants and the nature of the constraint, the best point on the isoquant map will always be one of tangency, whatever the actual level of the constraint.

Point $c$ is the point of tangency. What are the characteristics of this point? Obviously the slope of the 1250 isoquant is equal to the slope of the budget line at point $c$ since $ab$ is the tangent to the curve at that point. The slope of the isoquant gives the marginal rate of technical substitution between the two inputs while the slope of the budget line measures the ratio of the relative prices of the productive factors. (The slope of the budget line is given by $Oa/Ob$. But $Oa$ equals $Y/P_K$ while $Ob$ equals $Y/P_L$. Thus the slope of the budget line equals $Y/P_K$ divided by $Y/P_L$ equals $P_L/P_K$. This arithmetic simply repeats that of the consumer's budget line in Chapter 11.) It would seem, then, that the least-cost combination of factors of production is found when the marginal rate of technical substitution between the two factors is equal to the ratio of their relative prices. In terms of Figure 84 the least-cost combination in the face of a set of constraints given by $ab$ requires employment of $OK_1$ capital per time period and $OL_1$ labour per time period.

When the constraints are relaxed somewhat a higher level of output can be attained. Thus, as $ab$ shifts outwards in Figure 84 the output levels 1250, ₁600, etc. can be reached. Or, when the constraints are tightened and the budget line moves inwards towards the origin, output falls. But, whatever the level of outlay, once the constraint is fixed the least-cost combination is found

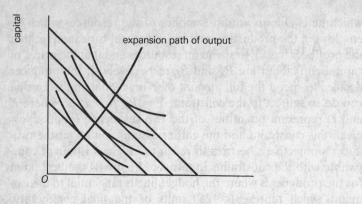

Figure 85

always by equating the marginal rate of technical substitution
with the ratio of relative prices. Figure 85 shows the path which
output follows as outlay on factors of production varies –
whether the locus of best points, the expansion path, inclines
towards the vertical or the horizontal axis will depend upon the
extent to which one factor of production is substituted for the
other as outlay varies.

# Part Four
## A Mathematical Interlude

In developing many of the arguments in this book we have had recourse to mathematical reasoning. We have not always provided rigorous proofs of our analysis, being content to illuminate our themes by juggling with shorthand symbols, yet often we have implied that more sophisticated techniques might be employed. Our aim here is to reproduce some of the major conclusions of the various chapters in a rather more elegant form. We are not about to plunge into the mainstream of pure mathematics but merely to *apply* some of the tools provided us by that branch of knowledge to the economic problems with which we have concerned ourselves. Economics is not mathematics and it is possible, although it may be difficult, to be a good 'non-mathematical' economist. Nevertheless, the language of mathematics provides us with both a shorthand to help us simplify mammoth problems to manageable proportions and a means of rigorously defining the models that we commonly employ in our economic analysis. Given these properties we would be extremely myopic not to make use of them. But for those so terrified by the title of this chapter as to resolve never again to deliberately open the book at this page, the chapter can be omitted without seriously damaging comprehension of basic economic theory. For those readers preparing the way for a more advanced study of economics we hope this chapter proves useful.

What mathematical concepts have we employed in our introduction to economic theory?

1 In the very first chapter we used the basic operations of *addition, subtraction, division* and *multiplication*. We also presented information in mathematical form, using the *table* as the basic format. Our tables presented *numbers* which in both absolute and relative (*percentage*) form conveyed information about prices, incomes, quantities and time. Furthermore, we plotted some of our information on a *graph* which gave us a two-dimensional picture of the behaviour of some of our data.

2 In Chapter 2 we introduced the concept of a *set* and we discussed the relationships between sets of wants, resources and goods. The theory of sets and relations is an important branch of mathematics and the techniques of formally describing relationships (or non-relationships) between sets of things can be of use to the economist. But many of these techniques are complex and the level of economic analysis at which we are aiming does not warrant an exploration of them.

3 In Chapter 3 we introduced the all-important concept of a *function*, that is the relationship(s) between the associated values of two or more variables. The functional relationship described in Chapter 3 was that between output and resource inputs – we called this 'the production function'. But production functions are not the only examples of this type of relationship used in our analysis. Indeed, almost every problem we have posed was simplified by abstracting the functional relationships between the variables within the problem. In so doing we have analysed problems by using simple pictures (graphs) which tell us at a glance something about associated values of the variables we have plotted and, with a little more effort on our part, something about the effects on one variable of changes in the other(s). Because functions are so important in economics this chapter presents a more rigorous exposition of some issues previously discussed with the aid of graphs and by toying with symbols. The branch of mathematics which helps us in this direction is the *calculus*.

4 Another occasion on which we incorporated mathematics directly into the main text was in Chapters 10 and 11 where we employed the algebra of *simultaneous equations* to demonstrate

the concept of market equilibrium. Little more need be said on this technique except to note that although it is a relatively simple one to employ, and probably one with which most readers are very familiar, its usage comes last in the logical ordering of our economic theory. This observation underlines again that economics is not mathematics and that our aim is to teach economics with the aid of mathematics and not the other way round. It should be clear from this preamble that we are here presenting those areas of mathematics not explicitly used in the main text.

## Functions

We commence with a tool employed on many occasions in our earlier chapters – the *function*. When two sets of things are functionally related then whatever values attach to the elements of one set, the values of the other set are uniquely determined. Consider the following diagram. In Figure 86 lots of cost–output combinations are plotted as a set of *xy* coordinates. As such, the diagram does not give us any precise information – for

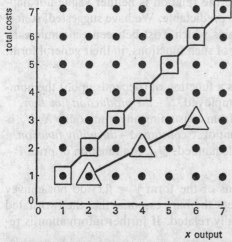

*x* output

Figure 86

each $x$-value there are at least six $y$-values. Suppose, however, that we know that $y = x$, then we can immediately identify the $xy$ coordinates which satisfy this equality. They are represented by rectangular shapes on the diagram and are seen to lie on a straight line. A similar exercise could be carried out for $y = \frac{1}{2}x$ (the relevant coordinates are represented by triangular shapes). Such unique $xy$ relationships are functional relationships – in both cases $y$ is a function of $x$, which we usually express as

$$y = f(x). \hspace{4cm} 1$$

It is important to note that although **1** may be read as '$y$ depends on $x$', the relationship does not imply causation. A function merely describes a relationship which exists, possibly by accident, between two variables and as such it can be expressed as **1** or as **2** without altering the nature of the relationship. When for each $y$ there is only one $x$ such that $y = f(x)$ we can write

$$x = f^{-1}(y). \hspace{4cm} 2$$

The variable which appears on the left-hand side of the expression we term the *dependent variable* and the variable on the right-hand side is termed the *independent variable*.[1]

The important thing to remember is that when two variables are functionally related the relation is neither vague nor haphazard but specific and predictable. We have suggested, so far, several such relationships which exist between economic variables. Three examples of such functions, in their general form, are listed below:

$Q = f(N)$: Output $Q$ is a function of (depends upon) the number of resource units employed, $N$ – *the production function*.

$U_x = f(X)$: The utility from consuming any commodity $X$, $U_x$, is a function of the amount of $X$ consumed – *the utility function*.

$Q_D = f(P)$: Quantity demanded, $Q_D$, is a function of price $P$ – *the demand function*.

But general expressions of the form $y = f(x)$ do not convey much information except the bare essential that the two stated variables are functionally related. If further information is re-

1.  A preliminary exploration of these concepts was made in Chapter 9.

quired about the relationship the specific form of the function must be referred to and, therefore, it is this form of the function that we employ when attempting to yield predictions from economic theories. Yet only rarely in our earlier chapters did we stipulate our functions in algebraic form, the reason being that for each specific function we can draw a picture, a graph, and pictures can be a very useful guide to the comprehension of basics.

However, the expository benefits from a picture are not sufficient reason for total reliance on this device as a means of drawing conclusions from economic analysis. Very often we might wish to place more reliance upon the mathematical formulae behind a set of graphs than on the graphs themselves, for two obvious reasons.

Firstly, there is the mundane point that graphs are usually drawn by hand and require interpretation by the naked eye. Rigorous mathematical specification protects us from human error in the construction of graphs and the visual interpretation of the models which employ them. Secondly, a more important drawback to a total reliance on visual aids is that when more than three sets of variables are functionally related a picture becomes impossible to construct. When we had two variables in our function we drew a two-dimensional diagram; if we had three variables we would draw a three-dimensional diagram; but we cannot draw four-or-more-dimensional diagrams.

What mathematical specifications underlie the economic relationship we have met so far? While the variables in an economic problem could take on any functional relationship most of the *basic* economic principles can be expressed in one of three functional forms:

The *linear function,*
The *quadratic function*,
The *cubic function*.

These three are not so frightening as they may appear to anyone a little out of touch with mathematics. Each function can be expressed as an equation which is either linear, quadratic or cubic. Now these terms merely refer to the *degree* of the equation which is determined by the highest *power* (or exponent) of the known variable in the equation. Let us have a brief look at each separate function.

1 *Linear function.* Such a function is expressed in the form of the linear equation, i.e. an equation of the first degree – the highest power of the known variable is *one*.

*Example.* $y = 7x + 10$ is a linear equation. The known variable is $x$ and its highest power is one – $x$ can be written $x^1$. Generally we use the form

$$y = a + bx \qquad\qquad 3$$

to express a linear function; where $a$ and $b$ are numerical constants. The graph of a linear function is a straight line with $a$ representing the intercept on the $y$ axis and $b$ the slope of the line. To understand this, consider the relationships between $y$ and $x$ when $x$ is zero.

The value of $y$ in this case is given by $a$. Since $a$ is a constant the relationship between different values of $x$ and $y$ is unaffected by it, i.e. $y$ varies directly with $x$ according to the constant $b$, thus $b$ is the slope of the function. When $b$ is positive the function slopes upwards to the right (a positive slope) since $y$ increases as $x$ increases; and when $b$ is negative the function slopes downwards from left to right (a negative slope) since $y$ decreases as $x$ increases. Two linear functions are graphed below. Figure 87a is the function $y = a + bx = 4x - 2$ (i.e. $a = -2, b = +4$). Figure 87b shows the function $y = a + bx = 2 - 4x$ (i.e. $a = +2$, $b = -4$).

Prime examples of linear functions are given by the straight line demand and supply curves of Chapter 9.

2 *Quadratic functions.* This type of function is expressed as a quadratic equation, i.e. an equation of the second degree – the highest power of the known variable is 2.

*Example.* $y = 7x^2 + 10x + 5$ is a quadratic equation. The known variable is $x$ and its highest power is 2. Generally such a function is expressed by the form

$$y = ax^2 + bx + c. \qquad\qquad 4$$

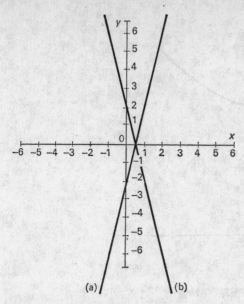

(a)                    (b)

Figure 87

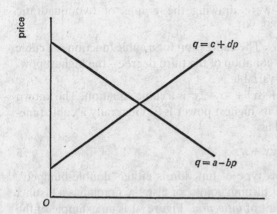

$q = c + dp$

$q = a - bp$

quantity demanded and supplied per unit of time

Figure 88

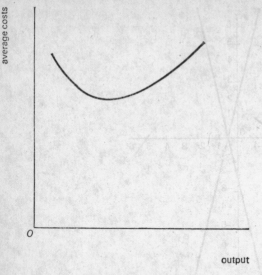

Figure 89 The average-cost curve $y(AC) = 12 + x^2 - 4x$

The graph of this type of function is either 'U-shaped' or 'hump-shaped' (it is a parabola). Thus, when we plotted an average-product curve in Chapter 3 and an average cost-curve in Chapter 12 we were drawing the graphs of two quadratic functions (Figs. 89, 90).

3 *Cubic functions.* The expression for a cubic function is a cubic equation, i.e. an equation of the third degree – the highest power of the known variable is 3.
*Example.* $y = 5 + 8x^3 + 4x - 2x^2$ is a cubic equation. The known variable is $x$ and its highest power is 3. Generally a cubic function is expressed as

$$y = ax^3 + bx^2 + cx + d. \qquad 5$$

The graph of this type of function is either 'double-humped', i.e. it has distinct turning points, or else the graph has a distinct bend in it – a point of *inflection*. Figure 91 is an example of the first type of graph. We have not as yet had recourse to this sort of relation in our economic theory. We have, however, made use of graphs like Figure 92. If the $y$-axis of this graph were to represent total costs and the *x*-axis to represent output, Figure 92 would be an example of the total variable cost as constructed in Chapter 12.

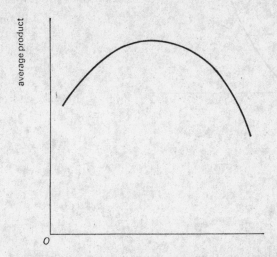

Figure 90  The average-product curve $y(AP) = 12 - x^2 + 4x$

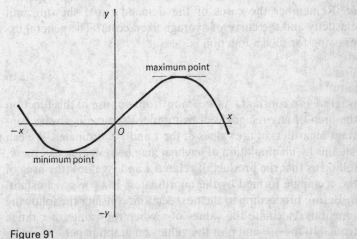

Figure 91

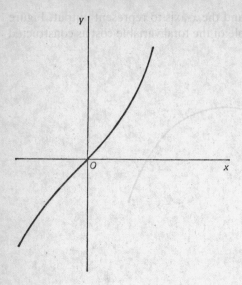

Figure 92

These three functions, then, are the main ones employed so far. Have we made specific reference to any others? Perhaps we should mention one further type of function which has appeared twice so far in our analysis – the *rectangular hyperbola*. Remember the cases of the demand curve showing unit elasticity and the curve of average fixed costs? The general expression for such a function is

$$y = \frac{k}{x},\qquad\qquad 6$$

where $k$ is a constant. As we know from our use of this function the area of any rectangle drawn under its curve is always constant regardless of the values of the $x$ and $y$ coordinates. We can see this by manipulation of **6** which may be rewritten as $yx = k$, telling us that the product of related $x$ and $y$ values (the area of the rectangle formed by the coordinates) is always a constant, $k$. Before proceeding to the next section, consider the following functions, calculate the values of $y$ when the values of $x$ range from $-10$ to $+10$ and plot the values on graph paper.

1 linear $\quad y = x + 1$,

2 quadratic $\quad y = x^2 + 2x + 3$,

5 cubic $\quad y = x^3 + 3x^2 + 13x + 15$.

# Chapter 14
# The Calculus

## Rates of change

The functions with which we have been dealing are smooth and *continuous* – their curves are free from breaks and kinks. From such functions we can readily calculate the related absolute values of the $x$, $y$ variables. But how can we calculate the effect on one set of values resulting from some *change* in the other set? Time and again in our economic analysis we have referred to *a rate of change*, how something changes value in response to a change in some other thing.

### Examples

1 In Chapter 3 we were concerned with how output might change in response to changes in man-hours employed – *marginal product*, i.e. the rate of change of output as employment changes.

2 In Chapter 11 we considered how utility might change in relation to changes in quantity consumed – *marginal utility*, i.e. the rate of change of utility as consumption changes.

3 In Chapter 12 we considered how costs might vary in response to output changes – *marginal cost*, i.e. the rate of change of cost as output changes.

These are just three examples of the concept of the *margin* and, therefore, three examples of our implicit use of the *calculus*

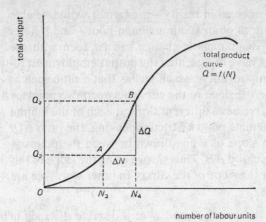

Figure 93 Total product curve $Q = f(N)$

which is that branch of mathematics employed to calculate rates of change of continuous functions. To fully appreciate the uses of this mathematical tool let us build up from a familiar diagram, Figure 8 of Chapter 3 which depicts a total-product curve. When we first used this diagram we said that the marginal product of an additional unit of resource is given by the slope[1] of the total-product curve between the two points (co-ordinates) at which the measurements are taken. This slope is defined as the ratio of change in total output to change in employment, or $\Delta Q / \Delta N$. Thus for a given change in employment, $N_3$ to $N_4$, marginal product is equal to $Q_3$ minus $Q_2$.

Marginal product, $\Delta Q / \Delta N = (Q_3 - Q_2)/(N_4 - N_3)$
$$= Q_3 - Q_2,$$
when $N_4 - N_3 = 1$.

In order to get this result we employed a little harmless trickery, a ploy we have resorted to often when analysing movements along curves. To enable our comprehension of the economics involved we depict a *discrete change* in the value of the two variables. It makes sense to discuss the effects of changes

1. The terms 'slope' and 'gradient' are used to mean the same thing.

which could be perceived in reality – the farmer would be able to measure the output of an additional man-hour – and it helps exposition if the diagrammatic change can be seen with the naked eye. But we have represented the output/employment relationships as a smooth curve which means that a ratio such as $\Delta Q/\Delta N$ cannot be the slope of the curve between two points $A$ and $B$ since the curve has a different slope at each of the infinite number of intermediate points. Strictly speaking, the ratio $\Delta Q/\Delta N$ measures the slope of a line drawn between the points $A$ and $B$, that is, the chord $AB$. Thus we are using the slope of this line as a proxy for the slope of the curve. In other words we are saying:

We have spaced the points $A$ and $B$ at a discrete distance in order to demonstrate an economic proposition; but since these points lie on a curve we are really assuming them to be an infinitesimally small distance apart so that a chord drawn between the two points approximates very closely to the slope of the curve.

### The concept of the limit

If instead of *assuming* points $A$ and $B$ to be an infinitesimally small distance apart, we actually depicted them as such then what would we construct? The answer is a *point* on the total-product function (the total-product curve) since when two points are such a minute distance apart, to all intents and purposes they must coincide. This suggests that a marginal increment (marginal product, marginal utility, etc.) is actually given by the slope at a point on the total function (total-product curve, total-utility curve, etc.). But how can a point on a curve have a gradient? What we really mean is that we measure the slope of a curve at a particular point by the slope of the *tangent* to the curve at that point. In Figure 94 the slope of the function $Q = f(N)$ at point $A$ is given by the slope of the tangent $Z$ and the slope at $B$ by the slope of the tangent $W$.

Now, for expositional purposes, we 'blow up' points such as $A$ (as we did in Figure 94) so that it appears not as a point but as

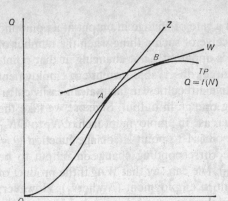

Figure 94

a discrete distance $AB$ on the curve although we assume the distance to be non-discrete. This seems a clumsy way of doing things: since we know that the marginal concept relates to points on the total function, is it not better to derive some useful formula which can always be applied, instead of continuing to explode diagrams in order to understand what we are doing?

The means whereby we discover such a short cut is to use the concept of the *limit*. To explain this idea we must persevere, for a little longer, with our diagrammatic methods, in particular with the manipulating of chords and tangents. Consider again a production function, $Q = f(N)$, which gives us a graph of the form previously employed and choose some point, $A$, on this function.

Suppose that we set ourselves the problem of finding marginal product using only the diagram when $ON_1$ man-hours are employed. Let us further suppose that we do not know that the slope of the function at point $A$ (the point corresponding to $N_1$ labourers) is given by the slope of the tangent $AZ$. Is there some method which we might employ to lead us automatically to the discovery that the slope of $AZ$ provides us with our answer? There is indeed such a method and it is described in the following paragraphs.

Our concern is with a rate of change in output at a point and we find it hard to conceive of such a thing when the number of man-hours employed is apparently not changing at that point. But if we take some large, observable increase in employment then we have no intuitive difficulties, in fact we can easily calculate the corresponding change in output. Suppose we take the starting point as an increase in employment from $ON_1$ to $ON_{10}$ which takes us from point $A$ to point $A'$ on the function $Q = f(N)$. We observe the corresponding change in output to be $WA'$ ($= OQ_1$ to $OQ_{10}$). We can say that $WA'$ is the product of the marginal increment in employment $(N_{10} - N_1)$. However, this increment in employment comprises several labour units and we are interested only in the output of the additional unit of labour. Thus the nearest approximation to what we want is given by the ratio $WA'/AW$ (change in output/change in employment) which measures the slope of the chord $AA'$ (the *tangent* of angle $A'AW$). This measure gives us an average of the marginal products for the $ON_1$ to $ON_{10}$ labour units, the nearest we can get to marginal product for such a large discrete employment increment.

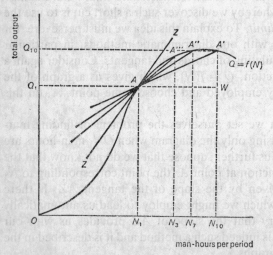

Figure 95

Suppose we now take a smaller increment in employment, say from $ON_1$ to $ON_7$. Again we can only obtain an average measure of marginal product, given by the gradient of the chord $AA''$, but this time our estimate is closer to the true measure (at point $A$) because the increment in employment is smaller. This fact is clearly shown on the diagram where the slope of the chord $AA''$ is seen to be steeper than the slope of the chord $AA'$, that is, the gradient of $AA''$ is nearer to the slope of the curve at point $A$ than is the slope of $AA'$. If we repeat this process, say for the employment increment $ON_1$ to $ON_3$, we obtain chord $AA'''$, which gives us an even closer approximation to the slope at point $A$.

It should now be clear that what is happening as we reduce the size of the increment in employment is that the gradient of the chord between the relevant coordinates approaches ever more closely to the slope of the function at point $A$. In Figure 95 the chords have been deliberately continued through point $A$ so that this process can be clearly observed. It can be seen from the figure that the original line through $A$ to $A'$ pivots about $A$ as the size of the employment increment reduces, until eventually it has pivoted to the position in which it just touches the curve $Q = f(N)$ at point $A$. At this point the slope of the line, which is now no longer a *chord* but a *tangent* (tangent $AZ$), is exactly equal to the slope of the curve, that is, to marginal product. We can say, then, that the slope of the tangent $AZ$ forms the limit to the slope of the chord $AA$ as the increment in employment approaches zero.

## The derivative

Let us now introduce some shorthand to reduce our reliance upon unwieldy diagrams. We may commence by restating the limit. Our analysis of the total-product function showed that, starting at point $A$ on the curve, as the increment in employment ($\Delta N$) gets even smaller, i.e. approaches zero ($\rightarrow 0$) the slope $\Delta Q/\Delta N$ (marginal product) approaches its limit (lim) which is the tangent to the total product curve at point $A$. In symbols

$$\lim_{\Delta N \to 0} \frac{\Delta Q}{\Delta N} = \text{slope of tangent to curve at } A.$$

In the language of the calculus this limit, this rate of change, is called the *derivative* of the function and its symbolic representation adopts the letter $d$ (to denote infinitesimally small change) instead of the more general symbol $\Delta$. Our analysis so far, then, has demonstrated that marginal product is the first derivative of the total product function, the rate of change of total product with respect to changes in employment. In symbols, we write

$$\frac{d}{dN}(Q) = \lim_{\Delta N \to 0} \frac{\Delta Q}{\Delta N},$$

and we usually adopt $dQ/dN$ for $(d/dN)(Q)$ although sometimes $Q'(N)$ is used, i.e.

$$\frac{dQ}{dN} = \frac{d}{dN}(Q) = Q'(N).$$

Before taking a closer look at derivatives we should remind ourselves that the concept can be applied to many different functions. We have taken the total-product function and demonstrated marginal product as the first derivative of this function, but we could easily have used a total-utility function or a total-revenue function or any other total function and repeated the procedure to obtain the corresponding marginal measures. To entrench this general applicability in our minds it might be useful to revert briefly to our general expression $y = f(x)$ where $y$ and $x$ may be any two related variables. Our general expression then is

$$\frac{dy}{dx} = \lim_{\Delta x \to 0} \frac{\Delta y}{\Delta x}. \qquad \qquad \textbf{1}$$

### The rules of differentiation

So far we have related the marginal concept to the mathematical concept of a derivative. Now, the process of *differentiation* (i.e. the process which gives us the derivative) of a function is subject to certain rules. We are asking that these rules be accepted on trust. A mathematical proof underlies each one but such proofs are complex and not essential to our understanding of economics. Remember that we are primarily interested in applying mathematical tools to economic problems, and somewhat less interested in the tools themselves. However, in order to gain the trust we want, the first simple rule is elaborated below.

## The general rule for power functions

How would we differentiate the simple functions that we have used several times already, $y = x^2$? The process follows our earlier description of the limit. Consider the definition of the first derivative as presented in **1**. If we spell out the right-hand side of this identity in more detail, the key to the process can be seen. Since $y$ depends on $x$, so must $\Delta y$ depend upon $\Delta x$. Thus we may write

$$\Delta x = (x + \Delta x) - x,$$

and $\quad \Delta y = f(x + \Delta x) - f(x),$

thus $\quad \dfrac{\Delta y}{\Delta x} = \dfrac{f(x + \Delta x) - f(x)}{\Delta x}.$ \hfill **2**

Substituting the right-hand side of **2** into our earlier definition **1**, we have

$$\frac{dy}{dx} = \lim_{\Delta x \to 0} \frac{f(x + \Delta x) - f(x)}{\Delta x}. \hspace{2em} \textbf{3}$$

### Procedure

(a) General case, $y = f(x)$.

$$\frac{dy}{dx} = \lim_{\Delta x \to 0} \frac{f(x + \Delta x) - f(x)}{\Delta x}.$$

(b) Specific case, e.g. $y = x^2$.

$$\frac{dy}{dx} = \lim_{\Delta x \to 0} \frac{(x + \Delta x)^2 - x^2}{\Delta x},$$

$$= \lim_{\Delta x \to 0} \frac{x^2 + 2x\Delta x + (\Delta x)^2 - x^2}{\Delta x},$$

$$= \lim_{\Delta x \to 0} \frac{2x\Delta x + (\Delta x)^2}{\Delta x},$$

$$\text{or } \frac{dy}{dx} = \lim_{\Delta x \to 0} \left\{ \frac{2x\Delta x}{\Delta x} + \frac{(\Delta x)^2}{\Delta x} \right\}.$$

If we now cancel the $\Delta x$s we are left with

$$\frac{dy}{dx} = \lim_{\Delta x \to 0} (2x + \Delta x). \qquad\qquad 4$$

What this final expression says is that at the limit, as $\Delta x$ tends to zero, the whole expression $2x + \Delta x$ will approach $2x$, that is

$$\frac{dy}{dx} = \lim_{\Delta x \to 0} (2x + \Delta x),$$

$$= 2x.$$

The result of our process, then, is that the derivative of the function $y = x^2$ is $2x$. Substitute any other value for power 2 in the example we have just considered and the resultant derivative will always conform to the general rule:

$$\text{If } y = x^n, \text{ then } \frac{dy}{dx} = nx^{n-1}, \qquad\qquad 5$$

and we can extend this rule to the function $x$ *times* a constant: $y = ax^n$, where $a$ is a constant, in which case

$$\frac{dy}{dx} = nax^{n-1} \qquad\qquad 6$$

(note that the first function, $y = x^n$, could be written as $y = 1x^n$ and its derivative as $dy/dx = n1x^{n-1}$).

Examples:

1  If $y = x^{10}$, then $\dfrac{dy}{dx} = 10x^9$.

2  $y = 4x^5$, $\dfrac{dy}{dx} = 20x^4$.

3 For practice, differentiate the following functions:

(a) $y = x^6$,

(b) $y = x^{150}$,

(c) $y = ax^{3/4}$,

(d) $y = 7x^{-7}$.

4 Suppose we have a variable-cost function

$$Cv = q^3,$$

where $Cv$ is total variable costs and $q$ is output. The derivative of this function is

$$\frac{dCv}{dq} = 3q^2,$$

which gives the rate of change of total variable costs ($Cv$) with respect to changes in output ($q$), in other words *marginal cost*. We can thus restate the definition of marginal cost as the first derivative of the total variable-cost function:

$$MC = \frac{dCv}{dq}.$$

But what about fixed costs? In our chapter on costs we said that marginal cost is the rate of change in *total* costs (fixed plus variable) as output changes by one very small unit. Remember, however, that we also pointed out that since fixed costs cannot vary with output (by definition) they do not enter into the calculation of marginal costs. Let us now try to express this point more rigorously in terms of the differentiation technique. To do so requires us to move on to our second and third rules, regarding the derivatives of constants and the differentiation of sums and differences, because a total-cost function takes the following form,

Total costs = total fixed costs + total variable costs, or in symbolic form,

$$C = a + q^3,$$

7

where $C$ represents total costs; $a$, fixed costs (a constant); and $q$, output ($q^3$ is variable costs).

## The derivative of a constant

Since a derivative is a rate of change and since a constant cannot change, by definition the derivative of a constant must be zero Fixed costs are thus independent of changes in the labour force, quantities of raw materials, etc., in other words, independent of the level of output. Given this constancy the rate of change of fixed costs in any set of circumstances must be zero, or put another way, the slope of the total fixed cost curve must be zero. This means that when calculating the rate of change of total cost with respect to a unit change in output, any constant term in the total function can be ignored. But before differentiating **7**, we must consider a third rule.

## Differentiation of sums and differences

The rule for differentiating a function containing additive terms is a simple extension of the general rule for differentiating power functions. This new rule merely demands that the separate derivatives be summed (or subtracted). Thus for any function:

$$y = x^n + x^m,$$

$$\frac{dy}{dx} = \frac{d}{dx}(x^n) + \frac{d}{dx}(x^m)$$

$$= nx^{n-1} + mx^{m-1},$$

or, for the function $y = u + v$,

where $u = f(x), \quad v = g(x),$

$$\frac{dy}{dx} = \frac{du}{dx} + \frac{dv}{dx}$$

8

*Examples:*

1 If $\quad y = x^{25} + x^{13}$,

then $\quad \dfrac{dy}{dx} = 25x^{24} + 13x^{12}$.

2 If $\quad y = x^6 + 3x^2 - 4x^9$,

then $\quad \dfrac{dy}{dx} = 6x^5 + 6x - 36x^8$.

3 $C = a + q^3$

Now we can return to the problem of deriving marginal cost from the total cost function. We now know that $da/dq = 0$ and our third rule is that

$$\frac{dC}{dq} = \frac{d}{dq}(a) + \frac{d}{dq}(q^3).$$

$$= 0 + 3q^2$$

$$= 3q^2,$$

where $dC/dq$ is the rate of change of total cost with respect to change in output, i.e. marginal cost. But we have already demonstrated that

$$\frac{dCv}{dq} = 3q^2,$$

so we may write $\quad MC = \dfrac{dC}{dq} = \dfrac{dCv}{dq}$,

which expresses the familiar result that variable, and not fixed, costs affect the margin.

## The product rule

The rule for differentiating a product is a little more complex than the other rules so far considered. By a product we mean a function of the form

$y = f(x)g(x),$

and to make the task easier we reform such a product into

$$y = uv,\tag{9}$$

where $u = f(x)$ and $v = g(x)$.

We now sum the product of the second term ($v$) and the derivative of the first ($du/dx$) and the product of the first term ($u$) and the derivative of the second ($dv/dx$);

$$\frac{dy}{dx} = v\,\frac{du}{dx} + u\,\frac{dv}{dx}.\tag{10}$$

Examples:[2]

1 If      $y = (4x^2)(10x^5)$,

   then   $u = 4x^2$ and $du/dx = 8x$,

   and    $v = 10x^5$ and $dv/dx = 50x^4$.

Thus   $\dfrac{dy}{dx} = (10x^5)(8x) + (4x^2)(50x^4)$,

$$= 80x^6 + 200x^6,$$

$$= 280x^6.$$

2 If      $y = (6x + 8)(7x^3)$,

   then   $u = 6x + 8$ and $du/dx = 6$,

   and    $v = 7x^3$ and $dv/dx = 21x^2$.

Thus   $\dfrac{dy}{dx} = (7x^3)(6) + (6x + 8)(21x^2)$,

$$= 42x^3 + 126x^3 + 168x^2,$$

$$= 168x^3 + 168x^2.$$

Although the product rule has many applications in economics

---

2. It is often very useful to employ the product rule but note that when dealing with power functions the multiplication process can be completed before differentiating. Thus $y = (4x^2)(10x^5)$ is $40x^7$ and $dy/dx = 280x^6$.

most of these uses can only be appreciated after a course of study at a higher level than our present aims. However, there is one important use to which we can put the rule at this stage. In Chapter 7 we first pointed out that marginal revenue must vary with price-elasticity of demand but we appealed more to intuition than rigour as a means of demonstrating this relationship. The product rule of differentiation allows us to show that our intuitive appeal was well-founded. Firstly let us reform the expression for price-elasticity of demand. In Chapter 7 we presented the form

$$e = - \frac{\Delta Q}{\Delta P} \left( \frac{P}{Q} \right).$$

Remember that this measure refers to point-elasticity,[3] elasticity at a point on the demand curve. Thus that part of the expression which relates to the slope of the demand curve, $-\Delta Q/\Delta P$ can now be more correctly presented as $-dQ/dP$. We now write

$$e = - \frac{dQ}{dP} \left( \frac{P}{Q} \right).$$

Now consider the concept of marginal revenue. Basic calculus tells us that marginal revenue $MR$ is the first derivative of the total revenue function $TR$ – marginal revenue is the rate of change of total revenue with respect to changes in output $Q$:

$$MR = \frac{dTR}{dQ}.$$ **11**

However, we know that $TR = P.Q$ (where $P$ represents price) so that finding $MR$ involves differentiating a product:

$$TR = P.Q,$$

$u = P$ and $du/dQ = dP/dQ$,

$v = Q$ and $dv/dQ = dQ/dQ = 1$.

3. Recall how, in Chapter 7, we constructed a tangent to the demand curve in order to illustrate the concept of point elasticity.

Differentiating gives

$$\frac{dTR}{dQ} = Q \frac{dP}{dQ} + P,$$

$$= P\left(1 + \frac{Q}{P} \cdot \frac{dP}{dQ}\right). \tag{12}$$

But does the expression within the bracket not seem familiar? In fact $Q/P.dP/dQ$ is no more than the reciprocal of the expression for price elasticity of demand:

$$- \frac{Q}{P} \cdot \frac{dP}{dQ} = - \frac{1}{p/Q.dQ/dP} = \frac{1}{e}.$$

We can now present **12** in a neater form. Replacing the negative sign:

$$MR = P(1 - 1/e). \tag{13}$$

Defining marginal revenue as in **13** we can see at a glance its relationship with price and with price-elasticity of demand. Marginal revenue is less than price by the amount of $P/e$: multiplying out the bracket in **13** gives $P - (P/e)$. Thus the larger is $P/e$ the greater the difference between marginal revenue and price; and the smaller is $P/e$ the smaller is the difference. This relationship is a very important discovery although its significance will only be fully appreciated in later chapters. In the meantime we can note that for a given $P$ the size of $P/e$ is determined by the size of $e$. Since the size of $e$ has two limits, zero and infinity, what are the effects on marginal revenue as $e$ approaches either of these limits?

1 As $e$ approaches infinity $P/e$ approaches zero and, therefore, at the limit marginal revenue equals price. Since $e$ is infinite when the demand curve is horizontal then marginal revenue is equal to price for any producer when the demand curve for his product is horizontal.

2 As $e$ approaches zero, $P/e$ approaches infinity which means that at the limit marginal revenue 'disappears', it ceases to have

meaning. This would be the case when the demand curve for a product is vertical.

3 Equally interesting are the in-between values of *e*. Given 1 and 2 it follows that so long as *e* is less than infinity and greater than zero, marginal revenue is less than price – the demand curve slopes downwards from left to right.

4 When *e* = 1 then marginal revenue = 0.

*The quotient rule*

The rule for differentiating a quotient appears complex at first sight but with practice proves to be straightforward. When

$$y = \frac{f(x)}{g(x)},$$

we let such a relationship be represented as

$$y = \frac{u}{v},$$

where $u = f(x)$ and $v = g(x)$ and differentiate as follows:

$$\frac{dy}{dx} = \frac{v(du/dx) - u(dv/dx)}{v^2}. \qquad \qquad \textbf{14}$$

Example:

If $y = \frac{3x^2}{5x^4}$,

then $u = 3x^2$ and $du/dx = 6x$,

and $v = 5x^4$ and $dv/dx = 20x^3$.

Thus $\dfrac{dy}{dx} = \dfrac{(5x^4)(6x) - (3x^2)(20x^3)}{(5x^4)^2}$,

$$= \frac{30x^5 - 60x^5}{25x^8},$$

$$= -\frac{30x^5}{25x^8} = \frac{-6}{5x^3} = \frac{-6x^{-3}}{5}.$$

An obvious use to which such a rule might be put is to tell us something about the rate of change of the average-cost function with respect to the rate of output change. Suppose we had the total-cost function 7:

$$C = a + q^3.$$

The corresponding average total-cost function $AC$ would be

$$AC = \frac{a + q^3}{q},$$

since average total cost is total cost divided by output $q$. Now suppose we wanted to know how $AC$ changes with respect to $q$:

$$\frac{dAC}{dq} = \frac{d}{dq}\frac{(a + q^3)}{q}.$$

$u = a + q^3$ and $du/dq = 3q^2$,

$v = q$ and $dv/dq = dq/dq = 1$.

$$\frac{dAC}{dq} = \frac{q(3q^2) - (a + q)^3\, 1}{q^2},$$

$$= \frac{3q^3 - a - q^3}{q^2}.$$

## Questions

1 A farmer has a given acreage of land on which he can employ labourers. The relationship between total output and the level of employment is given by

$$Q = 100 + 20L - L^2,$$

where $Q$ represents total output, and $L$ the number of man-hours employed.

(a) What is the average-product function?

(b) What is labour's marginal product when five man-hours are employed?

2 A producer can make and sell $q$ units of his commodity per week at a total cost (in £s) given by

$$TC = 3q^3 + 2q^2 + 10q + 45.$$

(a)  What is the producer's average-cost function?
(b)  What is the marginal cost when producing twenty units?

3  The market demand for coffee is given by

$$Q = 100 - P,$$

where $Q$ is the quantity purchased, in thousands of kilograms per week, and $P$ is the price per kilogram.
(a)  What is the total-revenue function?
(b)  What is the marginal-revenue function?
(c)  If consumers decide to buy five times their normal amount, whatever the price (and they continue to purchase the increased amounts for some time), what is the value of marginal revenue when 20 000 kilograms of coffee is being bought?

## Higher order derivatives

The list of rules we have presented should provide an aid to deeper understanding of economic principles. It is not a complete list but we feel it to be adequate for our present purpose. But our manipulation of functions of one variable is incomplete until we have considered second derivatives, i.e. the derivative of a first derivative.

Why should we wish to calculate the rate of change of a rate of change? In fact such a calculation has many uses in economics, one of which we can well appreciate at this level of analysis – the test for maxima, minima, and points of inflection. Earlier we described quadratic and cubic functions, noting that the graph of the former is either U-shaped or hump-shaped and the graph of the latter has a point of inflection. Our most usual examples of these types of functional relationships have been the marginal-cost ($MC$) curve and marginal-product ($MP$) curve, representing quadratic functions, and the total-cost ($TC$) curve, representing cubic functions. Much of our interest in these curves centres around their turning points, for example in Chapters 3 and 12 we saw that when the $MC$ curve turns then $MC$ is at a *minimum*, and when the $MP$ curve turns then $MP$ is at a *maximum*. Yet how can we be sure that this is always true? Do we always have to construct a graph or is there a test which will quickly tell us whether or not a function has a point of inflection or a turning point and if so whether that turning point is a maximum or minimum?

## Maxima and minima

1 *Use of the first derivative*: The first test to discover whether a function has a maximum or minimum turning point is to ask 'does the function have a *stationary value*?' When the function has a maximum turning point the slope of the graph of the function changes from positive to negative as the function passes through the turning point. At the point itself, however, the slope is neither positive nor negative, but equal to zero (the graph of the function is horizontal at the turning point). We thus define a stationary value as that value ($\bar{x}$) of $x$ in the function $y = f(x)$ for which $dy/dx = 0$.

A function with a minimum turning point will also have a stationary value since the slope of the function is negative before the turning point, positive after the point and equal to zero at the point itself. We have now arrived at the first test for a maximum or minimum turning point – does the function possess a stationary value? In other words, the existence of a stationary value is a *necessary condition* for a function to possess a turning point which is either a maximum *or* a minimum. Parts (a) of Figures 96 and 97 summarize this condition: When marginal product is at a maximum the marginal-product curve ($MP$) of Figure 96a has a slope equal to zero – output level $\bar{x}$ is the stationary value of the function $y = f(x)$; and when marginal cost is at a minimum the marginal-cost function ($MC$) of Figure 97a has a slope equal to zero (again a stationary value at $\bar{x}$).

2 *Use of the second derivative*: The necessary information, $dy/dx = 0$, does not enable us to distinguish between maximum and minimum turning points since both have stationary values. In order to make the distinction we require information about the gradient of the function before and after the turning point. Now, the first derivative gives us the information we require

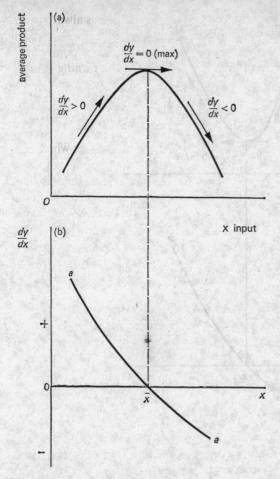

Figure 96

since $dy/dx$ changes sign when the function passes through a turning point. But using the first derivative can often be a clumsy method of testing for maxima and minima, even when the function is fairly straightforward. For example, suppose we attempt the following exercise:

$$y = x^2 - 10x + 5.$$

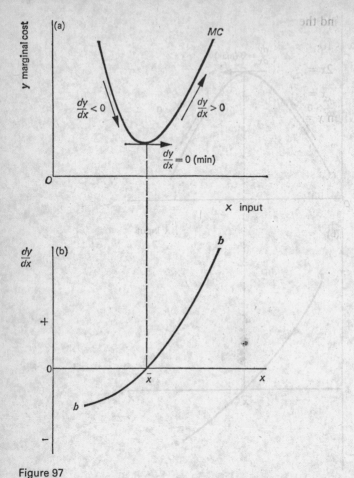

Figure 97

1 Find the turning point of this function.

2 Test whether this point is a maximum or minimum.
Proceed as follows:

1 $y = x^2 - 10x + 5$,

$$\frac{dy}{dx} = 2x - 10.$$

2 To find the stationary value set $dy/dx = 0$.

$$2x - 10 = 0,$$
$$2x = 10,$$
$$x = 5.$$

3 When $x = 5$, $y = 5^2 - 10(5) + 5$,
$$= 25 - 50 + 5,$$
$$= -20.$$

There is a stationary value at coordinates $x = 5$ and $y = -20$.

4 What happens to the sign of $dy/dx$ as the function passes through $x = 5$? Consider the sign when $x$ takes a value slightly lower than 5 and then when its value is slightly higher than 5.

When $x = 4.9$,

$$\frac{dy}{dx} = 2(4.9) - 10,$$
$$= 9.8 - 10,$$
$$= -0.2.$$

When $x = 5.1$,

$$\frac{dy}{dx} = 2(5.1) - 10,$$
$$= 10.2 - 10,$$
$$= +0.2.$$

The coordinates $(5, -20)$ give a minimum turning point since $dy/dx = 0$ and $dy/dx$ changes sign from negative to positive as the function passes through the point.

There exists however a better tool for pursuing such tests – the second derivative. As mentioned earlier this is the slope of the first derivative function and it measures, therefore, the rate of change of $dy/dx$ with respect to changes in $x$:

$$\frac{d^2y}{dx^2} = \frac{d}{dx}\left(\frac{dy}{dx}\right).$$

15

This is the notation for second derivatives. Note that since we could also differentiate **15** or indeed any derivative of the function $y = f(x)$ we may also form third, fourth etc., derivatives $(d^3y/dx^3; d^4y/dx^4; \ldots$ gives the appropriate notations). The procedure for differentiating derivatives is precisely that followed for differentiating any function, hence:

$$y = 4x^3,$$

$$\frac{dy}{dx} = 12x^2,$$

$$\frac{d^2y}{dx^2} = 24x.$$

Now, the second derivative helps us with our present task since its sign differs according to whether the turning point is a maximum or a minimum. When the function has a maximum turning point, as in the case of the marginal product curve, the slope of the function $y = f(x)$ decreases as $x$ increases, i.e. $dy/dx$ falls as $x$ increases. The graph of $dy/dx$, therefore, slopes downwards from left to right, as shown by curve *aa* in Figure 96 – note that this graph crosses the horizontal axis at $\bar{x}$, the stationary value.

The fact that $dy/dx$ slopes downwards from left to right means that its gradient, the second derivative of $y = f(x)$, is negative. Thus, for the types of functions used so far, we now have the *necessary and sufficient* condition for the existence of a maximum turning point:

$$\frac{dy}{dx} = 0; \text{ and} \frac{d^2y}{dx^2} < 0.$$

Consider, now, a function with a minimum turning point. In this case the gradient of the function changes from negative to positive as it passes through the minimum point. This means that the graph of $dy/dx$ slopes upwards from left to right, as represented by *bb* in Figure 97b. Therefore, the gradient of $dy/dx$ is *positive* and the necessary and sufficient condition for a minimum point to exist is:

$$\frac{dy}{dx} = 0; \text{ and} \frac{d^2y}{dx^2} > 0.$$

## Summary

*Necessary and sufficient condition*

Turning point a maximum; $dy/dx = 0$; and $d^2y/dx^2 < 0$.

Turning point a minimum; $dy/dx = 0$; and $d^2y/dx^2 > 0$.

N.B. $dy/dx = 0$ is termed the *first order* condition and $dy^2/dx^2 \lessgtr 0$ the *second order* condition.

Using first and second order conditions we can now reconsider the earlier exercise.

$$y = x^2 - 10x + 5.$$

Procedure:

1 $dy/dx = 2x - 10$.

2 Set $dy/dx = 0$,

$$2x - 10 = 0,$$

$$x = 5.$$

3 When $x = 5$, $y = 5^2 - 10(5) + 5$,

$$= -20.$$

5 and –20 are the coordinates of the turning point. Is the point a maximum or a minimum?

$$d^2y/dx^2 = 2.$$

Thus when $dy/dx = 0$, $d^2y/dx^2 > 0$. The function has a minimum turning point at $x = 5$, $y = -20$.

Now let us try a more interesting example. A supplier faces a total cost function

$$TC = 100x - 10x^2 + x^3$$

where $x$ is output. Find the output which minimizes average costs.

Procedure:

1  $AC = \dfrac{TC}{x}$,

$\quad\quad = \dfrac{100x}{x} - \dfrac{10x^2}{x} + \dfrac{x^3}{x}$,

$\quad\quad = 100 - 10x + x^2.$

2  $\dfrac{dAC}{dx} = 2x - 10.$

3  Set  $\dfrac{dAC}{dx} = 0,$

$\quad\quad 2x - 10 = 0.$

$\quad\quad\quad x = \dfrac{10}{2} = 5.$

The $AC$ function has a turning point at $x = 5$. But before calling this output level that which minimizes costs we should make sure that the turning point is a minimum.

4  $d^2AC/dx^2 = 2.$

Since $dAC/dx = 0$ and $d^2AC/dx^2 > 0$, the turning point is indeed a minimum, and the output level which minimizes average costs is five units.

*Points of inflection*

Another use for the second derivative is the test for a point of inflection. But first let us consider a function which contains an inflectional point the test for which does not require more than the first derivative. It is interesting to consider this function first since, as we shall see, the necessary condition for the existence of its inflectional value does not distinguish this value from maxima and minima. Consider the function $y = f(x)$ illustrated in the following figure, Figure 98.

An inflectional point $z$ exists at $x$-value $\bar{x}$. As can be seen, the slope of the function is zero at $\bar{x}$, i.e. $x$ is a stationary value. How, then, can we distinguish this inflectional point from maxi-

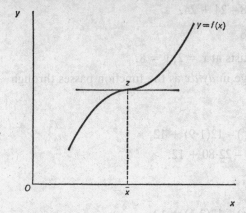

Figure 98

ma and minima? In all three cases $dy/dx = 0$. But note that the slope of the function is positive before and after point $z$, i.e. unlike maxima and minima $dy/dx$ does not change sign as the function passes through the point of inflection. Thus some points of inflection can be identified when $dy/dx = 0$ and is not changing sign.

Example:

Test for a point of inflection in the function

$$y = x^3 - 6x^2 + 12x.$$

*Procedure*

1  $y = x^3 - 6x^2 + 12x,$

   $dy/dx = 3x^2 - 12x + 12.$

2  Set $dy/dx$ equal to 0,

   $3x^2 - 12x + 12 = 0,$

then  $x^2 - 4x + 4 = 0,$

   $(x - 2)(x - 2) = 0,$

   $x = 2.$

3 When $x = 2$, $y = 8 - 24 + 24$,

$$= 8.$$

A stationary value exists at $x = 2$, $y = 8$.

4 Test the sign change in $dy/dx$ as the function passes through $x = 2$.

(a) When $x = 1.9$,

$$dy/dx = 3(1.9^2) - 12(1.9) + 12,$$
$$= 10.83 - 22.80 + 12,$$
$$= 0.03.$$

   When $x = 2.1$,

(b)   $$dy/dx = 3(2.1^2) - 12(2.1) + 12,$$
$$= 13.23 - 25.20 + 12,$$
$$= 0.03.$$

Thus $dy/dx$ is positive for both values of $x$ and the point ($x = 2$, $y = 8$) is a point of inflection.

Unfortunately, not all inflectional points are so easy to deal with. Consider now the function $y = f(x)$ which gives the graph shown in Figure 99.

Point $z$ in Figure 99a is a point of inflection but in this case there is no stationary value $-dy/dx \neq 0$. How, then, can we test for this sort of inflectional point? To do so we must consider the second derivative. In Figure 99b which depicts the graph of $dy/dx$, we can see that for $x$ values below $\bar{x}$, $dy/dx$ is falling and for values greater than $\bar{x}$, $dy/dx$ is rising. This means that the $dy/dx$ function has a stationary value at $x = \bar{x}$ and, therefore, $d^2y/dx^2$, the rate of change of $dy/dx$, is zero at $\bar{x}$.[4] Figure 99c which depicts the graph of the second derivative, shows this clearly.

Thus the test for an inflectional point is that $d^2y/dx^2 = 0$ and is changing sign.

Example:

1 $y = x^3 - 12x^2 + 10$.

4. Point $z$ is the minimum point on the graph of the first derivative.

(a)

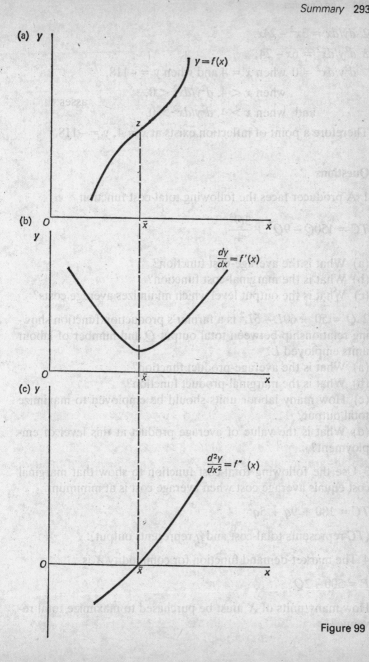

Figure 99

2  $dy/dx = 3x^2 - 24x.$

3  $d^2y/dx^2 = 6x - 24,$

$d^2y/dx^2 = 0$ when $x = 4$ and when $y = -118,$

when $x < 4$, $d^2y/dx^2 < 0,$

and  when $x > 4$, $d^2y/dx^2 > 0.$

Therefore a point of inflection exists at $x = 4$, $y = -118.$

## Questions

1  A producer faces the following total-cost function

$$TC = 150Q - 9Q^2 + \frac{3Q^3}{4}.$$

(a)  What is the average-cost function?
(b)  What is the marginal-cost function?
(c)  What is the output level which minimizes average costs?

2  $Q = 50 + 60L - 5L^2$ is a farmer's production function showing relationship between total output $Q$ and number of labour units employed $L$.
(a)  What is the average-product function?
(b)  What is the marginal-product function?
(c)  How many labour units should be employed to maximize total output?
(d)  What is the value of average product at this level of employment?

3  Use the following total-cost function to show that marginal cost equals average cost when average cost is at minimum.

$$TC = 180 + 9q + 5q^2$$

(*TC* represents total-cost and $q$ represents output).

4  The market-demand function for commodity $X$ is

$$P = 500 - 2Q.$$

How many units of $X$ must be purchased to maximize total revenue?

5 Does the following total-cost function have a point of inflection?

$$TC = 80 + 6 - 4 + \frac{2Q^3}{3}.$$

## Functions of several variables

So far we have confined our excursion into mathematics to problems relating only two variables, $y = f(x)$. Since many of the economic problems we have considered have concerned such a simple relationship the mathematics we have looked at so far suffices quite often. But what of all those problems involving more than one independent variable, of the form

$$y = f(x_1, x_2, x_3, \ldots, x_n).$$

What do we do in these cases? The mathematical technique involved is no more than what we have termed a 'simplifying' technique when facing such a function in economics. A good example of this is again provided by the production function.

In Chapter 3 we first introduced the concept of a production function, in the form

$$P = f(x_1, x_2, \ldots, x_n; T),$$

where $P$ represents output, $x_1, \ldots, x_n$ are inputs, and $T$ represents technology. Having expressed the function in this form we proceeded to analyse it by isolating the effects of only one independent variable, holding the values of the other variables constant (the infamous assumption of 'other things remaining unchanged'). This technique not only simplified the problem but also enabled us to consider the effects on production of changes in the magnitude of any single independent variable. As such the technique performed an invaluable service – an employer is often interested in the output effects of changes in his labour force, or in the amount of capital equipment used, or in the state of technology; but rarely does he need to calculate the output effects of all these changes occurring simultaneously.

The technique of isolating the effects of single independent variables has been repeated several times since we considered the production function. What, then, is the mathematical procedure involved? We have usually tried to begin the explanation of basic concepts with the aid of a graph and we can continue with this technique for three-dimensional diagrams (although they are often difficult to interpret) but when more than three variables are involved we can no longer rely on diagrams.

Consider the function $y = f(x, z)$. A diagram representing such a function is given by the 'quarter-igloo' picture below, the function being represented by the *surface* (instead of a curve) $y = f(x, z)$. The calculus, as we have seen, is concerned with the gradients of curves. If we are to contrive its use in the context of three (or more) variables we must somehow reduce the surface $y = f(x, z)$ (which is bulging out from the page) to more manageable proportions. We can do this by measuring the gradient of 'slices' of the figure, that is, by holding the value of one variable constant we can isolate the rate of change of a second vari-

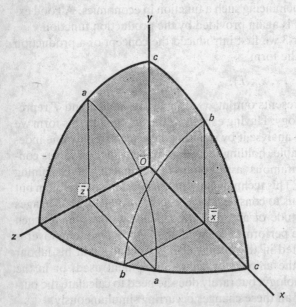

Figure 100

able with respect to changes in the value of a third. For example if $z$ is held constant at $\bar{z}$, $dy/dx$ is given by the gradient of the curve $aa$ (the curved edge of the slice $aa\bar{z}$); if $x$ is held constant at $\bar{x}$, $dy/dz$ is given by the slope of curve $bb$.

The process of differentiating $y$ with respect to $x$ or $z$ while holding the value of the other variable constant is termed *partial* differentiation and the symbol $\partial$ is adopted to distinguish it from the process of differentiating the function $y = f(x)$. Thus the *partial derivative* of $y$ with respect to $x$ is represented by $\partial y/\partial x$; and the partial derivative of $y$ with respect to $z$ is given by $\partial y/\partial z$.

Although this new technique may appear on the surface to be rather difficult, to find a partial derivative involves no rule that we have not previously met. By treating the other variable(s) as constant(s), finding $\partial y/\partial x$ is the same technique as deriving $dy/dx$ from $y = f(x)$. Generally, we can refer to: $y = x^n z^m$

then $\partial y/\partial x = nx^{n-1}z^m$,

and $\partial y/\partial z = mx^n z^{m-1}$.

Examples:

1     $y = 4x^3 + 3z - 10$,

    $\partial y/\partial x = 12x^2$,

    $\partial y/\partial z = 3$.

2     $y = 5x^5 z^2$,

    $\partial y/\partial x = 25x^4 z^2$,

    $\partial y/\partial z = 10x^5 z$.

3 $U^a = f(x^a, z^a)$ represents the utility function of an individual, $a$, where $x$ and $z$ are the two goods which $a$ consumes. The two *partials* (a shorthand version of partial derivatives) represent the marginal utility of each good to consumer $a$.

(a) $\partial U^a/\partial x^a$ is the marginal utility of $x$ to $a$ as the consumption of $x$ changes, consumption of $z$ held constant.

(b) $\partial U^a/\partial z^a$ gives the marginal utility to $a$ from consuming good $z$.

4 $P^y = f(L_a{}^y, L_b{}^y, K^y)$ is a production function showing that production, $P$, of good $y$ is a function of three inputs; land, $L_a$, labour, $L_b$, and capital, $K$. The three partials represent the three marginal products.

(a) $\partial P^y/\partial L_a{}^y$ shows the rate of change in $P^y$ with respect to change in $L_a{}^y$, the quantities of other inputs held constant, i.e. it gives the marginal product of land in the production of good $y$.

(b) $\partial P^y/\partial L_b{}^y$ gives the marginal product of labour in the production of good $y$.

(c) $\partial P^y/\partial K^y$ gives the marginal product of capital in producing $y$.

## Questions

1 Mr McSmith consumes two commodities, $x$ and $y$. The satisfaction ($U$) he gets from doing so is measured in utils and given by

$$U = 10x^4 + 2y^3.$$

(a) What is the marginal utility of $x$ when five units of $x$ are consumed?

(b) If his marginal utility from consuming $y$ is equal to 384 utils, how many units of $y$ has he consumed?

## The total differential

Partial differentiation enables us to discover the rate of change in the total function when a little bit of the relationship alters, a minute change in one independent variable. Thus, it might be interesting to round off our discussion of differentiation and its uses in economics by going one step further and considering what happens to the value of a function when *all* of the independent variables are changed by some small amount. What we shall be looking for in this case is something called the *total differential*.

As a first step we can specify a change in the dependent variable as the difference between the original value of the function and the new value created by the small changes in the values of the independent variables. Using again the function $y = f(x, z)$ we write:

$$\Delta y = f(x + \Delta x, z + \Delta z) - f(x, z) \qquad \textbf{16}$$

The interesting question now is the one which has been posed several times already in this chapter: what happens to $\Delta y$ as $\Delta x$ and $\Delta z$ become smaller and smaller? In other words, what is the limit value of $\Delta y$ as $\Delta x$ and $\Delta z$ approach zero? We can derive the answer by some clever manipulation of **16** but since we are more interested in application than derivation only the result of the manipulation is presented below. The result is as follows:

$$\lim_{\Delta x,\ \Delta z \to 0} \Delta y = \frac{\partial y}{\partial x} . \Delta x + \frac{\partial y}{\partial z} . \Delta z$$

And to emphasize that the changes in $x$ and $z$ are only minute increments we write:

$$dy = \frac{\partial y}{\partial x} . dx + \frac{\partial y}{\partial z} . dz \qquad \textbf{17}$$

where **17** represents the total differential of the function; it tells us that when the values of the independent variables in a function are changed by very small amounts the change in the total value of the function is found by multiplying each small variable change by the respective partial derivative of the function and then summing the resulting products.

Now, the above result has one application which we can find most helpful at this level of understanding of economic principles. At two stages in our earlier analysis we have employed iso-curves to demonstrate both maps of consumer preference and maps of production possibilities. In each case (indifference curves and isoquants) the dependent variable was a function of at least two independent variables (either commodities or factors of production). In each case, then, we were dealing with the three-dimensional problem discussed earlier in this chapter. We solved the problem by mapping onto a two dimensional surface, which meant that the value in the third plane of space was being held constant. Thus an indifference curve was used to link points of equal satisfaction in consumption – as amounts of one commodity were forgone amounts of some other were consumed to compensate and to keep satisfaction unchanged; an isoquant was used to link points of equal output – as the amount of one resource was reduced, the amount of some other one was increased to compensate and to keep output unchanged. We can now understand, with the help of the total differential, how to measure the slopes of these iso-curves.

Since the value of the function does not change as we move along the iso-curve we can use 17 as a condition to be fulfilled during such a movement. This condition is given by the total differential being set equal to zero:

$$dy = \frac{\partial y}{\partial x}.dx + \frac{\partial y}{\partial z}.dz = 0 \qquad\qquad \textbf{18}$$

If we now subtract $\frac{\partial y}{\partial z}.dz$ from both sides of 18 we obtain an equality:

$$\frac{\partial y}{\partial x}.dx = -\frac{\partial y}{\partial z}.dz$$

and by dividing each side by $dz$ and $\frac{\partial y}{\partial x}$ we arrive at

$$\frac{dx}{dz} = -\frac{\partial y}{\partial z}\bigg/\frac{\partial y}{\partial x} \qquad\qquad \textbf{19}$$

This result tells us that the slope of the iso-curve $\frac{dx}{dz}$ is negative and equal to the ratio of the two partial derivatives.

Suppose we look more closely at an indifference curve in order to illustrate our result. Figure 101 presents a familiar picture. On the vertical axis we measure quantities of some good $x$ and on the horizontal axis quantities of some other good $z$. Satisfaction (or 'utility' if we want to use that particular interpretation) is constant (the total differential does not change) as we move along the indifference curve $II'$. Satisfaction is represented by $y$; thus we are using $y = f(x, z)$.

Continuing with the 'blow-up' technique used earlier, we choose any point on $II'$, say $p$, and we can see the slope of the tangent to the curve (slope of the curve) at that point to be

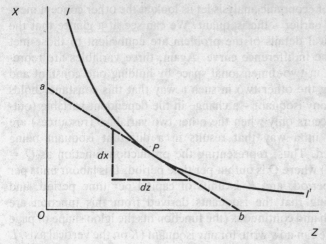

Figure 101

given by $\dfrac{dx}{dz}$. But we know from **19** that in order for satisfaction to remain unchanged along $II'$, $dy = 0$ and $\dfrac{dx}{dz} = \dfrac{\partial y}{\partial z} \big/ \dfrac{\partial y}{\partial x}$. However, in Chapter 11 we said that the slope of an indifference curve is given by the marginal rate of substitution between the two commodities being consumed. We can now see that this marginal rate of substitution is defined by the ratio of the two partial derivatives – the rate of change in satisfaction or utility with respect to a minute change in consumption of $z$, divided by the rate of change in satisfaction or utility with respect to a minute change in $x$. Indeed, we can go a little further than this, for our earlier introduction to partial derivatives tells us that if $y$ represents utility then $\dfrac{\partial y}{\partial z}$ and $\dfrac{\partial y}{\partial x}$ are the marginal utilities from consuming $z$ and $x$ respectively. We conclude that the slope of an indifference curve is given by the marginal rate of substitution between the two commodities which in turn is measured by (minus) the ratio of the marginal utilities from the two commodities.

To make sure that we can apply our new technique to other

areas of economic analysis let us look at the other concept mentioned earlier – the isoquant. We can see at a glance that the analytical details of the problem are equivalent to those met with the indifference curve. Again, three variables are represented in two-dimensional space by holding one constant and varying the other two in such a way that this constancy holds along any isoquant – a change in the dependent variable (output) occurs only when the other two variables (resources) are varied in a way that results in a different isoquant being attained. Thus, representing the production function as $Q = f(K, L)$ where $Q$ is output per time period, $L$ is labour units per time period, and $K$ is units of capital per time period, and assuming that the isoquants derived from this function are smooth and continuous (the function fits the igloo shape of page 296) we can now write for any isoquant ($K$ on the vertical axis, $L$ on the horizontal axis)

$$dQ = \frac{\partial Q}{\partial K} . dK + \frac{\partial Q}{\partial L} . dL = 0$$

and therefore

$$\frac{dK}{dL} = - \frac{\partial Q}{\partial L} \bigg/ \frac{\partial Q}{\partial K}$$

We conclude that the slope of the isoquants is given by minus the ratio of the two partial derivatives of output with respect to the two resource inputs. In Chapter 13 we defined the slope of the isoquant as the marginal technical rate of substitution and on page 301 of the present chapter we saw that the two partial derivatives of the production function are the respective marginal (physical) products. Thus, we now see that the marginal rate of technical substitution in production is given by (minus) the ratio of the marginal (physical) products of the two inputs.

As a final step along this excursion into the uses of mathematical techniques we make one further use of the total differential. We do so because economic concepts discussed in relation to the total differential do not by themselves constitute the economic problem. The preference map, comprising a set of indifference curves, and the production map, comprising a set of isoquants, are but one side of the scarcity picture. The real economic problem consists of matching these sets of possible combinations of goods or resources against the constraints which operate to ration their uses. Thus, the consumer chooses the highest difference curve compatible with the constraints imposed by his income and the relative prices of the two commodities; while the producer chooses the highest isoquant compatible with his available outlay and the relative prices of resources. Both agents maximize an objective within the confines of a set of constraints.

How can mathematics be used to show how these problems of *constrained maximization* (or, in other contexts, *constrained minimization*) can be resolved? The key to the analysis lies in the fact that the best position on either of the two maps mentioned is one of tangency. Consider Figure 101 once again. Let us suppose now that point $P$ represents the best point that can be reached on the indifference map, given the constraints imposed by the budget line $ab$. Since $P$ is a tangency point, the slope of the budget line and that of the indifference curve $II'$ are the same at that point. We have looked already and in some detail at the slope of the indifference curve so let us take a closer look at the slope of the budget line.

By assumption, the consumer spends all his income on the two goods $x$ and $z$. Thus, using $C$ to represent consumption expenditure (equals consumer income) and $px$ and $pz$ to represent the prices of $x$ and $z$ respectively we can write

$$C = px.x + pz.z$$

or, more conveniently for present purposes

$$F(x, z) = C - px.x - pz.z = 0 \qquad\qquad \textbf{20}$$

where $F(x, z)$ represents the general form of the constraint. Now, since income ($= C$) is given we know that its value is unchanged at all points along $ab$, in other words, the $F(x, z)$ function has a total differential equal to zero:

$$\frac{\partial F(x, z)}{\partial x} .dx + \frac{\partial F(x, 2)}{\partial y} .dy = 0$$

or, by differentiating **20** we can find the values for the specific case shown in Figure 101:

$$-px.dx - pz.dz = 0$$

from which we get $\dfrac{dx}{dz} = -\dfrac{pz}{px}$, the familiar result that the slope

of the budget line is equal to (minus) the ratio of relative prices.

Thus since $p$ is a point of tangency we may now write

$$\frac{dx}{dz} = -\frac{\partial y}{\partial z} \Big/ \frac{\partial y}{\partial x} = -\frac{pz}{px} \qquad\qquad 21$$

which tells us that in equilibrium (where the budget line is tangential to the highest possible indifference curve) the marginal rate of substitution, which measures the ratio of marginal utilities, is equal to the ratio of relative prices. Furthermore, by cross multiplying we obtain

$$\frac{\partial y/\partial z}{pz} = \frac{\partial y/\partial x}{px} \qquad\qquad 22$$

which explains in terms of partial derivatives the equi-proportional rule that in order to maximize utility the consumer should equate the ratios of marginal utility to price.

## Questions

1 A consumer of commodities $x$ and $z$ has a utility function of the form $U = x^3z^2$. Show that when the prices of $x$ and $z$ are £1 and £2 respectively the amount of $z$ he consumes is (minus) one-third of the amount of $x$ (in equilibrium).

2 Farmer Giles discovers that by combining man-hours ($L$) per week with tractor hours ($K$) per week he can harvest his weekly potato crop ($P$) according to the function

$$P = K^4L^2$$

If labour can be employed at £4 per hour and the cost of using a tractor is £6 per hour, show that Farmer Giles's option combination of factors of production is in the ratio of four man-hours to every three hours of tractor use.

After attempting the above questions some readers may be wondering about how to handle problems of constrained maximization and minimization when there are more than two independent variables involved. The mathematical technique involved in the solving of such problems is known as the 'Lagrangian multiplier',[5] a most useful piece of mathematics but a complex one and best left until a higher level of economic analysis is being tackled.

## Some final remarks

This interlude has been introduced to help throw some light upon some of the analytical concepts met in earlier chapters. It is hoped that when such concepts appear again in later chapters their mathematical characteristics will be remembered. It is hoped also that some readers have had their appetite whetted for further study of the application of mathematical techniques in economics.

We could have said a lot more and it will be appreciated that we have merely scratched the surface of the uses of mathematics in economic analysis. Perhaps we should reiterate, for the sake of those readers who like to read conclusions and summaries before they venture into the body of a chapter, that anyone reading this book in the hope of learning some basic economics and no more should find that the omission of this chapter leaves his comprehension of economic principles unimpaired. But for any reader using this text as a take-off to a higher level of economic analysis, this chapter should provide a useful introduction to some of the techniques he will employ later.

5. After a French mathematician, Joseph Louis Lagrange (1736–1813).

# Part Five
# The Social Institutions of Production

In the introduction to Part Two we looked at the relative merits of planning and the market as mechanisms for the allocation of resources and we put forward the tentative conclusion that we need both planning and the market in order to carry out different tasks. Which would be chosen – plan or market – would depend upon relative costs. In the intervening chapters we analysed the workings of markets. Now we return to the issue of planning, of which we can find many examples. Households are planning units: they produce children, a home, love and affection. There are also the giant corporations, such as ICI, Unilever and British Leyland, along whose corridors of power decisions are made which affect millions and in whose factories orders are issued which workers must obey or lose their jobs. Finally, there is the State which also produces what markets fail to provide and which can, through conscription, order its citizens to die so that such non-market goods as cultural heritage may be preserved.

There are in fact more planning units than markets – more firms than markets. It is the existence of these planners that we must now explain. Earlier economists sought to explain the workings of markets because for them markets were the novelty and were growing; now we look at the prior institutions whose persistence needs comment.

# Chapter 15
# The Social Institutions of Production

At the beginning of Part Two we drew a distinction between the plan and the market. Part Two then went on to discuss the market to the neglect of planning systems, but planning units do exist within markets and are called *firms*. We need to know why firms exist and to clarify the reasons for the choice of integration by administration, as opposed to integration by the market of various activities.

### The single process

Let us begin with the single process of production whereby some resources are, by a qualitative change, converted into something desirable. Now, as we saw in Chapter 3, all processes seem to require the cooperation of at least two different factors of production – be they men and machines or men and natural resources. It is only when one factor can produce something without the cooperation of other factors of production that no problem arises. For the problem is: how can the individual contributions of factors be assessed so as to pay them rewards from the total output? There must be some method of supervision so as to measure the relative contributions of different factors and there must be some method of supervision to coordinate their activities. The market can play a part but it cannot perform the necessary supervision to ensure that factors perform their tasks with the necessary efficiency. The institutional arrangement which brings about the requisite supervision is called a *firm*.

The firm is an institutional arrangement designed to cope with the collective goods problem that the existence of interdependence in the production function creates.

Consider the simple task of mending a boundary wall by two neighbours. The problem of 'how' can be handled by conferences. Whenever they hit a snag the neighbours can stop and discuss how the snag might be overcome. And since they constitute a small group they can check each other's efforts. But it is not always possible to hold conferences and in large groups supervision of each by all cannot be achieved, so there is a need to create a supervisor, a leviathan. It is the supervisor's task to monitor the work of each factor so as to determine rewards. When there is jointness in production and the rewards of factors depend upon their efficiency, then a supervision problem arises.

## Contracts

There is then a supervision problem of monitoring the performances of the various factors of production. The easiest method is, of course, for someone to own all the factors of production, but slavery is forbidden and the outright purchase of other factors may be costly. So there arises a need to establish contracts to obtain the use of factors. Each resource owner is faced with a double problem:

1 Either he can hire all the resources he needs to produce a commodity *or* he can hire his resources to others;

2 Either he can pay all the resources he hires at a fixed rate *or* he can allow them an uncertain (or variable) share in an uncertain outcome. (These possibilities also confront any lessee of resources.)

## The supervisor's reward

If a resource owner decides to hire other resources, then he seeks as his reward the residual – the difference between what he pays them and the value of the total product. The size of the residual will, in the first place, depend upon the vigour of his supervision and how it is implemented. In the case of labour the supervisor may need to know something about workers' motivation and the relative importance of monetary and non-monetary rewards.

The market can also help in determining supervisors' rewards. If they become abnormally large more people will set up as supervisors and rewards will decline. If some supervisors become lazy they will be eliminated because they will charge a higher price for what is produced than other supervisors. But within the limits set by the competition of others to become supervisors, there may exist a range of rewards – considerable differences in residuals.[1]

### Fixed versus variable payments

The second issue is that of fixed or variable payments to resource owners by the supervisor. In a world of certainty the problem would not arise: it would make little difference whether the hirer of resources paid his factors on a fixed or variable basis. His costs would remain constant. For if he found it cheaper to pay his resources at a fixed rate then some resource owners would set up in opposition and bid up the fixed rate until it yielded the same result as the variable rate. But in the real world certainty does not exist and we find preferences for one or other form of contract. Here we consider a few examples.

1 Suppose the hirer of resources wishes to reduce the costs of supervision or finds it difficult to establish a rigorous system of supervision. Then he may attempt to transfer the costs of supervision to the owners of the resources he has hired. He may, for example, pay his workers on a piece-rate basis; that is, he may pay a fixed price for each unit they produce and nothing if they produce nothing. Such a policy is efficient if the output can be

1. The problem of the supervisor's reward (what is sometimes called profit) will be discussed in Chapter 18 under the heading 'normal profit' and in Chapter 19 where the inefficiency of monopolists leads to other resource owners capturing some of the residual. Profit is also discussed in Chapter 25.

measured, its quality readily assessed and there are no break-downs which prevent workers earning their livelihood. If some of these condition are absent then the supervisor may be forced to pay workers on a time-rate basis and increase his control through the use of foremen.

2 A variation on simple piece rates and one that is tried when new processes are installed is to pay workers on a variable piece rate with the price falling per unit as output increases. The rationale for this policy is that not all the gains from improvements should go to workers, particularly those associated with learning by doing.

3 In agriculture tenancy agreements may specify who should own improvements (such as drainage schemes) installed by tenants, since landowners may claim them.

4 Situations where *all* resource owners take an uncertain share of an uncertain outcome – profit sharing is feasible when the number of participants is small. When the group becomes large it may be difficult to police each participant's effort and problems of free riders may emerge.

Workers' control represents an extension of the principle of profit sharing to the entire economy. Difficulties can arise. What happens if a worker leaves his firm? Does he take with him his right to a share in future income? If not might workers be reluctant to allow some income to be ploughed back to increase future income? Would workers risk putting all their eggs in one basket? What about the problem that arises when different enterprises differ in their profitability? Should some of the gains be passed on to others through price reductions? These are all important issues and involve a consideration of the role of ideology in the motivation of workers in socialist countries. Furthermore, they raise the question of whether any economy can institute some basic income (a social dividend) without encountering policing problems to prevent scrounging (social dividends are discussed in Chapter 28).

Resource owners may allow some of their rewards to be

ploughed back provided they can be allowed to sell their right to future income. This requires the establishment of a market in property rights (the stock market) and the effectiveness of such a market will be discussed in the next chapter. In the meantime let us note that if shareholders cannot effectively police their property rights then the appointed managers may divert the residual to their own ends. There may therefore be little difference between a property sharing socialist firm and a badly controlled capitalist firm.

*Nuisances as well as goods.* The incentive to seek to supervise resources applies to the production of nuisances as well as goods. People will seek to control the production of smoke, road accidents and injuries in factories.

### Consumption as well as production

We have emphasized the interdependence of factors in the production process and the need for cooperation of factors, but let us not forget the interdependence of consumers in the consumption process of collective goods. Where a good can be consumed equally by all then there must be a means of policing its consumption and financing. This was briefly discussed in Chapter 2 and will be re-examined in Part Nine.

### Sequential processes

To speak of a single process is an abstraction. Most firms control a sequence of operations, e.g. spinning and weaving and so on. The reasons for such integration by administration rather than integration by the market also lie in the costs of using the market – primarily the costs of time and uncertainty. Thus, it would be possible for each man on a car assembly line to sell his product to the next man down the line but it would be extremely inconvenient. Uncertainty presents a problem since it may not always be possible to ensure further supplies of resources through the market.

## What limits the size of firms?

Firms can grow by expansion of a single process, i.e. increasing the scale of a single process by increasing the scale of all inputs; by horizontal integration of a number of independent, identical single processes; by vertically integrating a series of sequential processes; or by some mixture of the various methods.

### Finance

The obvious limitation to the size or rate of growth of firms is finance – the resources, or the command over resources, necessary for growth. This is apparent in the case of one-man or family firms where abstention from immediate consumption of all current income may be dictated by the absence of an ability to borrow against future income. Financial limitations explain why the exploitation of the scientific and technological discoveries of the Renaissance and the Industrial Revolution had to await the contractual arrangement known as limited liability which allowed small savers to invest without the risk of losing their entire wealth. (The problems created by limited liability are dealt with in Chapter 16.)

### The will to grow

Finance is closely linked with the will to grow, especially in family firms. Alfred Marshall, the great English economist, likened firms to the trees of the forest, some of which were striving to grow whilst others were dying. In the case of family firms he felt that the initial stimulus and drive of the founder might be lost by his children and grandchildren who would dissipate his accumulated wealth. While joint-stock companies do not die, they could stagnate through loss of leadership.

### Technology

There may be limits to the size of firms set by technology but these may be rare since it is always possible to duplicate technological equipment.

## The market

The market may limit the growth of a firm by limiting the demand for its product. But this might be overcome by moving into another market. Multi-product firms are, of course, common and are an important method of overcoming the risks of specialization as well as the obstacles to growth. Market growth may, however, work in the opposite direction by enabling a firm to get rid of costly processes.

## Management

The production function is not technologically determined, is not given to management but is determined by management's strategy in the light of management's perception of profitable opportunities. We cannot, therefore, write $P = f(L,K)$ where $P$ is output, $L$ is labour and $K$ is capital without realizing that $(L,K)$ interact in a manner determined by management. Management can influence output through its structure of supervision. In the nineteenth century most firms were owner-managed. Growth of markets brought possibilities of growth of firms and the need for new management structures to cope with growth. The innovation was the functional structure in which each member of the board of directors was assigned a specific function – purchasing, sales, etc. But further growth in terms of diversity of products produced and geographical markets brought the need for a switch to the multi-divisional firm in which each product or geographical market was organized into a division. The last innovation permitted the board of directors to concentrate on broad issues of policy and avoid immersion in day-to-day detailed management (Figure 102).

## Power, the firm and the market

In our discussion of the firm we have emphasized the problems of communication, of the exchange of information. The market also exists to exchange information, so what is the difference between a firm and a market? What happens to the concepts of

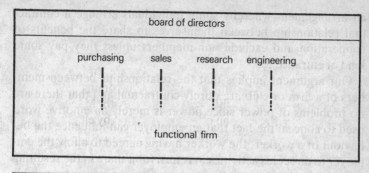

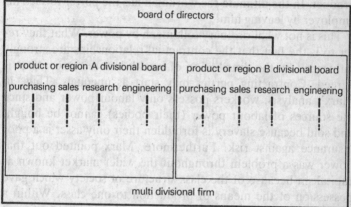

Figure 102

power, authority and status which are usually associated with people in organizations?

We begin with a bald statement. A firm is a market which emerges whenever there is failure in extremely decentralized markets. Thus market failures comprise spillovers of all kinds – the ability of one factor of production to obtain rewards in excess of its own contribution to output because there is no supervision of contributions; the ability of some consumers to benefit from the purchase of goods by others (the problem of collective goods that was discussed in Chapter 2 and will be looked at again in Part Eight). When spillovers occur then steps will be taken to eliminate them and so firms will be formed. The firm is an arrangement whereby some individuals arrange a contractual relationship between themselves to share the benefits of cooperation and exclude non-members unless they pay some kind of entrance fee.[2]

Our argument implies that the relationships between members of a firm or club are purely contractual and that there are no problems of power since power is merely an emotive word used to conceal the fact that an employer can influence the behaviour of a worker, the worker having agreed to allow the employer to direct his activities in return for a share in the resulting product. In the ultimate the workman has the power to sack his employer by leaving him!

This is not what ordinary folk mean by power. What they refer to is the fact that the contractual relationships are strongly influenced by the distribution of wealth before the contract is agreed. Contracting parties may start as unequals. Thus, in Marx's analysis, workers possess only labour power and since the sources of labour power (their bodies) cannot be bought and sold because slavery is forbidden their only asset is a poor insurance against risk. Furthermore, Marx pointed out that power was a problem throughout the wider market known as capitalism because of the class structure of society which gave possession of the means of production to one class. Within a firm power was personalized in the 'boss'; outside any firm it was depersonalized in the 'system'.

## Households

Households are production and consumption units: they produce meals, a home, children, love and affection. However, households have certain peculiarities which have become accentuated in the course of economic development. The first important feature is their small size. Since Victorian times the household has become stripped down to a core or nucleus of

2. Thus we can become members of the Heinz Beans Club or Firm by paying the entrance fee as indicated by the price of a tin of beans. In some cases there is a two-part fee – an initial charge and price per unit consumed.

parents and children. The tremendous emphasis upon individualism has reduced the roles of grandparents and spinster aunts that were a feature of nineteenth-century households. This individualism has been accompanied by disadvantages which make households dependent upon the environment in which they operate and often seriously dependent upon support from the State.

In market economies households acquire income from the sale of labour services which is then used to finance household activities. A characteristic of democratic societies is the prohibition on the sale of the sources of labour services: that is, the buying and selling of people. Slavery is forbidden and this makes it difficult for households to finance their activities. No one, for example, can sell his children to someone else in return for their being educated or in return for the money to buy a house, a car or a Continental holiday. Planning tends therefore to be restricted to what current earnings permit, unless the household has ample non-human assets to sell.

The typical household's life-time patterns of earnings and expenditure follow different paths as shown in Figure 103. Earnings tend to be low in the early years because of lack of skills. On the other hand, expenditures tend to be considerable – house purchase, and the maintenance of dependents such as wives and children. In the middle years earnings come to ex-

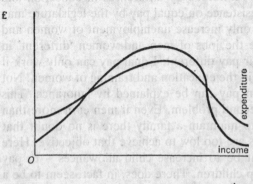

Figure 103

ceed expenditure as skills are acquired which lead to higher earnings, the children leave home and the house mortgage is paid off. Finally, there may be a stage in which earnings decline faster than expenditure and a second stage of low income may be encountered. Superimposed upon these trends may be major or minor dislocations caused by illness and accidents.

Within the household complex personal, social and economic changes have been taking place as a result of profound changes in society. The reduction in family size, assisted by the improvements in family planning, has reduced the amount of time spent by wives in motherhood. And the pulls and pressures on wives to seek a paid job outside the home have been helped by the emergence of labour-saving devices – the washing machine, the carpet cleaner, child nurseries, cafés and prepared foods. These forces have increased the potential lifetime earnings of wives but have, at the same time, increased tensions within the family and within society.

Two sources of tension can be detected. First, there is the problem of equal pay. Secondly, there is the problem of a wife's dependence upon her husband's earnings during motherhood. The two are not unrelated. As the length of time a woman can work in the labour market increases so does the demand for parity of pay with men. Traditionally men have been paid more than women because they were the breadwinners and this inequality has been reinforced by differences in education and training. Hence insistence on equal pay by the legislature may not work. It may only increase unemployment of women and pressures to make the jobs of men and women 'different' in order to keep their pay different. Equal pay can only work if there are changes in the education and training of women. Not all the disparity in pay can be explained by ignorance. This brings us to the second problem. Even if men earn more than women in order to maintain a family there is no doubt that many men's wages are too low to achieve that objective. Here the solution might be to increase child allowances – to pay women to bring up children. There does, in fact, seem to be a strong case for abolishing marriage tax allowances and treating married couples without children as two single people. The only case for giving marriage allowances seems to be to prevent people from falling into sin – but few believe in sin nowadays. What needs to be done is to get the property laws and tax laws into line with the changes that are taking place in the nature and behaviour of families.

## Questions

1 What are the implications of the technology of the production process for the organization of production?

2 Is the Soviet Union a firm? Is Leeds United a firm?

3 How would you account for the fact that the spinning and weaving of wool are carried out in the same firms whereas the spinning and weaving of worsteds are usually carried out in separate firms?

4 (a) How would you account for the existence of slavery in America in the nineteenth century?
(b) What was the difference between slavery and serfdom?
(c) How would you account for the abolition of serfdom in Europe in the eighteenth and nineteenth centuries?

# Chapter 16
# The Corporation

Among all the institutions that modern man has devised for the production of goods and services none has attracted more attention than the corporation. Just how important is the large corporation can be gleaned from a few facts. In 1907 the 100 largest firms in UK manufacturing were responsible for 15 per cent of total output; in 1970 they contributed 45 per cent.[1] And although large firms tend to be concentrated in manufacturing and manufacturing is tending to decline in importance, there are signs that their structure and mode of operation are spreading to other sectors of the economy, notably transport and services.

## Limited liability and the emergence of the corporation

The contrast in industrial organization between nineteenth and twentieth centuries is, in fact, quite marked. In the second half of the nineteenth century the cotton industry – the model for all theoretical work – had evolved its highly sectionalized structure with numerous competing firms at each stage of production. The industry contained no obvious forces leading to concentration and the market tended to grow faster than the size of firms.

What changed the pattern of industrial organization was the

1. L. Hannah, *The Rise of the Corporate Economy*, Methuen, London, 1976, p. 216.

emergence of limited liability, the development of new products and a changing economic environment. Limited liability means that if a person lends, say, £100 to a firm and the firm incurs debts of £1 million the total liability of the individual is confined to £100 and is not extended to embrace all his assets in order to pay off the firm's debts. As a result of financing, a firm acquires a legal existence distinct from its owners. It can own property and it can be sued in its own name – a fact which allows people to enter into contracts with it. The limited liability firm must appoint a board of directors and accounts must be presented annually to a meeting of shareholders. Limited liability makes it possible for large numbers of shareholders to invest their savings without endangering their livelihoods and it is also possible for individuals with ideas and drive, but no money, to acquire financial backing.

Although the concept of limited liability goes back at least to Roman times, it is nowadays felt to be a product of the nineteenth century. There was a period, in the seventeenth century, of experimentation with limited liability but the disastrous fiascos of John Law's schemes in France and America led to its suspension and finance for the Industrial Revolution came from personal or family savings, partnerships, loans from banks which had managed to channel the savings of the southern agricultural districts to northern industries and, to a limited extent, from governments. The railways, which required enormous amounts of finance, were built without the assistance of limited liability.

Joint stock, or limited liability, became available in the second half of the nineteenth century but its exploitation did not get under way until the last decades of the century. There was a wave of mergers in the period 1880–1914 which was assisted by the new methods of finance. There was also a shift of opinion towards large firms and amalgamations which began to surface in the First World War, with the need for planning, and continued afterwards. In the slump politicians and businessmen began to blame many of Britain's industrial ills on the sectional character of its industries and the small size of the individual firm. British industry contrasted badly with that of America,

Germany and Japan. There were moves towards rationalization and amalgamation, and opinion was still in favour of bigness after the Second World War despite the passing of anti-monopoly legislation. In many of the newer industries, such as chemicals, cars and aircraft, technological factors seemed to favour large plants. And even the creation of the European Economic Community was seen as a means whereby European firms could aspire to the sizes of their American rivals.

## The aims of the corporation
### The divorce of ownership from control

The sheer size and complexity of the modern corporation has tempted many observers to question whether their objective is the same as their nineteenth-century predecessors and the owner-managed firms of today. Beginning in the 1940s under the stimulus of the writing of Berle and Means there has emerged a body of opinion which states that the goal of profit maximizing has been displaced by other objectives. This shift, it is alleged, has occurred because of the *divorce of ownership from control*. Most modern companies have so many shareholders that it is impossible for them to combine to control the directors of their organizations; many do not turn up to the annual meetings of shareholders and the directors are able to collect their votes and use them to further their own ends. Thus, Baumol (1959) has put forward the theory that directors attempt to maximize sales, subject to a constraint on dividends. If dividends are regarded as too low then directors will attempt to maximize profits in order to increase dividends. If dividends are satisfactory then the firm concentrates on maximizing sales. What governs dividends is the dividends paid by other firms and if competition is weak then dividends can be low. Williamson (1964) postulated another goal – the number of employees under the control of a particular manager; the more employees responsible to a manager the more prestige he enjoys. Marris (1964) suggested that directors were interested in maximizing the growth of their firms and that the main problem was to avoid a takeover bid. Since share prices are influenced by dividends then a low dividend would imply low share prices. But if directors were ploughing back profits then the real value of the firms would be greater than the total value of shares and it would be possible for outsiders to buy up the firms cheaply. Hence, dividends have to be high enough to avoid a takeover bid.

The pursuit of goals other than profits has been allied to the notion that decision-making is difficult and therefore directors will aim not at maximum profits but satisfactory profits. *Satisficing*, rather than maximizing, behaviour characterizes the modern corporation.

Now the fact that there may be a large number of shareholders does not necessarily imply that shareholders have lost control. The existence of many shareholders may simply mean that there are available a large number of specialists, each of whom is capable of policing particular activities of directors. Tables 29 and 30 taken from the work of Nyman and Silberston show that there are a great variety of owners of the top 250 UK companies and that in many firms there does appear to be a group capable of exercising control.

But in addition to the statistics on shareholding there are other reasons why the divorce of ownership from control doctrine must be qualified. First, it must not be assumed that owner-managers only pursue profits. They will normally have a trade-off between income and leisure and at some point we should expect them to retire to the golf course or to indulge in other whims and fancies. Secondly, if investors believe that it is difficult to control directors then they will invest less and they would pay less for the shares of firms whose directors they suspected were less diligent in the pursuit of profits. The capital market is not perfect in the sense that everyone has complete knowledge of all events but it is efficient in the sense that given the information that is available then investors do tend to invest where the returns are highest. Of course, there are problems in the capital market. The information available to shareholders is not always as good as they would like and company reports can often be uninformative and misleading but these are problems associated with the costs of acquiring information and are common to all markets. And on the central issue of whether the returns on capital invested in large owner-managed and controlled firms is larger than that obtained on capital invested in large manager-controlled corporations, the available evidence suggests that there is little difference in rewards.

**Table 29** Ownership control of the U.K. 'Top 250' in 1975

| % of voting shares held by a single institution or by the board of directors and their families | Type of holder | | | | | | | | |
|---|---|---|---|---|---|---|---|---|---|
| | I | F | D | C | G | M | O | N | Total |
| Unquoted company | 3 | .. | 8 | 1 | 1 | .. | .. | 3 | 16 |
| Over 50% | 4 | .. | 15 | 1 | 1 | .. | 1 | .. | 22 |
| 40%–50% | 1 | .. | 5 | 1 | .. | .. | 1 | .. | 8 |
| 30%–40% | 1 | .. | 8 | 1 | 1 | .. | .. | .. | 11 |
| 20%–30% | 8 | 1 | 2 | .. | .. | .. | .. | 1 | 12 |
| 10%–20% | 5 | 4 | 17 | .. | .. | .. | .. | .. | 26 |
| Other holdings greater than 10% | .. | .. | 2 | .. | .. | 4 | .. | .. | 6 |
| 5%–10% | 1 | 4 | 5 | .. | .. | .. | .. | .. | 10 |
| Total | 23 | 9 | 62 | 4 | 3 | 4 | 2 | 4 | 111 |
| Family chairman or M.D. (but less than 5% shareholding by individual or group) | | | | | | | | | 15 |
| *Total* owner-controlled | | | | | | | | | 126 |
| No known control | | | | | | | | | 98 |
| *Total* firms | | | | | | | | | 224 |
| % owner-controlled | | | | | | | | | 56·25 |

Notes:
Types of holder I = Another industrial company.
F = Financial institution.
D = Directors and their families.
C = Charitable trust.
G = Government or quasi-government agency.
M = Mixed control type.
O = Other control type.
N = Not classifiable due to lack of information.
Source: S. Nyman and A. Silberston, 'The Ownership and Control of Industry', *Oxford Economic Papers*, 1978

**Table 30** Ownership control and industry

| Industrial group | Total no. companies in 'Top 250' | No. companies owner-controlled |
|---|---|---|
| Food | 15 | 12 |
| Drink | 7 | 4 |
| Tobacco | 3 | 1 |
| Oil | 5 | 2 |
| Chemicals | 12 | 3 |
| Metal manufacturing | 5 | 3 |
| Mechanical engineering | 15 | 8 |
| Electrical engineering | 13 | 8 |
| Vehicles | 8 | 5 |
| Metal goods (N.E.S.) | 9 | 3 |
| Textiles | 6 | 3 |
| Building materials | 12 | 4 |
| Paper, printing and publishing | 7 | 4 |
| Other manufacturing | 6 | 3 |
| Construction | 9 | 7 |
| Transport | 8 | 3 |
| Retailing | 17 | 13 |
| Merchanting | 17 | 11 |
| Miscellaneous services | 7 | 7 |
| Conglomerates | 24 | 11 |
| Unclassified | 19 | 11 |
| Total | 224 | 126 |

Source: S. Nyman and A. Silberston

## Management in the large corporation

For the divorce of ownership from control to have substance there would not only have to be apathetic shareholders but there would also have to be a monolithic management intent upon one goal, but most managements are not monolithic; they often appear to be full of conflict. Large firms are, in fact, markets in which some aspects of market behaviour have been eliminated in order to provide more exact information. Selection, training and promotion can be more easily controlled. Moreover, managers who aspire to quick promotion by joining other firms are likely to prove themselves by their performance with existing companies.

## Hierarchical control and property rights

Although large corporations may guarantee their shareholders at least the same return as owner-managers obtain, they may not get a greater return. Furthermore, the fact that they are large means that they will tend to suffer from the problems associated with hierarchical control which we touched upon in the previous chapter. Control of subordinates becomes progressively more difficult as the span of control and the chain of command becomes longer. Hence, although directors and employees may have their monetary rewards fixed by contract, there may exist opportunities for them to supplement their incomes; there may be opportunities for pilfering. But if shareholders are aware of these problems then the implication will be that there may be a greater *variety* of rewards in large corporations with dispersed shareholdings than in small, closely controlled firms. Employment contracts will take into account the problems of controlling managers but without necessarily reducing the wealth of shareholders.

## A corporate economy, a corporate world

Although we have expressed some reservations about the divorce of ownership from control thesis, the sheer size and complexity of the corporate sector does raise important political, as well as economic issues. According to Galbraith (1967) there is now a very long time lag between the emergence of a new idea and its fruition into the sale of consumer goods. Consequently, careful planning has to be carried out at all stages of production and selling. This planning cannot be carried out by the market and it also requires governments to stabilize the economy and not produce erratic fluctuations in economic activity. And because the corporations are large employers of labour, governments are inclined to offer them assistance if they encounter difficulties. Thus, the activities of governments and corporations become intertwined. Governments may, in their pursuit of full employment, be tempted to prop up obsolete firms which are large employers of labour.

Another feature of contemporary society has been the emergence of the multinational corporation. Foreign investment has tended to become the province of the firm rather than the market. Firms in the advanced countries will pioneer some new piece of technology and then look around for the cheapest place to produce it. They will then invest in the construction of plant in developing countries, such as Taiwan and Korea. Such countries often acquire methods of production which seem out of place with their relative backwardness and they become highly dependent upon foreign investment. Governments may then become subservient to foreign based firms.

There are, therefore, problems associated with the growth of corporations which require solutions. It might be possible to curb the pervasive influence of their advertising by taxation and the dissemination of information about the properties of products. In cases where monopoly power rests upon the fact that only one or a few firms can exist then consideration might be given to nationalizing them or exposing them to foreign competition. And there could be international agreements governing the behaviour of multinational corporations. But the fears expressed in the sixties and seventies are now less pressing given the greater awareness of the issues.

# Part Six
# Market Structures

In this section we shall discuss the behaviour of firms in different market situations. Firms exist as we saw in Chapter 15 because of the costs of using the market; they are islands of conscious planning. But what are firms attempting to do? In a nutshell they are trying to maximize the utilities of their owners: maximizing utilities is a sufficiently broad concept to cover the activities of families, multinational corporations and the state. But sometimes it is suggested that firms attempt to maximize profits and it must be remembered that this assumption covers only a limited range of firms – it excludes, for example, hospitals and schools – and must be regarded as a proxy for utilities. Money is a universal medium of exchange and the maximization of money profits means that the owners of a firm can have a large income to spend on goods which yield them utility. Money profits can also be easily measured and monitored. Interest in profit maximizing therefore stems from the historical fact that some firms are interested in profits and profits can be measured and provide a means of measuring utilities.

Profit maximizing is, of course, subject to reservations and criticisms. In the first place it is sometimes alleged that firms cannot maximize profits. What this often means is that uncertainty makes it difficult for firms to maximize profits. A second argument is that firms do not attempt to maximize profits; that the directors of firms do not attempt to maximize the income of the owners, but pursue their own goals. This criticism draws attention to the problems of control. Because of the expansion of the capital market it is difficult for shareholders to combine to safeguard their interest. A third criticism is that profit maximization may be against the community's interest and thus draw attention to problems of monopoly.

We shall concentrate on market situations in which firms are attempting or supposed to be attempting to maximize profits. This embraces four trading situations:

Perfect competition
Pure monopoly
Oligopoly
Bilateral monopoly

In the trading situation known as perfect competition there are numerous buyers and sellers: so numerous that though each comes to the market with his own trading price, none can feel that his will be the clearing price. In pure monopoly there is only one seller and the important question is: how does the monopolist decide on his trading price? In oligopoly there are a few sellers. Will they conspire to announce a common price so that they can be regarded as a single seller? If so, how do they decide to divide the spoils?

Trading situations in which profits are the goal are common but they are not the only trading situations. Profit maximization does not appear to describe the behaviour of churches, youth clubs, charities and nationalized industries. And such organizations are involved in a considerable part of economic activity. Armchair reasoning suggests that such firms will obey the basic laws of demand and supply. When, for example, there is an increase in demand for their services they will increase their output. But how can we be sure that they are efficient? There is a difficulty once we move away from something as easily measurable as money profits. And because measurement is difficult, control is difficult. In this section of the book we emphasize the difficulties of defining the goals of nationalized industries and hence the difficulties of controlling them, but it is easy to multiply the list of difficult cases – universities, schools, hospitals, etc. A task that economists have not yet successfully solved is how to devise practical measuring rods of the utilities flowing from such firms – particularly when so many appear to be in monopoly situations.

# Chapter 17
# Organizational Behaviour

Our reply to the question 'why firms?' was centred upon reasons for the suppression of the market. Similar reasoning prevails when we discuss the question '*how* do firms behave?' Sometimes market suppression may extend to the control of households by one huge firm, the state, dictating how much of a commodity must be consumed and at what price. The costs of such an exercise are usually prohibitive and the most that any firm can expect to achieve is control of the price of its product, leaving the amounts purchased at various prices to be determined by consumer preferences.

Markets, as the section introduction suggested, can take various forms and the behaviour of firms within the varying market structures makes a fascinating study. However, before we embark upon it we must first note some of the more general responses of firms to their environment, whatever its nature. This is the aim of this short chapter.

## The firm's objective

Our first task is to decide upon a common motivation for the firms we are to discuss. If we are to make a comparative analysis of firms' market responses then we must assume that they all pursue the same objective. As we saw in Chapter 15 firms may pursue several objectives depending on the desires of the decision-making unit. Fortunately there is one particular objective which most firms pursue although sometimes in a modified form. This common aim is the maximization of the firm's *net worth*, often referred to as 'profit maximization'.

## Net worth

Let us now attempt to define the firm's objective more rigorously. At any point in time a firm holds many things of value, termed *assets*, which enable the firm to produce and sell its commodity. However, although the firm may be in possession of these things it does not necessarily own them all. Some of the things are owned by outsiders (individuals and institutions), having been leased to the firm or sold to it on credit, and these things are termed *liabilities*. Thus, the true value of the firm at any one time is the difference between the values of these two sets of things – the difference between the value of assets and the value of liabilities. The difference is the firm's net worth. A shorthand definition is given by identity 1 set out below, where $W$ represents net worth; $V^A$ represents the value of total assets; and $V^L$ represents the value of total liabilities.

$$W \equiv V^A - V^L. \qquad\qquad 1$$

The accountant's breakdown of the composition of $W$ is given in the firm's balance sheet. Remember from Chapter 12 that the accountant measures costs objectively so that the *true* measure of net worth, which is subjective, is not given by the balance sheet.

It is essential to realize that net worth is a *stock* concept – it relates to the true value of an enterprise at *only one point in time*. Whether or not net worth differs at a future point in time depends upon the activities of the firm in the intervening period. During this interval additions to, or subtractions from, the original net worth will determine the future value of net worth. Thus we can now refine our identity into the form of 2 below, where $W_t$ represents net worth at time point $t$; $W_{t-1}$ represents net worth at time point $t-1$ (i.e. the previous date at which net worth was calculated); and $\Delta W$ represents additions to, or subtractions from, net worth between $t-1$ and $t$.

$$W_t \equiv W_{t-1} + \Delta W,$$

$$\Delta W \equiv W_t - W_{t-1}.$$

**2**

Note that $\Delta W$ is a *flow* concept; it represents the flow of net returns to the firm from its original net worth stock. Clearly then, maximization of net worth also requires maximization of net returns between any two points in time. Consider the firm at time point $t - 1$ with a given net worth stock of $W_{t-1}$. Its future plans are now geared to making $W_t$ as large as possible, an objective which can only be realized by making $\Delta W$ as large as possible.

### Profit as a residual

Before continuing to refine the firm's objective, let us take a closer look at the composition of $\Delta W$. As the firm's net income, or surplus, for a given period, it represents the difference between the value of output for the period and the value of relevant inputs for the period. The alternative term for net income in the present context is the more often employed one of *profit*. Information regarding the firm's performance between two points in time would be given in the profit-and-loss account or 'income statement', but remember that this statement does not measure *true* present values (see Chapter 6). The disadvantage of using the term 'profit' instead of, say, 'net income' is that it does not readily convey the generality of the concept. We have tried to minimize the differences between the various social institutions of production and have acknowledged that the same rules govern the economic activities of them all. Thus a household is a firm and changing the label reflects other institutional arrangements within society rather than any significant differences in economic behaviour. 'Net income' is the better term to maintain this general applicability of economic concepts and it is difficult for those unfamiliar with economics to imagine households aiming to maximize something labelled 'profit'. Yet we have adopted this term since most readers are familiar with it and with its relevance to something called a 'firm'.

We must note that 'profit' has not always meant the same

thing in economic literature and we shall later devote a small chapter (Chapter 25) to the concept. In the meantime let us remember that *our* use of the term is to describe the net income[1] flow which can be enjoyed, for a given period, by *any* social institution of production. The precise definition will be easier recalled if we continue that habit of using shorthand expressions. In identity **3**, then, $P$ represents profit for the given period; $R$ represents total revenue from all goods sold during the period; and $C$ represents the total costs of producing all goods sold during the period.

$$P \equiv R - C. \tag{3}$$

## Present values

Finally, we note that the plans formulated for net-worth maximization are based upon *expected* costs and revenues. It is this fact, above all others, which emphasizes the subjective nature of net worth. Since decisions are made now, but costs and revenues are expected in the future, the latter flows must be discounted to obtain their *present values*. We can, therefore, even further refine the firm's motivation to that of maximizing the present value of future profits. Referring again to identity **2** the objective of the firm at time point $W_{t-1}$ is to maximize the present value of $W_t$, i.e. to maximize the value of

$W_{t-1}$ plus the present value of $\Delta W$.

The object of the firm is to maximize its net present worth and this involves discounting future revenues and costs.

## Long run and short run

At any time the firm's net worth is given, determined by past events; only future events can be influenced. Thus, for the

1. Or, even more generally, 'net benefit', to remind us of the seemingly varied objectives previously referred to. All of these objectives can be collapsed into that of maximizing the utility of the firm's decision-maker(s), this utility being a function of many different things – money profit, sales, prestige, etc.

most part, our study of the firm concerns its market plans. As we saw in Chapter 8, we can distinguish two planning periods – the short-run and the long-run. There is a third production period, the immediate, but this is not really a planning period. Rather, it is a point in time at which all the firm's data, including its net-worth value, is fixed. The short and long-run, however, do refer to planning periods in so far as the firm plans for efficient output operations and estimates the resultant present values of costs and revenues. For the short run, the period during which it is only possible to vary the amounts employed of a few productive resources (labour, raw materials, short-term loans, etc.), present value estimates can be made with some degree of confidence and success rates in achieving short-run targets may be quite high. But the amount of information on which long-run plans are based is necessarily scanty and consequently the planning exercise becomes much more hazardous.

## *Making the best of any circumstances*

It should be made clear that any maximizing principle will be adhered to in both good times and bad times, in other words, the firm always aims to do the best it can in the circumstances. Thus in bad times, when costs outweigh revenues, the firm attempts to *minimize* its losses. In discounting terms we can say that the firm's objective is to maximize any *positive* present value of profit and to minimize any *negative* present value of profit. In some sets of circumstances the price–output choice which achieves the firm's objective will be a relatively simple one: there will be only one combination which guarantees maximum profit or minimum losses. In other circumstances the right price–output strategy may not be so clear-cut, facing the firm with a *range* of possibilities and a strong element of chance enters the decision-making process.

## The golden rule

By 'circumstances' we refer to the type of market in which the firm sells its output; the conditions within that market at the time the firm plans its production and sales programmes; and the prevailing conditions at the time those plans are executed. Generally, as suggested earlier, one would expect any firm to achieve a higher success rate in attempting short-run targets than long-run ones but even the short run is subject to some uncertainty and circumstances may change from day to day. Is there, then, a rule, a guideline, for the firm to follow in order to ensure that it will always be doing the best it can in the circumstances? If such a rule exists then it must in some way combine both the revenue and costs side of the output problem since both sides together determine the firm's net income. Costs, we have seen, refer to foregone benefits. Revenue is determined by the nature of the demand curve for the firm's product since this determines how much the firm can sell and at what price. The nature of the demand curve is, in turn, determined by the characteristics of the market in which the firm sells its product and the position of the firm relative to that of the other firms selling in that market. Such considerations are the subject-matter of the following chapters.

A rule such as that suggested above does exist and it defines a precise relationship between costs and revenues to satisfy the objective. The rule is that the firm should always equate marginal cost with marginal revenue. We know well by now that *marginal cost* is the cost of an additional unit of output and *marginal revenue* is the increase in revenue from an additional unit of output sold.[2] By adjusting output to equate these two marginal-values the firm will always ensure maximum income or minimum losses, depending on circumstances. Figure 104 should make this clear. *MC* represents the firm's marginal-cost curve and *MR* the firm's marginal-revenue curve. Now, assume the firm is currently producing eight units of output. If a ninth unit were to be produced the revenue the firm would receive from the sale of that unit would be greater than the cost of producing it. It is, therefore, in the firm's interest to produce the ninth unit. This is true, in fact, for any output level below ten

2. For the sake of emphasizing the relevance of this rule to *all* social institutions of production the marginal-revenue curve may be interpreted as a curve of *marginal benefits*.

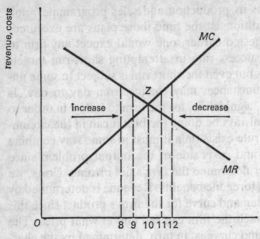

Figure 104

units of output per period

units. However, if the firm is currently producing say eleven or twelve units then it is in the firm's interest to contract output by at least one unit. The resulting reduction in cost will outweigh the resulting loss in revenue. Only when ten units are produced (when $MC = MR$) should the firm maintain a constant rate of output. This reasoning holds even when the firm is making a loss since the size of the loss will then be minimized.

In Figure 104 only the upward sloping part of the marginal-cost curve was drawn because the maximizing rule only applies to output levels in the range referred to by this section of the curve. To be more precise, equating marginal cost and marginal revenue only maximizes the firm's profit flow if the marginal-cost curve is cutting the marginal-revenue curve from *below*. If production is maintained at a level at which the marginal-cost curve cuts the marginal-revenue curve from *above* the firm's profit flow is not being maximized since a unit increase in output will add more to revenue than costs. Figure 105 illustrates this point.

As can be seen from the diagram, for the firm to maintain output at a level of three units, where marginal cost equals marginal revenue when the former is falling (point $A$), it should forego the income which would be generated by the sale of the

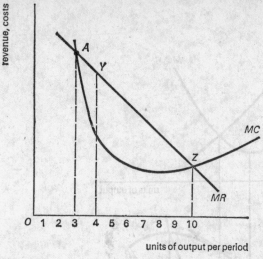

Figure 105

next seven units of output. Each additional unit from the fourth to the tenth adds more to revenue than it does to costs. Income is only being maximized when ten units are being produced, where marginal cost equals marginal revenue and the former is rising (point $Z$ is also the point of intersection in Figure 104). When the firm has reached this output level we say that it is in *equilibrium*; it cannot do any better in the existing circumstances.

*Using total functions.* Sometimes it is useful to represent equilibrium of the firm by the use of *total*-revenue and *total*-cost curves. Figure 106 presents such a situation and it includes a curve of total profits. The corresponding marginal curves are traced out in 106a.

In Figure 106 *TC* is our familiar total-cost curve. *TR* is a total-revenue curve and we know by now that its slope measures marginal revenue.[3] *TP* is a total-profit curve derived as the locus of all the vertical distances (positive and negative) between the

3. Note that since the slope of *TR* flattens as output increases, marginal revenue is falling; and that since the slope of *TC* decreases up to point *W* and then increases, marginal costs are falling prior to the output level given by *W* and afterwards they rise.

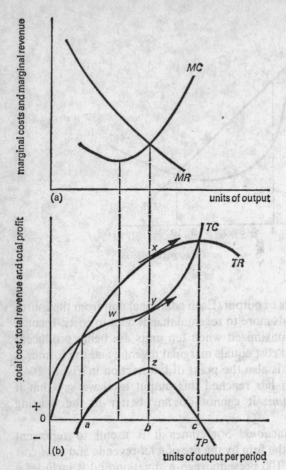

Figure 106

total-cost and total-revenue curves. Thus, when output is less than *Oa*, and total revenue is less than total cost, total profit is negative (the *TP* curve falls below the horizontal axis). Total profit is again negative when intended output exceeds *c* units; and in between output levels *a* and *c* total profit is positive. It can be seen from the *TP* function that profit is greatest at output level *b*. At this level of output total profit is *bz*, equal to the greatest vertical distance, *xy*, between the *TR* and *TC* curves.

It can also be seen that at this level of output *the slopes of the TR and TC curves are equal* – the curves are parallel at points *x* and *y*. In other words, at output level *b* marginal cost (given by the slope of *TC*) is equal to marginal revenue (given by the slope of *TR*) – *b* satisfies the golden rule. (Those readers who persevered with the 'mathematical interlude' should now turn to the appendix to the present chapter.)

## When to shut down

In the analysis so far it has been suggested that by following the maximizing rule the firm's profit would be as great as possible under favourable market circumstances *or* the firm's losses would be as small as possible when the market situation is not favourable. This latter observation begs the question of why a profit-maximizing enterprise is prepared to remain in the industry when it is making a loss, albeit one which is being minimized? The firm's owners will only choose to keep their assets in their current use if the return from doing so is at least as great as could be obtained in their best alternative use. This necessary return is sometimes referred to as 'normal profit', a somewhat misleading term since it refers to one of the firm's costs. (Chapter 25 discusses the concept in more detail.) If the firm's owners are not currently receiving this minimum and yet their assets stay put, this must mean that future circumstances are expected to be so favourable as to render net returns over the long run at least as large as could be earned elsewhere. The firm may expect either a shift in market demand and hence a rise in market price, or a fall in costs of production; either of these two changes would reduce losses and possibly turn them into a surplus. Such optimism may be quite blind or it may be founded in the firm's ability to change market circumstances. Depending on the nature of the market, some firms may be able to influence the price at which their product sells, others may have no choice but to accept a market-determined price over which they, as individual enterprises, have no control. Similarly with respect to inputs, some firms may be able to influence the prices at which they buy their productive agents while others must accept such prices as given. This important concept of market power is the basis of the following two chapters.

Even when the future is viewed optimistically a firm is only able to ride a short-run loss if the condition is met that running (variable) costs are being covered. Since fixed costs must be met even if the firm shuts down, it is in the firm's interest to continue production as long as it is covering such items as wages and raw-material bills. Indeed, shutting down itself involves costs which may prevent the firm ever recommencing operations. Not only does shutting down require the employment of security patrols or alternative protective measures for idle plant, it may also mean other substantial opportunity costs such as foregone good-will, and loss of a market foothold as consumers switch to available substitutes. We are now prepared for a discussion of the response of firms to specific market situations. Before doing so let us remind ourselves of some of the general points made in this chapter.

## Summary

1 We are assuming that over the long run firms attempt to maximize their *net worth*.

2 Net worth is a *stock* concept since it relates to a point in time. (Remember that the balance sheets of firms do not measure net worth, and that net worth must somehow be gleaned from the directors' statements about the future as well as past performances.)

3 The change in net worth between two points is determined by the amount of net revenue or profit earned by the firm during the interval. Thus, profit is a *flow* concept and is defined as the difference between the expected total revenue from the goods sold during the period and the expected total costs of producing all goods sold during the period.

4 It follows from the first three points that over the short run firms try to maximize their profit flows in present value terms (but remember that the income statements of firms do not measure these as such).

5 Maximizing profits is synonymous with minimizing losses when the market situation is not conducive to gains being made.

6 The profit-maximizing (loss-minimizing) guideline is *marginal revenue = marginal cost*. Output should not increase, in any given set of circumstances, beyond the level at which this equality is satisfied on the upward sloping section of the marginal-cost curve. When the firm is satisfying this condition it is in short-run equilibrium.

7 Firms may be prepared to maintain production in the face of short-run losses as long as expectations are optimistic and variable costs are being covered.

8 The short-run decision concerns price whereas the long-run decision involves investment. Short and long run are linked by expectations which determine whether or not net present value is positive.

## Questions

1 A University exists to promote teaching and research. How would you assess the efficiency of a University? Are teaching and research substitutes or complements? Can the golden rule be applied to these objectives?

2 How will a multi-plant firm or a multi-product firm ensure the efficiency of its different activities?

3 A newspaper produces 'news' and 'adverts'. What factors will determine the mix of 'news' and 'adverts'?

4 A firm donates annually to various charities. Is this compatible with the golden rule?

5 Can the golden rule be applied to the activities of the following:
(a) A hospital?
(b) A police station?

6 What is meant by net worth?

7 What are stocks and flows?

8(a) How will a businessman decide whether to work his plant on one or two shifts?

(b) When will a town and regional planner decide to build a new town instead of expanding an existing one?

(c) What factors determine the number of teams in the Football League?

(d) A group of firms decide to form a cartel. What factors will determine which plants are closed down or their output reduced or expanded?

## Appendix: the calculus of the golden rule

Using the calculus we can now calculate, for given total-cost and total-revenue functions, the profit-maximizing level of output. We can employ one of two methods of calculation.

### Method 1

Consider Figure 106 of this chapter. When profit is maximized the slope of the *TP* curve is zero, i.e. the first derivative of the total-profit function is zero. This fact enables us to find the profit-maximizing output level.

*Procedure.* Suppose we have the following total-revenue $R$ and total-cost $C$ functions:

$$R = 300Q - 6Q^2,$$
$$C = 400 + 3Q^2 + 30Q,$$

then total profit $P$ is given by

$$P = R - C,$$
$$= (300Q - 6Q^2) - (400 + 3Q^2 + 30Q),$$
$$= 270Q - 9Q^2 - 400.$$

Profit is maximized when $dP/dQ = 0$, (and when $d^2P/dQ^2 < 0$), i.e.

$$d/dQ(270Q - 9Q^2 - 400) = 0,$$
which gives $\quad 270 - 18Q = 0,$
$$\text{or } 18Q = 270.$$
$$\text{Thus} \quad Q = 15.$$

The profit-maximizing level of output is fifteen units. (Check that the second derivative is negative.)

### Method 2

Profits are maximized when marginal revenue is equal to marginal cost and when the marginal-cost curve cuts the marginal-revenue curve from below, i.e. when the second derivative of the total-cost function is positive.

*Procedure.* Marginal revenue is given by $dR/dQ$ and marginal cost by $dC/dQ$.

$$\frac{dR}{dQ} = 300 - 12Q,$$

and $\frac{dC}{dQ} = 6Q + 30.$

1 Let $\quad \frac{dR}{dQ} = \frac{dC}{dQ},$

then $300 - 12Q = 6Q + 30,$

$\qquad\qquad 18Q = 270,$

$\qquad$ and $\quad Q = 15.$

2 $\frac{d^2R}{dQ^2} = -12,$

$\quad \frac{d^2C}{dQ^2} = 6.$

Marginal cost equals marginal revenue when output is 15. Confirmation that this output maximizes profit is given by the fact that the second derivative of the total-revenue function is negative while the second derivative of the total-cost function is positive.

Perhaps as a final reminder we should work backwards through our example. What we have shown is that when output is fifteen units, profits are maximized since the first derivative of the total-profit function is then zero. Furthermore at this level of output marginal cost is equal to marginal revenue (and marginal costs are rising), i.e. when the first derivative of the total-profit function is zero, marginal cost equals marginal revenue. To summarize, we can present the rule in more general form:

$$P \equiv R - C,$$

where $P$ represents profit; $R$ represents total revenue; and $C$ represents total costs. Using $Q$ to denote quantity, $R = R(Q)$ and $C = C(Q)$, therefore $P = P(Q)$. When profit is maximized (the profit function is at a maximum) the first derivative of the profit function is zero and the second derivative is negative.

$$\frac{dP}{dQ} = 0, \left( \frac{d^2P}{dQ^2} < 0 \right),$$

$$P = R - C,$$

$$\frac{dP}{dQ} = \frac{dR}{dQ} - \frac{dC}{dQ},$$

and when $\dfrac{dP}{dQ} = 0,$

$$\frac{dR}{dQ} = \frac{dC}{dQ},$$

i.e. marginal revenue equals marginal cost.

# Chapter 18
# Perfect Competition

We begin our survey of the structures of markets in which private goods and services are sold by considering *perfect competition*. There are two good reasons for commencing with this model. Firstly, the study of perfect competition provides the best possible synthesis of basic economic concepts. Secondly, this model epitomizes the idea of a free market, to which we have referred on several occasions, by considering a host of apparently complex economic relationships, stripping them of their irrelevancies and revealing their underlying, clockwork simplicity.

Not only does the perfectly competitive model make positive predictions but it also has enormous normative implications. The normative aspects of perfect competition were uppermost in the minds of the early writers on economics. For economic philosophers like Adam Smith, the destruction of monopoly privileges and the enlargement of the sphere of market competition was the means towards greater personal liberty as well as increased efficiency. Such considerations are just as important for the latter half of the twentieth century. Political freedom is dependent upon economic freedom and many economists are emphatic in their definition of which economic system best maximizes political freedom – competitive capitalism.[1]

But of all concepts freedom is the most relative and it can only be defined according to the confines of personal experi-

1. A most cleverly argued exposition of this viewpoint is presented by Professor Milton Friedman of the University of Chicago (Friedman, 1962).

ence. By 'economic freedom' economists usually refer to freedom to buy and sell goods and services. Absolute economic freedom prevails when any individual may buy (and sell) what he wants, where he wants and when he wants. To many this does not spell freedom but misery – many goods are socially harmful and how do those with nothing to sell survive? The normative debate hinges on such issues and concerns the 'proper' role of the State. We intend to consider this debate later but first we must study in some depth that theoretical state of the world which is the nearest thing devised by economists to the conditions for absolute economic freedom.

## The assumptions of perfect competition

1 Producers aim to maximize their profits (as explained in the previous chapter) and consumers are interested in maximizing their utility.

2 There are a large number of actual and *potential* buyers and sellers.

3 All actual and potential buyers and sellers have perfect knowledge of all existing opportunities to buy and sell.

4 Although tastes differ, buyers are generally indifferent among all units of the commodity offered for sale, i.e. they view all units of the product as homogeneous.

5 Factors of production are perfectly mobile.

6 Productive processes are perfectly divisible, that is, constant returns to scale prevail.

7 Only pure private goods are bought and sold.

Having previously discussed the implications of maximizing behaviour we commence our analysis of these assumptions by considering the second one.

### Equal distribution of market power

Our second assumption implies that the number of actual and potential sellers is so large that it has a twofold effect. Firstly, neither the output of any existing seller, nor the potential output of any individual seller outside the market is great enough, relative to industry output, to affect the market price of the product. Secondly, collusive agreements among existing sellers, buyers, or between both sides of the market, to exert an influence over price, are precluded by the massive costs of seeking out traders of a like mind and of policing any agreement once arrived at. We might also note that the existence of a large number of potential entrants, albeit an uncoordinated mass, substantiates the first effect by even further precluding collusion among existing firms. This latter point is explained in the next paragraph.

## The attraction for new entrants

Part of the rationale behind the collusive checks also relates to our first assumption. Temporarily disregarding transaction costs, suppose the hundred or so producers in the sugar plum industry come to an agreement to restrict output in order to raise the price of sugar plums and hence raise their incomes. On our reasoning the industry would be swamped by hundreds of new producers entering the industry, *attracted by higher rewards than they could earn elsewhere*. The existing collusive arrangements would collapse as the price of sugar plums fell.

## Why entrance is easy

New firms are able to enter the industry so easily because there are no barriers to prevent them. This demonstrates the importance of assumptions 5 and 6. The fifth assumption refers to the absence of restrictions on the mobility of any productive agent and is self-explanatory.[2] Assumption 6 is equally important regarding entry to the industry but perhaps requires further explanation. It is often the case that engineering technology or

2. Note for readers who do not find this obvious: restrictions could range from family or neighbourhood ties, or loss of pension rights, in the case of workers, to the existence of patent or licensing laws in the case of innovations.

merely the confines of space necessitates the use of 'lumpy' inputs. For example transport systems require the construction of roads, railways and bridges. Such objects cannot be provided in little pieces, yet to provide more than one railway between London and Glasgow, or more than one bridge across the Humber estuary, may result in all of them running at a loss. Similarly, if cinemas can only be built in 200-seat sizes but there are 201 regular cinema-goers (at any price) in the locality then either two cinemas must be operated at well below their capacity, or there will always be at least one disappointed cinema-goer. In such situations, then, competition may be impossible and the product can only be provided under conditions of monopoly. We return to these questions in the following chapter and in our later discussion on the state.

### When to enter

Not only can new firms easily enter the perfectly competitive market but our third assumption ensures that they always know exactly when the time is ripe for doing so. Perfect knowledge means that potential entrants know immediately of a change in market circumstances which will yield them better rewards than can be earned elsewhere.

### A homogeneous product

The assumptions so far discussed also rule out collusive arrangements on the buyers' side of the market and the possibility of any concessionary price agreements between buyers and sellers. The assumption of perfect knowledge plays an extra role by linking up with assumption 4 to help further define the nature of the market. This makes reference to the tastes of consumers who regard all units of the industry's product as identical. Since we are also assuming perfect knowledge on both sides of the market all firms know their consumers' tastes and if one firm decides to produce a product slightly different to that of the other firms it can only be for a different market. In other words, product differentiation results in the market splitting up into several different competitive markets. A competitive market is therefore circumscribed by a gap in the chain of product substitutability.

## The absence of spillovers

The final assumption is designed to rule out spillovers. No one receives extra benefits or suffers nuisances unless he purchases them. If Smith can benefit from Jones' possession of a radio and Jones can similarly benefit if Smith owns one then each will hope that the other buys a radio and refrain from purchasing one himself – neither enjoys the benefits of a radio. Spillovers may also create nuisances. These are equally ruled out by assumption 7. Factories cannot dump smoke on people unless they pay the latter for the privilege of doing so, or unless there are people of perverse tastes who want to purchase smoke.

## The firm's short-run decision

The perfectly competitive firm is often referred to as a *price-taker/quantity adjuster*. The firm's course of action is dictated by forces outside its control, i.e. by the industry. It is industry supply matched against market demand which determines the price at which the individual firm can sell its output. Each firm must accept the market price as something given and unchangeable by individual action – the market is the 'price-marker'; each firm is a 'price-taker'. This means that although the market-demand curve slopes downwards (for reasons outlined in Chapter 7) the demand curve which faces the individual firm is horizontal, i.e. perfectly elastic. Since there is only one price which clears the market and every buyer (and seller) knows it, the firm can sell all it wants to at that price. If the firm charges a higher price, then no one buys its product: and what is the point of charging a price below that which is offered? Assuming the firm decides to produce, the only remaining decision is how much to produce in order to maximize profit. Given the circumstances of perfect competition this is very much a production engineering problem. The output decision is demonstrated by Figures 107a

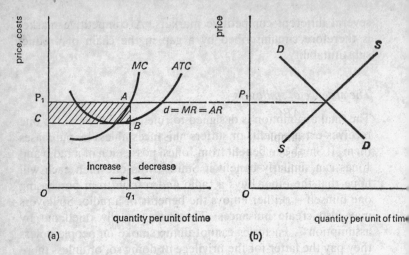

Figure 107 (a) The firm. (b) The market

and 107b. For purposes of exposition the diagrams for firm and market have been laid side by side, but remember that the scale along the horizontal axis differs greatly in each case.

The diagram shows the link between firm and industry and re-emphasizes the absence of a marketing problem. Market equilibrium is established at a price of $OP_1$ per unit of output. Remember that the firm can sell all it wants to at this price, as shown by the perfectly elastic demand curve $d$. As we saw in Chapter 7 this curve is also the firm's, marginal-revenue curve since each additional unit sold yields the same revenue (i.e. the market price) as all previous units. Thus, given price $OP_1$ the firm produces and sells $q_1$ units of the product thereby equating price (marginal revenue) with marginal cost. As we saw in the previous chapter, $Oq_1$ is the short-run equilibrium output since even a very small change in the number of units produced and sold would prevent the firm from maximizing profit. The actual size of the profit generated by the sale of output $Oq_1$ is shown by the shaded area $P_1ABC$ in Figure 107a. If this is not obvious recall identity **3** of the previous chapter:

$$P \equiv R - C.$$

In the example of Figure 107a total revenue $R$ is equal to $OP_1Oq_1$ (units sold multiplied by market price per unit); and $C$, total cost, is equal to $OC.Oq_1$ (units sold multiplied by average total costs of producing these units). Thus we may write

$$P = OP_1.Oq_1 - OC.Oq_1,$$
$$= \text{area } P_1 ABC.$$

Our initial example has depicted the firm as earning a surplus over costs, these costs including the return necessary to keep the assets of the firm's owners in that particular industry; the owner's transfer earnings or 'normal profit'. There is no guarantee that this is the short-run norm in such a market. It is quite conceivable that the firm may not be able to do more than cover total costs or, worse, only variable costs, in the short run. Both possibilities are depicted in Figures 108 and 109.

In Figure 109 the short-run market price is so low that the firm cannot earn a surplus. Again, the firm is doing the best it can and achieves equilibrium at output $Oq_2$ where price equals marginal cost. In this case however total revenue ($OP_2.Oq_2$) is just sufficient to cover total costs since marginal cost is also equal to minimum average total cost at the equilibrium level of output. In this situation the owners of the firm receive no sur-

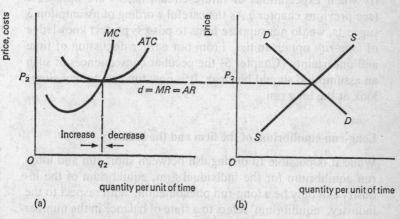

Figure 108 (a) The firm. (b) The market

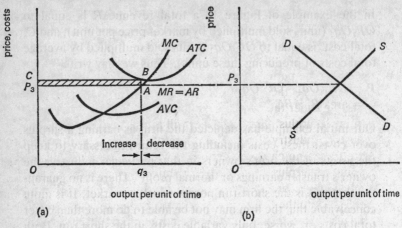

Figure 109 (a) The firm. (b) The market

plus above the amount they require to induce them to stay in the industry. In Figure 109a the firm cannot cover total costs but *is* covering variable costs. Again the firm does the best it can which in the circumstances means minimizing losses to the size of the area $P_3ABC$.

Remember that the covering of variable costs induces the firm to remain in production but it will only remain in the industry when expectations of future circumstances are optimistic (see previous chapter.) As the careful wording of assumption 3 suggests, we do not suppose firms to possess perfect knowledge of *long-run* opportunities. From our earlier discussion of time and uncertainty (Chapter 5) the peculiar consequences of such an assumption should be clear. It is now time we took a closer look at the long run.

## Long-run equilibrium of the firm and the industry

While it is possible to distinguish between short-run and long-run equilibrium for the individual firm, equilibrium of the industry can only be a long-run phenomenon. With respect to the industry, 'equilibrium' refers to a state of balance in the number of firms comprising the industry, that is, a state in which firms are neither entering nor leaving the industry. Obviously, the individual firm only achieves long-run equilibrium when this state is simultaneously reached by the industry.

Of the three possible short-run equilibrium positions we depicted for the perfectly competitive firm, only one is tenable in the long run – the one in which the firm is just covering total costs. Consider the first case we looked at, in which the firm is earning a surplus. Such surpluses will attract new firms into the industry. Industry supply will therefore increase and market price (given no change in demand) will fall. As price falls the amount of surplus which each firm enjoys will diminish; but as long as some profit remains new firms will continue to be attracted into the industry. The incentive for new firms to enter only disappears when price has been driven down to the level at which firms are just covering costs (the situation represented by Figure 108).

Consider the third situation, in which firms are making losses. If expectations turn out to have been unduly optimistic and these losses are sustained for a period of time, firms will leave the industry. Industry supply will therefore contract and market price will rise. However, as long as losses are being made firms will continue to leave the industry until market price is driven up to the level at which costs are being covered (Figure 108 again).

It appears, therefore, that the only long-run equilibrium position for the firm is the one in which it operates at minimum average cost and the owners of the enterprise do not earn any profit, any surplus over and above the amount required to induce them to remain in the industry.

## Supply curves

Our analysis of equilibrium behaviour gives some interesting clues about the nature of the supply curves of both the firm and the industry under perfectly competitive conditions. The industry-supply curve is particularly interesting but let us begin with the short run and try to build up slowly the long-run supply picture.

*Short-run supply curve of the firm.* The task of constructing the firm's short-run supply curve is made relatively simple by the nature of the market. As we saw in Chapter 8 a firm's supply curve shows how much a firm is willing or intends to supply at different market prices. As such the supply curve is an *ex ante* concept relating to output *plans* based on information concerning *expected* market prices. Now, given a set of expected market prices, we can immediately predict the output plans of the perfectly competitive firm since we know that such a firm will always aim at equating price with marginal cost. In other words, once information regarding costs has been collected and the firm's marginal-cost curve is constructed we have the firm's supply curve uniquely determined. The firm's supply curve is that section of the marginal-cost curve which lies above the curve of average variable costs, since the firm will not produce unless variable costs are being covered. Figure 110 illustrates this conclusion for a given set of costs.

Figure 110 illustrates the firm's cost structure, $AVC$ being the curve of average variable costs and $MC$ the marginal-cost curve. Figure 110 represents the firm's supply curve, point $A$ corresponding to point $A$ in (a). When the price is as low as $OP_1$ the best that the firm can possibly do is to produce $Oq_1$ units of output. Such an output would not yield sufficient revenue to cover variable costs and so the firm would not plan to produce any-

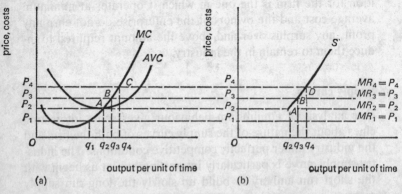

(a)

(b)

output per unit of time

output per unit of time

Figure 110

thing at this price. Only when the price rises to $OP_2$ is the firm prepared to commence production, producing $Oq_2$ to equate marginal cost with price. Thus point $A$ is the first point on the firm's supply curve showing that at a price of $OP_2$ the firm would plan to sell $Oq_2$ units. For any price above $OP_2$ the firm is always prepared to produce, hence, at price $P_3$, planned output is $Oq_3$ giving point $B$ on the supply curve; and at price $OP_4$ planned output is $Oq_4$ giving point $C$ on the supply curve. Thus the marginal cost curve from point $A$ upwards is also the firm's supply curve.

## The industry-supply curve

To construct the industry-supply curve we must underline the important distinction between *ex ante* and *ex post* supply curves. The *ex ante* supply curve refers to the intentions of the firms in the industry to produce certain quantities at given levels of market price, i.e. any point on the supply curve relates a market price to the quantity which the industry *intends to supply* at that price. The *ex post* supply curve relates to what the industry *actually does supply* in response to market prices.

*The ex ante supply curve.* The *ex ante* industry-supply curve, as we saw in Chapter 8, is a horizontal summation of the supply curves of individual firms. In a perfectly competitive industry this curve constitutes a horizontal summing of the marginal cost curves of existing firms, since, as we have already explained in detail, the firm's marginal-cost curve also represents the firm's willingness to supply at various prices. Figure 111 illustrates the construction of the *ex ante* curve.

Figure 111 attempts to simplify the demonstration by considering the supply curves of only two firms; the principle holds no matter how many producers. $MC_A$ and $MC_B$ represents the respective marginal-cost curves of firms $A$ and $B$. $A^*$ and $B^*$ refer to the respective points of minimum average variable costs. Now, at a market price of $OP_1$ firm $A$ would intend to sell $a_1$ and firm $B$ would intend to sell $b_1$ – both aiming to equate marginal cost with price. Intended market supply would thus be

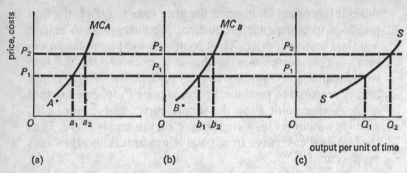

Figure 111(a) Firm *A*. (b) Firm *B*. (c) Intended market supply

$a_1 + b_1 (= OQ_1)$. At a higher price of $OP_2$ firm *A* would intend to produce $a_2$ and firm *B* $b_2$ giving a total of $a_2 + b_2 (= OQ_2)$ intended units for the market. The market curve, *SS*, would be flatter the greater the number of firms.

*The ex post curve.* A supply curve for the industry such as that drawn above never materializes *ex post* since not only do existing firms respond to price rises but so do potential firms, i.e. firms as yet outside the industry. As we saw earlier, as soon as price rises above the level of average total costs so that each firm earns a surplus, then new firms will enter the industry attracted by rewards which are higher than they can earn elsewhere. This will mean that existing firms will be intending to increase supply according to their marginal-cost curves but at the same time the *industry*-supply curve will also be shifting to the right as more units come onto the market, supplied by new entrants. Thus existing firms never realize their original expectations and intentions since market price moves from the level on which they based their original output plans, that is, *the* ex post *industry-supply curve does not coincide with the* ex ante *supply curve.*

The actual shape of the *ex post* industry-supply curve depends upon the availability of resources to the industry. If the supply curve of resources to the industry is perfectly elastic then the *ex post* supply curve of the industry's output will also be perfectly elastic; if the resources-supply curve is upward sloping then so will be the industry product-supply curve. In the former case cost conditions within the industry are unchanged as the size of the industry and its output expand, whereas in the latter case resource prices rise as the industry expands causing an upward shift in the firm's cost curves. The two cases are illustrated in Figure 112.

*Case 1 Constant costs.* There are of course many firms already in the industry but we are looking at one, firm $A$, for simplicity. At the existing market price of $OP_1$ firm $A$ will intend to supply $Oq_1$ units to maximize income. Suppose now that market price rises (as the result of a shift in demand to $D_2D_2$) to $OP_5$. At this high price firm $A$ wants to produce $Oq_1$ and hence earn a surplus over production costs. But at the same time this potential surplus is an incentive to new firms to enter the industry. Now, as new firms do enter, market supply increases, i.e. the market-supply curve $S'$ $S'$ shifts to the right. Thus firm $A$ never actually does produce quantity $Oq_5$ since market price $OP_5$ does not hold sufficiently long enough for $A$ to realize its output plans. As long as existing firms can earn the surplus, new firms will enter the industry. Consequently market supply continues to shift to the right, as shown by the movement from $S_1'$ $S_1'$ to $S_2'$ $S_2'$ to $S_3'$ $S_3'$ in Figure 112 until market price is re-established at its original level of $OP_1$. Once price has returned to this level the

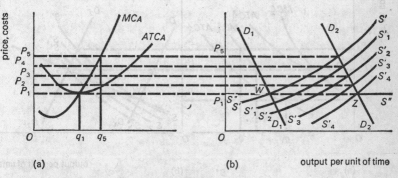

Figure 112(a) Firm $A$. (b) Market supply

incentive to new firms to enter the industry is removed. Points *W* and *Z* must, therefore, lie on the *ex post* supply-curve of the industry. Any tendency for market price to diverge from a level of $OP_1$, whether it be a rise or fall in price, is completely offset by a change in the number of firms in the industry and hence in the number of product units supplied to the market. If market price rises from $OP_1$ new firms enter the industry and market supply is increased. If market price falls below $OP_1$ (e.g. as a result of a *fall* in demand) then firms leave the industry and the resulting supply contraction drives up the price of $OP_1$ again. The industry long-run supply curve is thus perfectly elastic.

*Case 2 Rising costs*. In the above analysis we implicitly assumed that as new firms entered the industry nothing happened to existing cost conditions, i.e. the increased pressure of demand on productive resources did not cause a rise in resource prices. This could only mean that the demand of the industry for resources was extremely small in relation to the total demand for resources. In other words, we were assuming that the supply of resources was perfectly elastic. In Figure 113 we consider the case where the supply curve of resources is upward-sloping so that any increased demand for the use of productive resources by the industry results in a rise in the price of resources.

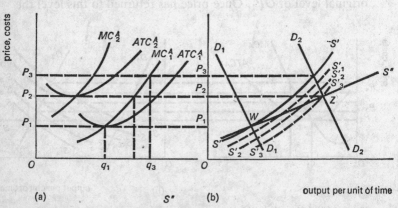

Figure 113(a) Firm *A*. (b) Market supply

Again, we assume that initially market price is at $OP$, at which level firm $A$ intends to produce $Oq_1$ and that this initial price is disturbed as the result of a rise in demand causing market price to rise to $OP_1$. At this new price firm $A$ intends to supply $Oq_3$ thereby earning a profit. This potential profit attracts new entrants which causes the industry-supply curve to shift to the right and depresses the market price below $OP_3$. However, this time price does not fall to its original level since the incentive for firms to enter the industry is removed at a much earlier stage as a result of a rise in the price of resources (due to the resultant demand pressure in the resource market), causing a rise in total costs. This rise in total costs, depicted by the vertical shift in the cost curves, means that the firm's surplus is eroded much earlier than it was in the first example. Market price settles at a new level which is higher than the original one but not as high as it would have been in the absence of new entrants to the industry. In our example the price settles at $OP_2$; and $W$ and $Z$ are both points on the upward sloping *ex post* industry-supply curve.

*Case 3 Falling costs*. Can there be a third case of falling costs? Our first reaction might be to dismiss such a possibility on the grounds that if firms regard a downward-sloping cost curve as a planning curve monopoly must inevitably result. This is where the distinction between *ex ante* and *ex post* becomes all import ant. If decreasing costs are to be compatible with perfect competition the downward-sloping supply curve can only be an *ex post* phenomenon – each individual firm continues to plan on the basis of its short-run marginal-cost curve. A falling industry-supply curve is illustrated in Figure 114 where $W$ and $Z$ represents two points on the curve.

The notion that an increase in output can be associated with falling costs goes back into the nineteenth century. In that period economists believed that agriculture was subject to diminishing returns (increasing costs) whereas manufacturing experienced increasing returns (diminishing costs). There is, of course, a grain of truth in this assertion. The dependence of agriculture upon climate means that its different operations

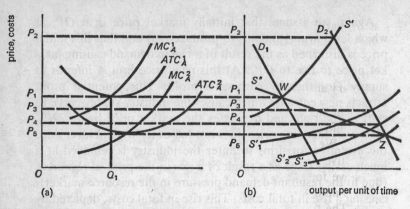

Figure 114(a) Firm *A*. (b) Market supply

cannot be operated simultaneously: they must be operated in sequence. In manufacturing there is no dependence on climate, and operations can be carried out in parallel *and* round the clock. There is less of a possibility of the co-existence of fixed factors in one operation and excess factors in another in manufacturing. There is also the possibility of more homogeneity of resources in manufacturing than when recourse has to be made to land.

Even if manufacturing industry was subject to increasing returns was it still possible to reconcile this with the existence of competition? Suppose one firm, by accident, received a lucky start, might it not quickly reap the scale economies, sliding down its average cost curve, buying up its competitors and creating a state of monopoly? Two sorts of answers were produced to deal with this problem. First, it was argued that the scope for increasing returns was extremely limited – in particular, firms would rapidly hit the bottleneck of a fixed management factor. This was an attempt to limit internal economies of scale. Secondly, it was allowed that all firms together might experience falling costs even though each individually was powerless to affect prices and costs. This was a reference to *external* economies of scale. Suppose that the industry expands in response to a price rise from an increase in market demand (Figure 114). As expansion takes place a reorganization of existing factor markets and of existing production functions may occur. This reorganization may reduce costs for *all* firms.[3]

## Summary and concluding remarks

In concluding this preliminary discussion of perfect competition we should remind ourselves of its social and political implications. We have tried to explore the conditions under which no productive institution enjoys an unequal share of market power and have found them to be most stringent; so stringent as to require modification if meant to provide us with a policy blueprint. The trouble with modified versions is that they tend to open the floodgates to a host of institutional problems which unrelentingly dog our efforts to construct the 'good society'.

The model yields two potential benefits – over the long run all firms produce at full capacity (minimum average cost) and consumers face a price per unit for a commodity which is just equal to the cost to any firm of producing that unit (marginal cost). Society would appear to receive maximum gains from the use of its resources and these gains are maintained by the checks of the market system which enforce firms to operate with maximum competence at all times in order to survive.

Against the potential benefits we must weigh the fact that there are many goods whose benefits would not be enjoyed in such a system. This is either because no one can obtain sole

3. This point is a very tricky one. If the reader can accept that 'somehow' reorganization takes place, all well and good. If not, then finding an example is exceedingly difficult. The following might suffice. Suppose that as a result of the initial expansion of market opportunities labour resources consider it worthwhile investing in new skills. This investment was not previously worthwhile since the scope for utilizing such skills was non-existent. Labour resources then offer these skills equally to all firms in the industry. As a consequence each firm reorganizes at the same time and costs for *all* fall by the same amount. The cost reductions are external to the firm but internal to the industry.

The notion of economies unattainable by an individual firm but attainable by the industry (the collection of firms) has led some writers to suggest that subsidies should be granted to such industries to allow these benefits to be realized. This proposal is an alternative to the creation of 'natural' monopolies which may internalize any benefits (as discussed in the following chapter).

property rights to the goods – the case of collective goods; or because the production of the goods involves indivisibilities. As we saw in Chapter 2 alternative arrangements to the market have to be made for the allocation of resources to particular goods like education, typhoid vaccinations, national defence, blood, etc. Furthermore, the competitive system is neutral and impersonal in doling out its rewards. A society accepting the free market system, because of its alleged efficiency *vis-à-vis* private goods, would be required simultaneously to accept the resultant distribution of incomes. Few societies have been prepared to go this far and alternative distributional arrangements have been devised.

The choice for society is not whether to embrace or to reject perfect competition. Rather, the important problem is how to devise a system which gleans the best features of the perfectly competitive model while avoiding the worst. Depending on the political and social values of the society concerned the adopted compromise may closely resemble the pure model of perfect competition or look more like the model of power which we discuss in the following chapters.

# Chapter 19
# Monopoly

We turn now to the opposite end of the market spectrum, to where competition does not exist. But where, one might ask, was the competition in the previous case? There was no price cutting on the part of individual firms; no advertising; no intrigue with some rivals in order to plot the downfall of others (collusive price cuts, buying up scarce factor supplies, etc.). It was precisely because competition was so 'perfect' that such activities were not undertaken. Remember that in such a market the individual firm wields no market power, it cannot influence the market price in any way. All firms are thus inward-looking and passive; taking the market price as given, they concentrate upon maximizing profits at that price. The most that any one firm can do to try and guarantee long-run existence is to keep an ever-watchful eye on costs of production – if it fails to do this then there is no possible price increase to save it.

In vivid contrast to this picture is the one in which all market power is concentrated in one source. Imagine a market in which there is only one seller; constrained only by the tastes and incomes of consumers this single enterprise has direct control over market price and can flood or starve the market of supplies according to its whims and objectives. If we further postulate that no new firms may ever enter the industry then, assuming no drastic changes in demand conditions, the position of the single seller appears impregnable, no rivals within the industry and no potential rivals without. Such a situation is usually described as *pure monopoly*, one firm constitutes the industry and that firm's demand curve is the market demand curve (downward-sloping), i.e. the firm can fix output or price, but not both simultaneously.

## Why monopoly?

Monopoly can arise through a variety of causes:

1 *Natural causes.* Some monopolies may arise either through the possession of land containing particular minerals, spa water or a desirable location. Other monopolies may reflect freakish ability – Maria Callas's voice; George Best's feet.

2 *Licensing.* The state may permit certain monopolies to exist or create them through its licensing laws. Typical of these are laws which restrict the number of pubs and newsagents within a given area; allow only the Post Office to deliver mail or the Central Electricity Generating Board to produce electricity; allow trade unions the right to strike and permit certain people to call themselves members of a profession. Let us consider the last two. It is extremely doubtful whether trade unions would be able to raise the wages of their members were they not able to picket and harass employers.[1] The right to strike and its associated weaponry of boycott, social ostracism of non-unionists and non-strikers and sympathetic strikes by other unions are very powerful weapons with which to lever up wages. Why then does the state permit unions? The answer seems to be the failure of the state to accept that income determination and income distribution should be functions of the state and should not be left to the vagaries of the market. In the absence of state intervention what happens is that the state permits unions to exercise some kind of countervailing power against employers. Unfortunately, unions may do relatively little for workers who are not union members, or for those who do not work, e.g. retirement pensioners.

1. Unions had this ability to harass employers in the days before trade-union legislation was passed because the law was not rigorously enforced. For a good account see Aspinall (1949).

Slightly more sophisticated than the trade unions of manual and white-collar workers are the professions – medicine, architecture, accountancy, the law, etc. Groups of workers in these professions are permitted to use particular titles in notifying the public that their services are available. Others can carry out similar services but they are not permitted to use the titles granted by the state. A man might practise medicine but if he has not been dubbed a doctor he may be considered a 'quack'. What is the reasoning behind professional licensing? The answer seems to be to protect the health, safety and morals of the public against incompetents and sharks. The public is not knowledgeable, consumer sovereignty is a myth. Therefore, the state allows the public to delegate decisions concerning health, safety and morals to others and indicates who the 'others' might be. However, the professions can sometimes behave like trade unionists or indeed any monopolists. They may control entry to the profession by insisting upon lengthy training, high entrance fees and high failure rates in examinations.

3 *Indivisibilities*. Indivisibilities are due to 'lumpiness' or discontinuities in the production process. It is impossible to have half a bridge, road or canal. One cinema in a town may earn its owner a handsome return; two cinemas would impoverish both owners if the demand was great enough for one cinema but insufficient for two. Indivisibilities are associated with economies of scale. If demand reaches a particular level then new techniques of production – mass production, buying – may be employed. Instead of constant returns to scale there may be increasing returns. We have two possibilities:

(a) Perfect divisibility – each production process can be replicated. If one plant can produce 500 units then two plants can each produce 500 units.

(b) Increasing returns – one plant can produce 500 units. With the finance available to produce 1000 units building a new plant using different production processes and 1500 units might be produced.

The kind of market structure resulting from indivisibilities depends upon demand. If demand for the product is low then only one firm may exist in the industry. However as demand increases other large firms enter and when a few firms co-exist in an industry the market structure is termed an *oligopoly*.

*How important are indivisibilities and the related economies of scale?* Clearly there is no point in going into detail on the nature and implications of indivisibilities if they are unimportant. Surprisingly little work has been done on this subject.

## Private sector indivisibilities

Table 31 reveals three approaches to the question of how important are plant indivisibilities and economies of scale in determining ease of entry and survival in industries in the private sector. Each has its limitations. The engineering approach tends to be simplistic and to overlook the impact upon market demand and the reactions of rivals. When a newcomer enters a market, output will expand and, depending upon the elasticity of demand, price will fall and profits may be affected. The survivor technique goes to the other extreme and overlooks the possibility that survival may be due to monopoly practices. For the outsider the crucial problem may be how long does he have to 'hang on' in order to survive – this is what the survival method tries to throw light upon. The third approach is to consider the size of plant which an established firm will choose to introduce if it were to expand. As such it takes for granted all the other economies – managerial, sales, finance, etc. – which would confront a newcomer. All three approaches have their limitations but they do agree on one important point. Technological factors may be relatively unimportant in determining ease of entry to many industries.

## Public sector indivisibilities

The public sector contains large numbers of examples of indivisibilities such as bridges, roads, canals, railways, health services and law and order. A peculiarity of these indivisibilities is that they have considerable spillover effects. A police force, army or fire service available for Smith tends to protect his next-

**Table 31** Optimum plant size, minimum efficient plant size and barriers to entry, 1968

| Industry | Engineer approach MEP as a percentage of UK output | Survivor technique Average optimum plant | | Second plant approach | |
|---|---|---|---|---|---|
| | | Size | Percentage of UK output | Size | Percentage of UK output |
| bread and flour | 1·0 | 592 | 0·4 | 228 | 0·15 |
| cocoa and chocolate | | 1287 | 1·5 | 192 | 0·24 |
| brewing | 3·0 | 1499 | 1·9 | 41 | 0·05 |
| vegetable and animal oils | | 48 | 0·7 | 46 | 0·52 |
| oils and greases | | 75 | 1·3 | 54 | 0·77 |
| dyes | 100.0 | | | 115 | 0·22 |
| fertilizers | | 833 | 3·8 | 154 | 0·80 |
| agricultural machinery | | 120 | 0·7 | 327 | 1·51 |
| watches and clocks | | 937 | 8·3 | 393 | 3·36 |
| engineers' small tools | | 95 | 0·2 | 68 | 0·10 |
| cotton spinning | | 517 | 0·6 | 150 | 0·18 |
| textile finishing | | 209 | 0·4 | 115 | 0·22 |
| hosiery | | 685 | 0·5 | 89 | 0·07 |
| women's outerwear | | 115 | 0·3 | 89 | 0·19 |
| leather goods | | 305 | 2·2 | 98 | 0·52 |
| bricks | 0·5 | 409 | 0·8 | 45 | 0·08 |
| pottery | | 531 | 1·0 | 194 | 0·35 |
| glass | | 1555 | 2·3 | 60 | 0·08 |
| cement | 10·0 | 298 | 2·2 | 187 | 1·35 |
| Paper and board | | 1170 | 1·6 | 240 | 0·32 |

Sources: Pratten (1971); Rees (1973); Lyons (1979)

door neighbour by its presence, because of these spillovers. These particular goods and services tend to be in the public sector. We shall therefore defer discussion until Part Eight.

### The closed monopoly

Let us concentrate, then, upon the polar case of absolute market power; when one firm has complete control of market supply of a product. In this case 'the firm' is synonymous with 'the industry', the firm's demand curve is the market demand curve for the product; and elasticity of demand for the firm's product is the same as market elasticity of demand. The firm is therefore the price-maker: faced with a downward sloping curve it sets price at that level which will maximize profits.

Profit, as we have seen, is maximized at the price–output combination which equates marginal cost with marginal revenue. But in the special case we are now considering, marginal revenue is not equal to price as it is in perfect competition. Marginal revenue is in fact less than price since the demand curve facing the firm is downward-sloping. Each unit increase in output can only be sold if the price asked for that unit is less than the price asked for any previous unit placed on the market. But, if one unit is offered at this lower price then all units must also be offered at this price (since all units are homogeneous). Thus the change in total revenue created by the unit increase in supply is less than the price received for that unit, e.g.[2]

50 units can be sold at 10p each; $TR^{(50)} = 500p$.
51 units can be sold at 9·95p each; $TR^{(51)} = 507·45p$

$$MR = TR^{(51)} - TR^{(50)} = 507·45p - 500p$$
$$= 7·45p.$$

The change in total revenue created by a unit increase in sales ($MR$) is only 7·45p which is less than the new price of 9·95p.

Given that the marginal curve lies below the average revenue

2. The relationship between total revenue and marginal revenue was fully analysed in Chapter 7.

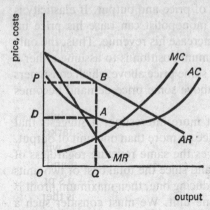

Figure 115

(demand) curve we may now proceed, in the usual fashion, to depict the equilibrium position of the firm. In order to do this we assume, for the time being, perfect knowledge on the buying side of the market – all potential consumers are aware of the existence of the product, the selling points at which it may be obtained, and the price at which it is being offered. (We are also assuming, as always, that the product is perfectly divisible, and can be offered for sale in minute units – the price–quantity demanded relationship is a smooth curve.) Equilibrium is shown in Figure 115. In this situation the firm is enjoying a surplus of total revenue over total cost by selling output *OQ* at price *OP*, thus equating marginal cost with marginal revenue. The surplus or profit is shown by area *DPBA*.

## The monopolist's demand curve

We have constructed the monopolist's demand curve as downward-sloping. Can we say any more about its nature? There are two cases which create difficulties for our analysis:

Demand for the monopolist's product is perfectly inelastic;
The monopolist's demand curve exhibits unit elasticity.

In the first case it is impossible, given our basic assumptions, to identify the optimum levels of price and output. If elasticity is zero at all prices then the monopolist can raise his price indefinitely and thus forever increase his revenue. Thus, the only way for us to depict an optimum position is to assume either a finite limit to price – there is some price above which consumers will not buy any – or that above some price demand becomes price-elastic.

The second case is rather more interesting: it suggests that the monopolist would produce no more than one unit of output. Since the monopolist receives the same revenue regardless of price and the quantity sold and since the total cost of two units exceeds the total cost of producing one, then maximum profit is obtained from producing one unit. We must consider such a situation as a curiosity rather than a norm in a market economy. Its analysis does, however, have interesting implications for that model which assumes the monopolist to be sole controller of the supply of *all* goods and services. Under such circumstances the demand curve would again show unit elasticity since all consumer outlay would be spent on the monopolist's (composite) product. However, in this model the inducement to produce only one unit of output is tempered by the fact that consumer expenditure is determined by factor incomes and if the monopolist's output is kept so low in one period then factor incomes will be correspondingly low and demand for the product in the ensuing period will plunge dramatically. Thus, discovering the optimal input–output balance is a severe problem for such a monopolist; and it is a problem epitomized by the central planning model of state control of all resources.

We can expect, then, that the normal monopolist's demand curve will be neither of the two cases described above. More precision than this is impossible except to say that, assuming marginal costs to be positive, a monopolist will never operate along that section of his demand curve where price-elasticity is less than unity. Remember (Chapter 7) that when price-elasticity of demand is less than one, marginal revenue is negative and, therefore, if the monopolist were to operate along such a section of his demand curve he could always increase his revenue by reducing output.

## The nature of the monopolist's supply curve

For any firm in a perfectly competitive market, marginal revenue is the same as average revenue. Since the optimizer equates marginal cost with marginal revenue there is a unique relationship between any price and the quantity the firm is willing to supply at that price. This unique relationship (supply curve) is traced out by the marginal-cost curve (as we saw in Chapter 13). When we turn to monopoly this price–quantity relationship is no longer determinate. Because the demand curve is downward-sloping, *MR* is no longer the same as *AR*. The monopolist himself sets the price and this is no longer equal to marginal cost (although *MR* is still equated with marginal cost).

In each set of circumstances, therefore, there is only a supply *point*, only one price–quantity position, and it follows that different quantities may be associated with one price and different prices may be associated with one quantity. This means that we cannot construct an *ex ante* supply curve since we cannot determine precisely how much the monopolist is willing to supply at each price. The marginal-cost curve still provides necessary information but this alone is not sufficient to determine quantity: we must also know the demand curve. The importance of this problem will be more obvious when we even-

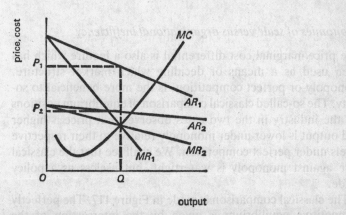

Figure 116

tually discuss the economy in macro terms (in the meantime think how you might construct an *aggregate* supply curve, i.e. one which relates to a whole economy).

Figure 116 demonstrates the lack of a unique price–quantity relationship under conditions of monopoly. Both the marginal-revenue curves $MR_1$ and $MR_2$ intersect the marginal-cost curve at the same point. The optimum output is therefore the same, $Q$, but the prices obtained, $OP_1$ and $OP_2$, are greatly different.

## The measurement of monopoly power

From the condition that profit maximization requires the equating of marginal revenue and marginal cost we can obtain a simple measure of monopoly power. Under perfect competition marginal revenue is equal to price and so price is equal to marginal cost. Under monopoly, price is greater than marginal revenue and hence marginal cost. So a measure of monopoly might be:

$$\frac{\text{price} - \text{marginal cost}}{\text{price}} = \text{degree of monopoly.}$$

Under perfect competition the degree of monopoly would be zero. In Chapter 19 we shall consider the usefulness of this formula.

## Economies of scale versus organizational inefficiency

The price/marginal cost differential is also a feature which has been used as a means of deciding which market structure, monopoly or perfect competition, is the more beneficial to society. The so-called classical comparison of equilibrium positions for the industry in the two cases observes that price is higher and output is lower under monopoly relative to their respective levels under perfect competition. We shall see that the classical case against monopoly is watertight, but useless as a policy guide.

The classical comparison is made in Figure 117. The perfectly competitive equilibrium is given by the intersection of the

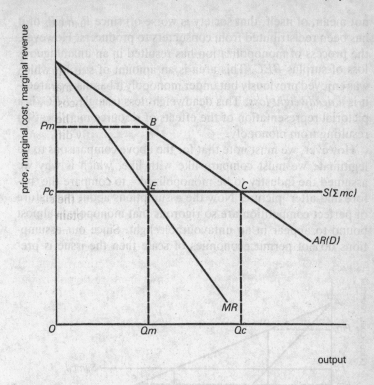

Figure 117

market-demand curve and the market-supply curve (summation of marginal costs) which for simplicity is assumed to be horizontal, output is $OQ_c$ and price is $OP_c$. Suppose now that the industry is 'monopolized' so that the equilibrium is determined by the intersection of the marginal cost and marginal revenue curves. Output is now $OQ_m$ and the price is $OP_m$; output has fallen and price has risen.

Another way to compare the relative benefits from the two price/output combinations is to measure the amount of consumer surplus which society enjoys from each one. In the case of the perfectly competitive case the amount of consumer surplus is $AP_cC$ but the higher price and lower output under monopoly reduce the surplus to $AP_mB$. A smaller consumer surplus does not mean, of itself, that society is worse off since $P_mBEP_c$ of it has been redistributed from consumers to producers. However, the process of monopolization has resulted in an unambiguous loss of surplus *BEC*. This area is an amount of surplus which was enjoyed previously but under monopoly it has disappeared – it is a *deadweight loss*. This deadweight loss triangle, *BEC*, is a pictorial representation of the effects of resource misallocation resulting from monopoly.

However, we must note that for the above comparisons to be legitimate we must compare like with like, which is why we assumed the industry to be monopolized – to compare the 'before and after' picture. Now the assumptions about the nature of perfect competition are so rigorous that monopoly is almost bound to appear in an unfavourable light. Since our assumptions do not permit economies of scale then the issue is pre-

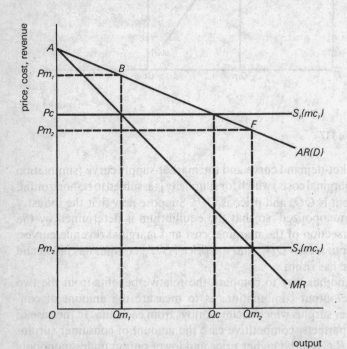

Figure 118

judged. If, on the other hand, we were to relax our assumptions and allow for the possibility of scale economies, then monopolization could well result in a lower price and a higher output as a result of falling costs, as shown by Figure 118.

In Figure 119 the economies of scale which help to create the monopoly situation succeed in pushing the marginal-cost curve down to the level of $S_2$. Output rises from $OQ_c$ to $OQ_{m_2}$ and price falls from $OP_c$ to $OP_{m_2}$ instead of being $OQ_{m_1}$ and $OP_{m_1}$. Note also, that the area of consumer surplus increases from $AP_cC$ to $AP_{m_2}F$. It is often claimed, however, that in spite of initial economies of scale a monopoly may become inefficient over the long run as a result of organizational slackness in the absence of market incentives continually to minimize costs. The strength of this argument really depends upon whether or not control of the firm resides with its owners. In our 'pure' models we have always assumed that the decision-maker(s) is also the owner(s) and on this assumption a rising cost curve may not necessarily reflect inefficiencies. Rather, it may be the result of a conscious decision on the part of the owner to employ prettier secretaries, to play more golf in the afternoons and so on. These activities yield a stream of net benefits to the owner and if we had maintained an approach to the theory of the firm that we mentioned in Chapter 17, namely, to assume the firm's objective is to maximize the utility of the owner, there would be no

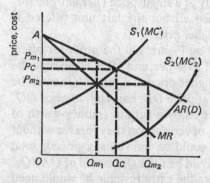

Figure 119

conflict between objectives and action. However, when the firm's owners are a group of shareholders whose aim is to maximize dividends then the controller's decision to permit longer tea-breaks and less office scrutiny conflicts with the owners' desires. This is the 'X-inefficiency' model. The monopolist is considered inefficient because the market provides no incentive for him to be efficient or else the shareholders are either ignorant or apathetic.

## Price discrimination

So far in our analysis we have imagined the monopolist to set only one price for his output. But if he could see some of his output at that price and *some at a higher price* (for the same outlay) would he not be much better off? It seems so intuitively obvious that he would be better off that the question appears trivial. But is it not true that this apparent triviality stems from the fact that we tend to take for granted the downward-sloping demand curve? Perhaps we should remind ourselves of some of its consequences.

The market demand curve for a private good is a horizontal summation of the demand curves of individual consumers. Thus for a given set of incomes and tastes the producer knows how much he can charge for each quantity he puts on the market. When he offers each quantity at a single price (*per unit*) he forgoes potential revenue since all but the last unit offered is valued by consumers at a higher price.

In the situation depicted by Figure 120 the producer offers quantity $OQ_4$ at a price of $OA$ per unit. But all except the $OQ_4$th unit is valued at a higher price, e.g. unit $OQ_3$ could be sold at price $OC$; unit $OQ_2$ at price $OE$, unit $OQ_1$ at price $OG$, and so on. Thus consumers enjoy a surplus (money-worth of utility) of $ZAB$ – an amount of satisfaction they receive without paying for it. If each unit could be individually priced, total revenue for the producer would be $OZBQ_4$ instead of $OABQ_4$.

For the producer to realize the extra revenue he would need to know the marginal utility schedules of all his consumers and be able to negotiate with each individual buyer. Furthermore,

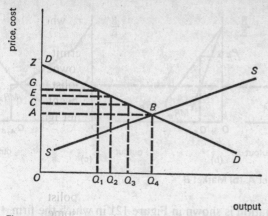

Figure 120

each individual buyer must be willing to buy units of the product one at a time or at least be willing to negotiate a price for each separate unit purchased. Thus the firm may be torn between finding the one price that will clear the market and the set of prices that will both clear the market and extract consumers' surpluses. The opportunity cost of searching for the latter prices could be too high since it would take an immense amount of time to discover the full nature of each individual's demand curve. Since expected receipts would be inadequate to warrant acceptance of such costs the producer settles for the market price and the resultant consumer surplus.

Nevertheless, the principle still holds and although the producer is not able to treat each individual buyer as a separate market, he may at least be able to isolate two or more individual buyers, or groups of buyers, charge a different price to each and hence 'tap' some of the consumer surplus enjoyed by some of the consumers when only one price is charged. The necessary condition for such a policy to be effective is that price-elasticity of demand for the product should differ in each of the separate markets (if this were not so then the two markets could not be considered as separate). One need only think of Harley Street specialists, 'cheap period' return rail tickets or 'off-peak' electricity pricing to realize that differential pricing is

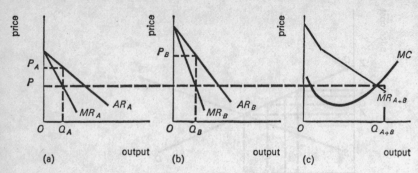

Figure 121  (a) Market A. (b) Market B

possible. The situation is shown in Figure 121 in which the firm is faced with two separate markets, A and B.

It is essential that goods purchased in market A cannot be resold in market B and vice versa. Figure 121c represents the production decision: as usual the output chosen is that which equates MC with MR (the horizontal sum of the MR curves for the two markets). Figures 121a and 121b represent the allocation problem – how much to allocate to each market in order to maximize profit? The quantities which will satisfy this objective must obviously be those which equate the marginal revenues of the two markets. If the revenue to be gained from selling one more unit in A is greater than that to be lost by selling one unit less in B then the firm will transfer a unit from B into A. If marginal revenues are equal then no further re-allocation can affect total profit. The prices charged in the two markets are $OP_A$ and $OP_B$.

## Open monopoly

The case of the closed monopoly is interesting but not always informative. A more typical case is where the monopolist has a temporary advantage which he may convert to a more secure basis by a variety of strategies such as advertising, not making maximum profits in the short run, having some reserve capacity with which he can threaten new entrants, fixing a price which will deter entrants. Consider, for example, the case of firm A planning its output and sales for years one to five inclusive. Suppose the firm anticipates that earning maximum profit of £100 in any one year will attract firm *B* into the market. The effect of *B*'s entrance is anticipated to reduce *A*'s annual revenue and hence *B*'s profit. Firm *A*, therefore, intends to produce an annual output which will not yield maximum (annual) profit and in this way 'scare off' firm *B*. By following this strategy, *A* is still maximizing net worth (in present value terms) in the light of anticipated circumstances (see Table 32).

Thus by keeping annual income below £100 (the maximum level which could be gained in any one year) firm A expects to earn income over the five-year period in excess of the level which could be earned if *B* was to enter the industry. *A* is still maximizing under the expected circumstances, although this no longer requires the equating of *MR* with *MC* for any short-run output period.

## Oligopoly, cartels and mergers

In many markets the number of firms is small and so each one becomes conscious of his rivals' behaviour. Thus, if one firm cuts its price then it may expect others to follow suit. Such a situation of conscious interdependence is called *oligopoly*. The existence of interdependence gives rise to the belief that the oligopoly problem is indeterminate in the sense that customary economic models and tools of analysis cannot provide a solution.

## The Cournot model

An early solution to the oligopoly problem was provided by Augustin Cournot in 1838 and his model remains the best way to demonstrate the basic oligopoly problem. He took the case of two firms (duopoly) and assumed that each firm believes that its rival's output will not be affected by changes in its output. In Figure 122 we measure *A*'s output along the horizontal axis and *B*'s output along the vertical axis. *A* fixes his output so as to maximize his output profits at *OL* on the assumption that *B* will

**Table 32**

| Year | Without potential entrants | | If firm B enters at end of year 1 | | If A deters B by not maximizing annual income | |
|---|---|---|---|---|---|---|
| | A's anticipated maximum profit £ | Present value at 10% discount rate £ | A's anticipated income[1] £ | Present value at 10% discount rate £ | A's anticipated income £ | Present value at 10% discount rate £ |
| 1 | 100 | 91 | 100 | 91 | 50 | 46 |
| 2 | 100 | 83 | 70 | 58·10 | 80 | 66 |
| 3 | 100 | 75 | 60 | 45·00 | 85 | 64 |
| 4 | 100 | 68 | 55 | 37·40 | 95 | 65 |
| 5 | 100 | 62 | 50 | 31·00 | 95 | 59 |
| Total present value | – | 379 | – | 262·50 | – | 300 |

1. A's anticipated income falls over the five-year period because firm B is expected to grow relative to A which has already exhausted most of the scale economies during the period.

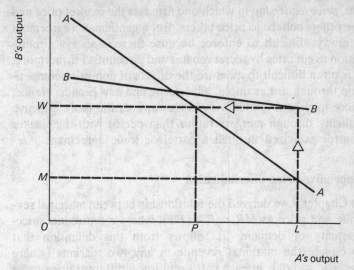

Figure 122

produce *OM*. But given *A*'s output, the best policy for *B* is to produce *OW*. If *B* produces *OW* this will cause *A* to reduce his output to *OP*. Thus, it is possible to derive two reaction curves, *AA* and *BB*. The curve *AA* traces out all the profit maximizing outputs for *A* on the assumption that *B*'s output is given and the curve *BB* traces out all the profit maximizing outputs for *B* on the assumption that *A*'s output is given. The intersection of the two curves gives the equilibrium output for both firms.

A minor objection to Cournot's model is that firms do not normally fix their outputs but set prices. This change however can easily be incorporated. A more serious criticism is that the theory assumes that firms do not learn from experience. If they do attempt to forecast a rival's behaviour then several possibilities present themselves.

1 Non-collusion: a firm will try to obtain the maximum profits given all the possible moves of its rivals. This amounts to minimizing the risk from a given policy.

2 Collusion: a firm may come to an agreement to share the market and achieve an orderly market situation by, for exam-

ple, *price leadership* in which one firm sets the market price and the others behave as price takers. But a gentleman's agreement is always difficult to enforce because there is always a temptation to cut price by secret rebates and discounts. Furthermore, it is often difficult to measure the effects of non-price competition through, for example, advertising and new brands. Hence, there may be a tendency to move towards the more effective policing through mergers rather than persist with the slacker control exercised through a cartel or trade agreement.

### Appendix: price discrimination

In Chapter 7 we derived the relationship between marginal revenue and price as $MR = P - (P/e)$, where $e$ represents price-elasticity of demand. It follows from this definition that to equate the marginal revenue in any two markets (where $0 < e < \infty$ holds in each case) requires a different price to be charged in each when the elasticities differ. Furthermore the price must be highest in the market where price-elasticity of demand is lowest:

Market 1 $MR_1 = P_1 - \dfrac{P_1}{e_1}$,

Market 2 $MR_2 = P_2 - \dfrac{P_2}{e_2}$.

If $MR_1 = MR_2$,

then $P_1 - \dfrac{P_1}{e_1} = P_2 - \dfrac{P_2}{e_2}$.

If $e_1 > e_2$,

then $P_1 < P_2$.

### Summary

Monopoly is the power to influence price or output. It arises through the existence of discontinuities of production possibilities which may be due to natural or legal causes. Though monopoly will give rise to a falling demand curve the monopolist will operate where his demand is price-elastic. Problems arise on the supply side because it is difficult to associate a unique output with a given marginal revenue. Whether a monopolist will be inefficient may turn upon his willingness to exploit any economies of scale available to him. Finally, a monopolist may obtain higher profit if he can divide his customers into separate markets.

## Questions

1 'The firm under perfect competition can sell as much as it wants at the going price. Should the same firm find itself in a monopoly position it would be faced with a downward-sloping demand curve and could only increase sales by reducing prices. Therefore monopolistic control benefits consumers.' Discuss.

2 'The demand curve of a monopolist is elastic.' Examine this statement.

3 What problems are raised by the concept of a monopolist's supply curve?

4 If in a market all firms charged the same price what conclusion would you draw?

5 Milk can be produced either for liquid consumption or for manufacture into cheese, butter, cream, milk powder, etc. What factors will determine the relative amounts of milk sold for different uses?

6 A monopolist producer of a service for which the marginal cost is zero faces the straight line demand curve shown in the figure below. *OB* represents one unit of output and *DF* = *FE*. Suppose the government grants a subsidy equal to *FM* per unit of output sold. The profit maximizing output will be:

(a) *OB*
(b) *OE*
(c) *OM*
(d) greater than *OB* but less than *OM*
(e) less than *OE* but greater than *OM*

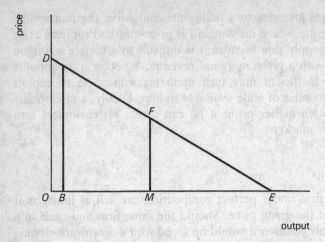

7 A monopolist faces the following demand and total cost functions:

$$p = 100 - 4Q$$
$$t = 50 + 20Q$$

where $p$ represents price and $t$ represents total costs and $Q$ represents quantity.

(a) What is the maximum level of profit?

(b) Suppose the government imposes a tax of 8 per cent on each unit of the monopolist's output. What will happen to price, output and profit?

(c) If, instead of a unit tax on output, the government levies a lump sum tax of 76 per cent on the monopolist, what will happen to price, output and profit? Compare your answers with the results obtained for the pre-tax and unit tax situations.

# Chapter 20
# Fix-Price Firms and Business Behaviour

Not all firms respond to short-run changes in demand by varying price as well as output and in this chapter we shall examine the behaviour of fix-price firms and link the discussion to business practice.

## Demand

The emergence of fix-price firms and fix-price markets became noticeable around the turn of the century and such market features spread as a result of factors on both the demand and supply sides of markets.

Given the tendency for industrial concentration to increase after 1900 there is a temptation to associate fix-price markets with the extension of monopoly to previously competitive markets. But monopoly is not synonymous with rigid prices and a monopolist may vary his price as much as a competitive firm in order to maximize his profits. Monopoly is, therefore, not synonymous with rigid prices.

Fixed prices may be preferred by customers. With the rise of real incomes it becomes more costly to shop around in order to find the lowest price in markets where prices are continually changing. 'Time is money' and for those for whom the opportunity cost of searching around or using the services of specialist buyers is too high the knowledge that some firms stand ready to sell at known prices may be a great convenience.

Fix-price labour markets have existed for a long time and

money wages have shown a high degree of rigidity over lengthy periods. At first fixed wages tended to be confined to markets for skilled workers but in the post-war years even the wages of unskilled workers have tended to become inflexible downwards.

The emergence of fix-price product markets was first observed in retail markets and was associated with the rise of standardization, branding and the advertising of goods.

## Costs

Given the need to supply a range of possible outputs at a fix-price, a firm will build a considerable amount of flexibility into its operations and its average and marginal costs curves will tend to be horizontal over a considerable range of output. Figure 123 shows the average variable and marginal cost curves of a plant designed to operate at an output $OQ$. The cost curves are U-shaped. In contrast, and on the same diagram, we show the marginal and average variable cost curves of a fix-price firm designed to produce at constant direct cost outputs which range from $OQ_2$ to $OQ_3$. At output $OQ$ the flex-price firm is clearly the most efficient but at other outputs the fix-price firm will be more efficient.

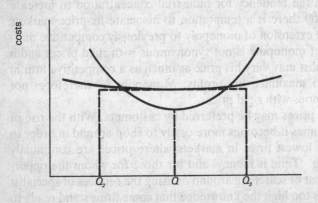

Figure 123

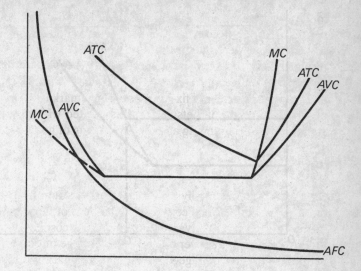

Figure 124

The fact that the direct cost curve is horizontal implies that the production function will not exhibit a stage of increasing returns but will have a constant slope. The fixed factor will be divisible in order to obtain flexibility in production but the average cost curve will still be U-shaped if some factor has to be bought in a fixed amount. Thus, in Figure 124 the average fixed cost will fall as output increases and give rise to a U-shaped average total cost curve.

## Market structures
### Perfect competition

The existence of a fix-price regime will introduce modifications to the model of perfect competition. In Figure 125 the firm takes the price *OP* as given and produces output *OQ*. If demand falls then the firm will cut back output but still sell at price *OP*. If demand rises then the firm may still sell at price *OP*.

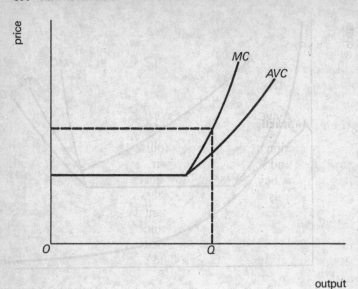

Figure 125

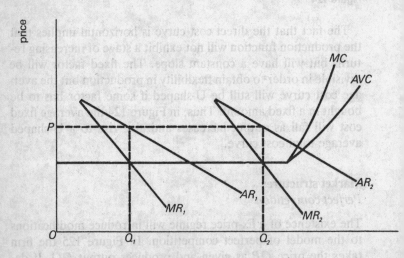

Figure 126

The fact that the direct cost curve is horizontal implies that the production function will not exhibit a stage of increasing returns, but will have a constant slope. The fixed factor will be varied in order to obtain flexibility in production and the average cost curve will still be U-shaped if some factor can be bought as a fixed amount. Thus, in Figure 126 we have an fixed cost ... still ... and ... shaped average cost curve ...

Market structure

Perfect competition

The existence of a fix-price regime will introduce modifications to the model of perfect competition. In Figure 125 the firm takes the price $OP$ as given and produces output $OQ$. If demand falls then the firm will cut back output but still sell at price $OP$. If demand rises then the firm may still sell at price

*Monopoly and oligopoly*

The case of fix-price behaviour under monopoly and oligopoly is illustrated in Figure 126. The firm's demand curve can shift from $AR_1$ to $AR_2$ without causing any revision of price.

## Accounting practice

The introduction of fix-price behaviour helps to explain much of accounting and business behaviour. Typically, accountants think of price being the sum of direct costs plus a mark-up to cover overheads and profit. Thus, there appears to be an exclusion of demand. What the accountant does is to regard direct costs as a linear function of output and fixed costs as a constant percentage. He then assumes that the firm can sell as much as it can produce at the existing price and so obtains the *break-even chart* shown in Figure 127.

The resulting intersection of total revenue and total costs as shown in Figure 127 yields what is known as a *break-even* point, *OA*. The break-even point *A* reveals the optimum output policy to lie to the right of output level *OA*. Figure 127 reveals a reason why many accountants have great difficulty in accepting the concept of marginal cost. If we derive the marginal- and average-cost curves from Figure 127 then we obtain the results

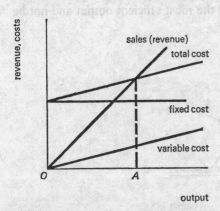

Figure 127

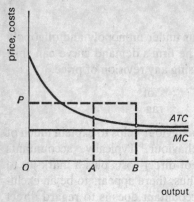

Figure 128

shown in Figure 128. Since marginal cost is below average cost the accountant cannot understand how overheads can be covered. Hence he imposes a price *OP* and produces *OB*.

The economist does not say that the businessman should charge a price equal to marginal cost. Indeed he says that only under special circumstances will the businessman be forced to accept a price equal to marginal-cost policy. This circumstance will be perfect competition where the firm can sell as much as it can produce at the market price but has no influence on market price. It should be noted that under perfect competition marginal cost will be rising at the most efficient output and not be constant as in Figure 128.

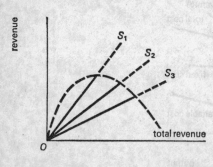

Figure 129

If pressed the accountant might admit that sales could vary with price charged. In other words, there is not one sales line as in Figure 128 but many as in Figure 129. Furthermore, he might concede that at each price there would be a maximum amount of sales. Hence through particular points on the sales lines of Figure 129 we can draw the locus of a total-revenue curve. From this curve can be derived average- and marginal-revenue curves and, as in economic analysis, the accountant will be interested in the falling sections of average- and marginal-revenue curves.

The accountant's assumption that total costs are a linear function of output is probably a simplification brought about by considering only small deviations from some planned capacity output and the effect of certain accounting practices. If a firm has been built with the objective of producing, say, one million tonnes steel per year then a risk factor of 10 per cent may be built into the plant design which would allow for outputs 10 per cent greater or less than one million tonnes to be produced without much change in costs. So in Figure 130 the effective output range *AB* can be produced at approximately constant average costs. The second group of reasons which may produce constant cost arises through, for example, the accountant's treatment of depreciation as a constant charge rather than allowing depreciation charges to vary with the degree of utilization of plant.

If we introduce the cost curve of Figure 130 to the total-revenue curve derived from Figure 129 we obtain a general

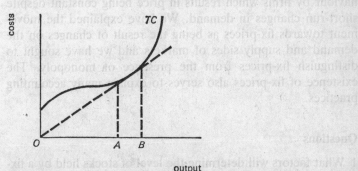

Figure 130

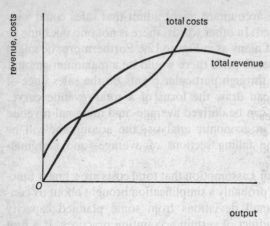

Figure 131

price–output decision model similar to that envisaged by economists. For the accountant the distance between the two curves will be dictated by the mark-up added to average costs and the percentage for overheads; for the economist the mark-up will emerge as a result of attempting to equate marginal revenue and marginal cost.

## Summary

In this chapter we have sought to take account of fix-price behaviour by firms which results in price being constant despite short-run changes in demand. We have explained the movement towards fix-prices as being the result of changes on the demand and supply sides of markets and we have sought to distinguish fix-prices from the presence of monopoly. The existence of fix-prices also serves to explain many accounting practices.

## Questions

1 What factors will determine the level of stocks held by a fix-price firm?

2 Why is fix-price behaviour compatible with perfect competition?

3 Can the accountant's break-even chart be reconciled with the economist's theory of pricing?

4 A businessman says that he bases his selling price upon his estimated average direct costs plus a percentage addition to cover his overheads and profit. Using the relationship between price, marginal cost and price-elasticity of demand (mentioned in the Mathematical Interlude) show how the businessman's pricing procedure is compatible with economic analysis.

# Chapter 21
# Workers' Control and Public Ownership

### Workers' control

Suppose, by a wave of a magic wand, the control of all firms was transferred to the workers employed in them. How would worker-controlled firms operate and what would a worker-controlled economy look like? In Figure 132 the horizontal axis

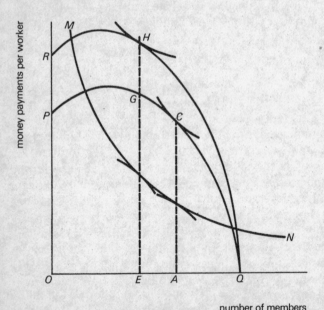

Figure 132 The worker cooperative

measures the number of members of a worker cooperative and the vertical axis measures the money payments per worker. The curve *MN* traces out the fixed cost of equipment per worker; being a rectangular hyperbola, *MN* maintains a constant total amount payable for the hire of equipment. The curve *PQ* traces out the average revenue per worker; that is, average output multiplied by the price of the product. Net earnings per worker are the vertical distance between curves *PQ* and *MN* and are maximized when the slopes of the two curves are equal as at *A*.

Note that the two curves (functions) *MN* and *PQ* are so shaped because of the reasoning involved in the law of diminishing returns. The transfer of the ownership of property rights from capitalists to workers does not alter the laws of production. Transfer of ownership may, as a result of psychological and sociological reasons connected with freedom from alienation, move the position of the curves although the evidence on the psychological and sociological effects of changes in the manner of participation in work activities is a matter of dispute. What we have done is to leave this debate on one side and assume that the curves remain constant although the distribution of the product changes hands.

Consider a rise in the product price such that the curve *PQ* is replaced by *RQ*. Now net earnings are maximized with *OE* workers; the slopes of *RQ* and *LM* are equalized. The value of output is maximized with a smaller group of members and this tendency to reduce the number of members outweighs any tendency to increase the number of members in order to minimize debt per worker.

We have the curious situation that when the demand for the product increases the worker-cooperative cuts back its output in order to maximize its profits. This is monopolistic behaviour and differs from that of the competitive firm in a market economy. The entrepreneur would maximize his income by increasing the labour and equipment he employed. The behaviour of the worker cooperative suggests that it will tend to be small and will not exploit any available economies of scale. Increases in output would therefore have to come from increasing the number of firms in the market. But freedom of entry with its associated risks is not a state of affairs most workers want to see happen when they argue for workers' control. Furthermore, there is the problem of the source of finance for new firms.

Because a worker obtains his income from the firm in which he works there may exist no capital market. Partners in a cooperative will be encouraged to consume their income and plough little back into the firm because they may leave the firm and so lose any rights to future income. They will also fear the risks of 'putting all their eggs in one basket'. This suggests another reason why worker cooperatives will tend to be small and will not grow rapidly. There may, of course, be offsetting advantages. Most workers may be immobile; they may never move from firm to firm, hence, they may be willing to plough back income. There may be the psychological and sociological advantages of working for oneself.

Economies of scale may be exaggerated and in industries such as construction, worker cooperatives may be efficient. But if economies of scale do exist then worker cooperatives may not be able to exploit them and it may be possible to remove the underlying causes of discontent by redistributing income and wealth so that workers could spread their risks through the capital market.

## Public ownership

A much more powerful rallying cry than that put forward by private ownership or workers' control is that which proclaims that all resources should be communally owned and used for the good of all. 'The dust does not belong to the dustmen' and 'the coal belongs to the nation' were proclamations of Morrisonian socialism,[1] enunciated in the 1930s and implemented in the nationalization statutes for coal, gas, electricity, railways, road transport and the post office. Morrisonian socialism stressed the needs of the consumer in a way neglected by both managerial

1. Herbert Stanley Morrison (1888–1965) was Minister of Transport in 1929–31, Home Secretary 1940–45 and Leader of the House of Commons, 1945–51.

capitalism and workers' control. It took the view that only under nationalization would it be truly possible to attain significant economies of scale and only if key industries were publicly owned could economic growth be increased.

The essence of Morrisonian socialism was as follows. The assets of private undertakings were to be purchased and transferred to the state. Once industries were nationalized a minister was to be appointed who would be responsible for seeing that the broad aims and long-term policy of an industry were to pursue 'the common good' as interpreted by Parliament. However, day-to-day operations and problems of commercial efficiency were to be entrusted to managers.

The problems of a nationalized industry are listed below.

## Mode of acquisition

1 If the assets of a firm or industry are acquired by purchase (compensation) then there is no gain to the community unless economies of scale are obtained. Since compensation is based upon share prices and share prices measure future earning power, then any unexploited economies of scale may be accounted for. The fact that a firm could, by expanding output in the future, lower its costs and increase its earnings may already be incorporated into the present share price. Hence, all the state may acquire through nationalization is the ownership of the assets but the income from those assets will remain with the former private owners in the form of compensation payments.

2 A more efficient method of acquisition would be through taxation (peaceful confiscation) achieved by running budget surpluses.

## Pricing policy

3 A nationalized industry could pursue an average cost pricing policy on the grounds that it should break even and neither exploit consumers nor workers. This would be sound commercial

policy. However, a problem can arise when, as in the case of roads, railways and power stations, fixed costs are large in relationship to running costs with the result that over considerable ranges of output marginal costs are below average costs. In Figure 133 an average cost pricing policy would mean a price of $OP$ and an output of $OQ$ and this would be less than the output $OQ_1$ which would minimize total costs.

4 Now an objection to the average cost pricing policy is that it merely reproduces the private monopoly solution to the problem of what price to charge when significant indivisibilities, large lumps of fixed equipment, exist; output is restricted to ensure that fixed costs are covered. But some writers have argued that as long as consumers can pay a price equal to marginal cost then output should be expanded. They state that marginal cost measures the cost of supplying an extra unit and that once a bridge or road is built the fixed costs become irrelevant. Since marginal cost measures the utility attaching to the use of scarce resources in their next highest valued use then marginal cost pricing should be the rule. In terms of Figure 133 this implies a

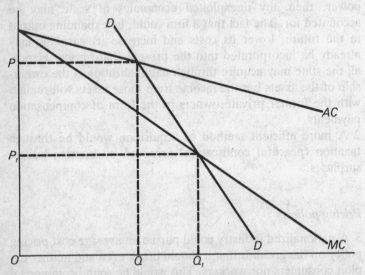

Figure 133 Marginal – and average – cost pricing

price $OP_1$ and an output $OQ_1$. Thus, there would be a much fuller use of assets and, in the extreme case, price could be zero as, for example, with parks, law and order and health and education.

5 Furthermore, if a nationalized industry equates price to marginal cost and sells to a monopolist in the private sector then it will increase the monopolists' profits. This is *the problem of second best*, of what to do when the rest of the economy, or the world, is not perfect. One solution would be for the nationalized industry to behave as a monopolist and make price greater than marginal cost. Another solution would be to break up the monopoly and create competition in the private sector.

6 One proposal that has been put forward to cover the deficits of nationalized firms which pursue marginal cost pricing policies is to meet the losses out of general taxation. But if fixed costs were met out of the revenue from an income tax then decisions about work and leisure could be affected, and if revenue was obtained by means of an expenditure tax then decisions about consumption and saving could be affected. A more general objection would be that those who pay the taxes might not be the same people as those who benefit from the commodity provided by the nationalized industry.

7 Total costs might be covered by means of a two-part tariff. A portion of the fixed costs might be allocated as a lump sum payment charged to each consumer and then a price charged for each unit consumed. Two-part tariffs are used for telephone services. The case for the two-part tariff is that the lump sum payment could be extracted out of the consumers' surplus without causing any reduction in the amount consumed. This argument seems doubtful and in the cases of widows and pensioners the fixed charge might be so high as to result in their abstention from consumption.

8 Given the variety of pricing and financing policies available it is always possible for the decision to be made that price should be zero in order to alter the distribution of income and wealth and to subsidize the consumption of particular goods or individuals. Of course, it is always possible for the state to subsidize

some group directly by giving them cash but the transfer payment may be spent on alcohol instead of bread. Hence, commuters and pensioners may be given cheap transport. What then becomes important is the treatment of the subsidy in the industry's accounts. Subsidies should be apparent and a charge upon the state – lest they become a means towards inefficiency.

## Wages

9  Nationalization may be a means of providing income security to workers and as such may slide imperceptibly into workers' control. Therefore it raises difficult problems of how to determine the wage level and how to prevent wages being financed out of taxation.

## Investment and finance

10  The investment policy of a nationalized industry could be to earn as much as could be earned in the private sector and to use the market rate of interest as a discount factor. But public sector industries may be safer than private ones from the investors' viewpoint and therefore a lower discount rate should be used. The real problem may be the measurement of the returns or benefits. How is it possible to measure the effects of a road programme or nursery schools?

11  Investment requires finance and a nationalized industry may use retained profits or borrow from the government. If retained profits were used the danger would be that the industry, being in a monopoly position, might raise prices and exploit existing consumers in order to benefit future consumers. If a nationalized industry borrows from the government and the government raises the money through taxes then future consumers will benefit at the expense of the current generation. If the government borrows and lends to the nationalized industry then future beneficiaries will pay for their benefits. Government borrowing may, however, be rejected because the market could refuse to finance projects.

## The abuse of rules

12 So far we have concentrated on rules for the efficient operation of a nationalized industry but these rules smack of an omniscient dictator. Practice suggests otherwise. The marginal cost pricing rule is an adaptation of a conclusion from market competition. In market competition a firm will attempt to maximize profits by trying to produce as much as it can at what it thinks is the prevailing market price. If it survives then it will find its marginal cost is equal to price. Thus marginal cost pricing is a conclusion rather than a starting point for behaviour. This contrasts sharply with the public enterprise which is often in a monopoly position and can therefore fix any price and costs for its product.

## Public ownership and private production

A way round the dilemmas of inefficient operation and financial difficulties would be for the state to own the assets but to auction the right to exploit them by private entrepreneurs. A competitive auction would yield the state revenue to finance schemes, such as defence and poverty programmes, without having to resort to taxation and it could mean that private producers would earn no more than a normal return. The concept of public ownership and private production is not a new one. It existed under the Tudors and Stuarts with their statutory monopolies, such as the East India Company. At the turn of the century, William Stanley Jevons, distinguished son of an illustrious father, proposed that the mineral rights in coal should be nationalized and politicians seriously considered the idea. Latterly, North Sea oil and gas have been the subject of leasing schemes but governments have sometimes intervened in the auctions to give preference to British firms.

## Conclusion

Workers' control and public corporations are methods of organizing production and consumption. They both have drawbacks but so do the private monopoly and the managerial firm under private ownership. And so does the firm operation in a more centralized socialist system, such as the Russian firm of the period 1920–60, which had to achieve, not financial targets, but physical output norms. There is also the more extreme case of the not-for-profit organization, such as a charity where the donors (shareholders) have no recognizable property right which can be bought and sold.

There are no obvious answers to the problems posed by various socio-economic organizations. What has to be done is to compare their relative advantages and disadvantages in the light of desired objectives, such as the distribution of income and wealth.

## Questions

1 Comment on the relative merits of public regulation and public ownership of a monopoly.

2 What are the main deficiencies of the marginal-cost pricing rule?

3 If the electricity industry is subject to increasing returns can it charge a price equal to marginal cost and still cover fixed costs?

4 What economic arguments can you advance for postal services being a government monopoly?

5 'Since the public sector invests in large numbers of projects it can afford to ignore the risk attaching to investments since risks will cancel out: the same policy could not of course be pursued by an individual.' Comment.

6 Transylvania's Railway Board is incurring a deficit on its rural passenger services. It can:
(a) close the services;
(b) raise fares on the services;
(c) cross-subsidize the services by raising the fares on main-line passenger and goods traffic;
(d) ask the State to cross-subsidize the services by raising taxes on the community.
Comment on the relative merits of these policies.

7 'London Transport should reduce fares in order to reduce road congestion.' 'London Transport should raise fares in order to cover costs.'
Comment on these two statements.

8 'The railway system confers benefits for which it cannot charge whilst road transport inflicts damages for which it cannot be made to pay.' Discuss.

9 The Post Office operates different price systems for mail and telephones. For letters a uniform price is charged irrespective of distance whereas telephone charges vary according to distance and the time at which phone calls are made. How would you justify these different price systems?

10 The Widget Corporation, a nationalized firm, is seeking to raise the price of widgets. Its arguments are:
(a) recent wage and raw-material price rises;
(b) British widget prices are below world prices;
(c) The Widget Corporation is importing widgets to cope with shortages and selling them at the lower British prices.
The price rise is opposed because:
(a) The prices of widget users' products will rise and intensify inflationary processes;
(b) The price of UK exports will rise and the balance of payments will deteriorate.
Carefully evaluate the above arguments. What policy recommendations would you make?

11 'Competition between gas and electricity should be banned as it has led to a waste of resources.' Comment.

12 On what grounds could a government justify earning a smaller rate of profit in nationalized industries than is available elsewhere in the economy?

13 'The aims of pricing policy in the nationalized industries should be that the consumer should pay the true cost of providing the goods and services he consumes' (*Nationalized Industries: Review of Financial and Economic Objectives, 1967*). Discuss, paying particular attention to the phrase, 'true cost'.

14 'I suggest that the only price a public enterprise or national-

ized industry can be expected to set is what we may as well call a *just price – a price which is set with some regard for its effect on the distribution of wealth* as well as for its effect on the allocation of resources' (J. de V. Graaf, 1967). Discuss.

15 Which of the following methods of financing the BBC do you consider to be the most efficient:

(a) a general subsidy out of taxes such as is used to finance overseas broadcasts;

(b) a pay-as-you-view or pay-as-you-listen system;

(c) continue the present licence system but increase the licence fees?

16 What criteria should the state use in compensating the owners of assets which it wishes to acquire?

17 Nationalization merely increases the size of the National Debt, it does not increase National Wealth, nor does it redistribute income. Do you agree with this statement? What does nationalization do?

# Part Seven
# The Theory of Distribution:
# A Preliminary Survey

In this section we enter one of the most disputed parts of economics. Many economists feel in fact that economics has no theory of distribution, only a few ill-assorted ideas. Let us therefore begin with some observations.

1 The general problem of any community is to decide how much of its production to devote to immediate needs (consumption) and how much to devote to future needs (savings leading to investment and the provision of greater consumption at a later date).

2 Arising out of this problem is how shall the community's decisions on the division of the product between immediate and future needs be implemented? Here we can distinguish between two methods. The first is the central planning approach and the second is the market procedure.

3 In the central planning procedure ethical considerations will enter immediately into the distribution of what is available whereas in the market system ethical considerations may tend to be neglected. Thus a market system will tend to reward a worker (the owner of labour services) according to his ability and will ignore the number of his dependents.

4 If a market economy produces rewards which fail to satisfy the broader considerations of fairness and needs it will convulse and explode into revolution unless some secondary mechanism is set up to correct disparities. The usual corrective is to redistribute some income through the tax regime.

5 A question that naturally arises is: why if market economies may fail to satisfy ethical standards is there a tendency to retain them instead of abandoning them completely? The answer is that it is believed that a market is the most efficient method of allocating resources. The compromise of market plus government-regulated tax redistribution is regarded as a means of reconciling equity and efficiency and coping with the essential tension inherent in a market economy.

6 A final point concerns the use of the surplus over immediate needs. In a central planned economy the use of the surplus is controlled either by the dictator or by a committee representative of (and presumably elected by) the people. On the other hand, in a market economy everyone can either decide how to divide and use his income into present and future use *or* he can hand over the use of the surplus to a private group of citizens known as capitalists.

7 We can now see that the sources of dispute about distribution theory are twofold. First, there is the feeling that nothing can be said about the ethical problems determining the rewards available to individuals. Secondly, there is the problem of seeing how the market solution is reconciled with a tax transfer scheme.

# Chapter 22
# The Demand for Productive Resources

In this and the next chapter we shall examine how demand and supply determine the rewards of factors of production. We begin with demand.

### Derived demand

The demand for a factor of production by an employer is a derived demand, i.e. it is dependent upon the demand for the commodity which the resource assists in producing. The precise nature of the derived demand depends to a large extent upon the objectives of the employer. We are assuming that our employer, the firm, is aiming to maximize net income or profit and just as we were able to establish a rule for achieving this goal with respect to sales of final output, so we can establish an equivalent rule with respect to purchases of inputs. As we shall see, the nature of a firm's demand for productive resources depends upon prevailing conditions in both product and factor markets.

An equally important determinant of resource demand is the technical aspects of the firm's production process, i.e. the nature of the firm's production function. Whatever the characteristics of the markets in which the firm sells its product and buys its resources, its demand for resources must be partly determined by the engineering techniques it employs in production. As we saw in Chapter 3 the proportions in which resources are used in production processes can be varied or fixed; each case will give rise to different patterns of resource demand. For the most part of our analysis we shall concentrate upon the variable proportions case. The case of fixed proportions creates some technical difficulties best left for discussion at a more advanced theoretical level, and since we are interested here in the discovery of general laws of efficiency relating to the use of productive resources, the case of variable proportions suits our purpose.

Consider first the technical features of resource demand, since these are independent of the nature of markets. We have said that resource demand depends to a large extent upon an input-output relationship, but as we saw in Chapter 3 this relationship may not be one to one. Indeed, over the short run (the period we are mainly concerned with in this chapter) output targets are dogged by diminishing returns. Output rises but at an ever-decreasing rate in response to increased resource employment since only some, and not all, inputs are readily available in increased amounts in the short run. We shall continue the technique of isolating one factor of production and considering its employment, given that the employment of other resources remains fixed.

*The efficiency rule.* In our earlier analysis of diminishing returns we constructed three curves: the total-product curve; the average-product curve; and the marginal-product curve. For the firm the most important guide to the employment of a factor is the marginal product of that factor. It is the marginal-product curve which shows the contribution made to total output by each additional unit of a factor of production. Since we are assuming the employer to be a profit-maximizer, such marginal output contributions are of prime importance in the employers' input-output calculations. The important decisions are always marginal decisions – in this case whether or not it is worthwhile employing an additional resource unit – and the answer must partly lie in the nature of the marginal-product curve.

To be more precise it is the *downward sloping section* of the marginal-product curve which is of importance to the employer, for reasons outlined in Chapter 3, but now viewed from a different angle. Applying the profit-maximizing output rule to *employment* decisions we can say that an employer should continue hiring resource units until the potential gain from hiring an additional unit is just equal to the cost of hiring that unit, i.e. until the marginal cost of employment is equal to the marginal benefit. For present purposes it is convenient to assume that the marginal cost of employment is constant (i.e. the supply curve of resources to the firm is horizontal at a given factor price) in order to isolate the importance of the marginal-product curve. In Chapter 26 we shall consider the implications of a rising marginal-cost curve of employment.

We illustrate the employment efficiency guide by Figure 134 and assume initially that resource units are paid in kind, an assumption we adopted in our earlier discussion of the over-population problem (see Chapter 3).

In Figure 134 *MP* represents the marginal-product curve for a factor of production. Consider first a price of $OP_1$ for each unit of factor. (Perhaps it is easiest for the reader to think in terms of agricultural labourers being paid in bushels of corn; in our case $OP_1$ bushels is the price of each labourer.) Which employment level will the employer desire at this price? The maximizing rule appears to be satisfied at two output levels, $ON_1$ and $ON_6$: which should the firm choose?

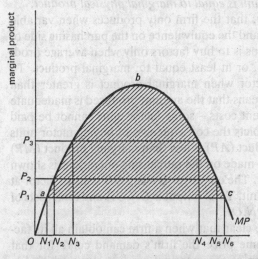

Figure 134                    units of resource employed

The problem is akin to that met earlier with respect to the two points on the marginal-cost curve which appeared to satisfy the output rule; and the answer to the employment question is similar to the one advanced there. $ON_1$ is ruled out because the potential gain from employing one additional resource unit is greater than the resource price $OP_1$. Indeed, this is true for the whole range of employment levels up to $ON_6$. Only when $ON_6$ units are being employed is the rule satisfied – the product of the $N_6$th unit is equal to the resource price. If the point needs further emphasis, note that the employer enjoys an output surplus over the costs of hire for employment levels $ON_1$ to $ON_6$. The total output produced by this number of units is equal to the area under the $MP$ curve between input levels $ON_1$ and $ON_6$, i.e. area $N_1abcN_6$. However, total employment costs of these units is only $N_1acN_6$ leaving a surplus output of $abc$ (shaded area of the diagram).

The above analysis also holds for other resource prices. For example, consider prices $OP_2$ and $OP_3$ – in each case it is the employment level given by the downward-sloping section of the $MP$ curve which satisfies our rule. So far, then, we have shown that *for a given factor price an employer will hire units of factor until the price per unit is equal to marginal physical product.*

Recall, however, that the firm only produces when variable costs are covered: and the equivalence on the purchasing side of the firm's operations is to buy factors only when average product is greater than, or at least equal to, marginal product. To buy units of a factor when marginal product is greater than average product means that the amount produced is inadequate to cover employment costs – some factor units cannot be paid for. Figure 135 depicts the consequences of buying factor units when average product $(AP)$ is less than marginal product $(MP)$ and the size of loss made on the purchasing operations is shown by the shaded area. The employer is using $ON$ units of factor at a price of $OP$ per unit. Total output is $ON.OA$ and total costs of employment are $ON.OP$.

It should now be clear that when a firm can obtain all its factor units at the same price the firm's demand curve for that factor is the section of the marginal-product curve which lies

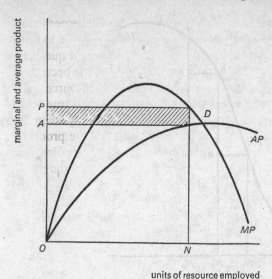

Figure 135

below the average-product curve. In Figure 135 the demand curve commences at $D$.

## Marginal revenue product

The analysis so far has assumed payments in kind so it must now be refined to take account of the existence of money. In a money economy most factors of production receive monetary payments as opposed to rewards in kind. Furthermore, in a money economy each employer is not interested merely in the *physical* output of each additional unit of resource but also in the *monetary value* of that output, i.e. how much revenue the employer can earn from selling the output of the additional unit of resource. This value is often referred to as *marginal revenue product* and is illustrated in Figure 136. Average revenue product ($ARP$) is also shown in the diagram.

In Figure 136 a $TRP$ is the total-revenue-product curve. It is the money value of the total-physical-product curve and as such

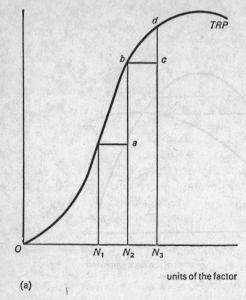

(a)

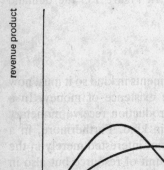

(b)

Figure 136

it is shaped by the law of diminishing returns. Suppose employment of factor of production $x$ is increased by one unit, say from $N_1$ to $N_2$, total revenue product increases by $ab$, i.e. marginal revenue product, the revenue to be gained from the sale of the output of the extra unit, is $ab$. For an increase in employment from $N_2$ to $N_3$, the resultant increase in revenue (marginal revenue product) is $cd$. If we repeated the exercise for all additions to employment we could trace out the marginal-revenue-product curve ($MRP$) as shown in Figure 136b.

Since this curve shows the money value of the marginal-physical-product curve, the downward-sloping section below $ARP$ represents the resource-demand curve for an employer in a money economy. When the firm's product market is perfectly competitive, calculation of marginal revenue product is very straightforward: since each extra unit of output sells at the same price as previous units, marginal revenue product equals marginal physical product multiplied by price per unit. When the firm's product market is monopolistic, calculations are more complicated since each additional unit of output results in a fall in product price (the demand curve for the product slopes downwards from left to right).

### Does the demand curve always have a downward slope?

The fact that the marginal-product curve of a factor of production slopes downwards seems to prejudge the issue of whether an employer will always buy more of a factor when its price falls. But this is not the case. In Chapter 11 we saw that a consumer might buy less of a good as the price falls, given the existence of superior substitutes. The same may be true in the case of an employer's demand for resources. So far we have looked at an individual resource in isolation, but firms combine several resources and our efficiency rule must be extended to consider these other resources. The rule is the equivalent of the equimarginal rule which we met in our earlier analysis of consumer behaviour. In the present case the employer maximizes the benefit from his outlay by spending on resources 1, 2, 3, . . . , $N$ until

$$\frac{MRP_1}{P_1} = \frac{MRP_2}{P_2} = \frac{MRP_3}{P_3} = \cdots = \frac{MRP_N}{P^N},$$

where $MRP$ refers to marginal revenue product, $P$ indicates factor price and the subscripts 1 to $N$ refer to specific factors.

Note that when more than one factor of production is variable the marginal-revenue-product curve of a factor ceases to be the firm's demand curve for that factor. A change in the price of one factor may lead to a substitution of that factor for the now relatively dearer factor(s) without a parallel change in output. This means that an employer's demand curve for a factor will be more elastic than the marginal-revenue-product curve: given the equi-marginal rule, the precise nature of an employer's demand response to a change in the price of any one factor of production will depend upon the ease with which factors can be substituted for one another within the firm's production function. In other words, the employer's response to a price change is determined by the relative strengths of the income, or in this context *output*, and the substitution effects.

*Substitution effect.* The fall in the price of one factor relative to the price of the other factors induces a substitution of the relatively cheaper factor for the one now relatively dearer.

*Output effect.* This is analogous to the income effect of consumer theory. The fall in the price of one productive resource means that costs have fallen and output can be profitably expanded. Three possibilities can be considered for implementing this increase in output:

Hire more of all factors;
Hire more of the factor whose price has fallen;
Hire more of the factors whose prices have not fallen.

The first possibility arises when factors can only be employed in fixed proportions or when there are limits to factor substitution. The second case, buying more of the new relatively cheaper factor, is consistent with the rules of optimizing behaviour. It is, however, the third case which is most interesting since it raises the question of whether an upward-sloping demand curve is possible – we encountered such a possibility in the earlier chapter on consumer behaviour.

It was assumed, in the case of the consumer, that his income was fixed so that a fall in the price of one good was equivalent to an increase in his income. He could therefore spend this increased income either on the good whose price had fallen or on the goods whose price had not fallen. The firm, however, is in a different position since, assuming a perfect capital market, its spending is not restricted by a given budget but by the benefit of buying more of a factor in relation to the cost (price of that factor). If the firm faces a perfect capital market it can borrow funds with which to buy factors as long as the expected revenue from using those factors exceeds their costs. This being so there is no reason why a firm should spend any of the increased income (resulting from a fall in one factor's price) on a factor whose price has not fallen. If it was previously not worthwhile buying more of that factor then there is no conceivable reason why more should be bought when its price has risen (relative to that of the factor whose price has fallen).

We can now see why the theory of consumer behaviour can give odd results. The theory gives the consumer a fixed income, and does not permit him to borrow because he possesses no assets nor buys any assets with which he can earn an income. If, however, we switch from a consumer to a household which obtains income by the sale of labour services then the rigid constraint would seem to disappear since the household could enter the capital market and borrow against future income. By borrowing, households may avoid having to buy some inferior goods, but the amount that they can borrow is limited by their prospects – they buy middle-price cars but not Rolls-Royces.

Differences in ease of access to the capital market of households and firms (corporations, partnerships) may be a reasonable assumption, given the problems that arise if a household goes bankrupt – the assets (labour services) of such a bankrupt cannot be owned by another person in a democratic society. There may be no restrictions on a person working harder or longer and income (work) may be dictated by consumption.

## The price-elasticity of derived demand

We have established that more of a factor will be bought if its price falls and it now remains for us to consider the factors determining the strength of the response of demand to a change in price, i.e. the elasticity of derived demand.

1 *The price-elasticity of demand for the product.* If a particular factor of production, say labour, pushes up its price then production costs and the product price may rise. If consumers cannot switch to another product then the producer will be under no compulsion to resist the demand of a resource owner for a price increase and the price-elasticity of demand for the factor will be low.

2 *Substitutability of factors.* If an employer can easily substitute one factor for another then the price-elasticity of demand for those factors will be high.

3 *Elasticity of supply of factors.* If one factor has only one use

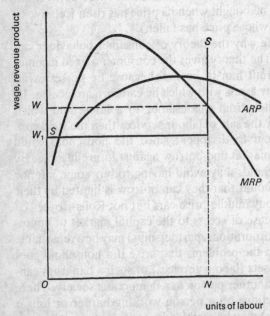

Figure 137

then it may find that its earnings may be reduced because other resource owners obtain increased rewards at the expense of it. Thus if a group of workers are immobile it may be possible for the owners of capital to reduce wages, below the marginal product of labour, down to the supply price as in Figure 137 where the wage is pushed down from $OW$ to $OW_1$.

4 *The percentage of total costs.* Supposing labour costs are 10 per cent of total costs, then a 10 per cent increase in wages will add only 1 per cent to total costs and hence to prices. So the effect on product demand may be slight.

### Shifts in derived demand

Since demand for a productive factor is a derived demand, shifts in the demand curve for the final product will, other things being equal, induce shifts in the demand curve for the factor. Using the illustration of perfect competition in both product and factor markets, suppose the demand curve for the product shifts to the right resulting in a rise in product price. This means a rise in marginal revenue product – marginal physical product is unchanged but price has risen – and the marginal-revenue-product curve shifts to the right.

Product price changes, however, are not the sole cause of shifts in the derived demand curve. Even when product price has not changed, marginal-revenue product can still rise or fall as a result of changes in marginal physical product. Some technological change may cause a factor's productivity to rise (or fall) and the marginal-revenue-product curve to shift to the right (or left). There will eventually be a product price reaction to the change in productivity and this will create yet another shift in the marginal-revenue-product curve.

Finally, a change in the price of other factors will cause a shift in the marginal-revenue-product curve. (Ask yourself why.)

### The industry's derived demand

When we constructed the market-demand curve for a product as the horizontal summation of individual demand curves there was no *a priori* reason why market demand *ex post* should differ from *ex ante* market demand. This is not the case when we attempt to construct an industry's derived-demand curve for a factor of production. Since we can construct an *ex ante* industry-supply curve for the product as the horizontal summation of marginal-cost curves, we can similarly construct an intended derived-demand curve – a horizontal summation of individual marginal-revenue-product curves. Such a curve would show how many factor units all firms in the industry intended to buy at various factor prices. Constructing an *ex post* derived-demand curve for the industry, however, is not so simple. As the price of a productive factor falls the individual firm's demand curve shows the firm to buy more units of the factor *on the assumption that the output of all other firms remains constant*. But if factor price falls to one firm it falls to all and, therefore, every firm wants to employ more units. As a result, output of final product rises and, final demand being unchanged, its price falls. This price fall means that marginal revenue product falls for each employer and individual derived demand curves shift

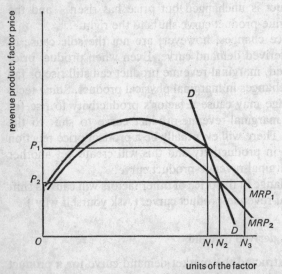

Figure 138

to the left. Thus, *ex post*, each employer buys less of the factor than he intended and the resultant industry-demand curve is steeper than the *ex ante* industry-demand curve.

Figure 138 depicts the construction of an *ex post* derived-demand curve for an individual firm. Horizontally summing all such curves gives the industry situation.

The original price in Figure 138 is $OP_1$. At this price the firm intends to hire $ON_1$ units of the factor, $MRP_1$ being the firm's original demand curve. Price now falls to $OP_2$ and the employer intends to hire $ON_3$ factor units. However, since the price has fallen to all employers, all hire more, produce more and product price falls. The resultant fall in marginal revenue product shifts the firm's factor-demand curve to the left, $MRP_2$, and, *ex post*, the firm hires $ON_2$ factor units instead of the intended $ON_3$ units. Repeating the analysis for all factor-price changes yields an *ex post* derived-demand curve $DD$.

## Summary

This chapter has not distinguished among different factors of production but has presented a general theory of what determines the demand for productive resources in a market system. The two major determinants were seen to be the price of the factor and its contribution to the employer's revenue, i.e. marginal revenue product. The demand for a factor of production is a derived demand and the nature of the demand curve for a factor depends upon the nature of the demand for the final product as well as the technical conditions of production.

## Questions

1 (a) Does a hump-shaped marginal-revenue-product curve imply a U-shaped marginal cost curve?
(b) A perfectly competitive firm employs only one variable factor of production. How could we distinguish its factor-demand curve from its supply curve of final output?

2 What happens to the firm's marginal-revenue-product curve

if the market-demand curve for the final product shifts to the left?

3  What determines the elasticity of the *ex post* industry demand curve for a factor of production?

4  If the price of factor $A$ used by a firm falls while the price of factor $B$ remains constant, will the firm adjust its use of factors so that the ratio of the marginal-product of $A$ to the marginal product of $B$ falls?

5  A firm can freely vary the amount of factor $X$ employed but the quantity available of other factors is fixed. The firm's product sells in a perfectly competitive market at a price of £2 per unit. The firm's production function is given by

$$Q = 20 + 24X - X^2.$$

(a)  Give an algebraic expression for average product.
(b)  Derive the marginal-product function.
(c)  How many units of $X$ must be employed to maximize total output?
(d)  If the unit price of $X$ is £8 how many units will the firm hire?
(e)  The price of final output falls to £1 per unit. How many units of $X$ will the firm hire now?

6  A farmer employs two factors of production – labour and land. His production function is given by

$$Q = 6AB - 10A^2 - 2B^2,$$

where $A$ represents the number of men employed per acre and $B$ represents the number of acres of land.

(a)  Derive the two marginal-product functions.
(b)  If labour's hiring-price is equal to that of land's, how many men per acre should the farmer employ?

7  'If, as we argued in the previous chapter, the distribution of income is of supreme importance to any society, then it is the demand for goods which is the derived demand and not that for factors.' Discuss.

# Chapter 23
# The Demand and Supply of Factors of Production

We can now bring demand and supply together in order to determine factor rewards. Demand is one determinant of factor rewards but without any indication of supply conditions it is but one blade of a pair of scissors. The simplest case of factor-price determination is where the supply of the productive resources is fixed and the resource has no production costs. Figure 139 shows the situation where $ON$ units of a factor are available irrespec-

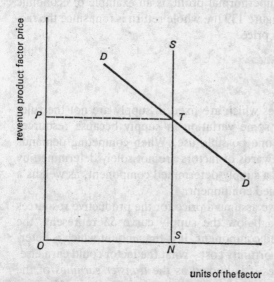

Figure 139

tive of the price per unit. The supply of the factor is therefore completely price-inelastic. In this instance the price of the factor, *OP*, is determined by the demand for the factor *DD*; and total return to the factor is *OPTN*.

The example shown in Figure 139 illustrates the theory of rent as propounded by David Ricardo (1772–1823). According to Ricardo, rent was the return to the owner of land. Since land was the gift of nature, it had no cost of production, it was fixed in supply, and so the return to land was demand-determined. In his general view of economic development Ricardo envisaged that as the demand for land shifted to the right, then the rents of landowners would rise.

The theory of rent, originally applied to land, was eventually extended to any factor of production in short supply. People with special abilities, footballers and opera singers, can earn rents. The generalized concept of *economic rent* is defined as *the amount of return to a factor over and above what is necessary to induce that factor to undertake its prevailing employment*. In other words, economic rent is a surplus over supply price (the entrepreneur's 'supernormal profit' is an example of economic rent). Thus, in Figure 139 the whole return is rent since the factor has no supply price.

## Variable supply

Cases of resources which are fixed in supply are not the rule. Usually there is some variation in supply because resources have more than one possible use. When competing demands occur then the rewards of factors are not solely determined by demand; there is a supply-determined component, as well as a demand-determined component.

In Figure 140 we assume a price for the productive resources of *OP*. The area below the supply curve *SS* represents the supply-determined component. It is the amount which is determined by the opportunity cost – what the factor could earn elsewhere. Sometimes it is known as the *transfer earnings* of the factor. The other area is the rent element. One way of looking

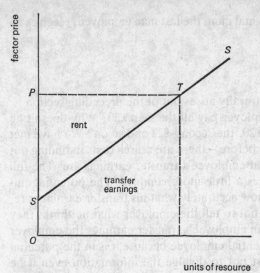

Figure 140

at the situation depicted in Figure 140 is to suppose that the horizontal axis refers to men willing to work at various rates of pay. We may suppose that the:

First man is willing to work for £20 per week;
Second man is willing to work for £22 per week;
⋮
Eighth man is willing to work for £25 per week;
⋮
Last man is willing to work for £30 per week.

As the diagram suggests that all men receive the same pay it follows that all receive £30, but for all but the last man his pay of £30 contains his transfer earnings and a rent. Thus:

First man has transfer earnings of £20 and a rent of £10;
Second man has transfer earnings of £22 and a rent of £8;
⋮
Eighth man has transfer earnings of £25 and a rent of £5;
⋮
Last man has transfer earnings of £30 and no rent.

Note that the marginal man, the last man employed, receives no rent.

### Why pay rent?

A question that naturally arises out of the preceding section is: why should an employer pay all the men £30? Why doesn't he pay the first man £20, the second £22 and so on? We have met part of the answer before – there are search costs in finding out what each potential employee's transfer earnings are. The full answer, however, is a little more complex. The potential employee may not know accurately what his transfer earnings are, but is determined not to tell the employer what he thinks they are. Thus to find an employee's transfer earnings the employer cannot ask his potential employee because it is in the potential employee's interest not to divulge the information even if he knows it accurately.

The other main part of the answer lies in the particular nature of *labour* as opposed to some inanimate factor of production. If the potential employees band together and offer to work only for £30 then the employer has the choice of an optimum sized labour force or *no* labour force. By banding together every potential employee stands to gain, except the last man, the man with transfer earnings of £30.

An interesting feature of this analysis is that for the first time we have dropped the assumption of homogeneous factors of production. Some workers have different tastes or abilities from others and thus have higher transfer earnings. We have now established an important point:

*When a factor is fixed in supply and has only one use then its reward will be demand-determined. It will obtain a rent. If, however, the factor has alternative uses then its reward will be dictated by its transfer earnings.*

In his early exposition of rent theory Ricardo assumed that land had only one use – the production of corn. Hence he was able to say that the price of land was high because the price of corn was high, that it was the strong demand for corn which led to an intense demand for land. For Ricardo, rent did not enter into production costs but was determined by demand. If the land had alternative uses, then the opportunity cost of using the land for some other purpose would have entered into the determination of the price of corn.

## Quasi-rent

In the short run resources are fixed and immobile. The decisions which have been made concerning their use were made in the past and so the costs have been incurred: 'bygones are bygones'. It follows therefore that in the short run any earnings of resources may be likened to a rent: they were called by Marshall 'quasi-rents'.

## Taxation

The notion that some resources are fixed in supply has been used as the basis for taxation and the financing of the state. Around the turn of the century Henry George pioneered the single-tax movement. He was impressed by the fact that, land being fixed in supply, landlords obtained an 'unearned increment' as the demand for land rose with economic development. He proposed that the unearned increment be taxed and argued that the proceeds would provide all the necessary state finances.

Apart from the problem that a single tax might bring insufficient revenue, the land tax runs into the difficulty of separating the economic rent from the return on capital invested in improvements. However, the basic idea behind the land tax does have relevance for fiscal policy. A Chancellor of the Exchequer who wished to raise finance without causing economic agents to change their decisions would try to impose taxes on commodities which were inelastic in demand, and on factors of production which were inelastic in supply; this is the essence of what is known as *optimum tax theory*. Furthermore, the land tax notion does contain the idea that resources which are a free gift of Nature might be owned by the state and the right to use them should be determined by auction. In effect, the auction would establish a tax upon the use of the resources. The problem, as policy on North Sea gas and oil has revealed, is that governments are often reluctant to allow free auctions but insist upon preferences being given to national firms.

## Questions

1 A professional footballer currently earning £200 per week faces the following employment opportunities.

| Occupation | Weekly earnings |
| --- | --- |
| garage mechanic | £20 |
| school teacher | £25 |
| sports writer | £40 |
| sales executive | £65 |

How much economic rent is he enjoying?

2 Distinguish between the effects (short-run and long-run) on factor supply of a unit tax on:
(a) A factor whose supply curve is perfectly elastic;
(b) A factor earning pure economic rent;
(c) A factor earning quasi-rent.

3 Colliery spoil heaps (which can provide road materials), scrap metals and antique furniture are examples of free gifts, not of Nature, but of the past. Does the reward to their owners constitute a rent?

4 Oil is discovered in the Irish Sea. Should the Government allocate quotas at a fixed price to producers or should it auction sites? What would be the effects of different pricing procedures?

5 A university professor is employed as a consultant by the Kruger Arms Company. His university claims that his fees constitute a rent to the Chair and as such should be surrendered to it. What do you think of the university's behaviour? Suppose the professor had worked as a consultant to the government and was awarded a knighthood. What should his university do? What do you think the professor will do? What do you think are

the implications of this problem for the conduct of university teaching and research?

6 'The price of cinema seats is high because the demand for cinema seats is high.' 'The price of cinema seats is high because the price of land is high.' Comment on these two statements.

# Chapter 24
# Interest

We have referred to the rate of interest in Chapter 6 and further discussion will take place in Part Nine. Hence, our present comments will be brief. The rate of interest is the price paid for a loan. The rate of interest is the price a borrower is willing to pay and is determined by his belief that he can use the loan in such a manner as to allow him to repay the principal and the interest charge and still leave him with a reward for his activities. Similar considerations will affect the willingness of a lender to make a loan. What the rate of interest does, therefore, is to provide a means by which future and present benefits can be compared. The crucial element, however, is the estimation of the future benefits. Thus, if an individual wishes to borrow today in order to buy wheat which he proposes to sell next year then he must first begin by estimating next year's price of wheat and then compare it with this year's wheat price before he can work out the rate of interest he is prepared to pay on a loan. Although the rate of interest appears to play an important part in economics, it must not be forgotten that the crucial element is the estimation of future prices. The lack of markets which yield future prices explains why uncertainty plays such an important role in determining economic activity.

In an industrial society loans are obtained to create or purchase capital goods such as lathes, bulldozers and power stations. Capital goods provide a future stream of benefits and these streams of benefits are subject to diminishing returns in the sense that successive additions to the stock of machines yields lower and lower returns. In seeking a loan an individual will compare the benefits discounted to the decision date with the price of a machine. If the discounted benefits are greater than the price of the machine then he will purchase a machine and the act of purchase is called *investment*. A fuller analysis of investment will be made in Part Nine.

## Money and real rates of interest

In a money economy we need to make a distinction between the money, or nominal rate of interest, and the real rate of interest. In equilibrium there would be no distinction between the two rates. But supposing an individual borrows £100 at 5 per cent. At the end of a year he would expect to pay back £105. If, however, the price level were to rise by 5 per cent then the effective or real rate of interest would be zero. It follows, therefore, that although the real rate of interest cannot be observed its magnitude can be inferred from the behaviour of the price level with respect to the money rate of interest.

*The real rate of interest is the difference between the money rate of interest and the rate of change of the price level.*

In discussing the distinction between real and money rates of interest it is important to distinguish anticipated movements of the price level from unanticipated price changes. If an inflation is anticipated then it is always possible to arrange contracts which take into account the movement of prices. Thus, if the real rate of interest is 5 per cent and the rate of change of prices is expected to be 10 per cent then it would be possible to fix the money rate of interest at 15 per cent. Failure to anticipate inflation can, of course, lead to the possibility that real rates of interest become negative – a state of affairs that did occur in the sixties and seventies.

### The rate of interest in a planned economy

The rate of interest is determined in a market economy through the interplay of demand and supply forces, but even in a

planned economy there would still be a need for rate of
interest to express the relative preference for present and future
benefits.

## Questions

1 Why are future prices so important and why do you think that
future prices and futures markets may not exist for many
goods?

2 Why do economists attach so much importance to the distinction between the real and money rates of interest?

# Chapter 25
# Profit

In everyday usage profit refers to the difference between the receipts and the costs of a firm and it is this profit which businessmen are supposed to maximize. This surplus does, however, differ from what economists have tended to call profit, for the following reasons.

In some circles the distinction is drawn between what is required for current consumption and what might be made available for investment and future consumption. This is a distinction between wages, on the assumption that all wages are spent on current consumption, and a surplus, which is also called *profit*.

Commercial profit may include the transfer earnings of the businessman. Frequently, and particularly in the case of the owner-managed firm, the owner(s) may fail to deduct from the surplus the amount which he (they) might have earned in some other line of activity. The reason for transfer earnings appearing in the commercial profit is because they are not considered in everyday usage to be costs. *Commercial profits will often include transfer earnings*.

There will also be a tendency to overlook the opportunity cost of the owner's capital. This can arise in the case of the self-proprietor who not only fails to exclude transfer earnings but neglects to allow for the interest he could have earned on his capital had he invested it elsewhere. For example, suppose a man invests £5000 in a shop and in a particular year he incurs expenditures of £2000 and receives £3000 from the sale of his output. From the £1000 surplus he should deduct his transfer earnings and an amount equivalent to that which he would have obtained had he invested his £5000 elsewhere. *Commercial profit will therefore tend to include foregone interest receipts*.

Finally, commercial profit will often include rent elements such as might arise when something owned by the firm is in scarce supply relative to the demands of other institutions and individuals. When the elements of transfer earnings, interest and rent are deducted there may be left a residual difference between revenue and costs and the explanation of the possible occurrences of discrepancies has been put down to a variety of causes.

### Ricardian theory (1817–?)[1]

David Ricardo began by explaining the origins of a surplus in an agrarian economy. He assumed that corn (a synonym for all agricultural products) was used to produce corn with the assistance of labour and land. Since corn took a year to produce workers were supported during the interval between sowing and reaping by advances of corn from a wage fund owned by capitalists. The basic features of this society can now be gleaned from Figure 141.

Along the vertical axis is measured the output of corn and along the horizontal axis is measured the balanced proportions of capital and labour applied to a given amount of land, *OA*. In the long run labour must be paid the subsistence wage, *OW*, and capitalists must earn the minimum rate of profit, *WS*. In the beginning, when capital (and labour) are scarce at *OF*, the share of rent is *DLM*, the share of wages is *OWBF* and the profits share is *WLMB*. The abnormally high profits cause capitalists to hire more workers, and thus temporarily pull up the wage, and also to invest. Initially, the wage is pulled up to *FP* and the subsequent behaviour of wages and profits is traced out by the *PE* curve. If labour supply were to increase faster than

1. The absence of a concluding date indicates that in economics old theories seldom die nor do they fade away.

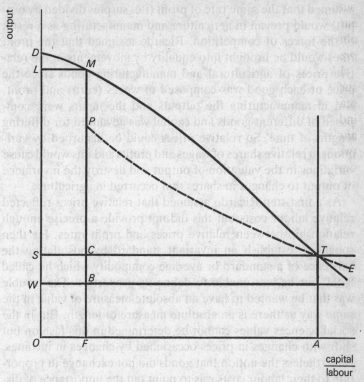

Figure 141

capital accumulation then the *PE* curve would be pushed closer towards the *WE* line and if capital were to increase faster than labour then the *PE* line would be pushed further away from the *PE* line. Eventually population expansion and capital accumulation propel the economy to the long-run equilibrium at *T* at which point labour earns its subsistence wage, capitalists earn their minimum profit and the landlords' share has become enlarged to *SDT*.

Problems arose when Ricardo attempted to extend the model to embrace manufactures. In agriculture the input and output are both measured in the same units, corn, and so there is no problem in measuring the value of profits. Now Ricardo assumed that the same rate of profit (i.e. surplus divided by output) would prevail in agriculture and manufacturing as a result of the forces of competition. Ricardo assumed that the profit rates would be brought into equality by movements in the relative prices of agricultural and manufacturing goods since the price of each good was composed of wages (corn) and profit. But in manufacturing the outputs and the inputs were composed of different goods and capital was advanced for differing lengths of time. So relative prices could be disturbed by variations in relative shares of wages and profits and this would cause variations in the valuation of output and destroy the invariance of output to changes in shares that occurred in agriculture.

As a first step Ricardo assumed that relative prices reflected relative labour costs but this did not provide a precise enough relationship between relative prices and profit rates. He then sought to establish an invariant standard by postulating the existence of a standard or average commodity which he called 'gold' but he was unable to define its properties. The trouble was that he wanted to have an absolute measure of value in the same way as there is an absolute measure of length. But in the social sciences values cannot be determined in this fashion but shift with changes in prices occasioned by changes in incomes. Nevertheless the notion that goods did not exchange in proportion to their labour costs was to point out the importance of distribution and to provide Marx with his political economy.

### Marxian theory (1867–?)

In Ricardo's theory the surplus arose from the bounty of nature but this proposition seemed inappropriate for an industrial economy and Marx attempted to resolve the problem of a surplus through his theory of exploitation. The worker worked ten hours but needed only the product of eight hours' work to provide for himself and his family. The capitalist pocketed the remaining two hours' work. This seemed to make sense in an industrial economy. For the characteristic of the late eighteenth and early nineteenth centuries was the massive increase in hours of work and the tremendous struggles to limit the length of the working day. These struggles were also intensified by the great expansion of employment of women and young children which meant that the working man had only to provide for himself.

The surplus was not spent in riotous living. As Keynes noted, the capitalists were allowed some of the cake but on condition that they did not consume it. The surplus was ploughed back because each capitalist feared being overtaken by his rivals. But if capitalists spent the surplus on building bigger and better factories might not that increase the demand for labour and raise real wages?

Wages might be held down by population expansion – the Malthusian terror. Marx did not like that idea. If wages were determined by biology what price socialism? So in Marx's theory wages were held down by a reserve army of unemployed created by the tendency of capitalists to buy labour-saving machines.

Marx also encountered Ricardo's problem of relating values to prices. But let us set out the basic information.

Let $u$ be total value of a commodity (or if aggregation is done, all commodities), $c$ be constant capital (machines used up in one period which do not create a surplus but merely transmit their own value to the final product), $v$ be variable capital (labour) and $s$ be surplus value created by labour. Then:

$$u = c + v + s.$$

This is no more than an accounting statement which says that the total value of a commodity can be broken down into the costs of machines, labour costs and a surplus or mark-up.

Now follow three crucial definitions:

The rate of surplus value or exploitation,

$$s' = s/v.$$

The rate of profit,

$$p' = s/c + v.$$

The organic composition of capital or capital–labour ratio,

$$q = c/v.$$

Marx assumed that organic compositions of capital would be dictated by technologies and would not be equal in all industries. But he did assume a tendency for rates of surplus value and rates of profit to be equalized through competition. This, it is alleged, constitutes a contradiction for all three ratios are related. Thus:

$$p' = \frac{s}{c + v} = \frac{s/v}{c/v + v/v} = \frac{s'}{1 + q} \ .$$

Hence if all $p'$ and all $s'$ are everywhere equal then all $q$ must everywhere be equal. So if organic compositions of capital are allowed to differ then rates of surplus values and profits must be allowed to differ and that could mean that constant capital was the source of surplus value. Worse still it might be that land, an element of constant capital, was responsible for surplus value.

Marx sought to resolve the problem between values and prices by assuming that prices diverged from values in a systematic manner and was related to some average organic composition of capital. This was Marx's solution to the problem of an invariable standard.

Before concluding this section it is worth noting that Marx linked up the discussion of real forces with monetary forces by pointing out that exploitation takes place in a monetary economy where capitalists spend sums of money in order to obtain larger sums of money. Hence the process of exploitation was intimately related to the control of finance since that ensured control over all other means of production.

### Neoclassical theory (1870–?)

By the 1870s Ricardian theory, based as it was on an agrarian society, had become untenable whilst Marxian theory was unpalatable. Almost simultaneously there arose in various countries a group of theorists who sought to explain the problems of distribution along alternative lines. These theorists – amongst whom were Jevons, Menger, Walras, Marshall, J. B. Clark, Bohm-Bawerk and Wicksell – are called neoclassical economists because they adopted certain elements from classical theory and gave them an emphasis which they had previously not been given.

In neoclassical theory the prices of factors of production are determined by the forces of demand and supply. And in the theory an important part is played by the marginal productivity doctrine. A factor of production will be employed up to the point at which the productivity of the last unit employed is measured by the factor price. Hence, there is a diminishing marginal productivity curve which is the demand curve for the factor. When the price of a factor falls more will be demanded and when the price rises more will be demanded. Given the existence of marginal productivity curves for each factor it was then established that, under perfect competition, if factors were paid in accordance with their marginal products then the sum of factor payments would just equal the total value of the product.

On the supply side the neoclassical economists explained the supply of labour in terms of the real wage offered to labour although they did recognize that there might be a backward sloping supply curve. In the case of capital an explanation was put forward in terms of the need to reward abstinence from current consumption.

After much refinement, neoclassical theory has come to decompose a factor's reward into:

1 A current reward consisting of two elements
(a) the payment necessary to keep a factor in its present employment – *transfer earnings*.
(b) a possible surplus above transfer earnings – *rent*.

2 In terms of the initial outlay incurred in creating the factor
(a) the *interest* on the original outlay; that is, the payment necessary to transfer resources from possible consumption in the past to increased consumption in the future.
(b) the *profit or loss* arising from the decision to invest resources in a particular activity whose outcome was clouded in uncertainty.

The theory appears to be most satisfactory if it is assumed that all resources exist at a point of time and there is a general auction which allocates them to various uses. Because this is extremely unrealistic and reduces economic activity to exchange and not production and exchange then the alternative is to postulate that the theory is valid in the long run when all resources are perfectly mobile and the proportions in which they can be used are variable. The reasons for such extreme assumptions are that an entrepreneur who cannot vary the proportions in which he employs factors cannot assess their efficiency. Thus, to take a famous problem. If twelve men are employed with twelve spades to dig a trench what would be the outcome if an extra man were employed? Unless he was provided with a spade then he would produce nothing and if he were provided with a spade then it would be impossible to disentangle his contribution from that of the spade. In the short run, therefore, when factors are employed in fixed proportions it might be impossible to measure productivities. In the long run, of course, it would be possible to use the depreciation allowances to buy thirteen cheaper spades. And it might also be possible to operate a shift system whereby thirteen men used twelve spades.

The problem of measuring productivities becomes most acute when an attempt is made to determine the shares of factors in the total product of an economy. This involves aggregating the amounts of various factors and is particularly difficult for capital. If we wish to measure a community's stock of capital then we cannot add the physical units together because they are heterogeneous. But if we wish to add the units together in value terms then we need a discount rate but the discount rate cannot be obtained until we know the stock of capital. This point can best be appreciated by considering an isoquant map with labour measured along one axis and capital measured along the other axis. We could assume units of skilled labour were multiples of unskilled labour and devise a subsistence wage. But what could we use to measure capital? In order to obtain a rate of interest we would need to know the amount of capital employed with the given labour force. The problem seems to be circular and this explains why it is resolved by assuming that the stock of capital and the rate of interest are simultaneously solved in a point-of-time auction or, in the very long run, by trial and error.

The marginal productivity doctrine assumes that a fall in the rate of interest would lead to the use of more capital intensive methods of production but this has been denied by some economists. Suppose, they argue, there are two methods of producing wine. In method A seven units of labour are employed two periods before the final output is produced, whereas method B employs two units of labour three periods earlier *and* six units one period earlier. Now the answer to the question: which is the more capital intensive method of production depends upon the rate of interest adopted. At rates of interest above 100 per cent method A will be preferred to method B and at very low rates of interest A will still be chosen instead of B. But at intermediate rates B will be found to be cheaper than A. This is the essence of the *capital reswitching* debate and the conclusion is that a fall in the rate of interest need not necessarily lead to a more capital intensive, more time intensive, method of production. Indeed it is impossible to say which is the more time intensive.

The reasoning behind such a startling conclusion lies in the compounded effects of interest rate changes on lengthy production processes when the capital intensity is high in the early stages of production. At very low rates of interest, close to zero, A will be preferred to B because $7 < 6 + 2$. As the interest rate rises it may, at first, be worthwhile cutting the length of the ageing process and so B will be chosen. But if interest rates were to rise still further the compounding effects of two units of labour for three periods will be greater than seven units for two periods and so A will be chosen. The conclusion is that if trades unions could alter the rate of interest then they could alter the distribution of income. But the importance of capital switching depends upon empirical evidence, upon the range in which interest rates vary, and the capital intensity of production.

## Neo-Keynesian theory (1936–?)

Neo-Keynesian theory is an outcome of the macroeconomic ideas of Keynes and Kalecki and as such it may not be appreciated without a prior reading of Part Nine. It seeks to establish a theory of distribution on the following assumptions.

1 Distribution theory cannot be divorced from economic growth.

2 Investment and capital accumulation are not sensitive to changes in the rate of interest but respond to the 'animal spirits' of entrepreneurs.

3 Workers cannot determine their real wages but only their money wages. This proposition stems from the fact that in a decentralized economy wage determination and product price determination take place in separate markets and frequently at different times. If workers agree to accept cuts in money wages in order to reduce their real wages and thereby combat unemployment they will not succeed. Instead they will reduce total demand because of the fall in purchasing power. If workers attempt to raise money wages too high then they will create inflation. In attempting to fix money wages workers will be influenced by notions of fairness; by what other comparable groups of workers are earning. If an employer attempts to pay too little then he will experience absenteeism, strikes and go-slows – *the productivity of labour is therefore not independent of the wage which was a crucial assumption of neoclassical theory*.

4 A characteristic feature of product markets is oligopoly. Product prices will be determined by a price leader who will fix a price on the basis of costs (which are assumed to be mainly wages) and a mark up. The mark up will determine the amount of savings necessary to finance projected investment.

5 Because of fixed proportions in production in the short run, wages do not determine employment but they do influence the amount of savings for investment. And because of fixed proportions it becomes difficult to assess the productivity of labour. Wages can therefore be determined by relative bargaining strength, by the power of trade unions. What collective bargaining does is to influence growth and future employment. But simple comparisons of present and future employment are not easy to make because of the impact of technical change.

These then are the basic elements of the Neo-Keynesian theory but which might be reasonably called the Ricardian–Marxian–Neo-Keynesian theory because of its emphasis upon the absence of a marginal productivity explanation of wages and profits, its stress upon the link between income distribution and growth and its reliance upon aggregate demand. To the main features of Neo-Keynesian theory can be added other propositions such as the view that money is passive and merely responds to changes in economic activity. Inflation is seen as a problem of income distribution and can only be resolved through an incomes policy. Finally, Neo-Keynesians argue that balance of payments deficits cannot be solved through deflation or devaluation because of their effects upon income distribution; they require the use of tariffs and incomes policies.

## An assessment

Many of the issues which we have raised concerning Classical, Marxian, Neoclassical and Neo-Keynesian theories are beyond the scope of an introductory text and some cannot be appreciated until after Part Nine has been read. Classical theory may be considered to have been refuted by the rise of real wages in the nineteenth century and the fall in the share of rent. Marxian theory may also be thought to have been refuted by the behaviour of wages, although its popularity in the sixties and seventies suggests that its strength lies less in its specific economic aspects and more in its sociological features, as well as its compelling attraction to the peasants of the underdeveloped agrarian economies. Neoclassical and Neo-Keynesian theory may be considered to be complementary with one stressing long-run behaviour and the other emphasizing short-run problems.

## Questions

1 What determines the share of rent in the national output of the Ricardian model? Supposing land was heterogeneous, would its presence make any difference to the theory?

2 What determines the wage in the Marxian model? Does it make any difference to the theory to assume that there are different types of labour?

3 Supposing the neoclassical theory was applied to a growing economy, what would be its predictions concerning wages, profits and rents?

4 Can any of the features of the Neo-Keynesian theory be incorporated into the neoclassical model without destroying the latter's usefulness? For example, trades unions, capital accumulation by firms, oligopoly, fixed proportions.

# Chapter 26
# Labour

Most people earn their livelihood through the sale of labour services and this is the reason why we have a separate chapter on the rewards of labour. What workers receive we shall call wages and consists, as we have seen in previous chapters, of transfer earnings, rents, interest and profit. The total presumably reflects the allocation of labour between jobs and this raises the question; can the labour market be treated like other markets? Is labour just another commodity? There are two important qualifications to be borne in mind.

## 1 *Personality*

Since the owners of labour services cannot detach themselves from their sale but must accompany them, a worker will be interested in the non-monetary aspects of employment. What this implies is that the distinction between an individual as a consumer and an individual as a worker must not be drawn too sharply; a worker may be prepared to forgo some money income in order to obtain pleasant working conditions and hence we should speak of the *net advantages of jobs*. We should not expect wages to be equalized through competition but we might expect net advantages to be equalized. The fact that those who enjoy high wages also enjoy pleasant working conditions suggests that labour markets are not perfectly competitive. Furthermore, we should also note that attitudes towards wages are strongly influenced by notions of justice and fairness.

## 2 *Human capital*

Because it is impossible, except in a slave society, to secure control of the assets embodied in an individual, investment in education and training become the responsibility of the individual or his parents. Thus, investment in human capital is strongly dependent upon the distribution of wealth. And because human capital cannot be easily bought and sold it is not as good a reserve against emergencies as non-human capital.

### The determinants of hourly pay

Whilst demand and supply are convenient shorthand expressions for the factors which determine earnings, the more interesting questions concern the things which lie behind those terms.

Table 33 reveals the importance of education, family background, length of time at work (on-the-job training), race, health and marital status in determining the hourly earnings of adult male workers in Great Britain in 1975. The table takes as its base line a man who left school at the age of 14 or under, had an unskilled father, has no work experience, is white but not Irish, has had no longstanding illness and earned £0·38 per hour. Thus, if he had stayed on at school he would have earned £0·51 per hour. Taken together, the factors itemized in the table explain 38 per cent of the difference in men's hourly earnings. Thus, there is still a great deal left to be explained. And what is particularly interesting is the apparently small influence exerted by family background – as measured by the father's occupation. However, it is possible that family background is important in determining the type and duration of education enjoyed by sons.

### *Sex differentials*

Women earn less than men; they also work fewer hours. Following the passing of the Equal Pay Act the differential rose from 64 to 74 per cent. The causes of pay disparity are numerous.

**Table 33** Percentage addition to hourly earnings resulting from various personal characteristics taken one by one
(The basic individual left school at 14 or under, had an unskilled father, has no work experience, is white and born outside Ireland, has no long-standing illness, is unmarried and has predicted earnings of £0·38 per hour.)

| Male full-time employees under 65 | % |
| --- | --- |
| Left full-time education at | |
| 15 | 11 |
| 16 | 34 |
| 17 | 46 |
| 18 | 52 |
| 19 + | 84 |
| Father's occupation | |
| Professional and managerial | 12 |
| Other non-manual | 12 |
| Skilled manual | 4 |
| Semi-skilled manual | −2 |
| Years of work experience | |
| 5–10 | 92 |
| 10–20 | 132 |
| 20–30 | 159 |
| 30–40 | 180 |
| 40–50 | 177 |
| 50 + | 151 |
| Coloured, W. Indies | −13 |
| Other coloured | −22 |
| Irish-born | −7 |
| Has long-standing illness | −4 |
| Is married | 14 |

Source: Royal Commission on the Distribution of Income and Wealth, Background Paper No. 5, *The Causes of Poverty*, HMSO, London 1978

## Pre-entry discrimination

Society still seems to believe that a woman's 'place' is in the home; daughters are expected to marry and withdraw from the labour market and so parents tend to invest less in their education and training than in the training of sons. Hence there are fewer job opportunities for girls and, because there are restricted outlets, there is a feedback – girls have little incentive to acquire skills. Girls, therefore, can get crowded into a few jobs where their supply forces down wages. Girls tend to be concentrated into casual jobs requiring little training, such as retailing and catering; they seldom become surgeons or barristers and when they do go into the professions they are often found in the lower rungs of the job hierarchies.

## Post-entry discrimination

Even when they obtain access to men's work they seldom earn as much. Women may be paid less because they produce less, are more likely to be absent through sickness, are reluctant to work overtime and because they often expect to have a lower station in life.

## Industry and region

The low paid industries tend to be agriculture, transport, catering, laundries and hairdressing whilst the high paid industries tend to be mining, insurance and banking. The high paid regions are London and the South East.

## Trade unions

The simplest case to consider when analysing the effects of trade unions on wages and employment is that of a monopsonist confronted by a rising supply curve of labour. Figure 142 depicts the employer's demand curve (marginal revenue product curve) and the supply curve of labour. Because the supply curve is upward sloping the marginal cost of labour will be above the average cost curve. Hence, a profit maximizing employer will equate the marginal revenue product of labour with the marginal cost of labour but will only pay labour its average cost.

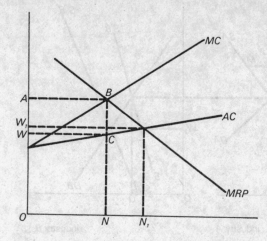

number employed

Figure 142 Monopsonistic exploitation.

Thus, $ON$ workers are paid a wage $OW$ and the area $WABC$ constitutes a producer surplus which the employer appropriates.

If now a union is formed and insists upon a wage $OW_1$ it can increase the wage without reducing employment. In effect, the union makes the average and marginal cost of labour equal. The importance of monopsony is difficult to ascertain. It may occur in occupations employing women because women workers may be very immobile. But low pay should not, of course, be taken to signify exploitation by monopsonists because there may be intense competition for labour by employers in low wage industries. Low wages may simply mean low productivity.

The more general case of unionism is illustrated in Figure 143. Initially, industries $A$ and $B$ pay wage $OW$ and employ $ON$ and $OQ$ workers respectively. A union is formed in industry $A$ and forces the wage up to $OW_1$. Employment falls to $ON_1$ and the displaced workers move to industry $B$ or else they become unemployed. If they drift to $B$ then they will shift the supply curve to the right and depress wages – $S'B$ shifts to $S''B$ and the wage falls to $OW_2$.

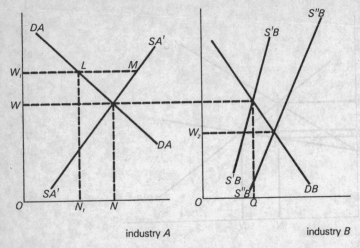

Figure 143 Effects of unions on relative wages and employment.

## The elasticity of derived demand

The degree to which unemployment falls when a union pushes up the wage will depend upon the factors governing the elasticity of derived demand. These conditions are

1 The elasticity of demand for the product produced by union labour should be low.

2 The ease of substitution between union labour and other factors should be low.

3 The percentage of total costs constituted by union labour should be low.

4 The elasticity of complementary factors should be low.

Conditions 1, 2 and 4 are straightforward. If the product elasticity of demand were low then union members could gain at the expense of consumers. If it is difficult to substitute other factors of production then unionists could gain at the expense of the employer. And if it was impossible for complementary factors of production to resist or move to other industries then unionists could gain at their expense. However, the third condition is ambiguous in its effects. Suppose, for example, coal is dug by miners with picks so that wages represent about 80 per cent of total costs. Then if a union were to push up miners' wages the employers might find it difficult to substitute coal-cutting machines for so large a body of workers. They might find the cost of buying machines rose steeply after a few were bought. Hence, even though consumers might be able to substitute gas or oil for coal, the workers could gain at the expense of their employers. Moreover, large unions of unskilled workers can often exert considerable political pressure so as to gain wage advantages.

Studies of the 1973 *New Earnings Survey* suggest that workers covered by national collective bargaining agreements enjoy little wage advantage over those non-unionists whereas those covered by national and local agreements can obtain a wage differential ranging from 12 to 33 per cent. Workers covered by local agreements may, of course, be able to exploit local monopoly situations. But the interesting question concerns those workers who are only covered by national agreements and appear to enjoy no wage advantage. In their case the sole reason for joining a trade union may lie in the difference in the working environment that a union can create. This difference may sometimes be referred to as 'restrictive practices' but no serious empirical work on this subject has yet been undertaken. It may be that the pace of work in unionized firms is lower because such firms enjoy, for example, lower accident rates. But there is a pressing need for investigations of this issue.

### The response of labour to economic incentives

The phrase 'labour supply' can refer to many things. Either it can mean the long-run supply of labour, when it is customary to ask whether the population and the proportion of the population seeking jobs responds to changes in wages or it can refer to the short-run response of workers to changes in wages – will they work longer or shorter hours? The other aspect of labour supply which needs to be analysed is the mobility of labour between occupations, industries and regions. And closely associated with these questions is the problem of defining the relevant decision-making unit; should it be the *individual* or the *family*? In view of the rise in the numbers of married women working and the increasing tendency of children to postpone entry into the labour market perhaps the question should be answered in terms of the family.

### Income and substitution effects

The response of an individual to an increase or decrease in wages can be analysed in terms of the income and substitution effects. On the one hand, a change in the wage alters the relative prices of income (work) and leisure and induces an individual to work longer or harder. On the other hand, the increase in the wage means that he could work less in order to obtain the same income as previously, or he could work longer or harder and reach a higher level of consumption of goods. *A priori* nothing can be said about the relative strengths of the income and substitution effects. This conclusion is illustrated in Figure 144. Along the vertical axis is measured the income from work and along the horizontal axis is measured hours available. The individual has *OA* hours and if he chooses to work them all

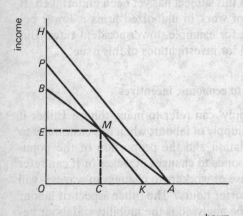

Figure 144 Supply of labour.

he could obtain $OB$ income. Hence the wage rate is $OB/OA$. Initially, we assume that he works $CA$ hours, earns $OE$ income and enjoys $OC$ hours of leisure. Now an increase in the wage from $OB/OA$ to $OH/OA$ gives rise to both income and substitution effects. $KP$ is a budget line which reflects the new relative price of leisure but passes through the original point $M$ to 'remove' the income effect. The resulting substitution effect will induce him to work more and not less because the points along $MP$ were previously not available to him whereas points along $MK$ were rejected. Hence, unless the supply curve has zero elasticity the substitution effect will cause him to move from a point on $AB$ to one on $AH$, but where will depend upon the sign of the income effect. The combined effect could result in more or less hours worked than at $M$.

The analysis of the effects of wage changes upon the supply of labour needs to be modified when considering the family because of the possibilities of substitution in the supply of labour between different members. A married woman may choose between housework, market work and leisure. If the market wage she is offered rises and her husband's wage remains constant she may consider taking a job and her husband may reduce his hours of work. And her decision will also be influenced by the number and ages of her children, whether the family is completed and what jobs are available.

The evidence collected in 1974 for the Royal Commission on the Distribution of Income and Wealth revealed the following facts.

In the case of married men:

1 An increase in the hourly wage of £1 leads to a reduction of about 8 hours per week.

2 An increase in the hourly wage of £1 earned by the wife leads, on average, to a reduction of about 7½ hours per week.

3 The effect of children is to increase hours worked.

In the case of married women

1 An increase in the hourly wage of £1 leads to an increase of about 2 hours per week.

2 An increase in the hourly wage of £1 earned by the husband leads to a fall of about 1 hour per week.

3 The age of the youngest child exercises a strong influence on the decision to start work. Once a child has started school a mother is more willing to seek a job.

4 Place of residence has a strong effect on participation in the labour market with Wales, Yorkshire, Humberside and East Anglia having low rates of participation in the labour market by married women.

5 Wives whose husbands are unemployed are less likely to work and this may have reflected the way in which social security payments operated in 1974. (Supplementary Benefit was reduced pound for pound for any earnings of the wife.)

The most striking feature of the evidence is the great difference in the response of married women to changes in their own wages as compared with the behaviour of their husbands.

*A backward sloping supply curve of labour exists for married men but not for their wives.*

## Mobility of labour
### Industrial mobility

One of the most interesting questions concerning the economist is whether the labour market does or should behave like any other commodity market. In a dynamic economy subject to changes in the demands for various goods and services it may be desirable for workers to change jobs. The question, therefore, arises does the distribution of the labour force change in response to changes in wages?

The evidence for the UK for the period 1924–50 is as follows:

1 Innovating firms had lower production costs and cut prices to expand sales.

2 In order to produce more, firms hired more labour and in order to get more labour they raised wages.

3 Stagnant firms lost labour but were compelled to pay those

workers they retained similar wages to those they could get elsewhere. (Salter, 1966)

These propositions are illustrated in Figure 145 where $A$ is the innovating firm and $B$ is the stagnant firm. Initially, both firms pay the same wage $OW$ for the same kind of labour. When the progressive firm shifts the demand curve from $DD$ to $D_1D_1$ in $A$ the wage rises from $OW$ to $OW_1$ and employment increases from $ON$ to $ON_1$. The stagnant firm loses $QQ_1$ workers (equal to $NN_1$) and has to pay its remaining workers $OW_1$. What the diagrams reveal is some interesting predictions. First, there is no correlation between changes in wages and changes in employment: all workers get the same wage increases. Now the period 1924–50 was one in which trade unions were relatively weak so we cannot attribute the fact that all workers got the same wage increases to unionism. Comparable wage increases were an aspect of a fairly competitive labour market in which unionism was weak. Secondly, the gains from increasing productivity were partly passed on to consumers in the form of lower prices and partly to workers in the form of wage increases.

Since 1950 the interrelations of wages, prices, productivity

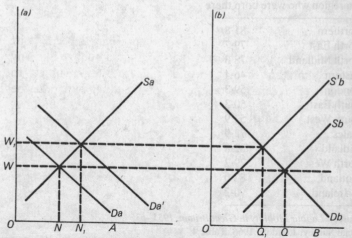

Figure 145 Technological change, wages and the distribution of labour

and employment have altered as a result of full employment, the spread of trade unionism and the effects of government policies towards full employment and inflation.[1] When firms innovate, their workers tend to want a larger share of the productivity gains and this restricts the expansion of sales and employment. Workers in static firms then demand similar wage increases and this causes unemployment. Because of their commitment to full employment, governments increase monetary demand. This restores full employment in the static sector but creates inflation in the innovating sector. The net effect is inflation and imports rise. The rise in imports causes a balance of payments deficit which governments try to correct by cutting back the money supply. Unemployment then rises in the static sector and workers are forced into the expanding sector or else they remain permanently unemployed.

*Geographical mobility*

A useful source of information on the geographical mobility of labour is the Social Survey study covering the period 1953–63.

**Table 34** Percentage of people living in a region who were born there

| Northern | 81·8 |
|---|---|
| North East | 79·7 |
| North Midland | 78·3 |
| Eastern | 46·4 |
| London | 59·3 |
| South East | 50·3 |
| South West | 53·9 |
| Wales | 72·9 |
| Midland | 82·8 |
| North West | 79·2 |
| Scotland | 82·0 |
| N. Ireland | 90·2 |

Source: *Labour Mobility in Great Britain, 1953–63*, Social Survey, London, 1966, Table 4

1. cf. Richard Wragg and James Robertson (1978).

Table 34 shows that there was a considerable movement of people to the south of England and little movement into the north and west of the British Isles. Table 35 indicates that the majority of people moved in order to obtain better housing and that wages were not an obvious cause of movement; there was a movement towards greater net advantages. The low rating of wages may, however, be due to the manner and type of questions asked of movers. Many of the social reasons for moving may have been conditional upon getting higher wages and the areas to which people were moving were regions of high wages as well as better housing.

**Table 35** Main reason given by men and women for moving

|  | Both sexes (%) |
| --- | --- |
| marriage (including prospective marriage) | 11 |
| had to –slum/redevelopment | 6 |
| had to – given notice | 3 |
| wanted – better/modern accommodation | 24 |
| wanted – different size dwelling | 15 |
| wanted – home of their own | 8 |
| work reasons | 17 |
| to be near relatives/friends | 6 |
| better surroundings | 7 |
| rents, rates, etc. too high | 1 |
| other vague answers | 2 |
| number on which percentage based | 10 456 |

Source: *Labour Mobility in Great Britain*, 1953–63, Table 16

## Vertical mobility

So far we have concentrated upon horizontal mobility but many people are interested in vertical or social mobility. Do the sons and daughters of dustmen go to Oxbridge? The evidence is unclear, being clouded by the classifications of occupations. Some people seem to have climbed the greasy pole but few appear to have slid down. The explanation appears to lie in the expansion of white collar jobs which tend to be automatically designated middle class jobs.

## Summary

Workers may not respond to changes in money wages but to the net advantages of jobs. Men appear to reduce the hours worked when wages increase whereas women work longer. Trade unions do increase the wages of their members but little is known about their effect upon employment and the pace of work. The labour force does appear to re-allocate itself in response to wage changes although the process is complicated by the presence of trade unions. Labour does appear to move in response to differences in geographical net advantages. A low paid worker is usually a woman with limited education, whose parents were unskilled and who is not a member of a trade union and who works in the catering industry in East Anglia.

## Questions

1 Professional footballers have to be paid to play football whereas amateurs usually play for the privilege. Therefore men who do not like football become professionals.

# Chapter 27
# Distribution in Post-War UK

In a sense many of the forces discussed in the chapters on factor pricing lie at the core of our interest in economics, since, ultimately, it is the size of an individual's share of national output which determines the quality of life which he can expect to enjoy. Rents, dividends, profits, wages, inheritances and state subsidies are determined in the mixed economy by a combination of market forces, social and demographic influences and political decision-making and the resulting distribution of incomes from the various sources will exhibit a degree of equality which reflects the relative impact of these several forces. The details of calculating the size distribution of incomes in any economy are many and complex and we shall not attempt a deep analysis of these details in the present context. However, it is interesting to consider how the many forces at work have moulded the distribution pattern in the UK in the light of the social objective of reducing inequalities in the distribution of incomes and wealth to that level which is politically tolerable. The reasons why this should be a social objective are discussed later in Chapter 28.

## Income distribution before tax

We shall concentrate upon the post-war years since this has been the period of intense interest in the problems of distribution and poverty and it has also been a time when statistics have been collected of sufficient calibre to permit reasonable estimates of distribution patterns to be made. Of course this has been the period of the Welfare State and the effects of market forces have been tempered accordingly. The commitment to an ideal of equality has meant that distribution patterns have been monitored fairly closely and perhaps the greatest manifestation of this concern was the appointment, in 1974, of a Royal Commission[1] on the subject and the information published by this commission has presented a most comprehensive picture of the post-war distribution of incomes in the UK.

Other researchers, of course, have documented the pattern of income distribution and the incidence of poverty and in presenting the summary below we shall draw on all sources.[2] In some respects the results of the various surveys are disappointing. Despite the social and economic progress of the post-war years, including full employment for a quarter of a century, the distribution of incomes has changed rather slowly during certain periods and wealth concentrations have been even slower to disintegrate. However, this is not to deny that considerable progress towards equality has been made. Table 36 presents the distribution of incomes before tax for selected years.

As Table 36 demonstrates, a policy of full employment is not sufficient to guarantee a continual closing of the distribution gap. The existence of rigidities in the economic system, for example fixed dividend policies by firms and scarce supplies of land, impose a limit to the degree of equality automatically created by a growing economy. Coupled with changes in the occupational structure, such as an increase in the number of salaried workers relative to the number of wage-earners, and an increase in the supply of women onto the labour market, these rigidities can have a very significant impact on the pre-tax distribution of incomes.

Looking at the patterns which emerge from Table 36 the

1. Royal Commission on the Distribution of Income and Wealth under the chairmanship of Lord Diamond (The 'Diamond Commission').
2. For a fuller discussion of the issues involved in measuring the size distribution of incomes and a comprehensive survey of research in the area of distribution and poverty, see G. P. Marshall, *Social Goals and Economic Perspectives*, Penguin Books, 1980, chs. 4–11.

**Table 36** Cumulative distribution of personal income 1949 to 1977 before tax

| Quartile group of income recipients | Share of total personal income in year | | | | | | | |
|---|---|---|---|---|---|---|---|---|
| | 1949[a] | 1957[b] | 1959[b] | 1963[b] | 1967[a] | 1972–3[a] | 1973–4[c] | 1976–7[d] |
| | % | % | % | % | % | % | % | % |
| top 1% | 11·2 | 8·2 | 8·4 | 7·9 | 7·4 | 6·4 | 6·5 | 5·4 |
| 5% | 23·8 | 19·1 | 19·9 | 19·1 | 18·4 | 17·2 | 17·1 | 15·9 |
| 10% | 33·2 | 28·1 | 29·4 | 28·7 | 28·0 | 26·9 | 26·8 | 25·8 |
| 40% | 68·1 | 65·7 | 67·8 | 67·7 | 66·9 | 66·8 | 66·5 | 66·3 |
| 70% | 87·3 | 88·8 | 90·3 | 90·3 | 89·7 | 89·4 | 89·1 | 89·0 |
| Bottom 30% | 12·7 | 11·3 | 9·7 | 9·7 | 10·3 | 10·6 | 10·9 | 11·0 |

Sources: Royal Commission on the Distribution of Income and Wealth, *Report No. 1*; R. J. Nicholson, 'The Distribution of Personal Income,' *Lloyds Bank Review*, Jan. 1967; Royal Commission on the Distribution of Income and Wealth, *Report No. 4*; Royal Commission on the Distribution of Income and Wealth, *Report No. 7*

changes in distribution have not been evenly spaced. For the period 1949 to 1957 the share of the top 10 per cent of income recipients fell by more than a seventh while the share of the top 1 per cent fell by over a quarter. However, the position of the bottom 30 per cent worsened during the same period (from 12·7 per cent to 11·3 per cent) which makes unambiguous judgements about the movement towards equality during that period impossible. If we take a broader range of income we can see that there was a worsening of the relative position of the top 40 per cent of income recipients while the position of the top 70 per cent improved. In other words, re-distribution seems to have taken place from the top of the range towards the middle with the middle also making some gain upon the lower quantiles.

For the next decade, 1957–67, the apparent trend towards equality slowed down and the positions of the top percentile groupings changed very little – the share of the top 10 per cent fell by only one tenth of a percentage point. Indeed, if we take a broader grouping, say the top 40 per cent, the share of this group actually increased over the decade while the share of the bottom 30 per cent worsened still further.

The distribution pattern which emerges after 1967, for the most part, shows again some very small changes although it can be argued that the overall reduction in inequality is less ambiguous. Each of the percentile groups up to 40 per cent shows a reduced share while the share of the bottom 30 per cent increases slightly.

It is difficult to record an *impression* of the *general* trend in income distribution for the whole period which is unambiguous in its conclusion. It cannot be denied that income has been redistributed from the top quantile groupings but the share of the bottom 30 per cent was lower in the middle of the seventies than it was in 1949. A sizeable increase in the share of the bottom 30 per cent of income recipients between 1963 and 1967 has been followed by only a very small increase since that time, and the combined effect of these increases has proved to be insufficient to counteract the substantial fall in this group's share between 1949 and 1959.

To some extent the patterns which emerge in the size distribution of incomes are a reflection of the forces discussed in our chapters on factor pricing, and a brief look at the post-war pattern of factor shares might prove interesting. Comparisons over time are particularly difficult in this context, given the data problems; however, the period up to 1963 has been studied closely by H. Lydall and we can note some of his findings.[3] According to Lydall, post-war economic expansion and improved labour market opportunities accounted for much of the apparent trend towards equality up to 1957. During this period earned income rose faster than any other form of personal income. However, during the period 1957–63 this pattern changed and the rate of growth of employment income slowed down relative to that of self-employment income. Within employment income the rate of growth of wages slowed down relatively to that of salaries while rent, dividend and interest

3. H. F. Lydall, 'The Long-term Trend in the Size Distribution of Incomes', *Journal of the Royal Statistical Society, Series A*, 122, part 1, 1959.

together became the most rapidly growing sector of personal income.

For the years since 1963 we can refer to the reports from the Diamond Commission.

Table 38 suggests that over the period since 1963 there has been little change in the share of total income going to employment income, although there are some interesting trends within that category. From 1963 to 1967 the share of self-employment income remained fairly static but from then it increased steadily until it reached 10·6 per cent. Thereafter the share fell again but in 1976 still remained above the 1963 level. The share of 'non-labour income' fell substantially from 1968 onwards. However, the most marked change during the period was in the share of transfer incomes which increased by over 30 per cent.

It is worth underlining at this stage that the trends apparent since 1963 continue the longer term pattern of a rise in the share of labour relative to that of capital – 3:1 by the seventies compared to 1:1 at the beginning of the century.

**Table 37** Percentage shares of main components in total personal income, 1963–76

|  | 1963 % | 1968 % | 1970 % | 1972 % | 1974 % | 1976 % |
|---|---|---|---|---|---|---|
| *Labour (market) income* | | | | | | |
| (a) income from employment | 71·2 | 69·6 | 70·2 | 69·4 | 69·4 | 70·0 |
| (b) income from self-employment | 8·6 | 8·5 | 8·7 | 9·9 | 10·1 | 9·1 |
| (c) total employment income | 79·8 | 78·1 | 78·9 | 79·3 | 79·5 | 79·1 |
| *Non-labour (market) income* | | | | | | |
| Rent, dividends and net interest | 11·1 | 11·2 | 10·3 | 9·1 | 10·4 | 9·0 |
| *Transfer income* | | | | | | |
| National insurance and other cash benefits from public authorities | 8.3 | 10·1 | 10·0 | 10·7 | 10·4 | 11·4 |

## Distribution of income after income tax

Given the progressive ratio structure of the UK income tax we should expect the post-tax distribution of incomes to be less unequal than the pre-tax distribution. However, we find that the changes in the post-war pattern of post-tax income distribution have been very similar to those seen in the distribution of pre-tax incomes. Table 38 presents a summary of the post-war shares in income after tax.

The most striking feature to emerge from Table 38 is that although the table shows a levelling down of incomes as a result of the income tax, it shows also that the relative share sizes of the quantile groups changed very little over the period. It would seem that the pattern of shares over time has not been altered significantly by the operation of the income tax. But what more could be done by the tax system? It may not be possible to reduce inequality any further through the *rates* of income tax without seriously affecting economic incentives. In Chapter 26 we analysed how a change in the wage rate induces both a substitution effect and an income effect and, depending on the relative strengths of these two effects, the wage-earner may choose to supply either more effort or less. So it is with an increase in the rate of income tax; the net return from the marginal hour of effort is reduced and the resulting substitution effect (of leisure for work) might outweigh the income effect (work for leisure). Empirical findings do not lend a great deal of support to this

**Table 38** Cumulative distribution of personal income 1949–1976/77: after tax

| Quantile group of Income recipients | 1949 % | 1957 % | 1959 % | 1963 % | 1967 % | 1972–3 % | 1973–4 % | 1976–7 % |
|---|---|---|---|---|---|---|---|---|
| top  1% | 6·4 | 5·0 | 5·3 | 5·2 | 4·9 | 4·4 | 4·5 | 3·5 |
| 5% | 17·7 | 14·9 | 15·8 | 15·7 | 14·8 | 14·2 | 14·3 | 12·9 |
| 10% | 27·1 | 24·0 | 25·2 | 25·2 | 24·3 | 23·6 | 23·6 | 22·4 |
| 40% | 64·1 | 62·5 | 65·0 | 64·7 | 63·5 | 63·8 | 63·5 | 63·0 |
| 70% | 85·4 | 86·5 | 88·7 | 88·2 | 88·0 | 87·8 | 87·2 | 87·1 |
| bottom 30% | 14·6 | 13·5 | 11·2 | 11·8 | 12·0 | 12·3 | 12·8 | 12·9 |

Sources: as for Table 36

possibility but the risk of such a net effect occurring is likely to deter the policy-makers from ever increasing the marginal rate of tax in order to try and reduce income inequality.

Thus it may be that scope for further income redistribution must be looked for elsewhere. One possibility is a widening of the tax base into a more comprehensive definition of income so that tax revenues (to be re-distributed) might increase without any necessary change in rates. Another avenue which has been considered recently is that of changing the tax base completely to one of 'expenditure' rather than 'income'.[4] Or, it may be that less emphasis should be placed on *taxing* higher incomes and more placed on transferring resources to lower incomes. The Royal Commission on the Distribution of Income and Wealth has presented evidence that during the post-war period the effect of State benefits has led to a distribution of incomes after tax *and* benefits which is much more equal than the pattern which emerges from a consideration of taxes alone.[5]

## Inequality of wealth

Inequalities in the distribution of wealth have proved to be even more difficult to eradicate. Over the course of this century there has been a distinct levelling down of wealth shares but by the seventies the top percentile of the wealth-owning population were still enjoying a relative concentration of total wealth. Table 39 presents a summary of the findings of the Royal Commission on the Distribution of Income and Wealth.

It is clear from Table 39 that wealth concentration at the very top of the distribution has been reduced considerably. However, by the middle of the seventies around half of the total wealth share remained in the possession of only 10 per cent of

4. For a debated and provocative comparison of the two tax bases and their relative effects on both equity and efficiency in the tax system see *The Structure and Reform of Direct Taxation*, Report of a Committee chaired by Professor J. E. Meade (The Meade Report), Allen and Unwin (for the Institute for Fiscal Studies), London, 1978.

5. See Royal Commission on the Distribution of Income and Wealth, *Report No. 1*, p. 62, and *Report No. 51*.

**Table 39** Cumulative (percentage) shares of personal wealth owned by given quantile groups of the population, 1911–1975

| Quantile group | Cumulative percentage share of personal wealth | | | | | |
|---|---|---|---|---|---|---|
| | (a) 1911–13 | (a) 1936–38 | (b) 1960 | (b) 1965 | (b) 1970 | (c) 1976 |
| top  1% | 69 | 56 | 42 | 33 | 29 | 21·1 |
| top  5% | 87 | 78 | 75 | 58 | 56 | 41·2 |
| top 10 % | 92 | 88 | 83 | 73 | 70 | 55·2 |
| bottom 10% | 8 | 12 | 17 | 27 | 30 | 44·8 |

(a) – England and Wales
(b) – Great Britain
(c) – United Kingdom
Source: Royal Commission on the Distribution of Income and Wealth, *Report No. 1*, p. 97; *Report No. 5*, Table 33; *Report No. 7*, Table 4.15

wealth-holders. The reasons for wealth concentration range across the discussion of marginal productivity discussed earlier in this section but also take account of many social and demographic factors such as marriage and fertility patterns, the mode of inheritance, etc. Some of these influences are referred to in a little more detail in Chapter 30 on the State's role in economic life. But we can make one observation now regarding the role of the tax system in breaking up wealth concentration.

For the period up to 1974 the main instrument of wealth redistribution through the tax system in the UK was *estate duty*. Unfortunately this duty did not have a great impact on wealth concentration because it was never applied properly to discretionary trusts and also because the tax laws permitted exemption of gifts *inter vivos* unless such transfers took place within seven years prior to the donor's death. However, probably the main reason why estate duty failed significantly to attack wealth concentrations is that it was levied on the value of an estate rather than the value of an inheritance. Large estates do not perpetuate inequalities unless they are passed on as large inheritances and it is the latter which must be taxed if inequalities are to be reduced. Indeed we can go further and suggest that an inheritance tax provides an incentive to break up inheritances while a tax on estates does not.

The case for switching to a tax on inheritances is strengthened considerably by several empirical findings which point to inheritances as being the prime cause of wealth concentrations in the UK.[6] It should be noted that *capital transfer tax* which replaced estate duty in 1974 is an improvement on the latter in that it is levied on a cumulative basis, not just on wealth at death but also on bequests and gifts *inter vivos* – there can be no tax avoidance through gifts made prior to death – however the capital transfer tax remains based on the estates principle and does not provide the incentive to disperse wealth that is offered by an inheritance tax.

## Poverty in the UK

Separate from the question of income distribution but necessarily related to the same set of causes is the problem of poverty, defined according to the standard accepted by the community (an issue discussed in a later chapter). The standard accepted in the UK is that of *Supplementary Benefit* level which has its origins in the comprehensive anti-poverty programme laid down in the Beveridge Report [7] of 1942 and represents a development within the regime of the 'Welfare State' which that Report introduced. Backed by a government commitment to full employment it was widely assumed during the forties that poverty would be eradicated and during the fifties it was believed that this expectation had been warranted.

Given this background, the fact that poverty still existed on a large scale in the United Kingdom came as a rude shock to the nation in the early 1960s. The heady atmosphere of the preceding fifteen years with full employment backed by a comprehensive social-security system *à la* Beveridge had lulled the

6. See C. D. Harbury and P. C. McMahon, 'Inheritance and the Distribution of Personal Wealth in Britain', *Economic Journal*, 1973.
7. *Social Insurance and Allied Services*, Cmnd. 6406, London, HMSO, 1942.

community into the belief that poverty was just a bad memory. But illusions were shattered by the publication in 1965 of the findings of two sociologists (Abel-Smith and Townsend), showing that 3·8 per cent of the population in 1960 were living in poverty. Further reports, authorized by government[8] in the following years substantiated these earlier findings. Yet, despite this evidence and some piecemeal alterations in the state programme, those in poverty still constituted 4·9 per cent of the population in 1971.[9]

Why did the scheme envisaged by Beveridge not prevent this situation from arising? After all, the plan formulated in the Report, the principles of which were implemented in subsequent legislation, seemed all-embracing: a comprehensive social-insurance scheme; a national-assistance 'safety net' to catch those not covered by the insurance provisions; and family allowances to take care of the financial problems created by excessive family size. The major reason for the relative failure of the plan lies in the neglect of successive governments to maintain the aims of the Beveridge proposals. A scheme so comprehensive and discretionary requires constant revision and overhaul if it is to adapt to structural changes in the economy and in society at large. Such checks have not been exercised on the social-security system, despite many structural changes in the United Kingdom in the last twenty-five years. Demographic changes have resulted in proportional increases in the dependent sectors of population – the pre-school sector; those in full-time education; and the retired sector. Changes have occurred in the occupational structure and hence in the incidence of unemployment. Even the concept of poverty itself has undergone change as general living standards have risen.

Given these changes and the lack of government monitoring of the poverty situation, the post-war system has failed the Beveridge principles in one very important respect. The Report

8. Ministry of Pensions and National Insurance (1966); Ministry of Social Security (1967); Department of Health and Social Security (1971).
9. See C. C. Fieghehen, P. S. Lansley and A. D. Smith, *Poverty and Progress in Britain 1953–73*, National Institute of Economic and Social Research Paper XXIX, Cambridge University Press, 1977.

proposed that both retirement pensions and family allowances should be adequate to provide at least a subsistence level of income. Neither of these conditions has been satisfied, a major contributory factor in the concentration of poverty among the aged and among families with small children. In the latter case, small children, failing to satisfy one of the Beveridge principles has been compounded by the fact that one of the Report's important assumptions has not been borne out by reality. This was the assumption that, given full employment, work income would be adequate in all cases to provide for the needs of a one-child family. However, in 1966 25 per cent of families with incomes below the national assistance scale (the 'official' poverty line) had a father in full-time employment.[10] It would seem that a full-employment policy is not enough to protect the lowly skilled from inadequate remuneration.

## What is to be done?

The growing concern about the existence of poverty in a so-called advanced economy and the apparent failure of the post-war programme to solve the problem, has led many academics and policy-makers to call for a radical departure from the existing social-security arrangements. Very often this call has been for the implementation of some sort of negative income-taxation plan whereby individuals are not only compelled to transfer resources to the state when income rises above some defined level, but also they receive *automatic subsidies* from the state when incomes fall below some defined level.

The term *negative taxation* is an umbrella which covers many types of anti-poverty plan. Indeed the term can be applied to any earnings-related transfer scheme. But generally we may distinguish between two types of plan which are referred to under this heading:

*Negative-rates* taxation;
*Social-dividend* taxation.

10. Ministry of Social Security (1967).

## Negative rates

Negative-rates taxation represents a simple extension of the existing income-tax structure – above the level of minimum taxable income a tax unit pays positive taxes; below this level it receives transfers ('pays' negative taxes).

The relationships in Figure 146 relate to a tax unit of given size and structure. $OY$ represents a guideline – along $OY$ gross income and disposable income are identical ($OY$ has a slope of 45°). $AB$ represents the actual relationship between gross income and disposable income for the prevailing tax régime: thus the vertical distance between $OY$ and $AB$ at any point indicates the amount of tax, positive or negative, associated with that particular level of gross income. As can be seen, this distance diminishes as gross income approaches $D$, that is, as gross income approaches the level of minimum taxable (positive) income $C$. Hence the actual rate of negative tax is given by the ratio $A/C$; for example, if $A/C = \frac{1}{2}$, the negative tax rate is 50 per cent.[11] To summarize, $D$ is the 'break-even' level of gross

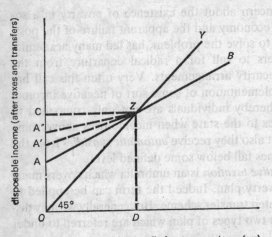

Figure 146

11. Note that our simple example assumes positive and negative rates to be identical. This may not be the case in a real world negative-rates plan.

income – when gross income is less than $D$ the tax unit is a net beneficiary from the scheme ($AB$ lies above $OY$); above this level the tax is a net contributor to the scheme ($AB$ lies below $Y$).

Negative-rates taxation epitomizes the 'selective' approach to the poverty problem – only the genuinely poor derive benefit from state transfers. As such, it faces the disclosure problem referred to in Chapter 28. A drawback of the Beveridge National Assistance programme ('supplementary benefit' as it is now termed) has been that eligibility for aid must be proven by a means test, a device notoriously deficient as a means of estimating true needs. In 1966, for example, an estimated 39 per cent of retirement pensioners who were eligible for National Assistance were not receiving it. Dislike of the means test accounted for at least a third (approximately) and possibly for as many as 50 per cent of those who did not apply for benefit.[12]

It is claimed that a negative-rates plan would avoid this difficulty since a tax return would be the only means test required. If this argument is assuming that a tax return under this sort of plan would not be viewed with hostility by potential transfer recipients, it is not very strong. Why should an individual with, say, zero income be more prepared to disclose this fact under this system than any other? However, if the argument is based on the fact that tax returns would be compulsory then it may carry some weight.

But whatever the basis to the argument it ignores an important point – how regular would negative-tax returns need to be? If such returns were made annually then alternative arrangements would be required for those suffering *unforeseen* hardship during the following tax year. Yet if some secondary mechanism were established to assess temporary needs of this kind the problem of eligibility disclosure reappears in full force. The alternative – to file tax returns regularly, say monthly or, better still, weekly – renders a compulsory scheme administratively impossible and the alternative of a voluntary system would be no improvement upon the current arrangements.

12. Ministry of Pensions and National Insurance (1966).

Neither is eligibility disclosure the sole problem under negative-rates taxation. Even more difficult to resolve are the problems surrounding the fixing of the break-even level of income, i.e. the income level at which negative-tax payments cease and positive payments commence. If this level is established as the poverty line then negative-tax rates of less than 100 per cent would not place tax units beyond poverty. Thus, in the example of Figure 146, if *OC* represents the official poverty line then the negative tax rate depicted by *AB* fills only a portion of the poverty gap. *A'Z* and *A"Z* represent rate improvements but only when the negative rate is depicted by *CZ* (when all the poverty gap is filled in) could the plan hope for a comprehensive attack on poverty. However, the price of filling the poverty gap this way is the disincentives likely to result since, under this alternative, marginal increments to income below *OD* would not improve disposable income beyond *OC*, so why work when *OC* disposable income is guaranteed for zero effort? While recognizing that we cannot predict on such matters in the absence of empirical information about income and substitution effects, the sheer size of the potential disincentive seems very likely to make it effective.

## Social dividend

The aim of social-dividend taxation is to provide a guaranteed minimum income (at least subsistence) for all – the social dividend – and to classify all income, including the social-dividend transfer,[13] as taxable. Such a scheme is illustrated in Figure 147 where a proportional tax rate is applied to all forms of income.

In the above diagram *OY* again represents a guideline. A guaranteed minimum income is fixed at *A* for the given tax unit. As the unit's gross income (income from other sources) rises above zero, positive tax payments are made. The rate at which these taxes are extracted (50 per cent for simplicity) is indicated

13. Some types of social-dividend scheme have been advanced in which the social dividend is excluded from the tax base, but such schemes do not satisfy the generally acceptable tax criteria.

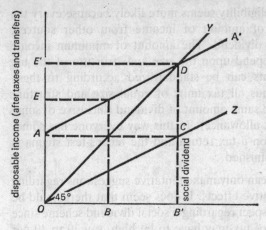

gross income (before taxes and transfers)

Figure 147

by $OZ$ – points on this line show income net of tax but not of transfer. To show income net of both taxes and transfer $OZ$ is shifted vertically by the amount of guaranteed minimum income, $A$. Thus points along $AA'$ show total disposable income, after allowing for both taxes and transfer. We can see, then, that the tax unit's break even level of income is $OB'$ gross (= $OE'$ net). At this point tax payments equal the minimum income guarantee ($AA'$ crosses $OY$); for gross income levels below $OB'$ the tax unit is a net beneficiary of the scheme but when gross income rises above $OB'$ the unit is a net contributor ($OY$ lies above $AA'$).

The concept of social dividend is more attractive than that of negative-rates taxation for three important reasons:

Disclosure of eligibility is more likely;
Despite *everyone* being guaranteed a minimum level of income, disincentive problems may be less severe;
By making the social dividend liable to income tax the scheme facilitates a movement towards a more comprehensive tax base and therefore towards achieving more horizontal, as well as more vertical, equity in the tax system.

1 Disclosure of eligibility seems more likely because every tax unit, regardless of amount of income from other sources, receives a social dividend. The amount of minimum income guarantee will depend upon the size and structure of the tax unit but payments can be standardized according to these basic criteria. Thus all tax units of equal size and structure would receive the same amount of dividend (inclusive of some standardized rent allowance). In this way everyone has something to declare on a tax return and the means-test stigma is consequently diminished.

2 As always, we can only make tentative suggestions regarding potential disincentive effects. It does seem that there could be dangers in this respect regarding a social dividend scheme since the *positive* rate of tax may have to be high, say 30 to 40 per cent, to help finance the scheme. But potential disincentives exist under any income-tax scheme, particularly, as we have seen, negative-rates taxation and it can be argued that such effects may be less severe at lower income levels under a social-dividend scheme. One reason for this cautious optimism is that since some minimum income level is guaranteed additions to the *gross* income above zero level also represent net additions to disposable incomes (assuming the *positive* tax rate to be less than 100 per cent); whereas under negative-rates taxation this was not the case when the break-even level equalled the poverty threshold since the negative-tax rate would then be 100 per cent.

A second possible argument is that providing a secure income floor may induce households to offer more labour hours than in the absence of such a guarantee. Consider Figure 146 again: in the absence of a minimum guarantee of $OA$ a household would need to earn $OB$ gross income to achieve this same amount. But under the social-dividend scheme a gross income level of $OB$ translates into disposable income of $OE$ – it may now appear worthwhile to offer the number of work hours necessary to yield $OB$ gross income whereas previously it did not. In other words the social dividend provides a foundation upon which it is worthwhile to build – in the absence of the foundation this incentive does not exist.[14]

3 Finally, a social dividend scheme may facilitate all-round improvements in the tax structure. A guaranteed minimum for all could replace all existing social-security benefits, some of which may not have been included in the definition of taxable income. Since the social dividend would be taxable this may be a means of achieving a more comprehensive tax base. In so far as any scheme did achieve this end it would immediately help create more horizontal equity in the tax structure and over the longer run more vertical equity as tax avoidance is reduced. This latter possibility would also alleviate the financing of the scheme – the broader the tax base the lower the tax rate for a given level of re-distribution.

Despite its relative attractiveness a social-dividend scheme suffers from a basic drawback – what to do about those individuals whose needs are not catered for by the transfer mechanism. The benefits from a social dividend derive from the *automatic* establishment of an income floor beneath every tax unit but to achieve this type of mechanism requires social-dividend payments to be standardized according to general circumstances, mainly the size and structure of the tax unit. However, many needs will be *specific* to the tax unit and will not be easily catered for by a tax return, very often because they cannot be foreseen. This problem would seem to return us full circle to some separate arrangement, some form of safety-net, and the problems of means testing. Yet, as previously hinted at, this is not a problem peculiar to social-dividend taxation.

Indeed, it must be faced by all types of tax/transfer mechanism since no system can cater for every individual need and circumstance by standardized transfers. The best that can be aimed for is a plan which gives as comprehensive a standardized coverage

14. There is some empirical evidence to suggest that savings are increased in similar fashion as a result of providing some secure floor such as a state pension. See, for example, Cagan (1965).

as possible, so minimizing the areas and occasions of specific needs.

## True to Beveridge

This question of stand-by arrangements must be faced, then, by the third alternative to existing arrangements which is to establish firmly for the first time a social-security system which is true to Beveridge principles. Such a plan would require all benefits, including retirement pensions and family allowances, to satisfy subsistence requirements. In this way families in and out of work could be given an income floor, thus lessening the need to rely on such schemes as minimum-wage legislation which has not been very successful in the UK, for reasons suggested by our theory in Chapter 26. The great drawback to such a scheme is that it is administratively unwieldy whereas a social-dividend plan can provide an income floor and create economies of scale in administration. These potential economies plus the other benefits from a social dividend which we discussed earlier are in large part dependent upon a general overhaul of the system of personal-income taxation. The social dividend seems the necessary longer-run objective, in the meantime the adoption of truly Beveridge principles may bring immediate gains.

## Questions

1 'Poverty is unacceptable whereas inequality is acceptable.' Discuss.

2 How can we say that one distribution of income (or wealth) is more unequal than another? Does our answer depend upon value judgements?

3 'The case for a social dividend or negative income tax founders upon the problem of incentives.' Discuss.

4 'The distribution of personal income depends upon genes and nothing can be done about them.'
'The distribution of personal income depends upon chance.'

'The distribution of personal income depends upon the "taste" for making money.'
'The distribution of ability is normally distributed whereas the distribution of incomes is skewed so making money has nothing to do with brains.'
Comment on these statements.

# Part Eight
## The State

That the state is a good and not a bad is something that the British school of economists, from Smith down to Keynes, has
always accepted. True, they could warn of dangers, but there
was never any doubt that they saw the state as something more
than an appendix. This view of the British tradition has come to
be rejected by one strand of contemporary British economists
and an influential group of American economists whose philosophic outlook, usually described as 'liberalism', seems to have
been influenced as much by continental thinkers as by aber-
rations of the British tradition. Briefly, in the opinion of these
latter groups, it is so difficult to control the state that a strong
preference is expressed for market production and distribution. So much so that every attempt is made to squeeze decision-
making into the confines of the market.

Science, so the history books demonstrate, has advanced by
solving the easy problems first. Physics appeared successful as
compared with the other natural sciences, because it found a
group of problems where classification and measurement made
prediction and understanding possible. The contrast with biology, chemistry and metallurgy was striking. Likewise economics among the social sciences seemed successful because it
appeared to indulge in measurement: psychology tended to follow the same path. Sociology and politics differ strikingly.
Sociology appears to be the residual legatee of all that is non-
quantifiable and politics appears to have languished since economics was severed from its Siamese twin, political economy.

But these were early and cheap successes. The willingness of physicists to move into a strange and difficult terrain like thermodynamics is, however, in sharp contrast to those economists who seem reluctant to consider institutions other than the market. 'Truth,' said William Blake, 'can never be told so as to be understood, and not be believed.' Perhaps we understand the market propagandists even if we do not believe them.

# Chapter 28
# The Role of the State

In a later chapter (Chapter 34) we discuss the impact of the government's revenue/expenditure processes on the level of employment and the general level of prices. But first we turn to a discussion of the need for government action to ensure a particular pattern of resource allocation and distribution of incomes. In this chapter, therefore, we are concerned with one of the longest-standing debates in economics: what constitutes the right 'mix' of economic activities undertaken by the public and private sectors of the economy?

The analysis of government's role is based upon a value judgement, arrived at through consensus, that society should aim at making the best possible use of its scarce resources which have alternative uses. Thus the study of government's economic role applies certain conclusions derived from *positive economics*, concerning the relative efficiencies of various institutional arrangements for production and distribution, to the field of *normative economics* which is concerned with discovering the best set of these institutional arrangements. Now since the state, as we saw earlier, is no more than another institutional mechanism for the transformation of scarce resources into goods, to refer (as people often do) to government's role in terms of 'interference' with the economic system is to deny the state's identity with that system. A system may comprise a sharing of the transformation processes between private and collective production; or it may comprise only one institution, the state, in which case all production is collective. Which system a society adopts is largely determined by the social and political, as well as the economic, desires of that society. In other words, the politico-economic system itself becomes a good, satisfying the philosophic ideals (wants) of the community which adopts it. Such goals, alongside all other community desires, constitute what the economist terms a 'social welfare function'.

## Objectives

Taking the role of the State to be the promotion of the best use of society's scarce resources, what constitutes the 'best'? Presumably the best use is that which maximizes community happiness or 'welfare'. But such a guideline is somewhat imperfect since the determinants of welfare constitute a multifarious array, creating severe measurement problems for the public decision-makers. The greatest problem facing the economist, as adviser to government, is that welfare is subjective. Now the economist usually makes objective calculations of things subjective via the use of the measuring rod of money; subjective motivations may promote activities which have a quantifiable impact on prices and incomes. In so far as welfare is determined by consumption of goods and services which carry market prices, then community welfare can also be measured in this way, i.e. in terms of national income. Indeed it is this measure of welfare which has traditionally been adopted by economists,[1] but total reliance upon it will always result in an inaccurate estimate of community welfare since the latter depends on many things which do not carry a market price. (We encountered some of these difficulties in the very first chapter of this book.)

The subjective nature of welfare also creates another serious problem – how to aggregate individual welfare levels. How can we measure the impact on community welfare of, say, an increase in the production of a particular good if some people benefit and others suffer as a result? Suppose the public decision-maker decides to promote an increase in the production

1. The term *economic welfare*, first coined by Pigou (1912), is usually employed.

of butter and a reduction in the production of ships. Suppose further that shipbuilders are totally unsuitable for employment in butter production without extensive re-training. Other things being equal, the income of factors involved in the production of butter will rise, while shipbuilders' short-run income will fall. On the narrow interpretation of welfare one group in society is made better off, another worse off; how then are we to measure the welfare effect of the policy change?

To avoid this problem of interpersonal welfare comparisons economists have adopted the *Pareto criterion*[2] which states that for a policy change to lead to an increase in community welfare it must make *at least one* community member better off and *no* community members worse off. In terms of Figure 148 a policy change which moves the community (two individuals) from welfare level $X$ to any level within the shaded area is acceptable, but not a change which results in a move from $X$ to a point outside the shaded area, e.g. $P$ or $Q$.

When discussing the theoretical complexities of analysing problems of welfare most of the current generation of economists accept the Pareto criterion, although not without reservations. The main foundation for this acceptance is a belief that

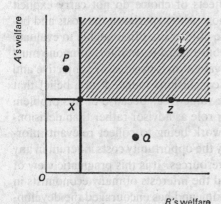

Figure 148

2. After Vilfredo di Pareto (1848–1923).

the Pareto criterion minimizes the ethical content of normative rules – it permits the least objectionable ethic and, therefore, appeals to the consensus within society. But the criterion also has its critics. Some would argue that any one normative rule is no more 'scientific' than any other and that the concept of a *minimum* ethical rule is meaningless. Others would claim that even if the criterion were acceptable on ethical grounds, the very characteristics making it palatable also render it impracticable. How does a normative rule which bases its appeal to the consensus upon a desire not to see anyone harmed by changes in policy, offer help to the decision-maker in a world in which someone is always going to be made worse off in some way, by virtual definition of the need for government policy? Any rigid adherence to the Paretian rule would always maintain the *status quo*.

Those who adopt the Pareto criterion are aware of the above criticisms but remain persuaded by the inherent appeal to the consensus which the criterion offers. Rather, supporters of the criterion see major problems as lying in the way of its practical application. Perhaps most serious of these obstacles is that of the difficulties involved in trying to measure aggregate costs and benefits. Many of the objects of choice do not carry explicit market prices and even those who experience the costs and benefits associated with these objects are often unable to evaluate them. Yet, to reach decisions regarding welfare, someone must place a value on actions, evaluation is necessarily subjective and a very real threat to any conclusions founded on a belief that policy decisions should be value-free. Because of this problem many economists see their role as advisor rather than decision-maker, the aim of their work being to collect relevant information and to help identify the opportunity costs inherent in any proposed reallocation of resources. It is this pragmatic view of things which has promoted the interests of many economists in public sector decision-making and has encouraged the development of analytical techniques such as 'cost-benefit analysis' (CBA) and planning frameworks such as 'planning, programming and budgeting' (PPB) systems.

Given the problems associated with its application the Pareto criterion needs to be handled with care. Nevertheless, it remains the dominant ethical framework in modern welfare economics and we shall adopt it as our yardstick in order to maintain a consistent reference point for studying real world policy problems.

### Private or public markets?

Turning to the definition of government's economic role we have two models to guide us – the market and the firm. Social welfare can be largely left to the results of private market activities or to the planning powers of the state. Acceptance of the Pareto criterion has led many to postulate competition as the blueprint for welfare maximization. In this system production and exchange take place in markets which are neutral regarding the interests of the parties concerned. Production is ultimately geared to the wants of households, each of which faces the same price for any particular product and the same financial reward for the rendering of factor services owned by the household. All producers face a common set of relevant factor prices and they equate the marginal cost of production with the price of their product. In this way society maximizes output from its given supply of scarce resources and consumers pay for the last unit of a commodity produced an amount exactly equal to the cost to the producer of producing that unit, i.e. to the cost to the community in foregone alternatives.

This extreme form of the market system merely minimizes the role of government, it by no means renders such a role unnecessary. No economic system can operate without some production activities being undertaken by the state. Even the perfectly competitive economy requires some minimum provision of government services since markets can only function properly against a backcloth of state protection. Such protection must at least include laws to prevent contractual default and violation of the institution of private property. Also required is the physical manifestation of these laws, both domestically and internationally, via a police force and a national defence network. (Equally important in a monetary economy is the maintenance of a stable value of the medium of exchange.)

Such goods as a legal system and a national defence network are examples of what we have termed 'collective goods'. A unit of national defence is equally available to all consumers – individual $A$'s consumption of that unit can in no way diminish the consumption by individual $B$ of that same unit. The private sector cannot undertake production of such goods since the exclusion principle cannot operate – no one can be excluded from the benefits of collective goods once they are supplied. In the absence of exclusion the price mechanism cannot operate since, in a free market, potential consumers would not reveal their true preferences, knowing that as long as one unit of the good is purchased by someone the benefits of that unit may be enjoyed by everyone. This difficulty is often referred to as the 'free-rider' problem. But the state possesses coercive powers to extract payment for such goods and can determine supply, assuming a democratic political framework, via reference to information collected in the ballot-box. Thus it is possible for the voting mechanism to constitute a proxy market-place wherein consumer preferences for various quantities of collective goods are expressed not in terms of money bids but in terms of votes.

We should note at this stage that 'public provision' merely refers to the fact that total supply of certain collective goods is determined by a political, rather than a market mechanism. The actual physical manifestation of these goods, in the form of inputs into the collective goods production process, may quite easily be undertaken by private enterprise. To continue with the example of national defence, it is not military hardware that constitutes this particular collective good but defence policies, the amount and nature of defensive protection. Production of the intermediate goods – machine guns, tanks and aircraft carriers (even trained manpower) – may be undertaken by the private sector in response to the placing of government contracts.

The provision of the two collective goods mentioned so far, a legal system and a defence network, is the necessary condition for an economy to operate smoothly. But is it sufficient? If, as suggested earlier, the perfectly competitive market system has so many attractive features, what is the case for extending state activity beyond the provision of law and order, defence of the realm and the financing of these provisions? The answer is twofold:

1 Several of the conditions necessary to achieve a perfectly competitive equilibrium are not features of the free enterprise system of reality.

2 The perfectly competitive model may be a world of allocative efficiency but it contains no in-built guarantees about an equitable distribution of incomes.

Let us now consider these problems and their consequences in some detail.

### Monopoly

A feature of the 'unregulated' market economy is that market-power may become concentrated in the hands of a few producers, or only one producer. As we saw in Chapter 18 this may result in a welfare loss for society. Because marginal cost is not equal to price under conditions of monopoly, consumer surplus is not being maximized. It is true, as we saw earlier, that output of a commodity may rise and its price be lowered when a perfectly competitive industry is 'monopolized'. This result obtains from the realization of economies of scale. But even if all monopolies were to be created via the reaping of scale economies a social optimum would still not be reached since marginal cost would still not equal price. As a result of increased output and a lower price consumer surplus from a particular commodity might be increased relative to the amount enjoyed under competition but unrealized consumer surplus would still exist. This is illustrated by Figure 149.

How might the State ensure maximum consumer surplus is enjoyed? One method would be for the community to subsidize the monopolist by an amount equal to $AFCP_m$ (the monopolist's surplus) to enable him to produce amount $OX_s$ and be no

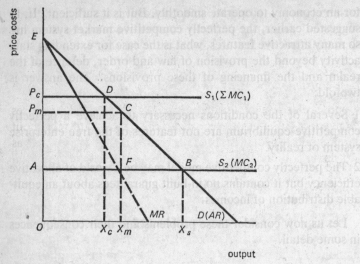

Figure 149

worse off. Alternatively the State could 'nationalize' the monopoly and operate a marginal-cost pricing policy, thus producing $OX_s$. Which method is chosen will depend partly on a comparison of relative costs – the subsidization costs of the first method compared to the acquisition costs of the second, including the extent of $X$ – inefficiency under public ownership. Choice will also depend upon prevailing views on income distribution since public ownership redistributes away from the monopolist to the community at large.

## Spillovers

The collective goods referred to earlier cannot be traded in the market place. But many goods which *are* produced and traded under market conditions also exhibit degrees of collectiveness. The case for perfect competition rests on the assumption that all goods are purely private, i.e. privately produced and privately consumed. In the real world, however, many goods are privately produced but few are absolutely privately consumed. Now, if most goods are collectively consumed free market allocation of resources could well lead to over-consumption of certain goods (bads) and under-consumption of others in terms of the optimum welfare level for the community.

## Over-consumption

Suppose, because of the nature of the production processes involved, it was not possible to produce steel cutlery without simultaneously producing (and distributing) soot, poisonous gas and noxious liquids. Such by-products, often termed *external effects, externalities* or *spillovers*, impose costs upon the community external to the costs borne by the producer, i.e. the social costs, or total community costs, of production outweigh the private costs (to the producer). In the cutlery example the producer chooses his output according to his private marginal production costs (labour, raw materials, etc.) but ignores the extra laundry bills and funeral outlays imposed on the community at large as a result of his activities. Free market allocation might ensure that the supply of knives and forks is optimal in terms of private costs and benefits, but in terms of *social* costs knives and forks are being over-produced.

Our analysis would seem to suggest that the rule to be followed to maximize community welfare is to produce units of a commodity until the marginal social costs of production are equal to the marginal social benefits from consumption. But choosing the most efficient mechanism for ensuring that this rule will be pursued is an exceedingly difficult task. Nor is it certain that an available mechanism will be adopted. The calculus of social costs and to a large extent the corrective mechanisms employed are largely determined by political and social considerations since the latter reflect the community's hierarchy of wants. The true (inter-generational) social costs of, say, despoliation of the countryside may be grossly underestimated or deliberately ignored by a community for which the major day-to-day concern is adequate food and shelter. We see evidence of this in Western Europe where current environmental problems are largely the inheritance of economic activities from an earlier period of relative under-development.

Measures taken to equate marginal social costs and benefits may operate through the market mechanism or they may take effect outside it. Where net social benefit from private production and/or distribution is likely to be negative for all ranges of output, then output may be controlled via an extension of that necessary collective good referred to earlier – the legal system. Hence in the UK we currently outlaw the private production (for purposes of market resale) of mustard gas and heroin. But where net social benefits from private production are likely to be positive for a considerable output range, products may be permitted to be bought and sold through the market mechanism subject to certain controls at the margin.

Controls on marginal outputs may again be physical although this can present problems. Referring again to noxious emissions, a method of control which has been tried in many western countries is the setting of legally permitted ceilings on the output of noxious materials. But this control mechanism presents serious scrutiny problems, e.g. how to discover which of a dozen firms established along the banks of a river exceeded the permitted noxious output limit and poisoned thousands of fish a hundred miles downstream. Obviously the larger the number of enterprises within an industry the greater the incentive for each one to ignore the law.

Alternatively the fitting of anti-pollution devices could be made compulsory on all outlets of noxious materials, both industrial (factory chimneys) and domestic (motor car exhaust systems). But if no such devices are available in the short term some alternative solution may initially be called for. Note that both the mechanisms referred to so far require the use of further resources. The pollution problem is not simply that the environment is unpleasant but also that resources must be diverted from production of goods to the reduction of nuisances. If we wish to rely upon the market mechanism to solve its own problems, presumably an ideal way is to encourage research into pollution-minimizing production techniques. The market itself might provide such an incentive via increased waste-disposal costs as the sources of free goods – disposal space – are gradually exhausted; or via consumer dissatisfaction with commodities which pollute. However, the market may be very tardy in providing such response, perhaps due to the availability of seemingly unlimited disposal space in the early stages of economic development; or due to reasons suggested earlier in relation to the hierarchy of wants. Despite over two hundred years of industrialization several areas of the world are only now discovering a shortage of waste-disposal space; and Nader's 'Raiders' are a recent phenomenon.

A possible means of speeding up market responses is to raise the costs of existing production methods by forcing firms to incorporate *all* their costs into their output calculations. The object of this would be to ensure that private costs, the costs actually borne by the polluter, are equal to social costs. This could be achieved by the imposition of a tax on each unit of output, the tax so calculated as to equal the difference between private and social costs, as in Figure 150.

Figure 150 depicts a polluter. *MPC* is the curve of marginal private costs; *MSC* the curve of marginal social costs; and *MSB* the curve of marginal social benefits. There is no divergence between private and social benefits (the *MSB* curve stands for both) but social and private costs do diverge (*MSC* lies above *MPC*). Left to its own devices the firm will want to produce

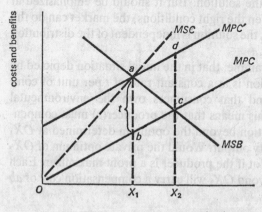

Figure 150

$OX_2$ units of output, equating $MPC$ with $MSB$. Yet this level of output is not optimal for society since $MSC$ is greater than $MSB$. Optimal output for society is $OX_1$ where $MSC$ and $MSB$ are equal. If a tax is imposed on each unit of output, equal to the difference between the private and social costs of each unit, then $MSC$ becomes the firm's effective marginal cost curve and production is cut back to $OX_1$ which is also the optimum output level for society.[3]

Since it would be impossible to apply a different tax rate to every tax unit produced, a compromise must be adopted. This could be achieved by levying, on each unit produced, a tax equal to the difference between the producer's costs and the cost to society at output level $OX_1$. By a vertical shifting of the producer's cost curve to $MPC'$ the optimum output level of $OX_1$ is produced. The gains in pollution reduction from moving to $OX_1$ outweigh the costs in terms of foregone output and the fact that the available output is offered at a higher price.

In the above example the optimum result is achieved by making the powers of the state impose penalties (in this case a corrective tax) upon those activities which do not conform to society's aims. Such powers are invoked when the market process is either unlikely to solve the problem or likely to be too slow in working towards the solution. But it should be emphasized at this stage that, given the right conditions, the market can do the job. Furthermore, the solution is independent of the distribution of property rights.

Suppose, for example, that in the initial situation depicted by Figure 150 pollution is at a constant rate of $t$ per unit of commodity output and that consumers own the environmental property right. This means that the producer(s) must compensate for any pollution beyond the optimum determined at $OX_1$ units of commodity output. Would the private optimum of $OX_2$ be maintained? Not if the producer is a profit maximizer. Each unit produced beyond $OX_1$ will carry a compensation cost of $ab$

---

3. This analysis and the illustrative diagram is applicable to all forms of congestion or pollution, e.g. road traffic, air traffic, effluence in rivers, over-population.

($= cd = t$), representing the difference between the social and private costs of that unit. Thus, total compensation costs at output $OX_2$ stand at *abcd*. Now, if the producer cuts back from $OX_2$ to $OX_1$ he foregoes net revenue of *abc* but he saves compensation costs of *abcd* and, therefore, enjoys a net gain of *acd* ($= abc$).

Suppose, instead, that the producer owns the property rights, so that the consumers have to bribe him to cut back output from $OX_2$ to $OX_1$. The maximum bribe per unit of output reduction that consumers will be willing to offer is again equal to the difference between the social and private costs of each unit, *ab* ($= cd = t$). If the producer accepts the bribe he moves back to $OX_1$ and receives payment of *abcd* in bribes which more than compensates him for the loss of revenue, *abc*. Again, the producer enjoys a net gain of *acd* in choosing the lower output. It would seem that the allocation of resources is unaffected by the distribution of property rights.

Before leaving this section we should recall that in the earlier analysis the powers of the state were invoked because the necessary conditions for the optimum to be reached by a market process were not present. These conditions, already outlined in earlier chapters on market processes, emphasize the role of property rights. For instance, the assumption of perfect knowledge in this context refers to property rights being clearly defined and recognized by all economic agents. Further, the distribution of these rights must be acceptable to all lest the result of the market process be unacceptable on distributional grounds. But equally important to the set of necessary conditions is the absence of transaction costs or at least an assumption that transaction costs are never high enough to preclude negotiations among affected parties and between this group and those who create the nuisance. Perfect competition in all markets is also assumed and the corollary that no production indivisibilities prevent marginal adjustments to output. Given the rigour of these assumptions it is not surprising that governments in the real world play a very active role in trying to correct, by both fiscal inducements and physical controls, the unwanted consequences of 'solutions' established in the market-place. For example, how are the millions who breathe air to negotiate with and extract compensation from the millions who poison that air by the emission of carbon monoxide from motor-car exhaust systems? And how are marginal adjustments to be made in the quantities of crude oil transported by ocean tankers when such vessels cannot be produced in little bits?

## Under-consumption

Just as too much of certain goods may be consumed, according to the prevailing aims and values of society, so it is possible for *too little* of many other goods to be consumed, according to the set of values. Such under-consumption may be general or specific. A household under-consumes *generally* when its means are inadequate to finance the enjoyment of a standard of living considered to be adequate by the majority of the population. The unfortunate who are in this position are usually classified as living in *primary* poverty. *Specific* under-consumption results when households consume too little of those goods and services which benefit everyone; a range including toothbrushes, milk, good quality housing, medical services, education and any other good which yields spillover benefits.

*Poverty and inequality.* The definition of 'adequacy' will be based upon value judgements reflecting both the cultural and moral standards of the majority of the population as well as the economic strength of the community as a whole. Thus, any definition of 'absolute poverty', a measure which aims to determine a minimum subsistence level, will prove difficult and is unlikely to help the policy-maker. Not only do basic requirements of nutrition, clothing, shelter, etc., vary with age and sex, but, within clearly defined categories of age and sex, individuals' requirements are likely to be heterogeneous because of physical shape and stature and nature of occupation. Furthermore, any concept of adequate functioning can only be defined with reference to the prevailing culture which means that an absolute standard will underestimate the true extent of poverty. This means, of course, that the policy-maker's problem is even more difficult, since the factors influencing relativity are even more varied than those which might be used in any concept of the absolute. It also means that cross-cultural and inter-temporal comparisons of living standards must be made with great caution because standards vary between cultures and over time.

*The causes*. What causes poverty? Primary poverty is not synonymous with inequality but it often reflects how incomes are distributed in the market-oriented economy. In principle the market system provides the basis for the satisfaction of everyone's material needs in so far as specialization and the division of labour enable Man to produce as much as he can from his given supply of resources. The market system helps members of society to enjoy the fruits of this efficiency by the provision of opportunities to earn income. However, principles are notorious for breaking down in practice and the guarantee of market opportunities is not enough to ensure that everyone can enjoy the fruits of the market place since not everyone is capable of *pursuing* these opportunities.

In the market system the standard of living of each individual household is circumscribed by its ownership of something marketable, either property or labour services. In other words how much a household can buy is largely determined by how much it can sell. But as we shall see in a later section the cyclical movements of aggregate demand in such a system prevent the guarantee that outlets for household services will always be plentiful. Furthermore, even if such a guarantee could be given, not all households possess something which markets desire – people are often limited in their capacity to learn; are subject to illness; and always grow old.

Not only does the market system provide opportunities to earn income but it also provides opportunities to accumulate wealth, i.e. a stock of net assets.[4] Such a stock provides a flow of benefits to its owner. The benefits thus derived are in excess of the regular flow of money income from the stock of assets since the ownership of wealth increases the household's range

4. 'Wealth' is synonymous with 'net worth', i.e. assets minus liabilities.

of expenditure opportunities – it provides protection against contingencies and enables periodic spending sprees; and magnifies the owner's total economic power giving access to privileges both economic, social and political.

But, as with earned income, there is no guarantee of equal access to wealth opportunities. Wealth derives initially from surplus income, that is, from income over and above consumption requirements. Thus, since opportunities for earning incomes are not equally distributed, neither are the opportunities for accumulating surplus income. Furthermore such inequality, left unchecked, is self-perpetuating. Once accumulated, a stock of wealth may be handed on from generation to generation. A household may thus enjoy a greater share of economic and political opportunities simply because it has inherited a stock of wealth.

It would seem, then, that to organize economic life in such a way as to permit purely market-determined results is to create two problems: a problem of inequality and a poverty problem. They are related but nevertheless distinct – it is possible (remember the example of Mauritius in Chapter 3) for the distribution of incomes to be perfectly equal within a community yet for everyone to be poor simply because community output is consistently very low. However, when poverty is the norm we no longer treat it as a spillover problem but as a problem of economic development. The role of the state in this respect has been discussed in earlier chapters.

Why should a community consider the distributional consequences of market activities to be problems? We can suggest two major reasons why there is concern:

1 Improvements in the distribution of incomes and wealth can lead to improvements in the allocation of resources since the latter is determined by effective demand, that is, demand backed by purchasing power, by income.

2 Utility functions are usually interdependent. Unless people wear blinkers they cannot exist in society without observing the plight of their fellows. Such awareness does not allow severe inequalities in income and wealth to persist indefinitely. The rich

eventually desire to improve the welfare of the poor. Such concern may derive from an altruistic or from a selfish basis. The rich may have a genuine unselfish desire to improve the lot of the poor but the desire for improvement could equally stem from a fear of revolution or a fear of the spread of contagious diseases, poverty and disease being long-standing bedmates.

*Market failure again.* If the rich are concerned about the welfare of the poor and the market is an efficient signalling device, why is the poverty problem not attacked via the market mechanism itself? To some extent it is, via private charitable institutions which provide information on the location of poverty. In the small group case, like the Bushmen of the Kalahari, or the local neighbourhood in a city, the information problem may not be severe since most individuals in these cases are aware of the location of poverty and can act accordingly. But in the large group of the modern mass society individuals are aware that poverty exists but are unaware of its precise location. It is in this context, then, that the market plays its role and charitable organizations are established to channel home transfers from the 'haves' to the 'have-nots'.

The reason the market fails to solve the poverty problem is that filling the information gap by the establishment of private charities is not enough. If the problem is to be overcome the actual amount of income transferred must suffice and it is in this respect that the market is unreliable, for two reasons: the absence of efficiency checks and the existence of free riders. Charitable organizations may be inefficient because only minimal efficiency checks operate upon them. An altruistic donor loses interest once he has donated; he does not pursue, like a tenacious shareholder, the organization's use of his donation. But even if charitable organizations were efficient in terms of minimizing the costs of giving to the poor, the amount of transfers from the rich would be unlikely to suffice for solving the poverty problem. The reason for this is that not all who wish to see the position of the poor improved will themselves actually donate an income transfer. A transfer of £1 from rich to poor presents a £1 increase in the incomes of the poor regardless of who actually effects the transfer. In other words, a charitable donation is a collective good, it confers an equal benefit on all potential donors and the total supply of voluntary transfers is likely to be inadequate.

*Some possible cures*. Thus, in the absence of effective private arrangements, the state may take on the responsibility for income-redistribution and for solving the poverty problem by pursuing policies to minimize those market tendencies which promote inequalities and by adopting the role of a collective transfer agency to channel income transfers from rich to poor. The state can apply coercion to raise revenue, thus ensnaring the free riders, and it is conceivable that through economies of scale the state may be able to channel aid to the poor at a lower cost than when private agencies effect such transfers. Private charitable organizations do, however, continue to play an important role in pinpointing any holes in the State's programme and in discovering new areas of need, that is, they are important as *pioneers* (a role which was recognized by the Charities Act of 1960).

Furthermore, the state's role is not that of a Robin Hood. Indeed, this gentleman found so much to keep him busy simply because the state at that time was not fulfilling its role as protector of everyone, including the lower income groups. Rather, we are assuming that the whole community, including the rich, is in favour of transfers to the poor and the state is *chosen* as the most efficient means of affecting such a programme.

## A necessary programme

In the context of market corrections there are certain minimum tasks which the state must perform if a positive attack is to be made upon the problems of poverty and inequality. First, any government must ensure that the level of aggregate demand is always sufficient to guarantee full employment (or else provide equivalent household means in the world of automation) and it must construct a programme whereby individuals can be helped to finance investment in new skills when their old ones become obsolete. The maintenance of stability in the value of money, the second task, is equally important since inflation breeds inequalities. It is essential also that the state destroy all unwarranted discriminatory practices which either prevent defined sections of the population acquiring market skills, or prevent other sections of the community from exercising skills which have already been acquired. Finally, the state must do all it can to iron out any undesirable inequalities (although the consensus may deem some amount of inequality as desirable) and this may involve using the tax mechanism to bring *disposable* incomes, both earned and inherited, in line with the desired distribution.

The above aims are no more than the necessary conditions for an effective programme against poverty and inequality; they are not sufficient. No matter how 'tight' the prevailing labour market nor how free from discrimination, there still remain the problems of the 'unemployables' (the chronic sick, the aged, the mentally subnormal); temporary loss of earning power; and excessive family size. These difficulties highlight how ineffective would be a redistributive programme which merely concentrated upon maximizing the number of market opportunities and upon reducing incomes from the top via the tax mechanism. If poverty is to be seriously tackled the amounts deducted from higher incomes must also be transferred to those on lower incomes. Not only is the tax *and* transfer method more effective for the recipients of the transfer – it is also cheaper for the donors, that section of society which is giving up some of its income. Consider a rich man with £10 and a poor man with £5. The rich man considers that an income gap of £5 is too great and the poor man requires at least £6 if he is to adequately feed, clothe and house his family. If the rich man lights his fire with one of his £1 notes then he immediately reduces the income gap to £4. But although the poor man may receive some slight psychological boost from the knowledge of this new state of affairs it is cold comfort to his hungry family. If, on the other hand, the rich man *gives* £1 to the poor man, not only is the poor man enabled to purchase extra household needs, but the rich man's desire for a more equitable income distribution is doubly satisfied since the income gap is closed to £3. Put another way – £1's worth of redistribution can be achieved for only 50p (assuming away administrative costs). In this way, then, society is able to pursue two objectives at the same time – to redistribute incomes and to relieve absolute poverty.

### The mechanics

The above example is deliberately simple for illustrative purposes and, consequently, it disguises a very thorny problem: *how* are transfers to be effected? There can be, and is, much conflict over the choice of transfer methods. If one group in society is to self-impose coercive transfers of a part of its income and wealth to another group, it is going to want the main say in how the transfer should be achieved. Thus the nature of the transfer mechanism will depend upon two things:

1 The motives of those who make the transfers. Altruistic motivations are likely to yield different policies to those based upon a fear of revolution or a belief in the doctrine of self-help. One set of principles gave Britain the Poor Law Amendment Act of 1834 and the consequent reliance upon the workhouse 'solution'. A quite different philosophy led to the Beveridge Report of 1942,[5] which laid the foundations of the post-war social security system.

2 The relative effectiveness of different methods of transfer. The best method of transfer is presumably that which channels a given amount of aid to those who need it most. To many this suggests the use of some form of means test. But in a society where social status is largely determined by economic success, potential recipients of state aid may be reluctant to disclose eligibility if this is dependent upon demonstration of inadequate household means.

The question of means-tested transfers has dominated the thoughts of both economists and social administrators for most of the post-war period. Much research time has been spent looking for an 'acceptable' selective tax/transfer mechanism.

5. *Social Insurance and Allied Services*, HMSO, Cmnd. 6404, 1942.

Currently, much thought is being devoted to the concept of *negative taxation* as a solution to the problem. We shall consider this concept in Chapter 29. In the meantime we should note that society has another powerful mechanism at its disposal, the *social contract*. Under this alternative system eligibility for aid is determined not by lack of means but according to the categorization of the *causes* of poverty – old age, sickness, etc. Such is the essence of the 'pay-as-you-go' social insurance system which the United Kingdom has operated since the Second World War. In this system the currently healthy provide for the sick, the currently employed provide for the unemployed and the young provide for the old; all out of general taxation with some help provided by national insurance contributions. The arrangement suits the donors (taxpayers) on the understanding that the next generation will do the same for them, in the belief that future governments will not renege on the contract. It is very tempting to pursue these arguments further at this point but in order that the basic principles may be digested and so that we may discuss all unsolved problems together, we shall leave further discussion on this topic also to Chapter 29.

## Spillover benefits

Finally, let us take a brief look at the problem created when commodities yield, in consumption, benefits to society in addition to those enjoyed by the individual. What we see here is the complete opposite of the problem of social costs discussed earlier in this chapter – in the case of goods such as education and health services, social benefits (i.e. total benefits) are in excess of private benefits. It is possible, therefore, for individuals to consume too little of these beneficial goods relative to the optimum consumption level for society. This specific underconsumption may have a primary cause, household income may simply be inadequate to purchase the socially desirable amounts of goods like education and health services, or even milk. But the problem can still prevail even when household means *are* sufficient to permit consumption of the socially optimum level, as the result of ignorance, self-interest, apathy or myopia. (Re-

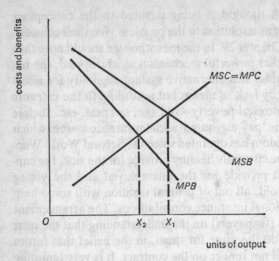

Figure 151

member that the individual may be maximizing his own, private benefit, not social benefit.)

When households do socially 'misspend' for these reasons the problem is often labelled as one of 'secondary poverty', a curious phrase since the rich are well capable of misspending, indeed in an increasingly congested environment they may well be the worst culprits. We can illustrate the problem of social under-consumption resulting from spillover benefits in a way analogous to the way we used to discuss the problem of over-production of spillover bads.

In Figure 151 marginal social benefit (MSB) exceeds marginal private benefit (MPB) at all levels of production and consumption. The social optimum is where MSB equals MSC (marginal social cost) at output $OX_1$. (We are assuming for convenience that MSC = MPC.) If we rely on private markets then consumption and output will be at $OX_2$, a lower total than the social optimum $OX_1$. Now we shall briefly discuss how we can move consumers from $OX_2$ to $OX_1$.

*Income transfers.* In so far as inadequate income is one root cause of under-consumption the answer may lie in an extension of the tax/transfer mechanism which aims at solving primary poverty. But if under-consumption results from ignorance, self-interest or apathy a cash transfer may be totally ineffectual in promoting a consumption rise. If Fred Smith receives cash but chooses to buy beer instead of extra education the social purpose of the transfer is defeated. To argue for cash transfers in the face of ignorance of spillover benefits, or decisions to ignore them because the individual is maximizing his private welfare is to expect people to spend in such a way as to (somehow) maximize social welfare. This expectation is based on two assumptions: that the individual knows what he wants and that allowing complete freedom of purchase (consumer sovereignty) will maximize community well-being. This latter argument is obviously ill-founded when we take the objectives of the donor into account – a cash transfer given in the hope that it will be spent on education can only reduce the welfare of the donor if it is spent on beer. Furthermore, the assumption that the consumers know what they want (and what is best for them) is extremely flimsy with respect to a highly technical environment which is befogged by persuasive advertising and where consumption decisions require specialist knowledge. How can the untrained individual always know the type and quality of medical services he requires?

*Transfers in kind.* Thus to induce extra consumption of goods which yield spillover benefits the state may effect transfers in kind by producing such goods in the public sector and then offering them at zero, or heavily subsidized, user prices (their production is, of course, financed by revenues provided by the community's citizens). Our consumer theory does indeed suggest that a price subsidy may induce a greater increase in consumption than a cash transfer because a price reduction results in two effects: an income effect *and* a substitution effect (which may operate in the same direction). A cash transfer, on the other hand, relies on only one effect – the income effect. The actual magnitude of the required price reduction will depend upon the nature and strength of individual tastes. When the commodity is very low on the individual consumers' hierarchies of wants a zero or even negative price may be required to promote the optimum level of consumption; but when the good is a little higher in their hierarchies the required price reduction may not be so massive.

*Other methods.* But even an offer at zero price may not be taken up if the good is considered highly inferior by individual consumers. This would seem to suggest two possible avenues by which the socially optimal level of consumption may be achieved. First, so long as individuals would be prepared to buy at least some units (no matter how few) of the commodity at zero price, the state can offer a choice to the individual of either consuming all the units offered by public provision, or none at all. Since the individual is prepared to consume some units without this choice he may not wish to lose these benefits and may opt for a big increase in his consumption as a result of the 'all or nothing' scheme. The second avenue is in fact the last re-sort – that of coercion. When the commodity is very high on the community's hierarchy of wants but believed to be so low on in-dividual hierarchies that even an all-or-nothing scheme would be unsuccessful, compulsory consumption will be the outcome. The United Kingdom has opted for this course of action with regard to education.

A final word on the all-or-nothing scheme. Many of the goods which rank high on the community's hierarchy of wants are sub-ject to constraints on the supply side. A lengthy time period is involved in building schools and hospitals and it takes a long time to train teachers, nurses and doctors. Thus even if the ignorance or self-interest problems could be overcome (by, say, a non-transferable voucher scheme) supply of these commodi-ties is likely to be highly inelastic in any short-run period. Thus, how can supply be rationed if the price mechanism is ruled out because of the massive spillover benefits involved and because access to supplies must be given to the poor as well as the rich? One method is to operate production in two sectors, a small pri-vate sector and a large public sector, giving the population equal access to each. Since supplies are relatively scarce and the price mechanism does not operate, a queue system serves to allocate resources in the public sector. Those who do not wish to queue and who have the means to pay for consumption can opt for the private sector where the price mechanism operates. In this way, access to essential services is guaranteed to all the population. The rich cannot gain a disproportionate share of scarce resources since the only queue-jumping permitted is that which involves a jump into a completely different sector. Britain's supply of medical services operates in this fashion with the National Health Service existing alongside private practice. The housing stock as we saw in Chapter 9 is also distributed along these lines in so far as two sectors operate side by side and the alternatives are to join a queue for public authority housing or pay a market price in the private sector. A cynical view might suggest that a qualitative all-or-nothing scheme operates with housing since the choice within the public sector is a characterless red-brick block or nothing, and the rich are not likely to starve the population of public housing resources, preferring to buy in the private market.

## Summary

Reaching conclusions on the topics discussed in this chapter is difficult. To say what society's problems are is one thing, to state categorically how they should be dealt with is quite another. As we have tried to underline, the way in which society chooses to deal with its problems depends upon the value judgements which are operative within the society at large. If people like to live in an environment in which essential services are offered free of direct charge, then they may opt for this form of provision despite the queues which go with it. If the consensus prefers alternative arrangements then these alternatives will be chosen. This chapter, then, has been very much a mixed bag; some positive economics has been used alongside a lot of analysis which is not quite so rigorous, but nevertheless important. Some of the problems referred to have been, or soon will be, solved; others *must* be solved if the future is going to be a pleasant time in which to live.

## Questions

1 What is the Pareto criterion? Do you think it is a universally acceptable criterion? Who decides whether someone might be made 'worse off' by a move from an optimum?

2 What criteria would you choose for deciding whether particular goods and services should be supplied free of charge by the government or provided through the market?

3 'The role of the state as defined in this chapter is so extensive that we may as well advocate complete central planning.' Discuss.

4 How could the model of perfect competition provide guidelines for a 'liberal socialist' economy in which the state owns all the means of production except labour services, a central planning unit decides what prices are to be charged for goods and services, but consumer preferences still dictate the use of productive resources?

5 This chapter has not made specific reference to *local* government. Do you think this is because local government is unimportant?

6 'Unless resources allocated to the public sector of the health services are legally prevented from transferring to the private sector (full time or part time) the rich can always command the lion's share of health services.' Discuss.

Is complete public ownership of health resources a better system?

7 Why is it that country villagers were able to shunt around the proposed sites for London's third airport while in most large cities hundreds of families live in close proximity to dirty, noisy factories and roadways?

8 Why is the 'free-rider' problem important?

9 Does the ethical behaviour of individuals depend upon the size of the group to which they belong?

10 What factors will determine the optimum mix of private and collective goods in an economy?

11 Is there any connection between indivisibilities in produc-

tion processes, joint supply of goods, externalities, exclusion in consumption and market failure?

12 'Economics is the study of the whole system of exchange relationships. Politics is the study of the whole system of coercive or potentially coercive relationships' (J. M. Buchanan). Discuss.

# Chapter 29
## Financing the State

The previous chapter concentrated upon the production side of the state's activities on the implicit assumption that the necessary finance was always available. But this assumption avoids many interesting questions regarding the determinants of how much finance the state can raise; what methods of fund-raising the state can adopt; and what economic effects are likely to result from the various methods. Only a simple guide to the answers to some of these questions can be attempted at first-year level. However, in a later chapter we discuss how a public sector can influence the allocation of resources and the distribution of incomes in an economy – by the way in which government spends and the means it chooses to finance such expenditure – under the heading of 'stabilization policy'.

At several stages in this book the point has been underlined that what distinguishes households, private firms and government (the public firm) is not only the products of these institutions but also their relative access to sources of finance. Of these three institutions the activities of government are the least circumscribed by financial constraints. Households and private firms rely upon two methods of financing their activities – the net revenue they gain from selling their goods and services, and net borrowing. Government also uses these sources of finance but has access to an additional source: governments can print money. Furthermore, the determinants of how much revenue can be raised from the first two sources differ in the case of the state from those affecting a private institution: the state can effect a *compulsory* transfer of resources from the private to the public sector and a government has access to an international capital market unrivalled by that enjoyed by private institutions.

## How the public sector gains resources

The government activities referred to in the previous chapter create a demand for productive resources and unless there are unemployed resources in the economy this demand must compete with the demands of the private sector. We can distinguish four methods by which the state may achieve a transfer of resources from the private to the public sector: taxation, borrowing, printing money and government directives (commandeering). What, then, determines which method the state will choose? For a given resource demand the method of finance should be chosen on a comparative costs basis, i.e. the least cost method should be chosen. The costs arise from any subsidiary reallocation of resources (which may include effects on inducements to work, save, take risks, etc.) plus any redistribution of incomes which accompanies the transfer of resources from private to public ownership. Thus the rule would seem to point to that method of finance which creates minimum disturbance of resource allocation (assuming this to be efficient) and has the most equitable impact on the distribution of incomes and wealth. Let us now take a closer look at the various methods of satisfying a government's demand for resources.

### Strong-arm tactics

The state could achieve a coercive transfer of resources to the public sector at prices below those prevailing in the private sector. Conscription into the armed forces is the prime example of this method of transfer. The obvious inequities that this method creates require little elaboration except to remind ourselves that the ramifications of resource commandeering by the government may spread the burden of finance well beyond those immediately affected. Indeed, in a situation of full employment the burden may extend its inequitable tentacles very far afield as a result of price inflation. Because a coercive transfer of resources to the public sector does not involve an automatic compensatory reduction in private demand, the prices of resources to the private sector will rise as a result of the newly denuded supplies to that sector. Commandeering in, say, a national emergency such as wartime may not have the same inflationary impact since, in such times, the transfer to the public sector is usually accompanied by price controls and/or physical rationing. Nevertheless, while recognizing that in such emergencies state directives might be necessary to speed up market processes, this does not excuse the state paying its resources rewards below what they could obtain in the private sector.

## The printing press

Since the central government controls the supply of money to the economy, including the issue of new notes and coins, why does it not always finance its activities with newly printed money? The reason is that unless there are unemployed resources in the economy the net impact of financing public expenditure by the printing of money is, like commandeering, inflationary and therefore constitutes no more than an inefficient and inequitable form of taxation.

When resources are idle, printing money may be the most efficient means of financing state activities since it is entirely neutral with regard to the allocation of resources and the distribution of incomes.[1] But when resources are already being fully utilized within the private sector the effect of increased resource demand from the public sector is to drive up resource prices unless a parallel contraction in private demand takes place. No such parallel adjustment takes place as a result of the government printing money. Resource prices rise in both sectors and a proportion of this increase in income is spent on

1. Assuming, of course, that the existing states of allocation and distribution are ideal, given the community's desires. Where this is not the case the community may deliberately choose a method of finance which interferes with the prevailing economic order.

goods and services produced in the private sector, thus causing a further rise in private-sector resource prices and, hence, in the prices of those goods produced by these resources.

Thus the financing of public expenditures with newly printed money is neither neutral nor equitable when resources are already fully employed. Indeed, inflationary finance, as we shall see in Chapter 41, creates a three-fold burden. Production planning becomes extremely hazardous in the face of unpredictable price movements. Some sections of the community, those consuming out of relatively fixed incomes, face a bigger consumption cut-back than other sections. Finally, as an unchecked inflation gathers so much momentum that the rate of price increases outstrips the rate of growth of the money supply, the community experiences ever-increasing transactions costs. This latter part of the burden might be viewed as a tax on cash balances. Chapter 41 explores further these arguments.

It would appear that any government which chooses to compete with the private sector by bidding up resource prices, financing the bidding with newly printed money, is choosing an inefficient and inequitable means of competition although, if subtly handled, it is potentially a method which minimizes the likelihood of public accountability.

### Loan finance

Another way the public sector can gain productive resources is for the government to finance its expenditure through borrowing and, given certain circumstances, this method may not bid up resource prices. The state can borrow from its citizens on the strength of a promised fixed rate of interest, using the funds so raised to purchase resources. If the community's supply of investment funds is financed (eventually) out of savings and the latter is a residual income remaining after consumption, the new issue of government bonds must compete alongside existing (low-yield) paper assets for the available supply of investment funds. The net effect on aggregate demand of any switching of assets within private portfolios depends upon the extent to which households and firms consider a purchase of government bonds to constitute an increase in net wealth. If such bonds are purchased because they are cheaper than private ones, or because they offer a safer return (they are 'gilt-edged') then buying them may result not only in a substitution of public debt for private debt but also an income effect which may induce spending on other things. On the other hand, if the income effect is very small then a simple shift of funds from the private to the public sector need have no net effect upon the general level of private expenditure.

However, there is another argument to suggest that government borrowing can lead to an increase in prices. The analysis of the paragraph above assumes that private households and firms purchase the government bonds. But what if the bonds are purchased by the banking sector? In this case acquisition of government liabilities can increase the reserve assets base of the commercial banks and permits the banks to increase their lending to the private sector. This is not true of all forms of government debt, some of which give rise to a single shift in the banks' deposit base, but it is true of, say, Treasury Bills, the purchase of which can have a secondary effect on the money supply by encouraging the banks to lend more to the private sector. The analysis of how this money supply mechanism works and how it can lead to price inflation is explained in Chapters 38 and 41.

Inflation aside, the national debt is often referred to as a burden in other senses. Two reasons have been put forward why loan finance imposes a burden on the community and in both cases the problem is considered to be an intergenerational one. The first reason refers to extra tax payments which a future generation may have to face in order to service the debt. This is not a very convincing argument for the existence of a burden of debt. 'Burden' must refer to the incidence (who actually bears the burden) of the taxes required to finance the interest payments on the original loan. As such the debt does not add to the general problem of tax incidence unless the state's use of the loan funds does not generate sufficient extra community income with which to finance the debt servicing. If the state's use of the original funds is sufficiently productive the debt can be serviced from existing taxes. (It should be noted also that raising taxes to service debt involves income redistribution.)

The second reason advanced for considering that public debt imposes a burden on a future generation presents a more complex argument. The analysis hinges on how the purchase of government bonds is financed, as the results of financing a loan by foregoing consumption will be different from those which will follow financing it out of savings. Since savings are a residual we can postulate that at any point in time the community's supply of investable funds (savings) is given. Now, as mentioned earlier, with a given supply of loanable funds a public loan will be largely financed out of a reduction in private capital formation, i.e. the community switches from one type of asset to another. This in itself cannot impose any burden on a future generation since the reduction in private capital is compensated for by the addition of publicly provided capital goods and the future generation merely inherits a different private/public capital mix. However, the total amount of capital goods inherited by the next generation is less than it would have been if the original expenditure had been financed by taxes. It is in this sense that loan financing might be considered to impose a burden. An increase in taxation reduces disposable incomes and assuming that households consume out of current disposable income (see Chapter 35, private consumption is likely to decrease. The new public expenditure is thus financed mainly out of a reduction in private consumption and hence the next generation inherits a larger capital stock than it would do following loan financing.

Perhaps we can summarize the above arguments by a simple example. Imagine a community which currently possesses capital worth £100 million. The community's government has decided to add to this stock by a new capital investment programme of £1 million. Let us assume that the community consumes, on average, 80 per cent of its disposable income and saves the remaining 20 per cent. If the government decides to finance the new programme via a voluntary loan it presents the community with a simple choice, either to ignore the new bonds or to buy them. The community's consumption of goods and services is unchanged since nothing has happened to disposable income (consumption remains at a proportional rate of 80 per cent). Thus, if the community decides to make the loan, it must do so out of existing loanable funds (20 per cent of disposable income). The government's capital expenditure is financed ultimately by a reduction in private capital expenditure. However, if the government chooses to increase taxes to finance the new project then the immediate impact will be a reduction of disposable income and therefore of private consumption. Tax financing thus enables a larger capital stock to be handed by one generation to another than is possible under loan financing.

It would seem from the above analysis that it can only be with reference to the *relative* effects of loan and tax finance that the former might constitute a burden. What the above analysis also highlights is the potential confusion surrounding the use of the term 'burden'. The use of this term conjures up a picture of future generations staggering, like Pilgrim, beneath a great weight, the Public Debt. Yet we have seen many times in this book that economic decisions involve *choice*, they require a sacrifice or cost to be realized. But this cost, gladly borne in expectation of an even greater benefit, cannot constitute a burden in the uncompensated sense. However, when the costs of obtaining given benefits are *greater than they might be*, then a true burden (previously referred to as an 'excess burden') does exist. It is in this context that the term 'burden' must be employed in relation to the relative results of loan and taxes, for if the term is meant to be merely synonymous with sacrifice then why should the reduced inheritance of a future generation, resulting from loan finance, be more of a burden than the reduced private consumption of the *present* generation as a result of tax financing?

Note that to consider the relative burden of debt in the manner of the above paragraph is to assume that the present generation is willing to make sacrifices for future generations. But why should one generation be prepared to do this for another? Why, for example, should people forfeit the use of resources which could provide them with consumption goods in order to provide young people with universities? When one generation expects to benefit, before it dies, from the education of another generation then part of the answer to this question is to be found in the collective-goods discussion of earlier chapters. But how can we explain such behaviour when practised by a generation which will not live to reap the spillover benefits of a well-educated society? The answer must have something to do with charity, albeit in an inter-generational sense. One generation derives psychic benefit from passing on goods and services to the next generation and just as parents provide for their children's future consumption of private goods so they may seek to provide for their children's future consumption of collective goods.

A final point that should be made in our discussion of government domestic borrowing concerns the possible impact of borrowing on interest rates, an effect which relates to our earlier remarks about the links between government spending and the monetary influences on the economy. If the government decides to change its borrowing it will affect the total demand for funds, the demand for money, and this will affect the level of interest rates. Other things being equal, an increase (decrease) in the level of government borrowing will raise (lower) interest rates. A change in the level of interest will affect consumption spending and savings decisions (Chapter 35), investment decisions (Chapter 36), and the balance of payments (Chapter 43), and thus, governments must take into account these ramifications.

## Foreign loans

Foreign borrowing may be preferred to domestic borrowing. At the time the loan is granted additional resources are made available from abroad without a consequent reduction in domestic resource use (normally such imports would need to be financed by exports). Thus, in a time of full employment of domestic resources a foreign loan may be of immense benefit. However, the adverse effect on the balance of payments that might result from a continuous reliance on such a means of financing government deficits has led some economists to challenge the wisdom of such a policy. Furthermore, when the debt has to be repaid real resources are drained from the domestic use. Of course, if the loan has been productively employed repayments may not present too great a problem unless the balance of payments is in difficulties for other reasons (the monetary adjustments which result from foreign loans and deficits in general are analysed in Chapter 43) and foreign loans may often be raised on very favourable repayment terms.

## Tax finance

Finally, let us turn to a discussion of taxation. Owing to the myriad complex issues raised in a study of taxation our analysis will be kept brief and somewhat restricted.

Currently the UK employs a whole range of different taxes but each one is an example of a particular form of taxation and the interesting question is: which form is best, given the state's concern for an efficient allocation of resources and an equitable income distribution? We broadly classify the two forms as taxes on income and taxes on outlay. In each case taxes are defined according to the *tax base*, i.e. the source at which the tax is aimed. Thus an income tax is aimed at releasing resources through a fall in private expenditure induced by a reduction in disposable income. An outlay tax, on the other hand, reduces private real expenditure by raising the prices of items of expenditure resulting in smaller quantities being purchased.

## The tax base

Why do we not term outlay taxes 'expenditure taxes'? The reason is historical rather than academic. Outlay taxes, as employed by the UK and by most of the other countries of the world, have always been levied on *specific* items of consumption rather than on *total* household expenditure for a given time period. At the present time the UK fiscal system exhibits both *ad valorem* outlay taxes (levied as a proportion of the sales value) such as value added tax; and unit taxes (levied per unit of measure) such as the tobacco tax. An *expenditure* tax, however, means precisely that to the economist. It is a tax levied on households' total expenditure for a specific time period. Now, if by 'total expenditure' we mean to include not only consumption expenditure but also savings (investment expenditure); and if we also adopt a comprehensive definition of income (see below) then income and expenditure become the same tax base since an expenditure flow during a given time period cannot exceed the income flow of the same period. However, defining savings as a residual – what is left after spending – means a rather different approach to the tax base which has attractions for some observers of taxation policy.

What do we mean by a 'comprehensive' definition of income? In a nutshell, we mean a true measure of *economic power*, the command over productive resources. Thus, income for a specified time period relates to all net additions to economic power between the beginning and end of that period. The major problem in defining income so comprehensively is one of computation: not all forms of income carry a monetary tag. Income which derives from the sale of market goods and services is readily calculable if in a monetary form, but if services are paid for in kind then the income of a particular resource owner may be exceedingly difficult to measure. Even more complicating is the case of 'imputed income', which is income derived from non-market resources. As such, imputed income includes any income in kind which does not constitute the result of a market transaction – receipt of a durable good as payment for work done does not constitute imputed income since it is a non-monetary reward for market services but the value of the flow of services from the good to its owner does constitute imputed income. A prime example of the concept is the flow of non-monetary returns from a dwelling to its owner-occupier.

It is apparent then that a truly comprehensive tax base would create such administrative complexities that the costs of collection would outweigh the benefits to society from the use of the proceeds. If the reader is not convinced, ponder on how leisure, an important source of imputed income, might be incorporated into the tax base. Thus a practical compromise must be adopted whereby a feasibly comprehensive definition of income is adopted. Such a definition would at least include those forms of income which are fairly readily translated into money form. Many payments in kind, plus gifts and bequests, could be so translated, as well as capital gains and all forms of wealth, including property and other material possessions (painting, antiques, etc.). The inclusion of sources of wealth is important since, as we saw in the previous chapter, wealth produces a flow of services to its owner and if this flow cannot be taxed comprehensively a tax on its source, the wealth stock, is an alternative means of transferring economic power to the public sector.

We should note finally that if a sufficiently comprehensive definition of income is not adopted then the aims of the state cannot be adequately pursued. The narrower the definition of income, the greater the scope for tax avoidance. For example, if a taxpayer faces the choice of receiving income in the form of £100 cash, or groceries valued at £100, and only money income is subject to tax, a strong incentive exists to choose the groceries. When the tax system contains many such loopholes, three results emerge. First, as tax units juggle their sources of income to avoid tax, the actual incidence of taxation may differ greatly from the intended incidence. Secondly, the certainty that a given amount of revenue can be raised is much reduced. Finally, as the actual tax base is steadily eroded, ever higher tax rates are required to raise a given level of income.

The above problems result from too narrow a definition of the tax base, whether or not prices are stable; but in an inflationary world the definition of the tax base faces even greater difficulties. When the general level of prices is rising the real value of assets (sources of real income) is falling and the contribution to real economic power made by various income components is diminished. In consequence, the tax base must be reviewed regularly to establish whether such things as capital gains are real or illusory, whether stocks are appreciating in real or money terms, whether debts are depreciating in real terms, etc. Such problems are part of the reason why some economists have advocated the adoption of consumption spending as the appropriate tax base for a world in which inflation is normal. Under such a base, no periodical adjustments to the definition are necessary since 'spending is spending' – it is never illusory. There remains, of course, the problem that household spending may rise in money terms between two points in time because prices have risen during the interval. However, under a simple proportional tax on spending this does not lead to major difficulties because the proportion of *potential* consumption foregone in tax is the same whether the base is calculated in real or in money terms. On the other hand, under a progressive rates structure (discussed below) price inflation can push spending into higher tax brackets and a system of indexing may have to be introduced to protect against this. The problem of indexing would prevail in the same circumstances under a progressive income tax and the point remains that the problem of base adjustments for inflation is very much reduced under an expenditure tax.[1]

*Under conditions of inflation a tax on all consumption spending may have advantages over an income tax.*

## The benefit principle

Why should taxation be such an apparently complex issue? Why can't the state simply charge a price for its services in the same way that other institutions do?

Such a system of taxation according to benefit has been advocated many times and there is a wealth of literature on the subject going back to the popular prevalence of the idea among seventeenth-century political and economic philosophers. The essence of the approach is that beneficiaries pay in direct proportion to the benefits they enjoy from publicly provided goods and services. It is claimed that this method of taxation is both fair and efficient since no one enjoys benefits without paying for them, and therefore, no one pays for benefits not received. Thus, no governmental expenditure is undertaken which is 'wasteful' since community demand and state supply meet, as in

1. For a thorough and lucid presentation of the case for an expenditure tax as it might be introduced into the UK tax system, see J. E. Meade, *The Structure and Reform of Direct Taxation*, Allen and Unwin, London, 1978.

the market place, to determine the optimal size of the public sector.

Figure 152 depicts a community of two taxpayers, a simple model of a much larger society. The curve $SS$ represents the supply curve of a state-provided good. As such it reflects marginal costs in terms of foregone private goods. Curves $D_A D_A$ and $D_B D_B$ represent the demand curves for the state-provided good by the taxpayers. These curves are assumed to reflect the marginal benefits to each consumer from consuming varying amounts of the services provided by the state good. Thus $D_A D_A$ shows the benefit which $A$ enjoys from successive amounts of the service and $D_B D_B$ shows the same for $B$. The combined benefits of the varying amounts are shown by the curve $D_{A+B} D_{A+B}$ which is constructed by the vertical summation of $D_A$ and $D_B$ and, as such, it shows the 'collective demand' for this particular state service. Demand and supply meet at output $OQ$. For this output taxpayer $A$ pays a unit price (tax) of $Oa$, i.e. he makes a contribution of forgone consumption of private goods to the value of area $OQda$. $B$ pays a unit price of $Ob$, making his contribution $OQeb$. The total contribution is thus $OQfc$.

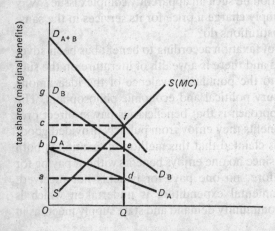

units of state provided services

Figure 152

In this way an 'optimum' output level is determined which is analogous to the market solution. But how true is it that the two individuals pay according to the benefits they receive? Since the state services are a collective good they are provided in a lump sum and individuals cannot consume more or less by offering different prices. In our example both $A$ and $B$ consume $OQ$ units once this amount is provided. Thus the total benefits enjoyed by $A$ equal the area $ObdQ$ and $B$'s benefits equal $OgeQ$. Yet $A$ pays only $OadQ$ and $B$ pays only $ObeQ$; apparently neither is paying according to the true magnitude of the benefits he receives and total benefits do not equal total costs.

The above problem is not the only drawback to the 'benefit principle' as a blueprint for taxation policy. Further difficulties surround whether or not consumers will reveal their true preferences for state-provided goods and services. (We assumed away this problem in order to construct Figure 152.) First, given the collective nature of state-provided services, preferences have to be somehow revealed via a political process (or else services are provided according to the dictates of a political authority, regardless of private preferences). But political processes are notoriously inefficient at determining true preferences, as discussed later in Chapter 30. Finally, even if all other problems surrounding the benefit approach could be solved, society might still want to reject it on the grounds that it does not fit in with the aims of a programme against inequality. A rich man may be able to afford to pay for his benefits, a poor man may not. Whereas society may find this acceptable in the case of toffee consumption it is unlikely to find it so regarding national defence. Thus, benefit taxation permits maintenance of the *status quo* and unless society considers this to be ideal, some alternative guide to taxation policy will be adopted.

Although payment according to benefit is not an acceptable principle on which to base a taxation system, certain taxes do approximate to this principle. The criterion is most likely to be adhered to when public services are considered to confer identifiable private benefits. In the UK for example, the television licence and the 'road tax' follow the benefit principle, representing payments for specific publicly provided services. Such payments are outlay taxes levied on items of expenditure. Despite the fact that revenues so raised disappear into the government's general pool, this does not prevent taxpayers from regarding such taxes as *earmarked* for a specific purpose. Earmarked taxes may of course be aimed not at specific benefits (goods) but at specific disbenefits (nuisances). Thus the gin tax of the eighteenth century was imposed to reduce consumption of cheap gin.

But to decide properly upon the relative merits of income and outlay taxes we must scrutinize more carefully the way in which taxation policy must be geared to fit the general aims of the state. Our discussion of the state's activities has always revolved around the basic aims of efficiency and equity – society's concern for the best allocation of resources and an equitable distribution of incomes. In terms of these basic objectives a tax on income wins hands down.[2]

## The goal of efficiency

At the beginning of this chapter we suggested that the best method of raising revenue would be that which interfered the least with the existing states of distribution and allocation, assuming these states to be the ones desired by society. Given this assumption we can employ Figure 153 to demonstrate the case for an income tax *vis-à-vis* a tax on a specific commodity. The diagram makes further use of the consumer-surplus concept employed in earlier chapters and in this case, perhaps more than in any of the others, we must beware of what the analysis presumes – that the specific circumstances have no ramifications beyond those reflected in the diagram.

The initial situation depicted in Figure 153 is one of market equilibrium, where the demand for a specific good equals supply of that good, at price *OP*. At this price consumer surplus is equal to area *FDI* and producer surplus to area *KDI*. A unit tax

2. At this point it might be useful to turn back and re-read Chapter 21 on the problems of pricing the goods produced by a nationalized industry where marginal cost-pricing can be interpreted as an application of the benefit principle.

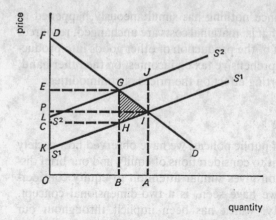

Figure 153

equal to *IJ*(= *HG*) is levied on the output of the commodity and the supply curve shifts vertically upwards by this amount. As a result, a new (post-tax) equilibrium is established at price *OE* and quantity *OB*. At this new equilibrium consumer surplus has been reduced to *FEG* and producer surplus to *KCH*, a total reduction equal to area *EGIHC*. But this loss of surplus is greater than the amount of revenue taken by the government. Tax revenue raised on output *OB* is equal to area *EGHC*, the number of units sold, *OB*(= *EG*), multiplied by the tax rate per unit, *GH*(= *IJ*). Thus the true burden of the tax is in excess of the resource transfer (*EGHC*) from private to public sector by an amount equal to *GHI*.

The existence of the excess burden is due to the distortion of relative prices which follows the imposition of the specific tax. In a perfectly competitive environment, market equilibria occur where marginal costs equal prices and marginal utilities. When a unit tax is imposed on one particular commodity, *X*, it drives a wedge between marginal cost and price – the post-tax price of the commodity is higher than the pre-tax price (i.e. the tax has been partially passed on) but marginal costs are unchanged. It would now benefit society if more were produced of *X* since its (post-tax) price has risen while other prices have remained the same. But since nothing has simultaneously happened to resource prices, that is, marginal costs are unchanged, resources will not move out of the production of other goods into production of $X$. A comprehensive tax on incomes, on the other hand, has no such distorting effect on the prices of commodities.

### The goal of equity

In our analysis of public policies we have observed how society gives much weight to considerations of equity and our brief discussion of taxation gives similar attention to equity considerations. Equity, we have seen, is a two-dimensional concept. Horizontal equity, which has been implicit throughout our analysis of state activities, relates to that concept of justice which most societies have readily accepted – *equal treatment of equals*. Vertical equity, to which we have already devoted considerable space, relates to society's ethical views on the distribution of economic power. As a guideline for taxation the concept of vertical equity roughly translates into *unequal treatment of unequals*.

### *Horizontal equity*

To aim at achieving horizontal equity is to accept a value judgement, but one unlikely to cause conflict. In the context of taxation, fairness demands that tax units possessing identical economic power face identical tax demands. Thus, if two tax units are in receipt of the same income (taken to be a measure of true economic power) then, under an income tax, they should each face the same tax demand from the state to ensure that post-tax incomes are also equalized. As in the case of the efficiency objective, it is essential that the tax base be comprehensively defined if horizontal equity is to be achieved. Therefore, if an outlay tax is not levied on all items of expenditure but only on some commodities, or groups of commodities, it will offend this criterion. For example, suppose the community comprises two sets of taxpayers, each possessing the same spending power but different tastes: one set has a strong preference for boiled sweets. Suppose, now, that the government decides to finance a particular level of expenditure by levying a tax on each ounce of boiled sweets supplied to retailers, who raise the price of boiled sweets accordingly. Consequently, the state extracts relatively more revenue from one section of the population simply because that section enjoys eating boiled sweets; and regardless of the fact that the economic power of this section is identical to that of those who abstain from consuming boiled sweets.

The need for a comprehensive base is equally important in the case of an income tax. If some forms of income are omitted from the income-tax base then taxpayers will not pay according to the magnitude of their income but according to its nature. Thus suppose two individuals receive income of £1000 p.a. but while all of the income of one is in monetary form, the income of the other is partly in kind – he works for a market gardener who pays him £750 p.a. plus fruit and vegetables which the recipient values at £250. If the revenue authorities, for administrative convenience, define 'income' to include only monetary returns, then the tax bill which each of our taxpayers must face will differ. If the tax rate applied is 25 per cent of income, as defined by the authorities, then the individual whose income is wholly in money form pays £250, while the other faces a demand for only £187·50, despite enjoying the same total amount of economic power.

## Vertical equity

It is in the context of vertical equity that the inferiority of specific-outlay taxes *vis-à-vis* a tax on incomes is really highlighted. If we are to continue with our assumption of a society committed, for whatever reason, to a more equitable distribution of incomes than that which results from market transactions, taxation policy must be brought into line with the general programme of redistribution. As we shall see, to tax items of expenditure is to pursue a policy which does not further such an aim.

If taxation policy is to reflect the community's desire for vertical equity then taxes must be levied according to the principle of *ability-to-pay*. Whereas the benefit principle seeks to link taxes paid with benefits received, ability-to-pay relates tax bills to true capacity to pay, thus, for a given level of state-provided services, yielding equal benefits to two individuals possessing different degrees of economic power, a relatively higher tax demand is made of the individual possessing the most economic power.[3] Under a comprehensive income-tax system a rich man pays more in tax than a poor man. But how much more? The ability-to-pay doctrine merely sets the tenor of an equitable taxation policy, it does not provide formal rules for the execution of such a policy. The obvious guide to formulating such rules is the range of tax *rates* which can be applied. Now, the range of rates at which resources are released to the public sector can be *regressive*, *proportional*, or *progressive*. The proportion of income (economic power) transferred to the public sector from any individual diminishes as his income rises, when tax rates are regressive. Under a proportional tax rate the proportion of income transferred remains constant as income rises. Finally, when tax rates are progressive an increasing proportion of any individual's income is transferred to public use

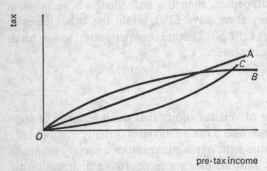

Figure 154

3. It is an interesting observation that when the rich want to live in a healthy environment, amidst a well-educated population, the distinction between the benefit and ability approaches tends to become blurred. The beneficiaries are also those with the ability-to-pay, i.e. the rich.

as his income rises. These various rates are illustrated in Figure 154.

*OA* represents a proportional rate: the slope of the schedule remains constant. A regressive-rates schedule is depicted by *OB* – the slope of this line flattens as income rises. *OC* represents a progressive-rates schedule – the slope of *OC* increases as income rises. (Progressive tax rates, then, do not simply require the rich to pay more than the poor. Indeed a rich man with income of £10 000 pays more than a poor man with income of £1000 under a regressive-rates schedule of 5 per cent and 10 per cent respectively.)

Of the three rate schedules briefly outlined economists usually recommend progression but their reasons for doing so are not always legitimate. In his advisory capacity an economist can adopt one of two attitudes on this issue. He can attempt to establish a 'scientific' case for progression via reference to areas of economic theory he believes to be relevant. Or he can swallow his pride, don the mantle of the pragmatist, and advance progression as one potential means of satisfying society's desire for a more equitable distribution of economic power.

## The sacrifice doctrine

Given our existing knowledge of the world, a truly scientific case for progressive taxation is impossible. The hypotheses upon which an analysis must be attempted are those which have never progressed beyond the armchair in which they were conceived: they are untestable. Such is the criticism aimed at the *sacrifice* doctrine. This doctrine was given a precise formulation in the heyday of marginal analysis after its fairly innocent beginnings as a seed sown in the writings of John Stuart Mill. As a general proposition the sacrifice principle is quite acceptable, suggesting no more than the idea that surrendering resources to the state involves a sacrifice for the taxpayers. Neither is its preliminary extension particularly objectionable: that, generally speaking, the greater a taxpayer's ability to pay, the less the sacrifice he suffers from paying a given amount of tax. But to refine the analysis beyond this, in the hope of ultimately making a case for progressive taxation, is fruitless.

We cannot at this level delve too deeply into the intricate formulation of the sacrifice concept, but we can consider its essence. The sacrifice assumed to be suffered in paying taxes relates to the forgone utility which could have been derived from the income surrendered to the state. A guideline for an equitable tax system would seem to be: equate the sacrifices made by all tax units.

In fact the guideline might be refined even further to the equating of *marginal* sacrifices,[4] that is, transferring resources from the community until the last unit of income taken from each represents the same sacrifice to each. In this fashion the total sacrifice of the community is minimized or, put another way, the total (after-tax) utility of the community is maximized. Suppose, for example, that the utility from the additional £1 of income differs for two tax units $A$ and $B$: $A$'s £1 represents 10 utils to $A$, whereas $B$'s has a subjective value of only 7 utils. Now, if £1 less were transferred from $A$ to the public sector and £1 more were transferred from $B$, then total money transfers to the public sector would be unchanged but total utility of the community would rise by 3 utils ($B$ loses 7 but $A$ gains 10).

At first sight, the analysis above seems quite harmless. Indeed it seems no more than a further application of the marginal rule that we have met several times in this book. Could it not be used to substantiate a case for progressive taxation? Some economists in the past have believed that it could be so used. Such an extension of our analysis requires one basic assumption – that the utility derived from additional units of income diminishes as total income rises. A curve of diminishing marginal utility of income is illustrated by $MM'$ in Figure 155.

Along the income axis of the above diagram $OS$ represents a

4. Students who eventually tackle more advanced literature will discover two other sacrifice measures: equal *absolute* sacrifice, and equal *proportional* sacrifice. For ease of exposition we have omitted consideration of these concepts from our analysis. The criticisms we shall aim at the equal marginal rule, which sets the limit to egalitarianism, also apply to those alternative concepts which are somewhat removed from the marginal limit.

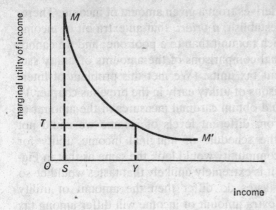

Figure 155

subsistence level of income. Additional units of income prior to this subsistence level being reached are assumed to have an infinite utility value, hence satisfaction from additional units, only begins to diminish when basic needs have been met. Now, if marginal utility of income declines for all potential tax units then the more income each one possesses, the less is the sacrifice of utility involved in a given transfer of income to public sector use. 'The richer the tax unit the smaller the sacrifice' seems to point to progression. If we now make a second assumption, that tastes of all within the community are identical, then *MM'* represents the marginal utility of income schedule for everyone in the community and the case for progression seems indisputable. Equal marginal sacrifice (say, *OT* utility in Figure 155) requires incomes to be levelled down from the top (say, to *OY* income in Figure 155). In other words, maximum progression should be used to equalize completely post-tax incomes.

## Some problems

However, despite the apparent rigour of this case for progression its core is somewhat hollow. In the first place there exists no mechanism by which to measure cardinally the amount of

utility a tax unit derives from a given amount of income. Therefore, we cannot establish, *a priori*, that an extra bit of income
means less to a rich tax unit than to a poor one; and we cannot
make interpersonal comparisons of the amounts of utility sacrificed by different tax units. (We met this problem of interpersonal comparisons of utility early in the previous chapter.)

Even if we could obtain cardinal measures of the amount of
utility derived from different levels of income we could not
guarantee that the schedule of marginal income utility for
everyone in the community would look the same as that in Figure 155. Indeed, it is extremely unlikely that tastes would be so
uniform. When tastes do differ then the amount of utility
derived from an extra amount of income will differ among tax
units – sober Mr Brown does not receive the same enjoyment
from an extra £1 of income as the riotous Mr Spender.

Finally, the basic assumption that marginal utility of income
schedules slope continually downwards is very open to challenge. While such a curve is conceivable in relation to a given
*level* of wants, in terms of a *hierarchy* of wants its shape is likely
to be very different. Although tax units may experience diminishing marginal utility from income within any particular
income bracket, it is quite probable that marginal utility rises
in the region of the threshold to each bracket. Figure 156
depicts a marginal utility of income schedule which exhibits
such characteristics.

$MM'$ is the marginal utility of income curve for a particular
tax unit. $OY_1$ is the subsistence level of income. Within each income bracket ($Y_1 - Y_2$; $Y_2 - Y_3$; etc.) the utility curve slopes
downwards until the tax unit is within sight of the following
bracket, at which point the curve slopes upwards until this
bracket is actually reached. (Effectively, the curve is shifting as
income rises, as shown by the dotted continuations in the diagram.) The major consumption item within the first bracket
may be a family car; within the second it may be foreign travel;
the third brings hope of a weekend cottage; and the fourth may
mean a yacht. Now, very often in economics (as we have seen
many times by now) we can legitimately iron out any minute
indivisibilities when the general relationship between two vari-

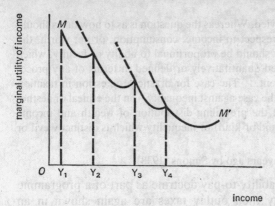

Figure 156

ables does at least approximate a smooth curve. But we cannot do so in the present example. Although we may postulate many steps in the hierarchy of wants the number of upturns in the marginal utility of income curve will always be discrete since each tax unit must spend considerable time within each income bracket. Thus, given such a schedule, a tax structure based on the utility sacrifice approach would require tax rates levied on certain levels of income (when the utility schedule slopes upwards) to be regressive.

## Some common sense

Lacking a rigorous analytical base on which to propose progressive tax rates the economist must again refer to the consensus within society which advocates a more equitable distribution of incomes. In principle, progressive tax rates further this end. After the almost pretentious apparatus displayed in our ramble through the sacrifice doctrine, the pragmatism of Henry Simons, the famous Chicago economist, is like a cooling blast of fresh air.

Tons of paper have been employed in teaching the world that taxes should be levied according to ability – perhaps for the reason that this word utterly defies definition in terms of any base upon which taxes are or ever might be levied. Whereas the question is as to how taxes should be allocated with respect to income, consumption, or net worth, the answer is that they should be proportional to ability or faculty, which cannot be conceived quantitatively or defined in terms of any procedure of measurement... The case for drastic progression in taxation must be rested on the case against inequality – on the ethical or aesthetic judgement that the prevailing distribution of wealth and income reveals a degree (and/or kind) of inequality which is distinctly evil or unlovely.

Written over forty years ago by Simons (1938).

If we accept the ability-to-pay doctrine as part of a programme against inequality then outlay taxes are again shown in an adverse light. An outlay tax, whether *ad valorem* or levied per unit of output, does not discriminate among taxpayers according to their ability-to-pay – the rich face the same tax rates as the poor. An attempt to reduce the regression may be made by exempting from tax those consumption items considered to be basic wants, e.g. food. But, given the interrelationships among markets, unless *all* the inputs which help produce basic goods are also exempt, then tax effects may filter through to the final price of these items of consumption. For example, if food were exempt but not petrol, if the tax on petrol were to be shifted forward (wholly or partly) food prices would still rise. Yet to exempt many goods greatly reduces the tax base, necessitating ever-increasing rates of tax to raise the same amount of revenue, thus creating further inequities. Furthermore, the very aim of protecting basic wants, like food, conflicts with the aim of raising a given amount of revenue when outlay taxes are designed to raise revenue objectives with minimum disincentive effects. Needless to say this requires that a comprehensive definition be applied to the tax base.

## Summary

We have succeeded in no more than briefly contemplating the tips of many icebergs. What should emerge from our discussion is that the state possesses several methods of raising finance each of which will have different consequences for the economy and society generally. Which method will be adopted depends upon the prevailing circumstances. Several observations have been made. We have seen that printing money is not necessarily the monster of popular thought. If there are unemployed resources in the economy this may be the best method of raising finance. Borrowing, as opposed to taxing, is a mechanism which could be used more often, particularly where inter-generational considerations are paramount. To rely on taxation as a major source of finance requires the adoption of a fully comprehensive tax base; taxing according to ability is not a sufficient principle to ensure satisfaction of general rules of fairness and efficiency unless such a base is adopted.

Finally, since different methods of transferring resources from private to public use can affect the prevailing states of allocation and distribution, they place at the disposal of governments various mechanisms for enabling society to reach desired ends. Thus, the raising of revenue may often be a secondary issue in the adoption of a particular method of reducing private consumption. This is very true, as we have previously implied, in the case of taxation where a tax may be imposed purely as a corrective mechanism. When discussing the relative merits of income and outlay taxes we have assumed most of the time that prevailing resource allocation is efficient, but when this condition is not met these taxes may appear in a different light in relation to their ability to change the course of economic events.

## Questions

1 Compare the relative merits of (a) confiscation, (b) printing money, (c) borrowing and (d) taxation as means of financing the goods and services provided by the state.

2 Can efficiency and equity be reconciled in a tax system?

3 What changes in the current UK tax system would seem to be required by the introduction of a comprehensive income-tax base or a comprehensive expenditure tax?

4 What tax principles can be derived from (a) the benefit principle, and (b) the least-sacrifice principle?

5 What do you understand by the concepts of (a) horizontal, and (b) vertical equity? How are these concepts implemented in the UK tax system?

6 Newtown is a commuter town near London. Its population consists of large numbers of 'business reps' who stay on average about three years. The council proposes to build a municipal golf course and swimming pool. A referendum is conducted to decide on the method of financing the projects. Which method of financing do you think will be chosen?

7 Given the existence of a hierarchy of wants certain inter-personal comparisons of income utility are possible. For example we may advocate income redistribution from those who own luxury yachts to those who are struggling to feed themselves but not to pony-trekkers. Discuss.

8 Since Hitler was defeated, in what sense can the government debt incurred as a result of the Second World War be considered a burden?

9 What effect do you think that government borrowing would have on the level of interest rates? Assuming that interest rates rose what effect would this have upon the balance of payments?

10 During and after the Second World War the UK borrowed from the US. Both countries were on a fixed exchange rate. How did the US manage to transfer resources to the UK? Were the Americans who lent made worse off? Were the Americans who did not lend made worse off? Did the UK citizens during the war feel better off? How was repayment effected?

# Chapter 30
# Political Processes

## The state and the market

So we come to the issue we have been avoiding: the efficiency of
the state. Whenever we encountered a problem – monopoly,
unemployment, collective goods and so on – we referred the
problem to the state for a solution. But we always avoided explaining what this thing called the state was and how it worked.
The state was introduced as an agent to solve problems beyond
the scope of the market. But even a casual glance at history
suggests that the state, the political process, is not above
reproach. And in this chapter we shall, in fact, stress the point
that both our instruments – market and state – are imperfect instruments and require careful use and continual improvement.
So if the impression is one of despair tinged with cynicism then
the reader should realize that the world is not perfect but needs
perfecting.

The state may be defined as a geographical segment of society
which is united by a common obedience to a sovereign. Of
especial importance to economists are the phrases 'common
obedience' and 'sovereign will'. Politics is concerned with problems of power, authority and legitimacy and these issues follow
from our earlier analysis of collective goods which demonstrated
that some goods cannot be provided by the market because of the
free rider problem. Some means must therefore be found whereby people can be coerced into accepting collective financing of
those goods. And this is in line with beliefs of the early political

theorists, Hobbes, Locke and Rousseau. For Rousseau, people had to force themselves to be free – in order, as economic jargon puts it, to get on to higher indifference curves. This viewpoint stands in contrast to much economics which is concerned with constructing theories of exchange from which power and coercion are absent. Indeed, economics may be regarded as an attempt to overcome or reduce the magnitude of the political problem by indicating areas where exchange might take the place of coercion or by suggesting rules which might most efficiently reduce the costs of coercion.

## *Rules for decision making*

The problems of political decision making are, of course, simplified if it is known in advance what should be done. Then there can be a simple rule: 'Implement decision $X$' and the people could elect or nominate someone to do $X$. Some economists do believe that such rules can be formulated and, as we shall see in Part Nine, there have been proposals to establish rules to govern the money supply. But, more commonly, there is a feeling that rules, at best, can only be guidelines and that what is required is a search process to find the most efficient methods of catering for wants. It is this search process that we call political processes and like the market solution, the political solution is a product of trial and error.

## *The constitution*

The set of rules governing the methods by which searches should be carried out is known as the *constitution* and may be written or unwritten. At the elementary level the UK constitution may be said to comprise the electorate and a group of institutions which includes parliament and the judiciary. The people, in effect, delegate the task of searching for optimum solutions to some of their number and exercise control over them through periodic elections.

## Problems of political processes
*Majority voting and the problem of group choice*

The essence of the democratic political process is the acceptance of the will of the majority with due consideration of the wishes of the minority. What is, however, interesting is the manner in which opinions are obtained for there is an apparent lack of any attempt to measure the relative intensities of preferences. The insistence on equality in democracies leads to the principle of one man – one vote. Unfortunately this insistence on equality can lead to the absence of clear-cut majorities. Consider, for example, the following problem. A report of a Monopolies Commission concludes that the lollipop industry is monopolistic and the government is therefore faced with the following courses of action:

Policy A – regulate prices;
Policy B – nationalize the lollipop industry;
Policy C – reduce tariffs in order to allow foreign competition
          to break up the domestic monopoly.

These three policies, we may suppose, are placed before the heads of the government departments most likely to be involved and we may imagine that they rank their preferences as follows:

**Table 40** Group choice

| Minister for | Regulate | Nationalize | Import |
|---|---|---|---|
| private industries | 1 | 2 | 3 |
| public sector | 2 | 3 | 1 |
| foreign trade | 3 | 1 | 2 |

What is apparent from Table 40 is that no basis exists for a group decision: each alternative receives as much support (i.e. votes) as every other one.

Now, coherence can be produced by either a dictatorship (note how this harks back to centralization discussed in Part

Two) or some way of trading preferences as in the market. This last solution points to the essential difference between political trading and private market trading. In the example given above each Minister behaves rationally in the sense that he ranks the alternatives and does not then behave inconsistently with respect to his preferences. Now this is what happens in the markets for private goods. A housewife may prefer meat to eggs or cheese and we would normally expect her always to purchase meat unless her tastes changed. Another housewife might prefer eggs to meat or cheese and we should always expect to observe her buying eggs. We could introduce further housewives but the general point is that what appears to be an identical situation does not produce stalemate. Why should this be so?

The answer to our question seems to lie in the lack of a means for expressing the relative strength of political preferences whereas in private markets money measures the intensity of preferences. As a result compromises are much more easily achieved in the markets for private goods.

## The efficiency of corruption

Of course money has been, and is, sometimes used in the political decision-making process. Stalemates and disequilibria are undesirable and methods must be found to obtain solutions. But the use of money for vote-buying is frowned upon on the grounds that the distribution of income and wealth should not be allowed to dictate the workings of a democracy. Paradoxically, it may be the 'back-door' use of money which yields political stability. Bribery and corruption can be efficient means of achieving ends – even if the means (or even the ends) are not always respectable to some.

## Small and large groups

Within a small group the problems posed by the paradox of voting can be overcome. Face-to-face contact allows group members the opportunity to gauge each other's intensity of preferences. But the state is a large group and the problem is compounded by further issues that the individual does not encounter in private markets:

1 The buyer of a private good is likely to be more knowledgeable about what he is being offered since he is continually shopping in the market. Moreover the goods are easier to judge in terms of the relationship between physical characteristics and presumed utilities. In contrast the political buyer may shop only once every four or five years.

2 In buying private goods the buyer is buying for himself whereas in buying political possibilities he may be buying for others. What this means is that market man and political man may have different frames of reference. Sometimes the political man may behave like the market man as, for example when he buys defence or law and order, but sometimes he may have in his mind the image of the good society.

3 In buying private goods the buyer is usually confronted by many sellers whereas in the political market there are usually a few sellers, and this difference in market situations can considerably affect the possibilities of many electors obtaining satisfaction at the polling booths.

## The similarity of political parties

The difficulties which we observe in political decision-making are increased by the strong similarities, which often exist, in the programmes of political parties and the power of governments to maintain themselves in office.

An important feature of British politics is that it is essentially two-party politics. And in most post-war elections there have been strong similarities in the election manifestos and actual policies of parties. During the 1950s the expression 'Butskellism' was coined to denote the similarities in the views of R. A. Butler (Conservative) and Hugh Gaitskell (Labour). And in the 1960s, despite the attempts at radicalism by Harold Wilson (Labour) and Edward Heath (Conservative) there were

similarities which became more pronounced as they modified
their policies when in office.

Now similarities in policies may arise from the distribution of
political attitudes in the electorate. Suppose, as in Figure 157,
the intensities of political attitudes are measured in either direction from the centre of the horizontal axis and the number of
people possessing a particular political point of view is measured along the vertical axis. Next assume that the frequency of
political attitudes has only one peak, then given the distribution
of preferences a party will frame its programme so as to maximize its votes. We may suppose that it attempts to appeal to all
voters to the right of *L* because any attempt to appeal to all
voters would result in conflict between the extreme right and
the extreme left. Once one party has chosen point *L* then the
best strategy for another party would be to move to *M*; that is,
immediately to the right of *L*. (What we have done is to use a
model similar to the Cournot duopoly model of Chapter 19.)
Given the second party's policy then the first party will move to
*N* and by successive moves parties will come to locate themselves close to *A* with both parties looking alike.

The model of party behaviour we have just outlined suggests
that the success of a political party in an election may be due to
chance. But once elected a party may be able to use a consider-

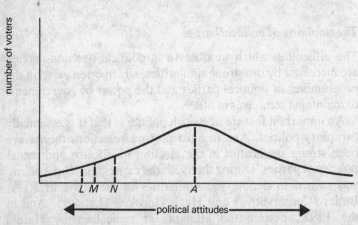

Figure 157

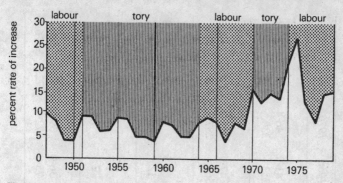

Figure 158 British wage increases and the election cycle. Source: H. A. Turner, 'The Wages of Fear', *New Society*, 1979.

able range of weapons in order to stay in office. A government can grant tax concessions or reduce the level of unemployment by monetary and fiscal policies. Such strategies have given rise to the concept of a *political cycle*, as opposed to a business cycle, in which fluctuations in economic activity are the result of government policies rather than businessmen's behaviour. Thus, Figure 158 shows a striking connection between the dates of elections and wage increases. Before an election there is a rise in wage advances. After an election, when the upsurge of wages has led to inflation, there is a tendency for governments to pursue restrictive policies.

## *Why vote?*

When we consider the obstacles in the way of political man obtaining what he wants the surprising thing is that he bothers to vote. Yet during the post-war period there have been ten general elections and the percentage of the electorate voting has never been less than 72 per cent and has been as high as 82·5 per cent (Table 41). Moreover, the difference in the votes cast for the winners and losers has usually been slight which suggests that many voters have been doomed to disappointment. The problem of wasted votes is associated with the existence of *marginal seats* and *wasted majorities*.

**Table 41** Voting behaviour at general elections, 1945–79

| | 1945[1] | 1950 | 1951 | 1955 | 1959 | 1964 | 1966 | 1970 | 1974 | 1979 |
|---|---|---|---|---|---|---|---|---|---|---|
| **Conservatives** | | | | | | | | | | |
| percentage votes cast | 39·8 | 43·5 | 48·0 | 49·7 | 49·4 | 43·4 | 41·9 | 46·4 | 35·8 | 43·9 |
| number of seats | 213 | 298 | 321 | 345 | 366 | 304 | 253 | 330 | 277 | 339 |
| **Labour** | | | | | | | | | | |
| percentage votes cast | 48·3 | 46·1 | 48·8 | 46·4 | 43·8 | 44·1 | 47·9 | 43·0 | 39·2 | 36·9 |
| number of seats | 393 | 315 | 295 | 277 | 258 | 317 | 363 | 287 | 319 | 268 |
| **Liberal** | | | | | | | | | | |
| percentage votes cast | 9·1 | 9·1 | 2·5 | 2·7 | 5·9 | 11.2 | 8·5 | 7·5 | 18·3 | 13·8 |
| number of seats | 12 | 9 | 6 | 6 | 6 | 9 | 12 | 6 | 13 | 11 |
| **Other** | | | | | | | | | | |
| percentage votes cast | 2·8 | 1·3 | 0·7 | 1·2 | 0·9 | ·1·3 | 1·7 | ·3·2 | 6·6 | 5·4 |
| number of seats | 19 | 4 | 3 | 2 | 6 | – | 2 | 7 | 26 | 17 |
| **total electorate** | | | | | | | | | | |
| (millions) | 32·8 | 34·3 | 34·7 | 34·9 | 35·4 | 35·9 | 36·0 | 39·3 | 40·0 | 40·5 |
| percentage voting | 73·3 | 84·0 | 82·5 | 76·8 | 78·7 | 77·1 | 75·8 | 72·0 | 72·8 | 76·0 |

Source: Butler and Pinto-Duschinsky (1971)

1. University seats excluded: other 1945 figures adjusted to eliminate the distortions introduced by double voting in the fifteen two-member seats then existing.

Elections are often decided by the results in a few marginal constituencies, that is, constituencies in which a change of allegiance of a few voters can dictate which party becomes the government. In contrast, there are other constituencies in which the successful candidate wins by a large majority and then discovers he is not a member of the victorious party. Hence, the situation in which a party can obtain the most votes and yet have the lowest number of seats. For example, the Labour Party obtained 48·8 per cent of the votes in 1951 but did not form the government. And the number of seats obtained by the Liberals bears no relationship to the number of votes they obtain.

## The irrelevance of elections

Yet it would be foolish to assume that political man only exercises his choice at elections. He can, through his trade union or trade association, exercise an influence on governments between elections. Indeed, it is possible to argue that since the turn of the century Britain has not experienced classical political democracy in which the voters elect a government which then rules with supreme power, but that there has been a *quasi-corporate state* in which governments rule with the assistance of numerous institutions and in which Parliament ceases to play an important role and elections become irrelevant.

Now such an interpretation of British politics does have a degree of plausibility but it leaves unanswered the question: why do people vote? One answer may be that universal suffrage is a relatively recent phenomenon. Another answer may be that people wish to affirm their commitment to a particular ideology.

There are many unanswered questions concerning political behaviour. Governments do not perpetuate themselves in office. There are dramatic shifts as in 1945 and 1979. Governments do make mistakes in locating the centre of gravity of the electorate. And Lincoln's dictum 'You can fool all the people some of the time and some of the people all the time, but you cannot fool all the people all the time' may explain why governments are sometimes able to maintain their positions but lose them on other occasions. Once the electorate realizes that a government's policy is inflationary then it may lose office. The voter does believe that elections matter and he also believes that he can influence governments between elections.

## Summary

The problems of ensuring efficiency in political processes are twofold. First, there is the simple point that voting processes can fail to reflect the intensity of voters' preferences. Secondly, the market so infiltrates the political sphere that appeals to the state to correct the imperfections of the market may be otiose.

## Questions

1 In countries where there is only one political party what purpose do you think is served by elections?

2 According to Marx the state would wither away with the emergence of socialism. Does your reading of Chapters 25 and 28 lead you to the same conclusion? Do you think that Marx employed a different definition of the state to that employed in those chapters?

3 The internal operations of a university are conducted without money. There is one fairly well-defined task of teaching and another objective, research, which is ill-defined. Consider how a university's constitution is framed so as to reconcile and permit the efficient pursuit of both objectives.

4 'Politics are, as it were, the market-place and the price mechanism of all social demands – though there is no guarantee that a just price will be struck; and there is nothing spontaneous about politics – it depends on deliberate and continuous individual activity' (Crick, 1962). Comment on this statement.

5 In his book, Crick (1962) sets out certain conditions for a stable political system. Examine these stability conditions in the light of your understanding of the workings of markets.

6 It has been suggested that (a) the political system produces

too much of some goods, such as defence, because of outmoded attitudes, and (b) too little of other goods, such as health, because of the attempts of people to avoid paying taxes. What do you think?

7 Can voting behaviour be analysed along the same lines as standard consumer behaviour (recall Chapter 11)?

8 What objections would you raise against the vote-maximizing theory of political party behaviour?

9 'It is impossible to construct a political constitution which is capable of resolving any interpersonal differences brought to it while at the same time satisfying certain reasonable and desirable assumptions.' Discuss and indicate whether the statement suggests that the lot of man is either civil discord or life under Big Brother.

10 In the political system the distribution of political money (votes) is equal yet the distribution of political power is unequal. Why should this be?

...increased of some goods, such as defence, because of unfounded fears or attitudes, and (b) too little of other goods, such as health, because of the unwillingness of people to avend paying taxes. What do you think?

7 Can voting behaviour be analysed along the same lines as standard consumer behaviour (recall Chapter 11)?

8 What objections would you raise against the vote-maximising theory of political party behaviour?

9 'It is impossible to construct a political constitution which is capable of resolving any interpersonal differences brought to it while at the same time satisfying certain reasonable and desirable assumptions.' Discuss and indicate whether the statement suggests that the lot of man is either civil discord or life under Big Brother.

10 In the political system the distribution of political money (votes) is equal yet the distribution of political power is unequal. Why should this be?

# Part Nine
# Macroeconomics

The subject matter of this part of the book is not in dispute though its interpretation has been a matter of serious contention for three decades. It is concerned with how the activities of various sectors or markets are coordinated and why it is that economies, as a whole rather than in parts, are subject to fluctuations in output, employment, prices and growth rates.

In previous chapters we assumed that decision making involved individuals attempting to maximize something called utility and that utility could be measured by a measuring rod of money. This theory of value in its varying forms – marginal utility, indifference analysis and revealed preference – was then applied to many situations where decisions were made and, in a slightly different form, was applied to the determination of factor rewards and so provided a theory of distribution. It did, however, tend to rest upon the assumption of a constant marginal utility of money income. It is true that the indifference and revealed preference approaches could incorporate income effects but only by excluding the possibilities of moving across the hierarchy of wants. Now the marginal utility of money income could vary either as a result of a fall in price or as a result of an increase in the quantity of money and both changes could break the relationship between utilities and prices.

### David Hume (1711–76) and the Quantity Theory of Money

The notion that changes in the quantity of money could disturb the decision-making process was severely qualified by David

Hume. What Hume suggested was that changes in the quantity of money could have a disturbing influence in the short run, but that in the long run money was neutral. What neutrality meant was that changes in the quantity of money would not cause changes in relative prices and the allocation of resources. This was an important insight because it removed any difficulties associated with changes in the measuring rod of money. A doubling of the quantity of money simply meant a doubling of the general level of prices and a halving of the value of money. A simple linear relationship was established between money and the price level. The task of monetary economics seemed, therefore, to be one of devising suitable index numbers to measure changes in the general level of prices and this involved finding representative bundles of goods and choosing between the arithmetic, geometric and harmonic means.

There was, of course, the problem of the short run effects of changes in the quantity of money. But this problem could not be analysed until the problem of market coordination had been resolved. Until, that is, economics had worked out the implications of disturbances in a barter economy. Similarly, the long run problems of introducing money into an economy where factor supplies and technical change were taking place seemed to require the prior analysis of a barter economy undergoing growth.

## Leon Walras (1834–1910) and General Equilibrium

The first economist to provide an explicit statement of market coordination was Leon Walras in his classic, *Elements of Pure Economics*. He showed the interaction of markets by means of simultaneous equations. The problem was: how was this set of simultaneous equations resolved so that all the plans of economic agents were reconciled? Walras presented a simple story in which the solution was achieved by an auctioneer. He imagined that everyone came to a central market with a list of prices at which they were prepared to buy and sell goods. They would hand their lists to the auctioneer who would shout out the prospective demands, supplies and prices. If the market was not cleared then everyone would retire from the market and revise his plans. The process would continue until the market was cleared.

Walras's story was a simplification. It assumed a degree of centralization which is not normally encountered in economies. It assumed away the existence of money by assuming that every good was money. It allowed most of the interesting activity to take place 'off stage' where individuals made and revised their plans. Walras was well aware that his story was a simplification and that economic activity was often attended by crises but he was not able to show how equilibrium was reached in the real world.

Nevertheless, Walras's portrayal of the interconnections of market activities was an achievement and in more recent times the system of simultaneous equations has been used to throw light upon a variety of interesting questions. In this connection the use of matrix algebra and the development of high speed computers has reduced the time in which rough conclusions can be reached.

## Alfred Marshall (1842–1924) and Partial Equilibrium Analysis

Alfred Marshall was well aware that all economic activity could be represented by a set of simultaneous equations but that such equations did not describe how an economy achieved equilibrium. Marshall was interested in the workings of a dynamic economy. He visualized an economy growing through time as a result of innovations and changes in factor supplies. This economy tended to a stable full employment equilibrium and all markets were linked together by the existence of money. Any disturbances of demand or supply would be damped down by the activities of speculators, who, using money, could switch between markets and buy up excess supplies of goods or release stocks to damp down excess demands. Of course, not all fluctuations could be erased and there was some unemployment of resources due to frictions in the workings of the economy.

Within the context of the dynamic economy Marshall chose to analyse the effects of disturbances in one market on the assumption that the repercussions on other markets would be minimal. This was the technique of *partial equilibrium* analysis which we used in Parts Two to Seven. Marshall divided the responses of market to a disturbance into two stages – the short run equilibrium and the long run equilibrium. In the short run supply was fixed and demand was the main determinant of price. Changes in demand led to changes in price, though Marshall did concede that in severe slumps price might not fall to the level of running costs. In the long run the major determinant of price was supply and changes in the demand led to changes in the amount of investment and disinvestment.

The short run, however, dominated the scene and the long run equilibrium was a kind of never-never land. This carried the implication that prices might not measure marginal utilities and marginal products. Marginal utilities could only be measured for those goods on which only a small portion of income was spent. Marginal utilities could not be measured in the case of comparisons of the present and the future because of uncertainty. Marginal utilities from work and leisure could not be easily measured because the utility from leisure and the disutility from work were not strictly comparable. Prices might not measure costs if there were increasing returns.

### John Maynard Keynes (1883–1946) and General Disequilibrium

What Keynes did was to take over the Marshallian short run equilibrium model and apply it to the whole economy. And whereas Marshall emphasized supply side problems, Keynes looked at the difficulties caused by demand. He analysed the total demand for goods and services, how it was influenced by expectations and how it determined not only the general level of prices but also the volume of output and employment.

Keynes's analysis contained problems and weaknesses. In a highly decentralized economy it will be the case that not all decisions take place simultaneously. There will be lags in reactions and these lags will be of different lengths. Marshall's analysis contained lags but they were confined to one industry and only occurred on the supply side. Keynes was aware of the existence of lags and in his *Treatise on Money* (1930) and in the years before the *General Theory* he had experimented with theories containing lags but found it difficult to say anything useful with lag or period analysis. In his *General Theory* he switched to the technique of *comparative statics*. What this amounted to was taking snapshots of an economy at various points of time. At one point the economy was in equilibrium and was then subjected to a disturbance and the consequences would be examined at a later time. The disturbances were variations in demand. Unfortunately, the technique meant that it was often difficult to see how the path to equilibrium was reached since everything appeared to happen instantaneously and it was also difficult to see how one short run was succeeded by another to produce a long run disequilibrium.

Although the *General Theory* is a general theory in the sense that it embraces both situations of unemployment and full employment, its basic message was that aggregate demand was often insufficient to guarantee full employment. This message seemed plausible in the thirties. The failure of market forces implied a failure of value theory; the prices that were supposed to clear the market did not exist and the prices that guided buyers were different from those influencing suppliers. On the one hand, wage earners based their supplies of labour services not on real wages over which they had no control but on money wages which were amenable to bargaining. On the other hand, employers based their demands for labour services on real wages because they had some control over product prices as well as money wages. On the one hand, lenders might be influenced by comparisons of present and future income, but could just as easily decide to hold command over future goods in the form of money as in the form of stocks and shares; there could be a reluctance to lend. On the other hand, borrowers based their investment decisions on extremely fragile assumptions about future profits. Value theory, which appeared to be set on a firm foundation by Walras, was qualified by Marshall and appeared to have been destroyed by Keynes. Moreover there was a strand in the *General Theory* which appeared to suggest that unemployment might persist forever; there might be secular stagnation. Wages might not fall because of trade union resistance or because social security benefits established a floor below which wages might not fall and even if they did fall then demand might also fall because wages were a source of income and hence demand. And even if the money rate of interest were pushed down businessmen might still be reluctant to borrow whilst lenders might consider the convenience of money more attractive than the uncertainty attaching to stocks and shares.

Although Keynes did not set out an explanation of how crisis might occur – there was, for example, no attempt at a detailed analysis of the upper turning point of business fluctuations – the *General Theory* can be read as giving support to the view that slumps are caused by real forces, principally a collapse of investment opportunities, and that changes in the money supply were not responsible for slumps. Money was a veil behind which real forces operated. In a slump, pumping money into an economy would do no good since the money would be held in idle balances. In a boom, attempting to hold back the supply of money would do no good since businessmen would find some way of getting finance. The money supply expands and contracts in response to the demands of industry. It is just this thesis which Milton Friedman attacked. He suggested that major fluctuations in activity are the result of changes in the money supply. He did not deny that real forces cause fluctuations but he believed that a mild recession in the thirties was converted into major catastrophe by a reduction in the money supply. The implications of Friedman's views are far reaching; they affect not merely theory but policy. Hence we need to take a look at the inter-war years.

## A monetary theory of history

Presented here is a point of view which contrasts sharply with that to be found in the newspapers, the history books and the television utterances of politicians and commentators. Consider, for example, the history of the UK, the USA, indeed of the world since 1914. The UK came out of the First World War with her major industries – coal and iron, textiles and engineering – ill-adapted to the changed patterns of demands and supplies. Before the war these industries had been adapting to overseas competition, but the war suspended the adjustment with the result that a much greater adaptation was needed afterwards.

The process of adjustment could have been eased by the lowering of export prices, for the foreign demands for UK goods might have been presumed to have some price-elasticity. Economists distinguished between two methods whereby these prices could be reduced: bankers and politicians were apt to see only one. Since UK goods had to be sold at foreign prices then *either* the initial UK price could have been altered *or* the conversion rate (exchange rate) whereby UK prices were translated into foreign prices could have been altered. That sounds a little complicated though an example should dispel the confusion. Assuming a conversion rate of $2 equalling £1, then a good priced at £1 on the home market would sell for $2 in America. If it were desired to lower UK prices to sell more this could be done *either* by lowering the domestic price to 50p and then, by conversion, selling at $1 in America *or* by altering the conversion rate from $2 equals £1, to $1 equals £1.

Both methods might be expected to yield the same result yet in the real world the paths to the final result are apt to give rise to the unexpected. To achieve the first result it would have been necessary to reduce the amount of money in the UK economy so as to press prices downwards: this is a process known as *deflation* and assumes that there is some link between the quantity of money and the level of prices and that prices are flexible. The other method, the alteration of the conversion rate, is known as *devaluation* and also assumes some control of money supply lest the alteration of the conversion rate be nullified by rising domestic prices.

In an ideal world either method of lowering the foreign price of domestic goods would work and the choice might be decided by a flip of a coin. But the world in 1919 was not ideal and the decision of the UK government to pursue a deflationary policy was to have profound implications. It meant that the brunt of the adjustment had to be borne by those in the export trades, leaving those in domestic trades to escape unscathed. Social justice was therefore involved and *the economic consequences of Mr Churchill* (Keynes, 1931) were the General Strike of 1926, the destruction of the first and second Labour Governments and the eventual devaluation of the pound sterling in 1931. Although organized labour was defeated in the battles of 1924, 1926 and 1931, it won the war. Deflation implied that wages bend to the dictates of a fixed ratio between pounds and other currencies, to the dictates of a Gold Standard, but in the end it was the Gold Standard that gave way to a Labour Standard: wages did not bend.

What of the rest of the world? In Germany there was inflation, prices rose dramatically, as the figures of Table 42 adequately indicate.

In America the twenties were the golden years of the motor car, jazz and prohibition. Apart from minor recessions in 1921, 1923, 1925 and 1927 the period was one of unprecedented prosperity. By 1927, however, there were signs that the boom was coming to an end: agriculture was in trouble and construction was entering the downswing of its long cycle of seventeen years. Yet the long spell of prosperity served to allow the Stock Market to develop its own fantasies until the euphoria broke in 1929. Then there occurred a most momentous decision. The governors of the Federal Reserve Banks began to reduce the money supply and thereby intensified the crisis.

**Table 42** Index of wholesale prices: 1913 = 1

| | |
|---|---|
| 1920 | 13·7 |
| 1921 | 14·3 |
| 1922 | 101·0 |
| 1923 January | 2875 |
| August | 944 041 |
| November | 750 000 million |

Source: Stolper (1967)

The rest of the world imported a slump from America. During the twenties loans from America propped up Europe but with the domestic crisis they were withdrawn. The reduction in industrial activity in Europe and the USA caused a fall in the demand for raw materials and foodstuffs and so the primary producers were embroiled in a world slump.

The world after the Second World War produced some variations on what had gone before. The difficulties of adaptation of the UK economy continued and were intensified by the loss of many overseas assets which had been sold to pay for the war. Europe was also exhausted. America emerged clearly as the greatest political-economic unit in the world. The world after the war was one that feared another Great Slump and so interest rates – the cost of borrowing – were kept low by cheap money policies so as to stimulate spending. Cheap money policies, the pent-up demands of people starved by war, and the great technological advances of thirty years conspired to produce a great technological boom.

The Second World War was a total war in the sense that there was extensive rationing and price control. The apparatus of controls and associated queues continued into the peace and so it was some time before people began to appreciate that they were living in an inflationary situation. Characteristic of the fifties and sixties was creeping rather than galloping inflation.

The UK commenced the peace with a cheap money policy and in 1949 a Labour Government, having absorbed the experiences of its pre-war ancestors, devalued the pound so that, at least until the mid-fifties, the problem of exports and economic adjustments were eased. However, the lack of control over the money supply, created by the adoption of a Labour Standard and policies aimed at maintaining full employment, led to upward pressure on wages and prices and hence to difficulties in selling goods in foreign markets. Consequently, successive Conservative Governments of the late fifties and sixties attempted to solve the economy's problems by deflationary policies. Meanwhile the rest of the world prospered until the Vietnam War created inflationary pressures in America. The inflation was then exported to the rest of the world.

The tendency to worldwide inflation as a result of the Vietnam War was superimposed upon an expansion of the public sector. Looking back to 1945 it is difficult to realize the structural changes that have taken place in most industrial economies. At the end of the Second World War most of them were predominantly market economies with a small public sector devoted to defence and a few odds and ends. And it was envisaged that this structure would continue with the additional requirement that the public sector engage in occasional bouts of contra-cyclical spending so as to iron out booms and slumps. But this view of the future failed to anticipate the big expansion of the public sector.

The public sector grew because of the high dependency ratio of too many young and old relative to the working population. It also grew because people wanted a better environment – better towns, roads and leisure facilities. Unfortunately, the British economy was unable to provide these collective goods without having to face a massive opportunity cost of foregone private goods and finance was often provided by printing money.

## Contemporary analysis

Keynesian theory came under attack because it rested upon a number of debatable assumptions and predictions. First, it assumed that in the short run consumer spending is a stable function of current income but this was subsequently refuted (see Chapter 35). Secondly, it assumed that spending on capital goods is highly volatile but later research has softened the force of this argument (see Chapter 36). Thirdly, it assumed that the demand for money is highly unstable and this assertion has been rejected (see Chapter 37). Fourthly, it assumed that the contraction in the money supply in the thirties was in response to a lack of demand for money brought about by a collapse of real forces rather than postulating that the cutback in the money supply caused the collapse in spending. Fifthly, it assumed that workers took little interest in real wages (see Chapter 41). Sixthly, it assumed that governments could steer economies along stable full employment paths by the use of discretionary monetary and fiscal policies (see Chapter 45). Now we are more aware that the short run cannot be divorced from the long run. But despite its failings Keynesian theory was a bold attempt to explain and suggest remedies for the slump of the thirties. And it was the first theory to bring real and monetary forces together in an analytical framework of great power and elegance.

Today our problems are different. Inflation as well as unemployment exists. Economic growth has become a problem. The optimum size of the public sector has become a problem. The distribution of income and wealth has become a problem. And the economic consequences of a declining population threaten to become a problem.

# Chapter 31
# Aggregate Demand and Supply

Macroeconomics is concerned with movements in the entire economy rather than with events in one industry. But we shall continue to make use of the tools of analysis of demand and supply which we developed in the microeconomics. We shall refer to *aggregate demand and aggregate supply* as determining the behaviour of total output and the general (or average) level of prices.

### Fix-price and flex-price

In examining the behaviour of the economy we shall make use of the distinction between fix-price and flex-price which we drew in Chapter 10. In the fix-price economy aggregate supply is perfectly elastic and changes in aggregate demand lead to changes in total output but not to changes in prices. Figure 159 illustrates the workings of a fix-price economy in which aggregate demand shifts from $AD$ to $AD_1$ without any change in the price level. On occasions, as in Chapter 33, we shall make use of an alternative method of describing the workings of a fix-price economy which dispenses with the redundant price level. Figure 160 illustrates the alternative procedure in which total output is measured along the horizontal axis and, instead of the price level, total expenditure is measured along the vertical axis. The curve $AD$ shows total expenditure rising as income rises and the 45 degree line traces out all points at which total expenditure is equal to total output.

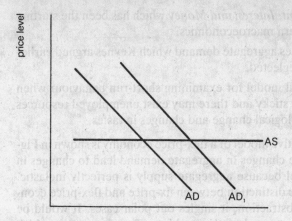

Figure 159

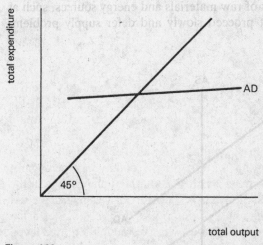

Figure 160

Through Chapters 33 to 39 we shall make use of the fix-price model. The justification for its adoption is as follows.

1 It has been derived from Keynes's book, *The General Theory*

*of Employment, Interest and Money* which has been the starting point of modern macroeconomics.

2 It emphasizes aggregate demand which Keynes argued earlier economists neglected.

3 It is a useful model for examining short-run behaviour when prices may be sticky and there may exist unemployed resources due to technological change and changes in tastes.

The alternative model of a flex-price economy is shown in Figure 161 where changes in aggregate demand lead to changes in the price level because aggregate supply is perfectly inelastic. Of course, the distinction between fix-price and flex-price economies is an abstraction; it singles out polar cases. It would be more plausible to analyse the workings of an economy in which price and output changed, as in Figure 162. And it is also important to consider the possibility of shifts in the supply curve as a result of trade unions attempting to obtain higher wages and of rises in the prices of raw materials and energy sources, such as oil. But we must proceed slowly and defer supply problems until later.

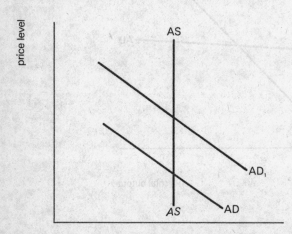

Figure 161

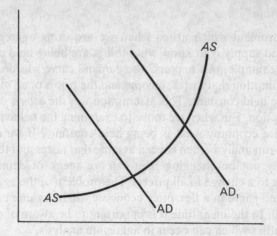

aggregate quantity demanded and supplied

Figure 162

## Aggregation

The attempt to describe an economy in terms of aggregate demand and supply has been severely criticized by F. A. von Hayek who argues that it involves too severe a distortion of reality. What, he argues, we must study is disaggregated phenomena and the effects of changes in the supply of money leading to disturbances of relative prices and outputs.

In order, therefore, to make aggregate analysis plausible we must either assume that the economy produces only one good or that the relative prices of all goods do not change. Either of these assumptions can be fitted into the fix-price model if there exist unemployed resources. If idle resources exist then it may be possible to expand output without changing relative prices. And in the case of a flex-price economy we can achieve a similar degree of simplification if we assume that all resources are fully employed and that changes in demand lead to all prices increasing by the same amount.

## *Ceteris paribus*

Another problem which arises when we are using aggregate demand and supply is to know what things are being held constant. For example, in Chapter 7 the demand curve was drawn on the assumption that tastes, income and the prices of all other goods were held constant. This assumption was the *ceteris paribus* assumption. But when we move to examining the behaviour of the entire economy what is being held constant? If we employ short-run analysis then we can assume that tastes and technology may not be changing. But can we speak of demand responding to a change in all prices? The problem of the aggregate demand curve in a flex-price economy will be examined in Chapter 40. In the meantime it is important to be aware of certain difficulties which can occur in aggregate analysis.

## Summary

Macroeconomics is about the behaviour of the entire economy rather than selected parts. We can distinguish between simple models which describe the behaviour of an economy when all prices are fixed and output can be varied, and of an economy in which output is fixed and the price level can vary.

# Chapter 32
# The Measurement of the National Income

In this chapter we shall discuss in more detail the concept of the national product or, as it is more usually called, the national income. We shall also examine how it can be measured. Therefore, the chapter is an important link between the basic ideas set out in the previous chapter and the more intensive analysis of the structure and functioning of macroeconomies which will follow in later chapters. The chapter will reveal many of the problems faced by statisticians in attempting to measure the national income.

## From gross national product to net domestic product

The basic concept of national income accounting is the *gross national product* (GNP) which measures the value of all final goods and services produced in an economy during a given period of time, usually a year, and measured at market prices. It includes such things as bread and haircuts but excludes activities performed within households because they do not involve market transactions.

Production gives rise to incomes for the owners of resources and the incomes so earned become the total expenditure on goods and services created during the production process. Output, income and expenditure are therefore interrelated and give rise to the concept of a *circular flow of output, incomes and spending*.

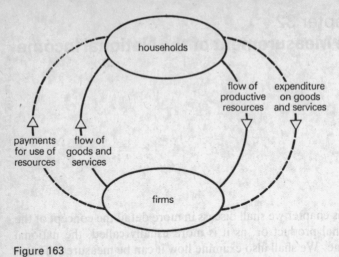

Figure 163

## Gross national product and net national product

Gross national product measures the value of goods and services produced during a period. Each commodity is valued at its market price and the total values for all commodities are added together to give the GNP. In a simple economy which produces 100 kilos of potatoes valued at 5 pence per kilo and 20 litres of beer, each litre being valued at 100 pence, then the GNP would be £25. By way of a contrast the UK gross national product was £225,522 millions in 1980 (Table 43).

The measurement of the GNP, however, contains snares and subtleties. First, there is the problem of *double counting*. If farmers produce and sell wheat to millers at a price of £100 and the millers sell flour to the bakers for £250 then the value of the millers' output is not £250 but £150 and the GNP is not £350 but £250. It is the *value added* by the millers which is counted by the national income statisticians. The reason is that the GNP measures the value of final goods and not intermediate goods such as the wheat used by the millers.

The second point to note is that the GNP measures the value of goods and services *currently produced*. Therefore, it excludes

Table 4.3 Gross national product

| | 1970 | 1971 | 1972 | 1973 | 1974 | 1975 | 1976 | 1977 | 1978 | 1979 | £ million 1980 |
|---|---|---|---|---|---|---|---|---|---|---|---|
| *At market prices* | | | | | | | | | | | |
| Consumers' expenditure | 31 778 | 35 599 | 40 183 | 45 759 | 52 668 | 64 749 | 74 952 | 86 001 | 98 947 | 116 717 | 135 403 |
| General government final consumption | 8 991 | 10 250 | 11 675 | 13 380 | 16 618 | 23 039 | 26 776 | 29 237 | 32 969 | 38 241 | 48 337 |
| Gross domestic fixed capital formation | 9 470 | 10 517 | 11 606 | 14 238 | 16 833 | 20 416 | 23 567 | 25 753 | 29 741 | 34 251 | 40 050 |
| Value of physical increase in stocks and work in progress | 421 | 158 | 44 | 1 448 | 1 263 | -1 483 | 847 | 1 950 | 1 075 | 2 539 | -3 596 |
| Total domestic expenditure | 50 660 | 56 524 | 63 508 | 74 825 | 87 382 | 106 721 | 126 142 | 142 941 | 162 732 | 191 748 | 220 194 |
| Exports of goods and services | 11 594 | 13 008 | 13 725 | 17 233 | 23 130 | 27 197 | 35 430 | 43 572 | 47 705 | 55 183 | 63 198 |
| Total final expenditure | 62 254 | 69 532 | 77 233 | 92 058 | 110 512 | 133 918 | 161 572 | 186 513 | 210 437 | 246 931 | 283 392 |
| *less* Imports of goods and services | -11 147 | -12 193 | -13 772 | -19 033 | -27 398 | -29 011 | -36 916 | -42 602 | -45 536 | -54 602 | -57 832 |
| Gross domestic product at market prices | 51 107 | 57 339 | 63 461 | 73 025 | 83 114 | 104 907 | 124 656 | 143 911 | 164 901 | 192 329 | 225 560 |
| Net property income from abroad | 554 | 502 | 538 | 1 257 | 1 415 | 773 | 1 365 | 104 | 592 | 846 | -38 |
| Gross national product at market prices | 51 661 | 57 841 | 63 999 | 74 282 | 84 529 | 105 680 | 126 021 | 144 015 | 165 493 | 193 175 | 225 522 |
| *Factor cost adjustment* | | | | | | | | | | | |
| Taxes on expenditure | 8 417 | 8 788 | 9 267 | 10 121 | 11 457 | 14 134 | 16 532 | 20 261 | 23 221 | 30 254 | 37 287 |
| Subsidies | 884 | 939 | 1 153 | 1 443 | 3 004 | 3 702 | 3 461 | 3 293 | 3 624 | 4 389 | 5 215 |
| Taxes *less* subsidies | 7 533 | 7 849 | 8 114 | 8 678 | 8 455 | 10 432 | 13 071 | 16 968 | 19 597 | 25 865 | 32 072 |
| *16* Capital consumption | -4 428 | -5 109 | -5 900 | -7 011 | -8 648 | -11 112 | -13 415 | -15 869 | -18 686 | -22 144 | -27 045 |
| *17* National income (*i.e.* net national product) | 39 700 | 44 883 | 49 985 | 58 593 | 67 428 | 84 136 | 99 535 | 111 178 | 127 210 | 145 166 | 166 405 |

Source: *National Income & Expenditure*, HMSO, 1981

antiques and such things as houses and factories unless they were produced during the period of observation.

The third point to observe is that the GNP is measured at *market prices*. Market prices include taxes which raise prices, and subsidies which lower prices. When taxes are subtracted from, and subsidies added to production costs we obtain *factor cost* which measures the true cost of production.

GNP also makes no allowance for the depreciation of the

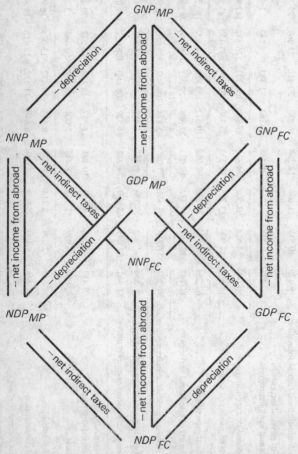

Figure 164

capital stock during the production process. If no allowance were made for wear and tear then the GNP could not be maintained at a given level. When a deduction is made for depreciation we arrive at *net national product* (NNP) at factor cost.

The interrelations between the various concepts of national product are illustrated in Figure 164 which is derived from Wilfrid Beckerman's excellent introductory book on national income analysis (Beckerman, 1968).

## National income

The total value of income is equal to the value of output because the revenue from the sale of output must accrue as income to someone. But the relationship between output and incomes is subject to two qualifications. First, the incomes which producers receive for their products do not include the taxes which are imposed upon them. Secondly, depreciation should not be counted as part of income. When these two items are deducted we arrive at *national income at factor cost* which is the income producers actually receive from productive activity.

## Disposable income

An important distinction for macroeconomics is that between income which the private market sector receives and that which the public sector obtains. Disposable income comprises national income minus direct taxes plus transfer and interest payments from the state. Direct taxes include income tax, corporation tax and national insurance contributions whilst the additions embrace pensions and family allowances.

## Expenditure

Because output is defined as equal to the value of incomes and expenditure, we can measure economic activity by looking at the flow of spending. Spending comprises consumption expenditure, business investment, government purchases and exports.

## Nominal and real GNP

Nominal GNP measures the value of output in a given period at the prevailing prices. Hence, a comparison of the size of GNP in two years may be difficult because of price changes, so the real GNP attempts to overcome this problem by valuing all goods and services produced in the two periods at the same price. But all prices do not move by the same amount and therefore we have to make use of the trend of average prices; this average is known as an *index number*.

The most well known index number is the *Index of Retail Prices* which measures changes in the price of consumer goods and is therefore used as a measure of changes in the cost of living. Thus, if the index for October 1980 was 304 (15 January 1974 = 100) then the average prices prevailing in October 1981 were 204 per cent higher than on 15 January 1974.

But prices vary between regions and the amounts spent on different goods by individuals also vary. Hence, the index attempts to reflect the importance of different goods as well as their prices. If, for example, the price of bread rose by 25 per cent and the price of caviar rose by 10 per cent then the average price rise would be 17·5 per cent but for the poor man who bought no caviar then the price rise would be 25 per cent and for the rich man the price rise would be between 10 and 25 per cent depending upon how much bread and how much caviar he bought.

In the calculation of price indices it is customary to use a *Laspeyre index* which compares the current and base year cost of a bundle of goods of fixed composition. If the base year quantities of goods are denoted by $\Sigma q_0$ and their prices by $\Sigma p_0$ then the cost of a bundle of goods in the base year is $\Sigma p_0 q_0$. The cost of the bundle in the following year becomes $\Sigma p_1 q_0$ and the ratio of the year's cost to the base year cost is

$$\frac{\Sigma p_1 q_0}{\Sigma p_0 q_0} \times 100$$

The alternative to the Laspeyre index is the *Paasche index* which uses as its reference point the quantities bought in the current period.

$$\frac{\Sigma p_1 q_1}{\Sigma p_0 q_1} \times 100$$

Although there is no theoretical reason for preferring one index number to another, the Laspeyre index has the advantage of using the same base period in all calculations whereas the Paasche index involves changing weights for each calculation.

## The best measure of price movements

Most people associate changes in prices with changes in the prices of consumer goods and the index of retail prices is therefore used to measure inflation. But the retail price index suffers from a number of defects. First, it 'weights' prices by assuming that consumers do not change the proportions in which they bought goods at some base date. Hence, the index fails to take into account the possibility that people will substitute goods whose prices are rising slowly for goods whose prices are rising quickly. By way of contrast, the *consumer expenditure deflator* allows for changing patterns of consumption and tends, therefore, to rise at a slower rate than the retail price index.

The second defect of the retail price index – and one which is also shared by the consumer expenditure deflator – is that it ignores about half the economy because it neglects spending by firms and government. The more broadly based *total final expenditure deflator* (sometimes known as the GNP deflator) measures the movement of all final prices.

But a criticism of the GNP deflator is that most people would not object to charging foreigners high prices for exports. Hence, the *total domestic expenditure deflator* might be considered a more acceptable measure of price movements. However, the total domestic expenditure deflator includes the movement of import prices and for some purposes we might want to measure domestically generated price movements arising, for example, from aggressive trade union wage policies.

For such purposes we could use the *implied index of total home costs*.

Table 44 shows the movements of the various price measures between 1956 and 1977. There are differences in their rates of increase. But which is the best measure of price movements depends upon the problem at hand. The national income statisticians tend to use the GNP deflator to measure real national income over time but there is no one indicator which gives satisfactory answers to all questions.

Table 44   Measures of price movements, 1959–80
(1975 = 100)

|  | *1959* | *1970* | *1980* |
| --- | --- | --- | --- |
| retail price index | 36·1 | 54·3 | 193·1 |
| consumers' expenditure | 36·7 | 55·0 | 189·5 |
| total final expenditure | 34·9 | 52·5 | 191·6 |
| total domestic expenditure | 34·1 | 52·2 | 192·1 |
| total home costs | 34·8 | 51·0 | 190·9 |

## The output gap

In the previous chapter we drew attention to the concept of full employment output and to the possibility that an economy may operate at less than full employment. A simple method of obtaining full employment national income is to measure output at constant prices in those peak years when output reaches a maximum. Thus, 1966 and 1973 appear to be years when gross domestic product at 1975 factor cost reached a peak. Through those peaks we can draw a line which we can call the *full employment growth path*. This path will have an upward slope because over time there will be an increase in factor supplies and the emergence of new ideas which will enable a greater output to be produced. Figure 165 shows the full employment growth path for the UK economy and it suggests that the economy might have been capable of growing at the rate of 3 per cent per annum. The diagram also reveals that the *output gap* – which is the difference between actual and potential output – has been

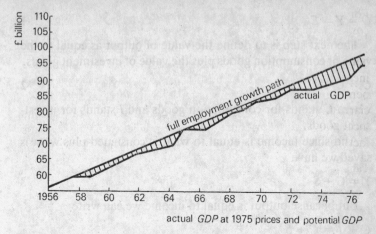

actual *GDP* at 1975 prices and potential *GDP*

Figure 165  Actual GDP at 1975 prices and potential GDP

growing larger over recent decades. What this suggests is that policies designed to keep aggregate demand equal to aggregate supply have not been successful. In subsequent chapters we shall examine the components of aggregate demand and suggest some reasons for the failure of demand policies. However, we should not ignore the fact that the difficulties of maintaining full employment may stem from movements of supply and in recent years there have been sharp increases in the prices of raw materials and over the period since 1945 there have been variations in the size of the labour force as a result of fluctuations in the birth rate.

## Accounting identities

In this final section we shall set out the basic relationships established earlier as a set of algebraic identities which will be used extensively throughout the remainder of our discussion of macroeconomics.

### A simple economy

Since the value of output is defined as equal to the value of income and expenditure we can write

$$O = Y = E \qquad\qquad 1$$

The next step is to define the value of output as equal to the value of consumption goods plus the value of investment goods.

$$O = C + I \qquad\qquad 2$$

where $C$ stands for consumption goods and $I$ stands for investment goods.

And since income is equal to what is consumed plus what is saved we have

$$Y = C + S \qquad\qquad 3$$

But because output is equal to income we can write

$$C + I = C + S$$

or $\quad I = S \qquad\qquad 4$

It should be noted that the proposition that investment is equal to savings is one which has been established as a result of the definitions adopted. Later, we shall encounter definitions where savings and investment are not equal and we shall examine the relationship between accounting identities and economic concepts.

### Government and foreign trade

We can now introduce government and foreign trade by adding government expenditure and exports minus imports to total demand.

$$Y = C + I + G + X - M \qquad\qquad 5$$

The next step is to establish the link between output and disposable income. As we have already observed, part of income is deducted as taxes and an addition is made in the form of transfers so that total disposable income is equal to

$$Y_d = Y - T + R \qquad\qquad 6$$

Disposable income is allocated between consumption and savings,

$$Y_d = C + S \qquad\qquad 7$$

and combining equations **5** and **6** enables us to write consumption as the difference between income plus transfers and savings

$$C + S = Y_d = Y + R - T \qquad\qquad 8$$

# Chapter 33
# The Fix-Price Economy

**A spending economy**

We are now in a position to analyse the workings of a fix-price economy in which there are unemployed resources and there is no technological change. We shall begin with a very simple version which contains only households and firms and there is no investment in new capital formation. In such an economy all income is spent. Figure 166 illustrates the basic features of such an economy. Firms produce goods and services and in doing so hire resources from households. The payments to households constitute the incomes out of which goods and services are

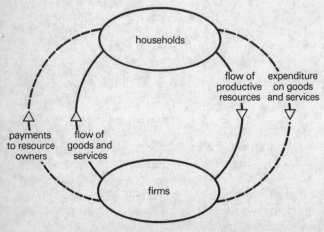

Figure 166

purchased from firms. In such an economy there is a circular flow of output, income and expenditure such that we can write

$$O = Y = E \qquad\qquad\qquad 1$$

where $O$ stands for the value of output, $Y$ is income and $E$ is expenditure. These three concepts correspond to those previously set out in the national income accounts.

## The savings economy

An economy in which all income is spent on consumer goods and no investment takes place is undoubtedly unrealistic, and in the savings economy we assume that households spend only part of their income and save the rest. We also assume that there are some firms which produce consumer goods and some which produce investment goods. Finally, to simplify the analysis we assume that all saving is undertaken by firms. The algebra of the savings economy is, therefore, as follows.

$$O = Y = E$$
$$O = C + I$$
$$Y = C + S$$

where $C$ stands for consumption, $S$ for saving and $I$ for investment.

### Autonomous and induced expenditures

We shall now make some assumptions about the nature of consumption expenditures, saving and investment. Households make plans about how much to spend on consumption and how much to save on the basis of their incomes. In the case of investment we shall assume that firms plan to make a constant addition to their fixed equipment each year and that inventories are held constant. What this means is that investment is independent of the magnitude of national income; investment is a form of *autonomous expenditure* and differs from consumption which is expenditure directly induced by the national income.

A question which we shall seek to answer later is: how autonomous is autonomous expenditure?

## Withdrawals and injections

Savings and investment are examples of two other general categories of expenditure called *injections and withdrawals*.

*An injection is an addition to the income of domestic firms that does not arise from the spending of households or, an addition to the income of domestic households that does not arise from the spending of firms. A withdrawal is any income that is not passed on in the circular flow of income and expenditure.*

## Lags in the circular flow

The question now arises: will injections always equal withdrawals so as to prevent an expansion or contraction in the national income? Will savings always be equal to investment? The reason the question arises is because our model of income and expenditure now looks as follows.

$$O = Y = E \qquad\qquad\qquad\qquad\qquad 1$$

$$O = C + I \qquad\qquad\qquad\qquad\qquad 2$$

$$Y = C + S \qquad\qquad\qquad\qquad\qquad 3$$

$$C = f(Y) \qquad\qquad\qquad\qquad\qquad 4$$

$$S = \psi(Y) = W \qquad\qquad\qquad\qquad\qquad 5$$

$$I = \bar{I} = J \qquad\qquad\qquad\qquad\qquad 6$$

where $\bar{I}$ denotes that investment is a constant and $W$ and $J$ are withdrawals and injections respectively.

As will be apparent from the equations there is no obvious and automatic mechanism for making savings and investment equal. If we treat equations as a set of simultaneous equations then we have no means of resolving them. In the flex-price economy we could invoke the rate of interest as the means of reconciling savings and investment. If savings were greater than investment then the rate of interest would fall and if investment were greater than savings then the rate of interest would rise. But in a fix-price economy the rate of interest cannot move. We could, of course, achieve equality by assuming that decisions to save and decisions to invest were made at the same time and place, but in a decentralized economy that would be unrealistic and we have to recognize the existence of lags in decision-making.

We can distinguish three possible causes of lags in the circular flow of income and expenditure.

1 An output lag occurs because it takes time to alter production plans in response to changes in demand.

2 A factor-payments lag occurs because some factor payments, such as dividends, are made at infrequent intervals.

3 An income-consumption lag may be unimportant for wage-earners but of considerable importance for those who receive dividends or who plan to purchase durable consumer goods.

As long as there are considerable amounts of unemployed resources we can ignore the output lag and assume that both consumer goods and investment goods can be produced

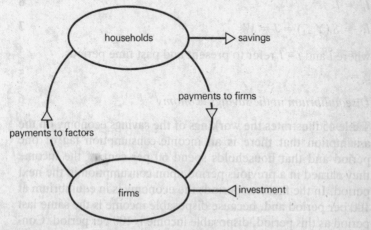

Figure 167

simultaneously and we can regard the second and third lags as constituting one spending lag. In the fix-price model it is the spending lag which is crucial and influences the reconciliation of injections and withdrawals, of savings and investment.

*The existence of lags serves to link the past with the present and the future and to indicate the possibilities of disequilibrium. Planned investment can be influenced by expectations about future profits and may not be equal to current savings which are dictated by past income.*

The behaviour of the circular flow of income in a savings economy with lags is illustrated in Figure 167.

Equilibrium in the circular flow requires equality of planned investment and planned savings and the equations of the model would, therefore, be

$$O_t = Y_t = E_t \tag{1}$$

$$O_t = C_t + I_t \tag{2}$$

$$Y_t = C_t + S_t \tag{3}$$

$$C_t = f(Y_{t-1}) \tag{4}$$

$$S_t = \psi(Y_{t-1}) \tag{5}$$

$$I_t = \bar{I}_t \tag{6}$$

$$I_t = S_t(Y_{t-1}) = J = W \tag{7}$$

where $t$ and $t-1$ refer to present and past time periods.

*Disequilibrium in the savings economy*

Table 45 illustrates the workings of the savings economy on the assumption that there is an income-consumption lag of one period and that households spend 60 per cent of the income they earned in a previous period upon consumption in the next period. In the first two periods the economy is in equilibrium at 100 per period and, because disposable income is the same last period as this period, disposable income is 100 per period. Consumption is 60 and saving is 40. Aggregate demand is for 60 of consumption goods and 40 of investment goods and it is just sufficient to purchase the total output of 100. Planned investment is equal to planned savings and there is no reason why anyone should change his plans.

In the third period planned investment rises to 80 and output rises to meet the new demand. As a result of the increase in output, national income rises to 140. Now this national income of 140 does not become disposable income until period 4.

In the fourth period households' consumption expenditures rise to 84 and savings rise to 56. The output of consumption goods rises immediately to 84 and total national income rises to 164 (consumption 84 and investment 80). In the fifth period income paid out to households is 164 and as a result expenditures rise once more.

Eventually, national income rises to 200 and the economy will be in equilibrium with consumption of 120 and investment of 80. The mechanism – the multiplier – which produces the final equilibrium national income will be discussed in the next chapter. However, a few minutes spent in substituting intermediate values will show that at any income less than 200 income will rise period by period and savings will be less than investment. But once income reaches to 200 planned investment will be equal to planned saving.

**Table 45** The effect of a spending lag upon the circular flow of income

| Period | disposable income $(Yd = Yt - I)$ | consumption $(0 \cdot 6\ Yd)$ | savings $(0 \cdot 4\ Yd)$ | investment | national income |
|---|---|---|---|---|---|
| 1 | 100 | 60 | 40 | 40 | 100 |
| 2 | 100 | 60 | 40 | 40 | 100 |
| 3 | 100 | 60 | 40 | 80 | 140 |
| 4 | 140 | 84 | 56 | 80 | 164 |
| 5 | 164 | 98·4 | 65·6 | 80 | 178·4 |
| 6 | 178·4 | 107 | 71·4 | 80 | 187·0 |
| $\vdots$ | | | | | |
| $n$ | 200 | 120 | 80 | 80 | 200 |

## Equalities and identities

Table 45 enables us to clear up a confusion between economic analysis and accounting measurement. Accountants measure income, output and expenditure at a point of time and make them equal by definition. Hence, savings are made equal to investment. In other words, an identity relationship is established and savings are made equal to investment for all values of investment.

In terms of Table 45 the accountant would measure national income in period 3 as 140 and factor incomes as 140. But since consumption was only 60 he would say that savings must have been 80 in order to equal the investment of 80. In effect, he would say that firms created 120 of income but paid out 100 (since factor payments are made in arrears) and therefore there exists unplanned savings of 40 which are temporarily held by firms for households.

Although the accountant's measurements can be interesting and informative and are used in the *National Income and Expenditure Blue Book* they tend to mask disequilibrium behaviour and direct attention away from the factors creating movement in the economy.

## A diagrammatic treatment of income determination in the savings economy

Although we have previously used a demand and supply diagram to illustrate income determination in a fix-price economy it has become customary to use what is known as the 45 degree diagram. In the top half of Figure 168 the vertical axis measures consumption and investment expenditures in real terms and the ͵orizontal axis measures national income in real terms. The 45 degree line represents all points at which total expenditure E is equal to national income. The 45 degree line is not considered to be a supply curve but it can be so regarded if it is assumed that factor prices were constant and that the productivities of factors remained constant as output increased. Because investment is assumed to be constant it can be illustrated by a line drawn parallel to the horizontal axis; OK measures the amount

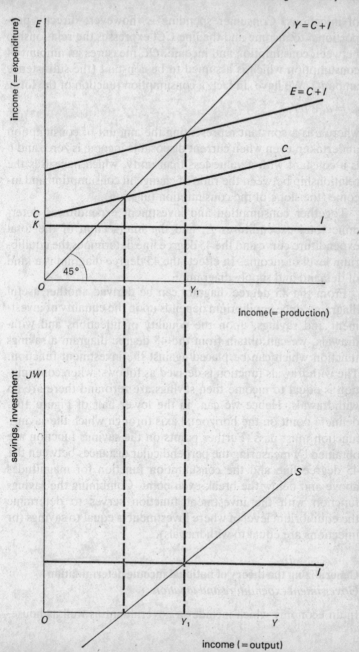

Figure 168

of injections. Consumer spending is, however, directly proportional to income and the line $CC'$ expresses the relationship between consumption and income. $OC$ measures an amount of consumption which is assumed to be constant (the subsistence amount). We have, in fact, a consumption function of the form

$C = a + bY$

where $a$ is a constant representing the amount of consumption undertaken even when current disposable income is zero; and $b$ is a constant with a value less than unity, which measures the relationship between the ratio of change in consumption and income (the slope of the consumption function).

Together consumption and investment expenditures determine total expenditures $E$, and the intersection of the total expenditure curve and the 45 degree line determines the equilibrium level of income. In effect, the 45 degree diagram is a kind of demand and supply diagram.

From the 45 degree diagram can be derived another useful diagram. Since equilibrium depends upon the equality of investment and savings, upon the equality of injections and withdrawals, we can obtain from the 45 degree diagram a savings function which can be placed against the investment function. The withdrawals function is derived as follows: when consumption is equal to income then savings are zero and there are no withdrawals. Hence we can, in the lower half of Figure 168, define a point on the horizontal axis through which the savings function must pass. Further points on the savings function are obtained by measuring the perpendicular distances between the 45 degree line and the consumption function for magnitudes above and below the break-even point. Combining the savings function with the investment function serves to determine the equilibrium level of where investment is equal to savings (or injections are equal to withdrawals).

## Generalizing the theory of national income determination
*Government expenditure and taxation*

In an economy which includes a government as well as households and firms total expenditure comprises consumption expenditures and injections of investment and government expenditure whilst withdrawals include savings and taxation. Algebraically

$O = Y = E$

$O = C + I + G$

$Y = C + S + T = E$

$C = f(Y)$

$I = \bar{I}$

$G = \bar{G}$

where $G$ is government expenditure and $T$ is taxation.

In Figure 169 government expenditure and taxation are added to the 45 degree diagram.

## The open economy

If a foreign trade sector is added to the economy then exports are included in the injections and imports are included in the withdrawals:

$O = Y$

$O = C + I + G + X$

$Y = C + S + T + M$

$J = I + G + X$

$W = S + T + M$

$C = f(Y)$

where $X$ stands for exports and $M$ denotes imports.

The full equilibrium of an open economy is shown in Figure 169. The total expenditure curve comprises consumption, investment, government spending and exports and intersects the 45 degree line to yield a national income of $OY$. In the bottom

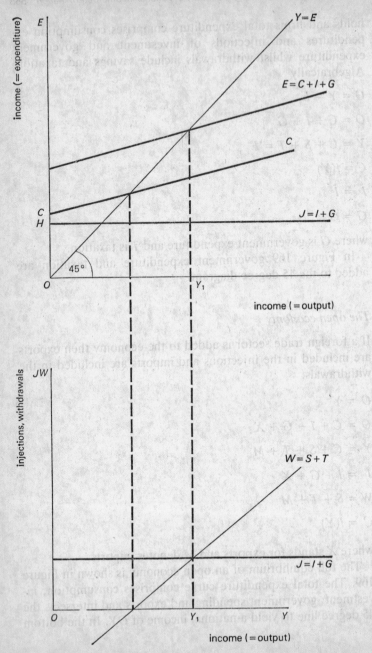

Figure 169

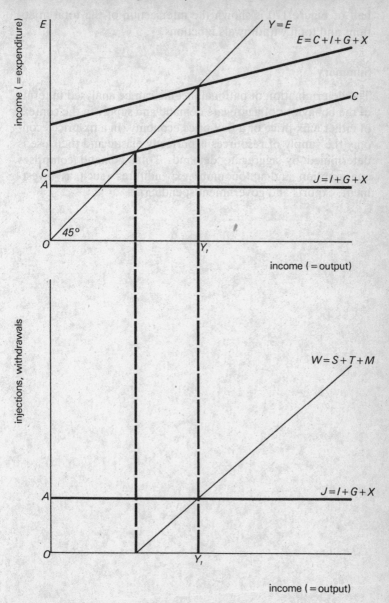

Figure 170

half of Figure 170 is shown the intersection of the total injections and total withdrawals functions.

## Summary

The determination of national income can be analysed in terms of the behaviour of aggregate demand and supply in the context of either a fix-price or a flex-price economy. In a fix-price economy the supply of resources is perfectly elastic and their use is determined by aggregate demand. Total demand comprises consumption and autonomous expenditures (such as investment, exports and government spending).

# Chapter 34
# Comparative Statics, Dynamics and the Multiplier

In the previous chapter we set out the basic framework of the fix-price economy in terms of flows of output, income and consumption and autonomous expenditures. We also stated the conditions for equilibrium in terms of either: (1) planned expenditure equals planned output or (2) planned injections equals planned withdrawals. Now what we shall do in this chapter is to carry the discussion further by examining the effects of changes in the behaviour of households, firms, government and exports upon the size of the national income.

## Increases and decreases in injections and withdrawals

We shall begin by considering the effects of injections and withdrawals in terms of the diagrammatic technique developed earlier. In Figure 171 the initial equilibrium is at $OY$ income. Subsequently, the injections curve rises to $J_1$ and the level of income rises to a new equilibrium of $OY_1$. Increases in injections raise the level of income and by the same line of reasoning reductions in injections lower national income.

In Figure 172 we shift the withdrawals function upwards and this has the effect of lowering the national income whilst a fall in the withdrawals function would raise the national income.

## The multiplier

Whilst it is apparent that changes in injections and withdrawals do alter the size of the national income, the crucial question is:

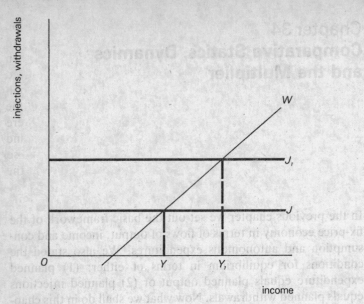

Figure 171

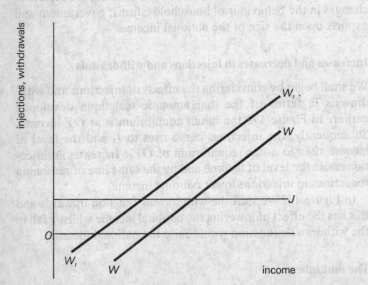

Figure 172

*by how much does national income alter*? This was the question which Mr Richard (now Professor Lord) Kahn attempted to solve during the slump of the thirties. The question was then posed in a slightly different fashion: If there exist unemployed resources in a country how effective would a public works policy be in removing the unemployment and how large must the government project be? Kahn assumed that the men who were employed on, say, road building would spend their wages and so create jobs for others, the latter would in turn spend and so the employment-creating process would snowball. This was the *employment multiplier*. But how large did the project have to be? At the time (1931) that Kahn was writing there were 2½ million unemployed. So the question then became, did the Government have to employ all of them or only some of them? The example given above suggests that the Government did not have to employ everyone since some would be sucked into employment by the spending of the roadbuilders. But could the Government solve the problem by employing only one man? Suppose one man was paid £20 and spent it all, and the person who received the £20 spent it all and that in like fashion everyone spent everything they received, then full employment could be restored. However, as Kahn recognized, not all income is spent and so the effectiveness of the multiplier is dependent upon what is spent.

Kahn's was an employment multiplier. Later Keynes was to switch to an investment multiplier, thereby emphasizing that it was spending that was important. Next came the foreign trade multiplier which stressed the importance of fluctuations in exports and imports. More recently, all forms of spending have been embraced by a general multiplier which refers to all injections.

## The mechanics of the multiplier

The essence of the multiplier is simplicity itself, but it has far-reaching implications. It rests on the interdependence of income and expenditure within the circular flow of income. It is because of this interdependence that an increase in injections increases total incomes by more than the income increase of the people who receive the initial extra injection of expenditure. What happens is that the increased expenditure of the initial income recipients becomes additional income for others who in turn spend. The process continues in this fashion, period by period, but successive income increments rapidly diminish because of the positive level of withdrawals in each period. The process finally ends and equilibrium is re-established in the circular flow when desired withdrawals again equal desired injections. The final stage however is only reached over a very large number of periods but this need not bother us because the arithmetic of a convergent series takes us close to the final value within the space of a fairly short number of periods. For many purposes it is often convenient to treat the multiplier as instantaneous.

Why does the equality of desired injections and withdrawals signify the end of the multiplier process? The answer is that as long as desired injections and withdrawals are unequal then the circular flow of income will be in disequilibrium and the level of income will be changing. If desired injections are greater than desired withdrawals then the level of income will be rising. The opposite is true when withdrawals exceed injections.

An alternative way of thinking about the process is to note that while actual injections and actual withdrawals are always equal desired injections and withdrawals are only equal when income stops changing. We shall now bring out the main features of the multiplier process by means of a little algebra and some geometry.

### Some algebra

The essence of the multiplier is that an increase in injections will lead to an increase in income. This can be expressed as:

$$k\Delta J_t = \Delta Y_t \qquad\qquad 1$$

where $\Delta Y_t$ is the increase in income, $\Delta J_t$ is the increase in injections and $k$ is the amount (the multiplier) by which injections must be multiplied to equal the resulting increase in income. On rearrangement equation 1 yields:

$$k = \frac{\Delta Y_t}{\Delta J_t}, \qquad\qquad 2$$

whence $k$ is revealed as the multiplier. Using equations 1 and 2 we can derive an expression for the determination of the value of the multiplier. When the circular flow is in equilibrium, income ($Y$) equals expenditure ($E$)

$$E_t = Y_t \qquad\qquad 3$$

where the subscript denotes the time period. We know that income arises as a result of domestic expenditure on consumption goods ($Cd$) and injections ($J$), so that:

$$Y_t = E_t = C_t + J_t \qquad\qquad 4$$

Furthermore we know that income received is either spent on domestic consumption goods ($C$) or lost from the circular flow as a result of withdrawals, ($W$), so that

$$Y_t = C_t + W_t \qquad\qquad 5$$

From equations 3, 4 and 5 we derive the equality of injections and withdrawals as follows:

$$J_t = Y_t - C_t$$
$$W_t = Y_t - C_t$$
therefore $J_t = W_t \qquad\qquad 6$

The marginal propensity to withdraw (mpw) is the term used to denote the relationship between a change in income and the change in withdrawals; the change in withdrawals gives rise to, symbolically,

$$\text{mpw} = w = \frac{\Delta W_t}{\Delta Y_t} \qquad\qquad 7$$

where $w$ stands for the marginal propensity to withdraw. Equation 1 tells us that a change in injections will give rise to a change in income which is $k$ times the change in injections,

$$\Delta Y_t = k\Delta J_t$$

From equation **6** we know that in equilibrium, desired injections equal desired withdrawals, so that it follows that in equilibrium, the change in injections ($\Delta J$) must equal the change in withdrawals ($\Delta W$), which allows us to rewrite equation **1** as

$$\Delta Y_t = k\Delta W_t \qquad\qquad\qquad 8$$

But the change in withdrawals is merely the change in income times the marginal propensity to withdraw, so we also have

$$\Delta Y_t = kw\Delta Y_t \qquad\qquad\qquad 9$$

which, on dividing both sides by $w$ and rearranging, yields the following expression for the multiplier:

$$k = \frac{1}{w}. \qquad\qquad\qquad 10$$

The multiplier is equal to the reciprocal of the marginal propensity to withdraw.

*The value of the multiplier varies inversely with the value of the marginal propensity to withdraw.*

### An example

We can illustrate our conclusion by means of an example. Suppose we have the following knowledge about an economy:

$$Y_t = C_t + J_t \qquad\qquad\qquad 11$$
$$C_t = 0 + 0 \cdot 8\, Y_t \qquad\qquad\qquad 12$$
$$J = 50. \qquad\qquad\qquad 13$$

Now let injections be increased by 50. The increase in income will be:

$$\Delta Y = k\Delta J \qquad\qquad\qquad 14$$
$$\Delta Y = k.50; \qquad\qquad\qquad 15$$

but $k = \dfrac{1}{w} = \dfrac{1}{0 \cdot 2}$,  **16**

because equation **12** tells us that $0 \cdot 8$ of every increase in income is spent and therefore $0 \cdot 2$ of every increase in income is withdrawn. So

$$\Delta Y_t = \frac{1}{0 \cdot 2} \times 50 = 250.$$  **17**

## Some geometry

Since the value of the multiplier depends upon the value of the marginal propensity to withdraw we can also illustrate the workings of the multiplier by means of the injections–withdrawals diagram which is reproduced below. Initially, planned

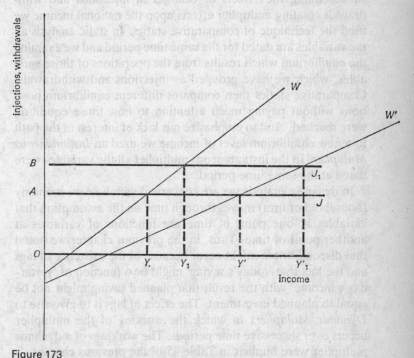

Figure 173

injections and planned withdrawals are equal and yield income level $OY$. Should injections increase by $AB$, this would result in a shift of the injections curve upwards from $J$ to $J_1$. The result is that the level of income rises from $Y$ to $Y_1$. The multiplier is the increase in income $(YY_1)$ divided by the increase in injections inducing the change $(AB)$; thus, the multiplier $k = YY_1/AB$. Notice in Figure 173 that the steeper the withdrawals function, i.e. the higher the marginal propensity to withdraw, the lower the value of the multiplier. A change in the position, as well as the slope, of the withdrawals function will also alter the equilibrium level of income.

## Comparative statics and dynamics

In describing the effects of changes in injections and withdrawals creating multiplier effects upon the national income we used the technique of comparative statics. In static analysis all the variables are dated for the same time period and we examine the equilibrium which results from the operations of those variables, which we have grouped as injections and withdrawals. Comparative statics then compares different equilibrium positions without paying much attention to how those equilibria were reached. And to emphasize our lack of interest in the path to a new equilibrium level of income we used an *Instantaneous Multiplier*. In the instantaneous multiplier all the variables were dated at the same time period.

In dynamic analysis we are concerned with how an economy (household or firm) moves through time on the assumption that variables at one point of time are functions of variables at another point of time. Thus, in the previous chapter we noted that disequilibrium might occur because of the existence of lags and the fact that 'today's saving' might be a function of 'yesterday's income' with the result that planned saving might not be equal to planned investment. The effect of lags is to give rise to *Dynamic Multipliers* in which the working of the multiplier occurs over successive time periods. The workings of a dynamic multiplier were implicit in Table 45 of the previous chapter.

Dynamic analysis is so obviously realistic that it would seem to be a waste of time using static analysis. But realism is not so easily gained. There are many lags and they may be of different lengths. The output lag may be longer than the income-consumption lag and the lags of different households and firms may vary considerably. Furthermore, the marginal propensity to withdraw may not be stable. Without recourse to complex computer simulations, comparative static analysis using an instantaneous multiplier may provide useful insights.

## Real versus money multipliers

So far the multiplier has been discussed in the context of unemployed resources. But what happens when there is an injection and resources are fully employed? An increase in spending would not lead to an increase in output but to a rise in prices. There would be a money multiplier and not a real multiplier.

## Summary

Changes in injections and withdrawals cause multiplier effects upon national income. The value of the multiplier depends upon the magnitude of the marginal propensity to withdraw and its stability. Where there are unemployed resources there will be a real multiplier giving rise to changes in output and income. When resources are fully employed there will be a money multiplier leading to rising prices.

# Chapter 35
# Households: Their Contribution to Aggregate Demand

Investigations into the determinants of consumption and saving have been a major field of activity since Keynes suggested that unemployment was a result of demand deficiency.[1] As consumption is a major component of aggregate demand, research was obviously necessary so that the resulting knowledge could be used to predict and manipulate the level of aggregate demand.[2] A second reason for examining the split between consumption and savings is that savings permit the diversion of resources from current consumption to capital accumulation upon which depends the future productive capacity of an economy. The third reason for examining the division between consumption and savings is that it strongly influences the distribution of income.

But having stressed the importance of households' decisions concerning savings we enter a caveat. The bulk of saving in a modern economy is undertaken by corporations and government and though they might be said to be acting on behalf of their owners – households – there is much evidence to suggest that control is not always rigorously exercised. In Chapter 16 we drew attention to the implications of the divorce of ownership

1. The terms 'household consumption', 'household consumption spending', 'consumption', and 'consumer spending' will be used as synonyms in this chapter and will refer to the amount that households spend on buying new goods and services.
2. In 1980 UK consumer spending accounted for 48 per cent of total demand.

from control in the modern corporation in determining the distribution of firms' profits.

## From micro to macro

We shall use the theory of household spending developed in earlier chapters to derive a theory of aggregate consumption. A theory of the determinants of how much one individual spends on one good will be used to derive a theory of how much all individuals spend on all goods.

In Chapters 7 and 11 we set out a theory of consumer's demand, which indicated that an individual derived utility from his consumption of goods and services. His choice is constrained by his income and the prices of goods and services. We then obtain the demand for any good as a function of all prices $P$, tastes $t$, his income $Y$:

$$d = f(P_a, \ldots, P_z, Y, t), \qquad\qquad 1$$

when the subscripts $a$ to $z$ refer to goods.

In Chapter 6 we noted that individuals could borrow and lend, so that they could consume more than their income 'today' and less than their income 'tomorrow', or vice-versa. Such a decision is influenced by the rate of interest $r$, and the individual's stock of assets $A$. So we can write:

$$d = f(P_{a_t}, \ldots, P_{z_t}, Y_t, t, A, r, P_{a_{t+1}}, \ldots, P_{z_{t+1}}, Y_{t+1}) \qquad 2$$

where the subscripts $t$, $t + 1$ indicate the time periods.

In Chapter 27 we indicated that an individual's income depended upon the allocation of his time between work and leisure, and that this choice might depend on the wage rate. With fixed working weeks quite common, the individual's income-leisure choice may take the form of training for a different type of job. This implies that in the long run, income is determined as much by consumption as consumption is by income: an individual will choose a job and (where possible) hours of work, so as to obtain an optimal combination of income and leisure.

However, in the short run, the individual is less free to choose his income, and he cannot, therefore, choose his consumption.

As well as his choice of private goods, an individual will consume public goods, provided collectively. But the individual cannot, by himself, choose his consumption of public goods, so in this chapter we ignore collective goods. The individual may however pay taxes to finance the provision of public goods if the government takes responsibility for their allocation, and his taxes reduce the amount of money he has left over to pay for private goods. In what follows, we use income to mean *disposable income* which is income after taxes have been paid.

What we have so far is a catalogue of all the factors which can influence a consumer's spending. As we are interested in total consumption, we can ignore relative prices, and hence concentrate on consumption as a function of individual incomes. Strictly speaking, this should be real incomes, which are money incomes corrected for price changes. We are mainly interested in consumption in relation to aggregate disposable income, and we shall hold the individual's stock of assets and rate of interest constant. We shall also assume that current prices are given. Hence we can write a relationship between consumption and current income,

$$c = d = f(y_t). \qquad\qquad 3$$

*Aggregation*

The final step is to aggregate the behaviour of all households into one macro household. This implies that though some households may be spending more than their current income they are offset by those who may be spending less. In addition, we shall be ignoring all internal transfers such as when parents give pocket money to their children. So we can write

$$D = F(Y_t), \qquad\qquad 4$$

or, replacing demand ($D$) by consumption ($C$) and inserting a suffix ($d$) to denote disposable income, we can write utility, $U$, as

$$U = G(C) = G\{F(Yd_t)\}, \qquad\qquad 5$$

or $\qquad C = F(Yd_t), \qquad\qquad\qquad\qquad$ 6

which is known as the *consumption function*.[3] This states that consumption is a function of real disposable income.

The consumption function which we have constructed contains a very important assumption concerning aggregation. It assumes that either all households have the same income elasticity of demand in which case changes in the distribution of income will have no effect upon total consumption *or* that the distribution of income tends to remain constant. If neither of these conditions is satisfied then shifts in the consumption function will occur. Shifts in the function will also occur if the ratio of disposable income to gross income is changed by changes in taxes, credit facilities and in consumers' expectations about future prices.

## The consumption function

We now have a theory which states that consumption depends upon real disposable income and, thus, that changes in consumption depend upon changes in real disposable income. We can test this theory by simply looking at the historical data on consumption and disposable income. If we use the data in the statistical appendix we get the result shown in Figure 174.[4]

It looks as though we can use the level of disposable income to explain consumption. More light is thrown on the relationship if we calculate the *average propensity to consume* (*APC* = consumer spending/disposable income). The figures for the *APC* in each year are shown in Figure 175 (row 3 of the statistical appendix). Whilst the overall trend was for the *APC* to fall from 1959 to 1980, there were quite marked fluctuations from

3. Thus the consumption function is related to the income–consumption curve of Chapter 11.

4. All the totals for spending and income are in constant price terms. The prices used are 1975 prices. Thus an income of £500 in 1955 would buy exactly the same bundle of goods as an income of £500 in 1963 or in 1973. This procedure reveals the *quantities* demanded and supplied.

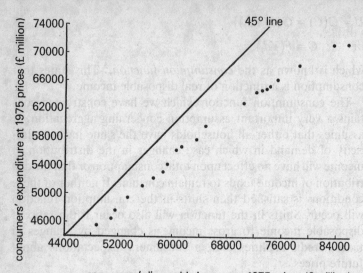

consumers' disposable income at 1975 prices (£ million)

Figure 174  Source: *Economic Trends*

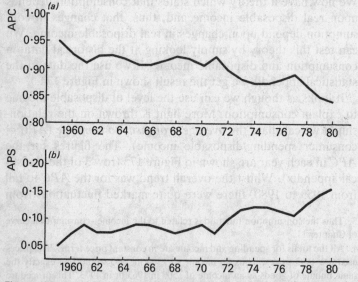

Figure 175

one year to the next. In the short run it seems as though something has disturbed the relationship between consumer spending and disposable income.

We can further examine the relationship if we compare the changes in disposable income from year to year with a change in consumption from year to year. The question being asked is, 'if we know that disposable income is £1000 million higher than last year, can we predict how much higher consumer spending will be, compared with the previous year?' The answer can be found in rows 5, 6 and 7 of the data. Row 5 shows the amount by which consumer spending exceeded that of the previous year. Similarly, row 6 is the increase in real disposable income. If the change in disposable income perfectly explains the change in consumer spending then the fraction, change in consumer spending/change in disposable income, should be a constant. Figure 176 (based on row 7) shows the ratio for each of the years 1960 to 1980.[5] What is immediately noticeable is that the fractions have not been constant, nor has there been a rising or falling trend. What we observe is apparently random fluctuations from year to year with values in the range 0·04 to 2·64. If disposable income rose by £1000 million from one year to the next then the first of these figures would predict a rise in consumer spending over the previous year of £40 millions whilst the other figure predicts a rise of £2640 millions – a difference between the estimates of £2600 millions. The ratios in row 7 are the estimates of the *marginal propensity to consume* (*MPC*) – that is, the fraction of an increase in income which is spent on consumption. What the fluctuations in the *MPC* from year to year clearly show is that we cannot explain the behaviour of household consumption solely in terms of current disposable income. The theory with which we started, that the level of consumption spending depended solely on current disposable income, has been tested and found wanting. We must now go back and consider whether we need to add more variables from our original catalogue.

5. In 1976 disposable income and consumption moved in opposite directions, falling and rising respectively.

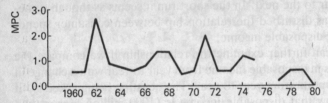

Figure 176

## A statistical digression

The points in the scatter diagram in Figure 174 appear to fall very closely along a straight line. Using the statistical technique called regression, a straight line has been estimated which most closely fits the scatter diagram for the years 1960–80. The result is equation

$$C_t = 9786 + 0.746\, Yd_t, \qquad\qquad 7$$

where $C_t$ is consumption spending in period $t$ and $Yd_t$ is disposable income in period $t$. Thus we predict that when disposable income was £63 709 millions (as in 1970), household consumer spending in that year would be:

$$C_t = 9786 + 0.746(63\ 709) = 57\ 313 \qquad\qquad 8$$

Since household consumption spending in 1970 was actually £57 814 million, this estimate was £510 million too low.[6] We can go on to calculate that for the years 1960–80 these annual estimates were in error by £630 million on average. This is the average absolute error.[7]

## A slightly more sophisticated theory of household consumption spending

A little introspection may lead to the formulation of a better

6. Whilst an error of £510 million seems small in a total of £57 814 million it makes a big difference to the level of unemployment when demand changes by £510 million.
7. The reader should note that the efforts to estimate consumption functions that are made in this book represent a very elementary beginning to what is statistically and economically a very difficult undertaking.

theory to explain what determines household consumer spending.

Because our standard of living has been rising steadily over a long period of time (remember this has been the case for perhaps at least two hundred years in Britain – see Chapter 1) it may have become one of those things that we take for granted. We may make spending decisions on the implicit assumption

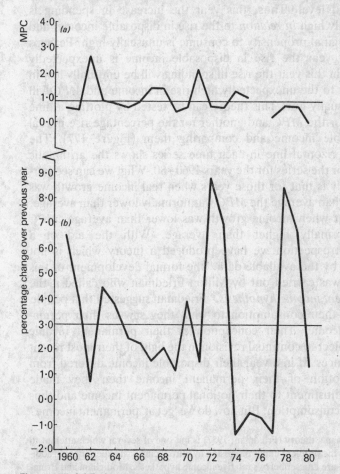

Figure 177 (a) Estimated marginal propensity to consumer. (b) Percentage change over the previous year of real disposable income.

that our real disposable income will rise by some 'average' amount, by an amount that we have come to expect. We may stick more or less to our spending plans even if for some reason disposable income only rises this year by very little. We are reluctant to lower our sights unless the low growth becomes the norm, and thus this year we only trim our spending plans slightly because of the shortfall of disposable income below the expected level. Thus, this year the increase in spending is unusually high *in relation* to the rise in disposable income, and the marginal propensity to consume is unusually high. Perhaps another year the rise in disposable income is unexpectedly large – in this year the rise in spending will be unusually low in relation to the unexpectedly high rise in income and *MPC* will be unusually low. This theory can be tested by plotting a time series for the *MPC* and another for the percentage rise in real disposable income and comparing them (Figure 177). The solid horizontal line in each time series shows the arithmetic mean for the series for the years 1960–80. What we can see fairly clearly is that for those years when real income growth was higher than average the *MPC* was normally lower than average, and that when income growth was lower than average, *MPC* was normally higher than average. With the aid of a little introspection we have produced a theory which is not refuted by the available data. The formal development of this theory was carried out by Milton Friedman who called it the *permanent income hypothesis*.[8] Friedman suggested that people related their consumption to what they saw as their permanent income. Their conception of their permanent income was subject to continual revision in the light of their most recent experiences. If in a year their disposable income differed from their notion of their permanent income then they made some adjustment to their notional permanent income and thus to their consumption. But how do we 'get at' permanent income?

8. Friedman's theory (Friedman, 1957) is but one of several which attempt to cope with the problem under discussion by introducing past experience. In addition there are Duesenberry's relative income hypothesis, Modigliani and Brumberg's life cycle hypothesis, and Clower and Johnson's endogenous income hypothesis.

It is not something that automatically reveals itself. The answer is by means of a lag analysis. We assume that permanent income will be reflected by previous consumption. Hence we can say that current consumption is determined by the interplay of current disposable income and past consumption. The theory can be summarized in the following equation:

$$C_t = a\beta + \alpha\beta Yd_t + (1-\beta)C_{t-1} \qquad\qquad 9$$

where $a$, $\alpha$ and $\beta$ are parameters.[9]

By again using regression analysis we can estimate the value of the constants using the historical data for the period 1960–80 included in the statistical appendix. The result obtained is

$$C_t = 7641 + 0\cdot564 Yd_t + 0\cdot245 C_{t-1} \qquad\qquad 10$$

Let us check how to use this result. As with our simple theory, let us try to predict consumer spending in 1970. Disposable income in that year was £63 709 million and consumer spending in the previous year was £56 313 million. Thus we predict that consumer spending in 1970 was

$$C_t = 7641 + 0\cdot564 \,(63\ 709) + 0\cdot245 \,(56\ 313)$$
$$= 57\ 369 \qquad\qquad 11$$

As consumer spending in 1970 was actually £57 814 million this is an error of only £445 million. The prediction error for 1970 using the first regression equation based on the simple theory was £510 million. Whilst the error for 1970 is smaller, the improvement over the whole period 1960–80 is more impressive, with an average annual error of £494 million as compared with £630 million with the simple theory. The gain in accuracy seems small and obviously we have not got to the bottom of what determines the level of consumer spending. There are several things we can do. First, we can abandon the theories on the grounds that they are not good predictors but before we do that we would have to consider what constitutes a good theory. Since the data may contain errors of observation should we not

9. The formal derivation of this equation is to be found in the appendix to this chapter.

say that the theory is in some sense all right? This question poses the further one of how we should lay down acceptable rules for testing and accepting theories. The second approach would be to attempt to obtain better data though even this strategy leads us back to a consideration of what constitutes a good test since we cannot expect error-free data. The third approach would be to disaggregate the data to see if there are any particular components of spending that need special treatment. This is what we shall do, but first we shall provide a diagrammatic exposition of the preceding analysis which some readers will find a useful generalization.

## Long- and short-run consumption functions

In the last section we investigated a complex consumption function which explicitly allowed for the fact that households take time to adjust to changed circumstances. The initial reaction of households to a change in income does not reflect their long-run normal pattern of behaviour. We can therefore distinguish between short- and long-run behaviour. The version of the permanent-income hypothesis that we investigated stated that households adjusted their consumption to changes in their permanent income $(P_t)$. Thus,

$$C_t = a + \alpha P_t. \qquad\qquad \textbf{12}$$

The fraction of any change in their permanent (long-run) income that they spend on consumption is $\alpha$; that is, their long-run marginal propensity to consume is $\alpha$. We estimated the long-run marginal propensity to consume to be $0.747$.[10]

10. Thus from equation **9** on page 605

$$C_t = \alpha\beta + \alpha\beta\, Yd_t + (1-\beta)C_{t-1},$$

we estimated

$$C_t = 7641 + 0.564Yd_t + 0.245C_{t-1},$$

| | | | | |
|---|---|---|---|---|
| Thus | $1-\beta = +0.245$ | | | |
| i.e. | $\beta = +0.755$ | | | |
| and | $\alpha\beta = +0.564$ | | Thus | $\alpha = +0.564/+0.755,$ |
| hence | $\alpha = +0.564/\beta.$ | | | $= +0.747.$ |

The short-run consumption function was estimated as equal to 0·564. Thus if disposable income rose by £1000 million, consumer spending would rise in the short run by £564 million, but in the long run when consumers had incorporated the income increase into what they perceived as their permanent income, they would increase their consumption by a further £183 million, making a total rise of £747 million.

We can show the difference between the short- and long-run marginal propensities diagrammatically by drawing short- and long-run consumptions functions as in Figure 178.

Let us assume that initially income is at a level $OY_0$ with aggregate consumption $OC_0$. Now we increase income to $OY_1$. In the short run the community only partially adjusts and raises consumption to $OC'_0$. When the community has had time to adjust fully, consumption rises to $OC''_0$, so that it bears its normal long-run relationship to income. We could analyse a fall in income below $OY_0$ in a similar way.

The line $C_2C_2$ is a short-run consumption function and $C_1C_1$ is the long-run consumption function. After full adjustment when consumption is at point $K$ there will be another short-run consumption function $C_3C_3$ which cuts $C_1C_1$ at $K$ in Figure 179.

The short-run marginal propensity to consume in Figure 179 is the short-run change in consumption divided by the change in income, i.e. $C_0C'_0/Y_0Y_1$, and the long-run $MPC$ is $C_0C''_0/Y_0Y_1$.

The distinction between the short- and long-run consumption functions has implications for the workings of the multiplier. Although the value of the multiplier will depend upon all the

---

Using the regression equation we estimated consumption spending in 1970

$C_t = 7641 + 0·564(63709) + 0·245(56313)$,
$\quad = £57\,369$

Now assume that disposable income had risen £1000 million extra in 1970 to £64 709 million. Consumption would have then risen to

$C_t = 7641 + 0·564(64\,709) + 0·245(56\,313)$
$\quad = £57\,933$

an immediate rise of £564 million which is the value of the short-run consumption function.

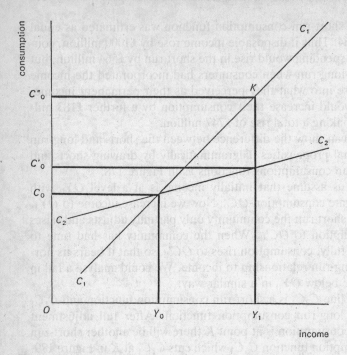

Figure 178

withdrawals (saving, imports and taxes), the existence of short-
and long-run consumption functions suggests that there may be
short- and long-run import and tax functions, and thus there
may be short- and long-run values to the overall multiplier.

### Further efforts to explain household consumer spending

Either we could try a little more introspection in an attempt to
find any factors which affect household consumer spending, or
we could try a fresh approach. Let us do the latter. The goods
and services that households purchase vary very much in their
characteristics. Some items are purchased frequently and are
quickly consumed as with food, public transport, heat and light.
Other items are purchased much less often and last for a long
time as with record players, new cars, washing-machines, etc. –

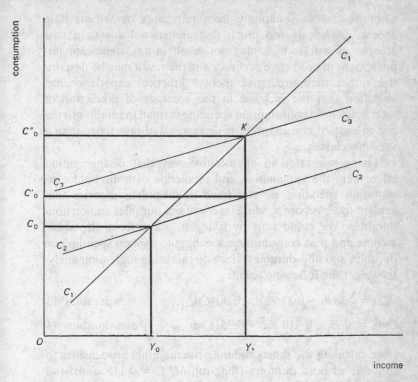

Figure 179

these are known as consumer durables. It seems intuitively reasonable to argue that the pattern of purchases of consumer durables will differ from the pattern for non-durables. If we pursue this line of inquiry, that is, trying to explain spending on durables and then trying to explain spending on non-durables separately, we are conducting a disaggregated analysis – we are disaggregating consumer spending.

Why stop at disaggregating household consumer spending into two sections; surely the factors influencing the purchase of record players differ from those influencing the purchase of cars, and even if they are the *same* factors, surely the relative importance of the factors will vary from good to good? If we went on disaggregating we would be analysing the purchase of

Cheshire cheese separately from purchases of Wensleydale cheese. Obviously too much disaggregation leads to a vast amount of work which may not result in any significant improvement in predictive accuracy and the result may be descriptive rather than predictive theory. Practical experience has indicated that the increase in the accuracy of prediction of total household consumption spending is small in relation to the rise in costs if consumption is disaggregated into more than a very few classes.

Having suggested in an intuitive way that disaggregation might help the explanation and prediction of household consumption spending we still have to formulate theories that explain the level of spending on consumer durables and on non-durables. We could start by trying to use current disposable income and past consumption spending to explain spending on durables and non-durables. If we do this using regression analysis we get the following result:

$$C_{D_t} = -3096 + 0{\cdot}116\ Yd_t - 0{\cdot}004 C_{D_{t-1}},\qquad\text{durables }\textbf{13}$$

$$C_{ND_t} = 8675 + 0{\cdot}410\ Yd_t + 0{\cdot}351 C_{ND_{t-1}}.\qquad\text{non-durables }\textbf{14}$$

If we calculate the short- and long-run marginal propensities to consume of both durables (long-run $MPC = 0{\cdot}115$, short-run $MPC = 0{\cdot}116$) and non-durables (long-run $MPC = 0{\cdot}631$, short-run $MPC = 0.410$) then we see that the way in which households respond to a change in their incomes differs as between durables and non-durables. Expenditure on non-durables increases much more slowly than spending on durables. This result has interesting policy as well as theoretical implications.

But we should be cautious. The equations may be imperfect, the data deficient and there are errors in the predictions of purchases of both durables and non-durables. We need more sophisticated theories and better data. Perhaps spending on durables depends on interest rates and hire-purchase conditions. The need to keep a balance in this book prevents us from going further both in theorizing and testing, but one point must be made very clearly. It is probably not possible to explain and predict consumption spending perfectly however much effort we put into our theorizing and statistical work. This is because the behaviour of groups is not entirely constant, and because there may be factors which are unpredictable such as hard winters, strikes, international crises, etc. Nevertheless, there is still considerable scope for theorizing and testing. Economics, as a quantitative subject, is yet in its infancy. We still need to establish the measurable area of the subject.

### Household spending on new dwellings: a special case of a durable good

An important injection from the household sector which creates effective demand and thus employment is the purchase of *new* dwellings (flats, houses, etc.). It is obvious that the purchase of second-hand houses does not create employment for builders – it only constitutes a swapping of existing assets, though we should perhaps note, in passing, that the purchase of a second-hand house does create employment for estate agents, solicitors, surveyors, etc. These people provide a service and consumer spending on their services is included in the 'consumer spending on services' figures.

If we look at real personal investment in new dwellings (row 11 of the statistical appendix) and plot it as a time series, as in Figure 180, what is immediately noticeable is the surprising irregularity of the series.

As a simple test we could plot the time series for the data on disposable income, interest rates and purchases of new dwellings that are set out in the appendix. Having done that we need to recognize that the investment data may reflect supply as well as demand conditions. It may be influenced by severe weather conditions and by possible changes in productivity in building. We have, in short, an identification problem of the kind discussed in Chapter 10. The problem in relation to the historical data on new dwellings is too complex to unravel in this book.

### Explaining consumption spending by investigating saving

So far we have concentrated on trying to explain consumer

spending by framing questions and theories as though the sole concern of households was with current consumption. The implication has almost been that savings are a residual, something that is not adjusted deliberately. Yet savings decisions are just as deliberate as consumption decisions. It may therefore be useful to explore the behaviour of savings data in order to provide a check on our theories of consumer behaviour. Unfortunately, savings data are unreliable. They are not calculated directly, but are obtained as residuals from the estimates of income and consumption. Hence any errors in the calculations of consumption and income tend to be magnified in the savings figures.

Before we leave savings a comment is in order on the years 1973–80. During this period the average propensity to save (the fraction of total income saved = the savings ratio) was at record high levels, see Figure 180. These very high savings were de-

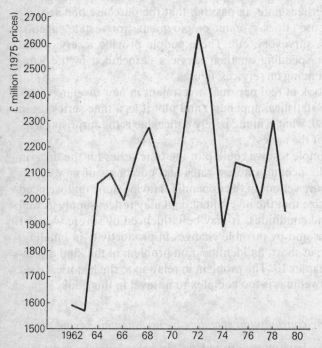

Figure 180   Personal investment in new dwellings (at 1975 prices)

spite very low levels of the real rate of interest (real rate of interest = money rate of interest *less* the rate of price increase) and some years (1974–7 and 1980) when increases in real disposable income was very low. These low real interest rates and low income increases would normally be expected to depress the savings ratio. Theoretical and empirical work since the mid 1970s has shown that it has been complex reactions to the record inflation rates that has caused the higher savings ratio.

## Summary and conclusions

We have discussed in this chapter the behaviour of households as this affects the level of demand for new goods and services and, through production, the level of employment. Households were separated from a discussion of firms' and government's expenditures because households have some features that uniquely distinguish them from the other economic agencies. They act purely out of self-interest which one hopes governments do not, and their ability to borrow is much more constrained than that of firms.

Households were discussed as a group because the group seems to behave in a consistent, predictable way as the eccentricities of individual households are averaged out. Our discussion has had three aims. First, we discussed the erection and development of theories of household behaviour. Secondly, elementary ideas of testing were introduced. Finally, we tried to give some idea of the problems, both theoretical and statistical, which are particularly developed in more advanced courses.

We found that the principal factor controlling household spending on goods was disposable income and we went on to show that the power of the theory was increased by including past consumption as an explanatory variable. Later sections went on to suggest that the theories could be improved by a measure of disaggregation and by a consideration of savings. A consideration of savings suggests that interest rates might be influential in explaining consumption. No direct testing of the effects of interest rates was attempted though they were implicit in the permanent income hypothesis.

An important assumption made in our analysis was that households take time to adjust fully to changed circumstances. This assumption was one that we used in Part Two when we examined short- and long-run responses in particular markets. It testifies to the power of Marshall's partial equilibrium analysis with its stress on the time lags. This difference in responses implied that the long-run and short-run multipliers will take on different values and may be difficult to predict accurately. However, before accepting that conclusion we noted that the multiplier is also dependent upon the behaviour of imports and taxes and that their behaviour may offset any waywardness in the income-consumption multiplier. Moreover, the crudeness in our theories and data suggested that more work needed to be done on refining both.

## Questions

1 It is suggested that the aggregate consumption function was derived from the micro behaviour of households in Chapters 7, 11 and 26. Indicate how this is done.

2 If we aggregate all incomes and spending do we have to assume that all individuals have identical tastes and incomes in order to derive a meaningful theory of the consumption function?

3 What is the connection between the consumption function and the income–consumption curve of Chapter 11?

4 What is the connection between the analysis of Chapter 7 and Friedman's consumption function?

5 Does the empirical testing of the consumption function suggest the need for new theories or new facts?

6 Using the data in the statistical appendix, test for any possible relationship between investment in dwellings and the change from the previous year in household disposable income.

7 Can you explain the marked difference between the short and long run *MPC* for durables and non-durables?

8 In 1970 household disposable income was £63 709 million and

in the previous year consumption spending was £56 313 million. Assume that disposable income rose by £1000 millions in 1971 and remained unchanged for six years. Using the consumption function

$$C_t = 7641 + 0.564Yd_t + 0.245C_{t-1}$$

calculate the level of consumption in 1971, 1972, 1973 and 1974.

9 How would you expect a change in future prices to affect current consumption?

## Appendix: Derivation of the Permanent Income Equation

We can write that consumption in time period $t(C_t)$ depends upon permanent income in period $t(P_t)$:

$$C_t = a + \alpha P_t. \hspace{4cm} 1$$

This is the type of equation that we found when we used actual current disposable income to explain current consumption. The change in permanent income is seen as a fraction ($\beta$) which is greater than zero and less than one of the differences between current disposable income and the previously perceived level of permanent income. That is,

$$P_t - P_{t-1} = \beta(Yd_t - P_{t-1}). \hspace{3cm} 2$$

If we rearrange 2 we get

$$P_t = \beta Yd_t - \beta P_{t-1} + P_{t-1} \hspace{3cm} 3$$

$$= \beta Yd_t + P_{t-1}(1 - \beta). \hspace{3cm} 4$$

Now we have an expression for the permanent income in time period $t(P_t)$ which we can substitute in equation 1. Thus,

$$C_t = a + \alpha[\beta Yd_t + P_{t-1}(1 - \beta)]. \hspace{2.5cm} 5$$

Now if we can write equation 1 we can also write that consumption in an earlier time period depends upon permanent income in that earlier time period. Thus

$$C_{t-1} = a + \alpha P_{t-1}. \hspace{3.5cm} 6$$

## Statistical Appendix

| Row number | 1959 | 1960 | 1961 | 1962 | 1963 | 1964 | 1965 | 1966 | 1967 |
|---|---|---|---|---|---|---|---|---|---|
| 1 Consumers' expenditure at 1975 prices (£ million) | 43 911 | 45 623 | 46 680 | 47 653 | 49 725 | 51 274 | 52 131 | 53 184 | 54 385 |
| 2 Personal disposable income at 1975 prices (£ million) | 46 134 | 49 143 | 51 131 | 51 499 | 53 767 | 55 781 | 57 205 | 58 498 | 59 385 |
| 3 Average propensity to consume | ·952 | ·928 | ·913 | ·925 | ·925 | ·919 | ·911 | ·909 | ·916 |
| 4 Average propensity to save | ·048 | ·072 | ·087 | ·075 | ·075 | ·081 | ·089 | ·091 | ·084 |
| 5 Change in consumers' expenditure (row 1) from the previous year ($\triangle C$) | | 1712 | 1057 | 973 | 2072 | 1549 | 857 | 1053 | 1201 |
| 6 Change from the previous year of personal disposable income (row 2) ($\triangle Y$) | | 3009 | 1989 | 368 | 2268 | 2014 | 1424 | 1293 | 887 |
| 7 Marginal propensity to consume ($\triangle C/\triangle Y$) | | 0·57 | 0·53 | 2·64 | 0·91 | 0·77 | 0·60 | 0·81 | 1·35 |
| 8 Percentage increase of disposable income (row 2) over the previous year | | 6·52 | 4·05 | 0·72 | 4·40 | 3·75 | 2·55 | 2·26 | 1·52 |
| 9 Consumers' expenditure on durable goods at 1975 prices | 2692 | 2768 | 2663 | 2793 | 3249 | 3534 | 3510 | 3452 | 3680 |
| 10 Consumers' expenditure on non-durable goods at 1975 prices | 41 219 | 42 855 | 44 017 | 44 860 | 46 476 | 47 740 | 48 621 | 49 732 | 50 705 |
| 11 Personal investment in new dwellings at 1975 prices | | | | 1591 | 1573 | 2056 | 2099 | 2005 | 2168 |
| 12 Building society interest rates on loans, annual average | 5·98 | 5·89 | 6·28 | 6·61 | 6·27 | 6·16 | 6·63 | 6·98 | 7·20 |

Sources: *National Income and Expenditure*, various issues, HMSO; *Economic Trends*, various issues, HMSO;
*Annual Abstract of Statistics*, various issues, HMSO.

| 1968 | 1969 | 1970 | 1971 | 1972 | 1973 | 1974 | 1975 | 1976 | 1977 | 1978 | 1979 | 1980 |
|---|---|---|---|---|---|---|---|---|---|---|---|---|
| 56 026 | 56 313 | 57 814 | 59 724 | 63 270 | 66 332 | 65 113 | 64 749 | 64 815 | 64 583 | 68 222 | 71 409 | 71 454 |
| 60 613 | 61 244 | 63 709 | 64 643 | 70 349 | 75 250 | 74 241 | 73 880 | 73 359 | 72 362 | 78 436 | 83 728 | 84 867 |
| ·924 | ·919 | ·907 | ·924 | ·899 | ·881 | ·877 | ·876 | ·884 | ·892 | ·870 | ·853 | ·842 |
| ·076 | ·081 | ·093 | ·076 | ·101 | ·119 | ·123 | ·124 | ·116 | ·108 | ·130 | ·147 | ·158 |
| 1641 | 287 | 1501 | 1910 | 3546 | 3062 | −1219 | −364 | 66 | −232 | 3639 | 3187 | 45 |
| 1228 | 631 | 2465 | 934 | 5706 | 4901 | −1009 | −361 | −521 | −997 | 6074 | 5292 | 1139 |
| 1·34 | 0·45 | 0·61 | 2·04 | 0·62 | 0·62 | 1·21 | 1·01 |  | 0·23 | 0·60 | 0·60 | 0·04 |
| 2·07 | 1·04 | 4·02 | 1·47 | 8·83 | 6·97 | −1·34 | −0·49 | −·70 | −1·36 | 8·39 | 6·75 | 1·36 |
| 3927 | 3667 | 3987 | 4774 | 5797 | 6064 | 5302 | 5367 | 5641 | 5224 | 5932 | 6595 | 6337 |
| 52 099 | 52 646 | 53 827 | 54 950 | 57 473 | 60 268 | 59 811 | 59 382 | 59 174 | 59 359 | 62 290 | 64 814 | 65 117 |
| 2278 | 2116 | 1974 | 2351 | 2634 | 2398 | 1898 | 2146 | 2128 | 2007 | 2299 | 1959 |  |
| 7·46 | 8·07 | 8.58 | 8·59 | 8·26 | 9·59 | 11·05 | 11·08 | 11·06 | 11·05 | 9·19 | 11·94 |  |

Rearranging **6** we get

$$C_{t-1} - a = \alpha P_{t-1},$$

and dividing both sides by $\alpha$ gives

$$(C_{t-1} - a)/\alpha = P_{t-1}. \qquad \qquad \textbf{7}$$

We can substitute the expression for $P_{t-1}$ in equation **7** into equation **5**, thus obtaining

$$
\begin{aligned}
C_t &= a + \alpha[\beta Y d_t + ((C_{t-1} - a)/\alpha)((1 - \beta)] \\
&= a + \alpha\beta Y d_t + (C_{t-1} - a)(1 - \beta) \\
&= a + \alpha\beta Y d_t + C_{t-1} - \beta C_{t-1} - a + \alpha\beta \\
&= (a - a + a\beta) + \alpha\beta Y d_t + C_{t-1}(1 - \beta) \\
C_t &= a\beta + \alpha\beta Y d_t + (1 - \beta)C_{t-1}. \qquad \qquad \textbf{8}
\end{aligned}
$$

What we have finished with is an expression (a function) which says that changes in current household consumption spending depend upon changes in current disposable income and changes in past consumption spending. The equation was implied when we suggested that consumption depends upon current disposable income and our expectation about disposable income – our expectation was based on past disposable income received and this in turn influenced past consumption. Thus current consumption reflects current disposable income and past consumption.

# Chapter 36
# Aggregate Demand: Investment by Firms

In this chapter we discuss the impact of firms' behaviour on aggregate demand. Like households or government (local and national) firms make both injections and withdrawals which contribute to the aggregate level of demand in the economy. Firms add to aggregate demand by demanding plant and machinery and other assets to be used to add to, and to maintain, the level of production, and they reduce aggregate demand to the extent that they have undistributed profits (business savings). As with households in the previous chapter, we consider the behaviour of firms as a group, not seeking to explain the exact behaviour of a particular firm but seeking to explain the behaviour of the typical firm and firms as a group. Again we justify this approach by a resort to the so-called 'law of averages', which suggests that the grouping will average out the behaviour of eccentric firms. But first we draw attention to two important distinctions. The first concerns the difference between gross and net investment whilst the second relates to the difference between stocks and flows.

## Gross and net investment

Not all spending by firms constitutes addition to their capital stocks of buildings and machines. A great deal is concerned with replacing or maintaining existing equipment. This is referred to as replacement investment and will be carried out as long as it yields a greater return than can be obtained from doing something else. From the point of view of an entire community 'doing something else' would mean consuming more presently and allowing the capital stock to fall. Hence we must subtract replacement investment from gross investment in order to arrive at net investment. Net investment will tend to take place when profit expectations increase, when technical change arises, when machine costs fall and when labour costs rise.

## Stocks and flows

At various points in this book we have drawn attention to the distinction between stocks and flows. *Stocks are quantities at a point of time whereas flows are quantities spread over a period of time.* Thus in a theory of demand and supply (Part Three) and in the theory of market structures (Part Five) we used the distinction between stocks and flows as a means of distinguishing the short- and long-run responses of supply to changes in demand.

Ideas about stocks and flows are important in the theory of investment. Firms purchase capital goods (machines, buildings, etc.) which are a stock but which yield a flow of services over time. And the relationship between the stock and flow may be variable as, for example, when machines are worked on one, two or three shifts. There is also another flow – the time rate of demand for capital goods – and it is this time rate which we refer to as investment.

### The marginal productivity of capital

In the second quadrant of Figure 181 is depicted the marginal productivity curve of capital, $D_{ko}$, of a typical firm. Along the horizontal axis is measured the stock of capital whilst the vertical axis measures the price of capital and the marginal productivity of capital. The marginal productivity curve slopes downwards from left to right because of diminishing returns to successive additions to the capital stock. But note that the marginal productivity of the capital curve is *not* an intended

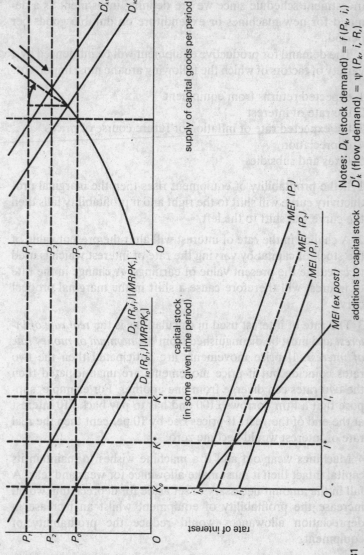

**Figure 181**

Notes: $D_k$ (stock demand) $= f(P_k, i,)$

$D'_k$ (flow demand) $= \psi(P_k, i, R,)$

investment schedule since we are defining investment as a demand for new machines or expenditure on durable goods per period.

The demand for productive equipment will be influenced by a variety of factors of which the following are the most important:

1 expected returns from equipment
2 the rate of interest
3 the expected rate of inflation or future course of prices
4 depreciation
5 taxes and subsidies

1 If the profitability of equipment rises then the marginal productivity curve will shift to the right and if profitability falls then the curve will shift to the left.

2 A change in the rate of interest will alter the present value of the stock of capital by varying the rate of interest which is used to calculate the present value of earnings. A change in the rate of interest will therefore cause a shift in the marginal product curve.

3 The rate of interest used in calculations is the *real rate of interest* and must be distinguished from the *nominal or money rate of interest*. If price movements are anticipated then the two rates coincide but if price movements are unanticipated then the two rates can diverge from one another. For example, suppose that a firm borrows £100 and has to pay back £10 interest at the end of the year. If prices rise by 10 per cent then the real rate of interest would become zero.

4 Machines wear out and if a machine wishes to maintain its capital intact then it must make allowance for wear and tear. A fall in the amount necessary to set aside for depreciation would increase the profitability of equipment whilst an increase in depreciation allowances would reduce the profitability of equipment.

5 An increase in taxes on profits would reduce the profitability of a stock of capital whilst the introduction of subsidies to purchase would raise the profitability of machines.

## The marginal efficiency of investment (*MEI*)

Suppose that the nominal rate of interest falls from $i_0$ to $i_1$. The marginal productivity of capital curve will shift upwards from $D_{k0}$ to $D_{k1}$. With an unchanged stock of capital, $OK_0$, the price of machines will rise from $OP_0$ to $OP_1$ and create quasi-rents of $OK_0.P_0P_1$. The emergence of quasi-rents will stimulate a flow of orders (investment) for new machines.

Now the rate of investment will depend upon two things. First, there will be the conditions of supply in the machine-making industry. If the supply of machines is perfectly elastic then ultimately $OK_1$ machines will be installed. In other words, the shift in the marginal product curve will cause a temporary rise in the price of machines from $OP_0$ to $OP_1$ but price will soon fall back to $OP_0$. However, in the first quadrant of Figure 181 we have shown an upward sloping supply curve in the machine-making industry – indicating that supply is not perfectly elastic. For simplicity, we assume that the eventual equilibrium price is $OP_2$. Hence, quadrant one shows a flow demand curve, $D^f K_0$, intersecting the supply curve at price $OP_0$. When the rate of interest falls the flow demand curve shifts upward to $D_{k1}$. There is a temporary equilibrium at $A$ and a final equilibrium at price $OP_2$.

The third quadrant shows the *marginal efficiency of investment curve*. This is an intended or ex ante investment curve (hence the superscript $a$) which links investment to the rate of interest. The curve $MEI^a(P_0)$ shows the curve which a businessman would move along if the rate of interest fell but the price of machines remained constant at $OP_0$. Now the effect of the rise in the price of machines to $OP_1$ is to cause the $MEI$ curve to shift downwards to $MEI^a(P_1)$ and to choke off investment despite the fall in the rate of interest. But this choking off is only temporary because of the rise in quasi-rents and because the machine industry can supply machines at less than $OP_1$. The supply industry can supply $K_0K_1$ machines at a marginal cost of $OP_2$.

When the rate of interest falls a businessman would like to move along $MEI^a(P_0)$. But because the increase in demand ap-

plies to all firms then price will rise initially to $OP_1$ and then fall
to $OP_2$. Hence he will move along the curve $MEI^a(P_2)$. The fact
that he cannot move along $MEI^a(P_0)$ reminds us of the distinction between ex ante and ex post factor demand curves which
we met in Chapter 22. Hence, we have drawn in the ex post
demand curve for investment which joins points on the two
ex ante investment curves.

One final point that needs to be noted is that the *MEI* curves
are not a simple mirror image of the supply conditions in the
machine-making industry but also embody *adjustment costs*
which have to be made when firms acquire new equipment.

## Expectations and the volatility of investment

In drawing the *MEI* curve we emphasized the connection between investment and changes in the rate of interest on the
assumption that expectations about profits could be taken for
granted. But some economists, notably Keynes, have emphasized the fragile nature of the beliefs underlying investment
decisions. They view investment curves as being highly interest

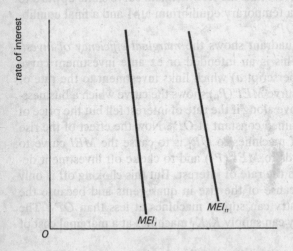

Figure 182

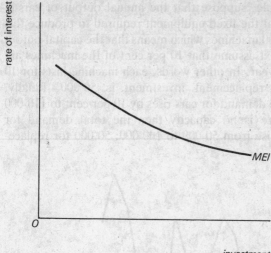

Figure 183

inelastic and subject to violent shifts such as are indicated in Figure 182. This point of view contrasts with that of other economists who regard the investment (*MEI*) curve as highly stable and interest elastic. They consider the violent shifts to be due to frequent changes in monetary and fiscal policy which cause large movements along the investment curve (Figure 183).

Tests to distinguish between these two hypotheses are difficult to construct but frequent changes in interest rates in the post-war period lend support to the second hypothesis.

### The acceleration principle

One method of examining the role of expectations in investment decisions is to analyse the relationship between changes in consumers' expenditure and changes in firms' fixed capital formation. A strong form of this relationship is the *acceleration principle* which states that: *Changes in the rate of increase in the demand for consumers' goods cause magnified changes in the demand for capital goods.*

As an example, suppose that the annual output of cars is
100 000 and that the fixed equipment required to produce this
output is 500 000 machines which means that the capital-output
ratio is 5:1. Next assume that 10 per cent of the machines are
replaced each year. In other words, each machine lasts for 10
years. Hence, replacement investment is 50 000. Finally,
assume that the demand for cars rises by 10 per cent to 110 000
a year. If there is no capacity then the total demand for
machines will rise from 50 000 to 100 000; 50 000 for replace-

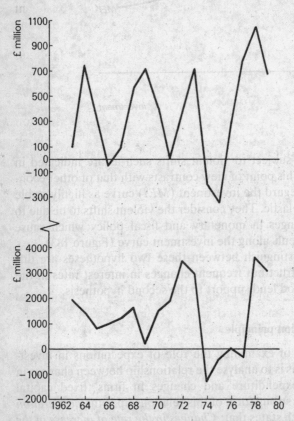

Figure 184 (a) Change in firms' GDFCF from the previous year (at 1975
prices). (b) Change in consumers' expenditure from the previous year (at
1975 prices)

ment and 50 000 to meet new demand. So an increase in the demand for cars by 10 per cent results in a 100 per cent increase in the demand for machines.

Figure 184 attempts a simple test of the acceleration principle. It shows time series data for annual changes in consumers' expenditure and annual changes in firms' gross fixed capital formation, both measured in real terms. The two series show similar patterns of fluctuations. Furthermore, the peaks in investment follow those in consumer spending. But the degree of association is not always strong; for example, the investment boom of 1968–9 followed a modest rise in consumer spending in 1966–8.

The acceleration principle contains a simple theory about expectations. It assumes no problems of finance, it ignores technological change and it rules out possibilities of firms responding to increases in demand by overtime and shift-working. These factors can account for the absence of a strong correlation between changes in final demand and changes in investment and suggest that firms consider permanent changes in demand rather than temporary changes as being the major influence upon their decisions to invest. *Firms' investment decisions may be influenced by their expectations about permanent income; they have a permanent income hypothesis analogous to that held by households.*

## Inventory investment

When we discussed the components of demand we mentioned inventory investment which may be defined as the value of the net physical change in stocks of finished goods, raw materials and work in progress. The desire to add to stocks increases aggregate demand, and the ability to reduce stocks means that, in the short run, demand can exceed production for finished goods, work in progress and raw materials.

Firms hold stocks because the benefits from holding stocks exceed their cost. Profits are considered to be higher when stocks are held than when they are absent. The costs of holding stocks are the cost of borrowing the money necessary to buy the stocks held plus the wages of warehouse staff and the rental value of warehouses. In the absence of stocks unexpected increases in demand cannot be met and profits are lost.

It follows from what has been said that the *levels* of stocks of finished goods, work in progress and raw materials which producers will wish to hold will be a positive function of demand and uncertainty, and a negative function of the rate of interest (the price of capital), the rental cost of storage facilities and the wages of warehousemen.

Earlier we saw that there was an accelerator effect for gross domestic fixed capital formation resulting from the relationship of investment to changes in demand and a similar relationship exists for inventory investment

planned net inventory investment $= g(Y_t - Y_{t-1})$

where $Y$ stands for national income, $g$ is the ratio of stocks to output and $t$ is the time subscript.

The effect of this relationship is that the level of inventory investment will fluctuate if income (demand) does not grow at a constant rate.

Figure 184 shows the current price value of the physical increase of stocks and work in progress for UK industrial and commercial companies between 1967 and 1980. The instability in the level of inventory investment is very marked.

Other things being equal we might expect a stable relationship between changes in output and changes in stocks. This hypothesis is partially examined in Figure 184 which shows the level of stocks plotted against the level of output for the period 1967–80 at constant 1975 prices. What the figure clearly demonstrates is that stock levels and output levels *are* related but not so closely that output levels can be used to predict stock levels. We could, however, estimate a constant value of $g$ by taking the arithmetic mean of the ratios of stock to output for each year and then treating divergences from the mean as unanticipated changes in stocks arising from unexpected changes in demand and supply. And, of course, one source of discrepancy may be that changes in demand lead to increases in imports and not to increased domestic production. Hence, there

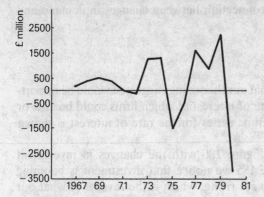

Figure 185a: Value of the physical increase in stocks and work in progress (current prices)

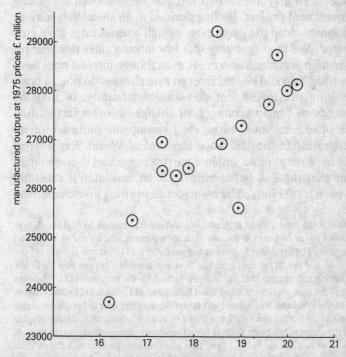

Figure 185b: Stocks and work in progress (value of year and stocks in manufacturing) at 1975 prices

may be no strong connection between changes in demand and changes in stocks.

### The rate of interest

Another variable that our theorizing suggested would be import-ant was the real rate of interest at which firms could borrow or lend money.[1] The time series for the rate of interest is shown in Figure 186.

If we compare Figure 186 with the changes in investment spending in Figure 185 we notice that investment is booming when interest rates are rising, which is the reverse of what our theorizing leads us to expect. The answer may be a practical one. We suggest that as investment planning takes time, businessmen may use current rates of interest when appraising an investment project. Having decided to go ahead they may be reluctant to drop the plans even though interest rates have now changed. We are suggesting that low interest rates *this* year re-sult in high investment *next* year even though interest rates have then risen. It could be that interest rate changes do not, in prac-tice, influence investment decisions significantly, or that the influence of demand changes, or changes in other factors (the state of expectations, costs, etc.) swamp the influence of in-terest rates. In the UK since the Second World War interest rates have only varied within a narrow range and thus we might argue that the link between investment and interest rates has not been tested fully. The coincidence of rising investment with

1. What is the 'real' rate of interest? We will use an example to explain. A firm borrows £100 at 10 per cent for one year for a project which finishes at the end of the year. The firm's net income at the year end is £110 – it can just pay off the £100 loan and the 10 per cent interest. Now assume that all prices rose by 10 per cent during the year so that net income earned by the firm was £121. The firm pays off the loan and interest and has a balance of £11, that is £121 – 100 – 100 = £11. In the first case, when there was no inflation, if the firm did not have to pay interest on the loan it would have had £10 after the loan of £100 was repaid. Thus the effect of the price rise has been the same as a zero-interest-rate loan. A 10 per cent rise has made the 10 per cent nominal interest rate into a zero 'real' interest rate. The difference of £1 between £11 and £10 benefit results from the 10 per cent inflation.

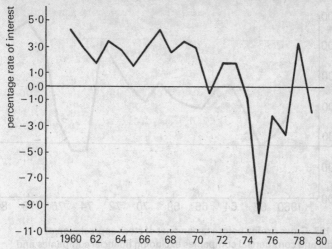

Figure 186 Perceived real rate of interest

rising interest rates may reflect the effect that an increased demand for investment funds has on the capital market.

More work needs to be done on testing the many possible hypotheses, some of which are suggested above, but this must wait on more advanced courses. An important implication of our doubts about the impact of interest rates on investment must be noted. If interest rates and investment are unlinked or only weakly linked then governments should not try and stimulate investment by changing the level of interest rates: a more effective policy would seem to lie in influencing investment indirectly by increasing consumer demand for final products.

## Company profits[2]

Since the role of profits was not discussed in the theoretical part of the chapter, why should it be introduced now? The reason is

2. 'Company' is almost identical with the 'firm' that we have discussed previously. The only reason that company profits and not firms' profits have been used is that the latter is not available and the former is known to be almost identically the same as firms' profits. We are using company profits as a proxy for firms' profits.

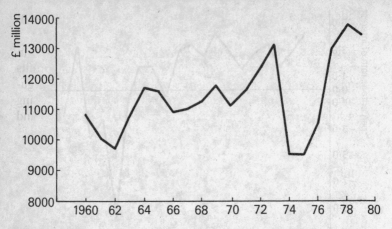

Figure 187  Gross profits before tax and net of stock appreciation of industrial and commercial companies excluding financial companies and institutions (at 1975 prices)

very practical. Recent econometric research has indicated that the inclusion of profits improves the predictive power of our theories. Let us try now to produce some theoretical foundation to support this observation. There are at least three reasons why changes in profits should be associated with changes in firms' investment in plant and machinery.

1 Firms may consider that rising (falling) profits indicate good (poor) future prospects and thus be encouraged to invest in more (less) plant and machinery. The effect here seems to be largely through the role of changes in profits in shaping optimism/pessimism.

2 If profits rise then firms can increase dividend payments, lend out the extra profits, or increase investment in plant and machinery. A manufacturing firm will probably have a 'mental block' against loaning money even if the return on the money was greatest in this use. Thus they are thrown back on more investment or higher dividends. Because of the way the Stock Exchange works, firms usually try and keep the growth of their

dividends steady, thus the outlet for increased profits is at least partly in increased investment.[3]

3 It may be that investment is strongly related to changes in consumer demand (as seems to be the case) and that profits happen to be high when demand is growing rapidly. This argument says that the causation is from rising demand to rising investment, and that rising profits are a result of rising demand but not a cause of rising investment.

## Summary

Investment has been regarded as the most volatile element of total spending and in this chapter we have set out what are believed to be the main influences upon investment. Spending upon plant and equipment – fixed capital formation – responds to a variety of influences, such as changes in the national income, the rate of interest and expectations. The accelerator theory attempts to link changes in investment with changes in the level of national income or consumers' spending. It is not a complete theory because it ignores such things as inventions but it does provide interesting insights. It is, however, important to note that investment consists of plant and equipment, inventories and housing and each of these categories may respond to different influences.

## Questions

1 Why is the distinction between the marginal product of capital and the marginal efficiency of investment so important?

2 How would you attempt to incorporate expectations into a theory of investment?

3. It is important to realize that retained profits are the major source of savings to finance firms' investment – the savings of households are a comparatively small source of saving for firms' investment. Additionally, approximately 11 per cent of company investment in the UK during 1967–77 was financed by Government capital grants.

# Chapter 37
# The Demand for Money[1]

People presumably hold money because it is useful to do so, because it represents a general command over goods and services. The existence of and the general acceptability of money, as a medium of exchange and a store of value, has permitted an enormous extension of the division of labour and a consequent increase in output. Indeed, so important and useful is money that even in the greatest of all inflations – often called hyper-inflation because of the exceptionally rapid rise in prices involved – people have still found it desirable to use money even though its value in terms of goods and services has been falling. For example, during the German inflation of the twenties, the Hungarian inflation of the forties, and the Latin American inflation of the fifties and sixties, people still continued to use a currency whose value depreciated with each second that ticked away. Of course, given a sufficiently high rate of inflation people will abandon a depreciating currency. But they will not necessarily resort to barter. Instead, they will adopt another stable currency. Such is the usefulness of money.

## Why do people use and hold money?

Money is apparently useful, but why? Answers were given in Chapter 5 and so we will merely recapitulate since our primary task is to examine more deeply the implications of the use of money.

1. Before reading this chapter it may be useful to re-read Chapter 5.

## Time and uncertainty

Most people are paid weekly or monthly but spend their income continuously so money is presumably held because of a lack of synchronization of payments and receipts. Such an answer could be wrong. If everyone possessed perfect foresight then all contracts concerning future payments and receipts could be arranged upon a given day. And from that day to eternity money need never be used. The techniques of transactions are therefore not sufficient to explain the existence of money. We could, and some do, contrive to lend out our money as soon as we get it, earn interest and recover our funds as and when we need them, but it is often inconvenient to do so. There are costs involved in investing money in small amounts and of reconverting it into cash as and when the latter is needed. There is also a loss of leisure in continually going to the market. Money cannot always or efficiently be disposed of in driblets.

The existence of money is incompatible with perfect foresight, but is compatible with our having a high degree of knowledge about the future. We may know with reasonable certainty the size of next year's national income, but we may not know the detailed manner of its attainment. Money will be held even when *general expectations* are likely to be fulfilled because it takes time to make up our minds about what we want to do.

We need not, of course, hold money since it yields no income. We could hold the alternative form of government debt – bonds. But if interest rates vary then the resale price of bonds will vary in the opposite direction. Hence, we may hold money because of the *specific uncertainty* attaching to the future price of apparently risk-free government bonds. We may also hold money because of specific uncertainty about the timing of future transactions.

## The quantity theory of money

Because it serves as a universal medium of exchange, money becomes the basic unit of account and this enables economists to speak of a general level of prices. In a barter economy, where money does not exist, the price of one good is measured in terms of the amount of another good for which it can be exchanged; that is, relative prices exist. However, it becomes impossible to speak of a general price level, or price level which is an average of two prices, unless one of the commodities is so generally acceptable that it becomes in fact money. Two sheep may exchange for one cow and it might therefore be possible to measure all prices in terms of cows or sheep, but that presupposes that cows or sheep act as money.

By virtue of its use as a unit of account there is established a link between money and the general level of prices. What is the nature of this link? This is the starting point of the quantity theory of money. In its simplest form the quantity theory postulates a strict proportionality between the quantity of money and the level of prices: if the quantity of money rises, for example, by 10 per cent, then the price level will rise by 10 per cent. It is doubtful if anyone holds the theory in this strict form and most economists would recognize that there are occasions when changes in the quantity of money exert no influence on prices and may in fact be accompanied by an increase in output. Perhaps the crucial feature of a quantity theory of money is, however, the amount of money that is required to effect transactions. Since the quantity theory emphasizes the role of money as a medium of exchange it points to the importance of the amount of money required to carry out exchanges. We might envisage a situation in which a single note could perform all the transactions desired by a community if it passed from hand to hand at a very high speed. There are of course limitations on the speed at which money can be turned over, such as the amount of time needed to decide whether to make a purchase, and it becomes imperative to know just how stable or unstable is the speed at which transactions are performed. This speed of turnover is known as the *transactions velocity of circulation of money* $(V_T)$.

We are now in a position to set out the quantity theory of money in the form in which it was formulated by the great American economist, Irving Fisher (1867–1947). In equation **1** $M$ refers to the stock of nominal money, $V_T$ is the transactions velocity of circulation of money, $P_T$ is the transactions price level and $T$ is the total number of transactions to be carried out.

$$MV_T = P_T T \qquad\qquad 1$$

## The stock of nominal money ($M$)

The definition of money becomes important in so far as any definition determines whether the stock of money can be regarded as something that is given (that is, determined from outside the equational system) or whether the stock of money is something that changes in response to changes in the other variables. Suppose, for example, that money is defined as a particular commodity, say gold, then the distribution of that amount of money available would move automatically in response to its price, and the amount of gold available in any one country would depend upon its international distribution and the relative price levels in different countries (this issue is taken up in Chapter 43, where the gold standard is discussed). On the other hand, money might consist of something, say paper, the amount of which was arbitrarily fixed by the state and which might bear no relationship to events elsewhere. The amount of money also needs to be defined carefully so as to make it clear whether it includes privately produced money such as that provided by the commercial banks or whether it is provided solely by the state, or whether the state has control over private production as well. For the sake of exposition, money will be taken to mean state notes and coin plus bank deposits. (These issues will be dealt with in the next chapter.)

## The total number of transactions ($T$)

This is determined by the amount of resources available to an economy, the efficiency with which they are used, and the degree of integration of the economy. On this last point it should be noted that in a highly developed market economy the number of transactions will be greater than in a centrally planned economy.

Once a monetary economy has been established and full employment exists it is usually assumed that changes in $M$ do not cause changes in $T$; that is, $M$ and $T$ are independent.

### The price level ($P_T$)

The price level is the average price at which all transactions are made, though other price levels, e.g. wholesale, or consumer goods, can and are sometimes used.

It follows from what has been said that $P_T T$ is the money value of all transactions, each transaction taking place at some average price represented by $P_T$.

### The transactions velocity of circulation ($V_T$)

This represents the crucial element in the theory since *if* it is allowed to vary passively in response to the movement of the other variables in the equation then that equation becomes an identity and therefore only a means of classifying material rather than a means of predicting responses. The Fisher version of quantity theory stresses spending and therefore $V$ *appears* to be determined by such institutional arrangements as payments systems (weekly, monthly, etc.) rather than acts of choice. Hence, the Fisher version of the quantity theory can be interpreted as emphasizing the need to hold money in order to finance transactions, given $P_T$, $T$ and $V_T$. This can be seen by rearranging equation **1** to yield the following expression for the demand for money ($M_D$),

$$M_D = M = \frac{P_T T}{V_T} \qquad\qquad \textbf{1a}$$

If $V$ and $T$ were assumed constant then equation **1a** would indicate that the demand for money was proportional to the transactions price level. On the other hand, and this is the more common form of the Fisher equation, equation **1a** can be rearranged so as to yield the following expression for the determination of the transactions (or general) price level,

$$P_T = \frac{M V_T}{T} \qquad\qquad \textbf{1b}$$

In this latter form it can easily be seen that if $V_T$ were assumed to be constant and $T$ were independent of $M$ then an increase in $M$ would cause a proportional change in $P_T$ and a decrease in $M$ would cause a proportional fall in $P_T$.

## The Cambridge approach

An alternative approach to the role of money in an economy does not ask what dictates the speed with which money changes hands but why people hold money when it obviously cannot be consumed like cakes and ale. This approach, the Cambridge approach, seeks to bring monetary theory into the fold of value theory by asking why is there a demand for money: why do people apparently 'consume' money?

$$M = M_D = P_R K R \qquad\qquad \textbf{2}$$

The Cambridge approach is summarized in equation **2**: $M$ is the stock of money, $P_R$ is the average price level of real output, $R$ is the national income on constant prices (that is, the real national income) and $K$ is the ratio of the money stock to income. Although $K$ might be regarded as the reciprocal of $V$ in the quantity theory there are several subtle differences between the two approaches which need to be recognized before any attempt is made to reconcile the two systems of thought.

1 The quantity theory stresses the spending of money whilst the Cambridge approach emphasizes that money is a temporary abode of purchasing power or store of value. It is therefore conceivable that the definition of $M$ in the two equations may differ: in the Cambridge approach $M$ might include antiques.

2 The quantity theory looks at payments schemes whereas the Cambridge approach has regard to utility, uncertainty and the costs and returns from holding money (see page 642).

3 The quantity approach concentrates on all transactions while the Cambridge approach narrows analysis down to income

transactions for which data are usually more available. The number of transactions, $T$, may in fact rise or fall because of a change in the number of hands through which goods pass before they reach the final consumer.

4 The quantity theory adopts a flow approach to monetary phenomena whereas the Cambridge theory is a stock approach.

Given the clarification of the differences in the two approaches we can now state the prediction from the Cambridge approach. If $K$ is a constant or a stable function, and $R$ is given then an increase in $M$ will lead to a proportional rise in $P_R$ and a fall in $M$ will lead to a proportional fall in $P_R$. If $R$ is not at the full employment level then an increase in $M$ could lead to an increase in $R$. If $M$ were constant and $R$ were given then $P_R$ could still change if people decided to hold more or less money; that is, if $K$ changed. This latter possibility arises in the Cambridge approach because the emphasis is upon the factors which determine the demand for money. Thus, in addition to the influence of institutional factors, allowance is made for variations in individuals' evaluation of the costs and benefits of making do with more or less money when there are changes in the rate of interest and price expectations.

### Money, the rate of interest, and the price level

The fact that money is used both as a medium of exchange and store of value means there is an automatic link between money and the rate of interest. Money is an asset which yields benefits in the present and in the future. Indeed it is the most accepted form of asset because it is the most acceptable medium of exchange. The term *liquidity* is used to signify the ease with which an asset can be converted at its full value into money. Money itself is obviously the most liquid of all assets and is held because of its liquidity. With money one can readily purchase goods and services in the present and in the future. However, if people have a positive rate of time preference (see Chapter 6), and prices are expected to remain unchanged, they will value the liquidity of a certain sum of money today more highly than the liquidity of the same sum in the future. To induce people to hold less money today – part with liquidity – they must be compensated for foregoing liquidity today in exchange for money in the future. The rate of interest is the reward for parting with this liquidity and in this sense the rate of interest can be regarded as the price of money.

The implications of the previous paragraph are profound. In the first place, the contention of that paragraph is that the rate of interest is not a purely real phenomenon. The demand for and supply of money enters into the determination of the rate of interest as well as the so-called real forces of productivity and thrift. How all these forces enter into the determination of the rate of interest and how disturbances produced by variations in them are resolved lies outside the scope of our analysis. At this stage we can only suggest that since most people obtain their incomes in the form of money they have a threefold decision as to what to do with that money. Either they can hold the money, spend it on consumption goods, or buy a new asset such as a machine (or a claim on a firm) or government bond.

The second implication of the establishment of a link between money and the rate of interest is that the inclusion of money into an economy simultaneously determines both the price level and the rate of interest. Earlier we saw that the use of money as a unit of account enabled a move from relative prices to the absolute price level. We have seen that the rate of interest is influenced by money, but to say that both the rate of interest and the price level are simultaneously determined once a money economy is established does jump over the difficult problem of 'how'. This we cannot pretend to answer at this stage of your career, though we can illustrate what the problem is. The demand for money approach says that the amount of money held will be governed by the benefits from, and costs of, holding money.[2]

2. These benefits and costs cannot be evaluated until current and future prices are known and these depend upon the existence of money. Here there is a chicken and egg problem which is usually dodged by assuming simultaneous determination of the amount of money and prices.

$$\frac{mu_1}{p_1} = \frac{mu_2}{p_2} = \dots = \frac{mu_n}{p_n} = \frac{mu_m}{r}. \qquad\qquad 3$$

Though we cannot say anything about how money is introduced into a barter economy we can indicate the effects of a further increase in the quantity of money into an existing money economy by using the Cambridge approach modified to include the rate of interest as in equation 3. Here we take the case of an individual who is maximizing his satisfaction by consuming various goods including money services, the price of money being the rate of interest. Suppose he receives an increase in the amount of money he holds and suppose initially prices of all goods are fixed, then the marginal utility of money ($mu_m$) will fall and this will result in disequilibrium. He will want to spend some of his money on goods so that the marginal utilities of other goods ($mu_1, \dots, mu_n$) will fall.

If all individuals in the community receive an increase in the quantity of money they are holding then we must allow for the possibility that because other goods are scarce then their prices ($p_1, \dots, p_n$) will rise as people spend more. However, for any given initial decline in the marginal utility of money, the more the prices of other goods rise the less the marginal utility of the same goods must fall before equilibrium is re-established. Similarly if a part of the increase in the supply of money is not held directly but is placed in the money market the short-term rate of interest will be reduced and some of the equilibrium adjustment will occur on the right-hand side of the equation.[3]

3. Equation 3 sums up the difference between the monetarists and the Keynesians. The former stress the direct effect of a change in the marginal utility of money on the demand for all other goods whereas the latter stress the indirect effect via the rate of interest. The former believe that small changes in the quantity of money held lead to relatively large changes in the marginal utility of money so that small changes in the rate of interest are insufficient to re-establish equilibrium. The monetary changes thus spill over directly into the goods market. The Keynesians, on the other hand, believe that large changes in the supply of money lead to only small changes in the marginal utility of money so that small changes in the rate of interest are sufficient to restore equilibrium, the adjustment coming wholly on the right hand side of the equation. The influence of money supply changes on the demand for goods is limited to the indirect effects of the rate-of-interest change.

## Price and output effects

The quantity theory of money emphasizes the existence of a link between the quantity of money and the price level, but if there are unemployed resources then there may be an output effect and no price effect. We can therefore distinguish three possible effects:

1 *Pure price effect* which is most likely to occur when there is full employment.

2 *Pure output effect*. Most likely when there are unemployed resources.

3 *Mixed price/output effect*. A probable occurrence because of the existence of *some* unemployed resources or because of price rigidities due to lack of information or monopolies. If there is an increase in money then unemployed resources can be employed but there may be bottlenecks in terms of scarce skilled labour and so some prices rise. If the money supply is reduced some prices may not fall but output may fall and result in unemployment.

## The optimum quantity of money

Discussion of the quantity theory suggests that there may be an *optimum quantity of money* which does not disturb relative prices nor cause changes in output but which acts as a mere lubricant to exchange. Such a quantity of money would keep the price level stable and would make the money rate of interest mirror the real rate of return on capital which governs businessmen's decisions to invest.[4] The stable price level need not be a constant price level, it could be rising or falling as long as it was fully anticipated. For example, the price level could be held constant and money wages could be increased as productivity increased or money wages could be held constant and prices

4. The money rate of interest would accurately reflect the real cost of borrowing; i.e. the money and real rates of interest would be identical. This ceases to be true when the price level is rising or falling. Under these conditions the money rate of interest may still reflect the true cost of borrowing if the behaviour of the price level is fully anticipated.

allowed to fall as productivity increased. In the former case the money rate of interest would be unaffected by the behaviour of the price level. In the latter case the money rate of interest would be lower than the real rate of interest by the anticipated rate of deflation.

But even if the monetary authorities did not produce arbitrary changes in the money supply, money need not be neutral. There could still be disturbances arising out of real forces – changes in tastes and inventions. The most that the monetary authorities could do would be to minimize the disturbances from the monetary side of the economy. However, there will still remain disturbances from the real side of the economy and some economists have sought to minimize the impact of real disturbances by changing the money supply whilst others have argued that the effects of real forces must be corrected directly by improving the mobility of resources.

### Inflation: a prefatory note

The quantity theory of money suggests that inflation – a situation in which the general level of prices is rising – is due to an increase in the quantity of money.[5] But the crucial question then arises as to what causes the quantity of money to increase? The quantity theory provides no answer to this question. Increases in the quantity of money can come about because governments choose to print more money rather than raise taxes or because trade unions are trying to alter the distribution of income. Changes in the quantity of money may be an essential ingredient of inflation but the money supply may be responding passively to political pressures.

### *The determinants of the demand for money*

In the preceding discussion of the quantity theory approaches

---

5. A clear distinction needs to be drawn between a once-and-for-all rise in the general level of prices and a situation in which prices are rising continuously. Only the latter can be described as inflation.

to the demand for money we introduced the rate of interest as one of the determinants of the demand for money and then went on to consider how it influences the velocity of circulation of money and hence the link between money and prices. While this possibility was recognized by exponents of the quantity theory of money it was given little weight before the publication of *The General Theory of Employment, Interest and Money* (Keynes, 1936). What Keynes did was to analyse the factors determining the demand for money more fully than previously and this, in turn, led him to argue that the demand for money could be highly variable. In particular, Keynes pointed to the possibility that in conditions of severe unemployment $V$ or $k$ could become so variable as to break the link between the quantity of money and the general level of prices. In this situation very large increases in the quantity of money would have such a negligible effect on the marginal utility of money that they would be held without any offsetting variations in the rate of interest or in the other determinants of the demand for money. To understand why this could occur we need to examine Keynes's theory of the demand for money.

Keynes divided the reasons for holding money into three categories or motives:

1 the transactions motive
2 the precautionary motive
3 the speculative motive

He labelled the first of these two motives the $M_{D1}$ demand and the third the $M_{D2}$ demand for money. The total demand for money was the product of these 'separate' demands.

$$M_{DT} = M_{D1} + M_{D2}$$

But note carefully: the equation should not be read as implying that people hold amounts of money in separate compartments with one container holding transactions holdings and another holding speculative holdings. Rather it should be taken as indicating the forces influencing total money holdings.

## The transactions demand for money

The transactions demand for money refers to the need for money to finance regular (predictable) transactions. For example, suppose an individual is paid weekly but buys consumer goods continuously during the week; then a saw-tooth pattern of income and expenditure will result, as is shown in Figure 188. Each Friday the individual would receive his wage of $OY$ out of which he would save $XY$ and he would continuously run down to zero the remainder of his money income by the following Friday. On average, therefore, his transactions money balance would be one-half of his planned expenditure and we can infer that if he is paid monthly (or at longer intervals) then his average transactions balance will be greater than when he is paid weekly.

The transactions demand for money will be determined by the frequency of payments and receipts, the general level of prices which measures the purchasing power of money and, although it was not emphasized by Keynes, the rate of interest which represents the opportunity cost of holding money as opposed to income yielding assets and which therefore serves to determine the distance $XY$ in Figure 188.

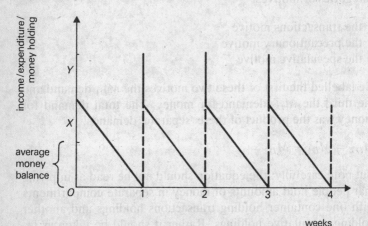

Figure 188  The transactions demand for money (regular income/payments flow)

## The precautionary motive for holding money

The precautionary motive, as developed by Keynes, also relates to the demand for money for transactions purposes but recognizes that both income and some payments may be unpredictable so that individuals may increase the size of their average money balances to allow for this uncertainty. It could, of course, be argued that individuals and firms might meet sudden and unforeseen demands for money by drawing on past savings or by borrowing. But withdrawal of savings involves a loss of interest and the incurring of other transactions costs. There are also costs involved in borrowing. Hence, there is a motive for holding precautionary balances. Subsequent refinements of the theory of the demand for money have developed the precautionary motive further by noting that it may even be sensible to hold 'barren' money in a portfolio of assets to offset some of the variability of return on interest yielding assets. This implies that the precautionary demand for money is interest sensitive. However, to simplify his analysis Keynes assumed that the transactions and precautionary demands for money were mainly determined by the level of income (expenditure) and allowed for the influence of the rate of interest on the demand for money through his speculative motive.

## The speculative motive

Because money can be held as a general store of value there is a link between the amount of money held and the rate of interest. Keynes gave special emphasis to this connection in his treatment of the speculative demand for money. He suggested that people would have in mind some normal or long-term rate of interest and that their holdings of money would be regulated by reference to any divergences between the actual rate of interest and the normal rate of interest, and at extremely low rates of interest he conjectured that people would prefer to hold money rather than safe income-bearing assets issued by governments. Two reasons for such behaviour should be noted. First, the cost of purchasing securities would place a floor on any downward movement of the rate of interest. Secondly, if the rate of interest was low and people expected it to return to its normal level then bond holders would incur a capital loss. For example, if the actual rate of interest was 2½ per cent then the holder of a £100 government bond would receive £2·50 but if the rate of interest rose to 5 per cent then the bond holder would only be able to sell his bond for £50 because anyone who wished to earn an annual income of £2·50 need only spend £50 to do so.

For irredeemable fixed-interest bearing securities, such as those issued by governments, with a nominal denomination of £100 the actual yield or interest rate is given by the formula:

$$\text{Actual yield} = \frac{£100}{\text{price of bond}} \times \text{fixed interest payment per year}$$

Such speculative behaviour gives rise to the possibility that at extremely low rates of interest the demand for speculative money balances with respect to the rate of interest becomes completely interest-elastic and changes in the quantity of money have no effects on the rate of interest. This state of affairs is called the *liquidity trap*.

The nature of the liquidity trap is shown in Figure 189 which combines Keynes's three motives to yield the total demand for money function.

In part a the transactions and precautionary demand are combined and represented by the curve $MD_1$. This curve is shown as being completely interest-inelastic so as to reflect Keynes's assumption that the two demands are mainly determined by the level of income. The position of the curve with respect to the vertical axis is determined by the level of income. As income increases the whole schedule moves out to the right. Part b illustrates the speculative demand and is drawn sloping downwards from left to right so as to indicate that, as the rate of interest falls, the amount of speculative money balances will rise. At some low interest rate, $r_1$ in the figure, the demand curve becomes infinitely elastic and the entire schedule is liable to shift as individuals collectively alter their expectations about what constitutes a 'normal' rate of interest.

The total demand for money schedule, part c, is the horizon-

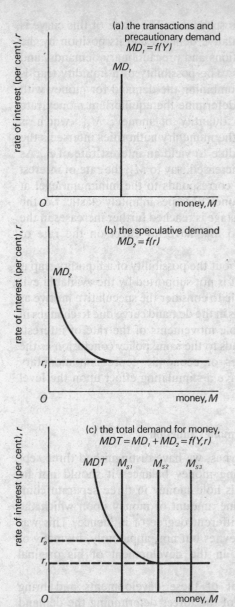

Figure 189 *The total demand for money and the liquidity trap.*

tal summation of the two schedules. The slope of this curve is determined by the speculative demand and its position by the level of income, transactions and precautionary demands, and the state of expectations. The possibility of a liquidity trap is illustrated in part c by combining the demand for money with the supply of money to determine the equilibrium money rate of interest. The initial quantity of money, $M_{s1}$, which is assumed to be given by the monetary authorities intersects the demand for money schedule to yield an interest rate of $r_0$. As the supply of money is increased, say to $M_2$, the rate of interest declines to $r_1$. This rate corresponds to the minimum level at which the demand for money becomes infinitely elastic; i.e. the liquidity trap. Once this stage is reached further increases in the supply of money, say to $M_3$, have no effect on the rate of interest.

Keynes's conjecture about the possibility of a liquidity trap is extremely interesting but is not supported by the available evidence. It seems preferable to consider the speculative motive as giving rise to violent shifts in the demand curve due to changes in opinion about the possible movements of the rate of interest. Such a state of affairs leads to the same policy conclusion as the liquidity trap – in times of economic depression monetary expansion may fail to have a stimulating effect upon the level of economic activity.

### The general demand for money function

Although, following Keynes, we have distinguished three separate motives for holding money balances it should not be imagined that individuals hold money in three separate compartments. They hold one amount of money upon which the three motives exert a different degree of influence. This was clearly recognized by Keynes but not, apparently, by many of those who participated in the development of his original contribution.

We can take account of these developments and bring together our discussion of the forces determining the demand for money by expressing the demand for money in terms of a generalized demand function. We can write

$$M_D = f(Y, r, r^e, P, P^e, T) \qquad\qquad 4$$

where $Y$ is income, $r$ is the money rate of interest, $r^e$ is the expected future rate of interest, $P$ is the price level, $P^e$ is the expected future price level and $T$ is the pattern of payments and receipts. A point to note about equation 4 is that $r - P^e$ measures the real rate of interest and is the relevant opportunity cost of holding money. Since the demand for money is for a real quantity of money, equation 4 can be expressed in real terms by dividing through by $P$,

$$\frac{M_D}{P} = f(\frac{Y}{P}, r, r^e, P^e, T) \qquad\qquad 4a$$

Now if an individual considers the future movement of prices and the rate of interest then he is also likely to consider the future movement of his income. Therefore, we can replace $Y$ in equation 4a by the discounted value of his income stream; that is, by wealth in real terms. This results in the following general demand for money function,

$$M_D = f(W, r, r^e, P^e, T) \qquad\qquad 5$$

What should now be appreciated is the intimate connections between the demand for money function, the consumption function, the investment function and the import function. For example, wealth appears in the demand for money function, the consumption function and the real value of money balances in the consumption function.

The generalized demand for money function provides a framework for estimating the actual demand for money function. Such estimates provide information on the sensitivity of the demand for money to changes in the variables on the right hand side of the equation and also the stability of the function. Both sorts of information are of vital importance in determining the nature, magnitude and efficiency of monetary policy.

## Monetary policy, the rate of interest and the level of income

Although we shall discuss monetary policy in more detail in Chapter 45 it is worthwhile observing how a change in the money supply can influence the level of economic activity via the rate of interest. This is revealed in Figure 190.

Part a which corresponds to c of the previous figure illustrates the determination of the equilibrium value of the money rate of interest. It differs from the previous example in that no liquidity trap is shown. The government increases the money supply from $M_{s1}$ to $M_{s2}$ so as to stimulate aggregate demand. If the demand curve remains unchanged then the rate of interest falls

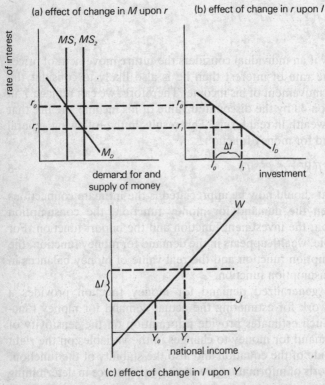

(a) effect of change in *M* upon *r*    (b) effect of change in *r* upon *I*

demand for and supply of money        investment

(c) effect of change in *I* upon *Y*

Figure 190

from $r_0$ to $r_1$. Assuming that the investment demand schedule is interest-elastic then there will be an increase in investment from $I_0$ to $I_1$. This is illustrated in b. Because the increase in investment is an injection it will lead via the multiplier process to an increase in the equilibrium level of income from $Y_0$ to $Y_1$. This is illustrated in part c.

Whether or not monetary policy is effective in this way depends upon a large number of factors, not all of which we have considered. For example, it is important to know whether there exists excess capacity in the economy which can be used to produce extra output and we need to know whether investment is sensitive to changes in the rate of interest.

## Summary

People use money to overcome some of the disadvantages associated with a barter economy. How much money they will choose to hold will depend upon such factors as the general level of prices, the rate of interest and expectations about their future movements. Changes in the quantity of money can, in the short run, cause changes in relative prices and output but in the long run monetary changes merely raise the general level of prices. Attempts to overcome disturbances arising from changes in the money supply should, however, recognize that changes in the value of money can occur through changes in the real forces, such as innovation and productivity.

## Questions

1 'It is nonsense to say that people have a demand to hold money. They simply hold money because they receive their wages on a Friday and the shops are closed until Monday.' Comment.

2 'People hold money because of a lack of synchronization of payments and receipts.' Comment.

3 'If people had perfect knowledge then they would not hold

money so the only reason for holding money must be the existence of uncertainty.' Discuss.

4 'It is ridiculous to hold non-interest-bearing money as long as interest is paid on other financial assets.' Discuss.

5 Which of the following statements gives the clearest statement of the functions of money?
(a) 'We can't afford to pay for the Channel Tunnel';
(b) 'I keep my money in stocks and shares';
(c) 'If I didn't keep cash in my pocket or a cheque book handy, I would always be running to the bank before I could buy a packet of cigarettes.'

6 'The theory of the demand for money is but a special case of the general theory of choice.' Comment.

7 In what circumstances will an increase in the quantity of money lead to an increase in (a) the general level of prices and (b) the volume of output?

8 What factors determine the velocity of circulation of money?

9 One of the most subtle concepts in economics is enshrined in the symbol $K$. What do you think $K$ expresses?

10 From the equation $MV_T = P_T T$ is it possible to deduce the value of $M$?

11 Express the effects of a change in the amount of money people possess in terms of the marginal utility approach.

12 What is meant by liquidity?

13 What is meant by the liquidity trap?

14 How would the existence of a liquidity trap influence the effectiveness of monetary policy?

15 In what ways, other than through the rate of interest, can an expansionary monetary policy influence the level of economic activity?

16 'I spend every penny I get, therefore my average money balance is zero.' Discuss.

17 'My saving depends upon the rate of interest but not my money holdings.' Discuss.

18 With reference to equation **5** in this chapter how would you expect the demand for money to vary in response to changes in each of the variables on the right hand side of the equation taken separately?

# Chapter 38
# The Supply of Money

The gist of the previous chapter was that people preferred to live in a monetary economy rather than a barter economy because there were advantages attaching to the use of money. These advantages were summarized under the headings of economizing on time and coping with uncertainty. What we then went on to examine was the effects of a change in the nominal amount of money (under the assumption that there was a stable demand for money relationship). We indicated that an increase in the nominal amount of money possessed by people would mean an imbalance in their holdings of goods and their portfolio holdings of money and other financial assets, and so they would attempt to increase their expenditure on goods and other financial assets in order to re-establish the desired ratio between them and their holdings of money. This effect of an increase in the nominal amount of money on people's behaviour is called the *real balance effect* because with an unchanged price level, people find that the real value of their money holdings increases as a result of the increase in the nominal quantity of money in circulation.[1] The next step was to inquire what happened to prices and output when the real value of the quantity of money differed from the desired quantity. If all resources were fully

1. The real balance effect was first evolved for a symmetrical case. Suppose people's money holdings remain constant while all prices fall. Then the real value of money holdings will rise and people will start spending. Our example is the case where prices do not change but the nominal amount of money does.

employed then we predicted that the price level would rise in proportion to the increase in the nominal quantity of money. This is the strong prediction of the quantity theory and is more likely to hold true in the long run than in the short run, since economies rarely operate at a level at which output is rigidly fixed in the short run. The weaker prediction, that prices will rise, allows for the possibility that output may also expand, at least in the short run. If, on the other hand, some resources were initially idle then output would increase in the short run and remain at the higher level even in the long run. In this case the effect on prices is less both in the short run and the long run.

If such changes in the nominal quantity of money can have temporary and permanent effects on output and prices, some of which may be destabilizing, then it would seem desirable to control the nominal quantity of money in circulation. The nominal quantity of money needs to increase over time as national income grows because, as we saw in the previous chapter, the velocity of circulation of money cannot be speeded up indefinitely (the interest elasticity of the demand for money is not infinite), and the increase should be such that it contributes to economic stability. But before we examine the production of money we need to define clearly the nature of the money commodity. This is an issue we have so far evaded. For in Chapter 37 we defined money as that which was generally acceptable as a medium of exchange and in settlement of debts: that was a *generic definition of money*. If everything is acceptable as money then we are in a barter world. Casual observation suggests that not everything is acceptable as money, so in the previous chapter we introduced a *specific* or *operational definition* of money. We defined money as state notes and coins plus commercial bank deposits. We did not advance any arguments for this definition: this we must now do.

### The definition of money

Figure 191 provides some assistance both to arriving at a specific definition of money and understanding the forms that money has taken over time

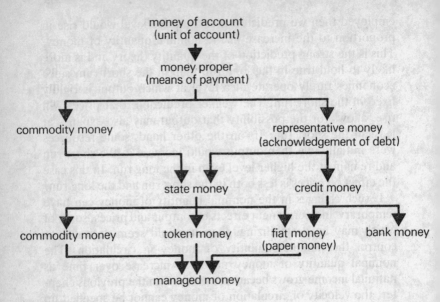

Figure 191 Based on a diagram in Keynes (1971b).

## Money of account

The intrinsic qualities of the different kinds of money, both spatially and over time, have little direct bearing on the question of the appropriate operational or specific definition of money. The starting point for an operational definition of money is in terms of its essential properties, namely that money is that which serves as a unit of account and as a means of payment. (A medium of exchange is not necessarily a means of payment. A credit card can be used as a medium of exchange, but is it a means of payment?) Once a monetary economy has been established there is a *money of account* which provides a *unit of account* in terms of which all transactions are valued or measured. Although this money of account need not be the actual money used in transactions (it may be abstract rather than concrete) the desire for efficiency in monetary transactions usually leads to the money of account also serving as *money proper* (the means of payment).

## Money proper

The actual money used in transactions serves as a medium of exchange and as a means of payment. It can either take the form of *commodity money* or *representative money* or a combination of the two. Today commodity moneys have been replaced in virtually all countries by representative money.

## Commodity money

Perhaps the earliest and simplest form of money was some commodity which had an alternative use but was sufficiently scarce that there was no possibility of frequent and large changes in its supply disrupting trade.[2] Gold has been perhaps the outstanding species of this large genus of commodity moneys. Coinage can be regarded as a means of ensuring homogeneity, divisibility and portability of commodity moneys though it was not essential to their development – think of the old prospectors settling debts with gold dust.

## Representative money

Commodity money is expensive to produce, using time and resources which might be put to alternative uses. And, as in all human activity, there has been a conscious attempt to reduce the costs of producing money, to release as many resources as possible from producing that which 'cannot be eaten, slept on or driven in'. So we have had the emergence of *representative moneys* of which paper is the most outstanding example. These moneys – paper notes and token coins – have a face value which is distinct from the intrinsic value of the materials from which they are made. Thus, the face value of a paper note is greater than its production cost, and in terms of the real resource cost (opportunity cost) of providing a nation's currency, society as a whole benefits from the substitution of low resource cost money

2. For an informative and somewhat unusual account of the development of a commodity money satisfying these requirements see Radford (1945).

commodities for high resource cost money commodities. Provided the monetary authorities exercise strict control over the production of 'paper' money, so as to avoid violent fluctuations in its exchange value or purchasing power – inflation and deflation – the resultant welfare gains accrue to society as a whole, not only at the time the substitution is made but throughout all subsequent time periods. Consequently, virtually all countries today have a *fiat* national currency based on paper notes rather than one based on precious metals. Hence the disappearance of gold, at least off the stage if not out of the theatre, from its star role as a monetary commodity.

Since all countries, other than those producing gold, would benefit from the introduction of a unified world paper currency and the final exclusion of gold from monetary affairs, one of the intriguing questions in international monetary economics is: why do countries still hold back from taking this step? There are several reasons, political as well as economic, but one of the major factors is the problem of deciding how to distribute the resultant welfare gains amongst the participating countries.

## Managed money

Commodity money has a value in terms of its alternative use whilst representative money appears to have none. The Bank of England one pound note bears the inscription 'I promise to pay the Bearer on Demand the sum of One Pound', a vestige of the times when such notes were convertible into gold of a specified amount. Nowadays the promise is empty, and all that the bearer can hope to obtain is perhaps a cleaner note. (Even this type of conversion is discouraged today by the Bank of England in an attempt to reduce the costs of maintaining the note issue in circulation.) Nevertheless there are occasions when the state may undertake to manage the production of fiat money in such a way as to ensure a determinate value of the fiat money in terms of some objective standard. Thus, the state may allow inconvertible fiat money to circulate internally whilst agreeing to its conversion at a fixed rate of exchange externally into other representative moneys or commodity moneys. This aspect of monetary management will, however, be ignored in this chapter and will be considered later in the context of international monetary relations (Chapter 43).

*Credit money*

We have established that state money proper (paper notes and coins) is a representative money (it represents an acknowledgement of debt by the state) and is thus also a form of *credit money*. Bank money is another form of credit money, since it represents an acknowledgement of debt on the part of the banks to their customers which the public apparently regard as equivalent to state money.

State-issued credit money serves as money proper because of the legal authority of the state – it determines the form of legal tender currency. As this legal authority does not apply to privately-issued acknowledgements of debt we come back to the question of why acknowledgements of debt issued by the banks (their deposits) serve as money proper while other privately-issued acknowledgements of debt do not.

Before answering this question we need to clarify what we mean by referring to bank deposits as money. We do not mean that bank deposits merely replace an equivalent amount of state money, albeit in a possibly more convenient form, as this would be a change of form lacking in substance. The composition of the money supply would be altered, bank deposits would re-place notes and coins, but the total value of the money supply would still be equal to that issued in the form of state money. We are concerned with the much more interesting case in which bank deposits serve not only as money proper, equivalent in all but form to state money, but are also additional to state money. Hence the total money supply is the sum of notes and coins in circulation with the public plus the value of their bank deposits; more accurately, those deposits transferable by cheque, i.e. current account deposits. For this implies that the commercial banks can in some way 'create' money and raises a second ques-tion: what limits the ability of the commercial banks to create money? Important as this question is, we must defer answering it until we have dealt with the earlier question of why bank deposits serve as money proper, since it turns out that the answer to the latter provides the key to the former.

To understand why bank deposits represent a form of money proper it is helpful to go back to the time when bank money did not exist. In the seventeenth century the goldsmiths, the forerunners of the modern commercial banks, began acting as safekeepers for people's gold bullion and coins. At some stage the receipts (acknowledgement of debt) which they issued against the deposits of gold began to circulate as a means of payment without the need for the gold deposits they represented actually to leave the vaults of the goldsmiths. Why? First, because the receipts were much more convenient to use than gold, and also much safer to carry. Secondly, because they were as good as gold provided the public had sufficient confidence in the ability of the goldsmiths to repay them on demand. This is the key to the next stage of development and the evolution of modern bank money.

The goldsmiths soon realized that they could grant credit, not by lending out part of the gold deposited with them, but by issuing additional receipts against themselves as the public regarded the receipts as equivalent to gold. Hence the goldsmiths could create money (credit money). As long as they did not over-issue such receipts, so that they were always able to pay out gold to those who demanded it, they were able to maintain the public's confidence in their liquidity and thus use their credit-granting ability to make an additional profit.

From this development the receipts evolved into bank notes which came to serve alongside state money as a generally accepted means of payment. *Bank money* has thus come to be sharply distinguished from other privately issued acknowledgements of debt and we have now a situation where the state has, by historical development rather than design, delegated the production of part of the nominal money supply to the commercial banks.

Although the commercial banks no longer issue their own bank notes and their reserves are held, in part, in the form of state money rather than in gold, their deposits serve as money because the public have confidence in the ability of the banks to convert their deposits into state money on demand. But given such confidence in the banks' liquidity the public have no reason to exercise this right to its full and hence today's commercial banks, like their predecessors the goldsmiths, can create credit in the form of additional bank deposits.

Because bank money represents by far the largest part of the total money supply in modern economies, it is important to understand fully why their deposits serve as money proper. Accordingly it is worth repeating the explanation in a different manner as follows:

1 Money is that which is usually acceptable as a medium of exchange and as a means of settling debts.

2 Privately-issued acknowledgements of debt will serve as money, alongside state money, provided they are freely transferrable *and* the general public have confidence in the ability of the issuers to convert their debts into state (legal tender) money on demand.

3 Current account commercial bank deposits satisfy these, and other, requirements and thus serve as money proper.

4 The deposits of other financial institutions do not serve as money because they either lack the required *general acceptability* as a means of payment and/or are not freely transferrable.

5 In choosing to regard commercial bank deposits as money, and holding them in preference to currency, the public enable the commercial banks to 'create' bank credit money.

6 All financial institutions have the potential to create credit money but only the commercial banks do so. The banks' ability to create credit money has been made legitimate by the public's willingness to accept the banks' deposit liabilities as money over a long historical period.

## The creation of bank credit money

Having established why bank deposits are money and that the commercial banks can in some sense 'create' credit money, we must next examine the process whereby they are created so as to answer the question: what factors limit the supply of bank credit money?

Historically, the central problem of money supply has been how to control the supply of credit money: that is, how to ensure that there is some link between state money and the amount of credit money. Bankers have frequently argued that there is no control problem since they only lend what is first deposited with them, i.e. that they cannot 'create' credit. This is the *cloakroom theory of banking* whereby banks are but 'cloakrooms' supplying receipts for the state money deposited with them. We have argued, however, that the banks can create credit by issuing receipts in excess of their holdings of state money. The control problem is thus tied up with the process of credit granting by the banks. If it turns out that the granting of credit also leads to the creation of credit then the banks and their critics may both be right and there is a money supply control problem.

The figures in Table 46 do, in fact, illustrate the magnitude of the 'money supply problem'. For whilst the supply of notes in circulation with the public is clearly under the direct control of the state, the supply of bank credit money, which is much greater, would appear to be determined by private producers. Is it possible therefore for the state to control bank credit money?

## Fractional reserve banking

Given public confidence in the moneyness of commercial bank deposits, and consequently their willingness to hold part of their desired money holdings in the form of bank deposits, the banks have no need to hold one hundred per cent reserves of state money to match their deposit liabilities. When a bank operates with less than one hundred per cent reserve backing it is referred to as a *fractional reserve bank*.

Imagine a banking system in which all the banks are required by law to hold one hundred per cent reserves of 'high-powered money' (another term for state money, the significance of which will become apparent shortly) against deposits. In such a world the banks can grant credit if they hold excess reserves but they cannot create credit money. More correctly, their ability to 'create' credit money as an alternative to state money is identically equal to their total holdings of high-powered money. Net credit money creation is thus impossible in a one hundred per cent reserve banking system, but in a system in which banks are not compelled to hold one hundred per cent reserves the net production of credit money becomes possible. All that is required for production to occur is that the public should not be able to distinguish, or should not choose to distinguish, between credit money backed by reserves of state money and credit money not backed by such reserves. As we have already seen, all that this requires is general acceptance of bank deposits as a medium of exchange.

In normal circumstances all current account bank deposits are accepted on an equal basis. It is the individual's credit worthiness, and not that of the bank, which is questioned. As long as each holder of bank deposits believes his credit balance is readily convertible into currency (high-powered money) all will be well. Given, therefore, the public's acceptance of bank credit money, and the desire of the banks to make profits, we can determine the amount of bank credit money which can be created since its production (the volume of bank deposits) depends upon the amount of high-powered money, the public's relative preference for bank deposits and the bank's cash reserve ratio.

*Public confidence in the 'moneyness' of bank deposits is the foundation stone of fractional reserve banking and hence of the 'creation' of bank credit money.*

### Credit money creation: some arithmetic

Let us now examine the process of producing bank credit money in some detail. We begin by emphasizing, because it is often not recognized, that commercial banks and other financial intermediaries are private firms intent on making profits.

Commercial banks produce and sell many financial services as well as accepting currency deposits and granting loans. Moreover, since their profits are linked to the full range of the services they sell and these are linked to the level of their deposits, they have an obvious interest in seeing their deposits grow by as much as possible.

Next, we make the simplifying assumption that there is only one banking firm (it could, of course, have many branches). This enables us to ignore the additional complexities which occur when there are movements of high-powered money between different banking firms. Simplicity is possible because the final result of the analysis will be the same regardless of the number of banks, provided each expands its deposits at the same rate in response to an increase in its holdings of high-powered money and provided they work to the same cash reserve ratio.

Now the public hold high-powered money (hereafter referred to as the public's cash holding) and bank deposits. In the previous chapter we analysed their total demand for money in terms of their desire to hold a portfolio of goods, services and assets which would yield maximum satisfaction (see equation 3 on page 642). People will be holding cash because it is the most liquid (the most marketable) of all assets. They will hold bank money because although it yields no interest, it offers security against loss and provides access to some of the financial services offered by banks. Over time the ratio of deposits to cash in each individual's portfolio will vary as deposits become more or less attractive relative to cash and all other goods. In the short run this ratio will tend to be constant. This ratio is the *public's cash-deposit ratio* and we shall use the symbol $\alpha$ to denote it.

We can analyse the commercial banks' demand for cash (high-powered money) in similar fashion to the public's demand for cash. The banks' desire for profit leads them to attempt to minimize their holdings of non-income-yielding cash. Profit also depends on staying in business and this requires the maintenance of the public's confidence in their solvency, in their ability to meet all demands for cash. The

**Table 46** Composition of the UK money stock, 1970–1980

| Year | Notes and coins in circulation with public, ($C_p$). mid December quarter figure £m 1 | Bank deposits: sterling current account end fourth quarter £m 2 | Bank deposits: sterling time deposit accounts end fourth quarter £m 3 | Money* stock: sterling $M_1$ end fourth quarter £m 4 | Money* stock: sterling $M_3$ end fourth quarter £m 5 | Notes and coins held by banks, ($C_B$) mid December figure £m 6 | Public's currency/ bank deposit ratio. $C_p/D$ 7 | Banks' currency/ bank deposit ratio $Cb/D$ 8 |
|---|---|---|---|---|---|---|---|---|
| 1970 | 3237 | 6315 | 8031 | 9635 | 17 666 | 707 | 0·225 | 0·049 |
| 1971 | 3470 | 7499 | 9023 | 11 088 | 20 111 | 665 | 0·210 | 0·040 |
| 1972 | 4006 | 8578 | 12 786 | 12 657 | 25 443 | 736 | 0·188 | 0·034† |
| 1973 | 4369 | 8926 | 18 743 | 13 303 | 32 046 | 806 | 0·158 | 0·029 |
| 1974 | 5068 | 9654 | 20 561 | 14 739 | 35 300 | 872 | 0·168 | 0·028 |
| 1975 | 5730 | 11 579 | 20 112 | 17 483 | 37 595 | 862 | 0·181 | 0·027 |
| 1976 | 6531 | 12 753 | 21 693 | 19 467 | 41 160 | 814 | 0·190 | 0·023 |
| 1977 | 7581 | 15 960 | 21 631 | 23 659 | 45 290 | 952 | 0·202 | 0·025 |
| 1978 | 8731 | 18 631 | 24 527 | 27 535 | 52 062 | 967 | 0·202 | 0·022 |
| 1979 | 9714 | 20 345 | 28 631 | 30 046 | 58 677 | 996 | 0·198 | 0·020 |
| 1980 | 10 255 | 20 805 | 38 361 | 31 230 | 69 591 | 1043 | 0·173 | 0·017 |

* Money Stock, $M$ = Col 1 + Col 2. Money Stock, $M_3 = M_1$ + Col 3.
† New system of monetary control introduced: competition and credit control. Commercial banks' cash reserve ratio reduced.
Source: Bank of England, *Quarterly Bulletin*, various issues

**Table 47** Relationship between currency outstanding (high-powered money) and the stock of money in the UK, 1963–1980

|  | Notes and coins outstanding, mid December figure £m | Ratio of notes and coins outstanding to $M_1$ money stock | Ratio of notes and coins outstanding to sterling $M_3$ money stock |
|---|---|---|---|
| 1963 | 2766 | 0·38 | 0·25 |
| 64 | 2969 | 0·40 | 0·25 |
| 65 | 3146 | 0·41 | 0·25 |
| 66 | 3261 | 0·43 | 0·25 |
| 67 | 3389 | 0·41 | 0·24 |
| 68 | 3524 | 0·41 | 0·23 |
| 69 | 3708 | 0·43 | 0·23 |
| 1970 | 3944 | 0·41 | 0·22 |
| 71 | 4135 | 0·37 | 0·21 |
| 72 | 4742 | 0·37 | 0·19* |
| 73 | 5175 | 0·39 | 0·16 |
| 74 | 5940 | 0·40 | 0·17 |
| 75 | 6592 | 0·38 | 0·18 |
| 76 | 7345 | 0·38 | 0·18 |
| 77 | 8533 | 0·36 | 0·19 |
| 78 | 9698 | 0·35 | 0·19 |
| 79 | 10 710 | 0·36 | 0·18 |
| 1980 | 11 298 | 0·36 | 0·16 |

* New system of monetary control introduced: competition and credit control. Commercial banks' cash reserve ratio reduced.
Source: Bank of England, *Quarterly Bulletin*

banks could be sure of solvency by always holding one hundred per cent reserves. This need not make banking unprofitable because banks would still be able to charge for their other services, but it would eliminate the extra profit to be earned from switching out of cash into other assets. Tables 46 and 47 show that banks do, in fact, manage with significantly less than one hundred per cent reserves: the question is, what determines their reserve ratio?

As long as the public believe in the 'moneyness' of bank deposits the banks will find that the calls for cash constitute only a small fraction of their total deposit liabilities. For most of the time their customers are content to receive and make payments with claims to bank deposits (cheques). In a bank credit money system credit transfers replace cash in many exchange transactions. Thus public usage enables the banks to operate with a *fractional cash reserve holding*. The actual cash reserve ratio will be determined by the banks reducing their cash holdings to the point where they feel they hold just enough cash to meet the normal volume of cash withdrawals at any point of time. Thus the banks' cash ratio may not be constant but vary over time in response to seasonal variations in the demand for cash. Because the actual level of cash withdrawal cannot be forecast with precision the banks are likely to hold secondary reserves in the form of highly liquid assets, i.e. financial assets which yield some return but which, because of their marketability, can be easily converted into cash. In practice, to ensure that the public do not lose confidence in the solvency of banks, the monetary authorities usually set a lower limit to the banks' cash reserve ratio by prescribing a minimum required cash reserve ratio. This ratio, or the one actually adopted by the banks if it is higher, gives us the banks' cash reserve ratio and we shall use the symbol $\beta$ to denote it.

The relationship between fractional reserve banking and the creation of bank credit money (deposit expansion) by banks (in the example represented by a single banking firm) is illustrated in Table 48. For the purpose of the example the public's cash-deposit ratio ($\alpha$) is assumed to be $0 \cdot 5$ and the minimum cash-deposit ratio (reserve ratio) of the bank ($\beta$) to be $0 \cdot 25$. The total supply of cash (high-powered money) in the economy is £200.

The first stage shows the public to be in equilibrium with regard to their desired cash-deposit holdings, but the bank is in disequilibrium because with a desired cash-reserve ratio of $0 \cdot 25$ it is holding excess cash. At this stage the bank's excess cash amounts to £100 and it will seek to convert this excess holding into an income yielding form by buying £100 worth of securities. To pay for the securities the bank will issue cheques drawn against itself so that when the sellers present these to the bank its deposit liabilities will decline by £100 and its assets by £100 of

**Table 48** The process of bank deposit expansion (bank credit money creation)

| Stage | Commercial bank Assets[1] (£) | Liabilities (deposits) (£) | Public Cash holdings (£) |
|---|---|---|---|
| 1 | 133 cash | 133 | 67 |
| 2 | 133 cash<br>100 securities | 233 | 67 |
| 3 | 100 cash<br>100 securities | 200 | 100 |
| 4 | 100 cash<br>150 securities | 250 | 100 |
| 5 | 83 cash<br>150 securities | 233 | 117 |
| 6 | 83 cash<br>173 securities | 258 | 125 |
| 7 | 75 cash<br>175 securities | 250 | 125 |
| ⋮ | ⋮ | ⋮ | ⋮ |
| n | 67 cash<br>200 securities | 267 | 133 |

1. For the purpose of this example, securities refer to all income-yielding assets including loans, held instead of cash. Figures do not add up exactly because of rounding.

The table is deliberately extended over a fairly large number of stages so as to make as clear as possible the process of bank credit money creation.

cash. This is what the bank expects but it need not happen. Suppose the public deposit the cheques with the bank and add the

£100 to their deposits. This is shown as stage 2. The bank's assets have grown by the addition of £100 worth of securities and its liabilities (its deposits) have grown by the same amount.

If the sellers of the securities withdrew the proceeds of their sales in full in the form of cash the bank would achieve its desired equilibrium. The composition of its assets would have altered but its total liabilities (deposits) would have remained the same. If, however, the bank achieved equilibrium in this way the public would necessarily be in disequilibrium with respect to their desired cash-deposit holdings. Unless they are to behave irrationally the public will not place themselves in a disequilibrium position by withdrawing the whole of their additional deposits in the form of cash. Consequently, the bank cannot dispose of its excess cash as intended. The process of adjustment will thus continue because the public will only withdraw as much cash as they require to maintain their desired cash-deposit holdings and the bank will be left with excess cash holdings *and* an increase in its deposit liabilities.

At the end of stage 2 the public must be in disequilibrium since their deposits have risen by £100 to £233·3, whilst their cash holdings have remained at £66·6. They will re-establish an equilibrium cash ratio by withdrawing cash from the bank. This decreases their deposit balances and increases their cash balances. Stage 3 depicts the public in equilibrium with deposits of £200 and cash balances of £100. Things are different for the bank. Stage 3 shows the bank to have free reserves of £50. And in stage 4 we see the bank attempting to reach equilibrium again by buying a further £50 of securities from the public. This increases the bank's portfolio of securities and deposits again, but throws the public into disequilibrium once more.

The growth of deposits and the persistence of free reserves at the bank are reconciled by the recognition of the public's willingness to hold additional deposits as deposits and not as cash. The moneyness of deposits means that while people will always withdraw cash from the bank to maintain their cash-deposit ratio they will not withdraw cash merely because their bank balance has increased. This is why the bank finds itself with excess cash even after it has made a purchase from the public equal in value to its free cash holding. The process only stops when both the public and the bank are in equilibrium. This is shown in the final line of Table 48. Total deposits stand at £267 and the bank's cash holding stands at one-quarter of this amount, namely, £67, and the public's cash holding is one half of the value of the deposits, namely, £133. The sum of the two cash holdings is £200 which is the amount of cash in the economy. Initially the total money supply was £200 (£133 with the public and the £67 with the banks). After the multiple expansion of bank deposits the total money supply is £400 (£267 in the form of bank credit money (deposits) and £133 in the form of cash held by the public).

In this example, the ability of the bank to create credit money is determined, given the public's acceptance of bank deposits as money, by the public's demand for cash as opposed to bank credit money (their cash-deposit ratio), the bank's demand for cash as a reserve asset (its cash-deposit ratio) and the total amount of cash in the economy. The role of cash in determining the total money supply such that the latter is a fixed multiple of the former (with a value of 2 in our example) explains why it is given the alternative, more descriptive, title of 'high-powered money'.

The above arithmetical example of bank deposit expansion (credit money creation) also serves to explain how the portfolio behaviour of the banks leads to the 'creation' of deposits, and hence money, despite the fact that they only lend or purchase securities with a part of the cash which they already hold against deposits.

Banks do not directly perceive that their actions lead to the creation of additional deposits because they expect them to result in an equivalent reduction in their cash holdings. But in practice they only experience a small reserve loss and thus find their deposits have increased as the public redeposit what is to them an excess cash holding. Given the use of cheques to transfer deposits between the banks and the public, the cash in question need not actually leave the banks, as is shown in our example.

## Credit money creation: some algebra

The determinants of the supply of bank credit money (the process of deposit expansion) can now be set down algebraically:

$c$ = total amount of cash (high-powered money)
$Cp$ = cash held by public
$Cb$ = cash held by commercial banks (cash reserves)
$C = Cp + Cb$
$D$ = total bank deposits (subject to cheque)
$\alpha = Cp/D$ = public's cash-deposit ratio
$\beta = Cb/D$ = banks' cash-deposit ratio (reserve ratio)

then $C = \alpha D + \beta D$

$$= D(\alpha + \beta)$$

therefore $D = \dfrac{C}{(\alpha + \beta)} = \dfrac{1}{(\alpha + \beta)} C$      **1**

and $\Delta D = \dfrac{\Delta C}{(\alpha + \beta)} = \dfrac{1}{(\alpha + \beta)} \Delta C$      **2**

Equation **1** indicates that the total amount of credit creation depends upon the total amount of cash and the cash-deposit ratios of the public and the banks. The expression $\dfrac{1}{(\alpha + \beta)}$ is the *bank credit multiplier* relationship and determines the numerical value of the volume of bank deposits generated by a given quantity of high-powered money in the economy. For normal values of $\alpha$ and $\beta$ the multiplier is greater than unity (it has a value of 1·33 in our example) but less than infinite. As with the income multiplier (Chapter 35) leakages from the multiplier process, in this case corresponding to the withdrawal of cash by the public and the banks at each round of the deposit expansion sequence, serve to ensure that the multiplier process converges to a finite limit.

Equation **1** can be used to verify the final line of the numerical example of credit creation with $C$ = £200. Substituting these values into equation **1** yields:

$$D = \frac{200}{(\frac{1}{2} + \frac{1}{4})} = \frac{200}{\frac{3}{4}}$$

$$= £266\cdot6 = £267 \text{ (if we round up again)}$$

This answer accords with the final line of the table in our previous example.

The bank credit multiplier is an important relationship as it allows us to answer the question: can the state control the production of bank credit money? Clearly it can since it directly controls the amount of high-powered money in the economy and this in turn, by the bank credit multiplier, determines the volume of bank deposits. Hence, by controlling the quantity of high-powered money the state can control the total money supply.

### The credit multiplier: some important qualifications

In practice the bank credit multiplier relationship is far more complex than the above example suggests. First, because the supply of high-powered money is never under the absolute control of the monetary authorities but varies positively with the demand for it, more so in an 'open' trading economy than in a 'closed' economy. Secondly, the banks' cash-deposit, or cash-reserve ratio, is not necessarily constant and as it varies so will the value of the bank credit multiplier. Even if the monetary authorities (the central bank) prescribe a minimum cash-reserve ratio the problem still exists. A legally required cash-reserve ratio only establishes a lower limit to the banks' cash-deposit ratio since the banks can choose to hold reserves in excess of the minimum required. Whether or not the banks hold such reserves, and hence whether or not in this situation their cash-reserve ratio is variable, depends upon their portfolio behaviour. But given that it is a choice variable it is obviously inappropriate to treat it as fixed in the multiplier relationship. Instead, in the extended version of the credit multiplier the fixed co-efficient $\beta$ is replaced by an expression which describes the determination of $\beta$ as a result of the bank's portfolio behaviour.

Finally, similar considerations apply to the public's cash-deposit ratio. The public is not faced with a simple choice between bank deposits and cash but a much wider one encompassing cash, bank deposits (current and time) and the diverse financial assets offered by the many other financial institutions found in modern economies. Moreover, the choice problem is not constant since an important feature of the development of mature economies is financial evolution, the expansion of the range of financial institutions and the assets they offer to the public. Thus the public's cash-deposit ratio, $\alpha$, is not fixed but varies, both in the short run and over time, as they alter the composition of their asset portfolios in response to changes in tastes, wealth and the relative yields on assets. Consequently, as with $\beta$, it is inappropriate to treat it as fixed. In the extended version of the credit multiplier relationship it is replaced by a detailed expression which describes the public's portfolio behaviour in determining the amounts of cash and bank deposits in their overall portfolio of assets.

Allowance for these factors does not rob the bank credit multiplier relationship of its predictive powers. Provided the monetary authorities can exercise control over the amount of high-powered money in the economy, albeit less than perfect, and provided the behavioural relationships describing the determination of $\alpha$ and $\beta$ are well defined, and stable functions of a small number of variables, there exists a predictable and measurable relationship between high-powered money and bank deposits. From the point of view of monetary control the predictability and stability of relationships is far more important than their complexity.

Some economists have challenged this view on the grounds that the spectrum of liquid assets available to the public, which at one end of the spectrum are so liquid as to be close substitutes for cash, robs the concept of money and hence monetary policy, of any practical significance. They argue that small changes in the yields on liquid assets are sufficient to induce the public, and the banks, to hold more or less cash in their portfolio of assets. This in turn means that policy-induced changes in the supply of money are neutral in their impact on economic activity because small interest rate changes have a negligible impact on expenditure decisions, or so it is claimed.

This argument, however, is essentially spurious in that it neglects the fundamental characteristic of money, namely that it is the only financial asset which serves as a generally acceptable medium of exchange. It also neglects the fact that it is also the only financial asset which all financial institutions must hold as a necessary prerequisite for staying in business. The argument confuses variability of behaviour with predictability of behaviour.

## Control of money supply: control of the economy

The bank credit multiplier relationship is the key by which the state can control the supply of money. Given the existence of a stable multiplier relationship, no matter how complex it might be, the principles of monetary control are simple. Despite their simplicity they have been hotly debated and at times veiled in a mist of confusion, and the mechanism of control has sometimes been ignored or rejected. The reasons for neglect will form the subject matter of another section. Meanwhile we will inform ourselves as to how the money supply can be controlled and, since money is presumed to have some influence on economic activity, how economic activity can be controlled.

We have seen that the principal creators of an effective substitute for money proper are the commercial banks. All other forms of credit have to be converted reasonably quickly into money proper. We have also established that the ability of commercial banks to create credit money rests on the practice of fractional reserve banking combined with the public's willingness to treat bank deposits as an alternative to money proper. Because this point is frequently misunderstood it is worth emphasizing that it is the combination of these two things, and not the fractional reserve nature of commercial banking as such, which allows the banks to create credit money. Other financial institutions also operate with a fractional cash reserve ratio but they do not create money because the public, in not regarding their deposits as a form of money, have a very low propensity to re-deposit funds received from such institutions back with them. Thus when such institutions expand their deposits they experience a much larger cash drain (leakage) than do the commercial banks. Technically, the public's cash to non-bank financial intermediaries' deposit ratio is much higher than their cash to banks' deposits ratio with the result that the non-bank financial intermediaries' credit multiplier has a much lower value than that of the banks. Despite their much greater ability to create credit, money banks do not completely abandon state money and there is a link between state money and bank money. Hence the banks' cash-reserve ratio can provide a fulcrum for monetary control. All that is required for monetary control is for the state, or its delegate, the central bank, to control the supply of high-powered money.

What methods of control of high-powered money are available? There seem to be two. First, the state can alter the cash base (the quantity of high-powered money in circulation) through alterations in the level of taxes and its expenditure. Secondly, the monetary authority can play the market game and exchange with the public and the commercial banks government securities for state money; this is known as *open market operations*.

Open-market operations are sales and purchases of government securities by the monetary authority.

In order to finance its own activities the state can either tax or borrow from the public.[3] If it borrows it sells interest-bearing securities to the public and these securities comprise what is known as the National Debt.[4] Since the public pay for the securities with money proper or, when they sell securities back to the

3. Further aspects of state borrowing and taxing were explored earlier in Chapter 29 and will also be considered in Chapter 45. It can also print money. This method of financing state expenditure is considered later in this chapter.
4. The National Debt is the paper legacy of government borrowing. It first grew into massive proportions as a result of the two World Wars. It has continued to grow since as a result of the rapid expansion of the public sector and its residual demand for finance.

state, are paid in money proper it follows that changes in the money supply will accompany the buying and selling of securities. When the securities are sold to raise money to finance government expenditure their sale only has a temporary impact on the supply of high-powered money and the total money supply since when the government spends the proceeds of its borrowing the stock of high-powered money returns to its previous level. Open market operations directed at controlling the money supply require the monetary authorities to retain the proceeds of an open market sale. Thus open market operations undertaken to control the supply of money need to be distinguished from debt financing sales. This suggests that the monetary authorities may face a conflict of interests if it is required to manage both the money supply and the government's debt financing.

## Variable cash-reserve ratio control

The bank credit multiplier expression suggests an alternative method of controlling the volume of bank deposits and hence the total money supply which does not involve any change in the quantity of high-powered money. Since the volume of bank deposits depends upon the value of the bank credit multiplier and the supply of high-powered money, it can alternatively be altered by varying the value of the bank credit multiplier which operates on an unchanged quantity of high-powered money. How? By virtue of the fact that the central bank controls one element of the bank credit multiplier expression, namely the minimum value of the commercial banks' cash-reserve ratio. This is known as the *variable cash-reserve ratio technique of monetary control*. In the UK this technique is not used formally but is used in practice through the technique of *Special Deposits*. These are compulsory deposits of cash made by the commercial banks at the Bank of England. From the commercial banks' point of view such deposits are equivalent to an increase in their required cash reserve ratio since, under appropriate behaviour by the Bank of England, they lead to a multiple reduction in the volume of bank deposits. From the government's point of view they are equivalent to the imposition of a higher required cash-reserve ratio on the banks not only with regard to their deposit reducing consequences but also in acting as a form of taxation on the banks, i.e. they are a form of subsidized government borrowing.

## Monetary control and the structure of interest rates

In the previous chapter we established a direct link between changes in the money supply and the general level of prices and/ or output. There may, however, be an indirect effect operating via the interest rate changes which accompany open market operations.

What we have to show now is how the indirect effect operating through interest rates influences the level of spending, particularly investment spending. Traditionally the authorities operate on the short end of the money and capital market (i.e. they buy and sell securities soon to be redeemed). Hence we must indicate how changes in short-term interest rates cause changes in long-term interest rates which are presumed to be the more important influence on investment. Figure 192 indicates why this might be so. We suppose that the monetary authority is seeking to reduce the money supply and so sells securities to the public and the banks. The effect of the transaction is to cause a fall in the cash reserves of the banks and so set in motion a contraction of bank deposits and cause short-term interest rates to rise. At the same time the banks and the public will find that not only are they short of cash but they are also holding long-term securities whose interest payment is now lower, relative to that of the short-term securities. Consequently they will sell long-term securities which will lower their price and raise their interest rates and thus long- and short-term interest rates will move together. The rise in long-term rates will serve to check investment.

We have now established that open-market operations working via the bank credit multiplier process link changes in the supply of high-powered money with changes in the total supply of money. The relationship between them in the UK

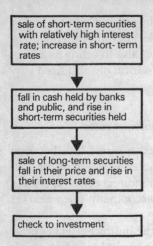

Figure 192  Control of the money supply through open market
operations also affects investment through the associated changes in
interest rates

economy is illustrated by the data plotted in Figure 193 and by
the more detailed data in Table 47. The data in Figure 193 relates the total amount of high-powered money outstanding to
the total money stock in the UK over the period 1881–1963.[5]
Inspection of the graph appears to confirm the predicted relationship between the two series and thus would seem to support
the theory of control outlined in this section. This conclusion
appears to be confirmed by the data for the post-1963 period
with respect to the relationship between the stock of high-
powered money and the narrow $(M_1)$ concept of the money
supply.

The relationship between the stock of high-powered money
and the broad (sterling $M_3$) concept of the money supply dis-
plays a more pronounced downward trend over this period,
especially after 1970, and this might be taken as evidence
against the theory of control we are considering. This is not in
fact the case since the decline, which is also apparent in the
ratio of high-powered money to the narrow money supply, can

5.  As of approximately 30 June each year.

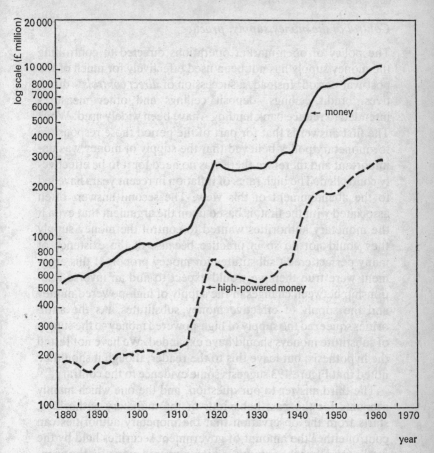

Figure 193

be explained by the many changes in the practice of monetary
control which occurred during this period. In particular, the
major reform in 1971 (known as Competition and Credit Control) led to a significant reduction in the banks' required and
actual cash to deposits ratio. The behaviour of the data in Table
49 is thus apparently consistent with the theory of cash-base
monetary control. A note of caution, however, is called for
since in interpreting data in this way it should be recognized
that association does not necessarily imply causation.

## Control of the money supply: practice

The policy of open-market operations directed to controlling the money supply has not been used effectively for much of the post-war period. Instead, a succession of *direct controls* – directives, credit ceilings, deposit ceilings and other measures intended to reduce bank lending – have been widely used. Why? The first answer is that for part of the period those responsible for monetary policy believed that the supply of money was unimportant and therefore there was no need for it to be effectively controlled. The high rates of inflation in recent years have led to the abandonment of this view. The second answer, often associated with the first, is based upon the argument that even if the monetary authorities wanted to control the money supply they could not do so in practice because of the existence of many perfect credit substitutes for money proper. If this argument were true then we would expect to find an inverse relationship between changes in the supply of high-powered money and the supply of effective money substitutes. As the authorities squeezed the supply of high-powered money so the supply of substitute moneys should have expanded. We have not tested the hypothesis, but leave this to the reader, though it should be noted that Figure 193 suggests some evidence to the contrary.[6]

The third answer to our question, and the one which mainly accounts for the past behaviour of the monetary authorities, starts from the observation that the monetary authorities can control either the amount of government securities held by the public (and thus the amount of high-powered money in the economy) *or* the price of those securities (i.e. the rate of interest) but not both. This is illustrated in Figure 194 where the public's demand curve for government securities is represented by $DD'$.

In terms of Figure 194 if the authorities release $OQ$ securities they will be sold at price $OP$ and if they release $OQ_1$ they will be sold at price $OP_1$. Alternatively, if the authorities fix price OP they will sell $OQ$ and so on. A concomitant of price is the rate

6. Figure 193 is not wholly conclusive since it leaves undisclosed the behaviour of the credit facilities of non-bank financial intermediaries.

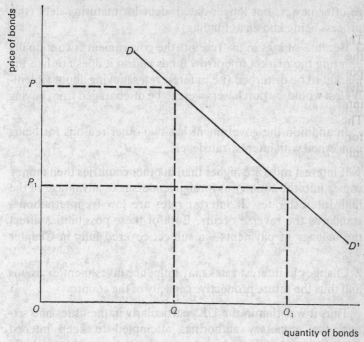

Figure 194

of interest: if the price of bonds rises then the rate of interest will fall, and if the price of bonds falls the rate of interest will rise. This can place the monetary authority in a dilemma since an attempt to reduce the money supply may move interest rates in an undesirable direction.

Why should the monetary authority be interested in the behaviour of interest rates? The answer lies partly in the existence of the National Debt. A government has several problems in managing the debt.

1 It has to ensure that the interest payments on the debt are kept as low as possible.

2 It has to control the conversion of securities into cash as each block of securities matures, otherwise there might be unwarranted increases in the money supply. One way of doing this is

to offer newer, but longer-dated, debt for maturing debt (this process being known as funding).

3 Because of lags in tax receipts the government is continually entering the market to borrow funds and so it does not like the market to be disturbed (i.e. interest rates moving about violently) lest would-be purchasers were to be discouraged from buying debt.

In addition the government has two other reasons for being concerned with interest-rate levels.

1 If interest rates are higher than in other countries then money comes into the country as foreign lenders take advantage of the high interest rates. If interest rates are low by international standards the reverse occurs. Both of these possibilities affect the balance of payments – a subject covered fully in Chapter 43.

2 Changes in interest rates may influence investment decisions and thus the future productive capacity of the country.

Thus it was that in the UK, particularly in the fifties and sixties, the monetary authorities attempted to keep interest rates low and stable which meant that the quantity of high-powered money and hence the total money supply were largely determined by the public. To maintain this interest-rate policy the monetary authorities had to purchase, at prevailing prices (interest rates) all government securities offered by the commercial banks wanting to obtain additional cash reserves. Thus, through choice, the Bank of England rendered open-market operations ineffective as a technique of monetary control. Although the monetary authorities tried to defend such a policy by arguing that the supply of money was unimportant, they apparently did not believe in their own argument since they introduced alternative techniques of monetary control. These included:

*Special deposits.* All commercial banks could be compelled to deposit an amount of their deposits, usually expressed as some percentage of their total sterling deposits, with the Bank of England. In effect this was a tax on the banks since, whilst the cash still belonged to the banks, they could not include it in their cash reserves and would otherwise have used the cash to purchase interest-bearing assets. The use of special deposits, at least in the 1960s, reflected the contradictory nature of monetary policy in the period. A call for special deposits is analytically equivalent to an open market sale of additional government securities. To be effective it must force the commercial banks to sell securities which means a rise in interest rates. Given that the Bank of England's interest-rate policy called for special deposits, it simply led to a sale of government securities by the commercial banks to the Bank of England which held the proceeds on special account. Thus special deposits failed to operate as an effective technique of monetary control. This, in turn, led to the introduction and use of other techniques.

*Directives*. Direct requests were issued from the Bank of England to the commercial banks asking them to behave in a particular way, e.g. to lend more to exporters and less to private consumers.

*Credit Ceilings*. A stronger restriction was to limit the annual growth of commercial bank lending to a percentage of the previous year's lending.

*Deposit Ceilings (the 'Corset')*. A stronger version of the credit ceiling directive which places the restriction on the rate of growth of bank deposits rather than their lending. When in operation this forces the banks to offer very low rates of interest on deposits to discourage the public from depositing with them.

The trouble with direct controls is not that they do not work – they certainly do – but that they do so by distorting the workings of the monetary system by only applying to some financial institutions (the commercial banks) and not others, and by not reflecting the interplay of market forces. They encourage inefficiency both within the banking sector and with respect to the use of funds, i.e. the banks resorted to non-price methods of allocating funds. Because the London Clearing Banks were subject to the main burden of direct controls in the 1960s they became less competitive and declined in importance relative to other deposit banks.

## Reform of the monetary system: competition and credit control

By the late 1960s the costs of the distortions introduced into the monetary system through the excessive use of direct controls combined with the re-emergence of the belief that inflation was essentially a monetary problem to create pressure for a reform of the UK system of monetary control. The reform came in September 1971 when the Bank of England introduced major changes in the system of monetary control and in its policy objectives. It was heralded in May of that year by the issue of a consultative document with the title *Competition and Credit Control*.[7]

The new arrangements involved two separate, but complementary, lines of change. One was intended to improve the efficiency of the monetary system by promoting competition between the London Clearing Banks and other financial institutions. Amongst other things this involved the abandonment of monopolistic pricing arrangements between the clearing banks, and of the common bid arrangement on the part of the discount houses. The other change was the introduction of a new method of monetary control which was designed to facilitate a change in the objective of monetary control away from excessive preoccupation with the level of interest rates and towards greater control of the money supply. This change was complementary to the first since it was intended to substitute a market form of control, designed to influence *all* financial institutions, for the previous battery of direct controls which operated mainly on the clearing banks.

The new method of monetary control centred on the 'classic' technique of open market operations. By making it the basis for the new control method the Bank of England signified its inten-

7. This was reprinted in the Bank of England *Quarterly Bulletin*, June 1971. Subsequent issues of the *Bulletin* should be consulted for other articles on the 1971 reform and its subsequent history.

tion of no longer managing interest rates to the exclusion of the money supply. Equity in operation was to be achieved by setting a common 'reserve asset ratio' of 12½ per cent for all banks and of 10 per cent for the finance houses.[8] Whilst ostensibly fixed, these ratios, which provided the fulcrum of control, were in fact variable in an upwards direction by virtue of the fact that the Bank of England could, in effect, request all institutions subject to reserve ratios to hold additional reserve assets in excess of the prescribed minimum amounts. This was achieved through calls for special deposits which, as explained earlier, can be an effective technique of monetary control if interest rates are allowed to vary.

Although long overdue, the new arrangements and techniques introduced by competition and credit control soon ran into difficulties. They were quickly overtaken by, and indeed contributed to, events which made them unworkable in practice. At the same time as competition (and hence deposit expansion) was encouraged in the banking sector, long-standing controls over hire-purchase and related forms of credit were abolished under a separate reform package, and the two together led to a spending boom which served to fuel the economy's accelerating inflation. Inflation in turn led to additional upward pressure on interest rates.[9] These developments are shown in Table 49.

Some rise in interest rates had been expected as a consequence of the new arrangements but the high levels of nominal

8. Reserve assets were defined in such a way as to apparently exclude high-powered money from the reserve base. However, since the banks still had to hold a proportion of their assets in the form of cash if they were to stay in business, an effective cash-reserve ratio still existed. The new cash ratio was significantly lower than the previous 8 per cent ratio.

9. In periods of sustained inflation interest rates tend to rise to include a mark-up which reflects the expected rate of inflation. Lenders need to be compensated for the erosion of the purchasing power of their money and borrowers are prepared to pay higher rates because they know they will be repaying money which has declined in purchasing power. Thus in periods of inflation a distinction has to be made between the *nominal* rate of interest (the rate which includes a mark-up for inflation) and the *real* rate of interest (the rate after allowing for inflation) which reflects the true costs of funds.

**Table 49**

| Year | Public sector borrowing requirement, P.S.B.R. £m. | Money stock: sterling $M_3$. End fourth quarter £m. | Annual rate of change of money stock % | Annual rate of inflation (Retail price index) % | Long-term rate of interest (long dated British Gov. Securities) % |
|------|------|------|------|------|------|
| 1970 | 4 | 17 666 | 8·7 | 6·3 | 9.25 |
| 1971 | 1382 | 20 111 | 13·8 | 9·4 | 8·90 |
| 1972 | 2054 | 25 443 | 26·5 | 7·3 | 8·97 |
| 1973 | 4209 | 32 046 | 26·0 | 9·1 | 10·78 |
| 1974 | 6437 | 35 300 | 10·2 | 16·0 | 14·77 |
| 1975 | 10 480 | 37 595 | 6·5 | 24·2 | 14·39 |
| 1976 | 9128 | 41 160 | 9·5 | 16·5 | 14·43 |
| 1977 | 5996 | 45 290 | 10·0 | 15·9 | 12·73 |
| 1978 | 8357 | 52 062 | 15·0 | 8·3 | 12·47 |
| 1979 | 12 608 | 58 677 | 12·7 | 13·4 | 12·99 |
| 1980 | 12 213 | 69 591 | 18·6 | 18·0 | 13·79 |

Sources: *Economic Trends Annual Supplement*, 1982 Bank of England *Quarterly Bulletin*

rates between 1974 and 1976 proved too much for the government. It failed to acknowledge that the high level of nominal rates were, in part, a reflection of its own excess demand for funds and an inevitable consequence of accelerating inflation.[10] The Bank of England, caught between the desire to restrain

10. This experience points to one of the major limitations of interest-rate control, in contrast to control of the money supply, as the policy variable of monetary control. In periods of accelerating inflation, rising nominal interest rates provide no indication of the behaviour of the real rate of interest and hence of the tightness or ease of monetary policy. Thus high nominal interest rates cannot be interpreted as indicating a restrictive monetary policy, as was presumed by those responsible for advocating interest-rate control.

monetary expansion on the one hand and prevent nominal interest rates rising on the other, reverted to its interventionist policies with respect to the control of interest rates. Continued inflation and balance of payments difficulties led to the floating of sterling and increased government intervention in the economy, first to deal with inflation and then with unemployment, as the economic situation deteriorated further and brought the emergence of a new state of affairs, *stagflation*. Against this background the new system of monetary control stood little chance of success. The spirit of competition and credit control rapidly withered as the Bank of England reintroduced directives as a means of controlling the growth of bank deposits and the money supply.

## Monetary targets

Sadly, governments cannot be relied upon to refrain from using the printing presses as an alternative means of financing their activities. Despite their good intentions central bankers are not infallible when it comes to matching the money supply with the needs of the community. Consequently, some economists have proposed that discretionary variations in the money supply should be abandoned in favour of specific monetary growth rules. Such a rule would be of the form that the money supply should grow on average by a stated percentage amount per period of time.

The money supply would then behave in a regular and predictable way and a concomitant of this stability of supply is that the general price level, while free to vary in both an upwards and downwards direction, would do so in a gradual and predictable fashion. Just how it would vary in the long run would depend upon the annual percentage increase in the money supply as specified in the rule relative to the rate of growth of real output and the income-elasticity of demand for money. If, for example, the income-elasticity of demand for money is unity and the annual rate of increase of real output is 5 per cent, a monetary rule of 5 per cent annual increase in the supply of money should lead to a stable general level of prices in the long run.

The success of the monetary rule would seem to depend on three things. Firstly, a link between money and real output. Secondly, that the country should be able to pursue an independent monetary policy. Thirdly, that other economic forces operate so as to lead to steady growth in output in the absence of de-stabilizing monetary actions. The second requires that if the country be small it should be able to operate floating exchange rates (on which see Chapter 43) whilst the first and third would seem to require a world of free competition.

However, despite these objections to a rigid monetary rule, there is little doubt that a policy which restricts the range of variations of the rate of monetary expansion is definitely superior to one which involves large and unpredictable variations, as can result when interest rates are chosen as the policy variable.

The UK moved some way towards the adoption of a monetary growth rule and a reduction in monetary instability with the introduction of *Monetary Targets* in 1976. As practised in the UK, the monetary target is a weak form of monetary rule. Each year the government announces a target rate of monetary expansion for the following twelve month period. The target is not a single figure but a target range, i.e. upper and lower limits for the rate of growth of the money supply are specified. The target range is not constant over time but is subject to periodic revisions. These features reduce the usefulness of monetary targets in comparison with a fixed monetary growth rule but still make them preferable to discretionary money supply variations provided, that is, that the rate of monetary expansion lies within the target range.

Initially, monetary targets were successful both in the sense of restricting the rate of monetary expansion to within the target range, and in the delayed impact of this slow down in monetary growth on the rate of inflation, as evidenced by the data in Table 49. Unfortunately, and in spite of a government committed to effective control of the money supply, the rate of monetary expansion in the period 1979–81 showed a marked tendency to exceed the upper limit of the target range, even when the target was revised upwards!

A consequence of the Bank of England's failure to keep the

growth of the money supply within the government's target range was another reform of the monetary control system.

## The new system of monetary control

The purpose and possible nature of the proposed changes to the system of monetary control were set out in a Green Paper entitled *Monetary Control*,[11] published in March 1980. The prime objective of the proposed reform was to bring about a system of monetary control which worked. This was to be achieved through greater reliance upon *monetary base* (high-powered money) control, using the technique of open market operations, than had hitherto been practised. But, true to form, the Bank of England still sought to retain its right to manage interest rates at its discretion and the new system, which came into effect in August 1981,[12] is not a fully fledged monetary base control system of the kind described earlier in this chapter. The fulcrum of control is the requirement that all banks above a certain size, maintain ½ per cent of these deposit liabilities in balances at the Bank of England. This replaces the 12½ per cent reserve asset ratio introduced by competition and credit control.

## Summary

The thing which is acceptable as money has passed through many stages of evolution from commodity money to token, and in a parallel and not unconnected evolutionary strand, instruments have developed for the acknowledgements of debts, one of which, bank debt, has come to be regarded as the same as money proper. The central problem of money supply, therefore, has been how to control the supply of bank money. The answer has been found by requiring banks to hold some high-powered money. The central bank, by buying and selling government securities in the open market, can control the amount

11. *Monetary Control*, HMSO, Cmnd. 7858.
12. Details of the new system are described in the March and September 1981 Bank of England *Quarterly Bulletins*.

of high-powered money in the economy and hence the volume of bank money. A consequence of this form of control is that interest rates are determined by market forces.

For much of the period since 1945 the UK money supply has been uncontrolled. This, we have argued, mainly reflects an unwillingness to accept the short-term consequences of effective monetary control rather than any inherent difficulty in attempting to exercise control.

## Questions

1 Why is it useful to have a knowledge of the history of the evolution of money?

2 What is (a) money proper; (b) commodity money and (c) token money?

3 Why must money be managed?

4 What is the difference between money proper, credit and credit money?

5 What are the main determinants of the commercial banks' ability to create credit money?

6 If banks were required to hold 100 per cent reserves would they survive?

7 What are the main determinants of the banks' demand for cash (high-powered money)?

8 What are the main determinants of the public's demand for cash? (You may wish to tackle this question after revising the chapter on the demand for money.)

9 Describe the mechanism of open market operations. Why might open market operations be ineffective?

10 In what respects do the activities of banks differ from those of a building society?

11 A banker said to an economist: 'Every pound that I lend has been deposited with me by someone else. How do I create money?' What reply should an economist make?

12 'The case for decentralized private production of money is

that it enables banks to cater for the needs of trade, but the same result can be achieved by centralized public production of money with private financial intermediaries improving the velocity of circulation.' Comment.

13 'Fine in principle, unworkable in practice.' Is this an apt description of the rise and fall of competition and credit control?

14 If, as some economists argue, the Bank of England does not control the money supply, who does?

# Chapter 39
# The *ISLM* Model

Given our discussion of money it is now possible to extend the analysis of the working of the fix-price economy and present a graphical version of a simple general equilibrium model which incorporates both goods and money. The model adopted is used extensively in more advanced treatments of macroeconomic theory and is called either the *Hicks-Hansen model*, in honour of the economists who first developed it, or the *ISLM model* in recognition of its constituent parts.

In a general equilibrium analysis the economy is viewed as a set of markets or sectors which together embrace all the main macroeconomic variables. Each market, in turn, is described by a demand equation, a supply equation and a market clearing (equilibrium) relationship. All the equations are then brought together and simultaneously solved to determine equilibrium values for each of the macroeconomic variables so that equilibrium values in one market are consistent with the simultaneous equilibrium of variables in other markets.

The *ISLM* is a simplified general equilibrium model because it is based on the assumption that the economy can be adequately represented by four distinct markets; a goods (output) market, a money market, a labour market and a bond (securities) market. This degree of aggregation immediately reveals the limitations of the model – it assumes that output can be described in terms of a single homogeneous commodity and it assumes that there is only one injection and one withdrawal. However, it does have the advantage of allowing the production side of the economy to be described by a single production function. What the assumption does, in effect, is to assume that there are sufficient unemployed resources to enable the simultaneous production of both consumption and investment goods. As for the criticism that the model contains only one injection and withdrawal (an injection of investment and a withdrawal of savings) it should be noted that the model can be extended to embrace other injections and withdrawals but that the geometry becomes a little more complicated. The additional refinements will, however, be found in subsequent chapters.

Although the model is based upon the existence of four markets, only two appear explicitly in the diagrammatic exposition; they are the goods and money markets. This condensation is achieved as follows. First, because of an absence of technological change, output and employment tend to move together. Hence, knowledge of the equilibrium value of output is sufficient to determine the value of employment and vice-versa. Secondly, the bond market can be ignored as a result of one of the 'Laws' of general equilibrium analysis. The law is known as *Walras's Law* and states that in any set of interdependent equations of markets, if equilibrium prevails in all but one market then it must necessarily obtain in the remaining market. Since the model serves to determine the equilibrium values of output (the goods market), the rate of interest ( the money market) and employment (the labour market), it follows that when these three markets are in equilibrium then the fourth market must also be in equilibrium. Hence, it is not necessary to represent the bond market in the model.

The validity of Walras's Law should be self-evident. In a money economy an excess supply of money necessarily implies an excess demand for commodities and an excess supply of commodities necessarily implies an excess demand for money. Thus, when one market is out of equilibrium, it means that at least one other market will be as well. Conversely, it follows that when all but one market are in equilibrium the remaining market must also be in equilibrium.

A possible cause for concern is why the bond market is selected to be the redundant market since Walras's Law is neutral as to which market is dropped. The reason, on the face of it, is quite straightforward. In partial equilibrium analysis we can examine the determination of the rate of interest either in terms of the supply and demand for money (money market), or the supply and demand for loanable funds (bond market). So in a general equilibrium model when the determination of the rate of interest also involves interaction between real and monetary variables, the choice of redundant market is between money and bonds. By tradition the bond market is dropped. This deliberate decision reflects the fact that money links all markets together so that it makes sense to treat it explicitly in the construction of the model.

This is perfectly reasonable so long as it is recognized that in general equilibrium analysis we are concerned with the equilibrium values of variables. Thus when general equilibrium prevails in an economy the equilibrium value of the rate of interest must be the same in the money and bond markets. So long as the general equilibrium model is used to derive comparative static propositions all is well. However, this does reveal another weakness of the *ISLM* curve model. It cannot be used to answer questions involving time, that is to analyse processes, such as the dynamics of adjustment from one equilibrium position to another. Out of equilibrium Walras's Law no longer holds, hence it is not possible to treat one market as redundant. Thus, for disequilibrium analysis both bond and money market processes need to be considered when analysing the behaviour of the rate of interest. Again this limitation of the *ISLM* model does not make the model useless, as long as it is borne in mind and the model is not used to analyse problems involving disequilibrium processes. The appendix to this chapter describes some of the problems which arise when this limitation is ignored, and the model is 'asked' to do too much.

To construct the *ISLM* model we have to set out the relationships which describe the real side of the model (the goods market), and the money side of the economy (the money market). The relationships for the two sides of the model are then solved to give two curves which plot the loci of combinations of the rate of interest and the level of real income which yield equilibrium in the respective markets. These two curves, the *IS* and *LM* curves, are then plotted on the same axes and their intersection point determines the unique pair of values for the rate of interest and the level of real income which allows the real and the money sides of the economy to be simultaneously in equilibrium.

Although the resultant diagram resembles the familiar supply and demand diagram, the differences are greater than the similarities. The *IS* and *LM* curves are not the graphical counterparts of behavioural relationships but the loci of equilibrium points established by the interaction of a larger number of behavioural relationships. The macroeconomic behavioural relationships of the economy lie 'behind' the *IS* and *LM* curves, and when using the model it is necessary to refer to them.

This feature of the model presents a minor difficulty in deriving the curves. Since all the relevant behavioural relationships have to be brought together to construct the curves, it is necessary to resort to composite diagrams and graphical devices for relating the different parts together.

## Construction of the *IS* curve

In Figure 195 we illustrate the derivation of the *IS* curve. Part (a) depicts the investment function. It shows, given the investment demand curve, *Id*, how the rate of investment per period of time increases as the rate of interest decreases. Part (c) of the diagram reproduces the investment and savings schedules of the 45° model of income determination. The savings schedule is derived from the familiar short-run consumption function and shows that the level of savings increases with real income. Three different levels of investment are illustrated by the investment schedules, $I_1$, $I_2$ and $I_3$, these correspond to the levels associated with the three different values of the rate of interest in part (a). Along the horizontal axis in part (c) are shown the three equilibrium income levels ($I = S$) associated with the three different levels of the investment function. Part (b) of the diagram brings together the information contained in the other two parts to yield the *IS* curve, the locus of pairs of

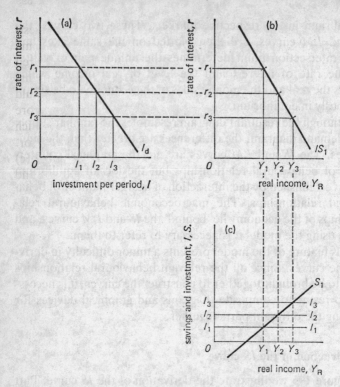

Figure 195 The derivation of the IS curve

values of the rate of interest and real income which yield equilibrium in the goods market. Only three points have been drawn, but it is obvious that by considering other values of the rate of interest, and hence investment, that additional equilibrium combinations of the rate of interest and real income could be established, and they would lie on the curve connecting the three points already drawn.

The resultant IS curve slopes down from left to right, indicating that, other things being equal, lower values of the rate of interest are associated with higher levels of real income. The intuitive explanation of the negative slope of the curve is that a fall in the rate of interest leads to a rise in the level of investment. An equilibrium level of real income requires that investment equals savings, so that as investment increases income must also increase, via the multiplier process, until the desired level of savings is increased to match the increase in investment.

Two things concerning the derivation of the *IS* curve should be apparent. Firstly, that the curve can also be derived for more general 'simple' models of income determination, in which other sources of injections and withdrawals are allowed for. This is easily seen by noting that the *S* and *I* schedules in part (c) merely have to be relabelled *W* and *J*. Secondly, the shape and position of the *IS* curve depends upon the shape and position of the underlying investment, and savings functions (injections and withdrawals functions).

For example, if business expectations improve and the investment demand curve shifts to the right, each value of the rate of interest is associated with a higher rate of investment, and the family of investment schedules in part (c) will shift upwards. With an unchanged savings schedule each value of the rate of interest is associated with a higher equilibrium level of real income. The *IS* curve shifts bodily to the right. Conversely, if expectations deteriorate and the investment demand curve in part (a) shifts bodily to the left, each value of the rate of interest is associated with a lower rate of investment and hence level of income, and the *IS* curve will shift bodily to the left. The *IS* curve will also shift in a similar fashion if the schedules for other categories of injections should shift bodily.

Likewise, if the consumption function should shift upwards (downwards) so that a larger (smaller) fraction of income is consumed for each level of income, the savings function will shift downwards (upwards). Hence with an unchanged investment demand schedule, and family of investment expenditure functions for different rates of interest, the equilibrium income points ($I_1 = S_1$, etc.) will alter and the *IS* curve move bodily to the right (left).

We can summarize these important results as follows:

*The* IS *curve will shift to the right (left) if the investment demand curve shifts to the right (left), other things being unchanged.*

*Likewise for similar changes in the functions for other categories of injections.*

*The* IS *curve will shift to the right (left) if the savings function shifts downwards (upwards).*
*Likewise for similar changes in the functions for other categories of withdrawals.*

Turning to the slope, or elasticity, of the *IS* curve it should be noted, and self-evident, that its slope will depend upon the slopes of the investment demand curve and the savings function. The steeper the slope of the investment demand curve, i.e. the lower the interest elasticity of investment, and the steeper the slope of the savings function, i.e. the higher the marginal property to save, the steeper the slope of the *IS* curve. Conversely, the more interest-elastic the investment demand curve, and the flatter the slope of the savings function, i.e. the lower the marginal property to save, the flatter will be the *IS* curve. As will become apparent later, these possibilities have important consequences for the relative efficiencies of monetary and fiscal policy changes.

**Construction of the *LM* curve**

The derivation of the *LM* curve is illustrated in Figure 196. The key to understanding the derivation of the *LM* curve is the distinction between the transactions demand for money ($M_{DT}$), which relates the demand for money to the level of income, and the asset demand for money ($M_{DA}$) which relates the demand for money to the rate of interest. It should be observed that the precautionary motive for holding money is subsumed into either the transactions or the asset demand for money.

In practice the demand for money functions are not separable, and for the economy as a whole we observe a total demand for money function, ($M_D$), which, at its most basic, is a function of the rate of interest and level of nominal income (or, if the demand for money is expressed in real terms, real income). For expositional purposes, it is convenient to treat the total demand as separable.

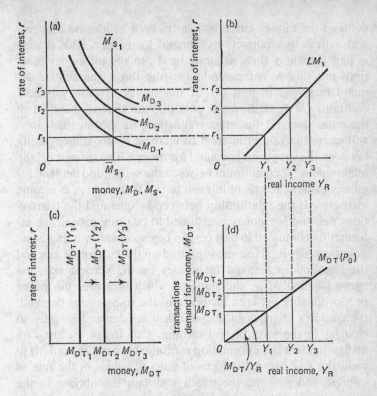

Figure 196 The derivation of the *LM* curve

Given the institutional framework of the economy the transactions demands for money depends solely upon the level of income, and thus when plotted against the rate of interest is completely interest-inelastic. This is illustrated in Figure 196 where three transactions demands for money functions are shown, corresponding to different levels of real income, $Y_1 < Y_2 < Y_3$. The asset demand for money, on the other hand, is an inverse function of the rate of interest, so that when the asset and transactions demands are combined to give the total demand for money function ($M_D$), this also slopes downwards from left to right against the rate of interest. The asset demand for money function may be constant, but the total demand for money curve will shift about as income changes, and with it the transactions demand for money. This is seen in part (a) where three separate total demand for money functions are shown, corresponding to the three transactions demand functions in part (c). If the supply of money is held constant, $(Ms)$, as shown in part (a), the shift to the right of the total demand for money function, as income increases, will cause the rate of interest to increase to maintain equality between the supply and demand for money. Thus in part (a) the maintenance of equilibrium between the supply and demand for money causes the rate of interest to rise from $r_1$ to $r_3$ as income increases. If the relationship between income and the transactions demand for money is assumed to be proportional, the information contained in part (c) can be expressed by a single line as in part (d). Real income is plotted on the horizontal axis and the transactions demand for money on the vertical axis, the curve labelled $M_{DT}$, the slope of which measures the factor proportionality between income and the transactions demand, then relates changes in the transactions demand directly to changes in the level of real income. Part (b) of the diagram brings together the information continued in parts (a) and (d) to yield the $LM$ curve, the locus of pairs of values of the rate of interest and real income which maintain equilibrium in the money market. As before, only three points have been drawn, but it is again obvious that other points could be added and that they would all lie along the curve labelled $LM$.

The resultant $LM$ curve slopes upwards from left to right, indicating that, other things being equal, higher levels (of real income) are associated with higher values (of the rate of interest). The intuitive explanation of the slope of the $LM$ curve is that, given a fixed supply of money, as income increases the growing transactions demand for money can only be satisfied by inducing people to hold less for asset purposes. People will only be prepared to reduce their asset demand for money as the rate of interest increases. Hence to maintain equilibrium between the supply of and total demand for money the rate of interest must increase as income increases. The derivation and general slope of the $LM$ curve are the same for different theories of the demand for money, provided they include the rate of interest and real income as determinants of the total demand. More importantly, the slope and position of the *LM* curve depend upon the slope and position of the underlying transactions and asset demand curves, and the supply of money.

For example, taking the latter first, if the demand for money curve remains unchanged but the supply of money is increased (decreased) the whole *LM* curve will shift bodily to the right (left). Because the demand for money balances is a demand for real rather than nominal money balances the position of the *LM* curve is also dependent upon the general price level. That is, a decrease in the general price level, with an unchanged nominal money supply, will cause the *LM* curve to shift to the right, and an increase in the general price level will cause the LM curve to shift bodily to the left. The similarity of effects for changes in the nominal money stocks and the general price level arises because both result in a change in the *real value* of the money supply. In analytical terms an increase in the nominal money supply, with a constant general price level, is equivalent to a decrease in the general price level, with a constant nominal money stock. In both cases, the initial effect of the change is an increase in the real value of the money stock. Likewise, a decrease in the nominal money supply, with the general price level held constant, is equivalent to an increase in the general price level, with the nominal money supply rate of interest and the level of real income. This is done in part (a) of Figure 197 in which both curves are drawn with slopes which indicate that the underlying functions are interest-elastic.

## The price level

In deriving these curves, the general price level is held constant, so that any change in the value of nominal income is necessarily a change in the value of real income, and it is real income which is measured along the horizontal axis. This allows us to introduce a maximum real output curve into the diagram, corresponding to the level of real output which is possible when labour and capital are fully employed. This is represented in

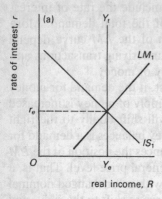
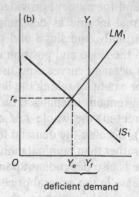

Figure 197(a) The *IS* and *LM* curve intersection – the simultaneous determination of equilibrium in the money and goods markets.
(b) Macro equilibrium at less than full employment

197 (a) by the vertical line labelled *Yf*. The *IS* and *LM* curves have been drawn to intersect at a point on the *Yf* line, which means that the situation depicted in part (a) is one of full employment general equilibrium. This is only one of many possible equilibrium positions, since the economy can be in equilibrium at less than full employment. If unemployment exists in the economy, in the sense that the equilibrium level of real output is less than *Yf*, the *IS* and *LM* curves will intersect to the left of the *Yf* line, as illustrated in part (b) of Figure 197. An indication of the deficiency in the level of aggregate demand is provided by the shortfall in real output *Ye – Yf*, which can be translated into a measure of unemployment by use of the aggregate production function. When analysing situations involving deficient aggregate effective demand it is reasonable to assume that the general price level is constant, so that no complications are introduced into the analysis by price induced shifts in the *LM* curve. However, this ceases to be true when we use the model to analyse excess demand situations, as represented by intersection points to the right of the *Yf* line.

This is illustrated in Figure 198, part (a). In such situations the general price level will rise. As the general price level rises,

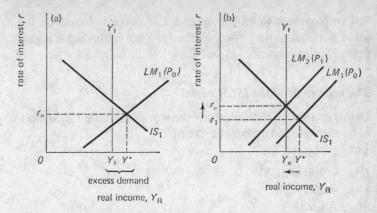

Figure 198(a)  The *IS* and *LM* curves – excess effective demand.
(b)  The *IS* and *LM* curves – elimination of excess demand. The general price level rises from $P_0$ to $P_1$ and the *LM* curve shifts leftward to $LM_2$

in response to excess demand pressures, it will affect the position of the *LM* curve by reducing the real value of the nominal money stock. It may also have an effect on the *IS* curve through the influence of rising prices on savings decisions, the distribution of income, and, if the exchange rate is fixed, the volume of imports and exports. Ignoring these latter effects, the influence of rising prices on the *LM* curve is illustrated in Figure 198. Initially the general price level is $P_0$, and the *LM* curve is $LM_1$. This intersects the *IS* curve to the right of the *Yf* line which indicates that the economy is suffering from excess demand, as indicated by the horizontal distance, $Ye - Y^*$. As in all supply and demand analysis the existence of excess effective demand leads to a bidding up of prices and a rise in the general price level. If the nominal money supply is held constant, the rise in the general price level will cause the real value of the money stock to fall and this will lead to a shift to the left in the *LM* curve. When the general price level has risen to $P_1$ the fall in the real value of the money stock, and the consequent rise in the rate of interest, will be such as to eliminate the excess demand and restore price stability. This is shown in the diagram by the second *LM* curve, $LM_2$, which intersects the *IS* curve at a point on the full employment line. The second *LM* curve is based on the same nominal money stock as the first, but embodies a higher general price level, i.e. $P_1 > P_0$.

## The arithmetic of the *ISLM* model

In this section we shall illustrate the workings of the *ISLM* model by means of an arithmetic example.
Let

$$C = 100 + 0.75Y$$
$$I = 275 - 25i$$
$$M_{DA} = 0.25Y$$
$$M_{DS} = 275 - 25i$$
$$M_S = 300$$

Monetary equilibrium exists when money supply equals money demand

$$M_S = M_{DT} + M_{DS}$$
$$300 = 0.25Y + 275 - 25i$$
$$25i = 0.25Y - 25$$

Equilibrium in the goods market requires

$$Y = C + I$$
$$Y = 100 + 0.75Y + 275 - 25i$$
$$25i = -0.25Y + 375$$

Simultaneous determination of equilibrium in goods and money markets obtains when $IS = LM$

$$25i = -0.25Y + 375$$
$$\text{(minus) } \underline{25i = 0.25Y - 25}$$
$$O = 0.50Y - 400$$
$$Y = 800$$

Putting $Y = 800$ into either the goods or money market equation gives an equilibrium rate of interest of 7 per cent. Equilibrium values for consumption (700), investment (100), the transaction demand for money (100) and the speculative or

asset demand for money (100) are obtained by putting the
equilibrium values for income and the rate of interest into the
appropriate equations.

# Chapter 40
# The Flex-Price Economy

So far we have analysed the workings of a fix-price economy. This has led to a neglect of the supply side of an economy and to the possibility that prices do vary in the long run. What we shall now do is to reformulate our analysis so as to take into account the interactions of prices and output. We shall proceed as follows:

1 Reconstruct the aggregate demand curve so as to make it a function of both the price level and autonomous expenditures.

2 Show the link between the ISLM model and the revised aggregate demand curve.

3 Derive the aggregate supply curves for the long run and the short run.

4 Examine the interactions of aggregate demand and aggregate supply.

### The aggregate demand curve

The microeconomic demand curve was developed earlier and made the market demand curve for a commodity depend upon the price of the commodity, the prices of other goods, incomes and tastes. The demand curve sloped downwards from left to right which implied that demand extended or contracted as price changed and the demand curve shifted to the left or right as income, tastes and the prices of other goods changed. The question that now arises is: can we construct an aggregate demand curve which is comparable to the microeconomic demand curve? We have, of course, constructed a total demand curve but on the assumption that prices remained constant and only income changed. What we now seek to do is to construct a total demand curve which admits of variations in the general level of prices.

In Figure 199 is shown an aggregate demand curve which relates planned demand for total output to the general level of prices. It is a function of autonomous expenditures, $A$, and the real value of money balances, $M/P$, *given the quantity of nominal money and fiscal policy*.

$$D_y = aA + b\ \frac{\bar{M}}{\bar{P}} \hspace{4cm} 1$$

where $A$ stands for autonomous expenditures, $M/P$ is the real value of money balances, $a$ and $B$ are constants and the bars over $M$ and $P$ denote that they are given.

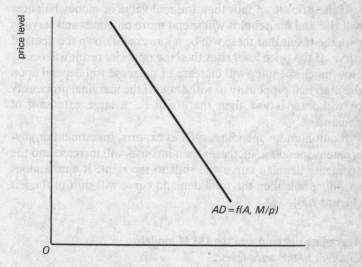

Figure 199

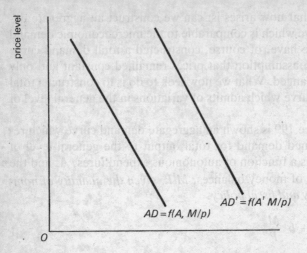

Figure 200

If the price level falls then the real value of money balances will rise and households will spend more on goods and services with the result that there will be a movement down the demand curve. If the price level rises then the opposite result will occur. How much spending will increase or decrease will depend upon the marginal propensity to withdraw. If the marginal propensity to withdraw is low then there will be a large extension of demand.

If autonomous spending, such as exports, investment or government spending, increases then incomes will increase and the aggregate demand curve will shift to the right. If autonomous spending falls then the total demand curve will shift to the left (Figure 200).

## Aggregate demand and the *ISLM* model
### Changes in the price-level

In the top half of Figure 201 we depict the *ISLM* model of an economy which is in equilibrium with output $Y_0$ and rate of in-

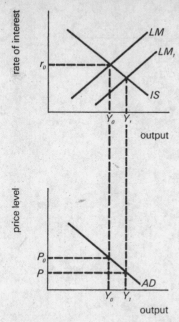

Figure 201

terest $r_0$. This equilibrium is associated with a price level $P_0$ which is shown in the bottom half of the diagram. Now if the price level falls the real value of money balances will rise and the *LM* curve will shift to the right, $LM_1$, and aggregate demand will extend. The new equilibrium will yield income $Y_1$, rate of interest $r_1$ and price level $P_1$. If the price level rises then real money balances will fall, the *LM* curve will shift to $LM_2$ and aggregate demand will contract until a new equilibrium is reached with income $Y_2$, interest rate $r_2$ and price level $P_2$.

## Changes in autonomous expenditure

Suppose now we consider cases of increases and decreases in autonomous spending. If, as in Figure 202, autonomous expenditures increase then the *IS* curve will shift to the right, $IS_1$, and the aggregate demand curve will also shift to the right until

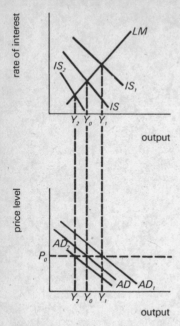

Figure 202

a new equilibrium is attained with income $Y_1$, interest rate $r_1$ and an unchanged price level $P_0$. If autonomous spending falls then the new equilibrium output will be $Y_2$.

### Changes in the money supply

If the quantity of money increases then the *LM* curve will shift to the right, $LM_1$, the interest rate will fall to $r_1$, spending will increase and the aggregate demand curve will shift to the right. A new equilibrium output, $Y_1$, will be achieved as in Figure 203. If the quantity of money falls the opposite process will occur.

The compatibility of the aggregate demand curve with the *ISLM* model arises because we have assumed that aggregate supply is perfectly elastic when we varied autonomous spending. And when we varied the price level we shifted the *LM* curve because each *LM* curve is constructed on the assumption

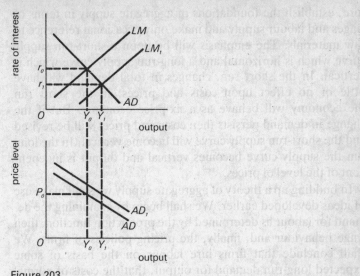

Figure 203

of a given price level. But if we can incorporate price level changes into the *ISLM* model why do we need to derive the aggregate demand curve? The answer, as we shall now proceed to elaborate is that, taken in conjunction with an aggregate supply curve, the total demand curve provides us with a more revealing analysis of the short- and long-run behaviour of an economy and permits us to move easily from fix-price to flex-price situations.

### Aggregate supply

The assumption that prices are fixed and that resources are perfectly elastic in supply may be a reasonable assumption for short periods of time, for an analysis of economic behaviour in the 1930s, and in the period 1945–65, but it had become less realistic by the 1970s.

The neglect of supply has meant that little or no theory of aggregate supply exists and what is available is mainly concerned with the behaviour of labour supply. We shall, therefore, establish the foundations of aggregate supply in terms of wages and labour supply and make only occasional reference to raw materials. The emphasis will be upon a short-run supply curve which is horizontal and a long-run supply curve which is vertical. In the short run, changes in total demand will have little or no effect upon costs and prices; in the short run the economy will behave as a fix-price economy. But if the change in demand persists then costs and prices will be revised and the short-run supply curve will become vertical. In the long run the supply curve becomes vertical and output is independent of the level of prices.

In building up a theory of aggregate supply we shall make use of ideas developed earlier. We shall begin by examining the demand for labour as determined by the production function, then wage behaviour and, finally, the pricing policies of firms. We shall conclude that firms hire labour on the basis of some expected long-run demand for output, that the costs of normal output are mainly wage costs, that wages are mainly influenced by the level of unemployment and that prices are determined by normal costs.

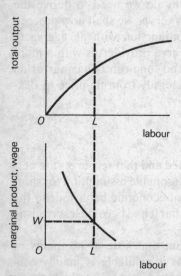

Figure 204

## The production function

Our starting point is the firm's demand for labour as determined by the production function. Because we have discussed the production function earlier, recapitulation will brief. In Figure 204 we depict the aggregate production for an economy on the assumption that the amount of capital equipment is fixed and that labour is the only variable factor of production. From the total product curve is derived a marginal product curve (MPL). Now in the long run the supply of labour is fixed at *OL* and if we assume that wages are perfectly flexible then the real wage will be *OW*. Equilibrium will result from the flexibility of the real wage.

## Equilibrium in the markets for goods and labour in a money economy

The next step is to recognize the existence of a money economy and a goods market. We have recognized the link between real and money wages and between money wages and prices. The

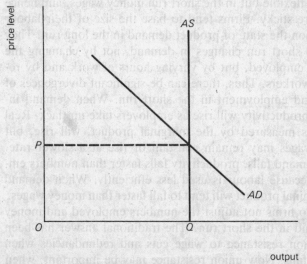

Figure 205

basic assumptions are that: (1) variations in the money wage cause corresponding changes in the real wage and produce equilibrium in the labour market and (2) changes in the money wage cause changes in the price level and produce equilibrium in the product market.

Figure 205 shows that aggregate demand for and supply of goods are in long-run equilibrium. The aggregate demand curve is downward sloping, for the reasons we have previously advanced, and the aggregate supply curve is vertical. In long-run equilibrium the price level is $OP$ and output is $OQ$. The existence of price level $OP$ serves to dictate the level of money wages. If, in equilibrium, the real wage level is too low then profits will be high and businessmen will bid for labour which will drive up the money wage. If the real wage is too high then money wages will fall.

### Short-run behaviour
*Employment*

In the long run it is assumed that money wages and prices are perfectly flexible but in the short run money wages, and hence prices, are sticky. Firms tend to base the size of their labour forces upon the state of product demand in the long run. They adjust to short run changes in demand, not by changing the numbers employed, but by varying hours of work and by re-grading workers. Thus, there can be significant divergences of output and employment in the short run. When demand increases, productivity will rise as employers take up slack. Real wages, as measured by the marginal product, will rise, but money wages may remain constant or rise at a slower rate. When demand falls, productivity falls faster than numbers employed because labour is used less efficiently. When demand falls marginal product will tend to fall faster than money wages.

Why do firms not adjust the numbers employed and money wages paid in the short run? The traditional answer has been trade union resistance to wage cuts and redundancies when demand falls. Now union resistance may be important, when demand falls it does not descend instantly and evenly over all industries but proceeds from one sector to another. Hence, an acceptance of a wage cut implies a redistribution of income from those who have suffered a wage reduction to those whose wages remain unchanged. The possibilities of short-run redistributions of income can create resistance to wage cuts and the structure of relative wages may remain constant. Ideas about fairness are involved in sectional wage changes.

There are, however, sound economic reasons, stemming from the demand side, why businessmen will not wish to reduce or dismiss workers when demand falls temporarily. There are costs in advertising, screening and training workers. The morale of the labour force may collapse if there are large-scale redundancies and workers may be reluctant to invest in skills if they fear unemployment or severe wage reductions. Money wage rigidity may, therefore, satisfy both employers and workers in the market for skilled labour. We, therefore, reach the following conclusion.

*The short-run demand for labour depends upon long-run expectations about product demand and the real wage (which in turn depends upon the level of money wage and the level of prices and notions of fairness).*

## Money wage

If the price level is given, then the general level of money wages will be determined by the degree of unemployment in the economy. In Figure 206 we measure the degree of unemployment along the horizontal axis and the rate of change of money wages along the vertical axis. The amount of unemployment, $OU$, is the *natural rate of unemployment* which is determined by 'frictions' in the labour market such as the mobility of labour and the costs of job changes; $OU$ is the amount of unemployment which would obtain in the long run. If unemployment were greater than $OU$ then the rate of change of money wages would fall. If unemployment were greater than $OU$ then the rate of wages would increase. Hence, the curve $WW$ traces out the be-

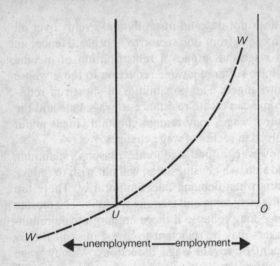

Figure 206

haviour of money wages as unemployment changes, given the level of prices. It is what is known as the *Phillips curve*, and we shall have more to say about it in the next chapter.

## Prices

Prices, as well as money wages, tend to rigidity in the short run. Firms will not change prices quickly to match short-run changes in demand because of the costs of changing prices. Customers may also prefer to shop in fix-price markets because of the costs of having to search through flex-price markets to find the lowest prices. Firms will adjust inventories in response to short-run changes in demand.

## Aggregate supply and demand

The relationship between short- and long-run supply and aggregate demand is shown in Figure 207. Initially, the economy is in equilibrium at output *OY* with aggregate demand curve *DD* and long-run aggregate supply curve *YT*. Now suppose aggre-

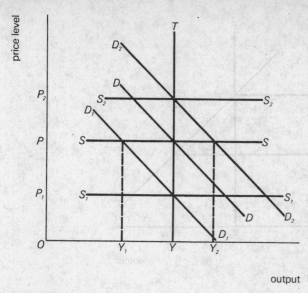

Figure 207

gate demand falls to $D_1D_1$ then the economy will move along the short-run supply curve $SS$ until an equilibrium is reached with output $OY_1$. If the fall in demand were expected to persist then long-run forecasts of product demand and employment would be revised downwards. Wages, costs and prices would fall, the short-run supply curve would shift downwards to $S_1S_1$ and the economy would return to long-run equilibrium with output $Y$ with the lower price level $P_1$.

Now consider the case where aggregate demand rises to $D_2D_2$. The economy will expand along the short-run supply curve $SS$ until the short-run equilibrium output $Y_2$ is reached. If this output were expected to persist then firms would revise their production processes and seek to hire more labour. In doing so they would bid up wages and costs, and prices would start to rise. The short-run supply curve would shift upwards to $S_2S_2$. The rise in prices would lower the real value of money balances and aggregate demand would contract until a new long-run equilibrium is attained with price level $P_2$ and output $Y$.

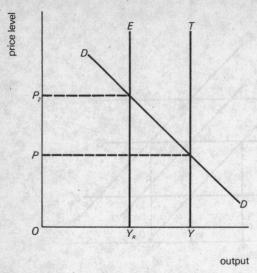

Figure 208

## The influence of raw material prices

So far we have assumed that the aggregate supply is mainly determined by labour supply. However, in the early 1970s there were rapid rises in raw material prices which suggested that the determinant of long-run equilibrium might be the supply of raw materials. In Figure 208 we show a long-run supply curve of raw materials $Y_R E$ to the left of the long-run labour supply curve $YT$. The implication is that long-run equilibrium output will be $OY_R$ and that long-run unemployment will be increased by $YY_R$, the wage will fall and the price level will rise to $P_2$. Of course, the economy might respond to raw materials shortages switching to labour-intensive, as opposed to raw-materials-intensive, methods of production but the response might be long delayed.

### How long is the short run?

Fix-price markets, particularly labour markets, have had a long history. British wages in the nineteenth century showed a high degree of rigidity and during the inter-war years wages also showed a high degree of rigidity despite considerable falls in demand and high levels of unemployment which persisted for two decades. So the short run can encompass a long period of clock time. The long run may be a kind of never-never land and economic activity may largely take place in the short run.

## Summary

Aggregate demand describes the relationship between total output and the price level. Movements along the demand curve are due to changes in real balances brought about by changes in the price level. Shifts of the demand curve are due to variations in autonomous expenditures. Aggregate supply is determined by the production function and the wage. Long-run equilibrium is determined by aggregate demand and aggregate supply. In the long run, aggregate supply is perfectly inelastic; in the short run it is highly elastic.

# Chapter 41
# Aggregate Supply and Inflation

Before we can consider inflation and the causes of inflation we need a working definition of inflation. Such a definition is '*a sustained rise in the general level of prices*', that is, a rise in some average or index of prices. Two things need to be emphasized about this definition. The first is that it defines inflation as a macroeconomic phenomenon and hence in terms of an average of all prices in the economy.[1] A rise in the price of a single commodity or even a group of commodities need not be inflationary if the commodities involved are only a small fraction of total output (or value of output), or if at the same time as they are increasing in price other commodities are falling in price. In the latter case the average of all prices could be constant or even falling. Variations in prices are a normal feature of a free market economy. The second point is that inflation need not be *open* as the definition implies, since inflation can exist without showing itself in changes in quoted prices. Such an inflation is termed *suppressed inflation*. In a situation of suppressed inflation upward pressure on prices is prevented from influencing quoted prices – this, of course, implies a controlled economy. Evidence of inflationary pressure reveals itself in other ways if prices are prevented from rising. Queues and rationing are one sign. Black market prices above quoted prices are another. De-

---

1. To be meaningful the index would have to be a *weighted* average of all prices. Ideally the commodities in the index should also be the same over time, otherwise price changes could reflect quality changes, and not inflation or deflation.

preciation of the country's currency in internal black markets for foreign exchange would also indicate inflationary pressure.

In what follows, however, we will be concerned explicitly with the case of open inflation but the analysis of the mechanics of inflation, and its cure, apply to suppressed inflation as well.

## The inflation problem

Why does inflation have a chapter all to itself? Why does it make the news and cause heated debate? Why does it cause governments to fall? What is wrong with inflation? Many books have been written for and against inflation but the short answer to the above questions is that inflation causes waste – the dissipation of scarce economic resources – and increases social conflict. Inflation is largely a problem in political economy. This is best illustrated by answering the question: *under what conditions would inflation not be a bad thing*? Inflation would not be a bad thing if:

1 People on fixed incomes – pensioners, students, etc. – could be compensated for the reduction in real incomes caused by inflation.

2 Freely floating exchange rates prevented balance-of-payments imbalances resulting from falling exports as the prices of export goods rose.

3 Inflation were slow and crawled rather than galloped. Creeping inflation permits anticipation of its effects.

4 The administrative costs of adjusting to inflation were low.

5 Expectations were fully realized and all processes of adjustment to inflation were instantaneous.

The last two reasons are the big giveaway. Even if a conscious attempt was made by society to alleviate *all* of the problems caused by inflation and the attempt was as successful as possible, inflation would still involve some direct hardship because of the time needed to implement offsets to the waste of resources. Society would be using resources purely to offset inflation. However, this by itself is not sufficient to warrant attempts to prevent inflation from starting, or to cure it if it does exist. The cure may be worse than the sickness, in which case effort should be concentrated on finding the best methods of offsetting the worse effects. So great is the dread of inflation in most mature economies that this is not often considered and a cure is always sought.

## The causes of inflation

Many books have been written for and against inflation but many more have been written on the subject of the causes of inflation. We are not so vain as to attempt to give what appears to be the definitive answer to the question, or to suggest that only economists are equipped to answer it, but we will outline what appear to be the basic economic features of all inflationary processes.

At root inflation is caused by an imbalance between demand and supply. Not demand and supply in the sense of a single demand-and-supply imbalance but in the macro sense of total or aggregate demand and supply. And not necessarily effective aggregate demand and supply! For at least in terms of prime causes, inflation may be the result of some group(s) in society trying to increase their share of total income, that is their real effective demands. This situation is a conflict situation in the sense of social conflict but then all inflation is the child of conflict.

### *Money not the prime mover*

Sustained inflationary processes are inseparable from monetary expansion. Because of this many economists call increases in the supply of money the cause of inflation, but this is only a half truth. Money itself cannot be the prime mover; it is the fuel of inflation but not the vehicle. The domestic money supply is based on the cash base – high-powered money – and cannot increase or decrease by itself; rather it has to be altered by the central bank, acting on behalf of the government. The causes of a sustained inflationary process lie behind increases in the supply of money; they are the forces explaining the increase.

Recognition of this helps to dispel much of the argument and confusion generated by economists, and others, in discussions of inflation. Control of the money supply is the obvious way of stopping inflation. Note we say stop and not cure. If money is not the prime mover, control of the supply of money does not eliminatè the cause of inflation. This explains why inflation is viewed by many as the major economic problem of the day, for it focuses attention on the fact that governments, committed to fighting inflation, still allow the money supply to increase despite the fact that it will add more fuel to the inflationary process. The dilemma results from the apparent incompatibility of the twin policy aims of full employment and stable prices.

## Demand-pull inflation

In Figure 209 we illustrate a typical case of demand-pull inflation – in which an increase in aggregate demand pulls up the general level of prices. The cause of the increase in demand may be due to a government financing its expenditure by printing money. Rather than raising taxes – which can be unpopular and could result in losing a general election – a government could resort to the printing press. Initially, there is a full employment level of income at $Y_f$. The aggregate supply curve is L-shaped indicating that below full employment, increases in demand lead to increases in output without raising prices, but once full employment is reached then increases in demand merely raise prices. Hence, at full employment, increases in aggregate money demand merely slide the aggregate demand curve up the vertical section of the aggregate supply curve.

The account of the inflationary process contained in Figure 209 contains several important assumptions which we must now consider. The first assumption concerns the source of the inflation. As drawn, Figure 209 implies that inflation stems from a movement of the demand curve. But inflation could start from a shift in the supply curve which forces an increase in the money supply and a consequent shift in the aggregate demand curve.

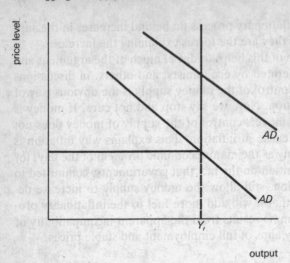

Figure 209

The second query concerns the nature of the aggregate supply curve. Is it, in fact, L-shaped? An L-shaped supply curve assumes a sudden move from fix-prices to flex-prices – it contains, therefore, an assumption about the aggregation of behaviour in all markets. Finally, the L-shaped supply curve suggests that there is one point – at the kink in the supply curve – at which full employment with stable prices is possible.

### The Phillips curve

The Phillips curve establishes a link between the rate of change of money wages and the level of unemployment (the measure of the demand for labour). It is named after A. W. Phillips who derived the curve from the time series data on money wages and unemployment for the UK for the period 1861–1957. Figure 210 illustrates the curve which Phillips derived. It suggests that as the demand for labour rises and unemployment falls then the rate of change of money wages increases. The Phillips curve is not a supply curve because it traces out the relationship between the supply of labour and the rate of change of money

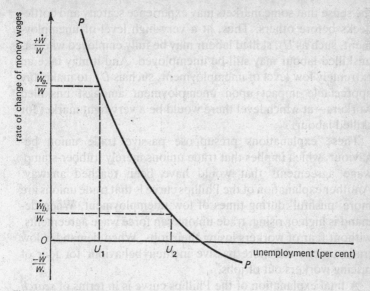

Figure 210  The Phillips curve

wages as the demand for labour changes, whereas a supply
curve would link supply of labour to the level of wages. Nevertheless, the Phillips curve does cast doubt upon the concept of
an L-shaped supply curve; there is no kink at full employment.
In addition, the curve appears to support a demand-pull explanation of inflation because of its apparent stability over a
long period despite great variations in trade unionism.

## Aggregation and expectations

The absence of a kink in the Phillips curve can be explained in
several, but not necessarily conflicting, ways. First, although
some labour markets are highly unionized and exhibit a high degree of money wage rigidity downwards, there are other labour
markets in which wages are highly flexible. Hence, a curve,
rather than a kink, may derive from the responses of different
labour markets to changes in demand. Secondly, changes in demand may exert a differential impact upon labour markets in

the sense that some markets may experience scarcity and bottle-necks before others. Thus, at a very high level of unemployment, such as $U_2$, skilled labour may be fully employed whereas unskilled labour may still be unemployed. And it may take an extremely low level of unemployment, such as $U_1$, to make any appreciable impact upon unemployment amongst unskilled workers – at which level there would be a very tight market for skilled labour.

These explanations presuppose passive trade union be-haviour, which implies that trade unions merely 'rubber-stamp' wage agreements that would have been reached anyway. Another explanation of the Phillips curve is that trade unions are more 'pushful' during times of low unemployment. When de-mand is high or rising, trade unions can force wage agreements, without fear of workers losing their jobs. When demand is low trade unions are more passive in their behaviour for fear of pricing workers out of jobs.

A final explanation of the Phillips curve is in terms of *search unemployment*. It is rarely optimal for an unemployed worker to take the first job offered him. In fact, an unemployed worker will adopt a *search strategy*. This involves balancing the ex-pected benefits and costs (in terms of lost wages) of holding out for a better job, with the costs of accepting a job now, and hence foregoing the chance of better paid employment. This strategy involves the worker having a *reservation wage*: this is the minimum wage at which he would accept a job. He will re-vise this minimum wage downwards in the light of subsequent experience. Now if aggregate demand rises, money wages rise, and, if all workers do not realize that money wages are rising, on average, unemployed workers searching for jobs will accept a job sooner than they would have done. Consequently all *unanticipated* increases in money wage rates will reduce the number of people searching for jobs.

Obviously there is no single explanation of the Phillips curve, and the three above seem to be the most important elements. All three *suggest* that money wages will rise by more than the rate of productivity increase if unemployment is held below *the natural rate of unemployment*.

## The natural rate of unemployment

What is meant by the *natural rate of unemployment*? The natural rate of unemployment, which is determined by labour mobility and job information is the rate of unemployment associated with stability of the general price level. It is given a special name because it is such a critical level of unemployment.

The name itself refers to the fact that price stability is regarded by many as a desirable or natural state of affairs, it does not imply that the level of unemployment is desirable or rigidly fixed.

## From wages to prices

To understand the natural level of unemployment more clearly, and better appreciate the bearing of the Phillips curve on the problem of inflation, it is helpful to translate the curve into one showing the relationship between the level of unemployment (excess demand) and the rate of change of prices. This is possible because wages make up a large fraction of manufacturing costs, so that changes in the general level of prices will closely mirror changes in money wages.

This is done in Figure 211. Part (a) is the same as before and shows the money wage Phillips curve, part (b) shows the alternative relationship, the price level Phillips curve. The difference in the two diagrams, other than the relabelling of the vertical axis in part (b), lies in the point of intersection of the Phillips curve with the horizontal axis. In part (a) the Phillips curve cuts the horizontal axis to the right of $\bar{U}$, the natural level of unemployment. Why? Because in going from changes in money wages to changes in prices it is necessary to allow for the existence of labour productivity growth. If the average rate of labour productivity is rising at say 3 per cent per annum then clearly money wages can rise at this rate without causing prices to rise. That is, stability of the general level of prices is consistent with rising money and real wages as long as the rate of increase in money wages does *not* exceed the average rate of productivity increase.

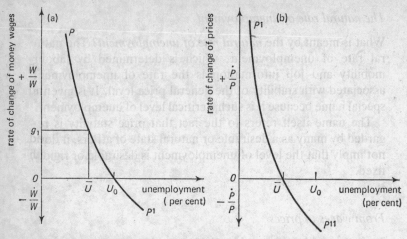

Figure 211 The Phillips curve. (a) The money wage Phillips curve.
(b) The price level Phillips curve

In part (a) let $Og_1$ indicate the rate of productivity growth, and hence the rate of change of money wages consistent with price stability. The level of unemployment associated with this rate of change in money wages is thus $\bar{U}$, the natural rate of unemployment, which, as long as productivity growth is positive, must lie to the left of $U_0$, the unemployment level associated with stable money wage. In part (b) the price level Phillips curve lies further to the left than the money wage Phillips curve, since it intersects the horizontal axis at $\bar{U}$, and not $U_0$. Looking at the price level Phillips curve we can see that if unemployment is held below the natural rate so that money wages rise faster than productivity growth, prices will rise. In addition, as unemployment falls, the average product of labour may begin to fall, and hence prices might also rise for this reason.

In algebraic terms we can summarize the above as follows:

$$\frac{\dot{W}}{W} = f(U) \qquad\qquad \textbf{1}$$

The rate of change of money wages $\left(\dfrac{\dot{W}}{W}\right)$ is a function of the level of unemployment, $(U)$.

$$\frac{\dot{P}}{P} = \frac{\dot{W}}{W} - \frac{\dot{PG}}{PG} = f(U) - \frac{\dot{PG}}{PG} \qquad \qquad 2$$

The rate of change of the general price level $\left(\frac{\dot{P}}{P}\right)$ depends upon the relationship between the rate of change of money wages and the rate of change of productivity $\left(\frac{\dot{PG}}{PG}\right)$.

When there is no productivity growth, the money wage and the price level Phillips curves are similar in that they will both intersect the horizontal axis at the same unemployment level.

## The collapse of the Phillips curve

The Phillips curve gave reasonable predictions of the behaviour of money wages before 1967 and thereafter its predictive power failed; money wages increased at a greater rate than that predicted by the Phillips curve. The Phillips curve appeared to have shifted to the right and a new phenomenon emerged – increasing unemployment and increasing inflation. This phenomenon came to be called *stagflation*. The nature of this problem can be gleaned from Table 50. Between 1969 and 1975, for example, the Index of Retail Prices rose by nearly 100 per cent whilst unemployment rose by 56 per cent. In the following five-year period, prices rose by about 100 per cent whilst unemployment increased by 115 per cent. It is left to the reader to explain the pattern of real output variations during the same period. (Hint: productivity changes and North Sea Oil.)

## Expectations

The explanation for the breakdown lies in expectations. Consider a trade union, negotiating for higher wages. Let us suppose that if prices are expected to stay the same, the union feels that it can squeeze *y* per cent out of employers, without jeopardizing the jobs of many of its workers (i.e. by pricing the product out of the market). Now let the union believe that all prices are going to rise by *x* per cent, it will now feel that it can

**Table 50** Unemployment and inflation in the UK 1965–1980

| Year | Index of retail prices, 1975 = 100 | UK unemployment rate, % | Real output. Index of G.D.P. (at factor cost) in 1975 constant prices. 1975 = 100 |
|------|------|------|------|
| 1965 | 43·4 | 1·5 | 81·4 |
| 1966 | 45·1 | 1·5 | 82·9 |
| 1967 | 46·2 | 2·3 | 84·6 |
| 1968 | 48·4 | 2·5 | 88·4 |
| 1969 | 51·0 | 2·5 | 90·5 |
| 1970 | 54·2 | 2·6 | 92·3 |
| 1971 | 59·3 | 3·4 | 93·7 |
| 1972 | 63·6 | 3·7 | 96·1 |
| 1973 | 69·4 | 2·6 | 103·0 |
| 1974 | 80·5 | 2·6 | 101·1 |
| 1975 | 100·0 | 3·9 | 100·0 |
| 1976 | 116·5 | 5·3 | 103·2 |
| 1977 | 135·0 | 5·7 | 105·1 |
| 1978 | 146·2 | 5·7 | 108·4 |
| 1979 | 165·8 | 5·4 | 109·9 |
| 1980 | 195·6 | 8·4 | 107·4 |

Source: *Economic Trends*

squeeze $x + y$ per cent out of the employers, before it begins to put the jobs of its workers at risk. Likewise, consider a worker searching for a job. If he expects wages in general to rise by $x$ per cent, the expected rate of inflation, he is much less likely to accept a job at a given money wage, than if he expected prices to remain constant. Finally, suppose that firms expect all prices to rise $x$ per cent. Then a firm wishing to attract workers will expect that it will have to offer wages $x$ per cent higher than it would have done. Since in aggregate prices and money wages rise together, we can conclude that the Phillips curve will shift bodily upwards, if the expected rate of inflation rises.

That is, the original Phillips curve relationship, summarized by equation 1 above, is an incomplete specification of the true wage/price unemployment relationship in that it fails to take account of the role of price expectations. It worked well for so long because the time periods for which it was derived were not periods of accelerating inflation, and hence price expectations were unimportant. But once inflation began to accelerate, as it did in the late 1960s, the original relationship ceased to hold. More precisely, the original relationship assumes that workers suffer from *money illusion*; that in wage negotiations they are only interested in the level of money wages and not in the real value of wages. This is nonsense as recent experience all too clearly demonstrates. Once inflation starts to accelerate and workers discover that increased money wages do not lead to increased real wages, they will begin to rectify matters by incorporating the expected rate of inflation into their money wage demands. As indicated above, unions and firms respond rationally to inflation.

In algebraic terms, the correct Phillips curve specification is:

$$\frac{\dot{W}}{W} = f(U) + \alpha \left( \frac{\dot{P}}{P} \right)^e \text{ , and } \frac{\dot{P}}{P} = f(U) + \alpha \left( \frac{\dot{P}}{P} \right)^e - \frac{\dot{PG}}{PG} \qquad 3$$

where $\left( \frac{\dot{P}}{P} \right)^e$ stands for the expected rate of inflation, and $\alpha$ is the coefficient of adjustment linking changes in money wages to the expected rate of inflation. If workers do not suffer from money illusions, and can fully adjust their money wages for the expected rate of inflation, $\alpha$ will be unity. In practice $\alpha$ is likely to be less than unity for a number of reasons. One of the most important of these is that starting from price stability, or even creeping inflation, it will take time for workers to adjust their expectations of inflation to the actual rate, as the actual rate continually accelerates.

### Adaptive expectations

What determines expectations? The most obvious answer is the previous rate of increase of prices. We can construct a scenario. Consider Figure 212. Let wages be increasing at the same rate as productivity so that wages and prices would be constant and people would not expect any inflation. The curve $E_0$ is the Phillips curve drawn on the assumption that the expected rate of inflation is zero. Now suppose that the government regards $U$ as an unacceptably high level of unemployment, and by monetary and fiscal stimulus, succeeds in reducing unemployment to $U_1$. The proportionate rate of wage increase is now $OB$, hence prices increase by $g_1B$. The Phillips curve will now shift

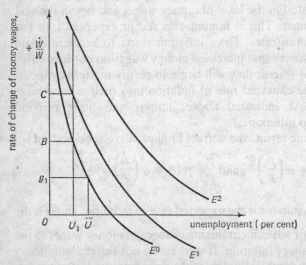

Figure 212  Price expectations and the 'breakdown' of the Phillips curve

upwards, by an amount depending on how quickly people incorporate the experience of price inflation into their expectations, $(0 < \alpha < 1)$. Suppose this gives the Phillips curve $E^1$ in the next period. If the government persists in maintaining unemployment at $U_1$, *validates* the rate of inflation by monetary expansion, wages would increase by $OC$ in the following periods which would give price inflation of $g_1C$, and as people reacted to this, the Phillips curve would shift upwards even further to a position such as $E^2$. The rate at which it will shift up will, again, depend on how rapidly expectations adjust.

### Accelerating inflation

In the orginal Phillips discussion of unemployment and inflation we have observed that it was possible to postulate a stable rate of inflation and that there was a stable trade-off between unemployment and inflation.

*A government can only maintain a given level of unemployment below the natural rate at the cost of a constant rate of inflation.*

By virtue of the reasoning embodied in Figure 212 E. S. Phelps and Milton Friedman replaced the Phillips hypothesis with the following:

*A government can only maintain a given level of unemployment below the natural rate at the cost of a constantly unanticipated rate of inflation.*

And given the assumption that anticipated inflation depends upon the past rate of inflation, this implies:

*A government can only maintain a given level of unemployment below the natural rate at the cost of a constantly accelerating rate of inflation.*

### Rational expectations

In fact matters may be even worse. If people realize that they have persistently underestimated inflation then they will cast around for additional information upon which to base their expectations. Thus, if people realize that the government is increasing the money supply in order to reduce unemployment, and that an increase in the money supply is likely to increase the rate of inflation in the future, then they will act rationally and use this information and not past inflationary experience to determine their inflationary expectations.

This conclusion suggests that the Phillips curve may be vertical in the short run if expectations are formed *rationally*.

*The Rational Expectations hypothesis states that economic agents form their expectations on the basis of the predictions, given all the information they possess, of their economic model of how the economy works. Unless government has access to additional information then individuals will not be misled by government policies and the Phillips curve may be vertical even in the short run.*

**The long-run Phillips curve**

Although we have suggested that the long-run Phillips curve might be vertical, a slope may result if there is random disturbance resulting from technological change and if there is resistance to wage cuts. The historical evidence does suggest that it is only severe unemployment which creates an acceptance of all-round wage reductions.

*The cycle of inflation and unemployment*

During the period since 1945 it is possible to observe a cycle of inflation and unemployment with periods when both unemployment and inflation were rising. This phenomenon can be explained by means of Figure 213. We assume that the economy is at point $h$, the natural rate of unemployment, with stable prices and expectations of no rise in prices. If the government decides to reduce the level of unemployment then the economy will move out along the curve $E_0$ which is the short-run Phillips curve denoting zero inflation expectations. The economy may

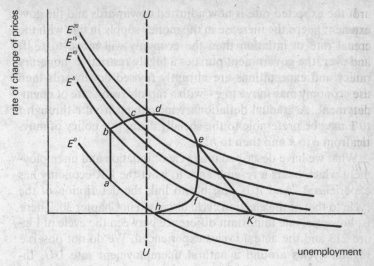

Figure 213

then move to point *a* at which position actual inflation is 5 per cent. If individuals become aware of the inflation rate they will revise all their contracts in order to incorporate a 5 per cent inflation rate. The result will be that the short-run Phillips curve will shift upwards and economy will reach *b*. But at *b* the actual rate of inflation may well be 10 per cent.

Now if the government becomes alarmed at the resulting inflation it will refuse to expand the money supply in order to validate the inflation rate. With a smaller increase in the money supply unemployment will rise. Inflation will, however, continue if expectations are based upon past experiences and everyone wants to be compensated for the previous fall in real income. And so the economy will move to *c* with an expected inflation rate of 10 per cent and an actual rate of 15 per cent. If the government still refuses to validate the inflation then the economy will move to *d*. If the expected rate now remains constant then the economy will move to *e* and the actual rate of inflation will start to decline. The expected rate will now tend to fall below the actual rate.

If the expected rate is now adjusted downwards and the government keeps the increase in the money supply in line with the actual rate of inflation then the economy will move to $f$. If, however, the government pursues a highly restrictive monetary policy and expectations are abruptly revised downwards then the economy may move to $g$ – with a rapidly rising rate of unemployment. A gradual deflationary movement from $e$ through $f$ to $h$ may be preferable to the socially disruptive policy of moving from $e$ to $k$ and then to $h$.

What we have described is a cycle of inflation and unemployment which bears a resemblance to what the UK economy has experienced. And it is possible to link the description of the cycle to that of the election cycle discussed in Chapter 30. There is, however, one important difference between the cycle of Figure 213 and the actual cycles experienced. We do not observe regular cycles around a natural unemployment rate $UU$. Instead, we observe cycles of increasing amplitude. This suggests that over time the natural unemployment rate has increased so that greater injections of money have had to be made in order to achieve a given level of unemployment. Now the natural rate of unemployment may have increased as a result of increases in labour supply. It may also have increased as a result of inflation-induced distortions which impair the efficient operation of the labour market.

### Cost-push inflation

So far we have examined the effects of an increase in aggregate demand upon wages, prices and employment. But we did not explain why demand increased.

Why the money supply was increased was left out of the discussion. The analysis concentrated upon the reactions of the market to an increase in demand. What we shall now do is to set out a theory of inflation which illustrates the increase in the money supply as a reaction to pressures from the supply side. The assumptions of the model are as follows.

1 Prices are based upon raw material prices, wages and a mark-up to cover overheads and profits.

2 Prices are not strongly influenced by demand because markets are oligopolistic.

3 Raw material prices may be determined in internationally competitive markets.

4 Setting aside raw materials, prices and the distribution of income are determined by bargaining between employers and trade unions.

5 Trade unions may ignore demand because they possess legal immunity from damages caused by strikes and can impose political pressure to guarantee full employment.

6 Employers seek that level of profits which will finance their investment.

7 Investment is not capable of rational analysis or influence by monetary policy.

8 Governments may respond to pressures in order to maintain themselves in power.

9 The public sector employs a large portion of the labour force and is not subject to market pressures.

The obvious solution might be anti-trade union and anti-monopoly legislation plus denationalization of the private sector in order to make markets competitive, governments less susceptible to pressures from big business and big unions, and to enable monetary and fiscal policy to control demand. But there may be strong resistance to such legislation and international trade may provide no corrective because international markets are dominated by multinational corporations. Hence, if unions attempt to increase their members' wages, then firms will increase their prices to protect profits and governments will expand the money supply to maintain full employment. The result is inflation.

## Policies

Control of inflation requires the control of the money supply, but control of the money supply requires changes in expectations and institutions. One solution often proposed has been incomes policies but these have tended to be short-lived and monetary-fiscal policy has not been geared to the wage target set in the incomes policy with the result that, following the rational expectations hypothesis, workers have demanded more than the norm. Furthermore, if there is no control on profits then workers become dissatisfied with falling relative incomes.

## Summary

A sustained rise in the price level is known as inflation and is associated with an increase in the money supply. Control of the money supply may require coping with the pressures on governments which cause them to increase the money supply. Incomes policies have been suggested as a cure but they must be operated in conjunction with an appropriate monetary-fiscal policy.

## Questions

1 Define inflation.

2 Outline a monetary theory of inflation.

3 What is the Phillips curve?

4 What is the natural rate of unemployment?

5 Does the rational expectations hypothesis mean that people never make mistakes?

6 Does a trade union wage-push inflation mean that inflation will be explosive?

7 What is the case for an incomes policy?

8 How can governments be prevented from causing inflation?

9 Does inflation impose a tax on money balances?

10 Is there a trade-off between unemployment and inflation in the long run?

11 How might inflation in one country be 'exported' to other countries?

12 'The inflation of the 1970s was a world phenomenon and cannot be explained in terms of cost-push pressures in one particular country.' Explain and discuss.

# Chapter 42
# Exports and Imports

The analysis we have been carrying out into the workings of a macroeconomy has proceeded on the assumption that it was a closed economy. Mention was made in Chapter 4 of exports and imports but thereafter they were ignored. But foreign trade is difficult to cast aside in the case of the UK economy when exports account for some 30 per cent of aggregate demand and a corresponding percentage of imports constitutes an important leakage. During the post-war period inflationary pressures have often been relieved by increased imports which then led to balance of payments crises. We cannot, therefore, delay an examination of foreign trade. In this chapter we shall review the basis of trade and examine the factors determining exports and imports. In the next chapter we shall consider alternative methods of coping with balance of payments problems.

## The basis of trade

The factors governing international trade are the same as those determining interpersonal and inter-regional trade but for one complicating factor – the necessity to pay for foreign goods in foreign currencies. In Chapter 4 we saw that the basis of trade lay in the principle of comparative advantage. Table 51 which is taken from that earlier chapter indicates the production possibilities of two countries. From the information contained in the table it is possible to derive opportunity cost ratios for each country as in Table 52.

**Table 51**

|  | Production possibilities | |
|  | Food | Clothing |
| --- | --- | --- |
| Country 1 | 800 | 500 |
| Country 2 | 1100 | 600 |

**Table 52**

|  | Opportunity cost of food in terms of clothing | Opportunity cost of clothing in terms of food |
| --- | --- | --- |
| Country 1 | 1·2 | 0·83 |
| Country 2 | 1·83 | 0·55 |

The next step is to introduce money and establish absolute (money) prices. Thus, suppose the price of food is £1 in Country 1 and $2 in Country 2 then we automatically know the price of cloth in both countries because, under perfect competition, prices are equal to marginal opportunity costs.

$$\frac{\text{money price of food}}{\text{money price of cloth}} = \frac{\text{marginal opportunity cost of food}}{\text{marginal opportunity cost of cloth}}$$

Table 53 reveals the domestic prices for both goods in the two countries.

**Table 53** Money prices of food and cloth in Countries 1 and 2

|  | Food | Cloth |
| --- | --- | --- |
| Country 1 | £1·2 | £0·83 |
| Country 2 | $3·66 | $1·10 |

## Some simple testing

On the basis of the analysis we have just outlined it is possible to conduct some simple tests of the behaviour of the markets for exports and imports. The demands for foreign goods will depend upon relative prices, incomes, tastes, the characteristics of goods and their availabilities. Characteristics of goods may be important, especially for manufacturers, because individuals may attach different utilities to, say, Japanese and German cars. Availability, or supply conditions, may also be important because the alternative to waiting for a particular commodity may be to buy a less favoured substitute.

### Exports

*Availability.* Although relative prices play a part in determining the demands for exports and imports, it is extremely difficult to provide a simple test of such a hypothesis. It is, however, possible to test the importance of supply conditions. Thus, we can test the hypothesis: 'Do UK exports flag when the home market becomes buoyant?' This hypothesis implies that when domestic demand rises, goods are switched from the export markets to the home market. Figure 214 provides a means of testing the hypothesis. If availability is important then we should expect a low (high) level of domestic demand to go with a high (low) volume of exports. Such a relationship seems to have occurred in 1964–72 but in the other years exports seemed to rise and fall in step with changes in domestic demand.

*Incomes.* In Figure 215 we examine the hypothesis that UK exports will increase when total incomes in the export markets are rising. As a proxy for incomes in export markets we use the value of total sales by UK rivals to UK markets for manufactures. The two time series suggest that UK exports rise when incomes increase but at a slower rate.

### Imports

Figure 216 provides a simple test of the hypothesis that changes

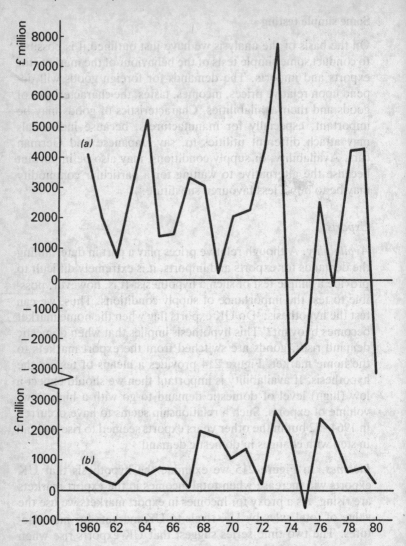

Figure 214(a) Change in total UK domestic demand from the previous year (1975 prices).
(b) Change in UK exports of goods and services from the previous year (1975 prices)

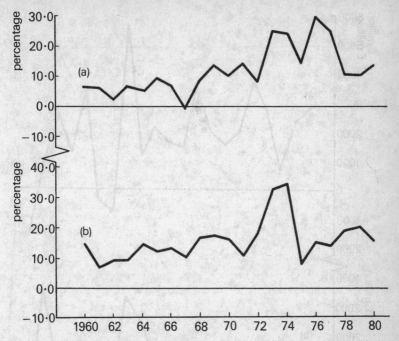

Figure 215(a) Percentage growth over the previous year of UK manufactured exports (current prices).
(b) Percentage growth over the previous year of non-UK manufacture exports to UK export markets (current prices)

in UK domestic income will lead to changes in imports. Clearly there is a positive relationship and if we disaggregated imports we should find that it was imports of manufactures and raw materials which provided the fluctuations in imports, whilst imports of foodstuffs grew in a more regular fashion.

## Summary

UK exports and imports do seem to respond to changes in demand in the manner in which the theory predicts. The relationships are, however, not always clear cut.

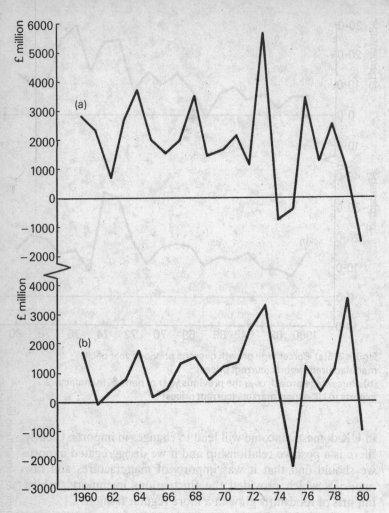

Figure 216(a)  Change from the previous year of UK Gross Domestic Product at 1975 factor prices.
(b)  Change from the previous year of UK imports of goods and services at 1975 prices

Statistical Appendix

| Row Number | 1960 | 1961 | 1962 | 1963 | 1964 | 1965 | 1966 | 1967 | 1968 | 1969 | 1970 | 1971 | 1972 | 1973 | 1974 | 1975 | 1976 | 1977 | 1978 | 1979 | 1980 |
|---|---|---|---|---|---|---|---|---|---|---|---|---|---|---|---|---|---|---|---|---|---|
| 1 Change in UK domestic demand from the previous year at 1975 prices (£ million) | 4135 | 1917 | 704 | 3047 | 5241 | 1395 | 1491 | 3345 | 3029 | 139 | 2097 | 2287 | 4226 | 7858 | -2623 | -2119 | 2580 | -222 | 4247 | 4325 | -3030 |
| 2 Change in UK exports of goods and services from the previous year at 1975 prices (£ million) | 711 | 422 | 218 | 703 | 516 | 741 | 702 | 147 | 2075 | 1836 | 1119 | 1472 | 270 | 2713 | 1853 | -687 | 2468 | 1929 | 602 | 827 | 293 |
| 3 Percentage growth over the previous year of UK manufactured exports at current prices | 6·6 | 6·5 | 2·4 | 6·9 | 5·6 | 8·5 | 7·3 | -0·2 | 8·8 | 13·8 | 10·0 | 14·1 | 7·8 | 25·1 | 24·4 | 14·0 | 29·8 | 25·7 | 10·5 | 10·1 | 12·8 |
| 4 Percentage growth over the previous year of non-UK manufactured exports to UK export markets at current prices | 15·0 | 7·1 | 9·1 | 9·5 | 15·1 | 12·7 | 13·6 | 9·9 | 16·6 | 16·0 | 16·0 | 11·1 | 18·3 | 33·1 | 34·4 | 7·8 | 15·6 | 13·7 | 19·1 | 19·4 | 15·9 |
| 5 Change from the previous year of UK GDP at 1975 factor prices (£ million) | 2821 | 2286 | 618 | 2717 | 3739 | 1993 | 1595 | 1997 | 3535 | 1438 | 1655 | 2170 | 1161 | 6820 | -730 | -430 | 3473 | 1292 | 2629 | 1088 | -1603 |
| 6 Change in UK imports of goods and services from the previous year (1975 prices, £ million) | 1680 | -114 | 326 | 750 | 1733 | 167 | 466 | 1326 | 1531 | 706 | 1210 | 1249 | 2507 | 3247 | 302 | -2232 | 1221 | 327 | 1199 | 3561 | -1175 |

Sources: *National Income and Expenditure*, various issues, HMSO
*National Institute Economic Review*, various issues
*Annual Abstract of Statistics*, various issues, HMSO

# Chapter 43
# Balance of Payments Adjustment Processes

Britons cannot buy foreign goods with pounds, they must first obtain foreign currencies. Similarly, foreigners cannot buy British goods without first obtaining pounds. Thus, the demands for internationally traded goods set up demands for different currencies, and payment problems can arise. In this chapter we analyse the factors which determine the demands and supplies of various currencies. These demands and supplies establish prices which are known as exchange rates; that is, the price or rate at which one currency exchanges for another. In order to simplify the analysis we shall concentrate on two currencies, pounds and dollars.

## The demand for sterling

We can distinguish two reasons why Americans may wish to buy sterling.

### *Consumption*

Americans wishing to buy holidays or whisky in the UK have to pay with sterling and even if they pay with dollars, the UK hoteliers or whisky salesmen will want to exchange their dollars for pounds so that they can conveniently spend their income in Britain. In either case, people with dollars will wish to exchange them for sterling. In order to derive a demand curve for sterling we shall take as an example the sale of cars to Americans. Sup-

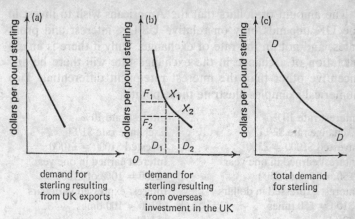

Figure 217

pose that the price of sterling is two dollars per pound; that is, if an American goes to a foreign exchange dealer he can buy £1 with $2. The UK cars that Americans wish to buy we may suppose are £5000 each which is equivalent to $10 000. At the price of $10 000 there will be a certain US demand for British cars. If the exchange rate were to become one dollar per pound then the US price of British cars would be $5000. Since demand theory tells us that fewer cars would be bought at higher prices then the demand curve might be expected to slope downward as in Figure 217a.

## Investment

Americans may observe that interest rates and profits are higher in the UK than in the US. In order to obtain the higher returns they will attempt to lend money to individuals and firms in the UK. Since the latter do not want dollars the Americans will have to buy sterling with their dollars. Thus, a demand for sterling arises. If UK industry is more profitable than US industry then Americans may want to benefit from this discrepancy by buying shares in UK companies, or even by starting a new firm in the UK. In both cases they need sterling. US investment in the UK gives rise to a demand for sterling.

The amount of dollars that the Americans wish to invest in the UK depends only on relative US/UK interest and profit rates, and not on the rate of exchange. Only if there is an expectation of a change in the exchange rate will there be any incentive other than the interest rate/profit differential. Two numerical examples illustrate these points.

| | |
|---|---|
| Interest rate 10% | Interest rate 10% |
| Exchange rate $2/£1 | Exchange rate $1/£1 |
| Invested $1000 = £500 | Invested $1000 = £1000 |
| Interest earned in one year | Interest earned in one year |
| £50 = 10% of £500 | £100 = 10% of £1000 |
| Interest expressed in dollars | Interest expressed in dollars |
| $100 = £50 times | $100 = 100 times |
| $2/£1 | $1/£1 |
| Rate of interest | Rate of interest |
| $= \dfrac{\$100}{\$1000} = 10\%$ | $= \dfrac{\$100}{\$1000} = 10\%$ |

In the first case, where the exchange rate was $2 per £1, if the exchange rate had changed at the end of the year from $10 to $20 per £1 then the £10 of interest would have converted into £10 × $20 per £1 = $200 return on an investment of $1000. An extra profit has been made simply by buying sterling at $10 per £1 and selling at $20 per £1. It is apparent therefore that if the value of the pound is expected to rise then people will buy in anticipation. Conversely, if the value of the pound is expected to fall then people will sell sterling at the high price and then buy it back at the lower price. This buying and selling of currency in anticipation of a change in its value is called *speculation*. No profit is made if the anticipated change in exchange rate fails to occur.

If we assume for the moment that exchange rate changes are not anticipated then the number of dollars that Americans wish to invest in the UK either long-term or short-term depends on the interest/profit rates in the UK relative to America and all other countries where investments could be made. The volume of dollars does not depend upon the level of the exchange rate. However, the sterling demanded does depend on the exchange rate, for example, if there are $100 to be invested at an exchange rate of $1 per £1 the demand is for £100. If the exchange rate is $2 per £1 then the demand is for £50. The relationship results in the demand for sterling by American investors being a rectangular hyperbola, as in Figure 217b.

The total demand for sterling in the course of a period of time is thus the demand arising from trade plus the demand arising from new investments made in the UK during that time period.

## Flow versus stock

We have discussed investment as though Americans have a stock of funds and put them into the country which offers the greatest reward. This is certainly part of the truth. Additionally we need to remember that saving is a continuous process and thus, at any time there is a *stock* of dollars which may or may not be used to buy sterling in order to hold UK assets, and in addition, there is a *flow* of savings also looking for outlets (forms of assets to hold) both in the US and in other countries.

In summary we can say that, per period of time, the demand for sterling will result from both UK exports of goods and services and overseas (US) desire to buy UK assets to hold in both the short run and the long run. The total demand for sterling is the sum of those demands. Thus Figure 217c is the horizontal summation of Figures 217a and 217b.[1]

## The supply of sterling

The supply of sterling depends upon a variety of factors.

### Importing

Let us say that a bottle of bourbon in the US costs $10. At the exchange rate of $1 per £1 a Briton would give £10 for a bottle.

---

1. The reader should note that we have here assumed that the supply of UK exports is perfectly elastic, that is, a fall in American demand for UK goods has no effect on prices within the UK. In the discussion of the supply of sterling we will similarly assume that the supply of American goods is perfectly elastic. Readers who wish to examine the consequences of dropping this simplifying assumption could read the early parts of Haberler (1969).

If the rate of exchange was $10 per £1 then the Briton has to give up £5 to buy a $10 bottle. The price has fallen and he will buy more bottles as a result. The sterling price is half what it was; if he more than doubles his purchases of bottles the supply of sterling will be greater than before the exchange rate change. If he doubles his purchases then supply of sterling is unchanged, and if he less than doubles his purchases the supply of sterling will fall. What happens to the supply of sterling after exchange rate changes depends upon the price-elasticity of demand. Let us examine the supply of sterling resulting from UK imports in more detail. Figure 218 shows the UK demand

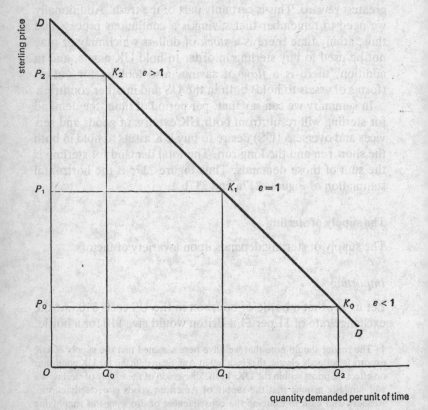

quantity demanded per unit of time

Figure 218

for bourbon at each of the sterling prices that the UK purchaser faces as the exchange rate varies.

At the initial exchange rate the sterling price is $OP_2$ and the demand is $OQ_0$, thus the expenditure (and the supply of sterling) is price times quantity = $OP_2 . OQ_0$ (represented by the area on the graph $OP_2K_2Q_0$). Now the number of dollars per pound is raised and so the sterling price falls to, say, $OP_1$ with demand rising to $OQ_1$. Thus the supply of sterling is the area $OP_1K_1Q_1$. If the price-elasticity of demand is greater than unity over the price range $OP_2$ to $OP_1$ then $OP_1K_1Q_1 > OP_2K_2Q_0$ and the supply of sterling has increased. Somewhere as we go down the demand curve the price-elasticity of demand will fall to unity and then to less than unity as we continue down the line. We see this if the number of dollars per pound again rises making the sterling price of bourbon even lower, the price falling to $P_0$. The total supply of sterling is now $OP_0K_0Q_2$ and is less than at $OP_1$ and the same as at $OP_0$. We can now draw Figure 219 which is a supply curve of sterling resulting from the UK purchases of bourbon.

This supply curve is an unusual shape, depending as it does on elasticity of demand for imports. Such evidence as we have suggests that demand elasticities for imports are characteristically in the range $0 \cdot 5$ to $1 \cdot 0$, but values outside this range cannot be discounted. If they fall in this range then only the upper part of the curve will be observed with the supply curve sloping downwards from left to right.

*Investment*

The supply of sterling arising from UK desires to invest overseas either in the long run or the short run will be unaffected by the level of the exchange rates, but solely by relative interest/profit rates. The supply of sterling by people buying foreign currency for speculative purposes will depend not upon the level of the exchange rate but upon expectations of a change in that level. Thus if for simplicity we assume that no exchange rate change is expected then there will be no speculation and the supply of sterling resulting from UK investment overseas will be

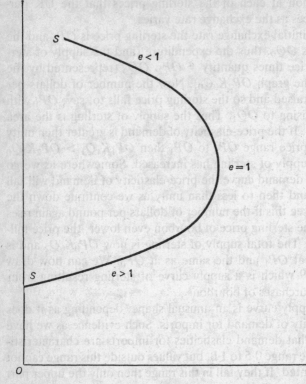

Figure 219

as in Figure 220: the vertical line will shift if relative interest/profit rates change between the UK and other countries.

The total supply of sterling in a given time period is thus the horizontal summation of Figures 220a and 220b, giving 220c.

Now that we have discussed the supply and demand curves for sterling (the flows) we can bring the two together in order to determine the equilibrium rate of exchange, the one at which the supply and the demand during a given time are equal.

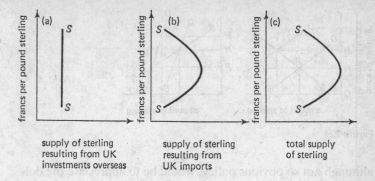

Figure 220

## Equilibrium rate of exchange

Figure 221a depicts a market for sterling in which the demand
and supply curves have the customary shapes; the demand
curve has a negative slope and the supply curve has a positive
slope. The market is in equilibrium with $OA$ pounds being supplied and demanded at exchange rate $OH$. Embodied in this
equilibrium is the *purchasing power parity theory* which says
that there is a connection between the exchange rate and the
prices of traded goods in alternative currencies. Thus, if a good
sells for £1 in Britain it must sell for $10 in the US if the ex-
change rate is £1 for $10.

Now suppose there is an increase in the demand for sterling.
The demand curve shifts to the right and a new equilibrium is
established at exchange rate $OM$. This accords with common
sense: an increase in demand will tend to raise price. In international trade theory the move from $OH$ to $OM$ is referred to as
an *appreciation* of sterling in terms of dollars and a *devaluation*
of the dollar. Now consider the case shown in 221b. The demand curve for sterling cuts a backward sloping segment of the
supply curve. The equilibrium at $A$ is therefore unstable. If the
dollar is devalued from $OH$ to $OM$ then the excess demand for
sterling increases rather than decreases. Indeed the correct,

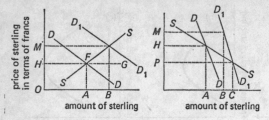

Figure 221

although not so obvious policy, would be to appreciate the dollar to $OP$. It is the possibilities of such perverse cases that have led some economists to suggest that balance of payments problems should be tackled by the use of tariffs.

The efficiency of the foreign exchange market can only be settled empirically. However, we should note that the perverse case rests upon the assumption that import demand elasticities are extremely low. As we have observed, a backward sloping supply curve of sterling can only be derived from a UK demand curve for US goods that has an elasticity less than unity. But it seems common sense to assume that as the dollar falls in value, Britons will purchase more dollars in order to buy the relatively cheaper US goods. Hence the supply curve of sterling would eventually twist round and assume an upward slope. It is also plausible to assume that at some adverse rate of exchange Americans will consider it advantageous to substitute domestic goods for British goods. Therefore, we would expect the demand and supply curves for sterling to intersect at some exchange rate. Such a result is indicated in Figure 221 and arises because at some exchange rate Americans would decide to become self-sufficient; the exchange rate $OC$ is dictated by the US comparative cost ratio. And a similar boundary is $OE$ which is dictated by the UK comparative cost ratio.

Before concluding that devaluations can work it is useful to consider Figure 222 where the demand curve cuts the supply curve from below; the distinction between Figures 221b and 222 lies in the fact that in Figure 222 the demand curve is more elastic than the supply curve. Figure 222 yields a stable equilibrium in

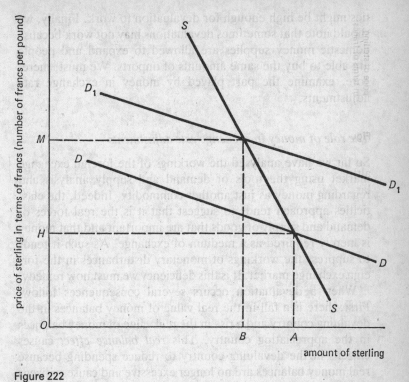

Figure 222

the sense that any arbitrary displacement from *A* will lead to a restoration of the equilibrium. In this example a shift of the demand curve to $D_1D_1$ will produce a new equilibrium at *B* and devaluation will work. So a backward sloping supply curve of a currency can be compatible with an efficiently working foreign exchange market.

We have three possible market situations and the question arises: which is the typical case? Early studies suggested that import demands were extremely low, and gave rise to 'elasticity pessimism' and the belief that devaluations will not work. Subsequent studies suggested that the low elasticities might have been due to the existence of tariffs. Studies of UK exports and imports after the 1967 devaluation have suggested that elasticities might be high enough for devaluation to work. Finally, we should note that sometimes devaluations may not work because domestic money supplies are allowed to expand and people are able to buy the same amounts of imports. We must, therefore, examine the part played by money in exchange rate adjustments.

## The role of money in exchange rate adjustments

So far we have analysed the workings of the foreign exchange market using the tools of demand and supply analysis and regarding money as just another commodity. Indeed, the elasticities approach tends to suggest that it is the real forces of demand and supply of goods that are important and that money is merely required as a medium of exchange. As such it tends to suppress the workings of monetary disturbances in the foreign exchange market. It is this deficiency we must now remedy.

When a devaluation occurs several consequences follow. First, there is a fall in the real value of money balances in the devaluing country and a rise in the real value of money balances in the appreciating country. This *real balance effect* causes citizens in the devaluing country to reduce spending because real money balances are no longer excessive and causes citizens in the appreciating country to reduce their excess real money balances by spending. Secondly, there is a *substitution effect*. Devaluation leaves domestic prices unchanged but the alteration of the exchange rate changes the foreign values of goods and causes citizens of the devaluing country to switch to buying domestic goods and citizens in the appreciating country to switch to buying foreign goods. Thirdly, there is a *portfolio effect* as citizens in the devaluing country switch to buying the cheaper domestic assets and because money balances are substitutes for assets there will be an interaction of real and monetary factors which is additional to that created by the substitution effect. The extent of switching will be determined by the relative elasticities of demand and supply of currencies and domestic and foreign assets and goods. Hence real and monetary forces interact. Fourthly, if there were unemployed resources then the various effects distinguished above will give rise to multiplier effects which will lead to expansions in output and incomes in the export sector and contractions in the import section of the exporting sector.

The elasticities approach appears to be most relevant when there are unemployed resources, rigid prices and wages, liquidity traps and constant supplies of currencies: that is, a Keynesian world. The emphasis upon monetary variables seems most appropriate when there is full employment and flexible prices; that is in a monetarist world. In the Keynesian world devaluation would lead via multiplier effects to full employment and an absence of balance of payments problems. In the monetarist world devaluation would lead via real balance effects to the elimination of balance of payments difficulties. But the real world is not always at the polar extremes and frequently the two models have to be combined for policy purposes. In an economy suffering from inflation and an adverse balance of payments, the first step may be to reduce the money supply which could lead to unemployment. The second step would be to devalue and switch the idle resources into the export sector.

The conclusion we reach therefore is that both the elasticities and monetary approaches to exchange rate adjustments are required. The elasticities approach emphasizes flows of money and goods whilst the monetary approach reminds us that stocks of money, as well as other assets, may be large in relation to any net additions per period of time. Finally, we observe that a country has a choice between altering its money supply or its exchange rate in order to achieve a real balance effect – which policy is most efficient will be considered later.

## Movements of curves

From the discussion above it will be apparent that shifts in the demand and supply curves for currencies will be a function of changes in national incomes, price levels, interest rates and real balance effects at any given exchange rate.

The analysis of the elasticities and monetary approaches to exchange rate adjustment serves to remind us that a complete understanding of economic activity requires a general equilibrium approach and that the elasticities analysis may be one of partial equilibrium. But it is impossible to construct a general equilibrium model which embraces *simultaneous* changes in prices and outputs.

## Balance of payments policy and control

We have seen earlier in the chapter that if relative interest rates, income levels or price levels change between countries then the supply and demand curves for currencies will move, other things being equal. If governments allow the curves to move, and new equilibrium prices to emerge quite freely, then these are called *freely floating exchange rates*. In this situation a balance of payments problem cannot exist because changes in the price of currencies will always ensure that demands and supplies are reconciled. Any excess supply or demand can only result from a failure of the exchange rate to adjust.

The actual processes that occur in the economy when the supply of or the demand for a country's currency are not equal on the foreign exchange market are quite complex as we have indicated in the earlier part of the chapter; the money supply changes, interest rates change, investment levels change with resulting multiplier effects on income and so on, all these changes inter-reacting on one another. But at this stage it is enough to have sketched their nature.

Now we shall look briefly at the possibility that a government will not let the exchange rate float freely for various policy reasons. We will examine the case of a country with a deficit on its balance of payments.

To some extent, given enough time the balance of payments will adjust itself, provided that the government can in the short run buy the excess sterling using its foreign currency reserves or borrowed funds. Some of this adjustment we have already met. If the flows of sterling out of the UK to buy foreign currency exceeds the flow into the country from those overseas buying UK imports and investing in the UK, then the supply of sterling (money) within the UK is declining. Earlier chapters have sug-

gested that the effect of reduction in the money supply is to reduce prices and force up interest rates. The first result improves
the competitive level of prices, raising exports and cutting imports; and the second attracts foreign investment into the UK
thus increasing the demand for sterling.

The rise in interest rates will discourage domestic investment
in plant and machinery and domestic consumption and this will,
through the multiplier, reduce the level of income and thus the
demand for imports. A related feature is that if the country's
prices have been rising relative to foreign prices (perhaps the
cause of the payments deficit) then exports will be reduced and
imports increased, both reducing domestic demand and,
through the multiplier, national income. Lower income means
lower imports and possibly lower prices (see the chapter on
inflation).

Over the last few years the money supply in the UK has
grown so strongly that the monetary effect of the balance of
payments deficit had no noticeable effect and thus automatic
adjustment became too slow in practice and deliberate non-
automatic policies were resorted to in order to restore equality
between the demand for and supply of sterling on the foreign
exchange market.

## Balance of payments policies

If some change in the economic environment causes the supply
and demand curves for a currency to shift, then at the initial
equilibrium exchange rate the supply of currency will not equal
the demand. This situation is shown in Figure 221, where the
demand excess exceeds the supply by an amount *FG*.

If the government chooses to maintain the old exchange rate
then it has a number of possible short- and long-run policies.
All the policies must either have the effect of reducing the supply of, or increasing the demand for, the currency. How can this
be done? We will list, and briefly discuss, a number of possible
policies which may be used singly or together.

1 In the short run the UK government can use its reserves of

foreign currency to buy up the excess sterling (to take an example), in the process providing the foreign currency that the sterling holders were trying to buy. This way of removing the sterling excess can only be used in the short run as the government will run out of reserves.

2 The government can deflate the economy. With this policy it reduces the level of demand for imports, or at least slows the rate of growth of imports relative to the rate of growth of exports. We have seen that a major determinant of imports is the level of income. Deflation reduces national income or slows its rate of growth. As the labour force normally grows continuously any fall in income or its rate of growth results in unemployment. The cost of this solution to a balance of payments problem is the output that could have been produced by the unemployed. An additional problem is that the solution may only be short run in that when the government allows income to grow again at its 'normal' rate, imports may again jump up to a level where the supply of sterling again exceeds the demand for it.

If the low level of activity in the economy reduces the level of UK prices or their rate of growth relative to other countries, then the benefit may be long lasting if UK prices continue at the reduced level relative to other economies even after the deflation ends.

The government can deflate the economy in a number of ways, by cutting government spending, by increasing taxation, by reducing the money supply or by increasing the rate of interest and thus discouraging investment, or by a combination of these and other possible policies.

The raising of interest rates may be introduced for reasons other than their deflationary effect – to increase the inflow of foreign investment.

3 We have already seen how a rise in UK interest rates will increase private lending to the UK and tend to reduce UK private investment overseas, thus increasing the demand for sterling and reducing its supply. This is again a short-run policy, unless high interest rates are maintained the loans will be

repaid and not replaced. Foreign loans may allow some parts of the economy to go on spending in excess of their income but the high interest rates will tend to discourage manufacturers from investing in plant and machinery, thus reducing future potential output.

4 Another possible solution which doesn't require a change of exchange rates is to borrow foreign currency with which to buy the excess sterling until such time as the 'good times' return. Again the policy will only work in the short run, it does not remove the cause of the initial imbalance in the exchange markets. It does, however, give you time for other policies to take effect which will alter the long-run position. Such borrowing has a natural limit; lenders must be sure that the loan and the interest can, and will, be repaid.

5 The fifth policy that we would mention relates to inflation as a cause of balance of payments crisis. If imports are rising and exports are falling because the price level is becoming uncompetitive, then a solution is to reduce or stop inflation. In the past deflation has been used and so have incomes policies. The new element not previously discussed is incomes policies where the rate of growth of incomes is acted upon directly by voluntary agreement or legislation. Whether such policies are a long-term or only a short-term cure for inflation and balance of payments difficulties is not clear to researchers.

There is a full discussion of inflation in Chapter 41, all we need to remember at this stage is that it may cause foreign exchange market disequilibrium and its removal or reduction will certainly affect that market. Finally, is there a cost to incomes policy? – many argue that there is, the chief of which is loss of freedom in wage negotiation.

6 The last policy that we would mention is that of physical controls. If tariffs are imposed on imports then their value falls. Similarly, subsidies on exports will boost them. On the capital account you may place various restrictions on investment overseas by your nationals.

These restrictive measures are not normally available to countries as most are bound by international agreements forbidding or discouraging the erection of obstacles to free trade and the free flows of capital.

## Floating versus fixed rates of exchange

During the period from the Second World War until the early 1970s, the world's major trading nations were committed to a system of fixed exchange rates, but since then an increasing number of economies have allowed their currency to float.

The reasons are complex but what we will do is indicate at least some of the advantages that countries saw in fixed exchange rates.

Firstly, many countries saw the aim of a stable fixed exchange rate as highly desirable after the economic chaos of the 1930s. If the international community could agree on fixed exchange rates, then the beggar-my-neighbour devaluation policies of the 1930s could not reoccur. Eventually this desire became a political objective, almost a sign of political virility – 'what did you think of a country which couldn't even control its own balance of payments?' Unchanged currency values became a point of political honour. Attitudes have changed on this point somewhat.

Secondly, it was felt that free floating rates would fluctuate sufficiently widely that there would be uncertainty about currency values and that this would limit world trade which was seen to be a 'bad' thing. Recent world experience of floating seems to have allayed this fear.

Thirdly, it was felt that fixed exchange rates provided a useful and important discipline especially in relation to inflation. With fixed rates, inflation causes balance of payments crises, therefore stamp out inflation! With floating rates the rate just floats down as you inflate, therefore inflation would not apparently need to be so tightly checked as under fixed rates.

Paradoxically, one of the disadvantages of floating rates is that if the rate floats down then the cost of imports rises and if you are an economy like the UK with huge imports of food and raw materials which are not domestically available then your prices are forced up unavoidably and inflation is that much harder to control. The size of the downward float necessary to restore equilibrium will depend partly on the slopes of the currency supply and demand curves – they could be such that to restore equilibrium, a massive rise in import prices would occur. This is a situation, some argue, that the UK was in in 1977.

The breakdown of the fixed exchange rate system was caused by a number of factors although there is still not complete agreement over all the factors and their relative importance.

Two major factors developed throughout the post-war period. Firstly, there was a very rapid and sustained growth in world trade which meant that the absolute magnitude of temporary balance of payments fluctuations tended to be bigger, thus requiring larger foreign currency reserves. But the reserves did not grow proportionately and the temporary disequilibrium could not readily be accommodated. The second feature was a change in the relationship of international prices. Price levels in countries tended to diverge by more than had previously been the case. In this situation balance of payments problems arose which required that both the surplus and the deficit countries made adjustments. Unfortunately, the pressure on surplus countries to adjust their policies was slight, and they tended not to make these changes. Thus all of the burden of adjustment fell on the deficit countries who, in a period of fixed exchange rates, used deflation, thus imposing slower growth and unemployment on their economies. Gradually these costs became less acceptable and floating conversely began to seem attractive.

Two other contributory factors leading to the breakdown of the fixed exchanges rate regime were the US involvement in Vietnam, which fuelled a world inflation, and the sudden sharp rise in world mineral oil prices which immediately made the value of oil imports rise very suddenly without a compensating increase in exports.

Thus continuing developments and sudden shocks found the fixed exchange rate system wanting and encouraged a number of countries to experiment with floating rates.

## Summary and conclusions

We have seen that exports and imports of goods and services depend upon relative price level and income levels. We have suggested that the flow of international private lending and borrowing depends upon the relative interest rates and rates of profit.

We have investigated how trade in goods and services and private lending and borrowing across international frontiers leads to supplies and demands for currencies which are reconciled in the foreign exchange market at a price for each currency in terms of the other currencies – a price which, if the market is left free to float, will equate supply and demand.

If the exchange rate is fixed, and we looked at some reasons why this has seemed a reasonable policy, then any imbalance between demand and supply for a currency has had to be met in the short run by buying up the excess, and in the long run by adopting policies which would shift the supply and demand curves relative to one another so that they intersect at the desired rate.

The only other acceptable policy was of devaluation – a discrete change in the exchange rate to what was estimated to be the new equilibrium rate. The difficulties of this policy were that speculative pressure grew in anticipation of the discrete change and the chosen new exchange rate had to be estimated, and it might prove not to be at a level where currency demand and supply were equal.

All of these policies have costs as well as benefits. It may well be properly a political question just what costs are borne by whom in order to gain the desired balance of payments situation.

Two topics have not been mentioned and clearly should be. We have made no real mention of countries with a balance of payments *surplus*, where there is an excess demand for their currency at the current exchange rate. The analysis here is really the analysis that we have examined for a deficit country, but simply put into reverse, inflating rather than deflating, lowering interest rates, increasing money supplies and so on. The problem of a surplus is very much an embarrassment of riches not needing immediate action. If your exchange rate is not floating then you *have* to do something about a balance of payments deficit.

The second topic not mentioned is that of government spending overseas on military matters, diplomacy, etc. These currency flows occur as a result of government carrying out their policy aims and even in a deficit situation it does not follow that they should be cut in order to restore equilibrium. The effect of this government spending can be analysed using the balance of payments analysis developed in this chapter.

In an appendix to this chapter the balance of payments accounts of the UK for recent years are set out and explained.

This may have seemed a long and hard chapter, but we would justify it in terms of the importance of trade to many countries (the UK exports about one quarter of all it produces) and the profound effect on economies of balance of payments policies.

## Appendix I: International Monetary Experience 1875–1981

In order to understand the relative merits of fixed and floating exchange rates it is necessary to examine international monetary history over the last century.

### Gold standard

In the last quarter of the nineteenth century, world trade tended to operate on the basis of what was known as the *gold standard*. What this meant was that countries fixed the values of their currencies in terms of a given amount of gold and they adhered to these exchange rates. Because all currencies were tied to gold there was an international currency and the existence of the fixed ratios gave rise to all the advantages that stem from the introduction of a monetary system, such as easier communications and greater division of labour. Gold was the international currency though it was not always used in transactions. By virtue of Britain's importance in world trade there was a tendency to use sterling as the unit of account and medium of exchange. Thus, the system was sometimes referred to as a *gold exchange standard*.

The gold standard was a fixed exchange rate system – all currencies had their values fixed in terms of gold – and this provided a discipline and a check to currency debasement; and the system seemed to work, though it is not clear how and why it worked.

In theory, the system worked as follows. A country which experienced a deficit – an outflow of currency because it was importing too much and exporting too little – was required to deflate and reduce domestic demand. The outflow of currency implied less currency inside the country as the banking system contracted deposits because reserves were contracting. The fall in demand was supposed to lead to a fall in prices and costs which would make the goods of the country less expensive for foreigners to buy. At the same time the inflow of currency into other countries would cause an expansion of demand and a rise in prices making it dear to buy from them but easy to sell to. In short, the gold standard adjustment process was nothing more than the quantity theory of money with monetary flows between countries, or even regions, causing changes in prices and costs. Thus, a fixed exchange rate system rather similar to the gold standard system operates within countries. When the demand for coal declined in the sixties there was a fall in the exports of coal from Northumberland and Durham and there was a balance of payments problem.

We must now consider why the gold standard worked in the nineteenth century and failed in the twentieth century.

1 The first reason that can be put forward for its apparent success is that it was never called upon to operate. Most of the industrial countries kept in step with each other in the sense that their booms and slumps coincided. And even where their rates of growth differed, it was never serious enough to matter or was controlled by the use of tariffs.

2 The second reason that can be advanced is that imbalances were only temporary and were covered by capital flows. When

a country had a balance of payments deficit it raised interest rates and this resulted in an inflow of short term capital.

3 The adjustment process overlooked the effects on the under-developed, primary-producing countries. When, for example, Britain had a deficit, there would be a fall in demand for agricultural goods and raw materials and a fall in the amount of capital flowing out to be invested in the underdeveloped world. Because of the high price inelasticities of demand and supply for their goods, primary producers were forced to deflate drastically and this, paradoxically, had the effect of turning the terms of trade in favour of Britain. Hence, the underdeveloped countries came to view the gold standard as a capitalist plot.

In the inter-war years the gold standard broke down, and Britain discarded it in 1931. To understand why it broke down it is necessary to look at certain features of that troubled period. During the First World War many countries suffered major inflations and rates of inflation varied from country to country. After the war attempts to establish a fixed exchange rate system, a gold standard, ran into the difficulties of deciding what the new exchange rates should be. Many countries experimented with fluctuating exchange rates in an endeavour to find the right level, but these experiments were not successful because many of them were still experiencing inflation. As a consequence, exchange rates seemed to oscillate wildly and this was attributed to fundamental instability in the foreign exchange markets. It was seldom acknowledged that the instability stemmed from inflation. In the case of Britain the decision to return to the gold standard at the wrong rate created problems throughout the twenties.

The fundamental reaction to the gold standard came in the thirties and, in restrospect, for the wrong reasons. The decision of the American authorities to cut back their money supply and to call in loans led to a general reduction in currencies and left a situation in which the volume of international transactions could not be sustained by the volume of moneys internationally acceptable as proxies for gold. Just as the introduction of money results in improved communications and a greater division of labour, so its contraction results in chaos and a return to barter. These consequences were not understood at the time. The collapse of the gold standard was attributed to wage and price rigidities but these were the short-run responses to a traumatic shock. Beggar-my-neighbour policies of devaluation and tariffs merely intensified the problem because such policies had the effect of improving one country's balance of payments at the expense of others – there was not enough international money to go round. The collapse was due to ignorance and inexperience. What was wanted in the inter-war years was for America to provide the gold exchange standard that Britain had offered in the nineteenth century.

## The dollar standard

After the Second World War there was an attempt to return to a gold standard. The Bretton Woods Agreement of 1944 attempted to establish a regime of fixed exchange rates and laid down the conditions under which exchange rate adjustments could take place. Countries which did experience a 'fundamental disequilibrium' were permitted to realign their currencies and could borrow gold or dollars from a newly established International Monetary Fund to tide them over short-run difficulties. The Fund was financed by member countries. In addition to the IMF there was also established an International Bank for Reconstruction and Development (often referred to as the World Bank) which was intended to assist in the movement of long-term capital and to provide loans to developing countries.

Between 1950 and 1970 the system seemed to work, though the reasons for its success were not always obvious or desirable.

1 There were very few exchange rate variations. After an initial phase of difficulties which were sorted out by currency variations in the late forties, most countries accepted the fixed exchange rate discipline.

2 America provided enough liquidity, enough currency, to provide a gold exchange rate system. America did not produce too

many dollars to induce a loss of foreign confidence nor so few as to cause severe domestic unemployment.

From the late sixties, however, problems began to arise and finally caused a collapse of the fixed exchange rate system.

1 The lowering of tariff barriers by countries exposed them to competition from the developing nations. Since the middle sixties, tariff reduction has virtually ceased. In the fifties the gold standard worked because tariffs provided some protection from necessary adjustments, but if tariffs are to be reduced can the gold exchange system survive the numerous and complex adjustments?

2 Towards the end of the sixties, American restraint broke down under the necessity of financing the Vietnam War and a domestic anti-poverty programme. The sharp expansion in the dollar supply caused a worldwide rise in prices and a loss of confidence in the dollar.

3 Surplus countries, such as Western Germany, were reluctant to allow their domestic price levels to rise or their currencies to be revalued.

4 The upsurge in oil prices which led to difficult financing and adjustment problems.

Today (1983) it is not clear how the international monetary system will evolve. The situation is very much like the 1920s with strong and weak currencies coexisting in an uneasy alliance. Some economists believe that there is nothing to worry about, a world of floating exchange rates has not proved disastrous. Some, however, maintain that sooner or later there will be a return to a fixed exchange rate system because people will prefer to make their transactions in terms of the currencies which fluctuate least. Others argue for a return to gold, but that might mean that South Africa would benefit from a revaluation of gold – an action which, on political grounds, many dislike. A fourth group would like to see the establishment of an international man-made currency provided by an international agency and not subject to the limitations of supply, as in the case of gold, or the vagaries of domestic policies, as in the case of the dollar.

## Appendix II: Balance of Payments Accounts

In the light of our discussions of exchange rates and adjustment processes we can briefly comment upon the UK balance of payments accounts. And for ease of exposition we shall concentrate upon 1980. The accounts are divided into a current account, a capital or investment account and a financing section. The current account is divided into trade in viable goods, such as plant and equipment, and invisibles, such as freight and insurance. The plus sign indicates that the demand for sterling exceeded the supply so that in 1980 the demand for sterling on current account was in surplus by £3206 million. On the capital account there was an outflow of sterling of £1475 million which went into overseas investment. The overall balance of payments was, however, in surplus and the surplus was reduced and the payments brought to equilibrium by buying foreign currencies and adding them to reserves and by lending, as well as by a rise in the exchange rate. The rise in the exchange rate is not shown in the accounts but was tending to take place automatically because Britain was on a floating exchange rate.

**Table 54** Summary balance of payments

|  | 1970 | 1971 | 1972 | 1973 | 1974 | 1975 | 1976 | 1977 | 1978 | 1979 | 1980 |
|---|---|---|---|---|---|---|---|---|---|---|---|
| *Current account* | | | | | | | | | | | |
| Visible balance | -34 | +190 | -748 | -2586 | -5351 | -3333 | -3929 | -2284 | -1542 | -3458 | +1178 |
| *Invisibles* | | | | | | | | | | | |
| Services balance | +481 | +625 | +701 | +786 | +1083 | +1519 | +2443 | +3254 | +3711 | +4039 | +4188 |
| Interest, profits and dividends balance | +554 | +502 | +538 | +1257 | +1415 | +773 | +1365 | +104 | +592 | +846 | -38 |
| Transfers balance | -178 | -193 | -244 | -438 | -420 | -480 | -760 | -1115 | -1822 | -2290 | -2122 |
| Invisibles balance | +857 | +934 | +995 | +1605 | +2078 | +1812 | +3048 | +2243 | +2481 | +2595 | +2028 |
| *Current balance* | +823 | +1124 | +247 | -981 | -3273 | -1521 | -881 | -41 | +939 | -863 | +3206 |
| Capital transfers | — | — | — | -59 | -75 | — | — | — | — | — | — |
| Investment and other capital transactions | +545 | +1790 | -684 | +166 | +1594 | +134 | -3073 | +4212 | -4260 | +2177 | -1475 |
| Allocation of SDRs (+) | +171 | +125 | +124 | — | — | — | — | — | — | +195 | +180 |
| Gold subscription to IMF (-) | -38 | — | — | — | — | — | — | — | — | — | — |
| Official financing | | | | | | | | | | | |
| Net transactions with overseas monetary authorities | -1295 | -1817 | +449 | — | — | — | +984 | +1113 | -1016 | -596 | -140 |
| Foreign currency borrowing (net) | — | +82 | — | +999 | +1751 | +810 | +1791 | +1114 | -187 | -250 | -941 |
| Official reserves (drawings on +/ additions to -) | -125 | -1536 | +692 | -228 | -105 | +655 | +853 | -9588 | +2329 | -1059 | -291 |
| Balancing item | -81 | +232 | -828 | +103 | +108 | -78 | +326 | +3190 | +2195 | +396 | -539 |

Source: *UK Balance of Payments Accounts 1981*

# Chapter 44
## Business Cycles

Economic activity does not generate uninterrupted growth; it proceeds in fits and starts. In decomposing the time series of prices and outputs some economists have claimed to find cycles of economic activity of varying length. These cycles have been associated with different forms of economic activity and have been named after their discoverers as follows.

1 An inventory cycle of four years in length which has been called the Kitchin cycle. This cycle seems to have been prominent over the last thirty years and is associated with changes in stocks.

2 A cycle in fixed capital equipment of about nine years in duration appears in the nineteenth century with peaks in 1872, 1882, 1906 and 1913. It may have re-emerged in the 1970s. This was the trade cycle or Juglar cycle.

3 A building cycle of about seventeen years in duration which had the effect of reducing the severity of every alternate trade cycle.

4 A long wave of about fifty years in duration which is associated with major innovations, the clustering of minor innovations and the rise of new industries, such as the steam engine and textiles, the use of steel, the internal combustion engine and synthetic fibres and electronics. The fact that there have only been four observations of long waves since the Industrial Revolution casts doubt on its existence. However, some econ-

omists regard the prolonged recession of the seventies and early eighties as the downswing of a long wave or Kondratiev as they are sometimes called. Finally, it should be noted that these waves are observed in manufacturing industry but would seem to require innovations in agriculture and mining for their continuance.

## Characteristics of the cycle

We can divide the characteristics of a typical cycle into two groups in terms of either: (1) the behaviour of key variables or (2) the main features of various phases of a cycle.

In a typical business cycle certain key variables appear to behave as follows.

1 There is a tendency for the outputs of all industries to rise and fall together.

2 The amplitude of fluctuations in the capital goods industries are greater than those in the consumer goods industries.

3 Business profits tend to fluctuate more than wages.

4 The general level of prices tends to rise in booms and falls in slumps.

5 The velocity of circulation of money moves pro-cyclically.

6 Short-term interest rates tend to move pro-cyclically.

In addition to the behaviour of these indicators we can divide a stylized cycle into four phases.

1 *Slump.* During a slump there is heavy unemployment, a low level of consumer demand in relation to the capacity to produce consumer goods and a lack of business confidence. The general level of prices will be tending to drift downwards although money wages may be sticky.

2 *Upswing.* A recovery from a slump may arise for a variety of reasons but once under way, business confidence will grow and generate demands for new investment. Employment, incomes and consumers' spending will all begin to rise.

3 *Recession*. The upper turning point of a cycle may have its origins in a slackening in the rate of growth of consumers' expenditures which arises from increasing product prices. The slowing down of consumption leads to a fall in investment and a cumulative contraction of incomes, output and expenditure.

### Causes of the cycle
*Real theories*

A real theory of the business cycle can be constructed from the interaction of the multiplier and the accelerator. The multiplier states that an increase in investment will give rise to an increase in income. The accelerator makes investment respond to an increase in the rate of increase of income. Since any increase in investment will give rise to an increase in income a self-contained theory of income movement can be generated. Table 55 provides an example of the interaction of the multiplier and accelerator. The table assumes that the marginal propensity to consume out of the previous period's income is 0·5 and that investment is proportional to the rate of increase of consumers' expenditure. Following the initial injection of 100 of autonomous investment or government expenditure the multiplier-accelerator interaction gives rise to cyclical movement of income through time. In period 4 the rate of increase of consumers' expenditures falls to 25 as compared with 50 over the previous periods and this causes investment to fall. The fall in the rate of increase of consumers' expenditure between periods 4 and 5 is sufficient to cause an absolute fall in investment – there is capital consumption. What then causes an upswing is the impact of autonomous investment which sets the multiplier off in an upward direction in period 9.

By varying the values of the marginal propensity to consume and the acceleration coefficient it is possible to produce a variety of time paths for national income. It is even possible to produce a cycle of regular shape and amplitude although it is extremely doubtful if the two coefficients would have stayed at a

**Table 55** Interaction of the multiplier and accelerator

| Period | Autonomous investment | Current consumption induced by previous income | Current investment proportional to change in consumption | National income |
|---|---|---|---|---|
| 1 | 100 | — | — | 100 |
| 2 | 100 | 50 | 50 | 200 |
| 3 | 100 | 100 | 50 | 250 |
| 4 | 100 | 125 | 25 | 250 |
| 5 | 100 | 125 | 0 | 225 |
| 6 | 100 | 112·5 | −12·5 | 200 |
| 7 | 100 | 100 | −12·5 | 187·5 |
| 8 | 100 | 93·8 | −6·3 | 187·5 |
| 9 | 100 | 93·8 | 0 | 193·8 |
| 10 | 100 | 96·9 | 3 | 193·9 |

particular set of values for 200 years. And of the other possibilities, only two have been singled out for special attention. The first is the case where the coefficients are low in value and give rise to *damped cycles* with the cycles being restarted by an external shock. The second case is where the coefficients take on high values and produce an explosive path for income which is constrained by a ceiling imposed by full employment of resources and a floor provided by autonomous investment.

Although the multiplier-accelerator model is capable of providing a cycle, it is doubtful whether it can be a complete explanation. The model neglects the supply side of the economy. Fluctuations are produced as a result of lags in consumers' expenditures but to obtain a cycle of four to seven year. would seem to require an output lag. The model contains no discussion of monetary factors although changes in the money supply might be the external force which gets the cycle under way. The model relies upon relationships (consumption function and acceleration principle) which have been heavily criticized.

## Monetary theories

Changes in the money supply could be responsible for business cycles by creating unanticipated divergences between real and money rates of interest as a result of price level movements. But the question arises, what causes the changes in the money supply? One school of thought takes the view that changes in the money supply are purely passive and are induced by changes in real forces. Hence, it is expectations about real forces which cause changes in the money supply. The alternative view is that it is inappropriate actions by central banks which cause minor disturbances to be converted into major crises.

## Political theories

The money supply may change because the authorities believe that they can control unruly real forces through monetary actions but instead end up creating a crisis because real forces are not volatile until they are provoked by inappropriate monetary injections. One reason why such injections are produced, and which has found favour in recent years, is that governments wish to create a favourable economic climate before an election. This theory has the attraction that it gears the four-year inventory cycle to the four-to-five-year period of office of a government.

## Summary

Fairly regular cycles in economic activity seem to occur in all countries and are called business cycles. They have been explained by a variety of theories although it is probable that no single or simple explanation will ever prove satisfactory.

# Chapter 45
# Stabilization Policy

## Targets and instruments

By stabilization policy we mean attempts by governments to reduce fluctuations in economic activity. These fluctuations may be seen as causing undesirable movements in national income, prices, balance of payments and the rate of economic growth, and removing them offers *targets* for economic policy. The *instruments* of policy which are capable of reducing disturbances are: monetary policy, fiscal policy, exchange rate policy; indicative planning; and various other non-price measures.

Table 56 presents some of the targets of macroeconomic policy over the last three decades and some of the instruments used to pursue them. A point to note at this stage is that the targets have been the subject of considerable controversy. Thus, the pursuit of full employment has been challenged on the grounds that it has led to a situation of underemployment – too many

**Table 56** Targets and instruments of macroeconomic policy

| Targets | Instruments |
|---|---|
| national income | fiscal policy |
| employment | monetary policy |
| price level growth | indicative planning |
| balance of payments | exchange rate policy |

people not working efficiently. And the preoccupation with full employment has led to a neglect of leisure. Furthermore, the pursuit of growth has been attacked by the environmentalists who have pointed to the dangers of pollution, and exhaustion of raw materials. The targets have also been criticized as being impossible. Thus, it has been alleged that full employment, stable prices and free collective bargaining (another desired target) are incompatible.

The central problems of stabilization policy concern the appropriate values for the targets – which may be considered to be political decisions – and the requirement that there be as many instruments as there are targets. If there are too few instruments then some targets may not be attained. Thus, if fiscal policy is used to control the level of employment then there will also need to be an instrument to correct balance of payments disturbances. A second step is to ensure that each target is associated with the most efficient target for its attainment. Thus, if a country has a balance of payments problem then it can use monetary policy, fiscal policy, exchange rate adjustments or tariffs or subsidies to correct it. The problem of choosing efficient instruments will be the subject of this chapter although we will have little to add to the problems of foreign trade beyond the discussion of Chapter 43.

## Fiscal policy

The use of fiscal policy to control macroeconomic variables is an outcome of the slump of the 1930s and the emergence of Keynesian economics. In the nineteenth century governments, like households, were expected to balance their budgets and governments' budgets were expected to be small because there existed the apparently overwhelming evidence that private spending yielded greater returns than public spending. A consequence of these assumptions was that when government receipts fell during the slump of the thirties, government expenditure was also expected to fall, with the result that the recession was intensified. Keynesian economics led to a rejection of public thrift and a greater awareness of the usefulness in controlling depressions. Later, Keynesian fiscal policy was applied to the control of wartime inflation.

## The effects of government spending and taxing

We shall begin our analysis of the effects of government spending and taxing by considering the nature of the government budget constraint. As we saw in Chapter 29 a government can finance its expenditures by taxing, borrowing or printing money.

$$G_c = T + B + M$$

where $G_c$ stands for the government budget constraint, $T$ for taxes, $B$ for borrowing and $M$ for issues of money.

If government expenditure is financed through taxation, and current revenue is equal to current tax receipts then the government has a *balanced budget*. If revenues exceed expenditure then there is a budget surplus and if spending is greater than receipts then there is a budget deficit.

## Financial deficits and surpluses and the public sector borrowing requirement

If the government spends more than it raises in taxes then a *financial deficit* occurs. There is, however, another term – *the public sector borrowing requirement* – which describes the total borrowing undertaken by the government during a given period. Since public borrowing is undertaken to finance both the difference between expenditures and receipts *and* to finance any loans made to the other sectors of the economy it is usually the case that the public sector borrowing requirement is greater than the financial deficit. The broader definition is also preferred by those economists who see a close link between the borrowing requirement and the money supply.

*The public sector borrowing requirement is equal to the financial deficit and loans raised to finance other sectors of the economy*.

In recent years the public sector borrowing requirement has

undergone both considerable expansion and fluctuation and its financing has been the subject of considerable controversy.

Broadly, there are three main ways to finance a deficit:

1 Borrowing from the non-bank private sector through the sale of long-dated gilt-edged stock.

2 Borrowing from the banking sector through the sale of Treasury Bills.

3 Borrowing from foreigners through the sale of long-dated stock to overseas residents and/or governments.

Now in the first case we may assume that there is simply a shift of funds from the private sector to the public sector with no overall effect upon the level of private sector spending. This conclusion, however, hinges upon the assumption that households and firms do not regard bonds as net wealth. The shift into bonds and away from private assets involves both a substitution effect and an income effect. If bonds are regarded simply as an alternative asset then there will be no change in the level of private sector spending. But if government bonds yield a higher return or, because they are gilt edged, they yield a safer return so that there is a risk effect which enhances the income effect then there may be a rise in the overall level of private spending. However, the impact of government borrowing upon private non-bank spending is unlikely to be very great as compared with effects which flow from the sales of Treasury Bills to the banks.

The acquisition of government short-dated debt by the banking sector enables it to expand its deposits by a multiple of the increased debt holding because bills are treated as if they are money (see Chapter 38 for a discussion of bank multipliers). And if the government borrows from the central bank then the latter will simply pay with an increase in the money supply. Hence, the increase in the money supply induced by government borrowing can, under conditions of full employment, lead to an inflationary rise in prices. And since an inflationary rise in prices constitutes a form of taxation, $T$, $B$ and $M$ in the government budget constraint may not be independent of each other.

*There may be a link between changes in the public sector borrowing requirement, changes in the money supply and changes in the rate of inflation.*

Interest in the third method of borrowing has arisen because domestic borrowing may finance only a small part of any deficit. Consequently, the burden of the problem is shifted to the balance of payments. Thus, a group of Cambridge economists has suggested that over the period 1954 to 1972 the UK private sector created a small but predictable surplus which was insufficient to finance rising government expenditures and the resulting recourse to foreign loans created a deterioration in the balance of payments. Hence, the unstable sectors of the economy were the government and foreign trade sectors and not the private sector.

### The crowding-out hypothesis

Having noted the interrelations of the various methods of financing government spending we can proceed to analyse the effects of an increase in such spending. At its simplest, an increase in government spending may constitute a net addition to aggregate demand or it may replace a similar amount of private demand. In the latter case, government spending will merely reallocate total expenditures between the various sectors and any reduction in private spending which results from the increase in government spending is *crowded-out*.

Figure 223 illustrates possible underlying conditions for *crowding-out*. In the upper half of the diagram, parts (a) and (b), the demand and supply curves for money are relatively inelastic whilst the aggregate demand schedule is interest-elastic. Hence, an expansionary fiscal policy will shift the aggregate demand curve from $AD$ to $AD_1$. But as spending increases, the transactions demand for money will rise and cause interest rates to rise. This will lead to a contraction of total spending from $AD_1$ to $AD_2$. The contraction $A_1A_2$ is the crowding-out effect and is large in relation to the final effect of $AA_2$.

In the bottom half of Figure 223, parts (c) and (d), the demand

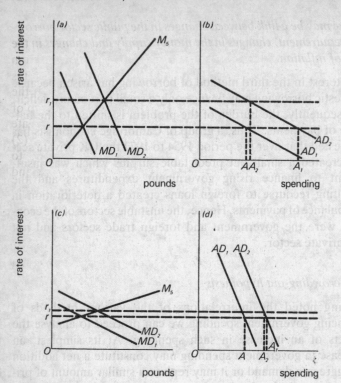

Figure 223

and supply curves for money are highly interest-elastic whilst the aggregate demand curve is interest-inelastic. An expansionary fiscal policy shifts total spending from $A$ to $A_1$. The transactions demand for money rises and the money supply responds in a fairly passive manner with the result that the crowding-out effect, $A_1A_2$, is small in relation to the total effect, $AA_2$.

There are, therefore, a variety of possible effects of an increase in government spending, ranging from the absence of any reduction in private spending to the other extreme where every pound of government spending reduces private spending by one pound.

## *The effects of taxes and expenditures on the national income*

On the assumption that there is no crowding out, then the effects of fiscal policy upon the national income follow on from the discussion contained in Chapter 39. Thus, in Figure 224 it is assumed that the full employment level of income is $OY$. If the actual level is $OY_1$ then there exists a deficient demand gap of $YY_1$ which can be eliminated either by (1) increasing aggregate demand from $AD_1$ to $AD_2$, holding tax rates constant, or (2) reducing tax rates sufficiently to cause aggregate demand to shift upward from $AD$ to $AD_1$. Similarly, if aggregate demand were given by the schedule $AD_2$ then there would be an excess demand gap of $YY_2$ which a government could eliminate either by (1) reducing expenditures, holding tax rates constant, or (2)

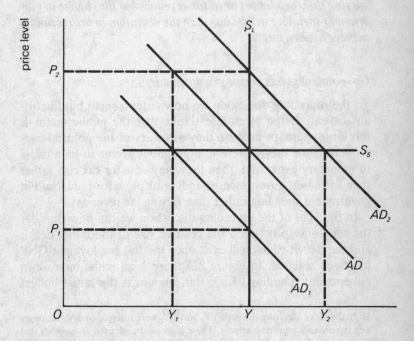

Figure 224

increasing tax rates.[1] Therefore, to eliminate deficient or excess demand, a government can either change its expenditure or its tax rates. Does it make any difference which?

Suppose the government raises its expenditures by £1 million and the multiplier is 2, then in conditions of unemployment the national income will rise by £2 million. But if, on the other hand, the government cuts tax rates sufficiently to reduce its receipts by £1 million then the private sector will have an extra £1 million of disposable income. But spending will rise by less than £1 million because part of the income will be saved and part will be spent on imports. Hence, we arrive at the following conclusion.

*A government can reduce unemployment or inflation either by varying its expenditures or its tax revenues but the change in government spending will be less than the alteration in tax receipts to achieve a given target.*

### Government goods versus private goods

To the preceding discussion we now enter a small but important caveat. If the electorate thinks that the public sector is too large, perhaps because they are wary of the political consequences, or they believe a large public sector to be a cause of monetary expansion, then they may vote for tax cuts rather than increased government spending or press for reductions in government spending rather than raising tax revenues.

In the light of the preceding discussion we can now consider the relationship between the relative size of the initial deficit and the deficit which will exist once the full employment GNP has been reached. In Figure 225 there is an initial increase in government spending of *ab*; this amount is the initial budget

1. In the older literature the gaps $YY_1$ and $YY_2$ were referred to as *deflationary and inflationary gaps* respectively. These gaps exist under the assumption that the price level remains constant and we could have used the 45 degree diagram to illustrate them. But our diagram brings out the point that fiscal policy may only be necessary in the absence of price flexibility which would yield full employment with price levels of $OP_1$ or $OP_2$.

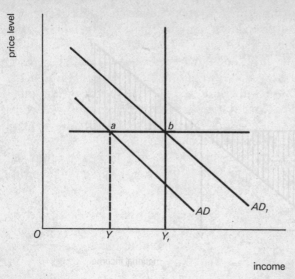

Figure 225

deficit. But with tax rates constant the rise in income will raise the tax yield and the budget deficit will fall below *ab*.

Will the deficit be eliminated? The answer is no. The increase in government spending represents a new injection and income will rise until there is an equivalent flow of withdrawals generated. Some of these withdrawals will be savings, some imports and some taxes. But only if all withdrawals are taxes will the deficit be eliminated.

The same analysis can be applied to a reduction of excess demand.

### The full employment balance

We can, therefore, draw a distinction between the *actual* budget deficit or surplus and the *potential* budget deficit or surplus at full employment with the latter being known as the *full employment balance*. Figure 226 illustrates the distinction. With tax rates given, total tax revenue varies with the level of income as is shown by the line *T*. Government expenditure is, however,

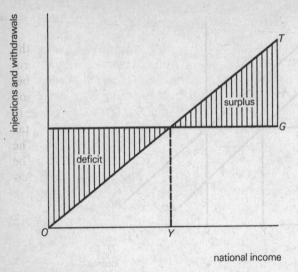

Figure 226

assumed to be autonomous and does not vary with the level of income and is indicated by the line $G$. The distance between $G$ and $T$ shows the size of the deficit or surplus corresponding to each level of income and only if the full employment level of income is $Y$ will there be budget balance at full employment. Clearly much depends upon whether $Y$ is the level of income generated by the natural level of unemployment.

## The balanced budget multiplier

So far we have considered the effects of either varying government expenditures or tax revenues. But what would happen if the government varied both so as to achieve budget balance? Although common sense suggests there to be no effect, our analysis indicates that a balanced budget might be expansionary. Thus, if the government raises £1 million in tax receipts and spends £1 million then aggregate demand would remain unchanged only if tax payers would have spent the £1 million on domestic goods. But if there had been withdrawals then a balanced budget would have a multiplier effect.

## The effects of alternative fiscal policies

From our preceding analysis it is now possible to evaluate the relative effects of different fiscal policies. Suppose the government wishes to increase aggregate demand and has a choice between (1) an increase in government expenditure of £1 million financed by printing money, or (2) a deficit financed increase in expenditure of £1 million, or (3) a £1 million reduction in tax revenues, or (4) a balanced budget increase of £1 million. The effect of the first two policies will, ignoring multiplier effects, be to raise income by £1 million, although the first policy is preferable to the second in a slump because the latter involves the administrative problem of collecting tax revenues to pay the subsequent interest payments on the debt. The effect of the third policy would be to raise income by that fraction of £1 million which would be spent on domestic goods. In the fourth case the effect depends upon the proportion of tax receipts which would not have been spent on domestic goods had the tax revenues remained in private hands.

*An increase in government spending of £x million will raise income by more than a tax cut of £x million and the latter will exert a greater effect than a balanced budget increase in spending of £x million.*

## Methods of implementing fiscal policy

Now that we have looked at fiscal policy as a means of combatting deflation and inflation, the question we must resolve is: how should fiscal policy be used and what degree of success can be expected from its use? During the fifties and sixties economic policy was dominated by three principles. First, there was the belief that fiscal policy was the only means of controlling the economy and that monetary policy was inoperable because of the existence of such factors as liquidity traps which meant that, at best, monetary policy should be confined to maintaining a steady rate of interest. Secondly, that fiscal policy could be used to iron out minor fluctuations in the economy; that is, fiscal policy could be used to *fine tune* the economy. Thirdly, that fiscal policy could be used with *discretion* instead of being governed by fixed or automatic rules. Because the first proposition involves some awareness of the workings of monetary policy we shall defer its consideration until later in this chapter and concentrate on the second and third principles.

## Fine tuning

The expression, *fine tuning*, means policies which involve frequent changes in government expenditure or tax receipts so as to hold the economy at full employment. In the late sixties the doctrine came under attack because of its failure to recognize the existence of lags in economic activity. The first problem which confronts fine tuning is the recognition lag. A considerable amount of time may elapse before a deviation from full employment is recognized and by the time it has been spotted, the deviation may have gathered momentum. Secondly, there is the *decision lag* which arises because fiscal changes have to be approved by Parliament and political processes tend to limit budgetary changes to no more than two a year. Thirdly, there is the *effect lag*. By the time that fiscal changes are implemented the economy may be set to change direction with the result that the fiscal changes accentuate the behaviour of the economy. Thus, a mild boom may be turned into a severe inflation and a mild recession be turned into a severe slump.

## Private sector reactions

A further problem with using discretionary fiscal policy to fine tune the economy lies in the private sector reactions to change. If households govern their spending by reference to their permanent incomes – and firms may well determine their investment decisions by a similar concept – then temporary fiscal changes are unlikely to exert much influence upon the economy. It is only those fiscal changes which are thought to be permanent which will exert much effect. Furthermore, the multiplier effects of fiscal changes are likely be spread out over a considerable period as a result of lagged responses by house-holds and firms.

### Severe and persistent slumps and booms

Since the private sector will tend to distinguish between tem-porary and permanent fiscal changes there is a strong case for using fiscal policy to deal with severe and permanent departures from the full employment path. Thus, to take a recent example, the sharp rise in oil prices between 1972 and 1974 and again in 1979 were unforeseen and involved a new and severe departure from the full employment path.

Figure 227 gives a simplified account of the behaviour of the UK economy in the early period with the aggregate demand curve, $AD$, intersecting the short-run supply curve, $AS'$, to the right of the long-run supply curve $S_L$. The effect of the oil price rise was to shift the supply curve from $AS'$ to $AS''$ – to reduce output and increase inflation as at point $E_1$. Point $E_1$ involves a severe departure from full employment. But observe that a gov-

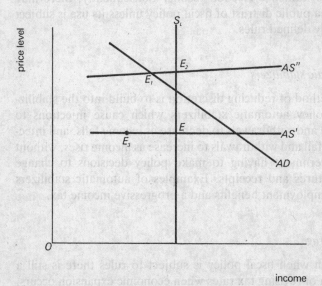

Figure 227

ernment has two policy options. First, it can increase aggregate demand so as to move the economy to point $E_2$ which would maintain full employment with increased inflation and from $E_2$ seek to move to $E$. Secondly, a government could move to $E_3$ through tough monetary policies and seek to control the inflation rate at the expense of reduced output – and later seek to move to $E$. The problem of which policy to pursue is mainly political. The UK economy tended to favour the first policy whilst other countries favoured the second policy. (Of course, in our analysis we have ignored monetary policy and also incomes policies which would shift the supply curve.)

## The political abuse of fiscal policy

Because of the powerful effects of fiscal policy and because these effects might be exercised at the wrong times there is a strong case against discretionary policy. This case may be felt to be even stronger if it is believed that governments use such policy to influence election results. Consequently, there may emerge a public distrust of fiscal policy unless its use is subject to clearly defined rules.

## Automatic stabilizers

One method of reducing discretion is to build into the stabilization policy automatic stabilizers which cause injections to increase and withdrawals to decrease as income falls, and injections to fall and withdrawals to increase as income rises, without the government having to make policy decisions to change expenditures and receipts. Examples of automatic stabilizers are unemployment benefits and a progressive income tax.

## Fiscal drag

But even when fiscal policy is subject to rules there is still a problem of revising tax rates when economic expansion occurs. A rise in income brought about by an increase in factor supplies, innovations or productivity advance will result in an increase in tax revenues which can slow down economic growth. *Fiscal drag* refers to the increase in the full employment surplus caused by economic growth which, in the absence of tax changes, is automatically diverted to the government. In the absence of increased government spending this fiscal dividend may slow down the rate of growth of the economy.

## A preliminary assessment of the effectiveness of fiscal policy

At the end of the Second World War Keynesian economics had led to the belief that through fiscal policy it would be possible to fine tune the economy. Subsequent experience has tempered these ambitious aims and it is no longer believed that fine tuning is possible nor that the problem of maintaining full employment is simply a matter of manipulating aggregate demand. Accordingly, some economists maintain that the budget should be balanced with reference to the social welfare function which would embrace collective goods such as poverty, income distribution, defence, law and order, housing and education. Such a proposal would leave the level of employment to be determined by markets and would yield a natural rate of unemployment. If the natural rate of unemployment was politically unacceptable then that would be just too bad. Of course, other economists pursuing the line of Keynesian economics might argue that unemployment was a component of the social welfare function and although demand-stimulation might not be the most efficient method of reducing unemployment, even supply-oriented methods, such as retraining, would involve finance. But whichever route is taken there is now an obvious need to consider monetary policy for at least two reasons. First, many fiscal policies, as we have noted, involve changes in the money supply. Secondly, even if fiscal policy is defined as policies which do not involve a change in the money supply, there is still a necessity to consider what kind of monetary policy is required to maintain the economy at the natural level of unemployment because market transactions would involve the use of money.

## Monetary policy

Monetary policy may be used to control the supply of money or the rate of interest. And although we tend to place primary emphasis upon income, governments are preoccupied with interest rates because high interest rates may intensify the problems of servicing (financing) interest payments of the national debt, and because interest rates which are higher than those prevailing in other countries may create balance of payments difficulties.

In seeking to control the targets of national income and the rate of interest governments can use as instruments the control of the money supply or direct control of interest rates.

### Controlling interest rates through monetary policy

Interest rates, as we observed in Chapter 38, can be controlled through open market operations. If the authorities buy bonds from the banks of the public then they will raise the prices of bonds and lower interest rates. If they sell bonds then they will lower bond prices and raise interest rates. The qualification to such a method of controlling interest rates is the Keynesian conjecture that at low rates of interest there may exist a liquidity trap in which the public will not be prepared to give up any of its holdings of money.

### Controlling the national income through monetary policy

In order to control the level of income through monetary policy the authorities must operate on the level of spending via the rate of interest, according to the Keynesians, and this runs into the difficulties of the liquidity trap and the possibility that the investment demand schedule may be interest-inelastic. However, critics of the Keynesian position argue that monetary policy may have a direct effect and does not need to operate through the rate of interest. Moreover, at full employment with inflation the liquidity trap argument tends to lose its strength.

## Conflicts over targets and instruments

Given that the money supply and the rate of interest are inter-related, does it matter which instrument is used to control, say, the national income? The answer, according to some economists, is that the *nominal* rate of interest is not a good guide to the direction – expansionary or contractionary – of monetary policy. The *real* rate of interest, which is equal to the nominal rate of interest minus the expected rate of inflation, is the relevant rate in the determination of investment. But a high nominal rate, together with a high expected rate of inflation, means a low real rate of inflation. Hence, monetary policy might be expansionary even though the nominal rate of interest is high.

A second criticism of an interest rate policy is that it might be destabilizing. Suppose the government decides that monetary policy should be expansionary and interest rates should be lowered. To do so the Bank of England buys bonds and increases the money supply. But the expansionary policy might raise the inflation rate and nominal interest rates as investors adjust their expectations about inflation to the actual inflation rate. Hence, the Bank would have to buy more bonds in order to keep nominal interest rates down – but that could lead to more inflation. Attempts to peg nominal interest rates result in a loss of control over the money supply.

However, we should not jump immediately to the conclusion that controlling the money supply is the solution because that may depend upon whether the demand for money function is stable.

## Lags in the use of monetary policy

Because the decision lag is shorter for monetary policy – it can be changed overnight – monetary policy has a more immediate impact upon the economy than does fiscal policy. But monetary policy may still be subject to long and variable lags in its effects. Hence, a monetary rule whereby the money supply is permitted to grow at a stipulated rate may be preferable to a discretionary monetary policy.

## Fiscal versus monetary policy

During the fifties and sixties monetary policy was used to control nominal interest rates. This meant that the authorities had no control over the money supply which expanded and contracted according to changes in aggregate demand fluctuations. Attempts were made to control inflation and deflation through fiscal policy but since the target rate for unemployment was below the natural rate there was a persistent tendency to inflation. To control inflation governments then resorted to non-price measures, such as credit rationing. But given the persistent inflation expansion of the money supply and discretionary fiscal policies, instability occurred. This led to a reappraisal of the roles of monetary and fiscal policy, reappraisal of Keynesian economics and the emergence of a body of doctrine known as *monetarism*.

### The monetarist controversy

The monetarist controversy had its origins in the pioneering work of Milton Friedman, at the University of Chicago, on the demand for money and the role of monetary policy. Friedman and his followers stressed the importance of the money supply in determining the behaviour of prices and the level of economic activity and hence argued the case for the revival of monetary policy, which at the time had fallen into disrepute. Consequently, they became known as *monetarists*. The participants on the other side of the controversy formed two distinct, but not unrelated, groups. Those who challenged the theoretical, empirical and methodological basis of the monetarists' arguments, and those who set themselves up as the defenders of fiscal policy, which they thought was under attack by the monetarists. This latter group became known as the Keynesians.

With hindsight it is clear that participants on both sides of the controversy were responsible for creating confusion. To avoid adding to this confusion we will describe the monetarist position, and the main issues involved in the controversy, by means of a set of straightforward propositions.

1 The demand for money function is a stable function of a relatively small number of economic variables.

2 The relationship between the demand for real money balances and the nominal supply of money is one of the key macroeconomic relationships.

3 There is a predictable relationship between changes in the supply of money and the level of nominal income, the *money multiplier relationship*.

4 The money multiplier relationship is at least as good a predictor of the response of the level of economic activity to changes in the supply of money, as the *fiscal multiplier* is for changes in the level of autonomous expenditure.

5 Changes in the supply of money exert their influence on nominal income with a long, and sometimes variable, lag.

6 In the long run, the influence of changes in the supply of money is mainly on the price level and not real output. Money is neutral in the long run.

7 The interest rate relevant to economic decision making is the *real* and not the *money* rate of interest. Because the real rate of interest depends upon price expectations, it is unobservable. Consequently, variations in the money rate of interest do not provide a good indication of variations in the real rate of interest, nor of the strength of monetary policy.

8 The target variable of monetary policy should be the supply of money (a monetary aggregate) and not the rate of interest (credit market conditions).

9 Because of lags in the transmission of monetary impulses, steady growth of the money supply is likely to be more stabilizing than discretionary variations.

10 Fiscal policy is important, but in using fiscal policy allowance must be made for the monetary consequences of different fiscal policy actions.

11 Monetary expansion is essential for the continuation of an inflationary process. Control of the money supply is an essential ingredient of any policy to stop inflation.

This rich menu of monetarist propositions clearly demonstrates why it is inappropriate to appraise the monetarist controversy solely in terms of monetary versus fiscal policy. It also dispels the myth that monetarism is synonymous with crude quantity theory predictions. Monetarism is concerned with the role of money in the economy, and the appropriate monetary policy for minimizing monetary and real disturbances in the economy. It does not imply that money alone is important, nor that monetary policy is more important than fiscal policy. It recognizes that both are important, but stresses that to use them effectively they must be used to attain the ends to which they are best suited. It further emphasizes that because changes in the supply of money, for whatever reason, exert specific and pronounced effects on the level of nominal income, the monetary consequences of fiscal policy actions must be allowed for. That is, monetarists recognize that in some cases the terms monetary and fiscal policy refer to the same policy actions, in that the policy actions involve changes in the supply of money.

## Indicative planning

Although monetary and fiscal measures for economic stabilization have been the main preoccupation of this chapter, it should be noted that other measures have been tried, among which *indicative planning* is perhaps the best known. By indicative planning a government attempts to bring together decision-makers in order to make better forecasts of future economic activity. Indicative planning is rather like a large Walrasian auction in which each decision-maker is asked to give a statement of his future consumption or production or information on some other crucial economic variable in which he is interested. When plans have been supplied they can be accumulated and compared with the total resources likely to be available in order to see whether the outcome would be inflationary or deflationary and what steps should be taken to revise plans in order to reconcile demands with supplies. The most interesting example of indicative planning in the UK was the National Plan of 1964 which, although it proved abortive, did have the merit of pointing out that all the plans of decision-makers rested upon an implicit assumption that productivity would increase by about 4 per cent per annum – a figure which had not been previously attained by the UK economy. Indicative planning has been used by the French and there exist sector plans for the UK economy.

Indicative planning does, however, have its problems. It is difficult to get all decision-makers together and therefore information has to be collected from representatives, such as trade associations. But not all the decision-makers will be available – some will not have been born! Moreover, the number of possible paths of the economy that might emerge from consultations might be enormously large.

## The framework of stabilization policy

Despite its limitations, indicative planning can provide a useful supplement to other instruments of economic policy. Thus, the instruments which might be used could be as follows.

1 *Indicative planning*. To provide insight into businessmen's expectations and to indicate whether projected spending will be excessive or deficient.

2 *Econometric forecasting*. To provide information on the responses of businessmen to policy variables in the past.

3 *Monetary and fiscal policy*. To provide a steady rate of change of the money supply and to cope with residual uncertainty through the provision of automatic stabilizers.

## Summary

In this chapter we have been concerned with the appropriate use of monetary and fiscal policies as means of dealing with macroeconomic instability. Both have been shown to have limitations but it is possible to suggest ways in which both might be used to provide methods of controlling the economy.

# Chapter 46
# Development and Growth

So we come back to the starting point of our investigation, the causes of the wealth of nations. We shall divide the subject into three parts. First, we shall examine the classical model of economic growth which provides an explanation of economic development in the eighteenth and early nineteenth centuries and which may throw some light upon the problems of the developing countries of today. Secondly, we shall consider the problems of keeping a mature economy on a full employment growth path. Thirdly, we shall comment upon the poor growth rate of the British economy as compared with those of other countries.

## Classical economic development: dualism

Classical economists envisaged economic development as taking place with unlimited supplies of labour. In Figure 228 we measure the marginal product of labour associated with given amounts of capital; the manufacturing sector along the vertical axis and the supply of labour along the horizontal axis. As a result of capital accumulation and innovation the marginal product of labour curve shifts to the right and the industrial sector expands. And as long as the supply of labour is perfectly elastic at the subsistence wage there is no reason why development should be checked by labour scarcity. Plentiful supplies of labour will, in fact, be available from three sources. First, high birth rates in the agricultural sector will produce an

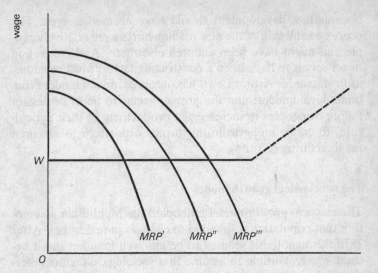

demand for and supply of labour in the industrial sector

Figure 228 The classical model of development

outflow of migrants whenever jobs become available in the manufacturing sector. Secondly, there will be internal growth of population in the towns whenever real wages rise above the subsistence level – this is the Malthusian proposition. Thirdly, innovations in the agricultural sector – which are necessary to feed the expanding labour force of the towns – will release labour.

The third point – agricultural innovations – provides a clue to the uneven pattern of development in the eighteenth and nineteenth centuries. For what stands out is that development displayed dualism within one country and between countries. Britain expanded her manfacturing sector relative to her agricultural base and it was also noticeable that the same pattern arose in other European countries and later the United States. They provided a core of industrializing countries which contrasted markedly with the agricultural periphery of the tropical areas. Internal dualism within Europe was matched by world dualism between Europe and the rest of the world. Now it is not obvious that development should have been so uneven. The processes and skill of the new manufactures were relatively simple and might have been adopted elsewhere. And motivation never seems to have been a constricting factor. Most religions, as Professor Sir Arthur Lewis has observed, do not hinder economic development, and the answer seems to lie in success or failure of peoples to increase the productivity of their agriculture, to create an agricultural surplus with which to sustain a manufacturing sector.[1]

## The neoclassical growth model

The classical growth model embodied the Malthusian assumption that population responded to changes in real wages. After 1870 this hypothesis seemed to be less well founded and it became more plausible to assume that sociological factors determined the birth rate and the problem was to ensure that capital accumulation took place at a rate equal to or greater than the rate of increase of the population. In practice this meant that savings had to increase at the same rate as the increase in the labour force. All savings were automatically invested because the rate of interest always moved so as to keep them equal and wages always moved to maintain full employment.

Neoclassical growth theory could be used to explain the so-called stylized facts of historical growth for the period 1870–1950. These facts were

1 Capital accumulation proceeded at a faster rate than population increase.

2 Real wages tended to rise.

3 Labour's share of national income tended to remain constant.

4 The rate of profit tended to remain constant.

5 The savings-income ratio tended to remain constant.

6 The capital-output ratio remained constant.

If capital accumulation were proceeding at a faster rate than

1. Sir Arthur Lewis (1978).

population increase then the real wage would rise. But labour's share in the national income could remain constant if the elasticity of substitution between capital and labour were unity. In other words, even though the return on capital might fall as it became more plentiful its share would remain constant as more of its units were substituted for labour. And the tendency of the rate of profit to decline might be offset by labour-saving innovations. As for the savings-income ratio and the capital-output ratio, the constancy of the former could be due to the life cycle factors which compelled individuals to consume and save at different rates over their lifetimes whilst the constancy of the capital-output ratio might be ascribed to technological factors.

From 1950 onwards the stylized facts have been the subject of much debate. In the industrialized countries, labour's share of the national income has risen and this has suggested that substitutability has become more difficult. However, this may be a temporary phenomenon associated with the unusually strong boom conditions of the fifties and sixties. But by the late sixties there were indications that the long delayed response to tight labour markets was emerging in the form of micro-processors and other electronic devices which threatened to create technological unemployment in the eighties and nineties.

### The Keynesian fix-price growth model

The slump of the thirties and the Keynesian revolution led to a reappraisal of growth economics in the 1950s. A new theory emerged which, at its simplest, can be stated as follows. In order to achieve equilibrium, planned injections must equal planned withdrawals. Now if they are equal and the volume of injections is sufficient to absorb all the labour-seeking jobs then a full employment equilibrium will be attained. This was the conclusion of previous chapters. The growth problem then emerges in two ways. First, it is not sufficient to solve the problem of unemployment at a point of time because the labour force may be growing over time and creating future unemployment. Secondly, investment creates employment in the short run but adds to capacity in the long run. There is, therefore, a growth in productive potential which must be absorbed by increasing demand if the economy is not to sink back to a low level of utilization of labour and equipment.

The construction of a growth model to solve the dilemma presented in the previous paragraph depends upon one's views on the workings of markets. If one assumes that all prices are flexible then the neoclassical flex-price model solves everything. But if one emphasizes that the long run emerges out of a succession of short-run disequilibria in which price movements are sluggish then a fix-price model emerges.

Let us begin by assuming that the population, and hence the labour force, $L$, is growing at a constant rate, $n$. Thus:

$$n = \frac{L_{t+1} - L_t}{L_t}. \qquad\qquad 1$$

Between two periods ($t$ and $t + 1$) the labour force grows at the rate $n$. That is, the growth rate is such that $L_{t+1}$ is equal in size to the labour force in the previous period plus some fraction ($n$) of its previous size.

$$L_{t+1} = L_t(1 + n). \qquad\qquad 2$$

Now if labour is to be fully employed then there must be an increase in the demand for labour from period to period. Let us, therefore, suppose that labour and capital are employed in fixed proportions so that we can switch from looking at the demand for labour to looking at the determinants of the demand for capital. We may suppose that investment is governed by the desire to begin each period with a stock of capital appropriate for the level of demand in that period. Hence investment, which is, of course, the change in the capital stock will be given by

$$\Delta K_t = K_{t+1} - K_t. \qquad\qquad 3$$

But how in one period can we determine the capital requirement of the next period? If there exists a fixed or desired relationship between the capital stock and output, called the capital–output ratio, $v$ (that is, the number of units of capital required to produce one unit of output), then $K_{t+1}$ will be $vY_{t+1}$ where $Y$ is income – the determinant of demand. This does not seem very helpful since in any period we do not know next period's income ($Y_{t+1}$). However, if a certain rate of growth of income is expected then we can have an expected value for next period's income. One way of arriving at an expected value would be to project the past trend of demand. What we can state, however, is that investment is governed by the expected rate of increase in demand and the desired capital–output ratio.

$$\Delta K_t = K^*_{t+1} - K_t = I_t = v(Y^*_{t+1} - Y_t) \qquad\qquad 4$$

where the symbol * denotes desired values. The right-hand side of the expression is the accelerator which we encountered in Chapter 36 but here it is the expected change in demand rather than the past change in demand which is the influential factor.

Increasing income will stimulate investment but will also be associated with withdrawals. If we assume for simplicity that savings are the only form of withdrawal and that they are a constant fraction of income, $s$, where $s$ is the marginal propensity to save, then we have:

$$S_t = sY_t. \qquad\qquad 5$$

We know that investment and savings are always equal, but that equilibrium only exists when desired savings and investment are equal, so our condition for stable equilibrium growth is the equality of desired savings and investment. We can, therefore, combine equations 4 and 5 as follows:

$$sY_t = v(Y^*_{t+1} - Y_t). \qquad\qquad 6$$

Equation 6 is more important than it might appear at first sight. To appreciate this we can divide both sides by $Y_t$ and $v$ to yield:

$$\frac{s}{v} = \frac{Y_{t+1} - Y_t}{Y_t} . \qquad\qquad 7$$

The expression on the right-hand side is the expected growth of income, $g^*$. But if the economy is in growth equilibrium then the expected growth rate must be equal to the actual growth rate, $g_a$. So for an equilibrium growth path we have the proposition that:

$$\frac{s}{v} = g^* = g_a = \frac{Y_{t+1} - Y}{Y_t}. \qquad\qquad 8$$

The rate of growth, $g^* = g_a$, is equal to the savings propensity divided by the desired capital–output ratio. Equation 7 and 8 therefore tells us a great deal. We can, in fact, go a little further by designating $s/v$ as dictating a warranted rate of growth, $g_w$.

At this stage a recapitulation should be useful. We have derived a variety of growth paths. One, the warranted rate of growth, refers to the potential growth rate as dictated by certain basic forces – savings and technology. A second growth rate refers to what is desired or expected. And a third growth rate refers to the actual or realized growth rate. Obviously, if an economy is on a stable equilibrium growth path then what is desired is equal to what is achieved and what is warranted:

$$g^* = g_a = g_w. \qquad\qquad 9$$

Equation 9 also implies that desired investment and savings are also equal and this may be accidental since the decisions to save and the decisions to invest are governed by different factors (recall the discussion of Chapter 35). The equilibrium growth path may in fact be highly unstable. If the expected rate does differ from the warranted rate then the economy will move further away from equilibrium since there are no forces to pull it back again.[2]

But there is another problem. If the labour force is growing at a rate different from the rate of growth of the capital stock then either there will be unemployment or there will be inflation. If the labour force grows faster than the capital stock there will be unemployment: if it grows at a slower rate there will be inflation. Both possibilities can lead to disequilibrium. Stable economic growth thus requires that the labour force should grow at the same rate as the warranted rate of growth and, in turn, at the desired rate of growth:

$$n = g_w = g^* = g_a. \qquad\qquad 10$$

2. The problem of instability is considered in Sen (1970).

The alarming picture of economic instability that we have drawn needs to be treated with caution. Real economies do not have a history of ever-increasing recessions nor do they soar upwards without restriction. And they do not exhibit smooth growth paths but cyclical variations around long-term upward trends. Within the context of the fix-price model it is possible to introduce modifications that go some way to meeting these objections.

1 An upper and a lower limit can be put on the tendency of the economy to shoot away in either direction by assuming the existence of a ceiling imposed by full employment of resources beyond which the economy cannot go and a floor created by investment which is not induced by recent changes in demand. Starting from the floor, an increase in investment could cause the economy to take off and move towards the ceiling. Once it hits the ceiling it bounces down again because the ceiling imposes a lower rate of increase of demand than previously and this causes investment to fall. The economy then moves towards the floor. By making various assumptions about the strength of consumption and investment it is possible to develop cycles of varying strength, some of which may not reach the ceiling. But, of course, the difficulty with this type of amended model is to discover what determines the trend of non-induced investment.

2 Another method of introducing stability into the model is to allow for changes in the distribution of income to occur. Thus, if capitalists wished to undertake more investment then product prices would be raised to permit a bigger mark-up to be achieved and this would generate sufficient savings to finance any required investment. However, the raising of prices would redistribute income away from wage earners and lead to attempts by workers to obtain compensatory wage increases. Similarly, if workers attempted to push up wages then savings would be squeezed and investment would decline and employment and wages would fall. Hence, the distribution of income determines the growth rate with the proviso that wages cannot fall below the subsistence level and profits cannot fall below the minimum required to overcome risk.

It will be apparent that the fix-price model assumes that it is income movements rather than price movements which generate growth and ensure stability. And the model can be developed in a variety of ways to include monopoly, trade unions and international trade. In fact, the discussion in this chapter complements that contained in the earlier chapter on profits where we emphasized the point that growth could not be divorced from income distribution.

## The energy and raw materials crisis

The neoclassical and Keynesian fix-price models assume that raw materials are plentiful. This was not an unreasonable assumption for the nineteenth century and the first half of the twentieth century. But since the 1970s, economists have become more aware of the limits to growth that may exist as the developed countries grow still further, and the developing countries try to imitate them. By the 1970s it was plausible to assume that the obstacle to full employment might be raw materials and not capital shortages.

Optimists, however, see no catastrophe emerging. In the case of exhaustible resources, such as coal and oil, they suggest that the rate of change of their prices should be equated with the rate of interest. Their reasoning is as follows. An exhaustible resource can be considered as a form of investment. It could, as in the case of oil, be pumped out of the ground and sold and the proceeds invested to yield a stream of income over time. But if the price were expected to rise then it would be more profitable to leave the oil in the ground and sell it later. Since the rate of interest purports to measure the rate of preference for consumption today as opposed to tomorrow, then equilibrium in the rate of usage of oil would be attained by equating the rate of change of oil prices with the rate of interest. In the case of metals, which could be re-cycled, then a similar process of reasoning would establish their optimum rate of consumption.

Pessimists, however, argue that the price mechanism cannot be expected to allocate resources over time because future generations are not present to bid against the present generation for the use of raw materials. And even when individuals do pay regard to the future it is unlikely to extend beyond the welfare of their grandchildren. And in the case of many goods there are no futures markets which establish a link between the present and the future.

## The periphery in the twentieth century

The classic economic model saw economic development and growth as taking place in a leading sector which gradually grew in size and importance and which drew from an agricultural sector, raw materials and labour. In the nineteenth century many countries failed to industrialize because they failed to raise the productivity of their agriculture or because they improved the production of the wrong kinds of crops. Hence the slow rate of development of the tropical countries. Some languished whilst others raised their living standards through supplying the industrial countries with commercial crops such as meat, wheat, rubber and also minerals.

Progress in the periphery was slow in the nineteenth century and was arrested in the slump of the thirties. But in the post-war period there have been significant improvements. The industrialized countries began to exhaust their surplus labour in agriculture and as their wage costs have risen they have been willing to invest in creating manufacturing industries in the developing countries and to import manufactures from them, particularly after the liberalization of trade in the sixties. The industrialization of the periphery has begun. Problems, however, remain. The development of the periphery is heavily dependent upon the creation of a surplus in agriculture and that, in turn, is dictated by stability in raw commodity prices which are strongly influenced by economic activity in the industrial countries. There is a need, therefore, for the advanced countries to control fluctuations in their own activity and to establish, in conjunction with the agricultural countries, buffer stock and price stabilization schemes. Public health measures have led to a population explosion which has increased urban unemployment and which can only be alleviated by increasing the productivity of agriculture and reducing the birth rate.

In the long run, however, it is likely that there will be a shift of manufactures towards the periphery.

### The UK economy

The third area of exploration has been the causes of the slow rate of growth of the UK economy. The growth rate in the period since 1945 has been about 2·5 per cent which has been higher than that of the golden period of the Victorian economy and even higher than in the early phases of the Industrial Revolution. But the growth rate has been lower than that of other countries.

From 1870 to 1914 there was continuous decline in the rate of growth of industrial production which was only partially offset by the growth of services and, much later, was offset by the rise in income from abroad. The fall in productivity resulted from too little investment. Savings flowed abroad which suggested that domestic industries were unprofitable although there seems to have been no great obstacle to British businessmen obtaining finance. The 1870s seem in retrospect to have been a climacteric. Before 1870 there was a long boom based on coal, iron and textiles. The boom ended in the 1870s and the industries of the earlier period were not replaced. After 1870 there was a failure to adopt new ideas and there was the striking fact that the productivity of British workers equipped with modern machines was very low.

Confronted by the strong competition of Germany and America and rising unemployment at home, Britain could have renounced free trade and sought to generate industries behind a tariff wall. But tariffs were an anathema and devaluation was out of the question in a country wedded to the gold standard. Textbook remedies were ruled out and would have required a change in the educational system and class attitudes.

The weaknesses of the nineteenth century persisted through the slumps of the twenties and thirties and into the post-war period. The low rate of investment has continued and has not been overcome by government subsidies. Furthermore, monetary disturbances have prevented businessmen from effectively planning investment. There has also been a tremendous expansion of the public sector which may have drained away resources from the private sector or may have been a response to rising unemployment – the public sector may have become the employer of last resort. The problems of the British economy have now been intensified by the industrialization of the periphery. In the light of the future pressures upon raw material it may be sensible for the British economy to have a larger public sector and to reduce its import bill – consuming more goods from the public sector and reducing its consumption of private goods. But whether future generations will find that sensible is debatable.

# References

Aspinall, A. (1949), *The Early Trade Unions*, Betchworth Press.

Baumol, W. J. (1959), *Business Behaviour, Value and Growth*, Harcourt Brace Jovanovich.

Beckerman, W. (1968), *An Introduction to National Income*, Weidenfeld & Nicholson.

Butler, D. E. and Pinto-Duschinsky, M. (1971), *The British General Election of 1970*, Macmillan.

Cagan, P. (1965), *Effect of Pension Plans on Aggregate Savings: Evidence from a Sample Survey*, National Bureau of Economic Research.

Crick, B. R. (1962), *In Defence of Politics*, Weidenfeld & Nicholson; Penguin (1969).

Deane, P. and Cole, W. A. (1960), *British Economic Growth 1685–1900*, Cambridge University Press.

Fieghehen, G. C., Langley, P. S. and Smith, A. D. (1977), *Poverty and Progress in Britain 1953–73*, NIESR Paper XXIV, Cambridge University Press.

Friedman, M. (1957), *A Theory of the Consumption Function*, Princeton University Press.

Friedman, M. (1962), *Capitalism and Freedom*, University of Chicago Press.

Galbraith, J. K. (1967), *The New Industrial State*, Houghton Mifflin.

Graaf, J. de V. (1967), *Theoretical Welfare Economics*, Cambridge University Press.

Haberler, G. (1969), Reading 5 in R. N. Cooper (ed.), *International Finance*, Penguin.

Hannah, L. and Kay, J. (1977), *Concentration in British Industry*, Macmillan.

**Harbury, C. D.** and **MacMahan, P. C.**, 'Inheritance and the Distribution of Personal Wealth in Britain', *Economic Journal*, 1973.
*Household Food Consumption and Expenditure* (1976), HMSO.
**Harrod, R. F.** (1951), *The Life of John Maynard Keynes*, Macmillan.

**International Monetary Fund** (1977), *Direction of Trade*.

**Keynes, J. M.** (1971a), *The Economic Consequences of the Peace*, Macmillan (first published in 1919).
**Keynes, J. M.** (1971b), *Treatise on Money*, Vol. I, Macmillan (first published in 1930).
**Keynes, J. M.** (1931), 'The Economic Consequences of Mr. Churchill' in *Essays in Persuasion*, Macmillan.
**Keynes, J. M.** (1936), *The General Theory of Employment, Interest and Money*, Macmillan.
**Knight, F. H.** (1971), *Risk, Uncertainty and Profit*, University of Chicago Press (first published in 1930).

**Lewis, W. A.** (1977), *Growth and Fluctuations 1870–1913*, Allen & Unwin.
**Lyons, B. R.** (1979), 'A New Measure of Minimum Efficient Plant Size in the United Kingdom', *Economica*.

**Malthus, T. R.** (1970), *An Essay on the Principles of Population*, Penguin (first published in 1798).
**Marris, R.** (1964), *Economic Theory of Managerial Capitalism*, Macmillan.
**Marshall, G. P.** (1980), *Social Goals and Economic Perspectives*, Penguin.
**Marx, K.** (1970), *Capital*, Vol. I, Penguin (first published in 1867).
**Meade, J. E.** (1961), 'Mauritius: a case study in Malthusian economics', *Economic Journal*.
**Meade, J. E.** (1977), *The Structure and Reform of Direct Taxation*, Allen & Unwin.
**Morris, V.** and **Ziderman, A.** (1971), 'The economic return on higher education in England and Wales', *Economic Trends*.

**Nicholson, R. J.** (1967), 'The distribution of personal income', *Lloyds Bank Review*.
**Nyman, S.** and **Silberston, A.** (1978), 'The ownership and control of industry', *Oxford Economic Papers*.

**Phillips, A. W.** (1958), 'Unemployment and wage rates', *Economica*.
**Pigou, A. C.** (1912), *Wealth and Welfare*, Macmillan.
**Pratten, C. F.** (1971), *Economies of Scale in Manufacturing Industry*, Cambridge University Press.
**Prest, A. R.** and **Coppock, D. J.** (1977), *A Manual of Applied Economics*, seventh edition, Weidenfeld & Nicholson.

**Radford, R. A.** (1945), 'The Economic Organization of a P.O.W. Camp', *Economica*.

**Rees, R. D.** (1973), 'Optimum Plant Size in United Kingdom Industries: Some Survivor Estimates', *Economica*.

**Revell, J.** (1967), *Wealth of the Nation*, Cambridge University Press.

**Robertson, D. H.** (1952), *Utility and All That*, Allen & Unwin.

**Royal Commission on the Distribution of Income and Wealth** (1976 to date), various reports.

**Salter, W. E. G.** (1966), *Productivity and Technical Change*, Cambridge University Press.

**Sen, A. K.** (1970), *Growth Economics*, Penguin.

**Sheppard, D. K.** (1971), *The Growth and Role of UK Financial Institutions 1880–1962*, Methuen.

**Simons, H. C.** (1938), *Personal Income Taxation*, University of Chicago Press.

**Stolper, W.** (1967), *The German Economy 1870 to the Present*, Weidenfeld & Nicholson.

**Turner, H. A.** (1977), 'The Wages of Fear', *New Society*.

**Williamson, D. E.** (1964), *The Economics of Discretionary Behaviour*, Prentice Hall.

**Wragg, J.** and **Robertson B. G.**, (1979), *Post-war trends in employment, productivity, output, labour costs and prices by industry in the United Kingdom*, Research Paper No 4, Department of Employment.

# Further Reading

American Economic Association/Allen & Unwin, London 1948–1972.
   *Readings in Business Cycles.*
   *Readings in Business Cycle Theory.*
   *Readings in Fiscal Policy.*
   *Readings in the Theory of Income Distribution.*
   *Readings in International Economics.*
   *Readings in the Theory of International Trade.*
   *Readings in Monetary Theory.*
   *Readings in Price Theory.*
   *Readings in the Economics of Taxation.*
   *Readings in Welfare Economics.*
E. H. Chamberlin, *The Theory of Monopolistic Competition*, Harvard University Press, 1933.
I. Fisher, *The Theory of Interest*, Macmillan, 1930.
N. Georgescu-Roegen, *Analytical Economics*, Harvard University Press, 1966.
N. Georgescu-Roegen, *The Entropy Law and the Economic Process*, Harvard University Press, 1970.
J. R. Hicks, *Value and Capital*, 2nd ed., Oxford University Press, 1946.
C. Hill, *Reformation to Industrial Revolution*, Penguin, 1970.
E. J. Hobsbawm, *Industry and Empire*, Penguin, 1970.
S. Jevons, *The Theory of Political Economy*, 1870; Penguin edition, 1971.
M. Kalecki, *Selected Essays on the Dynamics of the Capitalist Economy*, Cambridge University Press, 1971.
J. M. Keynes, *The Collected Writings of John Maynard Keynes*, Macmillan, 1971.
   vol II, *The Economic Consequences of the Peace.*
   vol IV, *A Tract on Monetary Reform.*
   vols V and VI, *A Treatise on Money.*
   vol VII, *The General Theory of Employment, Interest and Money.*
A. Marshall, *Principles of Economics*, 8th ed., Macmillan, 1920.

K. Marx, *Collected Works*, Penguin edition, 1973–5.
   *Grundrisse*, 1973.
   *The Revolution of 1848*, 1973.
   *Surveys from Exile*, 1973.
   *Early Writings*, 1975.
   *The First International and After*, 1974.
   *Capital vol. 1*, 1976.
   *Capital vol. 2*, 1977.
   *Capital vol. 3*, forthcoming.
J. E. Meade, *Efficiency, Equality and the Ownership of Property*, Allen & Unwin, 1964.
*The Structure and Reform of Direct Taxation*, Allen & Unwin, 1977.
J. S. Mill, *Principles of Political Economy*, University of Toronto edition, 1967.
R. A. Musgrave, *The Theory of Public Finance*, McGraw-Hill, 1959.
A. Nove, *An Economic History of the USSR*, Penguin, 1972.
A. C. Pigou, *The Economics of Welfare*, Macmillan, 1924.
M. M. Postan, *Medieval Economy and Society*, Penguin, 1975.
D. Ricardo, *The Works and Correspondence of David Ricardo*, Sraffa edition, Cambridge University Press, 1951–71.
J. Robinson, *The Economics of Imperfect Competition*, Macmillan, 1930.
P. A. Samuelson, *The Collected Scientific Papers of Paul A. Samuelson*, edited by J. Stiglitz and R. Merton, MIT Press, 1967–72.
J. Schumpeter, *History of Economic Analysis*, Allen & Unwin, 1954.
C. Shoup, *Public Finance*, Weidenfeld & Nicolson, 1970.
A. Smith, *An Inquiry into the Causes of the Wealth of Nations*, Cannan edition, Methuen, 1961.

*Penguin Modern Economics Readings*

A. H. Amsden, *The Economics of Women and Work*.
G. C. Archibald, *The Theory of the Firm*.
A. B. Atkinson, *Wealth, Income and Inequality*.
R. J. Ball and P. Doyle, *Inflation*.
H. Bernstein, *Underdevelopment and Development*.
J. Bhagwati, *International Trade*.
J. Bhagwati, and R. S. Eckaus, *Foreign Aid*.
M. Blaug, *Economics of Education*, vols. 1 and 2.
G. P. Clarkson, *Managerial Economics*.
R. W. Clower, *Monetary Theory*.
M. H. Cooper and A. J. Culyer, *Health Economics*.
R. N. Cooper, *International Finance*.
J. H. Dunning, *International Investment*.
M. Gilbert, *Modern Business Enterprise*.
G. C. Harcourt and N. F. Laing, *Capital and Growth*.
J. F. Helliwell, *Aggregate Investment*.

M. Hodges, *European Integration*.
R. W. Houghton, *Public Finance*.
M. C. Howard and J. E. King, *Economics of Marx*.
E. K. Hunt and J. G. Schwartz, *A Critique of Economic Theory*.
A. Hunter, *Monopoly and Competition*.
R. Jolly, E. de Kadt, H. Singer, F. Wilson, *Third World Employment*.
D. M. Lamberton, *Economics of Information and Knowledge*.
R. Layard, *Cost-Benefit Analysis*.
I. Livingstone, *Economic Policy for Development*.
B. J. McCormick and E. O. Smith, *The Labour Market*.
D. Munby, *Transport*.
L. Needleman, *Regional Analysis*.
A. Nove and D. M. Nuti, *Socialist Economics*.
E. S. Phelps, *Economic Justice*.
H. Radice, *International Firms and Modern Imperialism*.
P. Robson, *International Economic Integration*.
N. Rosenberg, *Economics of Technological Change*.
K. W. Rothschild, *Power in Economics*.
A. K. Sen, *Growth Economics*.
P. Temin, *New Economic History*.
H. Townsend, *Price Theory*.
K. A. Tucker and B. S. Yamey, *The Economics of Retailing*.
R. Turvey, *Public Enterprise*.
J. Vanek, *Self Management*.
A. A. Walters, *Money and Banking*.
B. S. Yamey, *Economics of Industrial Structure*.


*Penguin Modern Economics Texts*

C. M. Allan, *The Theory of Taxation*.
A. D. Bain, *The Control of the Money Supply*.
M. Barratt-Brown, *The Economics of Imperialism*.
M. Blaug, *Introduction to the Economics of Education*.
A. Bose, *Marxian and Post Marxian Political Economy*.
M. Bromwich, *Economics of Capital Budgeting*.
B. Carsberg, *Economics and Business Decisions*.
B. J. Cohen, *Balance-of-Payments Policy*.
G. Dalton, *Economic Systems and Society*.
P. Dorner, *Land Reform and Economic Development*.
W. Elkan, *Introduction to Development Economics*.
R. Findlay, *Trade and Specialization*.
C. Freeman, *The Economics of Industrial Innovation*.
H. J. Green, *Consumer Theory*.
H. G. Grubel, *The International Monetary System*.
E. K. Hawkins, *The Principles of Development Aid*.

G. K. Helleiner, *International Trade and Economic Development*.
M. B. Johnson, *Household Behaviour*.
B. J. McCormick, *Wages*.
D. Metcalf, *The Economics of Agriculture*.
H. Myint, *Southeast Asia's Economy*.
G. L. Reid and K. Allen, *Nationalized Industries*.
H. W. Richardson, *Elements of Regional Economics*.
H. W. Richardson, *Urban Economics*.
D. Swann, *The Economics of the Common Market*.
D. Swann, *Competition and Consumer Protection*.
J. M. Thomson, *Modern Transport Economics*.
M. A. Utton, *Industrial Concentration*.
D. M. Winch, *Analytical Welfare Economics*.

# Index

# FOR THE BEST IN PAPERBACKS, LOOK FOR THE

In every corner of the world, on every subject under the sun, Penguin represents quality and variety – the very best in publishing today.

For complete information about books available from Penguin – including Pelicans, Puffins, Peregrines and Penguin Classics – and how to order them, write to us at the appropriate address below. Please note that for copyright reasons the selection of books varies from country to country.

**In the United Kingdom:** For a complete list of books available from Penguin in the U.K., please write to *Dept E.P., Penguin Books Ltd, Harmondsworth, Middlesex, UB7 0DA*

**In the United States:** For a complete list of books available from Penguin in the U.S., please write to *Dept BA, Penguin, 299 Murray Hill Parkway, East Rutherford, New Jersey 07073*

**In Canada:** For a complete list of books available from Penguin in Canada, please write to *Penguin Books Canada Ltd, 2801 John Street, Markham, Ontario L3R 1B4*

**In Australia:** For a complete list of books available from Penguin in Australia, please write to the *Marketing Department, Penguin Books Australia Ltd, P.O. Box 257, Ringwood, Victoria 3134*

**In New Zealand:** For a complete list of books available from Penguin in New Zealand, please write to the *Marketing Department, Penguin Books (NZ) Ltd, Private Bag, Takapuna, Auckland 9*

**In India:** For a complete list of books available from Penguin, please write to *Penguin Overseas Ltd, 706 Eros Apartments, 56 Nehru Place, New Delhi, 110019*

**In Holland:** For a complete list of books available from Penguin in Holland, please write to *Penguin Books Nederland B.V., Postbus 195, NL–1380AD Weesp, Netherlands*

**In Germany:** For a complete list of books available from Penguin, please write to *Penguin Books Ltd, Friedrichstrasse 10 – 12, D–6000 Frankfurt Main 1, Federal Republic of Germany*

**In Spain:** For a complete list of books available from Penguin in Spain, please write to *Longman Penguin España, Calle San Nicolas 15, E–28013 Madrid, Spain*

*Published in Pelicans*

## ALMOST EVERYONE'S GUIDE TO ECONOMICS

### *J. K. Galbraith and Nicole Salinger*

'Economics preempts the headlines. It bears on everyone's life.'

Believing that 'the state of economics in general, and the reasons for its present failure in particular, might be put in simple accurate language that almost everyone could understand and that a perverse few might conceivably enjoy', Professor Galbraith has collaborated with Nicole Salinger in an entertaining dialogue.

She leads him through a step-by-step explanation of economic ideas with such clarity that all can understand the basic nature of classical, neo-classical and Marxian economics, the role of money and banking, the modus operandi of fiscal monetary policy, the part played by multinationals, the reasons for simultaneous inflation and unemployment and the causes of the present crisis in international economic and monetary affairs.

## THE GALBRAITH READER

### *J. K. Galbraith*

Here is the best of his writing, including selections from *The Affluent Society*, *The Great Crash*, *The New Industrial State*, and *Money*; together with more personal items, excerpts from his *Ambassador's Journal*, and letters to President Kennedy describing a nation and a world moving towards crisis. Here is a glittering prose mosaic of the Galbraith style, a portrait of a great man for ever challenging the beliefs of his generation.

'A singular delight . . . the delight of consistent good prose, and of a thinking man thinking' – *The New York Times*

*Peter Donaldson in Pelicans*

## GUIDE TO THE BRITISH ECONOMY

In the first part of this introductory guide, Peter Donaldson – who has revised and updated this edition – is mainly concerned with explaining matters of finance, including the stock market. After a full examination of industry, labour and trade, he goes on in the final section of the book to a general discussion of economic theories, their scope, and their limitations.

'Excellent . . . a most lucid and absorbing survey of the British Economy for the intelligent layman or for the beginning student of economics. It really cannot be faulted in either its scope or its exposition' – Professor Lomax in the *Economic Journal*.

## ECONOMICS OF THE REAL WORLD

Peter Donaldson describes here how a mixed economy is managed and (given the underlying market mechanisms) what can and what cannot be the subject of economic policy. Basically he argues that economics itself is strangely remote from the urgent problems of ordinary people and that policy-makers confuse ends and means. What matters, in his view, is not growth, but growth of what, for whom and at what cost; not full employment, but the nature of work; not just more wealth, but its more equitable distribution.

For *this* is the real world – a world of values and people – neglected by orthodox economics and evaded by policy-makers. Why? Because, suggests Peter Donaldson, if the real issues are to be tackled, there has to be a revolution in our whole outlook on economics and society.